INTRODUCTION TO ECONOMETRICS

INTRODUCTION TO
ECONOMETRICS

G. S. Maddala

University of Florida

Macmillan Publishing Company

New York

Collier Macmillan Publishers

London

Macmillan Publishing Company
866 Third Avenue, New York, New York 10022

Collier Macmillan Canada, Inc.

Library of Congress Cataloging in Publication Data

Maddala, G. S.
    Introduction to econometrics.

    Includes index.
    1. Econometrics.   I. Title.
HB139.M353 1988   330'.028   87-32638
ISBN 0-02-374530-4

Printing: 2 3 4 5 6 7 8   Year: 8 9 0 1 2 3 4 5 6

TO KAMESWARI, TARA AND VIVEK.

Preface

There have been many important developments in econometrics during the last two decades, but introductory books in the field still deal mostly with what econometrics was in the 1960's. The present book is meant to familiarize students (and researchers) with some of these developments, explaining them with very simple models without cluttering up the exposition with too much algebraic detail. Where proofs involve complicated expressions they are omitted and appropriate references are given. Ten of the more difficult sections have been marked with an asterisk indicating that they are optional. Beginning students can skip them and proceed. The book also contains several examples illustrating the techniques at each stage, and where illustrations are not given, some data sets have been provided so that students can compute the required results themselves.

Since the book covers quite a few topics, only a few examples have been given to illustrate *each* point. Giving too many illustrations for a single point might be boring for some students and would have made the book much too bulky. The study guide contains more illustrative examples, data sets, and questions and answers. The exercises given at the end of each chapter are somewhat challenging. However, the study guide contains answers or guidelines. The study guide also gives a "guided tour" of the material in each chapter as well as some detailed explanations for some points that are touched briefly in the book.

Some of the questions at the end of the chapters have been taken from the examinations at several U.S. and U.K. universities, and from P. C. B. Phillips and M. R. Wickens, *Exercises in Econometrics* (Cambridge, Massachusetts, Ballinger Publishing Co., 1978), Vol. I. (Many of the questions in that book are from examinations in the U.K. universities.) Since questions tend to get repeated with minor changes, I have not bothered to quote the exact source for each question.

There are many distinguishing features of the book, some of which are:

1. A discussion of aims and methodology of econometrics in Chapter 1.
2. A critique of conventional significance levels in Chapter 2.
3. A discussion of direct versus reverse regression and inverse prediction in Chapter 3.
4. A thorough discussion of several practically useful results in multiple regression (Chapter 4), some of which are not to be found even in specialized books on regression.

5. Discussion of several new tests for heteroskedasticity. Choice of linear versus log-linear models, and use of deflators (in Chapter 5).

6. A thorough discussion of the several limitations of the Durbin-Watson test, showing that it is almost useless in practice, and a discussion of Sargan's test, ARCH test, LM test, etc. (Chapter 6).

7. A critical discussion of the use and limitations of condition numbers, variance inflation factors (VIF's), ridge regression, and principal component regression in the analysis of multicollinearity (Chapter 7). Many of these techniques are often used uncritically, because computer programs are readily available.

8. The use of dummy variables to obtain predictions and standard errors of predictions, the relationship between discriminant analysis, and the linear probability model, the logit, probit and tobit models (Chapter 8).

9. Inference in under-identified simultaneous equation models, criteria for normalization and tests for exogeneity and causality (Chapter 9).

10. The discussion of partial adjustment models, error correction models, rational expectations models, and tests for rationality (Chapter 10).

11. Reverse regression, proxy variables (Chapter 11).

12. Different types of residuals and their use in diagnostic checking, model selection, choice of F-ratios in the selection of regressors, Hausman's specification error test, tests of non-nested hypotheses (Chapter 12).

These are not new topics for advanced texts but these topics (most of which are never dealt with in introductory texts) are important in econometric practice. The book explains them all with simple models so that students (and researchers) who have not had exposure to advanced texts and advanced courses in econometrics can still learn them and use them.

I have avoided any special discussion of computer programs. Nowadays, there are several computer packages available that one can choose from. Also, they change so rapidly that the lists have to be expanded and updated very often. The study guide will provide some guidance on this. I feel that it is more important to know the answers to the questions of what to compute, why to compute, how to interpret the results, what is wrong with the model, and how we can improve the model. Learning how to compute is rather easy. In the 1960's this last question received more attention because computer technology had not progressed enough and not many efficient computer programs were readily available. With the advances in computer technology and the large number of computer programs readily available, everyone can easily learn "how to compute." That is why I have tried to minimize the discussion of computer programs or the presentation of computer output. Moreover, there is no single program that will do all the things discussed in the book. But by simple adaptation many of the computer programs available will do the job.

Instructors using the book might find it difficult to cover all the material. However, it is always better to have some topics in the book that instructors can choose from depending on their interests and needs. Chapters 1 through 9 cover the basic material. The last three chapters, on models of expectations, errors in variables, and model selection, are topics that instructors can pick and choose from.

A one semester course would cover Chapters 1 to 6 (or 7). A two-semester course would cover Chapters 1 to 9 and parts of Chapters 10–12. In either case Chapter 2 need not be covered but can be used as a reference.

At some places I have a reference to my earlier book: *Econometrics* (New York, McGraw-Hill, 1977) for details. I saw no point in reproducing some proofs or derivations when they were not absolutely necessary for understanding the points being made. At several others, there is a footnote saying that the result or proof can be found in many books in econometrics, and I give a reference to my earlier book with page numbers. However, the same result can be often found in other standard references, such as:

J. Johnston, *Econometric Methods* (New York, McGraw-Hill), 3rd ed., 1984.

J. Kmenta, *Elements of Econometrics* (New York, The Macmillan Co.), 2nd ed., 1986.

H. Theil, *Principles of Econometrics* (New York, Wiley), 1971.

G. G. Judge, C. R. Hill, W. E. Griffiths, H. Lütkepohl and T. C. Lee, *Theory and Practice of Economics* (New York, Wiley), 2nd ed., 1985.

E. Malinvaud, "Statistical Methods of Econometrics" (Amsterdam, North Holland), 3rd ed., 1976.

Since I did not find it practicable to give detailed page numbers for every book, I have just referred to my earlier book.

I would like to thank Kajal Lahiri, Scott Shonkwiler, and Robert P. Trost for going through the whole manuscript and offering helpful comments.

G. S. M.

Contents

3

SIMPLE REGRESSION   27

4

MULTIPLE REGRESSION   89

5

HETEROSKEDASTICITY 159

6

AUTOCORRELATION 185

7

MULTICOLLINEARITY   223

8

DUMMY VARIABLES AND TRUNCATED VARIABLES   251

9

SIMULTANEOUS EQUATIONS MODELS   293

10

MODELS OF EXPECTATIONS   337

11

ERRORS IN VARIABLES   379

12

DIAGNOSTIC CHECKING, MODEL SELECTION, AND SPECIFICATION TESTING

APPENDIX: TABLES 453

INDEX 465

1

What Is Econometrics?

1.1 What Is Econometrics?

1.2 Economic and Econometric Models

1.3 The Aims and Methodology of Econometrics

1.4 What Constitutes a Test of an Economic Theory?

Summary and an Outline of the Book

1.1 WHAT IS ECONOMETRICS?

Literally speaking, the word "econometrics" means "measurement in economics." This is too broad a definition to be of any use because most of economics is concerned with measurement. We measure our gross national product, employment, money supply, exports, imports, price indexes, and so on. What we mean by *econometrics* is:

> The application of statistical and mathematical methods to the analysis of economic data, with a purpose of giving empirical content to economic theories and verifying them or refuting them.

In this respect econometrics is distinguished from mathematical economics, which consists of the application of mathematics only, and the theories derived need not necessarily have an empirical content.

The application of statistical tools to economic data has a very long history. Stigler [1] notes that the first "empirical" demand schedule was published in 1699 by Charles Davenant and that the first modern statistical demand studies were made by Rodulfo Enini, an Italian statistician, in 1907. The main impetus to the development

---

[1] G. J. Stigler, "The Early History of Empirical Studies of Consumer Behavior, "*The Journal of Political Economy*, 1954 [reprinted in G. J. Stigler, *Essays in the History of Economics* (Chicago: University of Chicago Press, 1965)].

of econometrics, however, came with the establishment of the Econometric Society in 1930 and the publication of the journal *Econometrica* in January 1933.

Before any statistical analysis with economic data can be done, one needs a clear mathematical formulation of the relevant economic theory. To take a very simple example, saying that the demand curve is downward sloping is not enough. We have to write the statement in mathematical form. This can be done in several ways. For instance, defining q as the quantity demanded and p as price, we can write

$$q = \alpha + \beta p \qquad \beta < 0$$

or

$$q = Ap^\beta \qquad \beta < 0$$

As we will see later in the book, one of the major problems we face is the fact that economic theory is rarely informative about functional forms. We have to use statistical methods to choose the functional form, as well.

1.2 ECONOMIC AND ECONOMETRIC MODELS

The first task an econometrician faces is that of formulating an econometric model. What is a model?

A *model* is a simplified representation of a real-world process. For instance, saying that the quantity demanded of oranges depends on the price of oranges is a simplified representation because there are a host of other variables that one can think of that determine the demand for oranges. For instance, income of consumers, an increase in diet consciousness ("drinking coffee causes cancer, so you better switch to orange juice," etc.), an increase or decrease in the price of apples, and so on. However, there is no end to this stream of other variables. In a remote sense even the price of gasoline can affect the demand for oranges.

Many scientists have argued in favor of simplicity because simple models are easier to understand, communicate, and test empirically with data. This is the position of Karl Popper[2] and Milton Friedman.[3] The choice of a simple model to explain complex real-world phenomena leads to two criticisms:

1. The model is oversimplified.
2. The assumptions are unrealistic.

For instance, in our example of the demand for oranges, to say that it depends on only the price of oranges is an oversimplification and also an unrealistic assumption. To the criticism of oversimplification, one can argue that it is better to start with a simplified model and progressively construct more complicated models. This is the

---

[2] K. F. Popper, *The Logic of Scientific Discovery* (London: Hutchinson, 1959), p. 142.
[3] M. Friedman, "The Methodology of Positive Economics," in *Essays in Positive Economics* (Chicago: University of Chicago Press, 1953), p. 14.

idea expressed by Koopmans.[4] On the other hand, there are some who argue in favor of starting with a very general model and simplifying it progressively based on the data available.[5] The famous statistician L. J. (Jimmy) Savage used to say that "a model should be as big as an elephant." Whatever the relative merits of this alternative approach are, we will start with simple models and progressively build more complicated models.

The other criticism we have mentioned is that of "unrealistic assumptions." To this criticism Friedman argued that the assumptions of a theory are never descriptively realistic. He says[6]:

> The relevant question to ask about the "assumptions" of a theory is not whether they are descriptively "realistic" for they never are, but whether they are sufficiently good approximations for the purpose at hand. And this question can be answered by only seeing whether the theory works, which means whether it yields sufficiently accurate predictions.

Returning to our example of demand for oranges, to say that it depends only on the price of oranges is a descriptively unrealistic assumption. However, the inclusion of other variables, such as income and price of apples in the model, does not render the model more descriptively realistic. Even this model can be considered to be based on unrealistic assumptions because it leaves out many other variables (like health consciousness, etc.). But the issue is which model is more useful for predicting the demand for oranges. This issue can be decided only from the data we have and the data we can get.

In practice, we include in our model all the variables that we think are relevant for our purpose and dump the rest of the variables in a basket called "disturbance." This brings us to the distinction between an economic model and an econometric model.

An *economic model* is a set of assumptions that approximately describes the behavior of an economy (or a sector of an economy). An *econometric model* consists of the following:

1. A set of behavioral equations derived from the economic model. These equations involve some observed variables and some "disturbances" (which are a catchall for all the variables considered as irrelevant for the purpose of this model as well as all unforeseen events).
2. A statement of whether there are errors of observation in the observed variables.
3. A specification of the probability distribution of the "disturbances" (and errors of measurement).

With these specifications we can proceed to test the empirical validity of the economic model and use it to make forecasts or use it in policy analysis.

---

[4] T. C. Koopmans, *Three Essays on the State of Economics Science* (New York: McGraw-Hill, 1957), pp. 142–143.
[5] This is the approach suggested by J. D. Sargan and notably David F. Hendry.
[6] Friedman, "Methodology," pp. 14–15.

Taking the simplest example of a demand model, the econometric model usually consists of:

1. The behavioral equation

$$q = \alpha + \beta p + u$$

   where q is the quantity demanded and p the price. Here p and q are the observed variables and u is a disturbance term.
2. A specification of the probability distribution of u which says that $E(u \mid p) = 0$ and that the values of u for the different observations are independently and normally distributed with mean zero and variance σ^2.

With these specifications one proceeds to test empirically the law of demand or the hypothesis that $\beta < 0$. One can also use the estimated demand function for prediction and policy purposes.

1.3 THE AIMS AND METHODOLOGY OF ECONOMETRICS

The aims of econometrics are:

1. Formulation of econometric models, that is, formulation of economic models in an empirically testable form. Usually, there are several ways of formulating the econometric model from an economic model because we have to choose the functional form, the specification of the stochastic structure of the variables, and so on. This part constitutes the *specification aspect* of the econometric work.
2. Estimation and testing of these models with observed data. This part constitutes the *inference aspect* of the econometric work.
3. Use of these models for prediction and policy purposes.

During the 1950s and 1960s the inference aspect received a lot of attention and the specification aspect very little. The major preoccupation of econometricians had been the statistical estimation of correctly specified econometric models. During the late 1940s the Cowles Foundation provided a major breakthrough in this respect, but the statistical analysis presented formidable computational problems. Thus the 1950s and 1960s were spent mostly in devising alternative estimation methods and alternative computer algorithms. Not much attention was paid to errors in the specification or to errors in observations.[7] With the advent of high-speed computers, all this has, however, changed. The estimation problems are no longer formidable and econometricians have turned attention to other aspects of econometric analysis.

---

[7] There was some work on specification errors in the early 1960s by Theil and Griliches, but this referred to omitted-variable bias (see Chapter 4). Griliches' lecture notes (unpublished) at the University of Chicago were titled "Specification Errors in Econometrics."

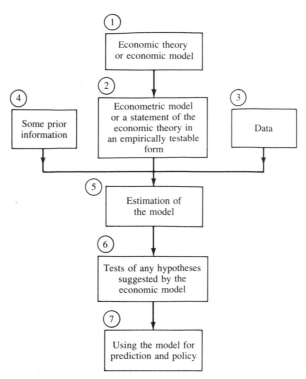

Figure 1.1. Schematic description of the steps involved in an econometric analysis of economic models.

We can schematically depict the various steps involved in an econometric analysis, as was done before the emphasis on specification analysis. This is shown in Figure 1.1. Since the entries in the boxes are self-explanatory, we will not elaborate on them. The only box that needs an explanation is box 4, "prior information." This refers to any information that we might have on the unknown parameters in the model. This information can come from economic theory or from previous empirical studies.

There has, however, been considerable dissatisfaction with the scheme shown in Figure 1.1. Although one can find instances of dissatisfaction earlier, it was primarily during the 1970s that arguments were levied against the one-way traffic shown in Figure 1.1. We will discuss three of these arguments.

1. In Figure 1.1 there is no feedback from the econometric testing of economic theories to the formulation of economic theories (i.e., from box 6 to box 1). It has been argued that econometricians are not just handmaidens of economic theorists. It is not true that they just take the theories they are given them and test them, learning nothing from the tests. So we need an arrow from box 6 to box 1.

2. The same is true regarding the data collection agencies. It is not true that they just gather whatever data they can and the econometricians use whatever data are given them. (The word "data" comes from the Latin word "datum," which means "given.") There ought to be feedback from boxes 2 and 5 to box 3.
3. Regarding box 6 itself, it has been argued that the hypothesis testing refers only to the hypotheses suggested by the original economic model. This depends on the assumption that the specification adopted in box 2 is correct. However, what we should be doing is testing the adequacy of the original specification as well. Thus we need an extra box of specification testing and diagnostic checking. There will also be feedback from this box to box 2, that is, the specification tests will result in a new specification for the econometric models. These problems, which have been one of the most important major developments in econometrics in the 1970s, are treated in Chapter 12.

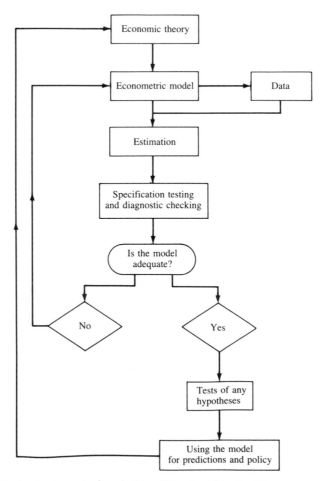

Figure 1.2.   Revised schematic description of the steps involved in an econometric analysis of economic models.

The new developments that have been suggested are shown figuratively in Figure 1.2. Some of the original boxes have been deleted or condensed. The schematic description in Figure 1.2 is illustrative only and should not be interpreted literally. The important things to note are the feedback

1. From econometric results to economic theory.
2. From specification testing and diagnostic checking to revised specification of the economic model.
3. From econometric model to data.

In the foregoing scheme we have talked of only one theory, but often there are many competing theories, and one of the main purposes of econometrics is to help in the choice among competing theories. This is the problem of model selection, which is discussed in Chapter 12.

1.4 WHAT CONSTITUTES A TEST OF AN ECONOMIC THEORY?

Earlier, we stated that one of the aims of econometrics was that of testing economic theories. An important question that arises is: What constitutes a test? As evidence of a successful test of an economic theory, it is customary to report that the signs of the estimated coefficients in an econometric model are correct. This approach may be termed the approach of *confirming* economic theories. The problem with this approach is that, as Mark Blaug points out [8]:

> In many areas of economics, different econometric studies reach conflicting conclusions and, given the available data, there are frequently no effective methods for deciding which conclusion is correct. In consequence, contradictory hypotheses continue to co-exist sometimes for decades or more.

A more valid test of an economic theory is if it can give predictions that are better than those of alternative theories suggested earlier. Thus one needs to compare a given model with earlier models. This approach of evaluating alternative theories has received greater attention in recent years. The problems associated with model comparison and model selection are dealt with in Chapter 12.

SUMMARY AND AN OUTLINE OF THE BOOK

The preceding discussion suggests some changes that have taken place during the last decade in the development of econometric methods. The earlier emphasis (during the 1950s and 1960s) was on efficient estimation of a *given* model. The emphasis has now shifted to specification testing, diagnostic checking, model comparison, and an adequate formulation of the expectational variables given the pervasive role of expectations in almost all economic theories.

[8] M. Blaug, *The Methodology of Economics* (Cambridge: Cambridge University Press, 1980), p. 261.

A large part of the book, however, will be devoted to developments that took place in the 1950s and 1960s because these developments form the basis for recent work. However, Chapter 12 is devoted to recent developments in the areas of specification testing, diagnostic checking, and model selection. In addition, the other chapters also describe recent developments. For instance, rational expectations models are discussed in Chapter 10, recent developments on tests for serial correlation are reviewed in Chapter 6 and so on.

The plan of the book is as follows:

Chapter 2 contains a review of some basic results in statistics. Most students will have covered this material in introductory courses in statistics.

Chapter 3 begins with the simple (two-variable) regression model. Some of the more complicated sections, such as those on inverse prediction, stochastic regressors, and regression fallacy, are denoted as optional and are marked with an asterisk. Beginning students may want to skip these.

In Chapter 4 we discuss the multiple regression model in great detail. It is the longest chapter in the book because it covers several issues concerning the interpretation of multiple regression coefficients. A detailed discussion of the model with two explanatory variables is given to fix the ideas.

Chapters 5 and 6 deal, respectively, with the problems of unequal error variances and serially correlated errors in the multiple regression model. Chapter 6, in particular, deals extensively with the usual approach of using the Durbin–Watson test and discusses several situations where its use would be undesirable.

Chapter 7 is devoted to the multicollinearity problem. A separate chapter on this problem is perhaps not necessary, but it was found that inclusion of this material in any other chapter would have made that chapter far too long.

Chapter 8 deals with dummy variables that are used as explanatory variables in several contexts. We also discuss special problems created when the dependent variable is a dummy variable or a truncated variable.

In Chapter 9 we give an elementary introduction to simultaneous-equations models and to the identification problem in econometrics.

In Chapter 10 we consider distributed lag models and models of expectations. We also give an elementary introduction to rational expectations models. Models with lags in behavior and expectations play an important role in most econometric models.

In Chapter 11 we consider errors in variables and proxy variables.

In Chapter 12 we present an introduction to some recent work on diagnostic checking, specification testing, and model selection.

Throughout, an attempt has been made to explain complicated material in simple terms. To avoid cumbersome algebra, many results have been stated without proofs although at times algebraic detail is unavoidable. Given readily available computer packages, even this algebraic detail may be unnecessary, but it is good for students to understand at least some minimal steps involved in the construction of computer packages. This will help in understanding the deficiencies and limitations of the various procedures.

2

Review Of Some Basic Results In Statistics

2.1 INTRODUCTION

In this chapter we review some basic results in probability and statistics that will be useful in later chapters. Most of the results in this chapter are generally covered in a course in introductory statistics. The present chapter serves two purposes:

1. As a review of some material covered in previous courses in statistics.

2. As a reference for some results when needed.

Proofs are omitted throughout and only the important results are stated.

2.2 SUMMATION AND PRODUCT OPERATIONS

Since the summation operator $\sum$ and the product operator π are frequently used throughout the book, we will review them here.

The summation operator $\sum$ is defined as follows:

$$\sum_{i=1}^{n} X_i = X_1 + X_2 + \cdots X_n$$

Some important properties of this operator are:

1. $\sum_{i=1}^{n} c = nc$, where c is a constant.
2. $\sum_{i=1}^{n} (x_i + y_i) = \sum_{i=1}^{n} x_i + \sum_{i=1}^{n} y_i$.
3. $\sum_{i=1}^{n} (c + bx_i) = nc + b\sum_{i=1}^{n} x_i$.

Where there is no confusion we will just write $\sum_i X_i$ or $\sum X_i$ to denote $\sum_{i=1}^{n} X_i$, that is, summation over all the X's.

Sometimes we use the double-summation operator, which is defined as follows:

$$\sum_{i=1}^{n} \sum_{j=1}^{m} X_{ij} = X_{11} + X_{12} + \cdots + X_{1m}$$
$$+ X_{21} + X_{22} + \cdots + X_{2m}$$
$$\cdots\cdots\cdots\cdots\cdots\cdots\cdots\cdots\cdots$$
$$+ X_{n1} + X_{n2} + \cdots + X_{nm}$$

Again, where there is no confusion that i runs from 1 to n and j runs from 1 to m, we will just write $\sum_i \sum_j X_{ij}$. Yet another notation is $\sum_i \sum_{j, i \neq j} X_{ij}$, which denotes summation over all values of i and j except those for which $i = j$. For instance, suppose that i goes from 1 to 3 and j goes from 1 to 2. Then

$$\sum_i \sum_j X_{ij} = X_{11} + X_{12} + X_{21} + X_{22} + X_{31} + X_{32}$$

But

$$\sum_{\substack{i \\ i \neq j}} \sum_j X_{ij} = X_{12} + X_{21} + X_{31} + X_{32}$$

That is, we have to omit all the terms for which $i = j$. As yet another example, consider

$$(X_1 + X_2 + X_3)^2 = X_1^2 + X_2^2 + X_3^2 + 2X_1 X_2 + 2X_2 X_3 + 2X_1 X_3$$

We can write this as

$$\left(\sum_i X_i\right)^2 = \sum_i \sum_j X_i X_j$$

$$= \sum_i X_i^2 + \sum_{\substack{i \\ i \neq j}} \sum_j X_i X_j$$

The product operator $\prod$ is defined as

$$\prod_{i=1}^{n} X_i = X_1 X_2 \cdots X_n$$

Again, where there is no confusion as to the limits if i, we will just write $\prod_i X_i$ or $\prod X_i$. As with the $\sum$ operator, we can also use the double-product operator, $\prod \prod$. For instance, if we have variables X_1, X_2, X_3 and Y_1, Y_2, then $\prod_i \prod_j X_i Y_j = X_1 X_2 X_3 Y_1 Y_2$.

2.3 RANDOM VARIABLES AND PROBABILITY DISTRIBUTIONS

A variable X is said to be a *random variable* (rv) if for every real number a there exists a probability $P(X \le a)$ that X takes on a value less than or equal to a. We shall denote random variables by capital letters X, Y, Z, and so on. We shall use lowercase letters, x, y, z, and so on, to denote particular values of the random variables. Thus $P(X = x)$ is the probability that the random variable X takes the value x. $P(x_1 \le X \le x_2)$ is the probability that the random variable X takes values between x_1 and x_2, both inclusive.

If the random variable X can assume only a particular finite (or countably infinite) set of values, it is said to be a *discrete* random variable. A random variable is said to be *continuous* if it can assume any value in a certain range. An example of a discrete random variable is the number of customers arriving at a store during a certain period (say, the first hour of business). An example of a continuous random variable is the income of a family in the United States. In actual practice, use of continuous random variables is popular because the mathematical theory is simpler. For instance, when we say that income is a continuous random variable, we do not mean that it is continuous (in fact, strictly speaking, it is discrete) but that it is a convenient approximation to treat it that way.

A formula giving the probabilities for different values of the random variable X is called a *probability distribution* in the case of discrete random variables, and *probability density function* (denoted by p.d.f.) for continous random variables. This is usually denoted by $f(x)$.

In general, for a continuous random variable, the occurrence of any *exact* value of X may be regarded as having a zero probability. Hence probabilities are discussed in terms of some ranges. These probabilities are obtained by integrating $f(x)$ over the desired range. For instance, if we want $\text{Prob}(a \le X \le b)$, this is given by

$$\text{Prob}(a \le X \le b) = \int_a^b f(x)\,dx$$

The probability that the random variable X takes on values at or below a number c is often written as $F(c) = \text{Prob}(X \le c)$. The function $F(x)$ represents, for different values of x, the cumulated probabilities and hence is called the *cumulative distribution function* (denoted by c.d.f.). Thus

$$F(c) = \text{Prob}(X \le c) = \int_{-\infty}^{c} f(x)\,dx$$

Joint, Marginal, and Conditional Distributions

We are often interested in not just one random variable but in the relationship between several random variables. Suppose that we have two random variables, X and Y. Now we have to consider:

1. The joint p.d.f.: $f(x, y)$.
2. The marginal p.d.f.'s: $f(x)$ and $f(y)$.
3. The conditional p.d.f.'s:
   (a) $f(x|y)$, which is the distribution of X given $Y = y$.
   (b) $f(y|x)$, which is the distribution of Y given $X = x$.

The joint density can be written as the product of the marginal and conditional densities. Thus

$$f(x, y) = f(x)f(y|x)$$
$$= f(y)f(x|y)$$

If $f(x, y) = f(x)f(y)$ for all x and y, then x and y are said to be *independent*. Note that if they are independent,

$$f(x|y) = f(x) \qquad \text{and} \qquad f(y|x) = f(y)$$

that is, the conditional distributions are the same as the marginals. This makes intuitive sense because for X, whether or not Y is fixed at a certain level, is irrelevant. Similarly, for Y it should be irrelevant at what level we fix X.

Illustrative Example

Consider, for instance, the discrete distribution of X and Y defined by the following probabilities:

y \ x	3	4	5	$f(y) \ne f(y\|x=3) \ne f(y\|x=4) \ne f(y\|x=5)$			
2	0.2	0	0.2	0.4	0.5	0	0.5
4	0	0.2	0	0.2	0	1.0	0
6	0.2	0	0.2	0.4	0.5	0	0.5
$f(x)$	0.4	0.2	0.4				

Since the conditional distributions of y depend on the values of x, X and Y cannot be independent. On the other hand, if the distribution of X and Y is defined as

x / y	3	4	5	$f(y) = f(y\|x = 3) = f(y\|x = 4) = f(y\|x = 5)$			
2	0.2	0.2	0.1	0.5	0.5	0.5	0.5
4	0.12	0.12	0.06	0.3	0.3	0.3	0.3
6	0.08	0.08	0.04	0.2	0.2	0.2	0.2
$f(x)$	0.4	0.4	0.2				

we see that the conditional distributions of y for the different values of x and the marginal distribution of y are the same and hence X and Y are independent.

2.4 THE NORMAL PROBABILITY DISTRIBUTION AND RELATED DISTRIBUTIONS

If we are given the probability distribution of a random variable X, we can determine the probability that X lies in an interval (a, b). There are some probability distributions for which the probabilities have been tabulated and which are considered suitable descriptions for a wide variety of phenomena. These are the normal distribution and the t, χ^2, and F distributions. We discuss these and also the lognormal and bivariate normal distributions. There are other distributions as well, such as the gamma and beta distributions, for which extensive tables are available. In fact, the χ^2-distribution is a particular case of the gamma distribution and the t and F distributions are particular cases of the beta distribution. We do not need all these relationships here.

There is also a question of whether the normal distribution is an appropriate one to use to describe economic variables. However, even if the variables are not normally distributed, one can consider transformations of the variables so that the transformed variables are normally distributed.

The Normal Distribution

The normal distribution is a bell-shaped distribution which is used most extensively in statistical applications in a wide variety of fields. Its probability density function is given by

$$f(x) = \frac{1}{\sigma\sqrt{2\pi}} \exp\left[-\frac{1}{2\sigma^2}(x - \mu)^2\right] \qquad -\infty < x < +\infty$$

Its mean is μ and its variance is σ^2. When x has the normal distribution with mean μ and variance σ^2, we write this compactly as $x \sim N(\mu, \sigma^2)$.

An important property of the normal distribution is that *any* linear function of normally distributed variables is also normally distributed. This is true whether the variables are independent or correlated. If

$$x_1 \sim N(\mu_1, \sigma_1^2) \qquad \text{and} \qquad x_2 \sim N(\mu_2, \sigma_2^2)$$

and the correlation between x_1 and x_2 is ρ, then

$$a_1 x_1 + a_2 x_2 \sim N(a_1 \mu_1 + a_2 \mu_2, a_1^2 \sigma_1^2 + a_2^2 \sigma_2^2 + 2\rho a_1 a_2 \sigma_1 \sigma_2)$$

In particular,

$$x_1 + x_2 \sim N(\mu_1 + \mu_2, \sigma_1^2 + \sigma_2^2 + 2\rho \sigma_1 \sigma_2)$$

and

$$x_1 - x_2 \sim N(\mu_1 - \mu_2, \sigma_1^2 + \sigma_2^2 - 2\rho \sigma_1 \sigma_2)$$

Related Distributions

In addition to the normal distribution, there are other probability distributions that we will be using frequently. These are the χ^2, t, and F distributions tabulated in the Appendix. These distributions are derived from the normal distribution and are defined as described below.

χ^2-Distribution

If $x_1, x_2, \ldots, x_n$ are independent normal variables with mean zero and variance 1, that is, $x_i \sim IN(0, 1)$, $i = 1, 2, \ldots, n$, then

$$Z = \sum_i x_i^2$$

is said to have the χ^2-distribution with degrees of freedom n, and we will write this as $Z \sim \chi_n^2$. The subscript n denotes degrees of freedom. The χ_n^2 distribution is the distribution of the sum of squares of n independent standard normal variables.

If $x_i \sim IN(0, \sigma^2)$, then Z should be defined as

$$Z = \sum_i \frac{x_i^2}{\sigma^2}$$

The χ^2-distribution also has an "additive property," although it is different from the property of the normal distribution and is much more restrictive. The property is:

> If $Z_1 \sim \chi_n^2$ and $Z_2 \sim \chi_m^2$ and Z_1 and Z_2 are *independent*,
> then $Z_1 + Z_2 \sim \chi_{n+m}^2$.

Note that we need independence and we can consider simple additions only, not any general linear combinations. Even this limited property is useful in practical applications. There are many distributions for which even this limited property does not hold.

t-Distribution

If $x \sim N(0, 1)$ and $y \sim \chi_n^2$ and x and y are independent, $Z = x/\sqrt{y/n}$ has a t-distribution with degrees of freedom n. We write this as $Z \sim t_n$. The subscript n again denotes the degrees of freedom. Thus the t-distribution is the distribution of a standard normal variable divided by the square root of an independent averaged χ^2 variable (χ^2 variable divided by its degrees of freedom). The t-distribution is a symmetric probability distribution like the normal distribution but is flatter than the normal and has longer tails. As the degrees of freedom n approaches infinity, the t-distribution approaches the normal distribution.

F-Distribution

If $y_1 \sim \chi^2_{n_1}$ and $y_2 \sim \chi^2_{n_2}$ and y_1 and y_2 are independent, $Z = (y_1/n_1)/(y_2/n_2)$ has the F-distribution with degrees of freedom (d.f.) n_1 and n_2. We write this as

$$Z \sim F_{n_1, n_2}$$

The first subscript, n_1, refers to the d.f. of the numerator, and the second subscript, n_2, refers to the d.f. of the denominator. The F-distribution is thus the distribution of the ratio of two independent averaged χ^2 variables.

2.5 CLASSICAL STATISTICAL INFERENCE

Statistical inference is the area that describes the procedures by which we use the observed data to *draw conclusions* about the population from which the data came or about the process by which the data were generated. Our assumption is that there is an unknown process that generates the data we have and that this process can be described by a probability distribution, which, in turn, can be characterized by some unknown parameters. For instance, for a normal distribution the unknown parameters are μ and σ^2.

Broadly speaking, statistical inference can be classified under two headings: classical inference and Bayesian inference. Classical statistical inference is based on two premises:

1. The sample data constitute the only relevant information.
2. The construction and assessment of the different procedures for inference are based on long-run behavior under essentially similar circumstances.

In Bayesian inference we combine sample information with prior information. Suppose that we draw a random sample $y_1, y_2, \ldots, y_n$ of size n from a normal population with mean μ and variance σ^2 (assumed known), and we want to make inferences about μ.

In classical inference we take the sample mean $\bar{y}$ as our estimate of μ. Its variance is σ^2/n. The inverse of this variance is known as the *sample precision*. Thus the sample precision is n/σ^2.

In Bayesian inference we have prior information on μ. This is expressed in terms of a probability distribution known as the *prior distribution*. Suppose that the prior distribution is normal with mean μ_0 and variance σ_0^2, that is, precision $1/\sigma_0^2$. We now combine this with the sample information to obtain what is known as the *posterior distribution* of μ. This distribution can be shown to be normal. Its mean is a weighted average of the sample mean $\bar{y}$ and the prior mean μ_0, weighted by the sample precision and prior precision, respectively. Thus

$$\mu\,(\text{Bayesian}) = \frac{w_1 \bar{y} + w_2 \mu_0}{w_1 + w_2}$$

where $w_1 = n/\sigma^2 =$ sample precision
$w_2 = 1/\sigma_0^2 =$ prior precision

Also, the precision (or inverse of the variance) of the posterior distribution of μ is $w_1 + w_2$, that is, the sum of sample precision and prior precision.

For instance, if the sample mean is 20 with variance 4 and prior mean is 10 with variance 2, we have

$$\text{posterior mean} = \frac{\frac{1}{4}(20) + \frac{1}{2}(10)}{\frac{1}{4} + \frac{1}{2}}$$

$$= \frac{10}{\frac{3}{4}} = 13.33$$

$$\text{posterior variance} = (\tfrac{1}{4} + \tfrac{1}{2})^{-1} = \tfrac{4}{3} = 1.33$$

The posterior mean will lie between the sample mean and the prior mean. The posterior variance will be less than both the sample and prior variances.

We do not discuss Bayesian inference in this book, because this would take us into a lot more detail than we intend to cover.[1] However, the basic notion of combining the sample mean and prior mean in inverse proportion to their variances will be a useful one to remember.

Returning to classical inference, it is customary to discuss classical statistical inference under three headings:

1. Point estimation.
2. Interval estimation.
3. Testing of hypotheses.

Point Estimation

Suppose that the probability distribution involves a parameter θ and we have a sample of size n, namely $y_1, y_2, \ldots, y_n$, from this probability distribution. In *point estimation* we construct a function $g(y_1, y_2, \ldots, y_n)$ of these observations and say that g is our estimate (guess) of θ. The common terminology is to call the function $g(y_1, y_2, \ldots, y_n)$ an *estimator* and its value in a *particular* sample an *estimate*. Thus an estimator is a random variable and an estimate is a particular value of this random variable. For instance, if θ is the population mean and $g(y_1, y_2, \ldots, y_n) = (1/n)\sum y_i = \bar{y}$ is the sample mean, $\bar{y}$ is an estimator of θ. If $\bar{y} = 4$ in a particular sample, 4 is an estimate of θ.

In *interval estimation* we construct two functions, $g_1(y_1, y_2, \ldots, y_n)$ and

---

[1] For more discussion of Bayesian econometrics, refer to A. Zellner, *Introduction to Bayesian Analysis in Econometrics* (New York: Wiley, 1971), and E. E. Leamer, *Specification Searches* (New York: Wiley, 1978).

$g_2(y_1, y_2, \ldots, y_n)$, of the sample observations and say that θ lies between g_1 and g_2 with a certain probability. In *hypothesis testing* we suggest a hypothesis about θ (say, $\theta = 4.0$) and examine the degree of evidence in the sample in favor of the hypothesis, on the basis of which we either accept or reject the hypothesis.

In practice what we need to know is how to construct the point estimator g, the interval estimator (g_1, g_2), and the procedures for testing hypotheses. In the classical statistical inference all these are based on *sampling distributions*. Sampling distributions are probability distributions of functions of sample observations. For instance, the sample mean $\bar{y}$ is a function of the sample observations and its probability distribution is called the sampling distribution of $\bar{y}$. In classical statistical inference the properties of estimators are discussed in terms of the properties of their sampling distributions.

2.6 PROPERTIES OF ESTIMATORS

There are some desirable properties of estimators that are often mentioned in the book. These are:

1. Unbiasedness.
2. Efficiency.
3. Consistency.

The first two are small-sample properties. The third is a large-sample property.

Unbiasedness

An estimator g is said to be *unbiased* for θ if $E(g) = \theta$, that is, the mean of the sampling distribution of g is equal to θ. What this says is that if we calculate g for each sample and repeat this process infinitely many times, the average of all these estimates will be equal to θ. If $E(g) \neq \theta$, then g is said to be biased and we refer to $E(g) - \theta$ as the *bias*.

Unbiasedness is a desirable property but not at all costs. Suppose that we have two estimators g_1 and g_2, and g_1 can assume values far away from θ and yet have its mean equal to θ, whereas g_2 always ranges close to θ but has its mean slightly away from θ. Then we might prefer g_2 to g_1 because it has smaller variance even though it is biased. If the variance of the estimator is large, we can have some unlucky samples where our estimate is far from the true value. Thus the second property we want our estimators to have is a small variance. One criterion that is often suggested is the mean-squared error (MSE), which is defined by

$$\text{MSE} = (\text{bias})^2 + \text{variance}$$

The MSE criterion gives equal weights to these components. Instead, we can consider a weighted average $W(\text{bias})^2 + (1 - W)\text{variance}$. Strictly speaking, instead of doing something ad hoc like this, we should specify a loss function that gives the loss in using $g(y_1, \ldots, y_n)$ as an estimator of θ and choose g to minimize expected loss.

Efficiency

The property of efficiency is concerned with the variance of estimators. Obviously, it is a relative concept and we have to confine ourselves to a particular class. If g is an unbiased estimator and it has the minimum variance in the class of unbiased estimators, g is said to be an *efficient* estimator. We say that g is an MVUE (a minimum-variance unbiased estimator).

If we confine ourselves to linear estimators, that is, $g = c_1 y_1 + c_2 y_2 + \cdots + c_n y_n$, where the c's are constants which we choose so that g is unbiased and has minimum variance, g is called a BLUE (a best linear unbiased estimator).

Consistency

Often it is not possible to find estimators that have desirable small-sample properties such as unbiasedness and efficiency. In such cases it is customary to look at desirable properties in large samples. These are called *asymptotic* properties. Three such properties often mentioned are consistency, asymptotic unbiasedness, and asymptotic efficiency.

Suppose that $\hat{\theta}_n$ is the estimator of θ based on a sample of size n. Then the sequence of estimators $\hat{\theta}_n$ is called a *consistent* sequence if for any arbitrarily small positive numbers ε and δ there is a sample size n_0 such that

$$\text{Prob}\,[|\hat{\theta}_n - \theta| < \varepsilon] > 1 - \delta \qquad \text{for all } n > n_0$$

That is, by increasing the sample size n the estimator $\hat{\theta}_n$ can be made to lie arbitrarily close to the true value of θ with probability arbitrarily close to 1. This statement is also written as

$$\lim_{n \to \infty} P(|\hat{\theta}_n - \theta| < \varepsilon) = 1$$

and more briefly we write it as

$$\hat{\theta}_n^p \to \theta \qquad \text{or} \qquad \text{plim}\,\hat{\theta}_n = \theta$$

(plim is "probability limit"). $\hat{\theta}_n$ is said to *converge in probability* to θ. In practice we drop the subscript n on $\hat{\theta}_n$ and also drop the words "sequence of estimators" and merely say that $\hat{\theta}$ is a consistent estimator for θ.

A sufficient condition for $\hat{\theta}$ to be consistent is that the bias and variance should both tend to zero as the sample size increases. This condition is often useful to check in practice, but it should be noted that the condition is not necessary. An estimator can be consistent even if the bias does not tend to zero.

There are also some relations in probability limits that are useful in proving consistency. These are

1. $\text{plim}\,(c_1 y_1 + c_2 y_2) = c_1 \text{plim}\, y_1 + c_2 \text{plim}\, y_2$, where c_1 and c_2 are constants.
2. $\text{plim}\,(y_1 y_2) = (\text{plim}\, y_1)(\text{plim}\, y_2)$.
3. $\text{plim}\,(y_1/y_2) = (\text{plim}\, y_1)/(\text{plim}\, y_2)$ provided that $\text{plim}\, y_2 \neq 0$.
4. If $\text{plim}\, y = c$ and $g(y)$ is a continuous function of y, then $\text{plim}\, g(y) = g(c)$.

2.7 SAMPLING DISTRIBUTIONS FOR SAMPLES FROM A NORMAL POPULATION

The most commonly used sampling distributions are those for samples from normal populations. We state the results here (without proof). Suppose that we have a sample of n independent observations, namely $y_1, y_2, \ldots, y_n$, from a normal population with mean μ and variance σ^2. Consider the following:

$$\bar{y} = \frac{1}{n} \sum y_i \qquad \text{sample mean}$$

$$\text{(2.1)}$$

$$S^2 = \frac{1}{n-1} \sum (y_i - \bar{y})^2 \qquad \text{sample variance}$$

Then

1. The sampling distribution of the sample mean $\bar{y}$ is also normal with mean μ and variance σ^2/n.
2. $(n-1)S^2/\sigma^2$ has a χ^2-distribution with degrees of freedom $(n-1)$. Further, the distributions of $\bar{y}$ and S^2 are independent.
3. Since

$$\frac{\sqrt{n}(\bar{y} - \mu)}{\sigma} \sim N(0, 1) \qquad \text{and} \qquad \frac{(n-1)S^2}{\sigma^2} \sim \chi^2_{n-1}$$

and these distributions are independent, we have (by the definition of the t-distribution as the distribution of a standard normal variable divided by the square root of an independent averaged χ^2 variable) that $\sqrt{n}(\bar{y} - \mu)/S$ has a t-distribution with degrees of freedom $(n-1)$.
4. Also, $E(\bar{y}) = \mu$ and $E(S^2) = \sigma^2$ and thus $\bar{y}$ and S^2 are unbiased estimators for μ and σ^2, respectively.

These sampling distributions will also be used to get interval estimates and for testing hypotheses about μ and σ^2.

2.8 INTERVAL ESTIMATION

In interval estimation we construct two functions $g_1(y_1, y_2, \ldots, y_n)$ and $g_2(y_1, y_2, \ldots, y_n)$ of the sample observations such that

$$\text{Prob}(g_1 < \theta < g_2) = \alpha \text{ a given probability} \qquad \text{(2.2)}$$

α is called the *confidence coefficient* and the interval (g_1, g_2) is called the *confidence interval*. Since θ is a parameter (or a constant that is unknown), the probability statement (2.2) is a statement about g_1 and g_2 and not about θ. What it implies is that if we use the formulas $g_1(y_1, y_2, \ldots, y_n)$ and $g_2(y_1, y_2, \ldots, y_n)$ repeatedly with different samples and in each case construct the confidence intervals using these formulas, then in 100α percent of all the cases (samples) the interval given will include the true value.

As an illustration of how to use the sampling distributions to construct confidence intervals, consider a sample $y_1, y_2, \ldots, y_n$ of n independent observations from a normal population with mean μ and variance σ^2. Then

$$\frac{(n-1)S^2}{\sigma^2} \sim \chi^2_{n-1} \quad \text{and} \quad \frac{\sqrt{n}(\bar{y} - \mu)}{S} \sim t_{n-1}$$

where $\bar{y}$ and S^2 are the sample mean and sample variance defined in (2.1).

If the sample size n is 20, so that the degrees of freedom $= n - 1 = 19$, we can refer to the χ^2 tables with 19 degrees of freedom and say that

$$\text{Prob}\left(\frac{19S^2}{\sigma^2} > 32.852\right) = 0.025 \tag{2.3}$$

or

$$\text{Prob}\left(10.117 < \frac{19S^2}{\sigma^2} < 30.144\right) = 0.90 \tag{2.4}$$

Also, referring to the t-tables with 19 degrees of freedom, we find that

$$\text{Prob}\left[-2.093 < \frac{\sqrt{n}(\bar{y} - \mu)}{S} < 2.093\right] = 0.95 \tag{2.5}$$

From equation (2.4) we get

$$\text{Prob}\left(\frac{19S^2}{30.144} < \sigma^2 < \frac{19S^2}{10.117}\right) = 0.90$$

and if $S^2 = 9.0$ we get the 90% confidence interval for σ^2 as $(5.7, 16.9)$. From equation (2.5) we get

$$\text{Prob}\left(\bar{y} - \frac{2.093S}{\sqrt{n}} < \mu < \bar{y} + \frac{2.093S}{\sqrt{n}}\right) = 0.95$$

If $\bar{y} = 5$ and $S = 3.0$ we get the 95% confidence interval for μ as $(3.6, 6.4)$.

These intervals are called *two-sided* intervals. One can also construct *one-sided* intervals. For instance, equation (2.3) implies that

$$\text{Prob}\left(\sigma^2 < \frac{19S^2}{32.852}\right) = 0.025$$

or

$$\text{Prob}\left(\sigma^2 > \frac{19S^2}{32.852}\right) = 0.975$$

If $S^2 = 9$, we get the 97.5% (right-sided) confidence interval for σ^2 as $(5.205, \infty)$. We can construct similar one-sided confidence interval for μ.

2.9 TESTING OF HYPOTHESES

We list here some essential points regarding hypothesis testing.

1. A statistical hypothesis is a statement about the values of some parameters in the hypothetical population from which the sample is drawn.

2. A hypothesis which says that a parameter has a specified value is called a *point hypothesis*. A hypothesis which says that a parameter lies in a specified interval is called an *interval hypothesis*. For instance, if μ is the population mean, then H: $\mu = 4$ is a point hypothesis. H: $4 \leq \mu \leq 7$ is an interval hypothesis.

3. A hypothesis test is a procedure that answers the question of whether the observed difference between the *sample value* and the *population value* hypothesized is real or due to chance variation. For instance, if the hypothesis says that the population mean $\mu = 6$ and the sample mean $\bar{y} = 8$, then we want to know whether this difference is real or due to chance variation.

4. The hypothesis we are testing is called the *null hypothesis* and is often denoted by H_0.[2] The alternative hypothesis is denoted by H_1. The probability of rejecting H_0 when, in fact, it is true, is called the *significance level*. To test whether the observed difference between the data and what is expected under the null hypothesis H_0 is real or due to chance variation, we use a *test statistic*. A desirable criterion for the test statistic is that its sampling distribution be tractable, preferably with tabulated probabilities. Tables are already available for the normal, t, χ^2, and F distributions, and hence the test statistics chosen are often those that have these distributions.

5. The *observed significance level* or *P-value* is the probability of getting a value of the test statistic that is as extreme or more extreme than the observed value of the test statistic. This probability is computed on the basis that the null hypothesis is correct. For instance, consider a sample of n independent observations from a normal population with mean μ and variance σ^2. We want to test.

$$H_0: \quad \mu = 7 \qquad \text{against} \qquad H_1: \quad \mu \neq 7$$

The test statistic we use is

$$t = \frac{\sqrt{n}(\bar{y} - \mu)}{S}$$

which has a t-distribution with $(n - 1)$ degrees of freedom. Suppose that $n = 25$, $\bar{y} = 10$, $S = 5$. Then under the assumption that H_0 is true, the observed value of t is $t_0 = 3$. Since high positive values of t are evidence against the null hypothesis H_0, the P-value is [since degrees of freedom $(n - 1) = 24$]

$$P = \text{Prob}(t_{24} > 3)$$

This is the observed significance level.

---

[2] This terminology is unfortunate because "null" means "zero, void, insignificant, amounts to nothing, etc." A hypothesis $\mu = 0$ can be called a null hypothesis, but a hypothesis $\mu = 100$ should not be called a "null" hypothesis. However, this is the standard terminology that was introduced in the 1930s by the statisticians Jerzy Neyman and E. S. Pearson.

6. It is common practice to say simply that the result of the test is (statistically) significant or not significant and not report the actual P-values. The meaning of the two terms is as follows:

Statistically significant. Sampling variation is an unlikely explanation of the discrepancy between the null hypothesis and sample values.
Statistically insignificant. Sampling variation is a likely explanation of the discrepancy between the null hypothesis and the sample value.

Also, the terms *significant* and *highly significant* are customarily used to denote "significant at the 0.05 level" and "significant at the 0.01 level" respectively. However, consider two cases where the P-values are 0.055 and 0.045, respectively. Then in the former case one would say that the results are "not significant" and in the latter case one would say that the results are "significant," although the sample evidence is marginally different in both cases. Similarly, two tests with P-values of 0.80 and 0.055 will both be considered "not significant," although there is a tremendous difference in the compatibility of the sample evidence with the null hypothesis in the two cases. That is why many computer programs print out P-values.[3]

7. *Statistical significance* and *practical significance* are not the same thing. A result that is highly significant statistically may be of no practical significance at all. For instance, suppose that we consider a shipment of cans of cashews with expected mean weight of 450 g. If the actual sample mean of weights is 449.5 g, the difference may be practically insignificant but could be highly statistically significant if we have a large enough sample or a small enough sampling variance (note that the test statistic has $\sqrt{n}$ in the numerator and S in the denominator). On the other hand, in the case of precision instruments, a part is expected to be of length 10 cm and a sample had a mean length of 9.9 cm. If n is small and S is large, the difference could not be statistically significant but could be practically very significant. The shipment could simply be useless.

8. It is customary to reject the null hypothesis H_0 when the test statistic is statistically significant at a chosen significance level and not to reject H_0 when the test statistic is not statistically significant at the chosen significance level. There is, however, some controversy on this issue which we discuss later in item 9. In reality, H_0 may be either true or false. Corresponding to the two cases of reality and the two conclusions drawn, we have the following four possibilities:

	Reality	
Result of the Test	H_0 Is True	H_0 Is False
Significant (reject H_0)	Type I error or α error	Correct conclusion
Not significant (do not reject H_0)	Correct conclusion	Type II error or β error

[3] A question of historical interest is: "How did the numbers 0.05 and 0.01 creep into all these textbooks?" The answer is that they were suggested by the famous statistician Sir R. A. Fisher (1890–1962), the "father" of modern statistics, and his prescription has been followed ever since.

There are two possible errors that we can make:

1. Rejecting H_0 when it is true. This is called the type I error or α error.
2. Not rejecting H_0 when it is not true. This is called the type II error or β error.

Thus

$$\alpha = \text{Prob}\,(\text{rejecting } H_0 \mid H_0 \text{ is true})$$

$$\beta = \text{Prob}\,(\text{not rejecting } H_0 \mid H_0 \text{ is not true})$$

α is just the significance level, defined earlier. $(1 - \beta)$ is called the *power* of the test. The power of the test cannot be computed unless the alternative hypothesis H_1 is specified; that is, H_0 is not true means that H_1 is true.

For example, consider the problem of testing the hypothesis.

$$H_0: \quad \mu = 10 \quad \text{against} \quad H_1: \quad \mu = 15$$

for a normal population with mean μ and variance σ^2. The test statistic we use is $t = \sqrt{n}(\bar{x} - \mu)/S$. From the sample data we get the values of $n, \bar{x}$, and S. To calculate α we use $\mu = 10$, and to calculate β we use $\mu = 15$. The two errors are

$$\alpha = \text{Prob}\,(t > t^* \mid \mu = 10)$$

$$\beta = \text{Prob}\,(t < t^* \mid \mu = 15)$$

where t^* is the cutoff point of t that we use to reject or not reject H_0. The distributions of t under H_0 and H_1 are shown in Figure 2.1. In our example α is the *right-hand* tail area from the distribution of t under H_0 and β is the left-hand tail area from the distribution of t under H_1. If the alternative hypothesis H_1 says that $\mu < 0$, then the distribution of t under H_1 would be to the left of the distribution of t under H_0. In this case α would be the left-hand tail area of the distribution of t under H_0 and β would be the right-hand tail area of the distribution of t under H_1.

The usual procedure that is suggested (which is called the Neyman–Pearson approach) is to fix α at a certain level and minimize β, that is, choose the test statistic

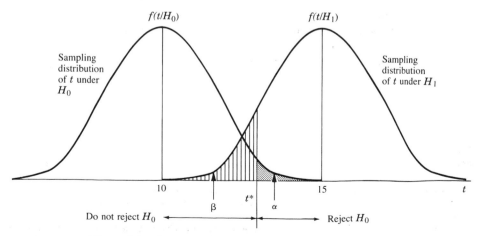

Figure 2.1. Type I and type II errors in testing a hypothesis.

that has the most power. In practice, the tests we use, such as the t, χ^2, and F tests, have been shown to be the most powerful tests.

9. There are some statisticians who disagree with the ideas of the Neyman–Pearson theory. For instance, Kalbfleisch and Sprott[4] argue that it is a gross simplification to regard a test of significance as a decision rule for accepting or rejecting a hypothesis. They argue that such decisions are made on more than just experimental evidence. Thus the purpose of a significance test is just to quantify the strength of evidence in the data against a hypothesis expressed in a (0, 1) scale, not to suggest an accept–reject rule (see item 7). There are some statisticians who think that the significance level used should depend on the sample size.

The problem with a preassigned significance level is that if the sample size is large enough, we can reject every null hypothesis. This is often the experience of those who use large cross-sectional data sets with thousands of observations. Almost every coefficient is significant at the 5% level. Lindley[5] argues that for large samples one should use lower significance levels and for smaller samples higher significance levels. Leamer[6] derives significance levels in the case of regression models for different sample sizes that show how significance levels should be much higher than 5% for small sample sizes and must lower than 5% for large sample sizes.

Very often the purpose of a test is to simplify an estimation procedure. This is the "pretesting" problem, where the test is a prelude to further estimation. In the case of such pretests it has been found that the significance levels to be used should be much higher than the conventional 5% (sometimes 25 to 50% and even 99%). The important thing to note is that tests of significance have several purposes and one should not use a uniform 5% significance level.[7]

2.10 RELATIONSHIP BETWEEN CONFIDENCE INTERVAL PROCEDURES AND TESTS OF HYPOTHESES

There is a close relationship between confidence intervals and tests of hypotheses. Suppose that we want to test a hypothesis at the 5% significance level. Then we can construct a 95% confidence interval for the parameter under consideration and see whether the hypothesized value is in the interval. If it is, we do not reject the hypothesis. If it is not, we reject the hypothesis. This relationship holds good for tests of parameter values. There are other tests, such as goodness-of-fit tests, tests of

---

[4] J. G. Kalbfleisch and D. A. Sprott, "On Tests of Significance," in W. L. Harper and C. A. Hooker (eds.), *Foundations of Probability Theory, Statistical Inference, and Statistical Theory of Science*, Vol. 2 (Boston: D. Reidel, 1976), pp. 259–272.

[5] D. V. Lindley, "A Statistical Paradox," *Biometrika*, 1957, pp. 187–192.

[6] E. E. Leamer, *Specification Searches: Ad Hoc Inference with Non-experimental Data* (New York: Wiley, 1978).

[7] A good discussion of this problem is in the series of papers "For What Use Are Tests of Hypotheses and Tests of Significance" in *Communications in Statistics, A. Theory and Methods*, Vol. 5, No. 8, 1976.

independence in contingency tables, and so on, for which there is no confidence interval counterpart.

As an example, consider a sample of 20 independent observations from a normal distribution with mean μ and variance σ^2. Suppose that the sample mean is $\bar{y} = 5$ and sample variance $S^2 = 9$. We saw from equation (2.4) that the 95% confidence interval was $(3.6, 6.4)$. Suppose that we consider the problem of testing the hypothesis

$$H_0: \quad \mu = 7 \quad \text{against} \quad H_1: \quad \mu \neq 7$$

If we use a 5% level of significance we should reject H_0 if

$$\left| \frac{\sqrt{n}(\bar{y} - 7)}{S} \right| > 2.093$$

since 2.093 is the point from the t-tables for 19 degrees of freedom such that $\text{Prob}(-2.093 < t < 2.093) = 0.95$ or $\text{Prob}(|t| > 2.093) = 0.05$. In our example $\sqrt{n}(\bar{y} - 7)/S = -3$ and hence we reject H_0. Actually, we would be rejecting H_0 at the 5% significance level whenever H_0 specifies μ to be a value outside the interval $(3.6, 6.4)$.

For a one-tailed test we have to consider the corresponding one-sided confidence interval. If $H_0: \quad \mu = 7$ and $H_1: \quad \mu < 7$, then we reject H_0 for low values of $t = \sqrt{n}(\bar{y} - 7)/S$. From the t-tables with 19 degrees of freedom, we find that $\text{Prob}(t < -1.73) = 0.05$. Hence we reject H_0 if the observed $t < -1.73$. In our example it is -3 and hence we reject H_0. The corresponding 95% one-sided confidence interval is given by

$$\text{Prob}\left[-1.73 < \frac{\sqrt{n}(\bar{y} - \mu)}{S} \right] = 0.95$$

which gives (on substituting $n = 20$, $\bar{y} = 5$, $S = 3$) the confidence interval $(-\infty, 6.15)$.

SUMMARY

1. If two random variables are uncorrelated, this does not necessarily imply that they are independent. A simple example is given in Section 2.3.

2. The normal distribution and the related distributions: t, χ^2, and F form the basis of all statistical inference in the book. Although many economic data do not necessarily satisfy the assumption of normality, we can make some transformations that would produce approximate normality. For instance, we consider log wages rather than wages.

3. The advantage of the normal distribution is that any linear function of normally distributed variables is normally distributed. For the χ^2-distribution a weaker property holds. The sum of independent χ^2 variables has a χ^2-distribution. These properties are very useful in deriving probability distributions of sample statistics. The t, χ^2, and F distributions are explained in Section 2.4.

4. A function of the sample observations is called a statistic (e.g., sample mean,

sample variance). The probability distribution of a statistic is called the sampling distribution of the statistic.

5. Classical statistical inference is based entirely on sampling distributions. By contrast, Bayesian inference makes use of sample information and prior information. We do not discuss Bayesian inference in this book, but the basic idea is explained in Section 2.5. Based on the prior distribution (which incorporates prior information) and the sample observations, we obtain what is known as the posterior distribution and all our inferences are based on this posterior distribution.

6. Classical statistical inference is usually discussed under three headings: point estimation, interval estimation, and testing of hypotheses. Three desirable properties of point estimators—unbiasedness, efficiency, and consistency—are discussed in Section 2.6.

7. There are three commonly used methods of deriving point estimators:
(a) The method of moments.
(b) The method of least squares.
(c) The method of maximum likelihood.
These are discussed in Chapter 3.

8. Section 2.8 presents an introduction to interval estimation and Section 2.9 gives an introduction to hypothesis testing. The interrelationship between the two is explained in Section 2.10.

9. The main elements of hypothesis testing are discussed in detail in Section 2.9. Most important, arguments are presented as to why it is not desirable to use the usual 5% significance level in all problems.

3

Simple Regression

3.1 INTRODUCTION

Regression analysis is one of the most commonly used tools in econometric work. We will, therefore, start our discussion with an outline of regression analysis. The subsequent chapters will deal with some modifications and extensions of this basic technique that need to be made when analyzing economic data.

We start with a basic question: What is regression analysis? Regression analysis is concerned with describing and evaluating the relationship between a given variable (often called the *explained* or *dependent* variable) and one or more other variables (often called the *explanatory* or *independent* variables). We will denote the explained variable by y and the explanatory variables by $x_1, x_2, \ldots, x_k$.

The dictionary definition of "regression" is "backward movement, a retreat, a return to an earlier stage of development." Paradoxical as it may sound, regression analysis as it is currently used has nothing to do with regression as dictionaries define the term.

The term *regression* was coined by Sir Francis Galton (1822–1911) from England, who was studying the relationship between the height of children and the height of parents. He observed that although tall parents had tall children and short parents had short children, there was a tendency for children's heights to converge toward the average. There is thus a "regression of children's height toward the average." Galton, in his aristocratic way, termed this a "regression toward mediocrity."

Something similar to what Galton found has been noted in some other studies as well (studies of test scores, etc.). These examples are discussed in Section 3.12 under the heading "regression fallacy." For the present we should note that regression analysis as currently used has nothing to do with regression or backward movement.

Let us return to our notation of the explained variable to be denoted by y and explanatory variables denoted by $x_1, x_2, \ldots, x_k$. If $k = 1$, that is, there is only one of the x-variables, we have what is known as *simple regression*. This is what we discuss in this chapter. If $k > 1$, that is, there are more than one x variables, we have what is known as *multiple regression*. This is discussed in Chapter 4. First we give some examples.

Example 1: Simple Regression

$$y = \text{sales}$$

$$x = \text{advertising expenditures}$$

Here we try to determine the relationship between sales and advertising expenditures.

Example 2: Multiple Regression

$$y = \text{consumption expenditures of a family}$$

$$x_1 = \text{family income}$$

$$x_2 = \text{financial assets of the family}$$

$$x_3 = \text{family size}$$

Here we try to determine the relationship between consumption expenditures on the one hand and family income, financial assets of the family, and family size on the other.

There are several objectives in studying these relationships. They can be used to:

1. Analyze the effects of policies that involve changing the individual x's. In Example 1 this involves analyzing the effect of changing advertising expenditures on sales.

Table 3.1 Classification of Variables in Regression Analysis

y	$x_1, x_2, \ldots, x_k$
(a) Predictand	Predictors
(b) Regressand	Regressors
(c) Explained variable	Explanatory variables
(d) Dependent variable	Independent variables
(e) Effect variable	Causal variables
(f) Endogenous variable	Exogenous variables
(g) Target variable	Control variables

2. Forecast the value of y for a given set of x's.

3. Examine whether any of the x's have a significant effect on y.

In Example 2 we would want to know whether family size has a significant effect on consumption expenditures of the family. The exact meaning of the word "significant" is discussed in Section 3.5.

The way we have set up the problem until now, the variable y and the x'variables are not on the same footing. Implicitly we have assumed that the x's are variables that influence y or are variables that we can control or change and y is the effect variable. There are several alternative terms used in the literature for y and $x_1, x_2, \ldots, x_k$. These are shown in Table 3.1.

Each of these terms is relevant for a particular view of the use of regression analysis. Terminology (a) is used if the purpose is prediction. For instance, sales is the predictand and advertising expenditures is the predictor. The terminology in (b), (c), and (d) is used by different people in their discussion of regression models. They are all equivalent terms. Terminology (e) is used in studies of causation. Terminology (f) is specific to econometrics. We use this terminology in Chapter 9. Finally, terminology (g) is used in control problems. For instance, our objective might be to achieve a certain level of sales (target variable) and we would like to determine the level of advertising expenditures (control variable) to achieve our objective.

In this and subsequent chapters we use the terminology in (c) and (d). Also, we consider here the case of one explained (dependent) variable and one explanatory (independent) variable. This, as we said earlier, is called simple regression. Further, as we said earlier, the variables y and x are not treated on the same footing. A detailed discussion of this issue is postponed to Chapter 11.

3.2 SPECIFICATION OF THE RELATIONSHIPS

As mentioned in Section 3.1, we will discuss the case of one explained (dependent) variable, which we denote by y, and one explanatory (independent) variable σ, which we denote by x. The relationship between y and x is denoted by

$$y = f(x) \tag{3.1}$$

where $f(x)$ is a function of x.

At this point we need to distinguish between two types of relationships:

1. A *deterministic* or mathematical relationship.
2. A *statistical* relationship which does not give unique values of y for given values of x but can be described exactly in probabilistic terms.

What we are going to talk about in regression analysis here is relationships of type 2, not of type 1. As an example, suppose that the relationship between sales y and advertising expenditures x is

$$y = 2500 + 100x - x^2$$

This is a deterministic relationship. The sales for different levels of advertising expenditures can be determined exactly. These are as follows:

x	y
0	2500
20	4100
50	5000
100	2500

On the other hand, suppose that the relationship between sales y and advertising expenditures x is

$$y = 2500 + 100x - x^2 + u$$

where $u = +500$ with probability $\frac{1}{2}$
$ = -500$ with probability $\frac{1}{2}$

Then the values of y for different values of x cannot be determined exactly but can be described probabilistically. For example, if advertising expenditures are 50, sales will be 5500 with probability $\frac{1}{2}$ and 4500 with probability $\frac{1}{2}$.

The values of y for different values of x are now as follows:

x	y
0	2000 or 3000
20	3600 or 4600
50	4500 or 5500
100	2000 or 3000

The data on y that we observe can be any one of the 8 possible cases. For instance, we can have

x	y
0	2000
20	4600
50	5500
100	2000

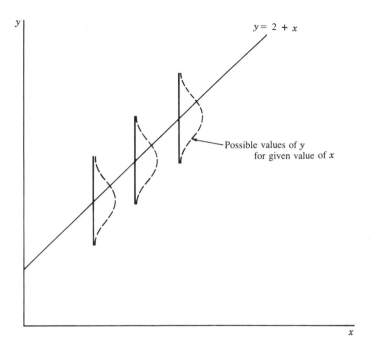

Figure 3.1. A stochastic relationship.

If the error term u has a continuous distribution, say a normal distribution with mean 0 and variance 1, then for each value of x we have a normal distribution for y and the value of y we observe can be any observation from this distribution. For instance, if the relationship between y and x is

$$y = 2 + x + u$$

where the error term u is $N(0, 1)$, then for each value of x, y will have a normal distribution. This is shown in Figure 3.1. The line we have drawn is the deterministic relationship $y = 2 + x$. The actual values of y for each x will be some points on the vertical lines shown. The relationship between y and x in such cases is called a *stochastic* or statistical relationship.

Going back to equation (3.1), we will assume that the function $f(x)$ is linear in x, that is,

$$f(x) = \alpha + \beta x$$

and we will assume that this relationship is a stochastic relationship, that is,

$$y = \alpha + \beta x + u \tag{3.2}$$

where u, which is called an *error* or *disturbance*, has a known probability distribution (i.e., is a random variable).

In equation (3.2), $\alpha + \beta x$ is the deterministic component of y and u is the stochastic or random component. α and β are called *regression coefficients* or *regression parameters* that we estimate from the data on y and x.

There is no reason why the deterministic and stochastic components must be additive. But we will start our discussion with a simple model and introduce complications later. For this reason we have taken $f(x)$ to be a linear function and have assumed an additive error. Some simple alternative functional forms are discussed in Section 3.8.

Why should we add an error term u? What are the sources of the error term u in equation (3.2)? There are three main sources:

1. *Unpredictable element of randomness in human responses.* For instance, if $y =$ consumption expenditure of a household and $x =$ disposable income of the household, there is an unpredictable elements of randomness in each household's consumption. The household does not behave like a machine. In one month the people in the household are on a spending spree. In another month they are tightfisted.
2. *Effect of a large number of omitted variables.* Again in our example x is not the only variable influencing y. The family size, tastes of the family, spending habits, and so on, affect the variable y. The error u is a *catchall* for the effects of all these variables, some of which may not even be quantifiable, and some of which may not even be identifiable. To a certain extent some of these variables are those that we refer to in source 1.
3. *Measurement error in y.* In our example this refers to measurement error in the household consumption. That is, we cannot measure it accurately. This argument for u is somewhat difficult to justify, particularly if we say that there is no measurement error in x (household disposable income). The case where both y and x are measured with error is discussed in Chapter 11. Since we have to go step by step and not introduce all the complications initially, we will accept this argument; that is, there is a measurement error in y but not in x.

In summary, the sources of the error term u are:

1. Unpredictable element of randomness in human response.
2. Effect of a large number of variables that have been omitted.
3. Measurement error in y.

If we have n observations on y and x, we can write equation (3.2) as.

$$y_i = \alpha + \beta x_i + u_i \qquad i = 1, 2, \ldots, n \tag{3.3}$$

Our objective is to get estimates of the unknown parameters α and β in equation (3.3) given the n observations on y and x. To do this we have to make some assumptions about the error terms u_i. The assumptions we make are:

1. *Zero mean.* $E(u_i) = 0$ for all i.
2. *Common variance.* $\text{var}(u_i) = \sigma^2$ for all i.
3. *Independence.* u_i and u_j are independent for all $i \neq j$.
4. *Independence of x_j.* u_i and x_j are independent for all i and j. This assumption automatically follows if x_j are considered nonrandom variables. With

reference to Figure 3.1, what this says is that the distribution of u does not depend on the value of x.

5. *Normality.* u_i are normally distributed for all i. In conjunction with assumption 1, 2, and 3 this implies that u_i are independently and normally distributed with mean zero and a common variance σ^2. We write this as $u_i \sim \text{IN}(0, \sigma^2)$.

These are the assumptions with which we start. We will, however, relax some of these assumptions in later chapters.

Assumption 2 is relaxed in Chapter 5.
Assumption 3 is relaxed in Chapter 6.
Assumption 4 is relaxed in Chapter 9.

As for the normality assumption, we retain it because we will make inferences on the basis of the normal distribution and the t and F distributions. The first assumption is also retained throughout.

Since $E(u_i) = 0$ we can write (3.3) as

$$E(y_i) = \alpha + \beta x_i \qquad (3.4)$$

This is also often termed the *population regression function.* When we substitute estimates of the parameters α and β in this, we get the *sample regression function.*

We will discuss three methods for estimating the parameters α and β.

1. The method of moments.
2. The method of least squares.
3. The method of maximum likelihood.

The first two methods are discussed in the next two sections. The last method is discussed in the appendix to this chapter. In the case of the simple regression model we are considering, all three methods give identical estimates. When it comes to generalizations, the methods give different estimates.

3.3 THE METHOD OF MOMENTS

The assumptions we have made about the error term u imply that

$$E(u) = 0 \quad \text{and} \quad \text{cov}(x, u) = 0$$

In the method of moments, we replace these conditions by their sample counterparts.

Let $\hat{\alpha}$ and $\hat{\beta}$ be the estimators for α and β, respectively. The sample counterpart of u_i is the estimated error $\hat{u}_i$ (which is also called the *residual*), defined as

$$\hat{u}_i = y_i - \hat{\alpha} - \hat{\beta} x_i$$

The two equations to determine $\hat{\alpha}$ and $\hat{\beta}$ are obtained by replacing population assumptions by their sample counterparts.

Population Assumption	Sample Counterpart
$E(u) = 0$	$\frac{1}{n}\sum \hat{u}_i = 0 \quad \text{or} \quad \sum \hat{u}_i = 0$
$\text{cov}(x, u) = 0$	$\frac{1}{n}\sum x_i\hat{u}_i = 0 \quad \text{or} \quad \sum x_i\hat{u}_i = 0$

In these and the following equations, $\sum$ denotes $\sum_{i=1}^{n}$. Thus we get the two equations

$$\sum \hat{u}_i = 0 \quad \text{or} \quad \sum(y_i - \hat{\alpha} - \hat{\beta}x_i) = 0$$
$$\sum x_i\hat{u}_i = 0 \quad \text{or} \quad \sum x_i(y_i - \hat{\alpha} - \hat{\beta}x_i) = 0$$

These equations can be written as

$$\sum y_i = n\hat{\alpha} + \hat{\beta}\sum x_i$$
$$\sum x_iy_i = \hat{\alpha}\sum x_i + \hat{\beta}\sum x_i^2$$

Solving these two equations, we get $\hat{\alpha}$ and $\hat{\beta}$. These equations are also called "normal equations." In Section 3.4, we will show further simplifications of the equations as well as methods of making statistical inferences. First, we consider an illustrative example.

Illustrative Example

Consider the data on advertising expenditures (x) and sales revenue (y) for an athletic sportswear store for 5 months. The observations are as follows:

Month	Sales Revenue, y (thousands of dollars)	Advertising Expenditure, x (hundreds of dollars)
1	3	1
2	4	2
3	2	3
4	6	4
5	8	5

To get $\hat{\alpha}$ and $\hat{\beta}$, we need to compute $\sum x, \sum x^2, \sum xy$, and $\sum y$. We have

Observation	x	y	x^2	xy	$\hat{u}_i$
1	1	3	1	3	0.8
2	2	4	4	8	0.6
3	3	2	9	6	−2.6
4	4	6	16	24	0.2
5	5	8	25	40	1.0
Total	15	23	55	81	0

The normal equations are (since $n = 5$)

$$5\hat{\alpha} + 15\hat{\beta} = 23$$
$$15\hat{\alpha} + 55\hat{\beta} = 81$$

These give $\hat{\alpha} = 1.0$, $\hat{\beta} = 1.2$. Thus the sample regression equation is

$$y = 1.0 + 1.2x$$

The sample observations and the estimated regression line are shown in Figure 3.2.

The intercept 1.0 gives the value of y when $x = 0$. This says that if advertising expenditures are zero, sales revenue will be $1000. The slope coefficient is 1.2. This says that if x is changed by an amount Δx, the change in y is $\Delta y = 1.2\Delta x$. For example, if advertising expenditures are increased by 1 unit ($100), sales revenue increases by 1.2 units ($1200) *on the average*. Clearly, there is no certainty in this prediction. The estimates 1.0 and 1.2 have some uncertainty attached. We discuss this in Section 3.5, on statistical inference in the linear regression model. For the present, what we have shown is how to obtain estimates of the parameters α and β. One other thing to note is that it is not appropriate to obtain predictions too far from the range of observations. Otherwise, the owner of the store might conclude that by raising the advertising expenditures by $100,000, she can increase sales revenue by $1,200,000.

We have also shown the estimated errors or the residuals, which are given by

$$\hat{u}_i = y_i - 1.0 - 1.2x_i$$

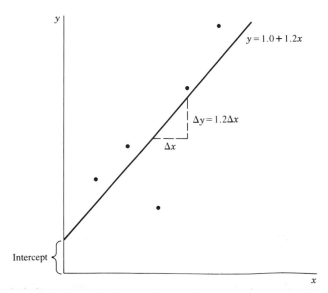

Figure 3.2. Sample observations and estimated regression line.

These are the errors we would make if we tried to predict the value of y on the basis of the estimated regression equation and the values of x. Note that we are not trying to predict any future values of y. We are considering only *within sample prediction errors*. We cannot get $\hat{u}_i$ for $x_i = 0$ or $x_i = 6$ because we do not have the corresponding values of y_i. Out of sample prediction is considered in Section 3.6.

Note that $\sum \hat{u}_i = 0$ by virtue of the first condition we imposed. The sum of squares of the residuals is

$$\sum \hat{u}_i^2 = (0.8)^2 + (0.6)^2 + (-2.6)^2 + (0.2)^2 + (1.0)^2 = 8.8$$

The method of least squares described in the next section is based on the principle of choosing $\hat{\alpha}$ and $\hat{\beta}$ so that $\sum \hat{u}_i^2$ is minimum. That is, the sum of squares of prediction errors is the minimum. With this method we get the same estimates of α and β as we have obtained here because we get the same normal equations.

3.4 METHOD OF LEAST SQUARES

The method of least squares is the automobile of modern statistical analysis; despite its limitations, occasional accidents, and incidental pollution, it and its numerous variations, extensions and related conveyances carry the bulk of statistical analysis, and are known and valued by all.

Stephen M. Stigler [1]

The method of least squares requires that we should choose $\hat{\alpha}$ and $\hat{\beta}$ as estimates of α and β, respectively, so that

$$Q = \sum_{i=1}^{n} (y_i - \hat{\alpha} - \hat{\beta}x_i)^2 \tag{3.5}$$

is a minimum. Q is also the sum of squares of the (within-sample) prediction errors when we predict y_i given x_i and the estimated regression equation. We will show in the appendix to this chapter that the least squares estimators have desirable optimal properties. This property is often abbreviated as BLUE (best least unbiased estimators). We are relegating the proof to the appendix so that readers not interested in proofs can proceed.

The intuitive idea behind the least squares procedure can be described figuratively with reference to Figure 3.2, which gives a graph of the points (x_i, y_i). We pass the regression line through the points in such a way that it is "as close as possible" to the points. The question is what is meant by "close." The procedure of minimizing Q in (3.5) implies that we minimize the sum of squares of vertical distances of the points from the line. Some alternative methods of measuring closeness are illustrated in Figure 3.4.

With the readily available computer programs, readers interested in just obtaining results need not even know how all the estimators are derived. However, it

[1] S. M. Stigler, "Gauss and the Invention of Least Squares," *The Annals of Statistics*, Vol. 9, No. 3, 1981, pp. 465–474.

is advisable to know a little bit about the derivation of the least squares estimators. Readers not interested in the algebraic detail can go to the illustrative examples.

To minimize Q in equation (3.5) with respect to $\hat{\alpha}$ and $\hat{\beta}$, we equate its first derivatives with respect to $\hat{\alpha}$ and $\hat{\beta}$ to zero. This procedure yields (in the following equations, $\sum$ denotes $\sum_{i=1}^{n}$)

$$\frac{\partial Q}{\partial \alpha} = 0 \Rightarrow \sum 2(y_i - \hat{\alpha} - \hat{\beta}x_i)(-1) = 0$$

or

$$\sum y_i = n\hat{\alpha} + \hat{\beta}\sum x_i$$

or

$$\bar{y} = \hat{\alpha} + \hat{\beta}\bar{x} \tag{3.6}$$

and

$$\frac{\partial Q}{\partial \hat{\beta}} = 0 \Rightarrow 2(y_i - \hat{\alpha} - \hat{\beta}x_i)(-x_i) = 0$$

or

$$\sum y_i x_i = \hat{\alpha}\sum x_i + \hat{\beta}\sum x_i^2 \tag{3.7}$$

Equations (3.6) and (3.7) are called the *normal equations*. Substituting the value of $\hat{\alpha}$ from (3.6) into (3.7), we get

$$\sum y_i x_i = \sum x_i(\bar{y} - \hat{\beta}\bar{x}) + \hat{\beta}\sum x_i^2$$
$$= n\bar{x}(\bar{y} - \hat{\beta}\bar{x}) + \hat{\beta}\sum x_i^2 \tag{3.8}$$

Let us define

$$S_{yy} = \sum(y_i - \bar{y})^2 = \sum y_i^2 - n\bar{y}^2$$
$$S_{xy} = \sum(x_i - \bar{x})(y_i - \bar{y}) = \sum x_i y_i - n\bar{x}\bar{y}$$

and

$$S_{xx} = \sum(x_i - \bar{x})^2 = \sum x_i^2 - n\bar{x}^2$$

Then (3.8) can be written as

$$\hat{\beta}S_{xx} = S_{xy} \quad \text{or} \quad \hat{\beta} = \frac{S_{xy}}{S_{xx}} \tag{3.9}$$

Hence the least squares estimators for α and β are

$$\boxed{\hat{\beta} = \frac{S_{xy}}{S_{xx}} \quad \text{and} \quad \hat{\alpha} = \bar{y} - \hat{\beta}\bar{x}} \tag{3.10}$$

The estimated residuals are

$$\hat{u}_i = y_i - \hat{\alpha} - \hat{\beta}x_i$$

The two normal equations show that these residuals satisfy the equations

$$\sum \hat{u}_i = 0 \qquad \text{and} \qquad \sum x_i \hat{u}_i = 0$$

The residual sum of squares (to be denoted by RSS) is given by

$$
\begin{aligned}
\text{RSS} &= \sum (y_i - \hat{\alpha} - \hat{\beta} x_i)^2 \\
&= \sum [y_i - \bar{y} - \hat{\beta}(x_i - \bar{x})]^2 \\
&= \sum (y_i - \bar{y})^2 + \hat{\beta}^2 \sum (x_i - \bar{x})^2 - 2\hat{\beta} \sum (y_i - \bar{y})(x_i - \bar{x}) \\
&= S_{yy} + \hat{\beta}^2 S_{xx} - 2\hat{\beta} S_{xy}
\end{aligned}
$$

But $\hat{\beta} = S_{xy}/S_{xx}$. Hence we have

$$\text{RSS} = S_{yy} - \frac{S_{xy}^2}{S_{xx}} = S_{yy} - \hat{\beta} S_{xy}$$

S_{yy} is usually denoted by TSS (total sum of squares) and $\hat{\beta} S_{xy}$ is usually denoted by ESS (explained sum of squares). Thus

$$
\underset{\text{(total)}}{\text{TSS}} = \underset{\text{(explained)}}{\text{ESS}} + \underset{\text{(residual)}}{\text{RSS}}
$$

Some other authors like to use RSS to denote regression sum of squares and ESS as error sum of squares. The confusing thing here is that both the words "explained" and "error" start with the letter "e" and the words "regression" and "residual" start with the letter "r." However, we prefer to use RSS for residual sum of squares and ESS for explained sum of squares.[2] We will reserve the word *residual* to denote $\hat{u} = y - \hat{\alpha} - \hat{\beta}x$ and the word *error* to denote the disturbance u in equation (3.3). Thus *residual is the estimated error.*

The proportion of the total sum of squares explained is denoted by r_{xy}^2, where r_{xy} is called the *correlation coefficient.* Thus $r_{xy}^2 = \text{ESS}/\text{TSS}$ and $1 - r_{xy}^2 = \text{RSS}/\text{TSS}$. If r_{xy}^2 is high (close to 1), then x is a good "explanatory" variable for y. The term r_{xy}^2 is called the *coefficient of determination* and must fall between zero and 1 for any given regression. If r_{xy}^2 is close to zero, the variable x explains very little of the variation in y. If r_{xy}^2 is close to 1, the variable x explains most of the variation in y.

> The coefficient of determination r_{xy}^2 is given by
>
> $$r_{xy}^2 = \frac{\text{ESS}}{\text{TSS}} = \frac{\text{TSS} - \text{RSS}}{\text{TSS}} = \frac{\hat{\beta} S_{xy}}{S_{yy}}$$

Summary

The estimates for the regression coefficients are

$$\hat{\beta} = \frac{S_{xy}}{S_{xx}} \qquad \text{and} \qquad \hat{\alpha} = \bar{y} - \hat{\beta} \bar{x}$$

---

[2] This is also the notation used in J. Johnston, *Econometric Methods*, 3rd ed. (New York: McGraw-Hill, 1984).

The residual sum of squares is given by

$$\text{RSS} = S_{yy} - \frac{S_{xy}^2}{S_{xx}} = S_{yy} - \hat{\beta}S_{xy} = S_{yy}(1 - r_{xy}^2)$$

and the coefficient of determination is given by

$$r_{xy}^2 = \frac{S_{xy}^2}{S_{xx}S_{yy}} = \frac{\hat{\beta}S_{xy}}{S_{yy}}$$

The least squares estimators $\hat{\beta}$ and $\hat{\alpha}$ yield an estimated straight line that has a smaller RSS than any other straight line.

The Reverse Regression

We have until now considered the regression of y on x. This is called the *direct regression*. Sometimes one has to consider the regression of x on y as well. This is called the *reverse regression*. The reverse regression has been advocated in the analysis of sex (or race) discrimination in salaries. For instance, if

$$y = \text{salary}$$

$$x = \text{qualifications}$$

and we are interested in determining if there is sex discrimination in salaries, we can ask:

1. Whether men and women with the same qualifications (value of x) are getting the same salaries (value of y). This question is answered by the direct regression, regression of y on x. Alternatively, we can ask:
2. Whether men and women with the same salaries (value of y) have the same qualifications (value of x). This question is answered by the reverse regression, regression of x on y.[3]

In this example both the questions make sense and hence we have to look at both these regressions. For the reverse regression the regression equation can be written as

$$x_i = \alpha' + \beta' y_i + v_i$$

where v_i are the errors that satisfy assumptions similar to those stated earlier in Section 3.3 for u_i. Interchanging x and y in the formulas that we derived, we get

$$\hat{\beta}' = \frac{S_{xy}}{S_{yy}} \quad \text{and} \quad \hat{\alpha}' = \bar{x} - \hat{\beta}'\bar{y}$$

Denoting the residual sum of squares in this case by RSS', we have

$$\text{RSS}' = S_{xx} - \frac{S_{xy}^2}{S_{yy}}$$

---

[3] We discuss this problem further in Chapter 11.

Note that

$$\hat{\beta}\hat{\beta}' = \frac{S_{xy}^2}{S_{xx}S_{yy}} = r_{xy}^2$$

Hence if r_{xy}^2 is close to 1, the two regression lines will be close to each other. We now illustrate with an example.

Illustrative Example

Consider the data in Table 3.2. The data are for 10 workers.

$$x = \text{labor-hours of work}$$

$$y = \text{output}$$

We wish to determine the relationship between output and labor-hours of work. We have

$$\bar{x} = \frac{80}{10} = 8$$

$$\bar{y} = \frac{96}{10} = 9.6$$

$$S_{xx} = 668 - 10(8)^2 = 668 - 640 = 28$$

$$S_{xy} = 789 - 10(8)(9.6) = 789 - 768 = 21$$

$$S_{yy} = 952 - 10(9.6)^2 = 952 - 921.6 = 30.4$$

$$r_{xy} = \frac{21}{\sqrt{28(30.4)}} \simeq \frac{21}{29} = 0.724 \qquad \text{or} \qquad r_{xy}^2 = 0.52$$

$$\hat{\beta} = \frac{S_{xy}}{S_{xx}} = \frac{21}{28} = 0.75$$

$$\hat{\alpha} = \bar{y} - \hat{\beta}\bar{x} = 9.6 - 0.75(0.8) = 3.6$$

Table 3.2

Observation	x	y	x^2	y^2	xy
1	10	11	100	121	110
2	7	10	49	100	70
3	10	12	100	144	120
4	5	6	25	36	30
5	8	10	64	100	80
6	8	7	64	49	56
7	6	9	36	81	54
8	7	10	49	100	70
9	9	11	81	121	99
10	10	10	100	100	100
Total	80	96	668	952	789

Hence the regression of y on x is

$$y = 3.6 + 0.75x$$

Since x is labor-hours of work and y is output, the slope coefficient 0.75 measures the marginal productivity of labor. As for the intercept 3.6, it means that output will be 3.6 when labor-hours of work is zero! Clearly, this does not make sense. However, this merely illustrates the point we made earlier—that we should not try to get predicted values of y too far out of the range of sample values. Here x ranges from 5 to 10.

As for the reverse regression, we have

$$\hat{\beta}' = \frac{S_{xy}}{S_{yy}} = \frac{21}{30.4} \simeq 0.69$$

and

$$\hat{\alpha}' = \bar{x} - \hat{\beta}'\bar{y} = 8.0 - 9.6(0.69) = 1.37$$

Hence the regression of x on y is

$$x = 1.37 + 0.69y$$

Note that the product of the two slopes $= \hat{\beta}\hat{\beta}' = 0.75(0.69) = 0.52 = r_{xy}^2$. These two regression lines are presented in Figure 3.3. The procedure used in the two regressions is illustrated in Figure 3.4. If we consider a scatter diagram of the observations, the procedure of minimizing

$$\sum_{i=1}^{n} (y_i - \alpha - \beta x_i)^2$$

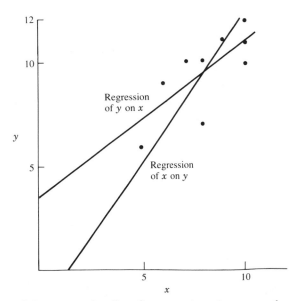

Figure 3.3. Regression lines for regression of y on x and x on y.

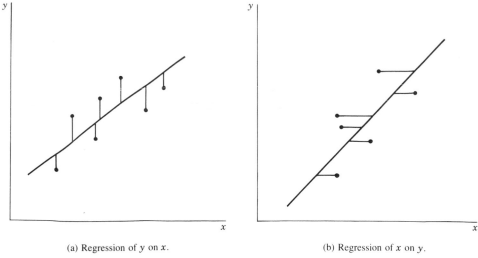

(a) Regression of y on x.   (b) Regression of x on y.

Figure 3.4. Minimization of residual sum of squares in the regression of y on x and x on y.

amounts to passing a line through the observations so as to minimize the sum of squares of the vertical distances of the points in the scatter diagram from the line. This is shown in Figure 3.4(a). The line shows the regression of y on x.

On the other hand, the procedure of minimizing

$$\sum_{i=1}^{n} (x_i - \alpha' - \beta' y_i)^2$$

amounts to passing a line through the observations so as to minimize the sum of squares of the horizontal distances of the points in the scatter diagram from the line. This is shown in Figure 3.4(b). The line shows the regression of x on y.

We can also think of passing a line in such a way that we minimize the sum of squares of the *perpendicular* distances of the points from the line. This is called *orthogonal regression.*

Since a discussion of orthogonal regression is beyond the scope of this book, we will confine our discussion to only the other two regressions: regression of y and x and of x on y. A question arises as to which of these is the appropriate one. Following are some general guidelines on this problem.

1. If the model is such that the direction of causation is known (e.g., if we say that advertising expenditures at time t influence sales at time t but not the other way around), we should estimate the regression using sales as the explained variable and advertising expenditures as the explanatory variable. The opposite regression does not make sense. We should estimate this equation whether our objective is to estimate sales for given advertising expenditures or to estimate advertising expenditures for given sales (i.e., always estimate a regression of an effect variable on a causal variable).
2. In problems where the direction of causation is not as clear cut, and where y

and x have a joint normal distribution, both the regressions y on x and x on y make sense and one should estimate a regression of y on x to predict y given x and a regression of x on y to predict x given y.

3. In models where y and x are both measured with error, we have to estimate both the regressions of y on x and x on y to get "bounds" on β. This problem is discussed in Chapter 11.

4. The case of salary discrimination mentioned earlier is an example where the problem can be posed in two different and equally meaningful ways. In such cases both regressions make sense.

5. Sometimes, which regression makes sense depends on how the data are generated. Consider the data presented in Table 3.2. x is labor-hours of work and y is output, and the observations are for different workers. Which of the two regressions makes sense depends on the way the data were generated. If the workers are given some hours of work (x), and the output they produced (y) was observed, then a regression of y on x is the correct one to look at. In this case x is the controlled variable. On the other hand, if the workers were assigned some amount of output (y) and the hours of work (x) that they took to produce that output was observed, it is a regression of x on y that is meaningful. In this case y is the controlled variable. Here what we are considering is an experiment where one of the variables is controlled or fixed. With experimental data which of the variables should be treated as dependent and which as independent will be clear from the way the experiment was conducted. With most economic data, however, this is not a clear-cut choice.

3.5 STATISTICAL INFERENCE IN THE LINEAR REGRESSION MODEL

In Section 3.4 we discussed procedures for obtaining the least squares estimators. To obtain the least squares estimators of α and β we do not need to assume any particular probability distribution for the errors u_i. But to get interval estimates for the parameters and to test any hypotheses about them, we need to assume that the errors u_i have a normal distribution. As proved in the appendix to this chapter, the least squares estimators are

1. Unbiased.
2. Have minimum variance among the class of all linear unbiased estimators.

The properties hold even if the errors u_i do not have the normal distribution provided that the other assumptions we have made are satisfied. These assumptions, we may recall, are:

1. $E(u_i) = 0$.
2. $V(u_i) = \sigma^2$ for all i.
3. u_i and u_j are independent for $i \neq j$.
4. x_j are nonstochastic.

We will now make the additional assumption that the errors u_i are normally distributed and show how we can get confidence intervals for α and β and test any hypotheses about α and β. We will relegate the proofs of the propositions to the appendix and state the results here.

First, we need the sampling distributions of $\hat{\alpha}$ and $\hat{\beta}$. We can prove that they have a normal distribution (proofs are given in the appendix). Specifically, we have the following results:

$\hat{\alpha}$ and $\hat{\beta}$ are jointly normally distributed with

$$E(\hat{\alpha}) = \alpha \qquad \text{var}(\hat{\alpha}) = \sigma^2 \left(\frac{1}{n} + \frac{\bar{x}^2}{S_{xx}} \right)$$

$$E(\hat{\beta}) = \beta \qquad \text{var}(\hat{\beta}) = \frac{\sigma^2}{S_{xx}}$$

and

$$\text{cov}(\hat{\alpha}, \hat{\beta}) = \sigma^2 \left(\frac{-\bar{x}}{S_{xx}} \right)$$

These results would be useful if the error variance σ^2 were known. Unfortunately, in practice, σ^2 is not known, and has to be estimated.

If RSS is the residual sum of squares, then

$$\hat{\sigma}^2 = \frac{\text{RSS}}{n - 2} \text{ is an unbiased estimator for } \sigma^2$$

Also

$$\frac{\text{RSS}}{\sigma^2} \text{ has a } \chi^2\text{-distribution with degrees of freedom } (n - 2)$$

Further the distribution of RSS is independent of the distributions of $\hat{\alpha}$ and $\hat{\beta}$. (Proofs of these propositions are relegated to the appendix.)

This result can be used to get confidence intervals for σ^2 or to test hypotheses about σ^2. However, we are still left with the problem of making inferences about α and β. For this purpose we use the t-distribution.

We know that if we have two variables $x_1 \sim N(0, 1)$ and $x_2 \sim \chi^2$ with degrees of freedom k and x_1 and x_2 independent, then

$$x = \frac{x_1}{\sqrt{x_2/k}} = \frac{\text{standard normal}}{\sqrt{\text{independent averaged } \chi^2}}$$

has a t-distribution with d.f. k.

In this case $(\hat{\beta} - \beta)/\sqrt{\sigma^2/S_{xx}} \sim N(0, 1)$. (We have subtracted the mean and divided it by the standard deviation.) Also, $\text{RSS}/\sigma^2 \sim \chi^2_{n-2}$ and the two distributions are independent. Hence we compute the ratio

$$\frac{\hat{\beta} - \beta}{\sqrt{\sigma^2/S_{xx}}} \bigg/ \sqrt{\frac{RSS}{(n-2)\sigma^2}}$$

has a t-distribution with d.f. $(n-2)$. Now σ^2 cancels out and writing $RSS/(n-2)$ as $\hat{\sigma}^2$ we get the result that $(\hat{\beta} - \beta)/\sqrt{\hat{\sigma}^2/S_{xx}}$ has a t-distribution with d.f. $(n-2)$. Note that the variance of $\hat{\beta}$ is σ^2/S_{xx}. Since σ^2 is not known, we use an unbiased estimator $RSS/(n-2)$. Thus $\hat{\sigma}^2/S_{xx}$ is the estimated variance of $\hat{\beta}$ and its square root is called the *standard error* denoted by $SE(\hat{\beta})$.

We can follow a similar procedure for $\hat{\alpha}$. We substitute $\hat{\sigma}^2$ for σ^2 in the variance of $\hat{\alpha}$ and take the square root to get the standard error $SE(\hat{\alpha})$.

Thus we have the following result:

$(\hat{\alpha} - \alpha)/SE(\hat{\alpha})$ and $(\hat{\beta} - \beta)/SE(\hat{\beta})$ each have a t-distribution with d.f. $(n-2)$. These distributions can be used to get confidence intervals for α and β and to test hypotheses about α and β.

$\hat{\sigma}$ is usually called the *standard error of the regression*. It is denoted by SER (sometimes by SEE.)

Illustrative Example

As an illustration of the calculation of standard errors, consider the data in Table 3.2. Earlier we obtained the regression equation of y on x as

$$\hat{y} = 3.6 + 0.75x$$

We will now calculate the standard errors of $\hat{\alpha}$ and $\hat{\beta}$. These are obtained by:

1. Computing the variances of $\hat{\alpha}$ and $\hat{\beta}$ in terms of σ^2.
2. Substituting $\hat{\sigma}^2 = RSS/(n-2)$ for σ^2.
3. Taking the square root of the resulting expressions.

We have

$$V(\hat{\alpha}) = \sigma^2 \left(\frac{1}{n} + \frac{\bar{x}^2}{S_{xx}} \right) = \sigma^2 \left(\frac{1}{10} + \frac{64}{28} \right) = 2.39\sigma^2$$

$$V(\hat{\beta}) = \frac{\sigma^2}{S_{xx}} = \frac{\sigma^2}{28} = 0.036\sigma^2$$

$$\hat{\sigma}^2 = \frac{1}{n-2}\left(S_{yy} - \frac{S_{xy}^2}{S_{xx}} \right) = \frac{1}{8}\left[30.4 - \frac{(21)^2}{28} \right] = 1.83$$

$$SE(\hat{\alpha}) = \sqrt{(2.39)(1.83)} = 2.09$$

$$SE(\hat{\beta}) = \sqrt{(0.036)(1.83)} = 0.256$$

The standard errors are usually presented in parentheses under the estimates of the regression coefficients.

Confidence Intervals for α, β, and σ^2

Since $(\hat{\alpha} - \alpha)/\text{SE}(\hat{\alpha})$ and $(\hat{\beta} - \beta)/\text{SE}(\hat{\beta})$ have t-distributions with d.f. $(n - 2)$, using the table of the t-distribution (in the appendix) with $n - 2 = 8$ d.f. we get

$$\text{Prob}\left[-2.306 < \frac{\hat{\alpha} - \alpha}{\text{SE}(\hat{\alpha})} < 2.306 \right] = 0.95$$

and

$$\text{Prob}\left[-2.306 < \frac{\hat{\beta} - \beta}{\text{SE}(\hat{\beta})} < 2.306 \right] = 0.95$$

These give confidence intervals for α and β. Substituting the values of $\hat{\alpha}, \hat{\beta}, \text{SE}(\hat{\alpha})$, and $\text{SE}(\hat{\beta})$ and simplifying we get the 95% confidence limits for α and β as $(-1.22, 8.42)$ for α and $(0.16, 1.34)$ for β. Note that the 95% confidence limits for α are $\hat{\alpha} \pm 2.306$ $\text{SE}(\hat{\alpha})$ and for β are $\hat{\beta} \pm 2.306\text{SE}(\hat{\beta})$. Although it is not often used, we will also illustrate the procedure of finding a confidence interval for σ^2. Since we know that RSS/σ^2 has a χ^2-distribution with d.f. $(n - 2)$, we can use the tables of the χ^2-distribution for getting any required confidence interval. Suppose that we want a 95% confidence interval. Note that we will write $\text{RSS} = (n - 2)\hat{\sigma}^2$.

From the tables of the χ^2-distribution with degrees of freedom 8, we find that the probability of obtaining a value < 2.18 is 0.025 and of obtaining a value > 17.53 is 0.025. Hence

$$\text{Prob}\left(2.18 < \frac{8\hat{\sigma}^2}{\sigma^2} < 17.53 \right) = 0.95$$

or

$$\text{Prob}\left(\frac{8\hat{\sigma}^2}{17.53} < \sigma^2 < \frac{8\hat{\sigma}^2}{2.18} \right) = 0.95$$

Since $\hat{\sigma}^2 = 1.83$, substituting this value, we get the 95% confidence limits for σ^2 as $(0.84, 6.72)$.

Note that the confidence intervals for α and β are symmetric around $\hat{\alpha}$ and $\hat{\beta}$, respectively (because the t-distribution is a symmetric distribution. This is not the case with the confidence interval for σ^2. It is not symmetric around $\hat{\sigma}^2$.

The confidence intervals we have obtained for α, β, and σ^2 are all very wide. We can produce narrower intervals by reducing the confidence coefficient. For instance, the 80% confidence limits for β are

$$\hat{\beta} \pm 1.397\text{SE}(\hat{\beta}) \quad \text{since} \quad \text{Prob}(-1.397 < t < 1.397) = 0.80$$

from the t-tables with 8 d.f.

We therefore get the 80% confidence limits for β as

$$0.75 \pm 1.397(0.256) = (0.39, 1.11)$$

The confidence intervals we have constructed are two-sided intervals. Sometimes we want upper or lower limits for β. In which case we construct one-sided intervals. For instance, from the t-tables with 8 d.f. we have

$$\text{Prob}(t < 1.86) = 0.95$$

and

$$\text{Prob}(t > -1.86) = 0.95$$

Hence for a one-sided confidence interval, the upper limit for β is

$$\hat{\beta} + 1.86\text{SE}(\hat{\beta}) = 0.75 + 1.86(0.256) = 0.75 + 0.48 = 1.23$$

The 95% confidence interval is $(-\infty, 1.23)$. Similarly, the lower limit for β is

$$\hat{\beta} - 1.86\text{SE}(\hat{\beta}) = 0.75 - 0.48 = 0.27$$

Thus the 95% confidence interval is $(0.27, +\infty)$.

We will give further examples of the use of one-sided intervals after we discuss tests of hypotheses.

Testing of Hypotheses

Turning to the problem of testing of hypotheses, suppose we want to test the hypothesis that the true value of β is 1.0. We know that

$$t_0 = \frac{\hat{\beta} - \beta}{\text{SE}(\hat{\beta})} \quad \begin{array}{l} \text{has a } t\text{-distribution with} \\ (n-2) \text{ degrees of freedom} \end{array}$$

Let t_0 be the observed t-value. If the alternative hypothesis is $\beta = 0$ then we consider $|t_0|$ as the test statistic. Hence if the true value of β is 1.0, we have

$$t_0 = \frac{0.75 - 1.0}{0.256} = -0.98 \quad \text{Hence } |t_0| = 0.98$$

Looking at the t-tables for 8 degrees of freedom, we see that

$$\text{Prob}(t > 0.706) = 0.25$$

and

$$\text{Prob}(t > 1.397) = 0.10$$

Thus $\text{Prob}(t > 0.98)$ is roughly 0.19 (by linear interpolation) or $\text{Prob}(|t| > 0.98) \simeq 0.38$. This probability is not very low and we do not reject the hypothesis that $\beta = 1.0$. It is customary to use 0.05 as a low probability and to reject the suggested hypothesis if the probability of obtaining as extreme a t-value as the observed t_0 is less than 0.05. In this case either the suggested hypothesis is not true or it is true but an improbable event has occurred.

Note that for 8 degrees of freedom, the 5% probability points are ± 2.306 for a two-sided test and ± 1.86 for a one-sided test. Thus if *both* high and low t-values are to be considered as evidence against the suggested hypothesis, we reject it if the observed t_0 is > 2.306 or < -2.306. On the other hand, if only very high *or* very low t-values are to be considered as evidence against the suggested hypothesis, we reject it if $t_0 > 1.86$ or $t_0 < -1.86$, depending on the suggested direction of deviation.

Although it is customary to use the 5% probability level for rejection of the suggested hypothesis, there is nothing sacred about this number The theory of significance tests with the commonly used significance levels of 0.05 and 0.01 owes its origins to the famous British statistician Sir R. A. Fisher (1890–1962). He is considered the father of modern statistical methods and the numbers 0.05 and 0.01 suggested by him have been adopted universally.

Another point to note is that the hypothesis being tested (in this case $\beta = 1$) is called the *null hypothesis*. Again the terminology is misleading and owes the origin to the fact that the initial hypotheses tested were that some parameters were zero. Thus a hypothesis $\beta = 0$ can be called a null hypothesis but not a hypothesis $\beta = 1$. In any case for the present we will stick to the standard terminology and call the hypothesis tested the null hypothesis and use the standard significance levels of 0.05 and 0.01.

Finally, it should be noted that there is a correspondence between the confidence intervals derived earlier and tests of hypotheses. For instance, the 95% confidence interval we derived earlier for β is $(0.16 < \beta < 1.34)$. Any hypothesis that says $\beta = \beta_0$, where β_0 is in this interval, will not be rejected at the 5% level for a two-sided test. For instance, the hypothesis $\beta = 1.27$ will not be rejected, but the hypothesis $\beta = 1.35$ or $\beta = 0.10$ will be. For one-sided tests we consider one-sided confidence intervals.

It is also customary to term some regression coefficients as "significant" or "not significant" depending on the t-ratios, and attach asterisks to them if they are significant. This procedure should be avoided. For instance, in our illustrative example the regression equation is sometimes presented as

$$y = 3.6 + 0.75*x$$
$$\quad (2.09) \quad (0.256)$$

The $*$ on the slope coefficient indicates that it is "significant" at the 5% level. However, this statement means that "it is significantly different from "zero" and this statement is meaningful only if the hypothesis being tested is $\beta = 0$. Such a hypothesis would not be meaningful in many cases. For instance, in our example, if y is output and x is labor-hours of work, a hypothesis $\beta = 0$ does not make any sense. Similarly, if y is a posttraining score and x is a pretraining score, a hypothesis $\beta = 0$ would imply that the pretraining score has no effect on the posttraining score and no one would be interested in testing such an extreme hypothesis.

Example of Comparing Test Scores from the GRE and GMAT Tests[4]

In the College of Business Administration at the University of Florida, two different tests are used to measure aptitude for graduate work. The economics department relies on GRE scores and the other graduate departments rely on GMAT scores. To allocate graduate assistantships and fellowships, it is important to be able to compare the scores of these two tests. A rough rule of thumb that was suggested was the following.

GRE score = 2(GMAT score) + 100

A question arose as to the adequacy of this rule.

[4] I would like to thank my colleague Larry Kenny for this example and the computations.

To answer this question data were obtained on 262 current and recent University of Florida students who had taken both tests. The GRE and GMAT scores were highly correlated. The correlation coefficients were 0.71 for U.S. students and 0.80 for foreign students.

If we have GRE scores on some students and GMAT scores on some others, we can convert all scores to GRE scores, in which case we use the regression of GRE score on GMAT score. Alternatively, we can convert all scores to GMAT scores, in which case we use the regression of GMAT score on GRE score. These two regressions were as follows (figures in parentheses are standard errors):

Students	Numbers	Regression	R^2
		Regression of GRE on GMAT	
All	255	$\widehat{GRE} = 333 + 1.470GMAT$ (0.087)	.53
U.S.	211	$\widehat{GRE} = 336 + 1.458GMAT$ (0.101)	.50
Foreign	44	$\widehat{GRE} = 284 + 1.606GMAT$ (0.183)	.64
		Regression of GMAT on GRE	
All	255	$\widehat{GMAT} = 125 + 0.363GRE$ (0.021)	.53
U.S.	211	$\widehat{GMAT} = 151 + 0.345GRE$ (0.024)	.50
Foreign	44	$\widehat{GMAT} = 60 + 0.400GRE$ (0.046)	.64

Although we can get predictions for the U.S. students and foreign students separately, and for the GRE given GMAT and GMAT given GRE, we shall present only one set of predictions and compare this with the present rule. The predictions, from the regression of GRE on GMAT (for all students) are as follows:

GMAT	$\widehat{GRE}$	Current Rule[a]
400	921	900
450	995	1000
500	1068	1100
550	1142	1200
600	1215	1300
650	1289	1400
700	1362	1500

[a] GRE = 2(GMAT) + 100.

Thus, except for scores at the low end (which are not particularly relevant because students with low scores are not admitted), the current rule overpredicts the GRE based on the GMAT score. Thus the current conversion biases decisions in favor of those students taking the GMAT test as compared to those taking the GRE test. Since the students entering the economics department take the GRE test, the current rule results in decisions unfavorable to the economics department.

3.6 ANALYSIS OF VARIANCE FOR THE SIMPLE REGRESSION MODEL

Yet another item that is often presented in connection with the simple linear regression model is the *analysis of variance*. This is the breakdown of the total sum of squares TSS into the explained sum of squares ESS and the residual sum of squares RSS. The purpose of presenting the table is to test the significance of the explained sum of squares. In this case this amounts to testing the significance of β. Table 3.3 presents the breakdown of the total sum of squares.

Under the assumptions of the model, RSS/σ^2 has a χ^2-distribution with $(n - 2)$ degrees of freedom. ESS/σ^2, on the other hand has a χ^2-distribution with 1 degree of freedom *only if* the true β is equal to zero. Further, these two χ^2 distributions are independent. (All these results are proved in the appendix to this chapter.)

Thus under the assumption that $\beta = 0$, we have the F-statistic (σ^2 cancels) $F = (ESS/1)/RSS/(n - 2)$, which has an F-distribution with degrees of freedom 1 and $(n - 2)$. This F-statistic can be used to test the hypothesis that $\beta = 0$.

For the data in Table 3.2 we are considering, the analysis of variance is presented in Table 3.4. The F-statistic is $F = 15.75/1.83 = 8.6$.

Note that the t-statistic for testing the significance of β is $\hat{\beta}/SE(\hat{\beta}) = 0.75/0.256 = 2.93$ and the F-statistic obtained from the analysis of variance Table 3.4 is the square of the t-statistic. Thus in the case of a simple linear regression model, the

Table 3.3 Analysis of Variance for the Simple Regression Model

Source of Variation	Sum of Squares	Degrees of Freedom	Mean Square
x	$ESS = \hat{\beta}S_{xy}$	1	$ESS/1$
Residual	$RSS = S_{yy} - \hat{\beta}S_{xy}$	$n - 2$	$RSS/(n - 2)$
Total	$TSS = S_{yy}$	$n - 1$	

Table 3.4 Analysis of Variance for the Data in Table 3.2

Source of Variation	Sum of Squares	Degrees of Freedom	Mean Square
x	15.75	1	15.75
Residual	14.65	8	1.83
Total	30.4	9	

analysis-of-variance table does not give any more information. We will see in Chapter 4 that in the case of multiple regression this is not the case. What the analysis-of-variance table provides there is a test of significance for all the regression parameters together. Note that

$$\text{ESS} = \hat{\beta}S_{xy} = r^2 S_{yy}$$

and

$$\text{RSS} = S_{yy} - \hat{\beta}S_{xy} = (1 - r^2)S_{yy}$$

Hence the F-statistic can also be written as

$$F = \frac{r^2}{(1 - r^2)/(n - 2)} = \frac{(n - 2)r^2}{1 - r^2}$$

Since $F = t^2$ we get

$$r^2 = \frac{t^2}{t^2 + (n - 2)}$$

We can check in our illustrative example that $t^2 = 8.6$ and $(n - 2) = 8$. Hence

$$r^2 = \frac{8.6}{8.6 + 8} = \frac{8.6}{16.6} = 0.52$$

as we obtained earlier. The formula

$$r^2 = \frac{t^2}{t^2 + (n - 2)}$$

gives the relationship between the t-ratio for testing the hypothesis $\beta = 0$ and the r^2. We will derive a similar formula in Chapter 4.

3.7 PREDICTION WITH THE SIMPLE REGRESSION MODEL

The estimated regression equation $\hat{y} = \hat{\alpha} + \hat{\beta}x$ is used for predicting the value of y for given values of x and the estimated equation $\hat{x} = \hat{\alpha}' + \hat{\beta}'y$ is used for predicting the values of x for given values of y. We will illustrate the procedures with reference to the prediction of y given x.

Let x_0 be the given value of x. Then we predict the corresponding value y_0 of y by

$$\hat{y}_0 = \hat{\alpha} + \hat{\beta}x_0 \tag{3.11}$$

The true value y_0 is given by

$$y_0 = \alpha + \beta x_0 + u_0$$

where u_0 is the error term.

Hence the prediction error is

$$\hat{y}_0 - y_0 = (\hat{\alpha} - \alpha) + (\hat{\beta} - \beta)x_0 - u_0$$

Since $E(\hat{\alpha} - \alpha) = 0$, $E(\hat{\beta} - \beta) = 0$, and $E(u_0) = 0$ we have

$$E(\hat{y}_0 - y_0) = 0$$

This equation shows that the predictor given by equation (3.11) is unbiased. Note that the predictor is unbiased in the sense that $E(\hat{y}_0) = E(y_0)$ since both $\hat{y}_0$ and y_0 are random variables.

The variance of the prediction error is

$$V(\hat{y}_0 - y_0) = V(\hat{\alpha} - \alpha) + x_0^2 V(\hat{\beta} - \beta) + 2x_0 \operatorname{cov}(\hat{\alpha} - \alpha, \hat{\beta} - \beta) + V(u_0)$$

$$= \sigma^2 \left(\frac{1}{n} + \frac{\bar{x}^2}{S_{xx}} \right) + \sigma^2 \frac{x_0^2}{S_{xx}} - 2x_0 \sigma^2 \frac{\bar{x}}{S_{xx}} + \sigma^2$$

$$= \sigma^2 \left[1 + \frac{1}{n} + \frac{(x_0 - \bar{x})^2}{S_{xx}} \right]$$

Thus the variance increases the farther away the value of x_0 is from $\bar{x}$, the mean of the observations on the basis of which $\hat{\alpha}$ and $\hat{\beta}$ have been computed. This is illustrated in Figure 3.5, which shows the confidence bands for y.

If x_0 lies within the range of the sample observations on x, we can call it within-sample prediction, and if x_0 lies outside the range of the sample observations, we call

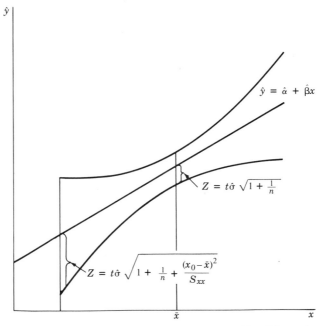

Figure 3.5. Confidence bands for prediction of y given x. [Confidence bands shown are $\hat{y} \pm Z$, where $Z = t\operatorname{SE}(\hat{y})$ and t is the t-value used].

the prediction out-of-sample prediction. As an illustration, consider a consumption function estimated on the basis of 12 observations. The equation is

$$y = 10.0 + 0.90x$$

where y = consumer expenditures

x = disposable income

We are given $\hat{\sigma}^2 = 0.01$, $\bar{x} = 200$, and $S_{xx} = 4000$. Given $x_0 = 250$, our prediction of y_0 is

$$\hat{y}_0 = 10.0 + 0.9(250) = 235$$

$$\text{SE}(\hat{y}_0) = \sqrt{0.01\left(1 + \frac{1}{12} + \frac{2500}{4000}\right)} = 0.131$$

Since $t = 2.228$ from the t-tables with 10 degrees of freedom, the 95% confidence interval for y_0 is $235 \pm 2.228(0.131) = 235 \pm 0.29$, that is, $(234.71, 235.29)$.

Prediction of Expected Values

Sometimes given x_0, it is not y_0 but $E(y_0)$ that we would be interested in predicting; that is, we are interested in the mean of y_0, not y_0 as such. We will give an illustrative example of this. Since $E(y_0) = \alpha + \beta x_0$, we would be predicting this by $\hat{E}(y_0) = \hat{\alpha} + \hat{\beta} x_0$, which is the same as $\hat{y}_0$ that we considered earlier. Thus our prediction would be the same whether it is y_0 or $E(y_0)$ that we want to predict. However, the prediction error would be different and the variance of the prediction error would be different (actually smaller). This means that the confidence intervals we generate would be different. The prediction error now is

$$\hat{E}(y_0) - E(y_0) = (\hat{\alpha} - \alpha) + (\hat{\beta} - \beta)x_0$$

Note that this is the same as the prediction error $\hat{y}_0 - y_0$ with $-u_0$ missing. Since the variance of this is σ^2, we have to subtract σ^2 from the error variance we obtained earlier. Thus

$$\text{var}\,[\hat{E}(y_0) - E(y_0)] = \sigma^2\left[\frac{1}{n} + \frac{(x_0 - \bar{x})^2}{S_{xx}}\right]$$

The standard error of the prediction is given by the square root of this expression after substituting $\hat{\sigma}^2$ for σ^2. The confidence intervals are given by $\hat{E}(y_0) \pm t\text{SE}$. Where t is the appropriate t-value.

Illustrative Example

Consider the example of the athletic sportswear store considered in Section 3.3 earlier. The regression equation estimated from the data from 5 months presented there is

$$\hat{y} = 1.0 + 1.2x \qquad \bar{x} = 3.0 \qquad \text{RSS} = 8.8$$

Suppose that the sales manager wants us to predict what the sales revenue will be if advertising expenditures are increased to $600. He would also like a 90% confidence interval for his prediction.

We have $x_0 = 6$. Hence

$$\hat{y}_0 = 1.0 + 1.2(6) = 8.2$$

The variance of the prediction error is

$$\sigma^2 \left[1 + \frac{1}{5} + \frac{(6 - 3)^2}{10} \right] = 2.1\sigma^2$$

Since

$$\hat{\sigma}^2 = \frac{\text{RSS}}{\text{d.f.}} = \frac{8.8}{3} = 2.93$$

the standard error of the prediction is

$$\sqrt{2.1(2.93)} = \sqrt{6.153} = 2.48$$

The 5% point from the t-distribution with 3 d.f. is 2.353. The 90% confidence interval for y_0 given $x_0 = 6$ is, therefore,

$$8.2 \pm 2.48(2.353) = (2.36, 14.04)$$

Thus the 90% confidence interval for sales revenue if advertising expenditures are $600 is ($2360; $14,040).

Consider now the case where the sales manager wants us to predict the *average* sales per month over the next two years when advertising expenditures are $600 per month. He also wants a 90% confidence interval for the prediction.

Now we are interested in predicting $E(y_0)$, not y_0. The prediction is still given by $1.0 + 1.2(6) = 8.2$. The variance of the prediction error is now

$$\sigma^2 \left[\frac{1}{5} + \frac{(6 - 3)^2}{10} \right] = 1.1\sigma^2$$

Substituting $\hat{\sigma}^2 = 2.93$ as before and taking the square root, we now get the standard error as

$$\text{SE}[\hat{E}(y_0)] = 1.795$$

The 90% confidence interval now is

$$8.20 \pm 2.353(1.795) = 8.20 \pm 4.22$$

Thus the 90% confidence interval for the *average* sales is ($3980; $12,420). Note that this confidence interval is narrower than the one we obtained for $\hat{y}_0$.

3.8 OUTLIERS

Very often it happens that the estimates of the regression parameters are influenced by a few extreme observations or outliers. This problem can be detected if we study the residuals from the estimated regression equation. Actually, a detailed analysis of residuals should accompany every estimated equation. Such analysis will enable us to see whether we are justified in making the assumption that:

1. The error variance $V(u_i) = \sigma^2$ for all i. This problem is treated in Chapter 5.
2. The error terms are serially independent. This problem is treated in Chapter 6.
3. The regression relationship is linear. This problem is treated in Section 3.9.

What we will be concerned with here is detecting some outlying observations using analysis of residuals. A more detailed discussion of analysis of residuals is given in Chapter 12. Actually, what we are doing is a diagnostic checking of our patient (regression equation) to see whether anything is wrong.

An *outlier* is an observation that is far removed from the rest of the observations. This observation is usually generated by some unusual factors. However, when we use the least squares method this single observation can produce substantial changes in the estimated regression equation. In the case of a simple regression we can detect outliers simply by plotting the data. However, in the case of multiple regression such plotting would not be possible and we have to analyze the residuals $\hat{u}_i$.

A good example to show that a simple presentation of the regression equation with the associated standard errors and r^2 does not give us the whole picture is given by Anscombe.[5] There are four data sets presented in Table 3.5. The values of x for the first three data sets are the same. All four data sets give the same regression equation.

For all of the four data sets, we have the following statistics:

$$n = 11 \qquad \bar{x} = 9.0 \qquad \bar{y} = 7.5$$

$$S_{xx} = 110.0 \qquad S_{yy} = 41.25 \qquad S_{xy} = 55.0$$

Table 3.5 Four Data Sets That Give an Identical Regression Equation

Data Set:		1–3	1	2	3	4	4
Variable:		x	y	y	y	x	y
Observation	1	10.0	8.04	9.14	7.46	8.0	6.58
	2	8.0	6.95	8.14	6.77	8.0	5.76
	3	13.0	7.58	8.74	12.74	8.0	7.71
	4	9.0	8.81	8.77	7.11	8.0	8.
	5	11.0	8.33	9.26	7.81	8.0	8.47
	6	14.0	9.96	8.10	8.84	8.0	7.04
	7	6.0	7.24	6.13	6.08	8.0	5.25
	8	4.0	4.26	3.10	5.39	19.0	12.50
	9	12.0	10.84	9.13	8.15	8.0	5.56
	10	7.0	4.82	7.26	6.42	8.0	7.91
	11	5.0	5.68	4.74	5.73	8.0	6.89

[5] F. J. Anscombe, "Graphs in Statistical Analysis," *The American Statistican*, Vol. 27, No. 1, February 1973, pp. 17–21.

The regression equation is

$$\hat{y} = 3.0 + 0.5x \qquad r^2 = 0.667$$
$$_{(0.118)}$$

regression sum of squares = 27.50 (1 d.f.)

residual sum of squares = 13.75 (9 d.f.)

Although the regression equations are identical, the four data sets exhibit widely different characteristics. This is revealed when we see the plots of the four data sets. These plots are shown in Figure 3.6.

Data set 1 shown in Figure 3.6(i) shows no special problems. Figure 3.6(ii) shows that the regression line should not be linear. Figure 3.6(iii) shows how a single outlier has twisted the regression line slightly. If we omit this one observation (observation 3), we would have obtained a slightly different regression line. Figure 3.6(iv)

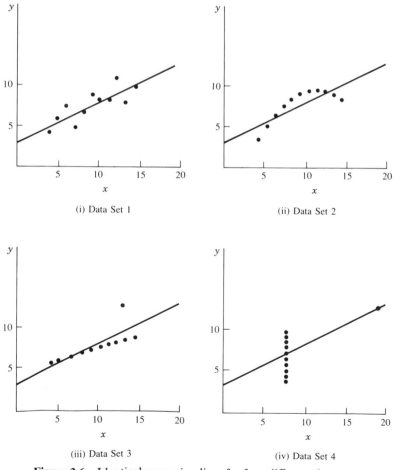

Figure 3.6 Identical regression lines for four different data sets.

shows how an outlier can produce an entirely different picture. If that one observation (observation 8) is omitted, we would have a vertical regression line.

We have shown graphically how outliers can produce drastic changes in the regression estimates. Next we give some real-world examples.

Some Illustrative Examples

Example 1

This example consists of the estimation of the consumption function for the United States for the period 1929–1984. Table 3.6 gives the data on per capita disposable income (Y) and per capita consumption expenditures (C) both in constant dollars for the United States. The data are not continuous. They are for 1929, 1933, and then continuous from 1939. The continuous data for 1929–1939 can be obtained from an earlier President's Economic Report (say, for 1972). But these data are in 1958 dollars and thus we have to link the two series.[6] We have not attempted this.

Table 3.6 Per Capita Personal Consumption Expenditures (C) and Per Capita Disposable Personal Income (Y) (in 1972 Dollars) for the United States, 1929–1984

Year	C	Y	Year	C	Y	Year	C	Y
1929	1765	1883	1957	2416	2660	1977	3924	4280
1933	1356	1349	1958	2400	2645	1978	4057	4441
1939	1678	1754	1959	2487	2709	1979	4121	4512
1940	1740	1847	1960	2501	2709	1980	4093	4487
1941	1826	2083	1961	2511	2742	1981	4131	4561
1942	1788	2354	1962	2583	2813	1982	4146	4555
1943	1815	2429	1963	2644	2865	1983	4303	4670
1944	1844	2483	1964	2751	3026	1984	4490	4941
1945	1936	2416	1965	2868	3171			
1946	2129	2353	1966	2979	3290			
1947	2122	2212	1967	3032	3389			
1948	2129	2290	1968	3160	3493			
1949	2140	2257	1969	3245	3564			
1950	2224	2392	1970	3277	3665			
1951	2214	2415	1971	3355	3752			
1952	2230	2441	1972	3511	3860			
1953	2277	2501	1973	3623	4080			
1954	2278	2483	1974	3566	4009			
1955	2384	2582	1975	3609	4051			
1956	2410	2653	1976	3774	4158			

Source: Economic Report of the President, 1984, p. 261.

[6] The data for 1929–1970 at 1958 prices have been analyzed in G. S. Maddala, *Econometrics* (New York: McGraw-Hill, 1977), pp. 84–86. These data are given as an exercise.

Table 3.7 Residuals for the Consumption Function Estimated from the Data in Table 3.6 (Rounded to the First Decimal)

Observation	Residual	Observation	Residual	Observation	Residual
1	75.0	17	24.2	33	24.1
2	152.4	18	41.6	34	−35.9
3	105.5	19	57.4	35	−37.1
4	82.8	20	18.8	36	20.5
5	−46.1	21	18.4	37	−67.9
6	−330.9	22	16.0	38	−60.2
7	−372.2	23	44.8	39	−55.4
8	−392.4	24	58.8	40	12.1
9	−239.4	25	38.7	41	51.0
10	11.0	26	46.0	42	37.4
11	132.4	27	59.7	43	36.7
12	68.4	28	20.1	44	31.5
13	109.4	29	5.0	45	2.1
14	70.5	30	7.6	46	22.5
15	39.5	31	−29.5	47	74.8
16	31.8	32	3.7	48	15.0

We will estimate a regression of C on Y. It was estimated by the SAS regression package. The results are as follows:

$$\hat{C} = -24.944 + 0.911Y \qquad r^2 = 0.9823$$
$$\underset{(58.124)}{\phantom{\hat{C} = -24.944 +}} \underset{(0.018)}{}$$

The t-value for β is $0.911/0.018 = 50.47$ and it can be checked that $r^2 = t^2/[t^2 + (n - 2)]$ and $n = 48$. (The figures have all been rounded to three decimal from the computer output.) The next step is to examine the residuals. These are presented in Table 3.7. One can easily notice the large negative residuals for observations 6, 7, 8, and 9. These observations are outliers. They correspond to the war years 1942–1945 with strict controls on consumer expenditures. We therefore discard these observations and reestimate the equation. The equation now is

$$\hat{C} = 85.725 + 0.885Y \qquad r^2 = 0.9975$$
$$\underset{(22.353)}{\phantom{\hat{C} = 85.725 +}} \underset{(0.007)}{}$$

Earlier the intercept was not significantly different from zero. Now it is significantly positive. Further, the estimate of the marginal propensity to consume is significantly lower (0.885 compared to 0.911). [7] The estimated residuals from this equation are presented in Table 3.8. We do not see any exceptionally large residual (except perhaps for observation 5, which is 1941), nor the long runs of positive and negative residuals as in Table 3.7.

---

[7] There is an increase in r^2 as well but the two r^2's are not comparable. To compare the two we have to calculate the r^2 between C and $\hat{C}$ from the first equation for just the 44 observations (excluding the war years). Then this recomputed r^2 will be comparable to the r^2 reported here.

Table 3.8 Estimated Residuals for the Consumption Function Omitting the War Years (1942–1945)

Observation	Residual	Observation	Residual	Observation	Residual
1	12.4	20	−24.2	35	−52.1
2	76.1	21	−24.4	36	8.3
3	39.6	22	−27.2	37	−74.5
4	19.2	23	3.2	38	−68.6
5	−103.7	24	17.2	39	−62.8
10	−39.7	25	−2.0	40	7.5
11	78.1	26	7.1	41	49.5
12	16.1	27	22.1	42	40.0
13	56.3	28	−13.4	43	41.1
14	20.8	29	−24.8	44	35.2
15	−9.6	30	−19.1	45	7.7
16	−16.6	31	−53.8	46	28.0
17	−22.7	32	−17.8	47	83.2
18	−5.8	33	4.3	48	30.3
19	12.6	34	−53.1		

Example 2

As a second example, consider the data presented in Table 3.9. They give teenage unemployment rates and unemployment benefits in Australia for the period 1962–1980. We will estimate some simple regressions of unemployment rates on unemployment benefits (in constant dollars) and present an analysis of the residuals. [8]

Defining

$$y_1 = \text{unemployment rate for male teenagers}$$

$$y_2 = \text{unemployment rate for female teenagers}$$

$$x = \text{unemployment benefit (constant dollars)}$$

we get the following regressions:

$$\hat{y}_1 = 2.478 + 0.212x \qquad r^2 = 0.690$$
$$\quad\;\;(1.234)\quad\;(0.035)$$

$$\hat{y}_2 = 3.310 + 0.226x \qquad r^2 = 0.660$$
$$\quad\;\;(1.410)\quad\;(0.039)$$

The equation suggests that an increase in unemployment benefit leads to an increase in the unemployment rate. However, the residuals from the two equations presented in Table 3.10 show very large absolute residuals for 1973, 1974, and 1977–1980.

---

[8] These are not the equations estimated by Gregory and Duncan. We are just estimating some simple regressions which may not be very meaningful.

Table 3.9 Teenage Unemployment Rates and Unemployment Benefits

Year	Teenage Unemployment Rate (%)		Unemployment Benefit for 16- and 17-Year-Olds	
	Males	Females	Nominal Dollars	Constant Dollars 1981
1962	4.5	5.9	3.50	13.3
1963	3.4	4.5	3.50	13.2
1964	2.5	4.4	3.50	12.7
1965	4.4	5.1	3.50	12.2
1966	3.1	5.5	3.50	11.9
1967	4.1	5.7	3.50	11.6
1968	4.7	6.0	3.50	11.3
1969	5.8	6.3	4.50	14.1
1970	5.7	5.1	4.50	13.4
1971	6.9	6.1	4.50	12.5
1972	8.6	9.3	7.50	20.0
1973	7.6	7.8	23.00	54.1
1974	11.9	12.3	31.00	62.7
1975	14.6	16.7	36.00	63.8
1976	13.6	15.6	36.00	55.8
1977	17.1	18.8	36.00	51.1
1978	16.4	18.8	36.00	47.4
1979	15.9	18.9	36.00	43.1
1980	15.7	17.6	36.00	39.5

Source: R. G. Gregory and R. C. Duncan, "High Teenage Unemployment: The Role of Atypical Labor Supply Behavior," *Economic Record*, Vol. 56, December 1980, pp. 316–330.

Suppose that as in Example 2, we delete these observations and reestimate the equations. The estimates are

$$\hat{y}_1 = 2.156 + 0.203x \qquad r^2 = 0.876$$
$$\phantom{\hat{y}_1 = }{\scriptstyle(0.610)} \quad {\scriptstyle(0.023)}$$

$$\hat{y}_2 = 2.799 + 0.225x \qquad r^2 = 0.955$$
$$\phantom{\hat{y}_2 = }{\scriptstyle(0.394)} \quad {\scriptstyle(0.015)}$$

The estimates of the coefficients of x did not change much. The r^2 values are higher but again to compare the r^2 values we have to compute the implied r^2 from the first equation using just these 13 observations. (The r^2 we compute is for y and $\hat{y}$.)

However, is the deletion of the six observations with high residuals the correct procedure in this case? The answer is "no." In Example 2 the deletion of the war years was justified because the behavior of consumers was affected by wartime controls. In this example there are no such controls. However, the large residuals are due to lags in behavior. First, with an increase in unemployment benefit rate, there will be an increase in the labor force participation. There will be time lags involved in

Table 3.10 Residuals from the Regressions of Unemployment Rates on Unemployment Benefits

Year	Regression of y_1	Regression of y_2
1962	−0.80	−0.42
1963	−1.88	−1.80
1964	−2.67	−1.78
1965	−0.67	−0.97
1966	−1.90	−0.50
1967	−0.84	−0.23
1968	−0.18	0.13
1969	0.33	−0.20
1970	0.38	−1.24
1971	1.77	−0.04
1972	1.88	1.47
1973	−6.34	−7.73
1974	−3.89	−5.20
1975	−1.42	−1.04
1976	−0.72	−0.33
1977	3.78	3.93
1978	3.86	4.77
1979	4.27	5.84
1980	5.04	5.35

this. Next there are the time lags involved in qualifying for benefits, filing of claims, receipt of benefits, and so on. Thus there are substantial time lags between x and y_1, and x and y_2. The large negative residuals in 1973 and 1974 and the positive residuals in 1977–1980 are a consequence of this. Further, one can see a trend in these residuals from 1973–1980. Thus the solution to this problem is not a deletion of observations as in the previous example of the consumption function but a reformulation of the problem taking account of labor force participation rates, time lags, and so on. This analysis is a lot more complicated for our purpose here. The example serves to illustrate the point that all "outliers" should not be deleted.

3.9 ALTERNATIVE FUNCTIONAL FORMS FOR REGRESSION EQUATIONS

We saw earlier with reference to Figure 3.6(ii) that sometimes the relationship between y and x can be nonlinear rather than linear. In this case we have to assume an appropriate functional form for the relationship. There are several functional forms that can be used which after some transformations of the variables, can be brought into the usual linear regression framework that we have been discussing.

For instance, for the data points depicted in Figure 3.7(a), where y is increasing more slowly than x, a possible functional form is $y = \alpha + \beta \log x$. This is called a

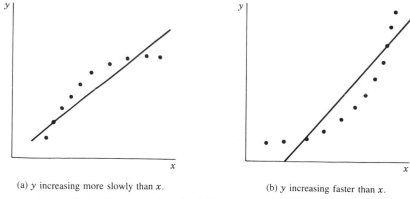

(a) y increasing more slowly than x.   (b) y increasing faster than x.

Figure 3.7.   Data sets for which linear regression is inappropriate.

semilog form, since it involves logarithm of only one of the two variables x and y. In this case if we redefine a variable $X = \log x$, the equation becomes $y = \alpha + \beta X$. Thus we have a linear regression model with the explained variable y and explanatory variable $X = \log x$.

For the data points depicted in Figure 3.7(b), where y is increasing faster than x, a possible functional form is $y = Ae^{\beta x}$. In this case we take logs of both sides and get another kind of semilog specification.

$$\log y = \log A + \beta x$$

If we define $Y = \log y$ and $\alpha = \log A$, we have

$$Y = \alpha + \beta x$$

which is in the form of a linear regression equation.

An alternative model one can use is

$$y = Ax^{\beta}$$

In this case taking logs of both sides, we get

$$\log y = \log A + \beta \log x$$

In this case β can be interpreted as an elasticity. Hence this form is popular in econometric work. This is called a *double-log specification* since it involves logarithms of both x and y. Now define $Y = \log y$, $X = \log x$, and $\alpha = \log A$. We have

$$Y = \alpha + \beta X$$

which is in the form of a linear regression equation. An illustrative example is given at the end of this section.

There is, of course, a difference between those functional forms in which we transform the variable x and those in which we transform the variable y. This becomes clear when we introduce the error term u. For instance, when we write the transformed equation with an additive error, which we do before we use the least squares method, that is, we write

$$Y = \alpha + \beta X + u$$

we are assuming that the original equation in terms of the untransformed variables is

$$y = Ax^\beta e^u$$

that is, the error term enters exponentially and in a multiplicative fashion. If we make the assumption of an additive error term in the original equation, that is,

$$y = Ax^\beta + u$$

then there is no way of transforming the variables that would enable us to use the simple methods of estimation described here. Estimation of this model requires nonlinear least squares.

Some other functional forms that are useful when the data points are as shown in Figure 3.8 are

$$Y = \alpha + \frac{\beta}{x}$$

or

$$Y = \alpha + \frac{\beta}{\sqrt{x}}$$

In the first case we define $X = 1/x$ and in the second case we define $X = 1/\sqrt{x}$. In both the cases the equation is linear in the variables after the transformation. It is

$$Y = \alpha + \beta X$$

If $\beta > 0$, the relationship is as shown in Figure 3.8(a). If $\beta < 0$, the relationship is as shown in Figure 3.8(b).

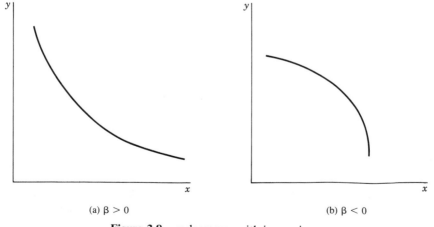

(a) β > 0   (b) β < 0

Figure 3.8. y decreases with increasing x.

Some other nonlinearities can be handled by what is known as "search procedures." For instance, suppose that we have the regression equation

$$y = \alpha + \frac{\beta}{x + \gamma} + u$$

The estimates of α, β, and γ are obtained by minimizing

$$\sum \left(y_i - \alpha - \frac{\beta}{x_i + \gamma} \right)^2$$

We can reduce this problem to one of simple least squares as follows: For each value of γ, we define the variable $Z_i = 1/(x_i + \gamma)$ and estimate α and β by minimizing

$$\sum (y_i - \alpha - \beta z_i)^2$$

We look at the residual sum of the squares in each case and then choose that value of γ for which the residual sum of squares is minimum. The corresponding estimates of α and β are the least squares estimates of these parameters. Here we are "searching" over different values of γ. This search would be a convenient one only if we had some prior notion of the range of this parameter. In any case there are convenient nonlinear regression programs available nowadays. Our purpose here is to show how some problems that do not appear to fall in the framework of simple regression at first sight can be transformed into that framework by a suitable redefinition of the variables.

Illustrative Example

In Table 3.11 we present data on output, labor input, and capital input for the United States for the period 1929–1967. The variables are

X = index of gross national product in constant dollars

L_1 = labor input index (number of persons adjusted for hours of work and educational level)

L_2 = persons engaged

K_1 = capital input index (capital stock adjusted for rates of utilization)

K_2 = capital stock in constant dollars

Since output depends on both labor and capital inputs we have to estimate a regression equation of X on L and K. This is what we will illustrate in Chapter 4. For the present let us study the relationship between output and labor input, and output and capital input. We will use L_1 for labor input and K_1 for capital input.

From the data it is clear that X has risen faster than L_1 or K_1. Hence we have a situation depicted in Figure 3.7(b). This suggests a semilogarithmic form or a double-logarithmic form. The advantage with the latter is that we can interpret the coefficients as elasticities. Moreover, even though X has been rising faster than L_1

Table 3.11 Output, Labor Input, and Capital Input for the United States, 1929–1967

Year	X	L_1	L_2	K_1	K_2
1929	189.8	173.3	44.151	87.8	888.9
1930	172.1	165.4	41.898	87.8	904.0
1931	159.1	158.2	36.948	84.0	900.2
1932	135.6	141.7	35.686	78.3	883.6
1933	132.0	141.6	35.533	76.6	851.4
1934	141.8	148.0	37.854	76.0	823.7
1935	153.9	154.4	39.014	77.7	805.3
1936	171.5	163.5	40.765	79.1	800.4
1937	183.0	172.0	42.484	80.0	805.5
1938	173.2	161.5	40.039	77.6	817.6
1939	188.5	168.6	41.443	81.4	809.8
1940	205.5	176.5	43.149	87.0	814.1
1941	236.0	192.4	46.576	96.2	830.3
1942	257.8	205.1	49.010	104.4	857.9
1943	277.5	210.1	49.695	110.0	851.4
1944	291.1	208.8	48.668	107.8	834.6
1945	284.5	202.1	47.136	102.1	819.3
1946	274.0	213.4	49.950	97.2	812.3
1947	279.9	223.6	52.350	105.9	851.3
1948	297.6	228.2	53.336	113.0	888.3
1949	297.7	221.3	51.469	114.9	934.6
1950	328.9	228.8	52.972	124.1	964.6
1951	351.4	239.0	55.101	134.5	1021.4
1952	360.4	241.7	55.385	139.7	1068.5
1953	378.9	245.2	56.226	147.4	1100.3
1954	375.8	237.4	54.387	148.9	1134.6
1955	406.7	245.9	55.718	158.6	1163.2
1956	416.3	251.6	56.770	167.1	1213.9
1957	422.8	251.5	56.809	171.9	1255.5
1958	418.4	245.1	55.023	173.1	1287.9
1959	445.7	254.9	56.215	182.5	1305.8
1960	457.3	259.6	56.743	189.0	1341.4
1961	466.3	258.1	56.211	194.1	1373.9
1962	495.3	264.6	57.078	202.3	1399.1
1963	515.5	268.5	57.540	205.4	1436.7
1964	544.1	275.4	58.508	215.9	1477.8
1965	579.2	285.3	60.055	225.0	1524.4
1966	615.6	297.4	62.130	236.2	1582.2
1967	631.1	305.0	63.162	247.9	1645.3

Source: L. R. Christensen and D. W. Jorgenson, "U.S. Real Product and Real Factor Input 1929–67," *Review of Income and Wealth*, March 1970.

66

(or K_1), it has not been rising that fast to justify a regression of $\log X$ on L_1 (or K_1). We will therefore estimate the equation in the double-logarithmic form:

$$\log X = \alpha + \beta \log L_1 + u$$

A regression of X on L_1 gave the following results (figures in parentheses are standard errors):

$$\hat{X} = -338.01 + 3.052 L_1 \qquad r^2 = 0.9573$$
$$\quad (23.55) \quad (0.106)$$

When we examined the residuals[9], they were positive for the first observations, negative for the middle 17 observations, and positive again for the last 10 observations. This is what we would expect if the relationship is as shown in Figure 3.7(b) and we estimate a linear function.

The results of a regression of $\log X$ on $\log L_1$ gave the following results (figures in parentheses are standard errors):

$$\log \hat{X} = -5.480 - 2.084 \log L_1 \qquad r^2 = 0.9851$$
$$\quad (0.226) \quad (0.042)$$

This equation still exhibited some pattern in the residuals, although not to the same extent as the linear form.

The log-linear form is more easy to interpret. The elasticity of output with respect to the labor input is about 2. This is, of course, very high, but this is because of the omission of the capital input. In Chapter 4 we estimate the production function with the capital input included.

In this particular example, estimation in the linear form is not very meaningful. A linear production function assumes perfect substitutability between capital and labor inputs. However, it is given here as an example illustrating Figure 3.7(b).

Note that r^2 is higher in the log-linear form than in the linear form. But this comparison does not mean anything because the dependent variables in the two equations are different. (This point is discussed in greater detail in Section 5.6 of Chapter 5).

Finally, in the case of a simple regression it is always easy to plot the points on a graph and see what functional form is the most appropriate for the problem. This is not possible in the case of multiple regression with several explanatory variables. Hence greater use is made of the information from the residuals.

*3.10 INVERSE PREDICTION IN THE LEAST REGRESSION MODEL

At times a regression model of y on x is used to make a prediction of the value of x which could have given rise to a new observation y. As an illustration suppose that we have data on sales and advertising expenditures for a number of firms in an

---

[9] To economize on space, we are not presenting the residuals here. We present residuals for some multiple regression equations in Chapter 12.
*Optional section.

industry. There is a new firm whose sales are known but advertising expenditures are not. In this case we would want to get an estimate of the advertising expenditures of this firm.

In this example we have the estimated regression equation

$$\hat{y} = \hat{\alpha} + \hat{\beta}x$$

and given a new value y_0 of y we have to estimate the value x_0 of x that could have given rise to y_0 and obtain a confidence interval for x_0.

To simplify the algebra we will write $x' = x - \bar{x}$ and $y' = y - \bar{y}$. Then the estimated regression equation can be written as

$$\hat{y}' = \hat{\beta}x' \tag{3.12}$$

We are given the value y_0 of y and we are asked to estimate the value x_0 of x that could have given rise to y_0. Define $y_0' = y_0 - \bar{y}$ and $x_0' = x_0 - \bar{x}$. The estimate of x_0' given from equation (3.12) is

$$\hat{x}_0' = \frac{y_0'}{\hat{\beta}} \tag{3.13}$$

The main problem is that of obtaining confidence limits for $\hat{x}_0'$ because both y_0' and $\hat{\beta}$ are normally distributed. One can use a method suggested by Fieller for this purpose.[10] This method can be used to obtain confidence intervals for ratios of estimators. These problems also arise in our discussion of simultaneous equation models and distributed lag models in later chapters. Another problem that falls in this same category is to estimate the value of x at which the value of y is zero. This is given by

$$\hat{x} = -\frac{\hat{\alpha}}{\hat{\beta}}$$

and $\hat{\alpha}$ and $\hat{\beta}$ have joint normal distribution.

Let us define $\theta = E(y_0'/\beta)$ (θ is just x_0' and is thus a constant). Then the variable $y_0' - \theta\hat{\beta}$ is normally distributed with mean zero and variance

$$\sigma^2\left(1 + \frac{1}{n}\right) + \theta^2\frac{\sigma^2}{S_{xx}} \tag{3.14}$$

[since $\operatorname{var}(y_0') = \operatorname{var}(y_0 - \bar{y}) = \sigma^2 + \sigma^2/n$ and $\operatorname{cov}(y_0, \hat{\beta}) = 0$]. Substituting the estimate $\hat{\sigma}^2$ of σ^2 derived earlier into (3.14), we get the estimated variance. Thus

$$t = \frac{y_0' - \theta\hat{\beta}}{\sqrt{\hat{\sigma}^2(1 + 1/n) + \theta^2(\hat{\sigma}^2/S_{xx})}}$$

has a t-distribution with degrees of freedom $(n - 2)$. This can be used to construct a confidence interval for θ, which is what we need. For instance, to get a 95% confidence interval for θ, we find a value t_0 of t (from the t-tables for $n - 2$ degrees of freedom) such that

$$\operatorname{Prob}(t^2 < t_0^2) = 0.95$$

[10] E. C. Fieller, "A Fundamental Formula in the Statistics of Biological Assay and Some Applications," *Quarterly Journal of Pharmacy*, 1944, pp. 117–123.

To get the limits for θ we solve the quadratic equation

$$(y_0' - \hat{\beta}\theta)^2 - t_0^2 \hat{\sigma}^2 \left(1 + \frac{1}{n} + \frac{\theta^2}{S_{xx}}\right) = 0 \tag{3.15}$$

The roots θ_1 and θ_2 of this equation give the confidence limits.

As an illustration, suppose that we have estimated a consumption function on the basis of 10 observations and the equation is [11]

$$y = 10.0 + 0.9x$$

and $\bar{x} = 200$, $\bar{y} = 185$, $\hat{\sigma}^2 = 5.0$, and $S_{xx} = 400$. Consider the predicted value of x for $y = 235$. This is clearly $\hat{x}_0 = 250$.

To get the confidence interval for x_0 we solve equation (3.15). Note that $y_0' = 235 - 185 = 50$ and $t_0 = 2.228$ from the t-tables for 10 degrees of freedom. Thus we have to solve the equation

$$(50 - 0.9\theta)^2 - (2.228)^2(5)\left(1 + \frac{1}{10} + \frac{\theta^2}{400}\right) = 0$$

or

$$2500 - 90\theta + 0.81\theta^2 = 27.3 + 0.072\theta^2$$

or

$$0.738\theta^2 - 90\theta + 2472.7 = 0$$

The two roots are $\theta_1 = 41.80$ and $\theta_2 = 80.15$. Thus, the 95% confidence interval for x_0' is $(41.80, 80.15)$ or for x_0 it is $(241.80, 280.15)$. Note that the confidence interval obtained by the Fieller method need not be symmetric around the predicted point value (which in this case is $x_0 = 250$.

If the samples are large, we can use the asymptotic distributions and this will give symmetric intervals. However, for small samples we have to use the method described here.

*3.11 STOCHASTIC REGRESSORS

In Section 3.2 we started explaining the regression model saying that the values $x_1, x_2, \ldots, x_n$ of x are given constants, that is, x is not a random variable. This view is perhaps valid in experimental work but not in econometrics. In econometrics we view x as a random variable (except in special cases where x is time or some dummy variable). In this case the observations $x_1, x_2, \ldots, x_n$ are realizations of the random variable x. This is what is meant when we say that the regressor is stochastic.

Which of the results we derived earlier are valid in this case? First, regarding the unbiasedness property of the least squares estimators, that property holds good

---

[11] We have changed the illustrative example slightly from the one we discussed in Section 3.6 because with $\hat{\sigma}^2 = 0.01$ and $S_{xx} = 4000$ we get a symmetric confidence interval for θ. We have changed the example to illustrate the point that we need not get a symmetric confidence interval.

provided that the random variables x and u are independent. (This is proved in the appendix to this chapter.) Second, regarding the variances of the estimators and the tests of significance that we derived, these have to be viewed as conditional on the realized values of x.

To obtain any concrete results, with stochastic regressors, we need to make some assumptions about the joint distribution of y and x. It has been proved that when y and x are jointly normally distributed, the formulas we have derived for the estimates of the regression parameters, their standard errors, and the test statistics are all valid. Since the proof of this proposition is beyond the scope of this book, we will not pursue it here. [12]

Thus, with stochastic regressors the formulas we have derived are valid if y and x are jointly normally distributed. Otherwise, they have to be considered as valid conditional on the observed x's.

*3.12 THE REGRESSION FALLACY

In the introduction to this chapter we mentioned a study by Galton, who analyzed the relationship between the height of children and the height of parents. Let

x = mid-parent height

y = mean height (at maturity) of all children whose mid-
parent height is x

Galton plotted y against x and found that the points lay close to a straight line but the slope was less than 1.0. What this means is that if the mid-parent height is 1 inch above $\bar{x}$, the childrens' height (on the average) is less than 1 inch above $\bar{y}$. There is thus a "*regression* of childrens' heights toward the average."

A phenomenon like the one observed by Galton could arise in several situations where y and x have a bivariate normal distribution and thus is a mere statistical artifact. This is why it is termed a "regression fallacy." To see this, first we have to derive the conditional distributions $f(x|y)$ and $f(y|x)$ when x and y are jointly normal. We will show that both these conditional distributions are normal.

The Bivariate Normal Distribution

Suppose that X and Y are *jointly* normally distributed with means, variances, and covariance given by

$$E(X) = m_x \qquad E(Y) = m_y \qquad V(X) = \sigma_x^2 \qquad V(Y) = \sigma_y^2$$

and

$$\text{cov}(X, Y) = \rho \sigma_x \sigma_y$$

---

[12] In the case of multiple regression, proof of this proposition, can be found in several papers. A clear exposition of all the propositions is given in: Allan R. Simpson, "A Tale of Two Regressions," *Journal of the American Statistical Association*, September 1974, pp. 682–689.

Then the joint density of X and Y is given by

$$f(x, y) = (2\pi\sigma_x\sigma_y\sqrt{1 - \rho^2})^{-1} \exp(Q)$$

where

$$Q = -\frac{1}{2(1 - \rho^2)}\left[\left(\frac{x - m_x}{\sigma_x}\right)^2 - 2\rho\frac{x - m_x}{\sigma_x}\frac{y - m_y}{\sigma_y} + \left(\frac{y - m_y}{\sigma_y}\right)^2\right]$$

Now completing the square in x and simplifying, we get

$$Q = -\frac{1}{2(1 - \rho^2)}\left(\frac{x - m_x}{\sigma_x} - \rho\frac{y - m_y}{\sigma_y}\right)^2 - \frac{1}{2}\left(\frac{y - m_y}{\sigma_y}\right)^2$$

Thus

$$f(x, y) = f(x \mid y)f(y)$$

where

$$f(y) = \frac{1}{\sqrt{2\pi}\,\sigma_y}\exp\left[-\frac{1}{2\sigma_y^2}(y - m_y)^2\right]$$

and

$$f(x \mid y) = \frac{1}{\sqrt{2\pi}\,\sigma_x\sqrt{1 - \rho^2}}\exp\left[-\frac{1}{2\sigma_x^2(1 - \rho^2)}(x - m_{x\cdot y})^2\right]$$

where

$$m_{x\cdot y} = m_x + \frac{\rho\sigma_x}{\sigma_y}(y - m_y)$$

Thus we see that the marginal distribution of y is normal with mean m_y and variance σ_y^2. The conditional distribution of x given y is also normal with

$$\text{mean} = m_x + \frac{\rho\sigma_x}{\sigma_y}(y - m_y)$$

and

$$\text{variance} = \sigma_x^2(1 - \rho^2)$$

The conditional distribution of y given x is just obtained by interchanging x and y in the foregoing relationships.

Thus for a bivariate normal distribution, both the marginal and conditional distributions are univariate normal.[13] Note that the converse need not be true, that is, if the marginal distributions of X and Y are normal, it does not necessarily

---

[13] This result is more general. For the multivariate normal distribution we can show that all marginal and conditional distributions are also normal.

follow that the joint distribution of X and Y is bivariate normal. In fact, there are many nonnormal bivariate distributions for which the marginal distributions are both normal.[14]

Galton's Result and the Regression Fallacy

Consider now the mean of Y for given value of X. We have seen that it is given by

$$E(Y \mid X = x) = m_y + \frac{\rho \sigma_y}{\sigma_x}(x - m_x)$$

The slope of this line is $\rho \sigma_y / \sigma_x$ and if $\sigma_x \simeq \sigma_y$, since $\rho < 1$ we have the result that the slope is less than 1, as observed by Galton.

By the same token, if we consider $E(X \mid Y = y)$ we get

$$E(X \mid Y = y) = m_x + \frac{\rho \sigma_x}{\sigma_y}(y - m_y)$$

Since we have assumed that $\sigma_x = \sigma_y$, the slope of this line is also less than unity (note that we are taking dx/dy as the slope in this case). Thus if Galton had considered the conditional means of parents' heights for given values of offsprings' heights, he would have found a "regression" of parents' heights toward the mean. It is not clear what Galton would have labeled this regression.

Such "regression" toward average is often found when considering variables that are jointly normally distributed and that have almost the same variance. This has been a frequent finding in the case of test scores. For example, if

$$x = \text{score on the first test}$$

and

$$y = \text{score on the second test}$$

then considering the conditional means of y for given values of x shows a regression toward the mean in the second test. This does not mean that the students' abilities are converging toward the mean. This finding in the case of test scores has been named a *regression fallacy* by the psychologist Thorndike.[15]

This, then, is the story of the term "regression." The term as it is used now has no implication that the slope be less than 1.0, nor even the implication of linearity, although we will be discussing linear functions at first.

---

[14] C. J. Kowalski, "Non-normal Bivariate Distributions with Normal Marginals," *The American Statistician*, Vol. 27, No. 3, June 1973, pp. 103–106; K. V. Mardia, *Families of Bivariate Distributions* (London: Charles Griffin, 1970).

[15] F. L. Thorndike, "Regression Fallacies in the Matched Group Experiment," *Psychometrika*, Vol. 7, No. 2, 1942, pp. 85–102.

SUMMARY

1. The present chapter discusses the simple linear regression model with one explained variable and one explanatory variable. The term regression literally means "backwardation," but that is not the way it is used today, although that is the way it originated in statistics. A brief history of the term is given in Section 3.1, but it is discussed in greater detail in Section 3.12 under the title "regression fallacy."

2. Two methods—the method of moments (Section 3.3) and the method of least squares (Section 3.4)—are described for the estimation of the parameters in the linear regression model. A third method, the method of maximum likelihood (ML), is presented in the appendix. For the normal linear regression model all of them give the same results.

3. Given two variables y and x there is always the question of whether to regress y on x or to regress x on y. This question can always be answered if we know how the data were generated or if we know the direction of causality. In some cases both the regressions make sense. These issues are discussed in the latter part of Section 3.4.

4. In Sections 3.5 and 3.6 we discuss the procedures of obtaining
(a) Standard errors of the coefficients.
(b) Confidence intervals for the parameters.
(c) Tests of hypotheses about the parameters.
The exact formulas need not be repeated here because they are summarized in the respective sections. The main results that need to be presented are:
(a) The estimates of the regression parameters with their standard errors. Sometimes the t-ratios are given instead of the standard errors. If we are interested in obtaining confidence intervals, the standard errors are more convenient. If we are interested in tests of hypotheses, presentation of the t-ratios is sometimes more convenient.
(b) The coefficient of determination r^2.
(c) SEE or SER. This is an estimate of the standard deviation σ of the error term. However, these statistics by themselves are not sufficient. In Section 3.8 we give an example of four different data sets that give the same regression output.

5. While considering the predictions from the linear regression model, it is important to note whether we are obtaining predictions for the particular value of y or for the mean value of y. Although the point prediction is the same for the two cases, the variance of the prediction error and the confidence intervals we generate will be different. This is illustrated with an example in Section 3.7. Sometimes we are interested in the inverse prediction: prediction of x given y. This problem is discussed in Section 3.10.

6. In regression analysis it is important to examine the residuals and see whether there are any systematic patterns in them. Such analysis would be useful in detecting outliers and judging whether the linear functional form is appropriate. The problem of detection of outliers and what to do with them is discussed in Section 3.8. In Section 3.9 we discuss different functional forms where the least squares model can be used with some transformations of the data.

7. Throughout the chapter, the explanatory variable is assumed to be fixed (or a

nonrandom variable). In Section 3.10 (optional) we discuss briefly what happens if this assumption is relaxed.

8. The last three sections and the appendix, which contains some derivations of the results and a discussion of the ML estimation method and the LR test can be omitted by beginning students.

EXERCISES

(More difficult exercises are marked with a*)

1. Comment briefly on the meaning of each of the following.
    (a) Estimated coefficient.
    (b) Standard error.
    (c) t-statistic.
    (d) R-squared.
    (e) Sum of squared residuals.
    (f) Standard error of the regression.
    (g) Best linear unbiased estimator.
2. A store manager selling TV sets observes the following sales on 10 different days. Calculate the regression of y on x where

    $$y = \text{number of TV sets sold}$$

    $$x = \text{number of sales representatives}$$

y	3	6	10	5	10	12	5	10	10	8
x	1	1	1	2	2	2	3	3	3	2

   Present all the items mentioned in Exercise 1.
3. The following data present experience and salary structure of University of Michigan economists in 1983–1984. The variables are

    $$y = \text{salary (thousands of dollars)}$$

    $$x = \text{years of experience (defined as years since receiving Ph.D.)}$$

y	x	y	x	y	y	x
63.0	43	44.5	22	45.0	18	51.3	12
54.3	32	43.0	21	50.7	17	50.3	12
51.0	32	46.8	20	37.5	17	62.4	10
39.0	30	42.4	20	61.0	16	39.3	10
52.0	26	56.5	19	48.1	16	43.2	9
55.0	25	55.0	19	30.0	16	40.4	7
41.2	23	53.0	19	51.5	15	37.7	6
47.7	22	55.0	18	40.6	13	27.7	3

Source: R. H. Frank, "Are Workers Paid Their Marginal Products," *The American Economic Review*, September, 1984, Table 1, p. 560.

Calculate the regression of y on x. Present all the items mentioned in Exercise 1. Give reasons why the regression does or does not make sense. Calculate the residuals to see whether there are any outliers. Would you discard these observations or look for other explanations?

4. Show that the simple regression line of y against x coincides with the simple regression line of x against y if and only if $r^2 = 1$ (where r is the sample correlation coefficient between x and y).

5. In the regression model $y_i = \alpha + \beta x_i + u_i$ if the sample mean $\bar{x}$ of x is zero, show the $\text{cov}(\hat{\alpha}, \hat{\beta}) = 0$, where $\hat{\alpha}$ and $\hat{\beta}$ are the least squares estimators of α and β.

6. The following are data on

$$y = \text{quit rate per 100 employees in manufacturing}$$

$$x = \text{unemployment rate}$$

The data are for the United States and cover the period 1960–1972.

Year	y	x	Year	y	x
1960	1.3	6.2	1967	2.3	3.6
1961	1.2	7.8	1968	2.5	3.3
1962	1.4	5.8	1969	2.7	3.3
1963	1.4	5.7	1970	2.1	5.6
1964	1.5	5.0	1971	1.8	6.8
1965	1.9	4.0	1972	2.2	5.6
1966	2.6	3.2			

(a) Calculate a regression of y on x.

$$y = \alpha + \beta x + u$$

(b) Construct a 95% confidence interval for β.

(c) Test the hypothesis H_0: $\beta = 0$ against the alternative $\beta \neq 0$ at the 5% significance level.

(d) Construct a 90% confidence interval for $\sigma^2 = \text{var}(u)$.

(e) What is likely to be wrong with the assumptions of the classical normal linear model in this case? Discuss.

7. Let $\hat{u}_i$ be the residuals in the least squares fit of y_i against x_i ($i = 1, 2, \ldots, n$). Derive the following results:

$$\sum_{i=1}^{n} \hat{u}_i = 0 \quad \text{and} \quad \sum_{i=1}^{n} x_i \hat{u}_i = 0$$

8. Given data on y and x explain what functional form you will use and how you will estimate the parameters if

(a) y is a proportion and lies between 0 and 1.

(b) $x > 0$ and x assumes very large values relative to y.

(c) You are interested in estimating a constant elasticity of demand function.

9. At a large state university seven undergraduate students who are majoring in economics were randomly selected from the population and surveyed. Two of the survey questions asked were: (1) What was your grade-point average (GPA)

in the preceding term? (2) What was the average number of hours spent per week last term in the Orange and Brew? The Orange and Brew is a favorite and only watering hole on campus. Using the data below, estimate with ordinary least squares the equation

$$G = \alpha + \beta H$$

where G is GPA and H is hours per week in Orange and Brew. What is the expected sign for β? Do the data support your expectations?

Student	GPA, G	Hours per Week in Orange and Brew, H
1	3.6	3
2	2.2	15
3	3.1	8
4	3.5	9
5	2.7	12
6	2.6	12
7	3.9	4

10. Two variables y and x are believed to be related by the following stochastic equation:

$$y = \alpha + \beta x + u$$

where u is the usual random disturbance with zero mean and constant variance σ^2. To check this relationship one researcher takes a sample size of 8 and estimates β with OLS. A second researcher takes a different sample size of 8 and also estimates β with OLS. The data they used and the results they obtained are as follows:

Researcher 1		Researcher 2	
y	x	y	x
4.0	3	2.0	1
4.5	3	2.5	1
4.5	3	2.5	1
3.5	3	1.5	1
4.5	4	11.5	10
4.5	4	10.5	10
5.5	4	10.5	10
5.0	4	11.0	10

$$\hat{y} = \underset{(1.20)}{1.875} + \underset{(0.339)}{0.750x}$$

$$r^2 = 0.45$$

$$\hat{\sigma} = 0.48$$

$$\hat{y} = \underset{(0.27)}{1.5} + \underset{(0.038)}{0.970x}$$

$$r^2 = 0.99$$

$$\hat{\sigma} = 0.48$$

Can you explain why the standard error of $\hat{\beta}$ for the first researcher is larger than the standard error of $\hat{\beta}$ for the second researcher?

11. Since the variance of the regression coefficient $\hat{\beta}$ varies inversely with the variance of x, it is often suggested that we should drop all the observations in the middle range of x and use only the extreme observations on x in the calculation of $\hat{\beta}$. Is this a desirable procedure?

12. Suppose you are attempting to build a model that explains aggregate savings behavior as a function of the level of interest rates. Would you rather sample during a period of fluctuating interest rates or a period of stable interest rates? Explain.

13. A small grocery store notices that the price it charges for oranges varies greatly throughout the year. In the off-season the price was as high as 60 cents per orange, and during the peak season they had special sales where the price was as low as 10 cents, 20 cents, and 30 cents per orange. Below are six weeks of data on the quantity of oranges sold (y) and price (x):

Oranges Sold, y (100s)	Price per Orange, x (cents)
6	10
4	20
5	30
4	40
3	50
1	60

Assuming that the demand for oranges is given by the linear equation

$$y = \alpha + \beta x + u$$

estimate the parameters of this equation. Calculate a 90% confidence interval for the quantity of oranges sold in week seven if the price is 25 cents per orange during that week.

14. In Exercise 9 we considered the relationship between grade-point average (GPA) and weekly hours spent in the campus pub. Suppose that a freshman economics student has been spending 15 hours a week in the Orange and Brew during the first two weeks of class. Calculate a 90% confidence interval for his GPA in his first quarter of college if he continues to spend 15 hours per week in the Orange and Brew. Suppose that this freshman remains in school for four years and completes the required 12 quarters for graduation. Calculate a 90% confidence interval for his final cumulative GPA. Suppose that the minimum requirements for acceptance into most graduate schools for economics is 3.25. What are the chances that this student will be able to go to graduate school after completing his undergraduate studies?

15. A local night entertainment establishment in a small college town is trying to decide whether they should increase their weekly advertising expenditures on the campus radio station. The last six weeks of data on monthly revenue (y) and radio advertising expenditures (x) are given in the accompanying table. What

would their predicted revenues be next week if they spent $500 on radio commercials. Give a 90% confidence interval for next week's revenues. Suppose that they spend $500 per week for the next 10 weeks. Give a 90% confidence interval for the *average* revenue over the next 10 weeks.

Week	Revenue, y (thousand of dollars)	Radio Advertising Expenditure, x (hundreds of dollars)
1	1.5	1.0
2	2.0	2.5
3	1.0	0.0
4	2.0	3.0
5	3.5	4.0
6	1.5	2.0

*16. In the model $y_i = \alpha + \beta x_i + u_i$, $i = 1, \dots, N$, the following sample moments have been calculated from 10 observations:

$$\sum y_i = 8 \qquad \sum x_i = 40 \qquad \sum y_i^2 = 26 \qquad \sum x_i^2 = 200 \qquad \sum x_i y_i = 20$$

(a) Calculate the predictor of y for $x = 10$ and obtain a 95% confidence interval for it.

(b) Calculate the value of x that could have given rise to a value of $y = 1$ and explain how you would find a 95% confidence interval for it.

*17. (*Instrumental variable method*) Consider the linear regression model

$$y_i = \alpha + \beta x_i + u_i$$

One of the assumptions we have made is that x_i are uncorrelated with the errors u_i. If x_i are correlated with u_i, we have to look for a variable that is uncorrelated with u_i (but correlated with x_i). Let us call this variable z_i. z_i is called an *instrumental variable*. Note that as explained in Section 3.3, the assumptions $E(u) = 0$ and $\text{cov}(x, u) = 0$ are replaced by

$$\sum \hat{u}_i = 0 \qquad \text{and} \qquad \sum x_i \hat{u}_i = 0$$

However, since x and u are correlated we cannot use the second condition. But since z and u are uncorrelated, we use the condition $\text{cov}(z, u) = 0$. This leads to the normal equations

$$\sum \hat{u}_i = 0 \qquad \text{and} \qquad \sum z_i \hat{u}_i = 0$$

The estimates of α and β obtained using these two equations are called the instrumental variable estimates. From a sample of 100 observations, the following data are obtained:

$$\sum y_i^2 = 350$$
$$\sum x_i y_i = 150 \qquad \sum x_i^2 = 400$$
$$\sum z_i y_i = 100 \qquad \sum z_i x_i = 200 \qquad \sum z_i^2 = 400$$
$$\sum y_i = 100 \qquad \sum x_i = 100 \qquad \sum z_i = 50$$

Calculate the instrumental variables estimates of α and β.

Let the instrumental variable estimator of β be denoted by $\beta*$ and the least squares estimator of β be $\hat{\beta}$. Show that $\beta* = S_{zy}/S_{zx}$ with S_{zy} and S_{zx} defined in a similar manner to S_{xx}, S_{xy} and S_{yy}. Show that

$$\text{var}(\beta*) = \sigma^2 \cdot \frac{S_{zz}}{(S_{zx})^2} = \frac{\sigma^2}{S_{xx}}\left(\frac{1}{r_{xz}^2}\right)$$

Hence, $\text{var}(\beta*) \geq \text{var}(\hat{\beta})$. To test whether x and u are correlated or not, the following test has been suggested (Hausman's test discussed in Chapter 12).

$$t = (\beta* - \hat{\beta})/\sqrt{\hat{V}(\beta*) - \hat{V}(\hat{\beta})} \sim N(0,1)$$

Apply this test to test whether $\text{cov}(x,u) = 0$ with the data provided.

*18. (*Stochastic regressors*) In the linear regression model

$$y_i = \alpha + \beta x_i + u_i$$

Suppose that $x_i \sim \text{IN}(0, \lambda^2)$. What is the (asymptotic) distribution of the least squares estimator $\hat{\beta}$? Just state the result. Proof not required.

*19. Consider the regression model

$$y_i = \alpha + \beta x_i + u_i$$
$$u_i \sim \text{IN}(0,1) \qquad\qquad i = 1, 2, \ldots, T$$

Suppose that the model refers to semiannual data, but the data available are either:

1. Annual data, that is,

$$\bar{y}_1 = y_1 + y_2$$
$$\bar{y}_2 = y_3 + y_4$$
$$\bar{y}_3 = y_5 + y_6, \text{ etc.}$$

with $\bar{x}_1, \bar{x}_2, \bar{x}_3, \ldots$, defined analogously (assuming that T is even), or
2. Moving average data, that is,

$$y_1^* = \frac{y_1 + y_2}{2}$$

$$y_2^* = \frac{y_2 + y_3}{2}$$

$$y_3^* = \frac{y_3 + y_4}{2} \qquad \text{etc.}$$

with $x_1^*, x_2^*, x_3^*, \ldots$ defined analogously.

(a) What are the properties of the error term in the regression model with each sets of data: (y_i, x_i), $(\bar{y}_i, \bar{x}_i)$, and (y_i^*, x_i^*)?
(b) How would you estimate β in the case of annual data?
(c) How would you estimate β in the case of moving average data?
(d) Would you rather have the annual data or moving average data? Why?

*20. Given data on y and x explain how you will estimate the parameters in the following equations by using the ordinary least squares method. Specify the assumptions you make about the errors.
(a) $y = \alpha x^\beta$
(b) $y = \alpha e^{\beta x}$

(c) $y = \alpha + \beta \log x$

(d) $y = \dfrac{x}{\alpha x - \beta}$

(e) $y = \dfrac{e^{\alpha + \beta x}}{1 + e^{\alpha + \beta x}}$

(f) $y = \alpha + \beta \sqrt{x}$

(g) $y = \alpha + e^{\beta x}$

(h) $y = \alpha + \dfrac{\beta}{x - c}$

APPENDIX TO CHAPTER 3

In the following proofs we will use the compact notation $\sum y_i$ for $\sum_{i=1}^{n} y_i$.

(1) Proof that the Least Squares Estimators are Best Linear Unbiased Estimators (BLUE):

Consider the regression model

$$y_i = \beta x_i + u_i \qquad i = 1, 2, \ldots, n$$

For simplicity we have omittted the constant term. We assume that u_i are independently distributed with mean 0 and variance σ^2. Since x_i are given constants, $E(y_i) = \beta x_i$ and $\operatorname{var}(y_i) = \sigma^2$.

The least squares estimator of β is

$$\beta = \frac{\sum x_i y_i}{\sum x_i^2} = \sum c_i y_i$$

where $c_i = x_i / \sum x_i^2$. Thus $\hat{\beta}$ is a linear function of the sample observations y_i and hence is called a *linear estimator*. Also,

$$E(\hat{\beta}) = \sum c_i E(y_i)$$

$$= \sum \left(\frac{x_i}{\sum x_i^2} \right)(\beta x_i) = \beta \frac{\sum x_i^2}{\sum x_i^2} = \beta$$

Hence $\hat{\beta}$ is an *unbiased linear estimator*. We have to show that it is the best (i.e., has minimum variance among the class of linear unbiased estimators). Consider any linear estimator.

$$\tilde{\beta} = \sum d_i y_i$$

If it is unbiased, we have

$$E(\tilde{\beta}) = \sum d_i E(y_i) = \sum d_i(x_i \beta) = \beta$$

Hence we should have $\sum d_i x_i = 1$. Since y_i are independent with a common variance σ^2, we have

$$\operatorname{var}(\tilde{\beta}) = \sum d_i^2 \sigma^2$$

We have to find d_i so that this variance is minimum subject to the condition that $\sum d_i x_i = 1$.

Hence we minimize $\sum d_i^2 - \lambda(\sum d_i x_i - 1)$, where λ is the Lagrangean multiplier. Differentiating with respect to d_i and equating to zero, we get

$$2d_i - \lambda x_i = 0 \qquad \text{or} \qquad d_i = \frac{\lambda}{2} x_i$$

Multiplying both sides by x_i and summing over i, we get

$$\sum d_i x_i = \frac{\lambda}{2} \sum x_i^2$$

But $\sum d_i x_i = 1$. Hence

$$\lambda = \frac{2}{\sum x_i^2}$$

Thus we get

$$d_i = \frac{\lambda}{2} x_i = \frac{x_i}{\sum x_i^2}$$

which are the least squares coefficients c_i. Thus the least squares estimator has the minimum variance in the class of linear unbiased estimators. This minimum variance is

$$\text{var}(\hat{\beta}) = \sum c_i^2 \sigma^2 = \sum \left(\frac{x_i}{\sum x_i^2}\right)^2 \sigma^2 = \frac{\sigma^2}{\sum x_i^2}$$

Note that what we have shown is that the least squares estimator has the minimum variance among the class of linear unbiased estimators. It is possible in some cases that we can find nonlinear estimators that are unbiased but have a smaller variance than the linear estimators. However, if u_i are independently and *normally* distributed, then the least squares estimator has minimum variance among all (linear and nonlinear) unbiased estimators. Proofs of these propositions are beyond our scope and hence are omitted.

(2) Derivation of the Sampling Distributions of the Least Squares Estimators

Consider the regression model

$$y_i = \alpha + \beta x_i + u_i \qquad u_i \sim \text{IN}(0, \sigma^2)$$

We have seen that the least squares estimators are

$$\hat{\beta} = \frac{S_{xy}}{S_{xx}} \qquad \text{and} \qquad \hat{\alpha} = \bar{y} - \hat{\beta}\bar{x}$$

To derive the sampling distributions, we will use the following result: If $y_1, y_2, \ldots, y_n$ are independent normal with variance σ^2, and if

$$L_1 = \sum c_i y_i \qquad \text{and} \qquad L_2 = \sum d_i y_i$$

are two linear functions of y_i, then L_1 and L_2 are jointly normally distributed

$$\text{var}(L_1) = \sigma^2 \sum c_i^2 \qquad \text{var}(L_2) = \sigma^2 \sum d_i^2$$

and

$$\text{cov}(L_1, L_2) = \sigma^2 \sum c_i d_i$$

We now write $\hat{\beta}$ and $\hat{\alpha}$ as linear functions of y_i. First we write

$$
\begin{aligned}
S_{xy} &= \sum (x_i - \bar{x})(y_i - \bar{y}) \\
&= \sum (x_i - \bar{x}) y_i - \bar{y} \sum (x_i - \bar{x}) \\
&= \sum (x_i - \bar{x}) y_i
\end{aligned}
$$

The last term is zero since $\sum (x_i - \bar{x}) = 0$. Thus

$$\hat{\beta} = \frac{S_{xy}}{S_{xx}} = \sum c_i y_i$$

where $c_i = (x_i - \bar{x})/S_{xx}$. Also,

$$\hat{\alpha} = \bar{y} - \hat{\beta}\bar{x} = \frac{1}{n} \sum y_i - \bar{x} \frac{\sum (x_i - \bar{x}) y_i}{S_{xx}} = \sum d_i y_i$$

where

$$d_i = \frac{1}{n} - \frac{\bar{x}(x_i - \bar{x})}{S_{xx}}$$

Thus

$$\text{var}(\hat{\beta}) = \sum c_i^2 \sigma^2 = \frac{\sigma^2}{(S_{xx})^2} \sum (x_i - \bar{x})^2 = \frac{\sigma^2}{S_{xx}}$$

$$\text{var}(\hat{\alpha}) = \sum d_i^2 \sigma^2$$

$$= \sigma^2 \sum \left[\frac{1}{n^2} + \left(\frac{\bar{x}}{S_{xx}} \right)^2 (x_i - \bar{x})^2 - \frac{2}{n} \frac{\bar{x}}{S_{xx}} (x_i - \bar{x}) \right]$$

But

$$\sum (x_i - \bar{x}) = 0 \qquad \sum (x_i - \bar{x})^2 = S_{xx} \qquad \sum \frac{1}{n^2} = \frac{1}{n}$$

Hence

$$\text{var}(\hat{\alpha}) = \sigma^2 \left(\frac{1}{n} + \frac{\bar{x}^2}{S_{xx}} \right)$$

$$\text{cov}(\hat{\alpha}, \hat{\beta}) = \sum c_i d_i \sigma^2$$

$$= \sigma^2 \sum \left(\frac{x_i - \bar{x}}{S_{xx}} \right) \left[\frac{1}{n} - \frac{\bar{x}(x_i - \bar{x})}{S_{xx}} \right]$$

$$= \sigma^2 \left(-\frac{\bar{x}}{S_{xx}} \right)$$

Also, $\hat{\alpha}$ and $\hat{\beta}$ are unbiased estimators. So $E(\hat{\alpha}) = \alpha$ and $E(\hat{\beta}) = \beta$. We can show this by noting that

$$E(\hat{\beta}) = \sum c_i E(y_i) = \sum c_i(\alpha + \beta x_i) = \beta$$

(since $\sum c_i \alpha = 0$ and $\sum c_i x_i = 1$). Also,

$$E(\hat{\alpha}) = E(\bar{y}) - \hat{\beta}\bar{x} = \alpha + \hat{\beta}\bar{x} - \hat{\beta}\bar{x} = \alpha$$

Thus we get the following results:

1. $\hat{\alpha}$ has a normal distribution with mean α and variance

$$\sigma^2\left(\frac{1}{n} + \frac{\bar{x}^2}{S_{xx}}\right)$$

2. $\hat{\beta}$ has a normal distribution with mean β and variance σ^2/S_{xx}.
3. $\text{cov}(\hat{\alpha}, \hat{\beta}) = \sigma^2(-\bar{x}/S_{xx})$.

(3) Distribution of RSS

Note that the derivation of the t-tests in the regression model depend on the result that RSS/σ^2 has a χ^2-distribution with $(n-2)$ d.f. and that this distribution is independent of the distribution of $\hat{\alpha}$ and $\hat{\beta}$. The exact proof of this is somewhat complicated.[16] However, some intuitive arguments can be given as follows.

The estimated residual is

$$\hat{u}_i = y_i - \hat{y}_i$$

Note that $\hat{y}_i = \hat{\alpha} + \hat{\beta}x_i$ and $\hat{y}_i$ and $\hat{u}$ are uncorrelated because

$$\sum \hat{y}_i \hat{u}_i = \hat{\alpha}\sum \hat{u}_i + \hat{\beta}\sum x_i \hat{u}_i = 0$$

by virtue of the normal equations. This proves the independence between $\hat{u}_i$ and $(\hat{\alpha}, \hat{\beta})$. Note that under the assumption of normality zero correlation implies independence.

The next thing to note is that $\sum u_i^2/\sigma^2$ has a χ^2-distribution with n d.f. and $\sum u_i^2$ can be partitioned into two components as follows:

$$\sum u_i^2 = \sum(y_i - \alpha - \beta x_i)^2 = \sum(y_i - \hat{y}_i + \hat{y}_i - \alpha - \beta x_i)^2$$

$$= \sum \hat{u}_i^2 + \sum[(\hat{\alpha} - \alpha) + (\hat{\beta} - \beta)x_i]^2 \qquad \text{(the cross-product term vanishes)}$$

$$= Q_1 + Q_2 \quad \text{(say)}$$

Q_1/σ^2 has a χ^2-distribution with $(n-2)$ d.f. and Q_2/σ^2 has a χ^2-distribution with 2 d.f. Presentation of a detailed proof involves more algebra than is intended here.

---

[16] It is easier to prove it with the use of matrix algebra for the multiple regression model. This proof can be found in any textbook of econometrics. See, for instance, G. S. Maddala, *Econometrics* (New York: McGraw-Hill, 1977), pp. 456–457.

(4) The Method of Maximum Likelihood

The method of maximum likelihoold (ML) is a very general method of estimation that is applicable in a large variety of problems. In the linear regression model, however, we get the same estimators as those obtained by the method of least squares.

The model is

$$y_i = \alpha + \beta x_i + u_i \qquad u_i \sim \text{IN}(0, \sigma^2)$$

This implies that y_i are independently and normally distributed with respective means $\alpha_i + \beta x_i$ and a common variance σ^2. The joint density of the observations, therefore, is

$$f(y_1, \ldots, y_n) = \prod_{i=1}^{n} \left(\frac{1}{2\pi\sigma^2} \right)^{1/2} \exp\left[-\frac{1}{2\sigma^2} (y_i - \alpha - \beta x_i)^2 \right]$$

This function, when considered as a function of the parameters $(\alpha, \beta, \sigma^2)$ is called the *likelihood function* and is denoted by $L(\alpha, \beta, \sigma^2)$. The maximum likelihood (ML) method of estimation suggests that we choose as our estimates the values of the parameters that maximize this likelihood function. In many cases it is convenient to maximize the logarithm of the likelihood function rather than the likelihood function, and we get the same results since $\log L$ and L attain the maximum at the same point.

For the linear regression model we have

$$\log L = \sum_{i=1}^{n} \left[-\frac{1}{2}\log(2\pi\sigma^2) - \frac{1}{2\sigma^2}(y_i - \alpha - \beta x_i)^2 \right]$$

$$= c - \frac{n}{2}\log \sigma^2 - \frac{Q}{2\sigma^2}$$

where $c = -(n/2)\log(2\pi)$ does not involve any parameters
$Q = \sum (y_i - \alpha - \beta x_i)^2$

We will maximize $\log L$ first with respect to α and β and then with respect to σ. Note that it is only the third term in $\log L$ that involves α and β and maximizing this is the same as minimizing Q (since this term has a negative sign). Thus the ML estimators of α and β are the same as the least squares estimators $\hat{\alpha}$ and $\hat{\beta}$ we considered earlier.

Substituting $\hat{\alpha}$ and α for $\hat{\beta}$ for β we get the likelihood function which is now a function of σ only. We now have

$$\log L(\sigma) = \text{const.} - \frac{n}{2}\log \sigma^2 - \frac{\hat{Q}}{2\sigma^2}$$

$$= \text{const.} - n\log \sigma - \frac{\hat{Q}}{2\sigma^2}$$

where $\hat{Q} = \sum (y_i - \hat{\alpha} - \hat{\beta} x_i)^2$ is nothing but the residual sum of squares RSS.

Differentiating this with respect to σ and equating the derivative to zero, we get

$$-\frac{n}{\sigma} + \frac{\hat{Q}}{\hat{\sigma}^3} = 0$$

This gives the ML estimator for σ^2 as

$$\hat{\sigma}^2 = \frac{\hat{Q}}{n} = \frac{RSS}{n}$$

Note that this is different from the unbiased estimator for σ^2 which we have been using, namely, $RSS/(n-2)$. For large n the estimates obtained by the two methods will be very close. The ML method is a large-sample estimation method.

Substituting $\hat{\sigma}^2 = Q/n$ in $\log L(\sigma)$ we get the maximum value of the log-likelihood as

$$\max_{\alpha,\beta,\sigma} \log L = c - \frac{n}{2}\log\frac{\hat{Q}}{n} - \frac{n}{2}$$

$$= c - \frac{n}{2}\log\hat{Q} + \frac{n}{2}\log n - \frac{n}{2}$$

This expression is useful for deriving tests for α, β, σ using the ML method. Since we do not change the sample size n, we will just write

$$\max \log L = \text{const.} - \frac{n}{2}\log\hat{Q}$$

or

$$\max L = \text{const.}\,(\hat{Q})^{-n/2} = \text{const.}\,(RSS)^{-n/2}$$

(5) The Likelihood Ratio Test

The likelihood ratio (LR) test is a general large-sample test based on the ML method. Let θ be the set of parameters in the model and $L(\theta)$ the likelihood function. In our example θ consists of the three parameters α, β, and σ. Hypotheses such as $\beta = 0$ or $\beta = 1$, $\sigma = 0$ impose restrictions on these parameters. What the likelihood ratio test says is that we first obtain the maximum of $L(\theta)$ without any restrictions and with the restrictions imposed by the hypothesis to be tested. We then consider the ratio

$$\lambda = \frac{\max L(\theta) \text{ under the restrictions}}{\max L(\theta) \text{ without the restrictions}}$$

λ will necessarily be less than 1 since the restricted maximum will be less than the unrestricted maximum. If the restrictions are valid, λ will be significantly less than 1. If they are not valid, λ will be close to 1.

The LR test consists of using $-2\log_e\lambda$ as a χ^2 with d.f. k, where k is the number of restrictions. Note that it is log to the base e (natural logarithm).

In our least squares model suppose that we want to test the hypothesis $\beta = 0$.

What we do is we obtain

$$URSS = \text{unrestricted residual sum of squares}$$

and

$$RRSS = \text{restricted residual sum of squares}$$

As derived in the preceding section we have the unrestricted maximum of the likelihood function $= C(URSS)^{-n/2}$ and the restricted maximum $= C(RRSS)^{-n/2}$. Thus

$$\lambda = \left(\frac{RRSS}{URSS}\right)^{-n/2}$$

Hence

$$-2\log_e \lambda = n(\log_e RRSS - \log_e URSS)$$

and we use this as a χ^2 with 1 d.f. In the case of our simple regression model, this test might sound complicated. But the point is that if we want to test the hypothesis $\beta = 0$, note that

$$RRSS = S_{yy}$$

$$URSS = S_{yy}(1 - r^2)$$

Hence, $-2\log_e \lambda = -n\log_e(1 - r^2) = n\log_e[1/(1 - r^2)]$. This we use as χ^2 with 1 d.f. Of course, in the simple regression model we would not be using this test, but the LR test is applicable in a very wide class of situations and is used in non-linear models where small sample tests are not available.

(6) The Wald and Lagrangian Multiplier Tests

There are two other commonly used large sample tests that are based on the ML method. These are the W (Wald) test and the LM (Lagrangian Multiplier) test. We will derive the expressions for these test statistics in the case of the simple regression model.

Note that the t-test for the hypothesis $\beta = 0$ is based on the statistic

$$t = \hat{\beta}/SE(\hat{\beta})$$

and in deriving $SE(\hat{\beta})$ we use an unbiased estimator for σ^2. Instead, suppose, we use the ML estimator $\hat{\sigma}^2 = RSS/n$ that we derived earlier. Then, we get the Wald test. Note that since this is a large sample test we use the standard normal distribution, or the χ^2-distribution if we consider the squared test statistic. Thus,

$$W = \hat{\beta}^2/[\text{Estimate of } var(\hat{\beta})]$$

which we use as χ^2 with 1 d.f. Estimate of $var(\hat{\beta}) = \hat{\sigma}^2/S_{xx}$ where

$$\hat{\sigma}^2 = \frac{S_{yy}(1 - r^2)}{n}.$$

Noting that $\hat{\beta} = S_{xy}/S_{xx}$ we get, on simplification,

$$W = \frac{nr^2}{1 - r^2}.$$

For the LM test we use the restricted residual sum of squares (i.e., residual sum of squares with $\beta = 0$). This is nothing but S_{yy} and $\hat{\sigma}^2 = S_{yy}/n$. Thus, the LM test statistic is

$$LM = nr^2$$

which again has a χ^2-distribution with a 1.d.

In summary, we have

$$
\boxed{
\begin{aligned}
LR &= n\log(1/(1 - r^2)) \\
W &= nr^2/(1 - r^2) \\
LM &= nr^2
\end{aligned}
}
$$

Each has a χ^2-distribution with 1 d.f. These simple formulae are useful to remember and will be used in subsequent chapters. There is an interesting relationship between these test statistics that is valid for linear regression models: This is

$$W \geq LR \geq LM.$$

Note that $W/n = r^2/(1 - r^2)$. Hence, $LM/n = r^2 = (W/n)/(1 + W/n)$. Also, $LR/n = \log(1/(1 - r^2)) = \log(1 + W/n)$. For $x > 0$, there is a famous inequality

$$x \geq \log_e(1 + x) \geq x/(1 + x).$$

Substituting $x = W/n$ we get

$$\frac{W}{n} \geq \frac{LR}{n} \geq \frac{LM}{n}$$

or

$$W \geq LR \geq LM.$$

What this suggests is that a hypothesis can be rejected by the W test but not rejected by the LM test. An example is provided in Section 4.12.

The LR test was suggested by Neyman and Pearson in 1928. The W test was suggested by Abraham Wald in 1943. The LM test was suggested by C. R. Rao in 1948 but the name Lagrangian Multiplier test was given in 1959 by S. D. Silvey. The inequality between the test statistics was first pointed out by Berndt and Savin in 1977.

For the LR test we need the ML estimates from both the restricted and unrestricted maximization of the likelihood function. For the W test we need only the unrestricted ML estimates. For the LM test we need only the restricted ML estimates. Since the last estimates are the easiest to obtain, the LM test is very popular in econometric work.[17]

---

[17] There is a lot of literature on the W, LR and LM tests. For a survey, see R. F. Engle, "Wald, Likelihood Ratio, and Lagrange Multiplier Tests in Econometrics," in Z. Griliches and M. D. Intrilligator (eds.), *Handbook of Econometrics*, Vol. 2 (North Holland Publishing Co., 1984).

(7) Stochastic Regressors

Consider the regression model

$$y_i = \beta x_i + u_i \qquad i = 1, 2, \ldots, n$$

u_i are independent with mean zero and common variance σ^2. x_i are random variables but x_i and u_j are independent for all i and j. We will show that the least squares estimator $\hat{\beta}$ is an unbiased estimator for β. We have

$$\hat{\beta} = \sum c_i y_i$$

where

$$c_i = x_i \Big/ \sum_{j=1}^{n} x_j^2$$

Substituting the value of y_i and simplifying we get

$$\hat{\beta} = \beta + \sum c_i u_i$$

Since x_i and u_j are independent for all i and j, we know that c_i and u_i are independent. Thus, $E(c_i u_i) = E(c_i) \cdot E(u_i) = 0$. Since $E(u_i) = 0$, we need not worry about evaluating $E(c_i)$. Hence, we get the result that

$$E(\hat{\beta}) = \beta + E\left(\sum c_i u_i\right) = \beta.$$

Thus, the least squares estimator is unbiased even if x_i are random variables, provided they are independent of the error terms.

However, when we consider the variance of $\hat{\beta}$, we have to evaluate $E(c_i^2) \cdot E(u_i^2)$. The latter term is σ^2 but the former term is rather cumbersome to compute in general. Hence, the conclusions stated in Section 3.11.

4

Multiple Regression

4.1 INTRODUCTION

In simple regression we study the relationship between an explained variable y and an explanatory variable x. In multiple regression we study the relationship between y and a number of explanatory variables $x_1, x_2, \ldots, x_k$. For instance, in demand studies we study the relationship between quantity demanded of a good and price of the good, prices of substitute goods and the consumer's income. The model we assume is

$$y_i = \alpha + \beta_1 x_{1i} + \beta_2 x_{2i} + \cdots + \beta_k x_{ki} + u_i \qquad i = 1, 2, \ldots, n$$

The errors u_i are again due to measurement errors in y and errors in the specification of the relationship between y and the x's. We make the same assumptions about u_i that we made in Chapter 3. These are:

1. $E(u_i) = 0$.
2. $V(u_i) = \sigma^2$ for all i.
3. u_i and u_j are independent for all $i \neq j$.
4. u_i and x_j are independent for all i and j.
5. u_i are normally distributed for all i.

Under the first four assumptions, we can show that the method of least squares gives estimators of $\alpha, \beta_1, \beta_2, \ldots, \beta_k$, that are unbiased and have minimum variance among the class of linear unbiased estimators. (The proofs are similar to those in Chapter 3 and are omitted.)

Assumption 5 is needed for tests of significance and confidence intervals. It is not needed to prove the optimal properties of least squares estimators.

In addition to these assumptions which are similar to those we make in the case of simple regression, we will also assume that $x_1, x_2, \ldots, x_k$ are not collinear, that is, there is no deterministic linear relationship among them. For instance, suppose that we have the regression equation

$$y = \alpha + \beta_1 x_1 + \beta_2 x_2 + u$$

but x_1 and x_2 are connected by the deterministic linear relationship

$$2x_1 + x_2 = 4$$

then we can express x_2 in terms of x_1 and get $x_2 = 4 - 2x_1$ and the regression equation becomes

$$y = \alpha + \beta_1 x_1 + \beta_2 (4 - 2x_1) + u$$
$$= (\alpha + 4\beta_2) + (\beta_1 - 2\beta_2) x_1 + u$$

Thus we can estimate $(\alpha + 4\beta_2)$ and $(\beta_1 - 2\beta_2)$ but not α, β_1, β_2 separately.

A case where there is an exact linear relationship between the explanatory variables is known as exact or *perfect collinearity*. In the case of the two variables we considered, the exact relationship implies that the correlation coefficient between x_1 and x_2 is $+1$ or -1. In our analysis in this chapter we rule out perfect collinearity but not the case where the correlation between the variables is high but not perfect. When it comes to the analysis of the effect of several variables $x_1, x_2, \ldots, x_k$ on y, we have to distinguish between joint effects and partial effects. For instance, suppose that we are estimating the effect of price and income on quantity demanded; then we have to consider the joint effect of income and price and the partial effects:

1. Effect of price on quantity demanded holding income constant.
2. Effect of income on quantity demanded holding price constant.

These are the problems that we will be dealing with in this chapter. If price and income are highly correlated with each other, it is intuitively clear that it would be difficult to disentangle the separate effects of the two variables.

We start our analysis with the case of two explanatory variables and then present the formulas for the case of k explanatory variables.

4.2 A MODEL WITH TWO EXPLANATORY VARIABLES

Consider the model

$$y_i = \alpha + \beta_1 x_{1i} + \beta_2 x_{2i} + u_i \qquad i = 1, 2, \ldots, n \qquad (4.1)$$

The assumptions we have made about the error term u imply that

$$E(u) = 0 \qquad \mathrm{cov}(x_1, u) = 0 \qquad \mathrm{cov}(x_2, u) = 0$$

As in the case of the simple regression model discussed in Section 3.3, we can replace these assumptions by their sample counterparts.

Let $\hat{\alpha}, \hat{\beta}_1,$ and $\hat{\beta}_2$ be the estimators of $\alpha, \beta_1,$ and $\beta_2,$ respectively. The sample counterpart of u_i is the residual

$$\hat{u}_i = y_i - \hat{\alpha} - \hat{\beta}_1 x_{1i} - \hat{\beta}_2 x_{2i}$$

The three equations to determine $\hat{\alpha}, \hat{\beta}_1,$ and $\hat{\beta}_2$ are obtained by replacing the population assumptions by their sample counterparts:

Population Assumption	Sample Counterpart		
$E(u) = 0$	$(1/n) \sum \hat{u}_i = 0$	or	$\sum \hat{u}_i = 0$
$\mathrm{cov}(u, x_1) = 0$	$(1/n) \sum x_{1i} \hat{u}_i = 0$	or	$\sum x_{1i} \hat{u}_i = 0$
$\mathrm{cov}(u, x_2) = 0$	$(1/n) \sum x_{2i} \hat{u}_i = 0$	or	$\sum x_{2i} \hat{u}_i = 0$

These equations can also be obtained by the use of the least squares method and are referred to as the "normal equations."

The Least Squares Method

The least squares method says that we should choose the estimators $\hat{\alpha}, \hat{\beta}_1, \hat{\beta}_2$ of α, β_1, β_2 so as to minimize

$$Q = \sum (y_i - \alpha - \hat{\beta}_1 x_{1i} - \hat{\beta}_2 x_{2i})^2$$

Differentiate Q with respect to $\hat{\alpha}, \hat{\beta}_1,$ and $\hat{\beta}_2$ and equate the derivatives to zero. We get

$$\frac{\partial Q}{\partial \hat{\alpha}} = 0 \Rightarrow \sum 2(y_i - \hat{\alpha} - \hat{\beta}_1 x_{1i} - \hat{\beta}_2 x_{2i})(-1) = 0 \qquad (4.2)$$

$$\frac{\partial Q}{\partial \hat{\beta}_1} = 0 \Rightarrow \sum 2(y_i - \hat{\alpha} - \hat{\beta}_1 x_{1i} - \hat{\beta}_2 x_{2i})(-x_{1i}) = 0 \qquad (4.3)$$

$$\frac{\partial Q}{\partial \hat{\beta}_2} = 0 \Rightarrow \sum 2(y_i - \hat{\alpha} - \hat{\beta}_1 x_{1i} - \hat{\beta}_2 x_{2i})(-x_{2i}) = 0 \qquad (4.4)$$

These three equations, as mentioned earlier, are called the "normal equations." They can be simplified as follows. Equation (4.2) can be written as

$$\sum y_i = n\hat{\alpha} + \hat{\beta}_1 \sum x_{1i} + \hat{\beta}_2 \sum x_{2i}$$

or

$$\bar{y} = \hat{\alpha} + \hat{\beta}_1 \bar{x}_1 + \hat{\beta}_2 \bar{x}_2 \qquad (4.5)$$

where

$$\bar{y} = \frac{1}{n} \sum y_i \qquad \bar{x}_1 = \frac{1}{n} \sum x_{1i} \qquad \bar{x}_2 = \frac{1}{n} \sum x_{2i}$$

Equation (4.3) can be written as

$$\sum x_{1i} y_i = \hat{\alpha} \sum x_{1i} + \hat{\beta}_1 \sum x_{1i}^2 + \hat{\beta}_2 \sum x_{1i} x_{2i}$$

Substituting the value of $\hat{\alpha}$ from (4.5) into this equation, we get

$$\sum x_{1i} y_i = n\bar{x}_1 (\bar{y} - \hat{\beta}_1 \bar{x}_1 - \hat{\beta}_2 \bar{x}_2) + \hat{\beta}_1 \sum x_{1i}^2 + \hat{\beta}_2 \sum x_{1i} x_{2i} \qquad (4.6)$$

We can simplify this equation by the use of the following notation. Let us define

$$S_{11} = \sum x_{1i}^2 - n\bar{x}_1^2 \qquad\qquad S_{1y} = \sum x_{1i} y_i - n\bar{x}_1 \bar{y}$$

$$S_{12} = \sum x_{1i} x_{2i} - n\bar{x}_1 \bar{x}_2 \qquad S_{2y} = \sum x_{2i} y_i - n\bar{x}_2 \bar{y}$$

$$S_{22} = \sum x_{2i}^2 - n\bar{x}_2^2 \qquad\qquad S_{yy} = \sum y_i^2 - n\bar{y}^2$$

Equation (4.6) can be written as

$$S_{1y} = \hat{\beta}_1 S_{11} + \hat{\beta}_2 S_{12} \qquad (4.7)$$

By a similar simplification, equation (4.4) can be written as

$$S_{2y} = \hat{\beta}_1 S_{12} + \hat{\beta}_2 S_{22} \qquad (4.8)$$

Now we can solve these two equations to get $\hat{\beta}_1$ and $\hat{\beta}_2$. We get

$$\hat{\beta}_1 = \frac{S_{22} S_{1y} - S_{12} S_{2y}}{\Delta}$$

$$\hat{\beta}_2 = \frac{S_{11} S_{2y} - S_{12} S_{1y}}{\Delta} \qquad (4.9)$$

where $\Delta = S_{11} S_{22} - S_{12}^2$. Once we obtain $\hat{\beta}_1$ and $\hat{\beta}_2$ we can get $\hat{\alpha}$ from equation (4.5). We have

$$\hat{\alpha} = \bar{y} - \hat{\beta}_1 \bar{x}_1 - \hat{\beta}_2 \bar{x}_2$$

Thus the computational procedure is as follows:

1. Obtain all the means: $\bar{y}, \bar{x}_1, \bar{x}_2$.
2. Obtain all the sums of squares and sums of products: $\sum x_{1i}^2, \sum x_{2i}^2, \sum x_{1i} x_{2i}$, and so on.
3. Obtain $S_{11}, S_{12}, S_{22}, S_{1y}, S_{2y}$, and S_{yy}.
4. Solve equations (4.7) and (4.8) to get $\hat{\beta}_1$ and $\hat{\beta}_2$.
5. Substitute these in (4.5) to get $\hat{\alpha}$.

In the case of simple regression we also defined the following:

$$\text{residual sum of squares} = S_{yy} - \hat{\beta} S_{xy}$$

$$\text{regression sum of squares} = \hat{\beta} S_{xy}$$

$$r_{xy}^2 = \frac{\hat{\beta} S_{xy}}{S_{yy}}$$

The analogous expressions in multiple regression are

$$\text{RSS} = S_{yy} - \hat{\beta}_1 S_{1y} - \hat{\beta}_2 S_{2y}$$

$$\text{regression sum of squares} = \hat{\beta}_1 S_{1y} + \hat{\beta}_2 S_{2y}$$

$$R_{y \cdot 12}^2 = \frac{\hat{\beta}_1 S_{1y} + \hat{\beta}_2 S_{2y}}{S_{yy}}$$

$R_{y \cdot 12}^2$ is called the *coefficient of multiple determination* and its positive square root is called the *multiple correlation coefficient*. The first subscript is the explained variable. The subscripts after the dot are the explanatory variables. To avoid cumbersome notation we have written 12 instead of $x_1 x_2$. Since it is only x's that have subscripts, there is no confusion in this notation.

The procedure in the case of three explanatory variables is analogous. The normal equations give

$$\hat{\alpha} = \bar{y} - \hat{\beta}_1 \bar{x}_1 - \hat{\beta}_2 \bar{x}_2 - \hat{\beta}_3 \bar{x}_3$$

and

$$S_{1y} = \hat{\beta}_1 S_{11} + \hat{\beta}_2 S_{12} + \hat{\beta}_3 S_{13}$$

$$S_{2y} = \hat{\beta}_1 S_{12} + \hat{\beta}_2 S_{22} + \hat{\beta}_3 S_{23}$$

$$S_{33} = \hat{\beta}_1 S_{13} + \hat{\beta}_2 S_{23} + \hat{\beta}_3 S_{33}$$

We can solve these equations by successive elimination. But this is cumbersome. There are computer programs now available that compute all these things once the basic data are fed in. Thus we will concentrate more on the interpretation of the coefficients rather than on solving the normal equations. Again,

$$\text{RSS} = S_{yy} - \hat{\beta}_1 S_{1y} - \hat{\beta}_2 S_{2y} - \hat{\beta}_3 S_{3y}$$

and

$$R_{y \cdot 123}^2 = \frac{\hat{\beta}_1 S_{1y} + \hat{\beta}_2 S_{2y} + \hat{\beta}_3 S_{3y}}{S_{yy}}$$

Note that $\text{RSS} = S_{yy}(1 - R^2)$ in all cases.

One other important relationship to note, which we have also mentioned in Chapter 3, is that if we consider the residual $\hat{u}_i$ we note that

$$\hat{u}_i = y_i - \hat{\alpha} - \hat{\beta}_1 x_{1i} - \hat{\beta}_2 x_{2i}$$

Thus the normal equations (4.2)–(4.4) imply that

$$\sum \hat{u}_i = 0 \qquad \sum \hat{u}_i x_{1i} = 0 \qquad \sum \hat{u}_i x_{2i} = 0 \qquad (4.10)$$

These equations imply that $\operatorname{cov}(\hat{u}, x_1) = 0$ and $\operatorname{cov}(\hat{u}, x_2) = 0$. Thus the sum of the residuals is equal to zero and the residuals are uncorrelated with both x_1 and x_2.

Illustrative Example

With many computer packages readily available for multiple regression analysis, one does not need to go through the details of the calculations involved. However, it is instructive to see what computations are done by the computer programs. The following simple example illustrates the computations.

In Table 4.1 we present data on a sample of five persons randomly drawn from a large firm giving their annual salaries, years of education, and years of experience with the firm they are working for.

$$Y = \text{annual salary (thousands of dollars)}$$

$$X_1 = \text{years of education past high school}$$

$$X_2 = \text{years of experience within the firm}$$

The means are $\bar{Y} = 30, \bar{X}_1 = 5, \bar{X}_2 = 10$. The sums of squares of deviations from the respective means are

$$S_{11} = 16 \qquad S_{12} = 12 \qquad S_{1y} = 62$$
$$S_{22} = 10 \qquad S_{2y} = 52$$
$$S_{yy} = 272$$

The normal equations are

$$16\hat{\beta}_1 + 12\hat{\beta}_2 = 62$$
$$12\hat{\beta}_1 + 10\hat{\beta}_2 = 52$$

Solving these equations, we get

$$\hat{\beta}_1 = -0.25 \qquad \hat{\beta}_2 = 5.5$$
$$\hat{\alpha} = \bar{Y} - \hat{\beta}_1 X_1 - \hat{\beta}_2 X_2 = 30 - (-1.25) - 55 = -23.75$$
$$R^2 = \frac{\hat{\beta}_1 S_{1y} + \hat{\beta}_2 S_{2y}}{S_{yy}} = \frac{271.5}{272} = .998$$

Thus the regression equation is

$$\hat{Y} = -23.75 - 0.25X_1 + 5.5X_2 \qquad R^2 = 0.998$$

This equation suggests that years of experience with the firm is far more important than years of education (which actually has a negative sign). The equation says that

Table 4.1 Data on Salaries, Years of Education and Years of Experience

Y	X_1	X_2	$Y - \bar{Y}$	$X_1 - \bar{X}_1$	$X_2 - \bar{X}_2$
30	4	10	0	-1	0
20	3	8	-10	-2	-2
36	6	11	6	1	1
24	4	9	-6	-1	-1
40	8	12	10	3	2

we can predict that one more year of experience, after allowing for years of education (or holding it constant) results in an annual increase in salary of $5500. That is, if we consider the persons with the same level of education, the one with one more year of experience can be expected to have a higher salary of $5500. Similarly, if we consider two people with the same experience, the one with an education of one more year can be expected to have a *lower* annual salary of $250. Of course, all these numbers are subject to some uncertainty, which we will be discussing in Section 4.3. It will then be clear that we should be dropping the variable X_1 completely.

What about the interpretation of the constant term -23.75? Clearly, that is the salary one would get with no experience and only high school education. But a negative salary is not possible. What of the case when $X_2 = 0$, that is, a person just joined the firm? Again, the equation predicts a negative salary! So what is wrong?

What we have to conclude is that the sample we have is not a truly representative sample from all the people working in the firm. The sample must have been drawn from a subgroup. We have persons with experience ranging from 8 to 12 years in the firm. So we cannot extrapolate the results too far out of this sample range. We cannot use the equation to predict what a new entrant would earn.

It would be interesting to see what the simple regressions in this example give us. We get

$$\hat{Y} = 10.625 + 3.875X_1 \qquad R^2 = 0.883$$
$$\hat{Y} = -22.0 + 5.2X_2 \qquad R^2 = 0.994$$

The simple regression equation predicts that an increase of one year of education results in an increase of $3875 in annual salary. However, after allowing for the effect of years of experience we find from the multiple regression equation that it does not result in any increase in salary. Thus omission of the variable "years of experience" gives us wrong conclusions about the effect of years of education on salaries.

4.3 STATISTICAL INFERENCE IN THE MULTIPLE REGRESSION MODEL

Again we will consider the results for a model with two explanatory variables first and then the general model. If we assume that the errors u_i are normally distributed, this, together with the other assumptions we have made, implies that $u_i \, IN(0, \sigma^2)$, the following results can be derived. (Proofs are similar to those in Chapter 3 and are omitted.)

1. $\hat{\alpha}$, $\hat{\beta}_1$, and $\hat{\beta}_2$ have normal distributions with means α, β_1, β_2, respectively.
2. If we denote the correlation coefficient between x_1 and x_2 by r_{12}, then

$$\text{var}(\hat{\beta}_1) = \frac{\sigma^2}{S_{11}(1 - r_{12}^2)}$$

$$\text{var}(\hat{\beta}_2) = \frac{\sigma^2}{S_{22}(1 - r_{12}^2)}$$

$$\text{cov}(\hat{\beta}_1, \hat{\beta}_2) = \frac{-\sigma^2 r_{12}^2}{S_{12}(1 - r_{12}^2)}$$

$$\text{var}(\hat{\alpha}) = \frac{\sigma^2}{n} + \bar{x}_1^2 \text{var}(\hat{\beta}_1) + 2\bar{x}_1\bar{x}_2 \text{cov}(\hat{\beta}_1, \hat{\beta}_2) + \bar{x}_2^2 \text{var}(\hat{\beta}_2)$$

$$\text{cov}(\alpha, \hat{\beta}_1) = -[\bar{x}_1 \text{var}(\hat{\beta}_1) + \bar{x}_2 \text{cov}(\hat{\beta}_1, \hat{\beta}_2)]$$

$$\text{cov}(\alpha, \hat{\beta}_2) = -[\bar{x}_1 \text{cov}(\hat{\beta}_1, \hat{\beta}_2) + \bar{x}_2 \text{var}(\hat{\beta}_2)]$$

Comments

1. Note that the higher the value of r_{12} (other things staying the same), the higher the variances of $\hat{\beta}_1$ and $\hat{\beta}_2$. If r_{12} is very high, we cannot estimate β_1 and β_2 with much precision.

2. Note that $S_{11}(1 - r_{12}^2)$ is the residual sum of squares from a regression of x_1 on x_2. Similarly, $S_{22}(1 - r_{12}^2)$ is the residual sum of squares from a regression of x_2 on x_1. We can now see the analogy between the expressions for the variances in the case of simple regression and multiple regression. In simple regression $\text{var}(\hat{\beta}) = \sigma^2/S_{xx}$. In multiple regression $\text{var}(\hat{\beta}_1) = \sigma^2/\text{RSS}_1$, where RSS_1 is the residual sum of squares after regressing x_1 on the other variable, that is, after removing the effect of the other variable. This result generalizes to the case of several explanatory variables. In that case RSS_1 is the residual sum of squares form a regression of x_1 on *all* the other x's.

Analogous to the other results in the case of multiple regression, we have the following results:

3. If RSS is the residual sum of squares then RSS/σ^2 has a χ^2-distribution with degrees of freedom $(n - 3)$. This result can be used to make confidence interval statements about σ^2.
4. If $\hat{\sigma}^2 = \text{RSS}/(n - 3)$, then $E(\hat{\sigma}^2) = \sigma^2$ or $\hat{\sigma}^2$ is an unbiased estimator for σ^2.
5. If we substitute $\hat{\sigma}^2$ for σ^2 in the expressions in result 2, we get the estimated variances and covariances. The square roots of the estimated variances are called the standard errors (to be denoted by SE). Then

$$\frac{\hat{\alpha} - \alpha}{\text{SE}(\hat{\alpha})} \qquad \frac{\hat{\beta}_1 - \beta_1}{\text{SE}(\hat{\beta}_1)} \qquad \frac{\hat{\beta}_2 - \beta_2}{\text{SE}(\hat{\beta}_2)}$$

each has a t-distribution with degrees of freedom $(n - 3)$.

In addition to results 3 to 5, which have counterparts in the case of simple regression, we have one extra item in the case of multiple regression, that of confidence regions and joint tests for parameters. We have the following results.

6. $F = \dfrac{1}{2\hat{\sigma}^2}[S_{11}(\hat{\beta}_1 - \beta_1)^2 + 2S_{12}(\hat{\beta}_1 - \beta_1)(\hat{\beta}_2 - \beta_2) + S_{22}(\hat{\beta}_2 - \beta_2)^2]$ has an F-

distribution with degrees of freedom 2 and $(n - 3)$. This result can be used to construct a *confidence region* for β_1 and β_2 together and to test β_1 and β_2 together.

We will state later results 1 to 6 for the general case of k explanatory variables. But first we will consider an illustrative example.

Illustrative Example

A production function is specified as

$$y_i = \alpha + \beta_1 x_{1i} + \beta_2 x_{2i} + u_i \qquad u_i \sim IN(0, \sigma^2)$$

where

$$y = \log \text{output}$$

$$x_1 = \log \text{labor input}$$

$$x_2 = \log \text{capital input}$$

The variables x_i are nonstochastic. The following data are obtained from a sample of size $n = 23$ (23 individual firms):

$$\bar{x}_1 = 10 \qquad \bar{x}_2 = 5 \qquad \bar{y} = 12$$

$$S_{11} = 12 \qquad S_{12} = 8 \qquad S_{22} = 12$$

$$S_{1y} = 10 \qquad S_{2y} = 8 \qquad S_{yy} = 10$$

(a) Compute $\hat{\alpha}$, $\hat{\beta}_1$, and $\hat{\beta}_2$ and their standard errors. Present the regression equation.

(b) Find the 95% confidence intervals for α, β_1, β_2, and σ^2 and test the hypotheses $\beta_1 = 0$ and $\beta_2 = 0$ separately at the 5% significance level.

(c) Find a 95% confidence region for $\hat{\beta}_1$ and $\hat{\beta}_2$ and show it in a figure.

(d) Test the hypothesis $\beta_1 = 1$, $\beta_2 = 0$ at the 5% significance level.

Solution

(a) The normal equations are

$$12\hat{\beta}_1 + 8\hat{\beta}_2 = 10$$

$$8\hat{\beta}_1 + 12\hat{\beta}_2 = 8$$

These give $\hat{\beta}_1 = 0.7$ and $\hat{\beta}_2 = 0.2$. Hence $\hat{\alpha} = \bar{y} - \hat{\beta}_1 \bar{x}_1 - \hat{\beta}_2 \bar{x}_2 = 12 - 0.7(10) - 0.2(5) = 4$.

$$R^2_{y \cdot 12} = \frac{\hat{\beta}_1 S_{1y} + \hat{\beta}_2 S_{2y}}{S_{yy}}$$

$$= \frac{0.7(10) + 0.2(8)}{10} = .86$$

The residual sum of squares RSS $= S_{yy}(1 - R^2) = 10(1 - 0.86) = 1.4$. Hence

$$\hat{\sigma}^2 = \frac{\text{RSS}}{n - 3} = \frac{1.4}{20} = 0.07$$

$$r^2_{12} = \frac{S^2_{12}}{S_{11} S_{22}} = \frac{64}{144}$$

Hence we have

$$S_{11}(1 - r^2_{12}) = 12\left(\frac{80}{144}\right) = \frac{80}{12} = \frac{20}{3}$$

Hence

$$\text{var}(\hat{\beta}_1) = \frac{\sigma^2}{S_{11}(1 - r^2_{12})} = \frac{3}{20}\sigma^2$$

$$\text{var}(\hat{\beta}_2) = \frac{3}{20}\sigma^2$$

and

$$\text{cov}(\hat{\beta}_1, \hat{\beta}_2) = \frac{-\sigma^2 r^2_{12}}{S_{12}(1 - r^2_{12})}$$

$$= \frac{-\sigma^2(64/144)}{8(80/144)} = -\frac{\sigma^2}{10}$$

Also, since $\bar{x}_1 = 10$ and $\bar{x}_2 = 5$, we have

$$V(\hat{\alpha}) = \sigma^2\left[\frac{1}{23} + (10)^2\left(\frac{3}{20}\right) - \frac{2(10)(5)}{10} + \frac{(5)^2(3)}{20}\right] = 8.7935\sigma^2$$

Substituting the estimate of σ^2, which is 0.07, in these expressions and taking the square roots, we get

$$\text{SE}(\hat{\beta}_1) = \text{SE}(\hat{\beta}_2) = \sqrt{\frac{0.21}{20}} = 0.102$$

$$\text{SE}(\hat{\alpha}) = 0.78$$

Thus the regression equation is

$$\hat{y} = 4.0 + 0.7x_1 + 0.2x_2 \qquad R^2 = 0.86$$
$$\quad (0.78) \quad (0.102) \quad (0.102)$$

Figures in parentheses are standard errors.

(b) Using the t-distribution with 20 d.f., we get the 95% confidence intervals for α, β_1, and β_2 as

$$\hat{\alpha} \pm 2.086\text{SE}(\hat{\alpha}) = 4.0 \pm 1.63 = (2.37, 5.63)$$

$$\hat{\beta}_1 \pm 2.086\text{SE}(\hat{\beta}_1) = 0.7 \pm 0.21 = (0.49, 0.91)$$

$$\hat{\beta}_2 \pm 2.086\text{SE}(\hat{\beta}_2) = 0.2 \pm 0.21 = (-0.01, 0.41)$$

The hypothesis $\beta_1 = 1.0$ will be rejected at the 5% significance level since $\beta_1 = 1.0$ is outside the 95% confidence interval for β_1. The hypothesis $\beta_2 = 0$ will not be rejected because $\beta_2 = 0$ is a point in the 95% confidence interval for β_2. Using the χ^2 distribution for 20 d.f., we have

$$\text{Prob}\left(9.59 < \frac{20\hat{\sigma}^2}{\sigma^2} < 34.2\right) = 0.95$$

or

$$\text{Prob}\left(\frac{20\hat{\sigma}^2}{34.2} < \sigma^2 < \frac{20\hat{\sigma}^2}{9.95}\right) = 0.95$$

Thus the 95% confidence interval for σ^2 is

$$\left(\frac{20(0.07)}{34.2}, \frac{20(0.07)}{9.59}\right) \qquad \text{or} \qquad (0.041, 0.146)$$

(c) The 5% point for the F-distribution with d.f. 2 and 20 is 3.49. Hence using result 6, we can write the 95% *confidence region* for β_1 and β_2 as

$$[S_{11}(\hat{\beta}_1 - \beta_1)^2 + 2S_{12}(\hat{\beta}_1 - \beta_1)(\hat{\beta}_2 - \beta_2) + S_{22}(\hat{\beta}_2 - \beta_2)^2] \leq 3.49(2\hat{\sigma}^2)$$

or

$$[12(0.7 - \beta_1)^2 + 16(0.7 - \beta_1)(0.2 - \beta_2) + 12(0.2 - \beta_2)^2] \leq 3.49(2)(0.07)$$

Or, dividing by 12 throughout and changing $\hat{\beta}_1 - \beta_1$ to $\beta_1 - \hat{\beta}_1$ and $\hat{\beta}_2 - \beta_2$ to $\beta_2 - \hat{\beta}_2$, we get

$$(\beta_1 - 0.7)^2 + \tfrac{4}{3}(\beta_1 - 0.7)(\beta_2 - 0.2) + (\beta_2 - 0.2)^2 \leq 0.041$$

This is an ellipse with center at $(0.7, 0.2)$. It is plotted in Figure 4.1. There are two important things to note: first that the ellipse will be slanting to the left if $\text{cov}(\hat{\beta}_1, \hat{\beta}_2) < 0$ as in our case, and it will be slanting to the right if $\text{cov}(\hat{\beta}_1, \hat{\beta}_2) > 0$. In the case of the two explanatory variables this will depend on the sign of S_{12}. The second point to note is that the limits for β_1 and β_2 that we obtain from the ellipse will be different from the 95% confidence limits we obtained earlier for β_1 and β_2 separately. The limits are $(-0.07, 0.47)$ for β_2 and $(0.43, 0.97)$ for β_1. This is because what we have here are *joint* confidence limits. If $\hat{\beta}_1$ and $\hat{\beta}_2$ are independent, the confidence coefficient for the joint interval will simply be the product of the confidence coefficients for $\hat{\beta}_1$ and $\hat{\beta}_2$ separately. Otherwise, it will be different.

This distinction between *separate intervals and joint intervals*, and between *separate tests and joint tests* should be kept in mind when we talk of statistical inference in the multiple regression model. We discuss this in detail in Section 4.8.

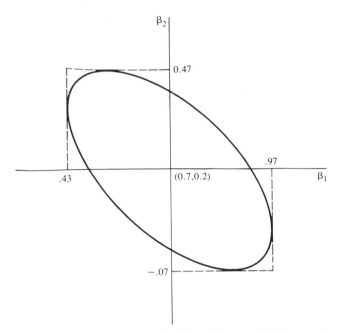

Figure 4.1. Confidence ellipse for β_1 and β_2 in multiple regression.

(d) To test the hypothesis $\beta_1 = 1$, $\beta_2 = 0$ at the 5% confidence level we can check whether the point is in the 95% confidence ellipse. But since we do not plot the confidence ellipse all the time, we will apply the F-test discussed in result 6 earlier. We have

$$F = \frac{1}{2\hat{\sigma}^2}[S_{11}(\hat{\beta}_2 - \beta_1) + 2S_{12}(\hat{\beta}_1 - \beta_1)(\hat{\beta}_2 - \beta_2) + S_{22}(\hat{\beta}_2 - \beta_2)^2]$$

has an F-distribution with d.f. 2 and $n - 3$.

The observed value F_0 is

$$F_0 = \frac{1}{2(0.07)}[12(0.7 - 1.0)^2 + 2(8)(0.7 - 1.0)(0.2 - 0) + 12(0.2 - 0)^2]$$

$$= 4.3$$

The 5% point from the F-tables with 2 and 20 d.f. is 3.49. Since $F_0 > 3.49$ we reject the hypothesis at the 5% significance level.

Formulas for the General Case of *k* Explanatory Variables

We have given explicit expressions for the case of two explanatory variables so as to highlight the differences between simple and multiple regressions. The expressions for the general case can be written down neatly in matrix notation, but since we are not assuming a knowledge of matrix algebra, we will state the results that do not need matrix notation.

In any case we get all the necessary results printed out from all the standard computer packages, and hence we do not need to bother about derivations of the formulas. It is more important to learn how to interpret the results.

If we have the multiple regression equation with k regressors, that is,

$$y_i = \alpha + \beta_1 x_{1i} + \beta_2 x_{2i} + \cdots + \beta_k x_{ki} + u_i$$

then we have to make the following changes in the earlier results: In result 2 earlier, in the expressions for $V(\hat{\beta}_1)$, $V(\hat{\beta}_2)$, and so on, the denominator now will be the residual sum of squares from a regression of that variable on *all* the other x's. Thus

$$\text{var}(\hat{\beta}_i) = \frac{\sigma^2}{\text{RSS}_i} \qquad \text{for } i = 1, 2, \ldots, k$$

where RSS_i is a residual sum of squares from a regression of x_i on *all* the other $(k-1)x$'s.

These k regressions are called *auxiliary regressions*. In practice we do not estimate so many regressions. We have given the formula only to show the relationship between simple and multiple regression. This relationship is discussed in the next section.

In results 3 to 5 we have to change the degrees of freedom from $(n-3)$ to $(n-k-1)$. In simple regression we have $k=1$ and hence d.f. $= n - 2$. In the case of two explanatory variables $k = 2$ and hence we used d.f. $= n - 3$. In all cases one d.f. is for the estimation of α.

Result 6 is now

$$F = \frac{1}{k\hat{\sigma}^2} \left[\sum_{i=1}^{k} \sum_{j=1}^{k} S_{ij}(\hat{\beta}_i - \beta_i)(\hat{\beta}_j - \beta_j) \right]$$

has an F-distribution with d.f. k and $(n-k-1)$.

Some Illustrative Examples

We will now present a few examples using the multiple regression methods. To facilitate the estimation of alternative models, we are presenting the data sets at the end of the chapter (Tables 4.7 to 4.14)

Example 1

In Table 4.7 data are given on sales prices of rural land near Sarasota, Florida.[1] The variables are listed at the end of the table. Since land values appreciated steadily over time, the variable MO (month in which the parcel was sold) is considered an important explanatory variable. Prices are also expected to be higher for those lots that are wooded and those lots that are closer to transportation facilities (airport, highways, etc.). Finally, the price increases less than proportionately with acreage, and hence price per acre falls with increases in acreage. The estimated equation was

---

[1] These data have been provided by J. S. Shonkwiler. They are used in the paper: J. S. Shonkwiler and J. E. Reynolds, "A Note on the Use of Hedonic Price Models in the Analysis of Land Prices at the Urban Fringe," *Land Economics*, February 1986.

(figures in parentheses are standard errors)

$$\log P_t = 9.213 + 0.148WL - 0.33DA - 0.0057D75$$
$$\quad\;\; (0.204) \quad\; (0.099) \qquad\quad (0.011) \qquad\quad (0.0142)$$

$$\quad - 0.203 \log A + 0.0141MO \qquad R^2 = 0.559$$
$$\qquad (0.035) \qquad\quad (0.0039)$$

All the coefficients have the expected signs although some of them are not significant (not significantly different from zero) at the 5% level.

Example 2

In Example 1 we had some notions of what signs to expect for the different coefficients in the regression equation. Sometimes, even if the signs are correct, the magnitudes of the coefficients do not make economic sense. In which case one has to examine the model or the data. An example where the magnitude of the coefficient makes sense is the following.

In June 1978, California voters approved what is known as Proposition 13 limiting property taxes. This led to substantial and differential reduction in property taxes, which led to an increase in housing prices. Rosen[2] studied the impact of reduction in property taxes on housing prices in the San Francisco Bay area. Besides property taxes, there are other factors that determine housing prices and these have to be taken into account in the study. Rosen therefore included the characteristics of the house, such as square footage, age of the house, and a quality index. He also included economic factors such as median income and transportation time to San Francisco. The estimated equation was (figures in parentheses are *t-values*, not standard errors).

$$\hat{y} = 0.171 + 7.275x_1 + 0.547x_2 + 0.00073x_3 + 0.0638x_4$$
$$\qquad\quad (2.97) \qquad\; (2.32) \qquad\;\; (1.34) \qquad\quad (3.26)$$

$$\quad - 0.0043x_5 + 0.857x_6 \qquad R^2 = 0.897 \qquad n = 64$$
$$\qquad (2.24) \qquad\;\; (1.80)$$

where y = change in post-Proposition 13 mean house prices
  x_1 = post-Proposition 13 decrease in property tax bill on mean house
  x_2 = mean square footage of house
  x_3 = median income of families in the area
  x_4 = mean age of house
  x_5 = transportation time to San Francisco
  x_6 = housing-quality index as computed by real estate appraisers

All the coefficients have the expected signs.

The coefficient of x_1 indicates that each $1 decrease in property taxes increases property values of $7. The question is whether this is about the right magnitude. Assuming that the property tax reduction is expected to be at the same level in the future years, the present value of a $1 return per year is $1/r$, where r is the rate of

[2] Kenneth T. Rosen, "The Impact of Proposition 13 on Housing Prices in Northern California: A Test of the Interjurisdictional Capitalization Hypothesis," *Journal of Political Economy*, February 1982, pp. 191–200.

interest (also expected to remain the same). This is equal to $7 if $r = 14.29\%$. The interest rates at that time were around this level and thus Rosen concludes: "The capitalization rate implied by this equation is about 7 which is precisely the magnitude that one would expect with an interest rate of 12–15%."

Example 3

In Table 4.8 data are presented on gasoline consumption in the United States for the years 1947–1969. Let us define

$$G = \frac{KC}{M(\text{POP})} = \text{per capita consumption of gasoline in gallons}$$

We will regress G on P_g and y. (The variables are defined in Table 4.8). The results we get are

$$\hat{G} = -117.70 + 0.373P_g + 0.156Y \qquad R^2 = 0.953$$
$$\quad\;\;(-1.14)\quad\;(0.44)\qquad(12.02)$$

(Figures in parentheses are t-ratios.) The price P_g has the wrong sign although it is not significant. Only per capita income appears to be the major determinant of demand for gasoline. In log form the equation is

$$\log \hat{G} = -8.72 + 0.535 \log P_g + 1.541 \log Y \qquad R^2 = 0.940$$
$$\quad\;\;(-3.00)\quad\;(1.23)\qquad\quad(11.21)$$

Again P_g has the wrong sign. Instead of population, suppose that we use labor force as divisor and define G as $G = K \cdot C/M \cdot L$. This can be justified on the argument that miles driven would be more related to L than to population. The results we get are

$$\hat{G} = -248.44 + 0.258P_g + 0.406Y \qquad R^2 = 0.925$$
$$\quad\;\;(-0.70)\quad\;(0.09)\qquad(9.15)$$

The variable P_g still has the wrong sign. In log form the results are

$$\log \hat{G} = -8.53 + 0.541 \log P_g + 1.636 \log Y \qquad R^2 = 0.907$$
$$\quad\;\;(-2.18)\quad\;(0.92)\qquad\quad(8.82)$$

Gilstein and Leamer [3] estimate the equation using the 1947–1960 data and obtain

$$\hat{G} = 799.1 - 2.563P_g + 0.0616Y$$
$$\quad\;(77.5)\quad\;(0.706)\qquad(0.0015)$$

(Figures in parentheses are standard errors.) Also, we get, using the 1947–1960 data,

$$\hat{G} = -439.4 - 2.241P_g + 0.662Y \qquad R^2 = 0.979$$
$$\quad(-2.92)(-1.64)\qquad(22.25)$$

(Figures in parentheses are t-ratios.) In log form we get

$$\log \hat{G} = -10.477 - 0.387 \log P_g + 2.472 \log Y \qquad R^2 = 0.974$$
$$\quad\;\;(-5.67)\quad\;(-1.16)\qquad\quad(20.04)$$

[3] C. Z. Gilstein and E. E. Leamer, "Robust Sets of Regression Estimates," *Econometrica*, Vol. 51, No. 2, March 1983, p. 330.

In summary, the period 1947–1960 shows a price elasticity of demand slightly negative and an income elasticity of demand significantly greater than unity. Estimation of the same equation over 1947–1969 shows no responsiveness to price but an income elasticity of demand again significantly greater than 1.

Further analysis using these data is left as an exercise. Students can experiment with this data set after going through this and the next two chapters.

Example 4

In Table 4.9 data are presented on the demand for food in the United States. Let us try to estimate the price elasticity and income elasticity of demand for food. A regression of Q_D on P_D and Y gave the following results:

$$\hat{Q}_D = 92.05 - 0.1421 P_D + 0.236 Y \qquad R^2 = 0.7813$$
$$\quad\;\; {\scriptstyle (15.76)} \;\; {\scriptstyle (-2.13)} \qquad\quad {\scriptstyle (7.56)}$$

(Figures in parentheses t-ratios.) The coefficients have the right signs. However, someone comes and says that the variables all have trends and we ought to account for this by including T as an extra explanatory variable. The results now are (all variables have the right signs).

$$\hat{Q}_D = 105.1 - 0.325 P_D + 0.315 Y - 0.224 T \qquad R^2 = 0.8812$$
$$\quad\;\; {\scriptstyle (18.47)(-4.58)} \qquad {\scriptstyle (9.85)} \qquad {\scriptstyle (3.67)}$$

Now the price variable is more significant than before. Also, a simple regression of Q_D on P_D gives a wrong sign for P_D:

$$\hat{Q}_D = 89.97 + 0.107 P_D \qquad R^2 = 0.044$$
$$\quad\;\; {\scriptstyle (7.89)} \quad {\scriptstyle (0.91)}$$

We have given four examples, the first two on cross-section data, the other two on time-series data. The results were more straightforward with the cross-section data sets. With the time-series data sets, we have had some trouble obtaining meaningful results. This is a common experience. The problem is that most of the series move together with time.

4.4 INTERPRETATION OF THE REGRESSION COEFFICIENTS

In simple regression we are concerned with measuring the effect of the explanatory variable on the explained variable. Since the regression equation can be written as

$$y - \bar{y} = \hat{\beta}(x - \bar{x})$$

this effect is measured by $\hat{\beta}$, where

$$\hat{\beta} = \frac{S_{xy}}{S_{xx}} \qquad \text{or} \qquad \frac{\text{cov}(x, y)}{V(x)}$$

In the multiple regression equation with two explanatory variables x_1 and x_2 we can talk of the *joint* effect of x_1 and x_2 and the *partial* effect of x_1 or x_2 upon y. Since the regression equation can be written as

$$y - \bar{y} = \hat{\beta}_1(x_1 - \bar{x}_1) + \hat{\beta}_3(x_2 - \bar{x}_2)$$

the partial effect of x_1 is measured by $\hat{\beta}_1$ and the partial effect of x_2 is measured by $\hat{\beta}_2$. By partial effect we mean holding the other variable constant or after eliminating the effect of the other variable. Thus $\hat{\beta}_1$ is to be interpreted as measuring the effect of x_1 on y after eliminating the effect of x_2 on x_1. Similarly, $\hat{\beta}_2$ is to be interpreted as measuring the effect of x_2 on y after eliminating the effect of x_1 on x_2.

This interpretation suggests that we can derive the estimator $\hat{\beta}_1$ of β_1 by estimating two separate simple regressions:

Step 1. Estimate a regression of x_1 on x_2. Let the regression coefficient be denoted by b_{12}. Denoting the residuals from this equation by W_i, we have

$$W_i = x_{1i} - \bar{x}_1 - b_{12}(x_{2i} - \bar{x}_2) \tag{4.12}$$

Note that W_i is that part of x_1 that is left after removing the effect of x_2 on x_1.

Step 2. Now regress y_i on W_i. The regression coefficient is nothing but $\hat{\beta}_1$, which we derived earlier in the multiple regression [see (4.9)]. To see this, note that the regression coefficient of y_i on W_i is nothing but $\text{cov}(y_i, W_i)/\text{var}(W_i)$. From (4.12) we have (since $\sum W_i = 0$)

$$nV(W_i) = \sum W_i^2 = S_{11} + b_{12}^2 S_{22} - 2b_{12}S_{12}$$

But $b_{12} = S_{12}/S_{22}$, hence $nV(W_i) = S_{11} - S_{12}^2/S_{22}$. Also,

$$n\,\text{cov}(y_i, W_i) = \sum y_i W_i$$
$$= S_{1y} - b_{12}S_{2y}$$

Now substitute $b_{12} = S_{12}/S_{22}$. We get, on simplification,

$$n\,\text{cov}(y_i, W_i) = S_{1y} - \frac{S_{12}S_{2y}}{S_{22}}$$

Hence we get

$$\frac{n\,\text{cov}(y_i, W_i)}{nV(W_i)} = \frac{S_{22}S_{1y} - S_{12}S_{2y}}{S_{11}S_{22} - S_{12}^2}$$

which is the expression for $\hat{\beta}_1$ we got in (4.9).

Suppose that we eliminate the effect of x_2 on y as well. Let V_i be the residual from a regression of y on x_2. If we now regress V_i on W_i, then the regression coefficient we get will be the same as that obtained from a regression of y_i on W_i. This is because

$$V_i = y_i - \bar{y} - b_{y2}(x_{2i} - \bar{x}_2)$$

where b_{y2} is the regression coefficient of y on x_2. However, x_2 will be uncorrelated with W (a residual is uncorrelated with a regressor). Hence,

$$\text{cov}(V, W) = \text{cov}(y, W).$$

Thus, a regression of V_i on W_i will produce the same estimate $\hat{\beta}_1$ as a regression of y_i on W_i. Of course, the standard errors of $\hat{\beta}_1$ from the two regressions will be different because

$$\text{var}(V) < \text{var}(y).$$

This result is important and useful in trend elimination and seasonal adjustment of time-series data. What it implies is that if we have an explained variable y and an explanatory variable x and there is another nuisance variable Z that is influencing both y and x, the "pure" effect of x on y after eliminating the effect of this nuisance variable Z on both x and y can be estimated simply by estimating the multiple regression equation

$$y = \alpha + \beta x + \gamma Z + u$$

The coefficient β gives us the "pure" effect needed. We do not have to run a regression of y on Z and x on Z to eliminate the effect of Z on these variables and then a third regression of "purified" y on "purified" x.

Although we have proved the result for only two variables, the result is general. x and Z can both be sets of variables (instead of single variables).[4]

Finally, the standard error of $\hat{\beta}_1$ obtained from the estimation of the multiple regression (4.1) is also the same as the standard error of the regression coefficient obtained from the simple regression of y_i on W_i. This result is somewhat tedious to prove here, so we will omit the proof.[5]

The correlation coefficient between y and W is called the *partial correlation* between y and x_1. It is partial correlation in the sense that the effect of x_2 has been removed. It will be denoted by $r_{y1 \cdot 2}$. The subscript after the dot denotes the variable whose effect has been removed. Corresponding to the relationship we have given in Chapter 3 (end of Section 3.5), we have the formula

$$r_{y1 \cdot 2}^2 = \frac{t_1^2}{t_1^2 + (n - 3)}$$

where $t_1 = \hat{\beta}_1 / \text{SE}(\hat{\beta}_1)$. The derivation of this formula is also omitted here since it is somewhat tedious.

The interpretation of $\hat{\beta}_2$ and the formulas associated with it are similar. Thus we have

$$r_{y2 \cdot 1}^2 = \frac{t_2^2}{t_2^2 + (n - 3)}$$

where $t_2 = \hat{\beta}_2 / \text{SE}(\hat{\beta}_2)$.

Illustrative Example

In the illustrative example in Section 4.3 we have

$$t_1 = \frac{0.7}{0.102} = 6.863 \qquad t_2 = \frac{0.2}{0.102} = 1.961$$

---

[4] For a general model this is proved in G. S. Maddala, *Econometrics* (New York: McGraw-Hill, 1977), p. 462 under the title "Prior Adjustment."

[5] The proof can easily be constructed using the result in Maddala, *Econometrics*, p. 462.

Hence

$$r_{y1\cdot2}^2 = \frac{(6.863)^2}{(6.863)^2 + 20} = \frac{47.10}{67.10} = 0.70$$

$$r_{y2\cdot1}^2 = \frac{(1.961)^2}{(1.961)^2 + 20} = \frac{3.846}{23.846} = 0.16$$

The General Case

In the general case of k regressors we define $t_i = \hat{\beta}_i/\text{SE}(\hat{\beta}_i)$ for $i = 1, 2, \ldots, k$. Then the partial r^2 for the variable x_i is

$$r_{yx_i}^2 \cdot \text{other } x\text{'s} = \frac{t_i^2}{t_i^2 + (n - k - 1)}$$

4.5 PARTIAL CORRELATIONS AND MULTIPLE CORRELATION

If we have an explained variable y and three explanatory variables x_1, x_2, x_3 and $r_{y1}^2, r_{y2}^2, r_{y3}^2$ are the squares of the simple correlations between y and x_1, x_2, x_3 respectively, then $r_{y1}^2, r_{y2}^2,$ and r_{y3}^2 measure the proportion of the variance in y that x_1 *alone*, x_2 *alone*, or x_3 *alone* explain. On the other hand, $R_{y\cdot123}^2$ measures the proportion of the variance of y that x_1, x_2, x_3 *together* explain. We would also like to measure something else. For instance, how much does x_2 explain *after* x_1 is included in the regression equation? How much does x_3 explain after x_1 and x_2 are included? These are measured by the partial coefficients of determination $r_{y2\cdot1}^2$ and $r_{y3\cdot12}^2$ respectively.[6] The variables after the dot are the variables already included. With three explanatory variables we have the following partial correlations: $r_{y1\cdot2}$, $r_{y1\cdot3}, r_{y2\cdot1}, r_{y2\cdot3},$ and $r_{y3\cdot1}$, and $r_{y3\cdot2}$. These are called partial correlations of the *first* order. We also have three partial correlation coefficients of the *second* order: $r_{y1\cdot23}$, $r_{y2\cdot13}$, and $r_{y3\cdot12}$. The variables after the dot are always the variables already included in the regression equation. The order of the partial correlation coefficient depends on the number of variables after the dot. The usual convention is to denote simple and partial correlations by a small r and multiple correlations by capital R. For instance, $R_{y\cdot12}^2, R_{y\cdot13}^2,$ and $R_{y\cdot123}^2$ are all coefficients of multiple determination (their positive square roots are multiple correlation coefficients).

How do we compute the partial correlation coefficients? For this we use the relationship between r^2 and t^2. For example, to compute $r_{y2\cdot3}^2$ we have to consider the multiple regression of y on x_2 and x_3. Let the estimated regression equation be

$$\hat{y} = \hat{\alpha} + \hat{\beta}_2 x_2 + \hat{\beta}_3 x_3$$

---

[6] We are using the word "coefficient of determination" to denote the square of the "coefficient of correlation."

Let $t_2 = \hat{\beta}_2/\text{SE}(\hat{\beta}_2)$ from this equation. Then

$$r_{y2 \cdot 3}^2 = \frac{t_2^2}{t_2^2 + \text{d.f.}}$$

The degrees of freedom d.f. = (number of observations) − (number of regression parameters estimated) = $(n - 3)$ in this case. The variables to be included in the multiple regression equation are all variables that are mentioned in the partial correlation coefficient. For instance, if we want to compute $r_{y4 \cdot 237}^2$, we have to run a regression of y on x_4, x_2, x_3, and x_7. Let $t_4 = \hat{\beta}_4/\text{SE}(\hat{\beta}_4)$, where β_4 is the coefficient of x_4. Then

$$r_{y4 \cdot 237}^2 = \frac{t_4^2}{t_4^2 + \text{d.f.}}$$

and d.f. = $(n - 5)$ in this case (one α and four β's).

Partial correlations are very important in deciding whether or not to include more explanatory variables. For instance, suppose that we have two explanatory variables x_1 and x_2, and r_{y2}^2 is very high, say 0.95, but $r_{y2 \cdot 1}^2$ is very low, say 0.01. What this means is that if x_2 alone is used to explain y, it can do a good job. But after x_1 is included, x_2 does not help any more in explaining y; that is, x_1 has done the job of x_2. In this case there is no use including x_2. In fact, we can have a situation where, for instance,

$$r_{y1}^2 = 0.95 \quad \text{and} \quad r_{y2}^2 = 0.96$$

but

$$r_{y1 \cdot 2}^2 = 0.1 \quad \text{and} \quad r_{y2 \cdot 1}^2 = 0.1$$

In this case each variable is highly correlated with y but the partial correlations are both very low. This is called *multicollinearity* and we will discuss this problem later in Chapter 7. In this example we can use x_1 only or x_2 only or some combination of the two as an explanatory variable. For instance, suppose that x_1 is the amount of skilled labor, x_2 the amount of unskilled labor, and y the output. What the partial correlation coefficients suggest is that the separation of total labor into two components—skilled and unskilled—does not help us much in explaining output. So we might as well use $x_1 + x_2$ or total labor as the explanatory variable.

4.6 RELATIONSHIP AMONG SIMPLE, PARTIAL, AND MULTIPLE CORRELATION COEFFICIENTS

To study the relationships among the different types of correlation coefficients, we need to make use of the relationship that at each stage the residual sum of squares RSS = $S_{yy}(1 - R^2)$. Suppose that we have two explanatory variables x_1 and x_2. Then

$S_{yy}(1 - R_{y \cdot 12}^2)$ = residual sum of squares after *both* x_1 and x_2 are included

$S_{yy}(1 - r_{y1}^2)$ = residual sum of squares after the inclusion of x_1 only

Now $r_{y2 \cdot 1}^2$ measures the proportion of this residual sum of squares explained by x_2. Hence the unexplained residual sum of squares after x_2 is also included is

$$(1 - r_{y2 \cdot 1}^2)S_{yy}(1 - r_{y1}^2)$$

But this is equal to $S_{yy}(1 - R_{y \cdot 12}^2)$. Hence we get the result that

$$1 - R_{y \cdot 12}^2 = (1 - r_{y1}^2)(1 - r_{y2 \cdot 1}^2)$$

If we have three explanatory variables we get

$$(1 - R_{y \cdot 123}^2) = (1 - r_{y1}^2)(1 - r_{y2 \cdot 1}^2)(1 - r_{y3 \cdot 12}^2) \tag{4.13}$$

The subscripts 1, 2, 3 can be interchanged in any required order. Thus if we need to consider them in the order 3, 1, 2, we have

$$(1 - R_{y \cdot 123}^2) = (1 - r_{y3}^2)(1 - r_{y1 \cdot 3}^2)(1 - r_{y2 \cdot 31}^2)$$

Note that the partial r^2 can be greater or smaller than the simple r^2. For instance, the variable x_2 might explain only 20% of the variance of y, but after x_1 is included, it can explain 50% of the residual variance. In this case the simple r^2 is 0.2 and the partial r^2 is 0.5. We are thus talking of the proportions explained of different variances.

On the other hand, the simple r^2 and the partial r^2 can never be greater than R^2 (the square of the multiple correlation coefficient). This is clear from the formulas we have stated.

Two Illustrative Examples

The following examples illustrate simple r^2, partial r^2, and R^2. The first example illustrates some problems in interpreting multiple regression coefficients when the explanatory variables are proportions. The second example illustrates the use of interaction terms.

Example 1: Hospital Costs

Consider the analysis of hospital costs by case mix by Feldstein.[7] The data are for 177 hospitals. The explanatory variables are *proportions* of total patients treated in each category. There are nine categories: M = medical, P = pediatrics, S = general surgery, E = ENT, T = traumatic and orthopedic surgery, OS = other surgery, G = gynecology, Ob = Obstretics, Other = miscellaneous others. The regression coefficients, their standard errors, t-values, partial r^2's, simple r^2's, and average cost per case are given in Table 4.2, page 110.

The entries in Table 4.2 need some explanation. The t-values are just the coefficients divided by the respective standard errors. The partial r^2's are obtained by the formula

$$r^2 = \frac{t^2}{t^2 + \text{d.f.}}$$

[7] M. S. Feldstein, *Economic Analysis for the Health Service Industry* (Amsterdam: North-Holland, 1967), Chap. 1.

Table 4.2 Hospital Cost Regressions

Variable	Regression Coefficient	SE	t Ratio	Partial r^2	Simple r^2	Average Cost per Case
M	44.97	18.89	2.38	0.0326	0.1423	114.48
P	−44.54	28.51	−1.56	0.0143	0.0074	24.97
S	−36.81	14.88	−2.47	0.0350	0.0343	32.70
E	−54.26	16.52	−3.28	0.0612	0.0947	15.25
T	−29.82	17.18	−1.74	0.0177	0.0062	39.69
OS	28.51	20.27	1.41	0.0117	0.0478	98.02
G	−10.79	21.47	−0.50	0.0015	0.0099	58.72
Ob	−34.63	16.34	−2.12	0.0261	0.0011	34.88
Other	0					69.51
Constant	69.51		$R^2 = 0.3076$			

Thus, for the variable M,

$$\text{partial } r^2 = \frac{(2.38)^2}{(2.38)^2 + 168} = 0.0326$$

The simple r^2 is just the square of the correlation of average cost per case and the proportion of the cases in that category. The two are presented together to illustrate how the partial r^2's can be lower or higher than the simple r^2's.

The regression coefficients in this example have to be interpreted in a different way. In the usual case, each regression coefficient measures the change in the dependent variable y for unit increase in that independent variable, *holding other variables constant*. In this example, since the independent variables are proportions in that category; an increase in one variable holding other variables constant does not make sense (in fact, it is impossible to do it). The proper interpretation of the coefficients in this case is this: Put the value of $M = 1$, all others 0. Then the estimated value of the dependent variable = (constant + coefficient of M) = 69.51 + 44.97 = 114.48. This is the average cost of treating a case in M. Similarly, constant + coefficient of $P = 69.51 − 44.54 = 24.97$ is the average cost of treating a case in P. Finally, putting $M, P, \ldots, Ob$ all = 0, we get the constant term = 69.51 as the average cost of treating a case in the "Other" category. These coefficients are all presented in the last column of Table 4.2. What the regression equation enables us to estimate in this case is the average cost of treating a case in each category. The standard errors of these estimates can be calculated as $SE(\hat{\alpha} + \hat{\beta}_i)$ if we know the covariance between the constant term $\hat{\alpha}$ and the other regression coefficient $\hat{\beta}$.

An important point to note is that we have not estimated a coefficient for the category "other." An alternative procedure in which we estimate coefficients for all the categories directly would be to include all the variables and *delete the constant term*. We have to delete the constant term because the sum of all the explanatory variables (which are proportions of cases treated in each category) is equal to 1 for all observations. Since the constant term corresponds to an explanatory variable that is identically equal to 1 for all observations, we cannot include it in the regression equation. If we do, we have a situation where one of the explanatory variables is identically the sum of the other explanatory variables. In this case we cannot estimate all the coefficients.

To see what the problem is, consider the equation

$$y = \alpha + \beta_1 x_1 + \beta_2 x_2 + \beta_3 x_3 + u$$

where $x_3 = x_1 + x_2$. We can easily see that we cannot get separate estimates of β_1, β_2, and β_3 since the equation reduces to

$$y = \alpha + \beta_1 x_1 + \beta_2 x_2 + \beta_3 (x_1 + x_2) + u$$
$$= \alpha + (\beta_1 + \beta_2) x_1 + (\beta_2 + \beta_3) x_2 + u$$

such a situation is known as "perfect multicollinearity" and is discussed in greater detail in Chapter 7.

A regression equation with no constant term is also called "regression through the origin" because if the x-variables are all zero, the y-variable is also zero. The estimation of such an equation proceeds as before and the normal equations are defined as in equations (4.7) and (4.8) except that we do not apply the "mean corrections." That is, we define

$$S_{11} = \sum x_{1i}^2 \text{ and not } \sum (x_{1i} - \bar{x}_1)^2$$
$$S_{12} = \sum x_{1i} x_{2i} \text{ and not } \sum (x_{1i} - \bar{x}_1)(x_{2i} - \bar{x}_2) \qquad \text{etc.}$$

After these changes are made, the solution of the normal equations proceeds as before. The definition of RSS and R^2 also proceeds as before, with the change that in S_{yy} as well, no mean correction be applied.

Cautionary Note: Many regression programs allow the option of including or excluding the constant term. However, some of them may not give the correct R^2 when running a regression equation with no constant term. If the R^2 is computed as $1 - \text{RSS}/S_{yy}$ and S_{yy} is computed using the mean correction, we might get a very small R^2 and sometimes even a negative R^2.

Note that with two explanatory variables, and no constant term, $\text{RSS} = \sum y_i^2 - \hat{\beta}_1(\sum y_i x_{1i}) - \hat{\beta}_2(\sum y_i x_{2i})$ and if S_{yy} is computed (wrongly) with a mean correction, so that $S_{yy} = \sum y_i^2 - n\bar{y}^2$, it can happen that $S_{yy} < \text{RSS}$ and thus we get negative R^2.

The correct R^2 in this case is $1 - \text{RSS}/\sum y_i^2$. Of course, if $\bar{y}$ is very high $\sum y_i^2$ will be very high compared with RSS and we might get a high R^2. But one should not infer from this that the equation with no constant term is better than the one with a constant term. The two R^2 values are not comparable. With a constant term, the R^2 measures the proportion of $\sum (y_i - \bar{y})^2$ explained by the explanatory variables. Without a constant term that R^2 explains the proportion of $\sum y_i^2$ explained by the explanatory variables. Thus we are talking of proportions of two different things, and hence we cannot compare them.

Table 4.3 Indexes of Food Consumption, Food Price, and Consumer Income[a]

Year	Food Consumption Per Capita, q	Food Price p^b	Consumer Income y^c
1927	88.9	91.7	57.7
1928	88.9	92.0	59.3
1929	89.1	93.1	62.0
1930	88.7	90.9	56.3
1931	88.0	82.3	52.7
1932	85.9	76.3	44.4
1933	86.0	78.3	43.8
1934	87.1	84.3	47.8
1935	85.4	88.1	52.1
1936	88.5	88.0	58.0
1937	88.4	88.4	59.8
1938	88.6	83.5	55.9
1939	91.7	82.4	60.3
1940	93.3	83.0	64.1
1941	95.1	86.2	73.7
(World War II years excluded)			
1948	96.7	105.3	82.1
1949	96.7	102.0	83.1
1950	98.0	102.4	88.6
1951	96.1	105.4	88.3
1952	98.1	105.0	89.1
1953	99.1	102.6	92.1
1954	99.1	101.9	91.7
1955	99.8	100.8	96.5
1956	101.5	100.0	99.8
1957	99.9	99.8	99.9
1958	99.1	101.2	98.4
1959	101.0	98.8	101.8
1960	100.7	98.4	101.8
1961	100.8	98.8	103.1
1962	101.0	98.4	105.5

[a] 1957–1959 = 100.

[b] Retail prices of Bureau of Labor Statistics, deflated by dividing by Consumer Price Index.

[c] Per capita disposable income, deflated by dividing by Consumer Price Index.

Table 4.4 Estimates of Demand for Food Equations[a]

	Equation 1			Equation 2[b]		
	1927–41	1948–62	All Obs.	1927–41	1948–62	All Obs.
α	4.555 (22.67)	5.052 (5.61)	4.050 (29.65)	4.058 (0.54)	16.632 (0.61)	8.903 (4.50)
β_1 (price)	−0.235 (−4.41)	−0.237 (−1.54)	−0.120 (−2.95)	−0.123 (−0.07)	−2.745 (−0.47)	−1.011 (−2.55)
β_2 (income)	0.243 (10.63)	0.141 (3.03)	0.242 (17.85)	0.368 (0.20)	−2.416 (−0.40)	−0.732 (−1.69)
β_3 (interaction)				−0.028 (−0.07)	0.554 (0.43)	0.214 (2.26)
n	15	15	30	15	15	30
R^2	0.9066	0.8741	0.9731	0.9066	0.8762	0.9775
F^c	58.2	41.7	489	35.6	26.0	377
$10^2 \times$ RSS	0.1151	0.0544	0.2866	0.1151	0.0535	0.2397
d.f.	12	12	27	11	11	26
$10^4 \times \hat{\sigma}^{2d}$	0.9594	0.4534	1.0613	1.0462	0.4866	0.9218

[a] Figures in parentheses are t-ratios, not standard errors.
[b] From Equation 2, all the partial r^2's are very low for 1927–41 and 1948–62, although the R^2's are high.
[c] F is an F-statistic for testing overall fit, that is, for R^2. This is discussed in Section 4.8.
[d] $\hat{\sigma}^2 = $ RSS/d.f. The importance of this is discussed in Section 4.9.

Example 2: Demand for Food

Table 4.3 presents data on per capita food consumption, price of food and per capita income for the years: 1927–1941 and 1948–1962.[8] Two equations are estimated for these data:

Equation 1: $\log q = \alpha + \beta_1 \log p + \beta_2 \log y$

Equation 2: $\log q = \alpha + \beta_1 \log p + \beta_2 \log y + \beta_3 \log p \log y$

The last term in Equation 2 is an interaction term that allows the price and income elasticities to vary. Equation 1 implies constant price and income elasticities.

The estimates of α, β_1, β_2, and β_3 for 1927–1942 and 1948–1962 separately and for both periods combined are presented in Table 4.4. *Note that we have presented the t-ratios in parentheses* because this is more convenient to interpret. If we are interested in significance tests, the t-ratios are more convenient and if we are interested in obtaining confidence intervals, it is convenient to have the standard errors.

The interaction term has a very low t-value in the equations for 1927–1942 and 1948–1962 separately. Hence we will consider only the equation for the combined data. For this equation the income coefficient has a low t-value and the sign also appears to be wrong at first sight. However, the equation does give positive income elasticities. The income elasticities are given by

$$\eta_{qy} = \frac{d \log q}{d \log y} = \beta_2 + \beta_3 \log p$$

$$= -0.732 + 0.214 \log p$$

$\log p$ ranges from 4.33 to 4.66 in the data. Thus the income elasticity ranges from 0.195 to 0.265.

The price elasticity is given by

$$\eta_{qp} = \frac{d \log q}{d \log p} = \beta_1 + \beta_3 \log y = -1.011 + 0.214 \log y$$

Thus, as income increases, demand for food becomes more price inelastic. For the data in Table 4.3, $\log y$ ranges from 3.78 to 4.66. Thus the price elasticity ranges from -0.202 to -0.014.

4.7 PREDICTION IN THE MULTIPLE REGRESSION MODEL

The formulas for prediction in multiple regression are similar to those in the case of simple regression except that to compute the standard error of the predicted value we need the variances and covariances of all the regression coefficients. Again

---

[8] The data are from Frederick V. Waugh, *Demand and Price Analysis: Some Example from Agriculture*, U.S.D.A. Technical Bulletin 1316, November 1964, p. 16. The value of y for 1955 has been corrected to 96.5 from 86.5 in that table.

we will present the expression for the standard error in the case of two explanatory variables and then the expression for the general case of k explanatory variable. But we do not need to compute this general expression because there is an easier way of generating the standard error which we will describe in Chapter 8. (see Section 8.5).

Let the estimated regression equation be

$$\hat{y} = \hat{\alpha} + \hat{\beta}_1 x_1 + \hat{\beta}_2 x_2$$

Now consider the prediction of the value y_0 of y given values x_{10} and x_{20} of x_1 and x_2, respectively. These could be values at some future date.

Then we have

$$y_0 = \alpha + \beta_1 x_{10} + \beta_2 x_{20} + u_0$$

Consider

$$\hat{y}_0 = \hat{\alpha} + \hat{\beta}_1 x_{10} + \hat{\beta}_2 x_{20}$$

The prediction error is

$$\hat{y}_0 - y_0 = \hat{\alpha} - \alpha + (\hat{\beta}_1 - \beta_1)x_{10} + (\hat{\beta}_2 - \beta_2)x_{20} - u_0$$

Since $E(\hat{\alpha} - \alpha)$, $E(\hat{\beta}_1 - \beta_1)$, $E(\hat{\beta}_2 - \beta_2)$, and $E(u_0)$ are all equal to zero, we have $E(\hat{y}_0 - y_0) = 0$. Thus the predictor $\hat{y}_0$ is unbiased. Note that what we are saying is $E(\hat{y}_0) = E(y_0)$ (since both $\hat{y}_0$ and y_0 are random variables). The variance of the prediction error is

$$\sigma^2\left(1 + \frac{1}{n}\right) + (x_{10} - \bar{x}_1)^2 \operatorname{var}(\hat{\beta}_1) + 2(x_{10} - \bar{x}_1)(x_{20} - \bar{x}_2)\operatorname{cov}(\hat{\beta}_1, \hat{\beta}_2)$$
$$+ (x_{20} - \bar{x}_2)^2 \operatorname{var}(\hat{\beta}_2)$$

In the case of k explanatory variables, this is

$$\sigma^2\left(1 + \frac{1}{n}\right) + \sum_{i=1}^{k} \sum_{j=1}^{k} (x_{i0} - \bar{x}_i)(x_{j0} - \bar{x}_j)\operatorname{cov}(\hat{\beta}_i, \hat{\beta}_j)$$

We estimate σ^2 by $\text{RSS}/(n - 3)$ in the case of two explanatory variables and by $\text{RSS}/(n - k - 1)$ in the general case.

Illustrative Example

Again consider the illustrative example in Section 4.3. The regression is

$$y = 4.0 + 0.7x_1 + 0.2x_2$$

Consider the prediction of y for $x_{10} = 12$, and $x_{20} = 7$. We have

$$\hat{y}_0 = 4.0 + 0.7(12) + 0.2(7) = 13.8$$

Note that

$$x_{10} - \bar{x}_1 = 12 - 10 = 2$$
$$x_{20} - \bar{x}_2 = 7 - 5 = 2$$

Using the expressions for $\text{var}(\hat{\beta}_1)$, $\text{var}(\hat{\beta}_2)$, $\text{cov}(\hat{\beta}_1, \hat{\beta}_2)$, and $\hat{\sigma}^2$ derived in Section 4.3, we get the estimated variance of the prediction error as

$$0.07\left(1 + \frac{1}{23}\right) + 4\left(\frac{3}{20} + \frac{3}{20} - \frac{2}{20}\right)(.07) = 0.129$$

The standard error of the prediction is 0.375. Thus the 95% confidence interval for the prediction is

$$13.1 \pm 2.086(0.359) \quad \text{or} \quad 13.1 \pm 0.75 \quad \text{or} \quad (12.35, 13.85)$$

Comment

In the case of simple regression we said (in Section 3.7) that the variance of the prediction error increases as we increase the distance of the point x_0 from $\bar{x}$. In the case of multiple regression we cannot say that the variance of the prediction error increases with the Euclidean distance $[(x_{10} - \bar{x}_1)^2 + (x_{20} - \bar{x}_2)^2]^{1/2}$. This is because there is the covariance term as well. For instance, in our example let us change x_{20} to 3. Now $x_{20} - \bar{x}_2 = -2$. The Euclidean distance is the same as before. It is $\sqrt{2^2 + (-2)^2}$. However, the variance of the prediction error is now

$$0.07\left(1 + \frac{1}{23}\right) + 4\left(\frac{3}{20} + \frac{3}{20} + \frac{2}{20}\right)(0.7) = 0.185$$

which is higher because of the last term turning positive. If x_1 and x_2 are highly correlated, we will observe wide discrepancies in the variances of the prediction error for the same Euclidean distance of the value of x_0 from the sample mean. Thus the simple relationship we found in the case of simple regression does not hold in multiple regression.

4.8 ANALYSIS OF VARIANCE AND TESTS OF HYPOTHESES

In Section 4.3, result 6, we discussed an F-test to test hypotheses about β_1 and β_2. An alternative expression for this test is defined by the statistic

$$F = \frac{(\text{RRSS} - \text{URSS})/r}{\text{URSS}/(n - k - 1)} \tag{4.14}$$

where URSS = unrestricted residual sum of squares
      RRSS = restricted residual sum of squares obtained by imposing the restrictions of the hypothesis
          r = number of restrictions imposed by the hypothesis

The derivation of this test is beyond the scope of our discussion. A proof can be found in graduate textbooks in this area.[9]

---

[9] See, for instance, G. S. Maddala, *Econometrics* (New York: McGraw-Hill, 1977), p. 457–460.

As an illustration, consider the hypothesis $\beta_1 = 1$, $\beta_2 = 0$ in the illustrative example in Section 4.3. The unrestricted residual sum of squares is URSS = 1.4. To get the restricted residual sum of squares RRSS, we have to minimize

$$\sum (y_i - \alpha - 1.0x_{1i} - 0.0x_{2i})^2$$

Since both β_1 and β_2 are specified, there is only α to be estimated and we get $\hat{\alpha} = \bar{y} - 1.0\bar{x}_1$. Thus

$$\begin{aligned} \text{RRSS} &= \sum [y_i - \bar{y} - (x_{1i} - \bar{x}_1)]^2 \\ &= S_{yy} + S_{11} - 2S_{1y} \\ &= 10.0 + 12.0 - 2(10.0) = 2.0 \end{aligned}$$

Also, we have $r = 2$, $n = 23$, $k = 2$. Hence

$$F = \frac{(2.0 - 1.4)/2}{1.4/20} = \frac{0.3}{0.07} = 4.3$$

which is exactly the value we obtained in Section 4.3.

In the special case where the hypothesis is

$$\beta_1 = \beta_2 = \cdots = \beta_k = 0$$

we have URSS = $S_{yy}(1 - R^2)$, and RRSS = S_{yy}. Hence the test is given by

$$F = \frac{[S_{yy} - S_{yy}(1 - R^2)]/k}{S_{yy}(1 - R^2)/(n - k - 1)} = \frac{R^2}{1 - R^2} \cdot \frac{n - k - 1}{k} \tag{4.15}$$

which has an F-distribution with degrees of freedom k and $(n - k - 1)$. What this test does is test the hypothesis that none of the x's influence y; that is, the regression equation is useless. Of course, a rejection of this hypothesis leaves us with the question: Which of the x's are useful in explaining y?

It is customary to present this test in the form of an *analysis of variance* table similar to Table 3.3 we considered for simple regression. This is shown in Table 4.5. What we do is decompose the variance of y into two components: that due to the explanatory variables (i.e., due to regression) and that which is unexplained (i.e., residual).

Table 4.5 Analysis of Variance for the Multiple Regression Model

Source of Variation	Sum of Squares, SS	Degrees of Freedom, d.f.	Mean Square, SS/d.f.	F
Regression	$R^2 S_{yy}$	k	$R^2 S_{yy}/k = \text{MS}_1$	$F = \dfrac{\text{MS}_1}{\text{MS}_2}$
Residual	$(1 - R^2)S_{yy}$	$n - k - 1$	$\dfrac{(1 - R^2)S_{yy}}{n - k - 1} = \text{MS}_2$	
Total	S_{yy}	$n - 1$		

Table 4.6 Analysis of Variance for the Hospital Cost Regression in Section 4.6

Source of Variation	Sum of Squares, SS	Degrees of Freedom, d.f.	Mean Square, SS/d.f.	F
Regression	10,357	8	1294.625	$F = \dfrac{1294.625}{138.756}$
Residual	23,311	168	138.756	$= 9.33$
Total	33,668	176		

As an illustration, consider the hospital cost regression in Section 4.6. The analysis of variance table is given in Table 4.6. This F value is highly significant. The 1% point from the F-tables with 8 and 168 d.f. is 2.51 and the observed F is much higher.

Of course we reject the hypothesis that $\beta_1 = \beta_2 = \cdots = \beta_k = 0$. All this means is that the case-mix variables are important in explaining the variation in average cost per case between the hospitals. But it does not say which variables are important.

Nested and Nonnested Hypotheses

The hypotheses we are interested in testing can usually be classified under two categories: nested and nonnested. Consider, for instance, the regression models

$$y = \beta_1 x_1 + \beta_2 x_2 + \beta_3 x_3 + u \qquad \text{model 1}$$

$$y = \beta_1 x_1 + \beta_2 x_2 \qquad\qquad + u \qquad \text{model 2}$$

A test of the hypothesis H_0: $\beta_3 = 0$ versus H_1: $\beta_3 \neq 0$ is a test of the hypothesis that the data are generated by model 2 versus that the data are generated by model 1. Such a hypothesis is called a *nested hypothesis* because the parameters in model 2 form a subset of the parameters in model 1. A hypothesis

$$H_0: \quad \beta_1 + \beta_2 + \beta_3 = 0 \qquad \text{versus} \qquad H_1: \quad \beta_1 + \beta_2 + \beta_3 \neq 0$$

can also be called a nested hypothesis because we can reparametrize the original equation as

$$y = (\beta_1 + \beta_2 + \beta_3)x_1 + \beta_2(x_2 - x_1) + \beta_3(x_3 - x_1) + u$$

$$= \gamma x_1 + \beta_2(x_2 - x_1) + \beta_3(x_3 - x_1) + u$$

where $\gamma = \beta_1 + \beta_2 + \beta_3$. Now consider the parameter set as $(\gamma, \beta_2, \beta_3)$ and H_0: $\gamma = 0$ versus H_1: $\gamma \neq 0$.

Similarly, if we have the hypothesis

$$H_0: \quad \beta_1 + \beta_2 + \beta_3 = 0, \beta_2 - \beta_3 = 0$$

we reparametrize the original equation by defining $\gamma_1 = \beta_1 + \beta_2 + \beta_3, \gamma_2 = \beta_2 - \beta_3, \gamma_3 = \beta_3$ so that $\beta_3 = \gamma_3, \beta_2 = \gamma_2 + \gamma_3, \beta_1 = \gamma_1 - \gamma_2 - 2\gamma_3$ and the original becomes

$$y = (\gamma_1 - \gamma_2 - 2\gamma_3)x_1 + (\gamma_2 + \gamma_3)x_2 + \gamma_3 x_3 + u$$

$$= \gamma_1 x_1 + \gamma_2(x_2 - x_1) + \gamma_3(x_3 + x_2 - 2x_1) + u$$

Now we consider the parameter set $(\gamma_1, \gamma_2, \gamma_3)$ and H_0 specifies the values of γ_1 and γ_2.
Suppose, on the other hand, that we consider the two regression models:

$$y = \beta_1 x_1 + u_1 \qquad \text{model 3}$$

$$y = \beta_2 x_2 + u_2 \qquad \text{model 4}$$

H_0: the data are generated by model 3

H_1: the data are generated by model 4

Now the parameter set specified by model 3 is not a subset of the parameter set specified by model 4. Hence we say that hypotheses H_0 and H_1 are *nonnested*.

In the following sections we consider nested hypotheses only. The problem of selection of regressors, for instance, whether to include x_1 only or x_2 only, is a problem in testing nonnested hypotheses. This problem is treated briefly in Chapter 12.

Tests for Linear Functions of Parameters

We have until now discussed tests for parameters. Very often we need tests for functions of parameters. The functions we need to consider can be linear functions or nonlinear functions. We discuss linear functions first.

Suppose that we have estimated a production function in a log-linear form:

$$\log X = \alpha + \beta_1 \log L + \beta_2 \log K + u$$

where X is the output, L the labor input, and K the capital input. Then a test for constant returns to scale is a test of the hypothesis $\beta_1 + \beta_2 = 1$. We can use a t-test to test this hypothesis as follows.

We get the least squares estimates $\hat{\beta}_1$ and $\hat{\beta}_2$ and define

$$\sigma^2 C_{ij} = \operatorname{cov}(\hat{\beta}_i, \hat{\beta}_j) \qquad i, j = 1, 2$$

Then, under the null hypothesis $\beta_1 + \beta_2 - 1 = 0$, we have the result that $\hat{\beta}_1 + \hat{\beta}_2 - 1$ is normally distributed with mean 0 and variance $\sigma^2(C_{11} + 2C_{12} + C_{22})$.

Since RSS/σ^2 has an independent χ^2 distribution with degrees of freedom $(n-3)$, the t-statistic to test the hypothesis is given by

$$t = \frac{\hat{\beta}_1 + \hat{\beta}_2 - 1}{\sqrt{C_{11} + 2C_{12} + C_{22}}} \Big/ \sqrt{\frac{\text{RSS}}{n-3}}$$

which has a t-distribution with degrees of freedom $n - 3$.

An alternative procedure is to derive URSS and RRSS and use the F-test. URSS is the residual sum of squares we obtain when we estimate α, β_1, and β_2. To get RRSS, we have to use the restriction $\beta_1 + \beta_2 - 1 = 0$. The way to do this is to eliminate β_2 since $\beta_2 = 1 - \beta_1$. Thus we get the regression equation as

$$\log X = \alpha + \beta_1 \log L + (1 - \beta_1) \log K + u$$

or

$$(\log X - \log K) = \alpha + \beta_1 (\log L - \log K) + u$$

Thus to get RRSS we regress $(\log X - \log K)$ on $(\log L - \log K)$. The residual sum of squares from this equation gives us the required RRSS.

The same procedure applies if we have two linear restrictions. Consider, for instance, the case of the multiple regression equation

$$y = \alpha_1 + \beta_1 x_1 + \beta_2 x_2 + \beta_3 x_3 + u$$

and we need to test the restrictions

$$\beta_1 + \beta_2 + \beta_3 = 1 \qquad \beta_2 - 2\beta_3 = 0$$

Note that these restrictions can be written as

$$\beta_2 = 2\beta_3 \quad \text{and} \quad \beta_1 = 1 - 3\beta_3$$

Substituting these in the original equation, we get

$$y = \alpha + (1 - 3\beta_3)x_1 + 2\beta_3 x_2 + \beta_3 x_3 + \varepsilon$$

or

$$(y - x_1) = \alpha + \beta_3(-3x_1 + 2x_2 + x_3) + \varepsilon$$

Thus we get the restricted residual sum of squares RRSS by running a regression of $(y - x_1)$ on $(-3x_1 + 2x_2 + x_3)$ with a constant term.

Illustrative Example

Consider again the illustrative example in Section 4.3. Suppose that the problem is to test the hypothesis:

$$H_0: \quad \frac{\beta_1}{\beta_2} = \frac{5}{3} \qquad \text{against} \qquad H_1: \quad \frac{\beta_1}{\beta_2} \neq \frac{5}{3}$$

at the 5% significance level. The hypothesis is $\beta_2 = 0.6\beta_1$. To compute the restricted estimates, we substitute $\beta_2 = 0.6\beta_1$ and estimate the equation

$$y = \alpha + \beta_1 x + \varepsilon$$

where

$$x = x_1 + 0.6x_2$$

We now have

$$S_{xx} = S_{11} + (0.6)^2 S_{22} + 2(0.6)S_{12}$$

$$= 12 + (0.6)^2(12) + 2(0.6)(8) = 25.92$$

$$S_{xy} = S_{1y} + 0.6S_{2y}$$

$$= 10 + 0.6(8) = 14.8$$

Hence

$$\hat{\beta}_1 = \frac{14.8}{25.92} \simeq 0.57$$

$$\text{RRSS} = S_{yy} - \hat{\beta}_1 S_{xy} = 10 - 8.45 = 1.55$$

Thus RRSS − URSS = 1.55 − 1.40 = 0.15 and the F-statistic is

$$F = \frac{0.15/1}{1.4/20} = \frac{0.15}{0.07} \simeq 2.1$$

which, with d.f. 1 and 20, is not significant at the 5% level.

By the alternative method, we consider $\hat{\beta}_2 - 0.6\hat{\beta}_1$. It is normally distributed with mean zero (under H_0) and using the expression for C we note that its variance is

$$\sigma^2 \left[\frac{12}{80} + (0.6)^2 \frac{12}{80} - 2(0.6)\left(-\frac{1}{20}\right) \right] = 0.324\sigma^2$$

Since

$$\hat{\beta}_2 - 0.6\hat{\beta}_1 = 0.2 - 0.6(0.7) = -0.22$$

we have the F-statistic

$$F = \frac{(-0.22)^2/0.324}{1.4/20} = \frac{0.15}{0.07}$$

which is the same as the one obtained earlier.

4.9   OMISSION OF RELEVANT VARIABLES AND INCLUSION OF IRRELEVANT VARIABLES

Until now we have assumed that the multiple regression equation we are estimating includes all the relevant explanatory variables. In practice, this is rarely the case. Sometimes some relevant variables are not included due to oversight or lack of measurements. At other times some irrelevant variables are included. What we would like to know is how our inferences change when these problems are present.

Omission of Relevant Variables

Let us first consider the omission of relevant variables first. Suppose that the true equation is

$$y = \beta_1 x_1 + \beta_2 x_2 + u \tag{4.16}$$

Instead, we omit x_2 and estimate the equation

$$y = \beta_1 x_1 + u$$

This will be referred to as the "misspecified model." The estimate of β_1 we get is

$$\hat{\beta}_1 = \frac{\sum x_1 y}{\sum x_1^2}$$

Substituting the expression for y from (4.16) in this, we get

$$\hat{\beta}_1 = \frac{\sum x_1(\beta_1 x_1 + \beta_2 x_2 + u)}{\sum x_1^2} = \beta_1 + \beta_2 \frac{\sum x_1 x_2}{\sum x_1^2} + \frac{\sum x_1 u}{\sum x_1^2}$$

Since $E(\sum x_1 u) = 0$ we get

$$E(\hat{\beta}_1) = \beta_1 + b_{21}\beta_2 \tag{4.17}$$

where $b_{21} = \sum x_1 x_2 / \sum x_1^2$ is the regression coefficient from a regression of x_2 on x_1.

Thus $\hat{\beta}_1$ is a biased estimator for β_1 and the bias is given by

$$\text{bias} = (\text{coefficient of the excluded variable})$$

$$\times \left(\begin{array}{l}\text{regression coefficient in a regression of the}\\\text{excluded variable on the included variable}\end{array}\right)$$

If we denote the estimator for β_1 from (4.16) by $\tilde{\beta}_1$, the variance of $\tilde{\beta}_1$ is given by

$$\text{var}(\tilde{\beta}_1) = \frac{\sigma^2}{S_{11}(1 - r_{12}^2)}$$

where

$$S_{11} = \sum x_1^2$$

On the other hand,

$$\text{var}(\hat{\beta}_1) = \frac{\sigma^2}{S_{11}}$$

Thus $\hat{\beta}_1$ is a biased estimator but has a smaller variance than β_1. In fact, the variance would be considerably smaller if r_{12}^2 is high. However, the estimated standard error need not be smaller for $\hat{\beta}_1$ than for $\tilde{\beta}_1$. This is because σ^2, the estimated variance of the error, can be higher in the misspecified model. It is given by the residual sum of squares divided by degrees of freedom, and this can be higher (or lower) for the misspecified model.

Let us denote the estimated variance by S^2. Then the formula connecting the estimated variances is

$$\frac{S^2(\hat{\beta}_1)}{S^2(\tilde{\beta}_1)} = \frac{1 - r_{12}^2}{1 - r_{y2 \cdot 1}^2}$$

Thus the standard error of $\hat{\beta}_1$ will be less than the standard error of $\tilde{\beta}_1$ only if $r_{12}^2 > r_{y2 \cdot 1}^2$.

We have considered the case of only one included and one omitted variable. In the case where we have $k - 1$ included variables and the kth variable omitted, formula (4.17) generalizes to

$$E(\hat{\beta}_i) = \beta_i + b_{ki}\beta_k \qquad i = 1, 2, \ldots, k - 1 \tag{4.18}$$

where b_{ki} is the regression coefficient of x_i in the auxiliary regression of x_k on x_1, $x_2, \ldots, k_{k-1}$. That is, we consider the regression of the omitted variable x_k on all the included variables.

In the general case[10] where we have several included variables and several omitted variables, we have to estimated the "auxiliary" multiple regressions of *each* of the excluded variables on *all* the included variables. The bias in each of estimated coefficients of the included variables will be a weighted sum of the coefficients of all the excluded variables with weights obtained from these auxiliary multiple regressions.

Suppose that we have k explanatory variables, of which the first k_1 are included and the remaining $(k - k_1)$ are omitted. Then the formula corresponding to (4.17) and (4.18) is

$$E(\hat{\beta}_i) = \beta_i + \sum_{j=k_1+1}^{k} b_{ji}\beta_j \qquad i = 1, 2, \ldots, k \qquad (4.19)$$

where b_{ji} is the regression coefficient of the ith included variable in a regression of the jth omitted variable on all the included variables. Note that we pick the coefficients of the ith included variable from the $(k - k_1)$ auxiliary multiple regressions.

The formulas (4.17)–(4.19) can be used to get some rough estimates of the direction of the biases in estimated coefficients when some variables are omitted because of lack of observations or because they are not measurable. We will present two examples, one in which the omitted variable is actually measured and the other in which it is not.

Example 1: Demand for Food in the United States

Consider the estimation of the demand for food in the United States based on the data in Table 4.9. Suppose that the "true" equation is

$$Q_D = \alpha + \beta_1 P_D + \beta_2 Y + U$$

However, we omit the income variable. We get

$$\hat{Q}_D = 89.97 + 0.107 P_D \qquad \hat{\sigma}^2 = 2.338$$
$$\quad\; (11.85) \quad (0.118)$$

(Figures in parentheses are standard errors.)

The coefficient of P_D has the wrong sign. Can this be attributed to the omission of the income variable? The answer is yes, because the coefficient of P_D is a biased estimate with the bias given by

bias = (coefficient of the income variable)

× (the regression coefficient of income on price)

The coefficient of income is expected to be positive. Also, given that the data are time-series data, we would expect a positive correlation between P_D and Y. Hence the bias is expected to be positive, and this could turn a negative coefficient to a positive one.

---

[10] We will not go through the derivation here because the use of matrix notation is unavoidable. Proofs can be found in many textbooks in econometrics. See, for instance, G. S. Maddala, *Econometrics* (New York: McGraw-Hill, 1977), p. 461.

In this case the regression equation with Y included gives the result

$$Q_D = 92.05 - 0.142P_D + 0.236Y \qquad \hat{\sigma}^2 = 1.952$$
$$\quad\;\; {\scriptstyle(5.84)} \quad\;\; {\scriptstyle(0.067)} \quad\;\; {\scriptstyle(0.031)}$$

(Figures in parentheses are standard errors.) Note that the coefficient of P_D is now negative. Also, note that the standard error of the coefficient of P_D is higher in the misspecified model than in the "true" model. This is so in spite of the fact that the variance of β_1 is expected to be smaller in the misspecified model. (Check the relationship between r_{12}^2 and $r_{y2\cdot1}^2$ with the data.)

Example 2: Production Functions and Management Bias

In the estimation of production functions we have to omit the quality of inputs and managerial inputs because of lack of measurement. Consider the estimation of the production function

$$y = \beta_1 x_1 + \beta_2 x_2 + \beta_3 x_3 + u$$

where

$$y = \text{log of output}$$

$$x_1 = \text{log of labor input}$$

$$x_2 = \text{log of capital input}$$

$$x_3 = \text{log of managerial input}$$

Now x_3 is not observable. What will be the effect of this on estimates of β_1 and β_2? From the formula (4.18) we have

$$E(\hat{\beta}_1) = \beta_1 + b_{31}\beta_3$$
$$E(\hat{\beta}_2) = \beta_2 + b_{32}\beta_3$$

where b_{31} and b_{32} are the regression coefficients in the regression of x_3 on x_1 and x_2. Now $\beta_1 + \beta_2$ is often referred to as "returns to scale." Let us denote this by S. The estimated returns to scale, $\hat{S}$ is $\hat{\beta}_1 + \hat{\beta}_2$. Thus

$$E(\hat{S}) = S + \beta_3(b_{31} + b_{32})$$

Since β_3 is expected to be positive, the bias in the estimation of returns to scale will depend on the sign of $b_{31} + b_{32}$. If we assume that managerial input does not increase proportionately with measured inputs of labor and capital, we would expect $b_{31} + b_{32}$ to be negative and thus there is a downward bias in the estimates of returns to scale.

Inclusion of Irrelevant Variables

Consider now the case of inclusion of irrelevant variables. Suppose that the true equation is

$$y = \beta_1 x_1 + u$$

but we estimate the equation

$$y = \beta_1 x_1 + \beta_2 x_2 + v$$

The least squares estimators $\tilde{\beta}_1$ and $\tilde{\beta}_2$ from this misspecified equation are given by

$$\tilde{\beta}_1 = \frac{S_{22}S_{1y} - S_{12}S_{2y}}{S_{11}S_{22} - S_{12}^2}$$

$$\tilde{\beta}_2 = \frac{S_{11}S_{2y} - S_{12}S_{1y}}{S_{11}S_{22} - S_{12}^2}$$

where $S_{11} = \sum x_1^2$, $S_{iy} = \sum x_1 y$, $S_{12} = \sum x_1 x_2$, and so on. Since $y = \beta_1 x_1 + u$ we have $E(S_{2y}) = \beta_1 S_{12}$ and $E(S_{1y}) = \beta_1 S_{11}$. Hence we get

$$E(\tilde{\beta}_1) = \beta_1 \quad \text{and} \quad E(\tilde{\beta}_2) = 0$$

Thus we get unbiased estimates for both the parameters. This result, coupled with the earlier results regarding the bias introduced by the omission of relevant variables might lead us to believe that it is better to include variables (when in doubt) rather than exclude them. However, this is not so, because though the inclusion of irrelevant variables has no effect on the bias of the estimators, it does affect the variances.

The variance of $\hat{\beta}_1$, the estimator of β_1 from the correct equation is given by

$$V(\hat{\beta}_1) = \frac{\sigma^2}{S_{11}}$$

On the other hand, from the misspecified equation we have

$$\text{var}(\tilde{\beta}_1) = \frac{\sigma^2}{(1 - r_{12}^2)S_{11}}$$

where r_{12} is the correlation between x_1 and x_2. Thus $\text{var}(\tilde{\beta}_1) > \text{var}(\hat{\beta}_1)$ unless $r_{12} = 0$. Hence we will be getting unbiased but inefficient estimates by including the irrelevant variable. It can be shown that the estimator for the residual variance we use is an unbiased estimator of σ^2. Thus there is no further bias arising from the use of estimated variance from the misspecified equation.[11]

4.10 DEGREES OF FREEDOM AND $\bar{R}^2$

If we have n observations and estimate three regression parameters as in equation (4.1), we can see from the normal equations (4.2)–(4.4) that the estimated residuals $\hat{u}_i$ satisfy three linear restrictions:

$$\sum \hat{u}_i = 0 \quad \sum x_{1i}\hat{u}_i = 0 \quad \sum x_{2i}\hat{u}_i = 0 \qquad (4.20)$$

or, in essence, there are only $(n - 3)$ residuals to vary because, given any $(n - 3)$

[11] See Maddala, *Econometrics*, p. 157.

residuals, the remaining three residuals can be obtained by solving equations (4.20). This point we express by saying that there are $(n - 3)$ degrees of freedom.

As we saw earlier, the estimate of the residual variance σ^2 is given by

$$\hat{\sigma}^2 = \frac{\text{RSS}}{\text{degrees of freedom}}$$

As we increase the number of explanatory variables RSS declines but there is a decrease in the degrees of freedom as well. What happens to $\hat{\sigma}^2$ depends on the proportionate decrease in the numerator and the denominator. Thus there will be a point when $\hat{\sigma}^2$ will actually start increasing as we add more explanatory variables. It is often suggested that we should choose the set of variables for which $\hat{\sigma}^2$ is the minimum. We discuss the rationale behind this procedure in Chapter 12. [12]

This is also the reason why, in multiple regression problems, it is customary to report what is known as *adjusted* R^2, denoted by $\bar{R}^2$. The measure R^2 defined earlier keeps on increasing (till it reaches 1.0) as we add extra explanatory variables and thus does not take account of the degrees-of-freedom problem. $\bar{R}^2$ is simply R^2 adjusted for degrees of freedom. It is defined by the relation

$$1 - \bar{R}^2 = \frac{n-1}{n-k-1}(1 - R^2) \tag{4.21}$$

where k is the number of regressors. We subtract $(k + 1)$ from n because we estimate a constant term in addition to the coefficients of these k regressors. We can write (4.21) as

$$\frac{(1 - \bar{R}^2)S_{yy}}{n-1} = \frac{(1 - R^2)S_{yy}}{n-k-1} = \hat{\sigma}^2 \tag{4.22}$$

Since S_{yy} and n are constant, as we increase the number of regressors included in the equation, $\hat{\sigma}^2$ and $(1 - \bar{R}^2)$ move in the same direction as $\hat{\sigma}^2$ and $\bar{R}^2$ move in the opposite direction. Thus the set of variables that gives minimum $\hat{\sigma}^2$ is also the set that maximizes $\bar{R}^2$.

Also, from Equation (4.21) we can easily see that if $R^2 < k/(n - 1)$, $1 - R^2 > (n - k - 1)/(n - 1)$ and hence $1 - \bar{R}^2 > 1$. Thus $\bar{R}^2$ is negative! For example, with 2 explanatory variables and 21 observations, if $R^2 < 0.1$, $\bar{R}^2$ will be negative.

There is a relationship between the t tests and F-tests outlined earlier and $\bar{R}^2$. If the t ratio for the coefficient of any variable is less than 1, then dropping that variable will increase $\bar{R}^2$. More generally, if the F-ratio for any set of variables is less than 1, then dropping this set of variables from the regression equation will increase $\bar{R}^2$. Since the single-variable case is a special case of the many-variable case, we will prove the latter result. Equation (4.21) shows the relationship between $\bar{R}^2$ and $\hat{\sigma}^2$. So, instead of asking the question of whether dropping the variables will increase $\bar{R}^2$, we can as well ask the question of whether $\hat{\sigma}^2$ will decrease.

---

[12] In the limiting case when the number of parameters estimated is equal to the number of observations, we get $\hat{\sigma}^2 = 0/0$.

Let $\hat{\sigma}_1^2$ be the estimate of σ^2 when we drop r regressors. Then

$$\hat{\sigma}_1^2 = \frac{\text{restricted residual sum of squares}}{n - (k - r) - 1}$$

Since the unrestricted residual sum of squares is $(n - k - 1)\hat{\sigma}^2$, the F-test outlined earlier is given by

$$F = \frac{[(n - k + r - 1)\hat{\sigma}_1^2 - (n - k - 1)\hat{\sigma}^2]/r}{[(n - k - 1)\hat{\sigma}^2]/(n - k - 1)}$$

Solving for $\hat{\sigma}_1^2/\hat{\sigma}^2$ yields

$$\frac{\hat{\sigma}_1^2}{\hat{\sigma}^2} = \frac{a + F}{a + 1} \quad \text{where} \quad a = \frac{n - k - 1}{r}$$

Thus $\hat{\sigma}_1^2 \lessgtr \hat{\sigma}^2$ according as $F \gtrless 1$. What this says is that if the F-ratio associated with a set of explanatory variables is < 1, we can increase $\bar{R}^2$ by dropping that set of variables. Since for 1 degree of freedom in the numerator, $F = t^2$, what this means is that if the absolute value of the t-ratio for any explanatory variable is less than 1, dropping that variable will increase $\bar{R}^2$. However, we have to be careful about t-ratios for individual coefficients and F-ratios for sets of coefficients and we will discuss the relationships between t and F ratios. There are two cases that create problems:

Case 1. The t-ratios are less than 1 but the F-ratio is greater than 1.
Case 2. The t-ratios are all greater than 1 but the F-ratio for a set of variables is < 1.

Case 1 occurs when the explanatory variables are highly intercorrelated. (This is called *multicollinearity*, which we discuss in Chapter 7.) In this case because all the t-ratios are less than 1 does not mean that we can increase $\bar{R}^2$ by dropping *all* the variables. Once we drop one variable the other t-ratios will change.

In case 2, though by dropping any one variable we cannot increase $\bar{R}^2$, it might be possible to get a higher $\bar{R}^2$ by dropping a *set* of explanatory variables. Suppose that we have a regression equation in which all the explanatory variables have t-ratios which are greater than 1. Obviously, we cannot increase $\bar{R}^2$ by dropping any one of the variables. But how do we know whether we can increase $\bar{R}^2$ by dropping some sets of variables without searching over all the sets and subsets?

To answer this question we will state a simple rule that gives the relationship between t and F ratios. Consider a set of k variables that are candidates for exclusion; and let $F(k, n)$ be the F-ratio associated with these variables (n is the sample size). Then the rule says: If $F(k, n) \leq c$, the absolute t-values of each of the k discarded variables must be less than $\sqrt{kc}$, that is, if $F(k, n) \leq 1$, the absolute t-value of each of the k variables is $< \sqrt{k}$. The converse, however, is not true.[13] Thus if we do not have at least k variables with absolute t-values less than $\sqrt{k}$, $\bar{R}^2$ cannot be increased by discarding k independent variables at a time.

---

[13] Potluri Rao, "On a Correspondence Between t and F Values in Multiple Regression," *American Statistician*, Vol. 30, No. 4, 1976, pp. 190–191. We just present the results here; those interested in the derivation can refer to Potluri Rao's paper.

However, if there are k or more independent variables with absolute t-values less than $\sqrt{k}$, the F ratio may or may not be less than 1, and hence we may or may not be able to increase $\bar{R}^2$ by discarding these variables. But if the $\bar{R}^2$ is increased, the variables to be discarded must come from the set of independent variables with absolute t-values less than $\sqrt{k}$.

As an illustration, consider the case $k = 7$. Since $\sqrt{7} = 2.6$, if the F ratio is less than 1, all we can say about the t-ratios is that the t-ratios are less than 2.6. But this means that we can have all the t-ratios significant and yet have the $\bar{R}^2$ rise by dropping all the variables.

As yet another example, consider a regression equation with five independent variables and t-ratios of 1.2, 1.5, 1.6, 2.3, and 2.7. Note that $\sqrt{2} = 1.414$, $\sqrt{3} = 1.732$, and $\sqrt{5} = 2.236$. We consider $k = 1, 2, 3, 4, 5$ and check whether there are k t-ratios $< \sqrt{k}$. We note that this is the case for only $k = 3$. Thus if we can increase $\bar{R}^2$ at all, it is by dropping the three variables x_1, x_2, x_3. Thus all we have to do is to run the regression with these three variables excluded and check whether $\bar{R}^2$ has increased.

The point in all this discussion is that in multiple regression equations one has to be careful in drawing conclusions from individual t-ratios. In particular, this is so for analyzing the effect on $\bar{R}^2$ of deletion or addition of sets of variables, often, in applied work it is customary to run a "stepwise" regression where explanatory variables are entered into an equation sequentially (in order determined by the maximum partial r^2 at each stage), and to stop at a point where $\bar{R}^2$ stops increasing. What the previous discussion shows is that it might be possible to increase $\bar{R}^2$ by introducing a set of variables together.

Thus there are problems with maximizing $\bar{R}^2$. But if one is going to do it, the relationship between t and F ratios we have discussed will be of some help. The rationale behind the maximization of $\bar{R}^2$ is discussed in Chapter 12.

A Cautionary Note on the Omission of Nonsignificant Variables: Finally, there is one other result that needs to be noted regarding the procedure of deleting variables whose coefficients are not "significant." Often researchers are perturbed by some "wrong" signs for some of the coefficients. In an effort to obtain hopefully "right" signs, statistically insignificant variables are dropped. Surprisingly enough, there can be no change in the sign of any coefficient that is more significant than the coefficient of the omitted variable. Leamer[14] shows that the constrained least squares estimate of β_j must lie between $(\hat{\beta}_j - ts_j, \hat{\beta}_j + ts_j)$ where

$$\hat{\beta}_j = \text{unconstrained estimate of } \beta_j$$

$$s_j = \text{standard error of } \hat{\beta}_j$$

$$t = \text{absolute } t\text{-value for the deleted variable}$$

We will not go through the proof here. It can be found in Leamer's article. The result enables us to predict the sign changes in the coefficients of the retained variables when one of the variables is deleted.

[14] E. E. Leamer, "A Result on the Sign of the Restricted Least Squares Estimates," *Journal of Econometrics*, Vol. 3, 1975, pp. 387–390.

As an illustration, consider the problem of estimation of the demand for Ceylonese tea in the United States. This example is discussed in Rao and Miller. [15] The following is the list of variables used.

$$\text{Tea} = \text{demand for Ceylonese tea in the United States}$$

$$y = \text{disposable income}$$

$$P_C = \text{price of Ceylonese tea}$$

$$P_B = \text{price of Brazilian coffee, considered a substitute}$$

Y, P_C, and P_B are delated by the price of food commodities in the United States. All equations are estimated in log-linear form. The results are

$$\log \text{Tea} = 3.95 + \underset{(0.14)}{0.14} \log P_B + \underset{(0.24)}{0.75} \log Y + \underset{(0.41)}{0.05} \log P_C$$
$$\scriptstyle (1.99)$$

(Figures in parentheses are standard errors.) The coefficient of $\log P_C$ has the wrong sign, although it is not significantly different from zero. However, dropping the variable P_B, we get

$$\log \text{Tea} = \underset{(2.02)}{3.22} + \underset{(0.25)}{0.67} \log y + \underset{(0.42)}{0.04} \log P_C$$

Another alternative is to drop the variable $\log P_C$ arguing that the demand for Ceylonese tea is price inelastic. This procedure gives us the result

$$\log \text{Tea} = \underset{(0.71)}{3.73} + \underset{(0.13)}{0.14} \log P_B + \underset{(0.14)}{0.73} \log Y$$

However, the correct solution to the problem of a wrong sign for $\log P_C$ is neither to drop that variable nor to drop $\log P_B$ but to see whether some other relevant variables have been omitted. In this case the inclusion of the variable

$$P_I = \text{price of Indian tea which is a close substitute for}$$
$$\text{Ceylonese tea}$$

produces more meaningful results. The results are now

$$\log \text{Tea} = \underset{(2.00)}{2.84} + \underset{(0.13)}{0.19} \log P_B + \underset{(0.37)}{0.26} \log Y - \underset{(0.98)}{1.48} \log P_C + \underset{(0.69)}{1.18} \log P_I$$

Note the coefficient of $\log P_C$ is now negative and the income elasticity has dropped considerably (from 0.73 to 0.26), and is not significant.

Of course, in this case the variable P_I should have been included in the first place rather than as an afterthought. The deletion of $\log y$ from the last equation will not change the signs of any of the other coefficients by Leamer's rule. The resulting equation is

$$\log \text{Tea} = \underset{(1.39)}{1.85} + \underset{(0.13)}{0.20} \log P_B - \underset{(0.39)}{2.10} \log P_C + \underset{(0.42)}{1.56} \log P_I$$

Now $\log P_C$ and $\log P_I$ are both significant, and have the correct signs.

[15] Potluri Rao and Roger Miller, *Applied Econometrics* (Belmont, Calif.: Wadsworth, 1971), pp. 38–40.

4.11 TESTS FOR STABILITY

When we estimate a multiple regression equation and use it for predictions at future points of time we assume that the parameters are constant over the entire time period of estimation and prediction. To test this hypothesis of parameter constancy (or stability) some tests have been proposed. These tests can be described as:

1. Analysis-of-variance tests.
2. Predictive tests.

The Analysis-of-Variance Test

Suppose that we have two independent sets of data with sample sizes n_1 and n_2, respectively. The regression equation is:

$$y = \alpha_1 + \beta_{11}x_1 + \beta_{12}x_2 + \cdots + \beta_{1k}x_k + u \qquad \text{for the first set}$$

$$y = \alpha_2 + \beta_{21}x_1 + \beta_{22}x_2 + \cdots + \beta_{2k}x_k + u \qquad \text{for the second set}$$

For the β's the first subscript denotes the data set and the second subscript denotes the variable. A test for stability of the parameters between the populations that generated the two data sets is a test of the hypothesis:

$$H_0: \quad \beta_{11} = \beta_{21}, \quad \beta_{12} = \beta_{22}, \quad \ldots, \quad \beta_{1k} = \beta_{2k}, \quad \alpha_1 = \alpha_2$$

If this hypothesis is true, we can estimate a single equation for the data set obtained by pooling the two data sets.

The F-test we use is the F-test described in Section 4.8 based on URSS and RRSS. To get the unrestricted residual sum of squares we estimate the regression model for each of the data sets separately. Define

$$\text{RSS}_1 = \text{residual sum of squares for the first data set}$$

$$\text{RSS}_2 = \text{residual sum of squares for the second data set}$$

$$\frac{\text{RSS}_1}{\sigma^2} \text{ has a } \chi^2\text{-distribution with d.f. } (n_1 - k - 1)$$

$$\frac{\text{RSS}_2}{\sigma^2} \text{ has a } \chi^2\text{-distribution with d.f. } (n_2 - k - 1)$$

Since the two data sets are independent $(\text{RSS}_1 + \text{RSS}_2)/\sigma^2$ has a χ^2 distribution with d.f. $(n_1 + n_2 - 2k - 2)$. We will denote $(\text{RSS}_1 + \text{RSS}_2)$ by URSS. The restricted residual sum of squares RRSS is obtained from the regression with the pooled data. (This imposes the restriction that the parameters are the same.) Thus RRSS/σ^2 has a χ^2-distribution with d.f. $= (n_1 + n_2) - k - 1$.

The F-test is

$$F = \frac{(\text{RRSS} - \text{URSS})/(k + 1)}{\text{URSS}/(n_1 + n_2 - 2k - 2)} \tag{4.23}$$

which has an F-distribution with degrees of freedom $(k + 1)$ and $(n_1 + n_2 - 2k - 2)$.

Example 1: Stability of the Demand for Food Function

Consider the data in Table 4.3, where we fitted separate demand functions for 1927–1941 and 1948–1962 and for the entire period. Suppose that we want to test the stability of the parameters in the demand function between the two periods. The required numbers are given in Table 4.4.

For Equation 1 we have

URSS = sum of RSSs from the two separate regressions for 1927–1941 and 1948–1962

$$= 0.1151 + 0.0544 = 0.1695 \quad \text{with d.f.} = 12 + 12 = 24$$

RRSS = RSS from a regression for the pooled data

$$= 0.2866 \text{ with d.f.} = 27$$

This regression from the pooled data imposes the restriction that the parameters are the same in the two periods. Hence

$$F = \frac{(0.2866 - 0.1695)/3}{0.1695/24} = 5.53$$

From the F-Tables with d.f. 3 and 24 we see that the 5% point is about 3.01 and the 1% point is about 4.72. Thus, even at the 1% level of significance, we reject the hypothesis of stability. Thus there is no case for pooling.

Note that if we look at the individual coefficients, $\hat{\beta}_1$ is almost the same for the two regressions. Thus it appears that the price elasticity has been constant but it is the income elasticity that has changed in the two periods. In Chapter 8 we discuss procedures of testing the stability of individual coefficients using the dummy variable method.

Consider now Equation 2. We now have

$$\text{URSS} = 0.1151 + 0.0535 = 0.1686 \quad \text{with d.f.} = 11 + 11 = 22$$

$$\text{RRSS} = 0.2397 \text{ with d.f.} = 26$$

Hence

$$F = \frac{(0.2397 - 0.1686)/4}{0.1686/22} = 2.32$$

From the F-Tables with d.f. 4 and 22 we see that the 5% point is about 2.82. So, at the 5% significance level, we do not reject the hypothesis of stability.

One can ask how this result came about. If we look at the individual coefficients for Equation 2 for the two periods 1927–1941 and 1948–1962 separately, we notice that the t-ratios are very small, that is, the standard errors are very high relative to the magnitudes of the coefficient estimates. Thus the observed differences in the coefficient estimates between the two periods would not be statistically significant. When we look at the regression for the pooled data we notice that the coefficient of the interaction term is significant, but the estimates for the two periods separately, as well as the rejection of the hypothesis of stability for Equation 1, casts doubt on the desirability of including the interaction term.

Example 2: Stability of Production Functions

Consider the data in Table 3.11 on output and labor and capital inputs in the United States for 1929–1967.[16] The variables are:

X = index of gross domestic product (constant dollars)

L_1 = labor input index (number of persons adjusted for hours of work and educational level)

L_2 = persons engaged

K_1 = capital input index (capital stock adjusted for rates of utilization)

K_2 = capital stock in constant dollars

We will estimate regression equations of the form

$$\log X = \alpha + \beta_1 \log L + \beta_2 \log K + u \qquad (4.24)$$

First, considering the two measures of labor and capital inputs, we obtain the following results:

$$\log X = -3.938 + 1.451 \log L_1 + 0.384 \log K_1 \qquad (4.25)$$
$$\quad\ \ (0.237)\quad (0.083)\qquad\ \ (0.048)$$

$$R^2 = 0.9946 \qquad \bar{R}^2 = 0.9943 \qquad \text{RSS} = 0.0434 \qquad \hat{\sigma}^2 = 0.001205$$

$$\log X = -6.388 + 2.082 \log L_2 + 0.571 \log K_2$$
$$\quad\ \ (0.294)\quad (0.100)\qquad\ \ (0.067)$$

$$R^2 = 0.9831 \qquad \text{RSS} = 0.1363$$

Figures in parentheses are standard errors. Since the dependent variable is the same and the number of independent variables is the same, the R^2's are comparable. A comparison of the R^2's indicates that L_1 and K_1 are better explantory variables than L_2 and K_2. Hence we will conduct further analysis with L_1 and K_1 only.

One other thing we notice is that all variables increase with time. Regressing each of the variables on time we find:

$$\log X = 4.897 + 0.0395t \qquad R^2 = 0.9549$$
$$\quad\ (0.032)\quad (0.0014)$$

$$\log L_1 = 4.989 + 0.0185t \qquad R^2 = 0.9238$$
$$\quad\ (0.020)\quad (0.0009)$$

$$\log K_1 = 4.171 + 0.0324t \qquad R^2 = 0.9408$$
$$\quad\ (0.031)\quad (0.0013)$$

We can eliminate these time trends from these variables and then estimate the production function with the trend-adjusted data. But this is the same as including t as an extra explanatory variable (see the discussion in Section 4.4 earlier).[17]

---

[16] The data are from L. R. Christensen and D. W. Jorgenson, "U.S. Real Product and Real Factor Input 1929–67," *Review of Income and Wealth*, March 1970.

[17] This result is commonly known as the Frisch–Waugh theorem.

Thus we get the result

$$\log X = -3.015 + 1.341 \log L_1 + 0.292 \log K_1 + 0.0052t$$
$$\quad\quad\quad\quad (0.091) \quad\quad\quad\quad (0.060) \quad\quad\quad\quad (0.0022)$$

$$R^2 = 0.9954 \quad\quad \bar{R}^2 = 0.9949 \quad\quad \text{RSS} = 0.0375 \quad\quad \hat{\sigma}^2 = 0.001072$$

Comparing this result with (4.25), we notice that $\hat{\beta}_1 + \hat{\beta}_2$ has gone down from $1.451 + 0.384 = 1.835$ to $1.341 + 0.292 = 1.633$. $\hat{\beta}_1 + \hat{\beta}_2$ measures returns to scale. Also, the $\bar{R}^2$ has increased, or equivalently, $\hat{\sigma}^2$ has decreased. This is to be expected because the t-value for the last variable is greater than 1.

Although we do not need to test the hypothesis of constant returns to scale, that is $\beta_1 + \beta_2 = 1$, we will illustrate it. The estimated variances and covariances (from the SAS regression package used) were

$$\text{estimate of } V(\hat{\beta}_1) = 0.008353 \quad\quad \text{estimate of } V(\hat{\beta}_2) = 0.003581$$
$$\text{estimate of } \text{cov}(\hat{\beta}_1, \hat{\beta}_2) = -0.001552$$

Thus

$$\text{estimate of } V(\hat{\beta}_1 + \hat{\beta}_2 - 1) = 0.008353 + 0.003581 - 2(0.001552)$$
$$= 0.008830$$

Hence

$$\text{SE}(\hat{\beta}_1 + \hat{\beta}_2 - 1) = \sqrt{0.008830} = 0.094$$

The t-statistic to test $\beta_1 + \beta_2 - 1 = 0$ is

$$t = \frac{(\hat{\beta}_1 + \hat{\beta}_2 - 1) - (0)}{\text{SE}(\hat{\beta}_1 + \hat{\beta}_2 - 1)} = \frac{0.633}{0.094} = 6.73$$

From the t-tables with 34 d.f. we find that the 5% significance point is 2.03 and the 1% significance point is 2.73. Thus we reject the hypothesis of constant returns to scale even at the 1% level of significance.

Suppose that we estimate the production function (4.24) for the two periods 1929–1948 and 1949–1967 separately. We get the following results:

1929–1948

$$\log X = -4.058 + 1.617 \log L_1 + 0.220 \log K_1 \quad\quad\quad\quad (4.26)$$
$$\quad\quad\quad (0.357) \quad (0.209) \quad\quad\quad (0.230)$$

$$R^2 = 0.9759 \quad\quad \text{RSS} = 0.03555 \quad\quad \text{d.f.} = 17 \quad\quad (4.27)$$

1949–1967

$$\log X = -2.498 + 1.009 \log L_1 + 0.579 \log K_1$$
$$\quad\quad\quad (0.531) \quad (0.144) \quad\quad\quad (0.055)$$

$$R^2 = 0.9958 \quad\quad \text{RSS} = 0.00336 \quad\quad \text{d.f.} = 16$$

Applying the test for stability (4.23), we get

URSS $= 0.03555 + 0.00336 = 0.0389$ with d.f. $= 17 + 16 = 33$

RRSS $= 0.0434$ [from (4.25) earlier] with d.f. $= 36$

Thus

$$F = \frac{(0.0434 - 0.0389)/3}{0.0389/33} = 1.27$$

From the F-tables with 3 and 33 d.f. we find that the 5% point is 2.9. Thus at the 5% significance level we do not reject the hypothesis of stability.

Again, looking at the individual coefficient estimates for the two periods, this result is perplexing. We will consider some other tests for stability and see whether these tests confirm this result.

Predictive Tests for Stability

The analysis-of-variance test that we have discussed is also commonly referred to as the Chow test, although it had been known much earlier.[18] Chow suggests another test that can be used even when $n_2 < (k + 1)$. This is the predictive test for stability. The idea behind is this: We use the first n_1 observations to estimate the regression equation and use it to get predictions for the next n_2 observations. Then we test the hypothesis that the prediction errors have mean zero. If $n_2 = 1$, we just use the method described in Section 4.7. If $n_2 > 1$, the F-test is given by

$$F = \frac{(RSS - RSS_1)/n_2}{RSS_1/(n_1 - k - 1)} \tag{4.28}$$

which has an F-distribution with d.f. n_2 and $n_1 - k - 1$. Here

RSS $=$ residual sum of squares from the regression based on $n_1 + n_2$ observations; this has $(n_1 + n_2) - (k + 1)$ d.f.

$RSS_1 =$ residual sum of squares from the regression based on n_1 observations; this has $n_1 - k - 1$ d.f.

We will omit the proof here because it is beyond the scope of our discussion.[19] In Chapter 8 we give a dummy variable method of applying the same test. We will first illustrate the use of this test and then discuss its advantages and limitations.

---

[18] G. C. Chow, "Tests of Equality Between Subsets of Coefficients in Two Linear Regression Models," *Econometrica*, 1960, pp. 591–605. The paper suggests two tests: the analysis-of-variance test and the predictive test. The former test, although referred to as the Chow test, was discussed earlier in C. R. Rao, *Advanced Statistical Methods in Biometric Research* (New York: Wiley, 1952) and S. Kullback and H. M. Rosenblatt, "On the Analysis of Multiple Regression in k Categories," *Biometrika*, 1957, pp. 67–83. Thus it is the second test—the predictive test—that should be called the Chow test.

[19] Proofs are given in several econometrics textbooks; see, for instance, G. S. Maddala, *Econometrics* (New York: McGraw-Hill, 1977), pp. 459–460.

Illustrative Example

Consider the example of demand for food that we considered earlier. We have, for Equation 1, from Table 4.4:

$$\text{For 1927–1941:}\quad \text{RSS}_1 = 0.1151$$

$$\text{For 1948–1962:}\quad \text{RSS}_2 = 0.0544$$

$$\text{Combined data:}\quad \text{RSS} = 0.2866$$

Considering the predictions for 1948–1962 using the estimated equation for 1927–1941, we have

$$F = \frac{(\text{RSS} - \text{RSS}_1)/n_2}{\text{RSS}_1/n_1 - k - 1} = \frac{(0.2866 - 0.1151)/15}{0.1151/12} = 1.19$$

From the F-tables with d.f. 15 and 12 we find that the 5% point is 2.62. Thus at the 5% level of significance, we do not reject the hypothesis of stability. The analysis of variance test led to the opposite conclusion.

For Equation 2 we have (from Table 4.4):

$$\text{RSS}_1 = 0.1151 \qquad \text{RSS}_2 = 0.0535 \qquad \text{RSS} = 0.2397$$

The F-test is

$$F = \frac{(0.2397 - 0.1151)/15}{0.1151/11} = 0.79$$

Thus at the 5% significance level we do not reject the hypothesis of stability. Thus the conclusions of the predictive test does not seem to be different from that of the analysis-of-variance test, for this equation.

However, for the predictive test, we can also reverse the roles of samples 1 and 2. That is, we can also ask the question of how well the equation fitted for the second period predicts for the first period. If the coefficients are stable, we should do well. The F-test for this is now (interchanging 1 and 2)

$$F = \frac{(\text{RSS} - \text{RSS}_2)/n_1}{\text{RSS}_2/n_2 - k - 1} \tag{4.29}$$

which has an F-distribution with d.f. n_1 and $n_2 - k - 1$. For Equation 2 we have

$$F = \frac{(0.2397 - 0.0535)/15}{0.0535/16} = 3.71$$

From the F-tables with d.f. 15 and 16 we see that the 5% point is 2.35 and the 1% point is 3.41. Thus, even at the 1% significance level, we reject the hypothesis of stability of the coefficients. Using this predictive test has led us to an opposite conclusion.

Chow suggested the predictive test for the case where n_2 is less than $k + 1$. In this case the regression equation cannot be estimated with the second sample and thus the analysis-of-variance test cannot be applied. In this case only the predictive test can be used. He also suggested that the predictive test can be used even when $n_2 > (k + 1)$ but that in this case the analysis-of-variance test should be preferred because it is more powerful.

In our example we have $n_2 > (k + 1)$, but we have also used two predictive tests. In practice it is desirable to use both predictive tests as illustrated in our example.

Comments

1. Wilson [20] argues that though the Chow test (the predictive test) has been suggested only for the case $n_2 < (k + 1)$, that is, for the case when the analysis-of-variance test cannot be used, the test has desirable power properties when there are some unknown specification errors. Hence it should be used even when $n_2 > (k + 1)$, that is, even in those cases where the analysis-of-variance test can be computed. We have illustrated how the predictive test can be used in two ways in this case.

2. Rea [21] argues that in the case $n_2 < (k + 1)$ the Chow test cannot be considered a test for stability. All it tests is that the prediction error has mean zero, that is, the predictions are unbiased. If the coefficients are stable, the prediction error will have zero mean. But the converse need not be true in the case $n_2 < (k + 1)$. The prediction error can have a zero mean even if the coefficients are not stable, if the explanatory variables have moved in an offsetting manner. Rea's conclusion is that "the Chow test is incapable of testing the hypothesis of equality against that of inequality. It can never be argued from the Chow test itself that the two sets [of regression coefficients] are equal, although at times it may be possible to conclude that they are unequal." This does not mean that the Chow test is not useful. Instead of calling it a test for stability we would call it a test for unbiasedness in prediction. Note that in the case both n_1 and n_2 are greater than $(k + 1)$, the two predictive tests that we have illustrated are tests for stability.

3. Another problem with the application of the tests for stability, which applies to both the analysis of variance and predictive tests, is that the tests are inaccurate if the error variances in the two samples are unequal. [22] The true size of the test (under the null hypothesis) may not equal the prescribed α level. For this reason it would be desirable to test the equality of the variances.

Consider, for instance, the error variances for Equation 1 in Table 4.4. The F-statistic to test equality of error variances is

$$F = \left(\frac{\hat{\sigma}_1}{\hat{\sigma}_2}\right)^2 = \frac{0.9594}{0.4534} = 2.12$$

[20] A. L. Wilson, "When Is the Chow Test UMP?" *The American Statistician*, Vol. 32, No. 2, May 1978, pp. 66–68.

[21] J. D. Rea, "Indeterminacy of the Chow Test When the Number of Observations Is Insufficient," *Econometrica*, Vol. 46, No. 1, January 1978, p. 229.

[22] This was pointed out in T. Toyoda, "Use of the Chow Test Under Heteroskedasticity," *Econometrica*, 1976, pp. 601–608. The approximations used by Toyoda were found to be inaccurate, but the inaccuracy of the Chow test holds good. See P. Schmidt and R. Sickles, "Some Further Evidence on the Use of the Chow Test Under Heteroskedasticity," *Econometrica*, Vol. 45, No. 5, July 1977, p. 1293–1298.

For the F-distribution with d.f. 12 and 12 the 5% point is 2.40. Thus we do not reject the hypothesis of equality at the 5% significance level.

For Equation 2 the corresponding test statistic is

$$F = \frac{1.0462}{0.4866} = 2.15$$

Again if we use a 5% significance level, we do not reject the hypothesis of equality of the error variances.

Thus, in both cases we might be tempted to conclude that we can apply the tests for stability. There is, however, one problem with such a conclusion. This is that the F-test for equality of variances is a pretest, that is, it is a test preliminary to the test for stability. There is the question of what significance level we should use for such pretests. The general conclusion is that for pretests one should use a higher significance level than 5%. In fact, 25 to 50% is a good rule. If this is done, we would reject the hypothesis of equality of variances in the case of both Equations 1 and 2.

*4.12 THE *LR*, *W*, AND *LM* TESTS

In the Appendix to Chapter 3 we stated large sample test statistics to test the hypothesis $\beta = 0$. These were:

$$LR = n \log_e \left(\frac{1}{1 - r^2} \right)$$

$$W = \frac{nr^2}{1 - r^2}$$

$$LM = nr^2$$

Each has a χ^2-distribution with 1 d.f. In the multiple regression model, to test the hypothesis $\beta_i = 0$ we use these test statistics with the corresponding *partial* r^2 substituted in the place of the simple r^2. The test statistics have a χ^2-distribution with d.f. 1.

To test hypotheses like

$$\beta_1 = \beta_2 = \cdots = \beta_k = 0$$

we have to substitute the *multiple* R^2 in place of the simple r^2 or partial r^2 in these formulae. The test statistics have a χ^2-distribution with d.f. k.

To test any linear restrictions, we saw (in the Appendix to Chapter 3) that the likelihood-ratio test statistic was

$$LR = n \log_e \left(\frac{\text{RRSS}}{\text{URSS}} \right)$$

where   RRSS = Restricted Residual Sum of Squares

and   URSS = Unrestricted Residual Sum of Squares

LR has a χ^2-distribution d.f. r where r is the number of restrictions. The test statistics for the Wald test and the LM test are given by

$$W = \frac{(\text{RRSS} - \text{URSS})}{\text{URSS}/n}$$

$$LM = \frac{(\text{RRSS} - \text{URSS})}{\text{RRSS}/n}$$

Both W and LM have a χ^2-distribution d.f. r. The inequality $W \geq LR \geq LM$ again holds and the proof is the same as that given in the Appendix to Chapter 3.

Illustrative Example

Consider example 1 in Section 4.11 (stability of the demand for food function). For equation 1 we have

$$\text{URSS} = 0.1695, \text{RRSS} = 0.2866, n = 30$$

and the number of restrictions $r = 3$. We get

$$W = 20.73$$

$$LR = 15.76$$

$$LM = 12.26.$$

Looking at the χ^2 tables for 3 d.f. the 0.01 significance point is 11.3. Thus, all the test statistics are significant at that level, rejecting the hypothesis of coefficient stability. As we saw earlier, the F-test also rejected the hypothesis at the 1 percent significance level.

Turning to Equation 2 we have

$$\text{URSS} = 0.1686, \text{RRSS} = 0.2397, n = 30, r = 4$$

We now get

$$W = 12.65$$

$$LR = 10.56$$

$$LM = 8.90$$

From the χ^2 tables with 4 d.f. the 5 percent significance point is 9.49. Thus, both the W and LR tests reject the hypothesis of coefficient stability at the 5 percent significance level, whereas the LM test does not. There is, thus, a conflict among the three test criteria. We saw earlier that the F-test did not reject the hypothesis at the 5 percent significance level either.

The conflict between the W, LR and LM tests has been attributed to the fact that in small samples the actual significance levels may deviate substantially from the normal significance levels. That is, though we said we were testing the hypothesis of coefficient stability at the 5 percent significance level, we were in effect testing it at different levels for the different tests. Procedures have been developed to correct this problem but a discussion of these procedures is beyond the scope of this book. The suggested formulae are too complicated to be discussed here. However, the elementary introduction of these tests given here will be useful in understanding some other tests discussed in Chapters 4, 5 and 6.

SUMMARY

This chapter is very long and hence summaries will be presented by sections.

1. Sections 4.2 to 4.5: Model with Two Explanatory Variables. We discuss the model with two explanatory variables in great detail because it clarifies many aspects of multiple regression. Of special interest are the expressions for the variances of the estimates of the regression coefficients given at the beginning of Section 4.3. These expressions are used repeatedly later in the book. Also, it is important to keep in mind the distinction between separate confidence intervals for each individual parameter and joint confidence intervals for sets of parameters (discussed in Section 4.3). Similarly, there can be conficts between tests for each coefficient separately (t-tests) and tests for a set of coefficients (F-test). (This is discussed in greater detail in Section 4.10.) Finally, in Section 4.5 it is shown that each coefficient in a multiple regression equation can be interpreted as the regression coefficient in a simple regression involving two variables after removing the effect of all other variables on these two variables. This interpretation is useful in many problems and will be used in other parts of the book.

2. The illustrative examples given at the end of Section 4.3 show how sometimes we can get "wrong" signs for some of the coefficients and how this can change with the addition or deletion of variables. (We discuss this in more detail in Section 4.10.) The example of gasoline demand represents one where the results obtained were poor and further analysis with the data was left as an exercise.

3. Section 4.6: Simple, Partial, and Multiple Correlations. In multiple regression it is important to note that there is no necessary relationship between the simple correlation between two variables y and x and the partial correlation between these variables after allowing for the effect of other variables. (see Table 4.2 for an illustration). There is, however, some relationship between R^2 and the simple r^2 and partial r^2's. This is given in equation (4.13). Also partial $r^2 = t^2/(t^2 + \text{d.f.})$ is a useful relationship. Some examples are given to illustrate these relationships.

4. Section 4.7: Prediction. In the case of the simple regression model (Section 3.7) the variance of the prediction increased with the distance of x_0 from $\bar{x}$. In the case of prediction from the multiple regression model this is not necessarily the case. An example is given to illustrate this point. Again, as in the case of the simple regression model, we can consider prediction of y_0 or prediction of $E(y_0)$. The predicted value will be the same in both the cases. However, the variance of the prediction error will be different. In the case of prediction of $E(y_0)$ we have to subtract σ^2 from the corresponding expression for the prediction of y_0. Note that we did not discuss the prediction of $E(y_0)$ here as we did this in the simple regression case (Section 3.7).

5. Section 4.8: Tests of Hypotheses. Tests of single parameters and single linear functions of parameters will be t-tests. Tests of several parameters and several linear functions of parameters are F-tests. These are both illustrated with examples. Note again that there can be conflicts between the two tests. For instance, the t-statistics for each coefficient can be nonsignificant and yet the F-statistic for a set of coefficients can be significant.

6. Section 4.9: Omitted Variables and Irrelavant Variables. The omission of relevant variables produces biased estimates. Expressions are given in equations (4.17)–(4.19) for the omitted variable bias. The variance of the estimated coefficient will be smaller, although the estimated variance (or standard error) need not be. These points are illustrated with examples. The case with the inclusion of irrelevant variables is different. There is no bias. However, the variance of the estimated coefficients increases. Thus we get unbiased but inefficient estimators. These are all only statistical guidelines regarding omission of relevant and inclusion of irrelevant variables.

7. Section 4.10: $\bar{R}^2$. The addition of explanatory variables always increases R^2. This does not mean that the regression equation is improving. The appropriate thing to look at is the estimate of the error variance. An equivalent measure is $\bar{R}^2$, the value of R^2 adjusted for the loss in degrees of freedom due to the addition of more explanatory variables. It is given by equation (4.21). A procedure usually followed is to keep on adding variables until the $\bar{R}^2$ stops increasing. Apart from the lack of any economic rationale, there are some pitfalls in this procedure. The $\bar{R}^2$ might increase by the addition (or deletion) of two or more variables even though it might not if one variable is added (or dropped) at a time. Some rules are given for the prediction of sign changes in the estimates of the coefficients of the retained variables when a variable is deleted. Although maximization of $\bar{R}^2$ and mechanical deletion of nonsignificant variables have serious pitfalls, these rules provide some useful predictions.

8. Section 4.11: Test for Stability. In multiple regression analysis we are often concerned with the stability of the estimated relationships across two samples of sizes n_1 and n_2. We discuss and illustrate two tests: the analysis-of-variance test (AV test) and the predictive test (Chow test). In practice it is desirable to use both tests. If either n_1 or n_2 is not greater than the number of regression parameters estimated, the AV test cannot be used but the Chow test can be. However, in this case the Chow test is not a test for stability. It is merely a test for unbiasedness of predictions.

EXERCISES

(More difficult exercises are marked with an *)

1. Define the following terms.
   (a) Standard error of the regression.
   (b) R^2 and $\bar{R}^2$.
   (c) Partial r^2.
   (d) Tests for stability.
   (e) Degrees of freedom.
   (f) Linear functions of parameters.
   (g) Nested and nonnested hypotheses.
   (h) Analysis of variance.

2. In a multiple regression equation, show how you can obtain the partial r^2's given the t-ratios for the different coefficients.

3. In the multiple regression equation

$$y = \alpha + \beta_1 x_1 + \beta_2 x_2 + \beta_3 x_3 + u$$

   Explain how you will test the joint hypothesis $\beta_1 = \beta_2$ and $\beta_3 = 1$.

4. The following regression equation is estimated as a production function.

$$\log Q = 1.37 + 0.632 \log K + 0.452 \log L \qquad R^2 = 0.98$$
$$ (0.257) (0.219)$$

   $\text{cov}(b_K, b_L) = -0.044$. The sample size is 40. Test the following hypotheses at the 5% level of significance.
   (a) $b_K = b_L$.
   (b) There are constant returns to scale.

5. Indicate whether each of the following statements is true (T), false (F), or uncertain (U), and give a brief explanation or proof.
   (a) Suppose that the coefficient of a variable in a regression equation is significantly different from zero at the 20% level. If we drop this variable from the regression, both R^2 and $\bar{R}^2$ will necessarily decrease.
   (b) Compared with the unconstrained regression, estimation of a least squares regression under a constraint (say, $\beta_2 = \beta_3$) will result in a higher R^2 if the constraint is true and a lower R^2 if it is false.
   (c) In a least squares regression of y on x, observations for which x is far from its mean will have more effect on the estimated slope than observations for which x is close to its mean value.

6. The following estimated equation was obtained by ordinary least squares regression using quarterly data for 1960 to 1979 inclusive ($T = 80$).

$$\hat{y}_t = 2.20 + 0.104 x_{1t} + 3.48 x_{2t} + 0.34 x_{3t}$$
$$\phantom{\hat{y}_t = } (3.4) (0.005) \phantom{x_{1t} + } (2.2) \phantom{x_{2t} + } (0.15)$$

   Standard errors are in parentheses, the explained sum of squares was 112.5, and the residual sum of squares was 19.5.
   (a) Which of the slope coefficients are significantly different from zero at the 5% significance level?
   (b) Calculate the value of R^2 for this regression.
   (c) Calculate the value of $\bar{R}^2$ ("adjusted R^2").

7. Suppose that you are given two sets of samples with the following information:

	Sample 1	Sample 2
n	$n = 20$	$n = 25$
$\bar{x}$	$\bar{x} = 20$	$\bar{x} = 23$
$\bar{y}$	$\bar{y} = 25$	$\bar{y} = 28$
S_{xx}	$S_{xx} = 80$	$S_{xx} = 100$
S_{xy}	$S_{xy} = 120$	$S_{xy} = 150$
S_{yy}	$S_{yy} = 200$	$S_{yy} = 250$

(a) Estimate a linear regression equation for each sample separately and for the pooled sample.
(b) State the assumptions under which estimation of the pooled regression is valid.
(c) Explain how you will test the validity of these assumptions using the data provided.

8. A researcher tried two specifications of a regression equation.

$$y = \alpha + \beta x + u$$
$$y = \alpha' + \beta'x + \gamma'z + u'$$

Explain under what circumstances the following will be true. (A "hat" over a parameter denotes its estimate.)

(a) $\hat{\beta} = \hat{\beta}'$.
(b) If $\hat{u}_i$ and $\hat{u}_i'$ are the estimated residuals from the two equations $\sum \hat{u}_i^2 \geq \sum \hat{u}_i'^2$.
(c) $\hat{\beta}$ is statistically significant (at the 5% level) but $\hat{\beta}'$ is not.
(d) $\hat{\beta}'$ is statistically significant (at the 5% level) but $\hat{\beta}$ is not.

9. The model

$$y_t = \beta_0 + \beta_1 x_{1t} + \beta_2 x_{2t} + \beta_3 x_{3t} + u_t$$

was estimated by ordinary least squares from 26 observations. The results were

$$\hat{y}_t = 2 + 3.5x_{1t} - 0.7x_{2t} + 2.0x_{3t}$$
$$\quad\quad (1.9) \quad\quad (2.2) \quad\quad (1.5)$$

t-ratios are in parentheses and $R^2 = 0.982$. The same model was estimated with the restriction $\beta_1 = \beta_2$. Estimates were:

$$\hat{y}_t = 1.5 + 3(x_{1t} + x_{2t}) - 0.6x_{3t} \quad\quad R^2 = 0.876$$
$$\quad\quad (2.7) \quad\quad\quad (2.4)$$

(a) Test the significance of the restriction $\beta_1 = \beta_2$. State the assumptions under which the test is valid.
(b) Suppose that x_{2t} is dropped from the equation; would the $\bar{R}^2$ rise or fall?
(c) Would the R^2 rise or fall if x_{2t} is dropped?

10. Suppose that the least squares regression of Y on $x_1, x_2, \ldots, x_k$ yields coefficient estimates $b_j(j = 1, 2, \ldots, k)$ none of which exceed their respective standard errors. However, the F-ratio for the equation rejects, at the 0.05 level the hypothesis that $b_1 = b_2 = \cdots = b_k = 0$.

(a) Is this possible?

(b) What do you think is the reason for this?

(c) What further analysis would you perform?

11. What would be your answer to the following queries regarding multiple regression analysis.

    (a) I am trying to find out why people go bankrupt. I have gathered data from a sample of people filing bankruptcy petitions. Will these data enable me to find answers to my question?

    (b) I want to study the costs of auto accidents. I have collected data from a sample of police auto accident reports. Are these data adequate for my purpose?

    (c) I am trying to estimate a consumption function and I suspect that the marginal propensity to consume varies inversely with the rate of interest. Do I run a multiple regression using income and interest rate as explanatory variables?

    (d) I am fitting a demand for food function for a sample of 1000 families. I obtain an R^2 of only 0.05 but the regression program indicates that the F-statistic for the equation is very significant and so are the t-statistics. How can this be? Is there a mistake in the program?

    (e) In the regression of Y on x and z, should I leave one of them out?

    (f) I know that y depends linearly on x but I am not sure whether or not it also depends on another variable z. A friend of mine suggests that I should regress y on x first, calculate the residuals, and then see whether they are correlated with z. Is she correct?

12. A student obtains the following results in several different regression problems. In which cases could you be *certain* that an error has been committed? Explain.

    (a) $R^2_{Y.123} = 0.89$, $R^2_{Y.1234} = 0.86$

    (b) $\bar{R}^2_{Y.123} = 0.86$, $\bar{R}^2_{Y.1234} = 0.82$

    (c) $r^2_{Y1.2} = 0.23$, $r^2_{Y1.3} = 0.13$, $R^2_{Y.123} = 0.70$

    (d) Same as part (c) but $r^2_{Y2.3} = 0$

13. Given the following estimated regression equations

$$\hat{C}_t = \text{const.} + 0.92Y_t$$

$$\hat{C}_t = \text{const.} + 0.84C_{t-1}$$

$$\hat{C}_{t-1} = \text{const.} + 0.78Y_t$$

$$\hat{Y}_t = \text{const.} + 0.55C_{t-1}$$

calculate the regression estimates of β_1 and β_2 for

$$C_t = \beta_0 + \beta_1 Y_t + \beta_2 C_{t-1} + u_t$$

*14. Instead of estimating the coefficients β_1 and β_2 from the model

$$y = \alpha + \beta_1 x_1 + \beta_2 x_2 + u$$

it is decided to use ordinary least squares on the following regression equation:

$$y = \alpha + \beta_1 x_1^* + \beta_2 x_2 + v$$

where x_1^* is the residual from a regression of x_1 on x_2 and v is the disturbance term.

    (a) Show that the resulting estimator of β_2 is identical to the regression coefficient of y on x_2.

(b) Obtain an expression for the bias of this estimator.

(c) Prove that the estimators of β_1 obtained from each of the two equations are identical.

*15. Explain how you will estimate a linear regression equation which is piecewise linear with a joint (or knot) at $x = x_0$ if

(a) x_0 is known

(b) x_0 is unknown.

*16. In the model

$$y_t = \beta_1 x_{1t} + \beta_2 x_{2t} + \beta_3 x_{3t} + u_t$$

the coefficients are known to be related to a more basic economic parameter α according to the equations

$$\beta_1 + \beta_2 = \alpha$$
$$\beta_1 + \beta_3 = -\alpha$$

Assuming that the x's are nonrandom and that $u_t \sim IN(0, \sigma^2)$, find the best unbiased linear estimator $\hat{\alpha}$ of α and the variance of $\hat{\alpha}$.

17. A study on unemployment in the British interwar period produced the following regression equation (data are given in Table 4.11):

$$U = 5.19 + 18.3(B/W) - 90.0(\log Q - \log Q^*)$$
$$\ (2.0)\quad\ \ (4.46)\qquad\quad (-8.3)$$
$$R^2 = 0.8 \qquad SER = 1.9$$

Sample period 1920–1938 ($n = 19$).

$$U = \text{unemployment rate}$$
$$B/W = \text{ratio of unemployment benefits to average wage}$$
$$Q = \text{actual output}$$
$$Q^* = \text{trend predicted output}$$
$$\log Q - \log Q^* = \text{captures unexpected changes in aggregate demand}$$

The authors [23] conclude that the high benefit levels are partly responsible for the high rates of unemployment. Critics of this study argued that when the single observation for 1920 is dropped the results change dramatically. [24] The equation now is

$$U = 7.9 + 12.9(B/W) - 87.0(\log Q - \log Q^*)$$
$$\ (3.0)\quad\ \ (2.4)\qquad\quad (8.3)$$
$$R^2 = 0.82 \qquad SER = 1.7$$

Sample period 1921–1938 ($n = 18$).

Test whether the results are significantly different from each other.

[23] D. K. Benjamin and L. A. Kochin, "Searching for an Explanation of Unemployment in Interwar Britain," *Journal of Political Economy*, June 1979, pp. 441–478.

[24] P. A. Ormerod and G. D. N. Worswick, "Unemployment in Interwar Britain," *Journal of Political Economy*, April 1982, pp. 400–409.

18. In a study on determinants of children born in the Philippines,[25] the following results were obtained:

Variable	Coefficient	SE	t-Ratio	Coefficient	SE	t-Ratio
ED	−0.177	0.026	−6.81	−0.067	0.024	−2.79
LWH	0.476	0.327	1.46	0.091	0.289	0.31
AMAR	—	—	—	−0.296	0.016	−18.50
SURV	−0.006	0.003	−2.00	−0.003	0.003	−1.00
RURAL	0.361	0.193	1.87	0.281	0.171	1.64
Age	0.123	0.024	5.12	0.155	0.021	7.36
Constant	5.650	3.180	1.78	9.440	2.820	3.35
R^2		0.096			0.295	

The variables are:

> ED = years of schooling of the woman
>
> LWH = natural logarithm of present value of husband's earnings at marriage
>
> $AMAR$ = age of the woman at marriage
>
> $SURV$ = survival probabililily at age 5 in the province
>
> $RURAL$ = residence in rural area (dummy variable); this variable is supposed to capture search and schooling costs
>
> Age = age of the woman

The explained variable is number of children born.
  (a) Do the coefficients have the signs you would expect?
  (b) Using the t-ratio for $AMAR$ and the R^2 for the two equations, can you tell how many observations were used in the estimation?
  (c) Looking at the t-ratio of $AMAR$, can you predict the signs of the coefficients of the other variables if $AMAR$ is deleted from the equation?
  (d) Given that the dependent variable is number of children born, do you think the assumptions of the least squares model are satisfied?

19. In a study of investment plans and realizations in U.K. manufacturing industries since 1955, the following results were obtained:

$$A_t = \text{const.} - \underset{(6.24)}{54.60} C_{t-1} \qquad R^2 = 0.89 \qquad DW = 2.50$$

$$I_t - A_t = \text{const.} - \underset{(4.44)}{19.96}(C_t - C_{t-1}) \qquad R^2 = 0.68 \qquad DW = 2.31$$

$$I_t = \text{const.} + \underset{(0.10)}{0.88} A_t - \underset{(5.15)}{16.32}(C_t - C_{t-1}) \qquad R^2 = 0.90 \qquad DW = 1.65$$

[25] B. L. Boulier and M. R. Rosenzweig, "Schooling, Search and Spouse Selection: Testing Economic Theories of Marriage and Household Behavior," *Journal of Political Economy*, August 1984, p. 729.

$$I_t = \text{const.} - \underset{(3.64)}{50.08}C_{t-1} - \underset{(3.32)}{14.60}(C_t - C_{t-1})$$

$$R^2 = 0.96 \qquad DW = 2.61$$

A_t = investment that firms anticipate they will complete in year t; these plans are held at the end of year $t-1$.

I_t = actual investment in year t

C_t = measure of average level of under utilization of capacity

Figures in parentheses are standard errors.

(a) Interpret these results and assess whether or not knowledge of firms' anticipated investment is helpful in explaining actual investment.

(b) How many observations have been used in the estimation?

(c) What is the partial correlation coefficient of I_t with A_t after allowing for the effect of $C_t - C_{t-1}$?

20. The demand for Ceylonese tea in the United States is given by the equation

$$\log Q = \beta_0 + \beta_1 \log P_C + \beta_2 \log P_I + \beta_3 \log P_B + \beta_4 \log Y + u$$

where Q = imports of Ceylon tea in the United States

P_C = price of Ceylon tea

P_I = price of Indian tea

P_B = price of Brazilian coffee

Y = disposable income

The following results were obtained from $T = 22$ observations.

$$\log Q = \underset{(2.0)}{2.837} - \underset{(0.987)}{1.481} \log P_C + \underset{(0.690)}{1.181} \log P_I + \underset{(0.134)}{0.186} \log P_B$$

$$+ \underset{(.370)}{0.257} \log Y \qquad RSS = 0.4277$$

$$\log Q + \log P_C = \underset{(0.820)}{-0.738} + \underset{(0.155)}{0.199} \log P_B + \underset{(0.165)}{0.261} \log Y \qquad RSS = 0.6788$$

Figures in parentheses are standard errors.

(a) Test the hypothesis $\beta_1 = -1$, $\beta_2 = 0$, and $\beta_3, \beta_4 \neq 0$ against $\beta_i \neq 0$ for $i = 1, 2, 3, 4$.

(b) Discuss the economic implications of these results.

Some Data Sets

Table 4.7 Sale Prices of Rural Land[a]

N	Price	WL	DA	D75	A	MO
1	5,556	1.00	12.1	4.9	36.0	33
2	5,236	1.00	12.1	4.9	38.2	30
3	5,952	1.00	12.0	4.9	21.0	15
4	7,000	0.00	16.0	1.2	40.0	44
5	3,750	0.00	15.5	3.2	40.0	43
6	7,000	0.00	13.7	3.2	20.0	25
7	5,952	0.00	14.5	2.5	21.0	24
8	2,009	0.00	16.1	0.1	656.0	19
9	2,583	1.00	15.2	3.0	60.0	18
10	2,449	0.00	15.5	1.0	156.0	18
11	2,500	0.50	15.2	2.0	40.0	3
12	3,000	0.00	15.5	3.2	13.0	3
13	3,704	0.00	13.5	2.5	27.0	3
14	3,500	0.00	15.5	1.0	10.0	3
15	3,500	0.00	17.5	5.4	20.0	38
16	4,537	1.00	18.0	5.9	38.0	24
17	3,700	0.00	17.2	5.1	5.0	3
18	2,020	1.00	34.2	22.0	5.0	27
19	5,000	0.00	11.1	5.1	3.5	13
20	4,764	0.00	14.2	2.0	237.6	40
21	871	1.00	14.2	2.0	237.6	7
22	3,500	1.00	11.1	3.1	20.0	41
23	15,200	1.00	14.7	2.4	5.0	36
24	4,767	0.00	12.1	4.1	30.0	22
25	16,316	1.00	14.8	2.5	3.8	21
26	9,873	1.00	14.8	2.5	7.9	17
27	5,175	0.25	14.2	2.0	40.0	13
28	3,977	0.00	11.4	2.9	8.8	10
29	5,500	0.20	18.5	5.9	10.0	38
30	7,500	0.00	16.5	3.9	8.0	42
31	4,545	1.00	16.8	4.5	97.0	36
32	3,765	0.72	18.7	6.4	178.0	29
33	5,000	1.00	18.4	6.1	10.3	25
34	3,300	0.00	16.2	4.0	525.7	25
35	5,500	0.00	18.0	5.4	6.0	21
36	5,172	0.00	15.0	2.4	29.0	20
37	3,571	0.00	15.1	2.5	21.0	20
38	4,000	0.00	18.2	6.0	10.0	15
39	4,000	0.00	18.4	6.1	15.0	18
40	2,625	0.00	15.5	2.9	80.0	10
41	2,257	0.00	42.8	30.5	171.0	14
42	15,504	0.00	4.0	4.5	38.7	39
43	5,600	0.00	3.8	4.0	30.0	25

Table 4.7 (*continued*)

N	Price	WL	DA	D75	A	MO
44	8,000	0.00	3.5	4.2	30.0	27
45	7,700	0.00	4.0	3.8	15.0	46
46	6,187	0.00	4.2	5.0	69.5	15
47	7,018	0.00	3.5	4.0	10.9	23
48	4,821	0.60	7.8	2.7	224.0	33
49	6,504	0.00	14.9	4.8	6.4	40
50	5,225	0.00	16.2	5.0	10.0	40
51	2,500	0.00	24.0	14.0	40.0	33
52	4,000	1.00	22.5	12.4	10.0	20
53	3,638	1.00	5.0	2.2	73.0	2
54	5,400	0.00	13.1	3.7	10.0	28
55	4,850	0.00	12.4	3.0	10.0	28
56	1,628	0.00	22.8	12.8	80.0	23
57	2,780	0.00	23.2	13.2	10.0	26
58	4,500	0.00	21.0	11.0	5.0	28
59	5,600	1.00	21.2	11.2	5.0	22
60	4,750	1.00	21.7	11.7	5.0	32
61	1,790	0.00	18.8	8.8	375.0	38
62	2,750	0.00	23.4	13.4	10.0	22
63	3,250	0.00	22.5	12.5	10.0	19
64	8,500	1.00	16.8	2.7	5.0	27
65	5,357	0.00	16.8	2.7	5.6	26
66	2,500	0.00	21.8	7.5	50.0	14
67	8,505	1.00	20.5	5.8	9.7	12

[a] Price, observed land price per acre excluding improvements; WL, proportion of acreage that is wooded; DA, distance from parcel to Sarasota airport; D75, distance from parcel to I-75; A, acreage of parcel; MO, month in which the parcel was sold.

Table 4.8 Data on Gasoline Consumption in the United States[a]

Year	K	C	M	P_g	P_T	Pop.	L	Y
1947	9732	30.87	14.95	97.0	.538	145	59.3	1513
1948	9573	33.39	14.96	100.8	.564	147	60.6	1567
1949	9395	36.35	14.92	105.4	.633	150	61.3	1547
1950	9015	40.33	14.40	104.3	.678	152	62.2	1646
1951	9187	42.68	14.50	98.0	.694	155	62.0	1657
1952	9361	43.82	14.27	97.3	.723	158	62.1	1678
1953	9370	46.46	14.39	100.0	.765	160	63.0	1726
1954	9308	48.41	14.57	101.4	.814	163	63.6	1714
1955	9359	52.09	14.53	101.8	.840	166	65.0	1795
1956	9348	54.25	14.36	103.3	.860	170	66.6	1839
1957	9391	56.38	14.40	103.2	.862	172	66.9	1844
1958	9494	57.39	14.30	98.5	.879	175	67.6	1831
1959	9529	60.13	14.30	98.1	.897	178	68.4	1881
1960	9446	62.26	14.28	98.6	.913	181	69.6	1883
1961	9456	63.87	14.38	96.4	.944	184	70.5	1909
1962	9441	66.64	14.37	95.0	.965	187	70.6	1968
1963	9240	69.84	14.26	93.2	.965	189	71.8	2013
1964	9286	72.97	14.25	91.8	.970	192	73.1	2123
1965	9286	76.63	14.15	92.6	.972	194	74.5	2235
1966	9384	80.11	14.10	92.7	.979	196	75.8	2331
1967	9399	82.37	14.05	93.1	1.000	199	77.3	2398
1968	9488	85.79	13.91	90.8	1.004	201	78.7	2480
1969	9633	89.16	13.75	89.0	1.026	203	80.7	2517

[a] K, miles traveled per car per year; C, number of cars (millions); M, miles per gallon; P_g, retail gasoline price index deflated by consumer price index (1953 = 100); P_T, price of public transport (1967 = 100); Pop., population (millions); L, labor force (millions); Y, per capita disposable income in 1958 prices.

Table 4.9 Data on Demand for Food and Supply of Food in the United States[a]

Year	Q_D	P_D	Y	Q_S	P_S	t
1922	98.6	100.2	87.4	108.5	99.1	1
1923	101.2	101.6	97.6	110.1	99.1	2
1924	102.4	100.5	96.7	110.4	98.9	3
1925	100.9	106.0	98.2	104.3	110.8	4
1926	102.3	108.7	99.8	107.2	108.2	5
1927	101.5	106.7	100.5	105.8	105.6	6
1928	101.6	106.7	103.2	107.8	109.8	7
1929	101.6	108.2	107.8	103.4	108.7	8
1930	99.8	105.5	96.6	102.7	100.6	9
1931	100.3	95.6	88.9	104.1	81.0	10
1932	97.6	88.6	75.1	99.2	68.6	11
1933	97.2	91.0	76.9	99.7	70.9	12
1934	97.3	97.9	84.6	102.0	81.4	13
1935	96.0	102.3	90.6	94.3	102.3	14
1936	99.2	102.2	103.1	97.7	105.0	15
1937	100.3	102.5	105.1	101.1	110.5	16
1938	100.3	97.0	96.4	102.3	92.5	17
1939	104.1	95.8	104.4	104.4	89.3	18
1940	105.3	96.4	110.7	108.5	93.0	19
1941	107.6	100.3	127.1	111.3	106.6	20

[a] Q_D, food consumption per capita; Q_S, food production per capita; P_D, food prices at retail level/cost of living index; Y, disposable income/cost of living index; P_S, prices received by farmers for food/cost of living; t, time.

Source: M. A. Girschick and T. Haarelmo, "Statistical Analysis of the Demand for Food," Econometrica, April 1947.

Table 4.10　Data on Housing Starts in Canada (1954–4 to 1982–4 Quarterly)[a]

T	HS	y	RR	T	HS	y	RR
54–4	28.73	101.8	3.92	65–1	40.63	169.9	3.68
55–1	29.83	103.3	4.25	–2	38.23	172.4	3.47
–2	31.22	107.4	4.42	–3	39.63	177.0	3.34
–3	32.61	113.7	4.63	–4	40.38	179.0	3.28
–4	30.47	110.8	4.90	66–1	41.12	183.4	3.17
56–1	31.34	117.2	4.63	–2	29.11	185.8	2.73
–2	32.42	118.3	5.16	–3	29.83	191.0	2.44
–3	30.56	116.8	4.64	–4	32.95	186.9	2.38
–4	22.01	121.7	4.09	67–1	30.04	190.3	2.29
57–1	17.75	122.8	3.12	–2	43.53	193.5	2.14
–2	29.41	122.5	2.79	–3	42.41	194.5	2.13
–3	28.76	118.8	2.96	–4	35.87	194.0	2.39
–4	30.39	121.8	3.47	68–1	46.34	197.4	2.83
58–1	36.67	121.5	3.71	–2	48.37	202.6	2.70
–2	41.27	124.2	3.38	–3	42.49	208.0	2.40
–3	36.18	123.2	3.04	–4	51.00	209.1	2.53
–4	37.46	127.7	3.07	69–1	66.32	211.7	2.93
59–1	32.99	127.2	3.42	–2	54.51	213.2	3.42
–2	32.49	128.8	4.52	–3	47.52	218.1	4.06
–3	32.98	128.4	4.87	–4	41.58	218.0	4.09
–4	33.32	131.5	4.59	70–1	40.85	218.3	4.25
60–1	21.95	133.4	4.41	–2	34.54	220.4	3.77
–2	23.54	130.5	4.52	–3	44.43	222.4	3.29
–3	27.05	133.3	4.54	–4	60.78	221.7	3.62
–4	27.34	133.8	4.55	71–1	49.18	227.8	3.36
61–1	31.90	132.5	4.54	–2	55.81	233.3	3.76
–2	29.88	137.1	4.36	–3	57.23	239.8	2.97
–3	30.07	135.1	4.47	–4	59.27	242.0	2.02
–4	27.39	141.5	4.45	72–1	62.12	243.8	1.93
62–1	30.58	143.3	4.34	–2	62.08	250.5	1.68
–2	31.97	143.3	4.05	–3	60.51	249.2	1.60
–3	31.53	148.4	4.38	–4	57.25	257.7	1.05
–4	28.36	148.2	3.96	73–1	62.39	264.7	0.88
63–1	31.94	148.2	3.72	–2	68.25	267.2	1.65
–2	32.78	150.1	3.63	–3	65.32	267.0	1.92
–3	34.97	157.1	3.84	–4	62.45	278.1	1.46
–4	39.12	157.7	3.85	74–1	68.48	280.6	1.21
64–1	42.82	160.7	3.75	–2	62.68	279.6	2.34
–2	32.84	162.2	3.69	–3	50.43	274.5	2.50
–3	37.40	165.2	3.81	–4	40.33	281.5	1.37
–4	46.10	166.6	3.90	75–1	37.28	278.9	–0.96

Table 4.10 (*continued*)

T	HS	y	RR	T	HS	y	RR
−2	51.37	280.4	−1.23	−2	48.53	322.3	3.73
−3	60.49	282.7	−0.09	−3	48.29	324.6	3.85
−4	67.14	286.8	0.78	−4	49.24	328.1	5.85
76−1	66.58	294.4	1.42	80−1	38.24	325.6	6.00
−2	70.57	298.9	1.87	−2	35.33	321.3	5.26
−3	64.94	299.0	2.54	−3	41.39	324.3	2.69
−4	63.81	299.0	2.88	−4	40.57	332.6	4.97
77−1	53.48	301.3	2.36	81−1	39.14	332.0	7.53
−2	61.83	302.5	1.65	−2	53.69	338.5	8.56
−3	61.79	304.9	0.71	−3	47.06	338.3	11.37
−4	59.81	307.9	0.54	−4	33.87	335.5	8.00
78−1	69.51	310.5	0.59	82−1	40.71	319.8	6.27
−2	50.31	312.7	1.62	−2	28.61	320.9	7.41
−3	55.22	318.4	2.28	−3	25.43	322.4	6.26
−4	53.05	318.9	4.00	−4	32.20	316.6	3.12
79−1	46.19	322.5	4.28				

[a] *T*, year and quarter; HS, housing starts; *y*, gross national expenditures (in 1971 $); RR, estimated real interest rate.

Source: R. Davidson and J. G. MacKinnon, "Testing Linear and Log-Linear Regressions Against Box–Cox Alternatives," *Canadian Journal of Economics*, Aug. 1985, Table 5, pp. 515–516. Data on *HS* and *y* have been rounded to four digit numbers.

Table 4.11   Wages, Benefits, Unemployment, and Net National Product: United Kingdom, 1920–1938

Year	Weekly Wages, W (s.)	Weekly Benefits, B (s.)	Unemployment Rate U (%)	Benefits/ Wages	NNP, Q^a (£ Million at 1938 Factor Cost)
1920	73.8	11.3	3.9	0.15	3426
1921	70.6	16.83	17.0	0.24	3242
1922	59.1	22.00	14.3	0.37	3384
1923	55.5	22.00	11.7	0.40	3514
1924	56.0	23.67	10.3	0.42	3622
1925	56.4	27.00	11.3	0.48	3840
1926	55.8	27.00	12.5	0.48	3656
1927	56.2	27.00	9.7	0.48	3937
1928	55.7	27.67	10.8	0.50	4003
1929	55.8	28.00	10.4	0.50	4097
1930	55.7	29.50	16.1	0.53	4082
1931	54.9	29.54	21.3	0.54	3832
1932	54.0	27.25	22.1	0.50	3828
1933	53.7	27.25	19.9	0.51	3899
1934	54.3	28.6	16.7	0.53	4196
1935	55.0	30.3	15.5	0.55	4365
1936	56.1	32.00	13.1	0.57	4498
1937	57.2	32.00	10.8	0.56	4665
1938	58.9	32.75	12.9	0.56	4807

[a] NNP, net national product; s = shilling = $\frac{1}{20}$£

Table 4.12 Weekly Closing Prices of Different Currencies, Commodities, and Financials, October 3, 1986 to January 23, 1987

Week	British Pound	Japanese Yen	Crude Oil	Gold	Treasury Bonds	S&P 500 Average	Dow Jones Industrial
1	142.75	64.75	14.87	433.70	97.06	232.40	1774.18
2	142.30	64.86	14.93	431.00	96.06	235.10	1793.17
3	141.90	64.92	14.80	419.30	94.18	237.95	1837.04
4	140.5	61.94	15.02	407.50	95.29	237.75	1832.26
5	139.80	61.34	15.27	403.60	98.03	244.70	1877.82
6	142.20	61.39	15.17	409.30	96.10	245.90	1886.54
7	142.50	62.01	15.64	398.00	98.05	245.30	1873.60
8	141.55	60.93	15.38	378.90	99.21	244.85	1893.57
9	143.15	61.82	15.00	390.90	99.23	248.65	1914.23
10	142.00	61.56	15.13	389.50	99.25	251.95	1924.78
11	142.90	61.42	16.10	392.80	99.27	247.05	1912.26
12	141.20	61.66	16.21	392.90	100.22	249.60	1928.85
13	144.55	63.01	17.27	390.20	100.08	247.70	1930.40
14	147.30	63.37	18.13	401.90	99.29	246.75	1927.31
15	146.40	63.44	18.77	406.00	101.19	259.50	2005.91
16	150.80	65.41	19.10	416.30	101.04	266.70	2076.64
17	151.55	65.72	18.76	404.90	100.12	269.30	2101.52

Table 4.13   Interest Rates in the United States

Year and Month	3-Month T-Bills	6-Month T-Bills	3-Year T-Bonds	10-Year T-Bonds	Federal Funds Rate
1980					
Jan.	12.04	11.85	10.88	10.80	13.82
Feb.	12.81	12.72	12.84	12.41	14.13
Mar.	15.53	15.10	14.05	12.75	17.19
Apr.	14.00	13.62	12.02	11.47	17.61
May	9.15	9.15	9.44	10.18	10.98
June	7.00	7.22	8.91	9.78	9.47
July	8.13	8.10	9.27	10.25	9.03
Aug.	9.26	9.44	10.63	11.10	9.61
Sept.	10.32	10.55	11.57	11.51	10.87
Oct.	11.58	11.56	12.01	11.75	12.81
Nov.	13.89	13.61	13.31	12.68	15.85
Dec.	15.66	14.77	13.65	12.84	18.90
1981					
Jan.	14.72	13.88	13.01	12.57	19.08
Feb.	14.91	14.13	13.65	13.19	15.93
Mar.	13.48	12.98	13.51	13.12	14.70
Apr.	13.64	13.43	14.09	13.68	15.72
May	16.30	15.33	15.08	14.10	18.52
June	14.56	13.95	14.29	13.47	19.10
July	14.70	14.40	15.15	14.28	19.04
Aug.	15.61	15.55	16.00	14.94	17.82
Sept.	14.95	15.06	16.22	15.32	15.87
Oct.	13.87	14.01	15.50	15.15	15.08
Nov.	11.27	11.53	13.11	13.39	13.31
Dec.	10.93	11.47	13.66	13.72	12.37
1982					
Jan.	12.41	12.93	14.64	14.59	13.22
Feb.	13.78	13.71	14.73	14.43	14.78
Mar.	12.49	12.62	14.13	13.86	14.68
Apr.	12.82	12.86	14.18	13.87	14.94
May	12.15	12.22	13.77	13.62	14.45
June	12.11	12.31	14.48	14.30	14.15
July	11.91	12.24	14.00	13.95	12.59
Aug.	9.01	10.11	12.62	13.06	10.12
Sept.	8.20	9.54	12.03	12.34	10.31
Oct.	7.75	8.30	10.62	10.91	9.71
Nov.	8.04	8.32	9.98	10.55	9.20
Dec.	8.01	8.23	9.88	10.54	8.95
1983					
Jan.	7.81	7.90	9.64	10.46	8.68
Feb.	8.13	8.23	9.91	10.72	8.51

Table 4.13 (*continued*)

Year and Month	3-Month T-Bills	6-Month T-Bills	3-Year T-Bonds	10-Year T-Bonds	Federal Funds Rate
Mar.	8.30	8.33	9.84	10.51	8.77
Apr.	8.25	8.34	9.76	10.40	8.80
May	8.19	8.20	9.66	10.38	8.63
June	8.82	8.89	10.32	10.85	8.98
July	9.12	9.29	10.90	11.38	9.37
Aug.	9.39	9.53	11.30	11.85	9.56
Sept.	9.05	9.19	11.07	11.65	9.45
Oct.	8.71	8.90	10.87	11.54	9.48
Nov.	8.71	8.89	10.96	11.69	9.34
Dec.	8.96	9.14	11.13	11.83	9.47
1984					
Jan.	8.93	9.06	10.93	11.67	9.56
Feb.	9.03	9.13	11.05	11.84	9.59
Mar.	9.44	9.58	11.59	12.32	9.91
Apr.	9.69	9.83	11.98	12.63	10.29
May	9.90	10.31	12.75	13.41	10.32
June	9.94	10.55	13.18	13.56	11.06
July	10.13	10.58	13.08	13.36	11.23
Aug.	10.49	10.65	12.50	12.72	11.64
Sept.	10.41	10.51	12.34	12.52	11.30
Oct.	9.97	10.05	11.85	12.16	9.99
Nov.	8.79	8.99	10.90	11.57	9.43
Dec.	8.16	8.36	10.56	11.50	8.38

Table 4.14 Money Stock, Liquid Assets, and Debt for the United States, 1959–1983[a]
(Billions of Dollars)

	M1	M2	M3	L	Debt
December					
1959	141.0	297.8	299.8	388.6	683.4
1960	141.8	312.3	315.3	403.6	718.7
1961	146.5	335.5	341.0	430.8	761.6
1962	149.2	362.7	371.4	466.1	814.5
1963	154.7	393.2	406.0	503.8	870.4
1964	161.9	424.8	442.5	540.4	934.0
1965	169.5	459.4	482.2	584.4	1002.8
1966	173.7	480.0	505.1	614.8	1070.1
1967	185.1	524.3	557.1	666.5	1147.1
1968	199.4	566.3	606.2	728.9	1242.4
1969	205.8	589.5	615.0	763.5	1330.7
1970	216.6	628.2	677.5	816.3	1420.5
1971	230.8	712.8	776.2	903.1	1555.5
1972	252.0	805.2	886.0	1023.0	1715.3
1973	265.9	861.0	985.0	1141.7	1906.3
1974	277.6	908.5	1070.5	1249.3	2081.8
1975	291.2	1023.3	1172.4	1367.9	2270.8
1976	310.4	1163.6	1311.9	1516.6	2513.3
1977	335.4	1286.7	1472.9	1704.7	2829.1
1978	363.1	1389.1	1647.1	1910.6	3200.0
1979	389.1	1498.5	1804.8	2117.1	3583.5
1980	414.9	1632.6	1990.0	2326.2	3926.1
1981	441.9	1796.6	2238.2	2599.8	4311.8
1982	480.5	1965.4	2462.5	2870.8	4710.0
1983	525.4	2196.3	2710.4	3183.1	5224.6

[a] M1, currency + demand deposits + travelers' checks and other checkable deposits; M2, M1 + savings and small deposits + overnight RPs and Eurodollars + MMMF balances; M3, M2 + large time deposits + term RPs + institutions only MMMF balances; L, M3 + other liquid assets; Debt, debt of domestic nonfinancial sectors (monthly average).

5

Heteroskedasticity

5.1 INTRODUCTION

One of the assumptions we have made until now is that the errors u_t in the regression equation have a common variance σ^2. This is known as the *homoskedasticity* assumption. If the errors do not have a constant variance we say they are *heteroskedastic*. There are several questions we might want to ask if the errors do not have a constant variance. These are:

1. How do we detect this problem?
2. What are the consequences on the properties of the least squares estimators, and what are the consequences on the estimated standard errors if we use OLS?
3. What are the solutions to this problem?

We will answer these questions in the following sections. But first, we will consider an example to illustrate the problem.

Illustrative Example

Table 5.1 presents consumption expenditures (y) and income (x) for 20 families. Suppose that we estimate the equation by ordinary least squares. We get

$$y = \underset{(0.703)}{0.847} + \underset{(0.0253)}{0.899x} \qquad R^2 = 0.986$$

$$RSS = 31.074$$

(Figures in parentheses are standard errors.) We can compute the predicted values and the residuals. In Table 5.2 we present the residuals for the observations which are ordered by their x-values. As we can easily see they are larger (absolutely) for larger values of x. Thus there is some evidence that the error variances are not constant but increase with the value of x. In Figure 5.1 we show the plot of the residuals. This shows graphically (perhaps more than Table 5.2) that there is a heteroskedasticity problem.

Table 5.1 Consumption Expenditures (y) and Income (x) for 20 Families (Thousands of Dollars)

Family	y	x	Family	y	x
1	19.9	22.3	11	8.0	8.1
2	31.2	32.3	12	33.1	34.5
3	31.8	36.6	13	33.5	38.0
4	12.1	12.1	14	13.1	14.1
5	40.7	42.3	15	14.8	16.4
6	6.1	6.2	16	21.6	24.1
7	38.6	44.7	17	29.3	30.1
8	25.5	26.1	18	25.0	28.3
9	10.3	10.3	19	17.9	18.2
10	38.8	40.2	20	19.8	20.1

Table 5.2 Residuals for the Consumption Function Estimated from Data in Table 5.1 (Ordered by Their x-Values)[a]

Observation	Value of x	Residual	Observation	Value of x	Residual
6	6.2	−0.32	8	26.1	1.18
11	8.1	−0.13	18	28.3	−1.30
9	10.3	0.19	17	30.1	1.38
4	12.1	0.37	2	32.3	1.30
14	14.1	−0.43	12	34.5	1.23
15	16.4	−0.80	3	36.6	−1.96
19	18.2	0.69	13	38.0	−1.52
20	20.1	0.88	10	40.2	1.80
1	22.3	−1.00	5	42.3	1.81
16	24.1	−0.92	7	44.7	−2.45

[a] Residuals are rounded to two decimals.

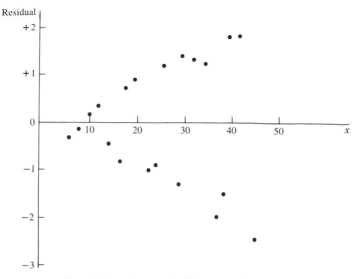

Figure 5.1. Example of heteroskedasticity.

Sometimes, the heteroskedasticity problem is solved by estimating the regression in a log-linear form. When we regress $\log y$ on $\log x$, the estimated equation is

$$\log y = 0.0757 + 0.9562 \log x \qquad R^2 = 0.9935$$
$$\quad\;\; (0.0574) \quad\; (0.0183)$$
$$RSS = 0.03757$$

(Figures in parentheses are standard errors.) The R^2's are not comparable since the variance of the dependent variable is different. We discuss the problem of comparing R^2's from linear versus log-linear form in Section 5.6. The residuals from this equation are presented in Table 5.3. In this situation there is no perceptible

Table 5.3 Residuals from the log-Linear Equation[a]

Observation	log x	Residual	Observation	log x	Residual
6	1.82	−0.12	8	3.26	0.44
11	2.09	0.04	18	3.34	−0.53
9	2.33	0.27	17	3.40	0.47
4	2.49	0.34	2	3.48	0.42
14	2.65	−0.33	12	3.54	0.38
15	2.80	−0.56	3	3.60	−0.59
19	2.90	0.35	13	3.64	−0.42
20	3.00	0.41	10	3.69	0.51
1	3.10	−0.54	5	3.74	0.50
16	3.18	−0.46	7	3.80	−0.56

[a] Log x rounded to two decimals and residual multiplied by 10.

increase in the magnitudes of the residuals as the value of x increases. Thus there does not appear to be a heteroskedasticity problem.

In any case, we need formal tests of the hypothesis of homoskedasticity. These are discussed in the following sections.

5.2 DETECTION OF HETEROSKEDASTICITY

In the illustrative example in Section 5.1 we plotted the estimated residual $\hat{u}_t$ against x_t to see whether we notice any systematic pattern in the residuals that suggests heteroskedasticity in the errors. Note, however, that by virtue of the normal equation, $\hat{u}_t$ and x_t are uncorrelated though $\hat{u}_t^2$ could be correlated with x_t. Thus if we are using a regression procedure to test for heteroskedasticity, we should use a regression of $\hat{u}_t$ on $x_t^2, x_t^3, \ldots$ or a regression of $|u_t|$ or $\hat{u}_t^2$ on $x_t, x_t^2, x_t^3, \ldots$. In the case of multiple regression, we should use powers of $\hat{y}_t$ the predicted value of y_t, or powers of all the explanatory variables.

The tests based on these ideas are:

1. The test suggested by Anscombe[1] and a test called RESET suggested by Ramsey[2] both involve regressing $\hat{u}_t$ on $\hat{y}_t^2, \hat{y}_t^3, \ldots$ and testing whether or not the coefficients are significant.
2. The test suggested by White[3] involves regressing $\hat{u}_t^2$ on all the explanatory variables and their squares and cross products. For instance, with three explanatory variables x_1, x_2, x_3, it involves regressing $\hat{u}_t^2$ on $x_1, x_2, x_3, x_1^2, x_2^2, x_3^2, x_1x_2, x_2x_3,$ and x_3x_1.
3. Glejser[4] suggested estimating regressions of the type $|\hat{u}_i| = \alpha + \beta x_i$, $|\hat{u}_i| = \alpha + \beta/x_i$, $|\hat{u}_i| = \alpha + \beta\sqrt{x_i}$, and so on, and testing the hypothesis $\beta = 0$.

The implicit assumption behind all these tests is that $\operatorname{var}(u_i) = \sigma_i^2 = \sigma^2 f(z_i)$ where z_i is an unknown variable and the different tests use different proxies or surrogates for the unknown function $f(z)$.

Illustrative Example

For the data in Table 5.1, using the residuals in Table 5.2 the Ramsey, White, and Glejser tests produced the following results. Since there is only one explanatory variable x, we can use x instead of $\hat{y}$ in the application of the Ramsey test. The test thus involves regressing $\hat{u}_i$ on x_i^2, x_i^3, and so on. In our example the test was not very useful. The results were (standard errors are not reported because the R^2 is very low

---

[1] F. J. Anscombe, "Examination of Residuals," *Proceedings of the Fourth Berkeley Symposium on Mathematical Statistics and Probability* (Berkeley, Calif.: University of California Press, 1961), pp. 1–36.
[2] J. B. Ramsey, "Tests for Specification Errors in Classical Linear Least Squares Regression Analysis," *Journal of the Royal Statistical Society*, Series B, Vol. 31, 1969, pp. 350–371.
[3] H. White, "A Heteroskedasticity Consistent Covariance Matrix Estimator and a Direct Test of Heteroskedasticity," *Econometrica*, Vol. 48, 1980, pp. 817–838.
[4] H. Glejser, "A New Test for Homoscedasticity," *Journal of the American Statistical Association*, 1969, pp. 316–323.

for sample size 20):

$$\hat{u} = -0.379 + 0.236 \times 10^{-2}x^2 - 0.549 \times 10^{-4}x^3 \qquad R^2 = 0.034$$

None of the coefficients had a t-ratio > 1 indicating that we are unable to reject the hypothesis that the errors are homoskedastic.

The test suggested by White involves regressing $\hat{u}^2$ on x, x^2, x^3, and so on. The results were:

$$\hat{u}^2 = -1.370 + 0.116x \qquad\qquad R^2 = 0.7911$$
$$\quad\;\; (0.390) \quad (0.014)$$

$$\hat{u}^2 = 0.493 - 0.071x + 0.0037x^2 \qquad R^2 = 0.878$$
$$\quad\;\; (0.620) \quad (0.055) \quad\;\; (0.0011)$$

The R^2's are highly significant in both the cases. Thus the test rejects the hypothesis of homoskedasticity. A suggested procedure to correct for heteroskedasticity is to estimate the regression model assuming that $V(u_i) = \sigma_i^2$, where $\sigma_i^2 = \gamma_0 + \gamma_1 x + \gamma_2 x^2$. This procedure is discussed in Section 5.4.

Glejser's tests gave the following results:

$$|\hat{u}| = -0.209 + 0.0512x \qquad R^2 = 0.927$$
$$\quad\;\;\; (0.094) \quad (0.0034)$$

$$|\hat{u}| = -1.232 + 0.475\sqrt{x} \qquad R^2 = 0.902$$
$$\quad\;\;\; (0.186) \quad (0.037)$$

$$|\hat{u}| = 1.826 - 13.78(1/x) \qquad R^2 = 0.649$$
$$\quad\;\;\; (0.155) \quad\;\; (2.39)$$

All the tests reject the hypothesis of homoskedasticity, although on the basis of R^2, the first model is preferable to the others. The suggested model to estimate is the same as that suggested by White's test.

The results are similar for the log-linear form as well, although the coefficients are not as significant. Using the residuals in Table 5.3 we get, for the White test,

$$\hat{u}^2 = -0.211 + 0.129x \qquad\qquad R^2 = 0.572$$
$$\quad\;\; (0.083) \quad (0.026)$$

$$\hat{u}^2 = -0.620 + 0.425x - 0.051x^2 \qquad R^2 = 0.600$$
$$\quad\;\; (0.385) \quad (0.273) \quad\;\; (0.047)$$

Thus there is evidence of heteroskedasticity even in the log-linear form, although casually looking at the residuals in Table 5.3, we concluded earlier that the errors were homoskedastic. The Goldfeld–Quandt test, to be discussed later in this section, also did not reject the hypothesis of homoskedasticity. The Glejser tests, however, show significant heteroskedasticity in the log-linear form.

Some Other Tests

The Likelihood Ratio Test

If the number of observations is large, one can use a likelihood ratio test. Divide the residuals (estimated from the OLS regression) into k groups with n_i observations in the ith group, $\sum n_i = n$. Estimate the error variances in each group by $\hat{\sigma}_i^2$. Let the estimate of the error variance from the entire sample by $\hat{\sigma}^2$. Then if we define λ as

$$\lambda = \prod_{i=1}^{k} (\hat{\sigma}_i)^{n_i} / \hat{\sigma}^n$$

$-2\log_e\lambda$ has a χ^2-distribution with degrees of freedom $(k-1)$. If there is only one explanatory variable in the equation, the ordering of the residuals can be based on the absolute magnitude of this variable. But if there are two or more variables and no single variable can provide a satisfactory ordering, then $\hat{y}$, the predicted value of y, can be used

Feldstein used this LR test for his hospital cost regressions described in Chapter 4 (Section 4.6, Example 1). He divided the total number of observations (177) into four groups of equal size, the residuals being ordered by the predicted values of the dependent variable. The estimates $\hat{\sigma}_i^2$ were 71.47, 114.82, 102.81, and 239.34. The estimate $\hat{\sigma}^2$ for the whole sample was 138.76. Thus $-2\log\lambda$ was 18.265. The 1% significance point for the χ^2-distribution with 3 d.f. is 11.34. Thus there were significant differences between the error variances. Next Feldstein weighted the observations by weights proportional to $1/\hat{\sigma}_i$. The weights normalized to make their average equal to 1 were 1.2599, 0.9940, 1.0504, and 0.6885. This would make the error variances approximately equal. The equation was estimated by OLS using the transformed data. This procedure is called *weighted least squares* and is often denoted by WLS. The new estimates of the variances from this reestimated equation, for the four groups were 106.34, 110.71, 114.99, and 117.06, which are almost equal. However, the regression parameters did not change much, as shown in Table 5.4. Although the point estimates did not change much, the standard errors could be different. Since Feldstein does not present these, we have no way of comparing them.

Goldfeld and Quandt Test

If we do not have large samples, we can use the Goldfeld and Quandt test.[5] In this test we split the observations into two groups—one corresponding to large values of x and the other corresponding to small values of x—fit separate regressions for each and then apply an F-test to test the equality of error variances. Goldfeld and Quandt suggest omitting some observations in the middle to increase our ability to discriminate between the two error variances.

Breusch and Pagan Test

Suppose that $V(u_t) = \sigma_t^2$. If there are some variables $z_1, z_2, \ldots, z_r$ that influence the error variance and if $\sigma_t^2 = f(\alpha_0 + \alpha_1 z_{1t} + \alpha_2 z_{2t} + \cdots + \alpha_r z_{rt})$, then the Breusch and Pagan test[6] is a test of the hypothesis

$$H_0: \quad \alpha_1 = \alpha_2 = \cdots = \alpha_r = 0$$

[5] S. M. Goldfeld and R. E. Quandt, *Nonlinear Methods in Econometrics* (Amsterdam: North-Holland, 1972), Chap. 3.
[6] T. S. Breusch and A. R. Pagan, "A Simple Test for Heteroscedasticity and Random Coefficient Variation," *Econometrica*, Vol. 47, 1979, pp. 1287–1294.

Table 5.4 Comparison of OLS and WLS Estimates for Hospital-Cost Regression

	Average Cost per Case	
Case Type	OLS	WLS
General medicine	114.48	111.81
Pediatrics	24.97	28.35
General surgery	32.70	35.07
ENT	15.25	15.58
Traumatic and orthopedic surgery	39.69	36.04
Other surgery	98.02	101.38
Gynecology	58.72	58.48
Obstetrics	34.88	34.50
Others	69.51	66.26

Source: M. S. Feldstein, *Economic Analysis for Health Service Efficiency,* North-Holland, Amsterdam, 1967, p. 54.

The function $f(\cdot)$ can be any function. For instance, $f(x)$ can be x, x^2, e^x, and so on. The Breusch and Pagan test does *not* depend on the functional form. Let

$$\hat{\sigma}^2 = \sum \frac{\hat{u}_t^2}{n}$$

S_0 = Regression sum of squares from a regression of $\hat{u}_t^2$ on $z_1, z_2, \ldots, z_r$

Then $\lambda = S_0/2\hat{\sigma}^4$ has a χ^2-distribution with degrees of freedom r.

This test is an asymptotic test. An intuitive justification for the test will be given after an illustrative example.

Illustrative Example

Consider the data in Table 5.1. To apply the Goldfeld–Quandt test we consider two groups of 10 observations each, ordered by the values of the variable x. The first group consists of observations 6, 11, 9, 4, 14, 15, 19, 20, 1, and 16. The second group consists of the remaining 10. The estimated equations were:

$$\text{Group 1:} \quad y = \underset{(0.616)}{1.0533} + \underset{(0.038)}{0.876x} \quad R^2 = 0.985$$
$$\hat{\sigma}^2 = 0.475$$

$$\text{Group 2:} \quad y = \underset{(3.443)}{3.279} + \underset{(0.096)}{0.835x} \quad R^2 = 0.904$$
$$\hat{\sigma}^2 = 3.154$$

The F-ratio for the test is

$$F = \frac{3.154}{0.475} = 6.64$$

The 1% point for the F-distribution with d.f. 8 and 8 is 6.03. Thus the F-value is significant at the 1% level and we reject the hypothesis of homoskedasticity.

Consider now the logarithmic form. The results are:

$$\text{Group 1:} \quad \log y = \underset{(0.079)}{0.128} + \underset{(0.030)}{0.934x} \qquad R^2 = 0.992$$

$$\hat{\sigma}^2 = 0.001596$$

$$\text{Group 2:} \quad \log y = \underset{(0.352)}{0.276} + \underset{(0.099)}{0.902x} \qquad R^2 = 0.912$$

$$\hat{\sigma}^2 = 0.002789$$

The F-ratio for the test is

$$F = \frac{0.002789}{0.001596} = 1.75$$

For d.f. 8 and 8, the 5% point from the F-tables is 3.44. Thus if we use the 5% significance level, we do not reject the hypothesis of homoskedasticity. Hence by the Goldfeld–Quandt test we reject the hypothesis of homoskedasticity if we consider the linear form but do not reject it in the log-linear form. Note that the White test rejected the hypothesis in both the forms.

Turning now to the Breusch and Pagan test, the regression of $\hat{u}_t^2$ on x_t, x_t^2 and x_t^3 gave the following regression sums of squares. For the linear form

$$S = 40.842 \text{ for the regression of } \hat{u}_t^2 \text{ on } x_t, x_t^2, x_t^3$$

$$S = 40.065 \text{ for the regression of } \hat{u}_t^2 \text{ on } x_t, x_t^2$$

Also, $\hat{\sigma}^2 = 1.726$. The test statistic for the χ^2 test is (using the second regression)

$$\frac{S}{2\hat{\sigma}^4} = \frac{40.065}{2(2.979)} = 6.724$$

We use the statistic as a χ^2 with d.f. $= 2$ since two slope parameters are estimated. This is significant at the 5 percent level, thus, rejecting the hypothesis of homoskedasticity.

For the log-linear form, using only x_t and x_t^2 as regressors we get: $S = 0.000011$ and $\hat{\sigma}^2 = 0.00209$. The test statistic is

$$\frac{0.000011}{2(0.00209)^2} = 1.259$$

using the χ^2 tables with 2 d.f. we see that this is not significant at even the 50 percent level. Thus, the test does not reject the hypothesis of homoskedasticity in the log-linear form.

An Intuitive Justification for the Breusch-Pagan Test

In Section 4.12 we discussed the LM, W and LR tests. There we showed that the LM test statistic was $LM = nR^2$ which has a χ^2-distribution. Arguing from analogy, we would get a test statistic nR^2 where R^2 is the multiple correlation coefficient in a regression of $\hat{u}_t^2$ on $z_{1t}, z_{2t}, z_{3t}, \ldots$, etc. To see the relationship between this and the

Breusch-Pagan test statistic, note that

$$nR^2 = \text{(Regression Sum of Squares from a regression of}$$
$$\hat{u}_t^2 \text{ on } z_{1t}, z_{2t}, z_{3t}, \ldots, \text{etc.)}/\text{var}(\hat{u}_t^2)$$

$$= S/\text{var}(\hat{u}_t^2)$$

Now, under the null hypothesis that the errors are homoskedastic, u_t^2/σ^2 has a χ^2-distribution with d.f. 1. Hence, $\text{var}(u_t^2/\sigma^2) = 2$ (because the variance of a χ^2 variable is twice the degrees of freedom). Thus,

$$\text{var}(u_t^2) = 2\sigma^4.$$

In large samples we can write $\text{var}(\hat{u}_t^2) = \text{var}(u_t^2)$ and $\hat{\sigma}^4 = \sigma^4$. Hence, we get $\text{var}(\hat{u}_t^2) \simeq 2\hat{\sigma}^4$. Thus, the test statistic is $S/2\hat{\sigma}^4$ as described earlier. The statistic can also be viewed as half the regression sum of squares from a regression of $g_t = \hat{u}_t^2/\hat{\sigma}^2$ on $z_{1t}, z_{2t}, z_{3t}, \ldots$, etc. Breusch and Pagan argue that in discussions of heteroskedasticity, *if one is going to plot any quantity*, it is more reasonable to plot g_t than quantities like $\hat{u}_t$.

5.3 CONSEQUENCES OF HETEROSKEDASTICITY

Before we attempt solutions to the heteroskedasticity problem, we will study the consequences on the least squares estimators. We will show that

1. The least squares estimators are still unbiased but inefficient.
2. The estimates of the variances are also biased, thus invalidating the tests of significance.

To see this, consider a very simple model with no constant term.

$$y_i = \beta x_i + u_i \qquad V(u_i) = \sigma_i^2 \tag{5.1}$$

The least squares estimator of β is

$$\hat{\beta} = \frac{\sum x_i y_i}{\sum x_i^2} = \beta + \frac{\sum x_i u_i}{\sum x_i^2}$$

If $E(u_i) = 0$ and u_i are independent of the x_i, we have $E(\sum x_i u_i / \sum x_i^2) = 0$ and hence $E(\hat{\beta}) = \beta$. Thus $\hat{\beta}$ is unbiased.

If the u_i are mutually independent, denoting $\sum x_i^2$ by S_{xx} we can write

$$V(\hat{\beta}) = V\left(\frac{x_1}{S_{xx}} u_1 + \frac{x_2}{S_{xx}} u_2 + \cdots + \frac{x_n}{S_{xx}} u_n\right)$$

$$= \frac{1}{S_{xx}^2}(x_1^2 \sigma_1^2 + x_2^2 \sigma_2^2 + \cdots + x_n^2 \sigma_n^2)$$

$$= \frac{\sum x_i^2 \sigma_i^2}{(\sum x_i^2)^2} \tag{5.2}$$

Suppose that we write $\sigma_i^2 = \sigma^2 z_i^2$, where z_i are known, that is, we know the variances up to a multiplicative constant. Then by dividing (5.1) by z_i we have the model

$$\frac{y_i}{z_i} = \beta \frac{x_i}{z_i} + v_i \tag{5.3}$$

where $v_i = u_i/z_i$ has a constant variance σ^2. Since we are "weighting" the ith observation by $1/z_i$, the OLS estimation of (5.3) is called weighted least squares (WLS). If β^* is the WLS estimator of β, we have

$$\beta^* = \frac{\sum (y_i/z_i)(x_i/z_i)}{\sum (x_i/z_i)^2}$$

$$= \beta + \frac{\sum (x_i/z_i)v_i}{\sum (x_i/z_i)^2}$$

and since the latter term has expectation zero, we have $E(\beta^*) = \beta$. Thus the WLS estimator β^* is also unbiased. We will show that β^* is more efficient than the OLS estimator $\hat{\beta}$.

We have

$$V(\beta^*) = \frac{\sigma^2}{\sum (x_i/z_i)^2}$$

and substituting $\sigma_i^2 = \sigma^2 z_i^2$ in (5.2), we have

$$V(\hat{\beta}) = \sigma^2 \frac{\sum x_i^2 z_i^2}{(\sum x_i^2)^2}$$

Thus

$$\frac{V(\beta^*)}{V(\hat{\beta})} = \frac{(\sum x_i^2)^2}{\sum (x_i^2/z_i^2) \sum x_i^2 z_i^2}$$

This expression is of the form $(\sum a_i b_i)^2/\sum a_i^2 \sum b_i^2$, where $a_i = x_i z_i$ and $b_i = x_i/z_i$. Thus it is less than 1 and is equal to 1 only if a_i and b_i are propositional, that is, $x_i z_i$ and x_i/z_i are propositional or z_i^2 is a constant, which is the case if the errors are homoskedastic.

Thus the OLS estimator is unbiased but less efficient (has a higher variance) than the WLS estimator. Turning now to the estimation of the variance of $\hat{\beta}$, it is estimated by

$$\frac{\text{RSS}}{n-1} \frac{1}{\sum x_i^2}$$

where RSS is the residual sum of squares from the OLS model. But

$$E(\text{RSS}) = E[\sum (y_i - \hat{\beta} x_i)^2]$$

$$= \sum \sigma_i^2 - \frac{\sum x_i^2 \sigma_i^2}{\sum x_i^2}$$

Note that if $\sigma_i^2 = \sigma^2$ for all i, this reduces to $(n-1)\sigma^2$. Thus we would be estimating the variance of $\hat{\beta}$ whose expected value is

$$\frac{\sum x_i^2 \sum \sigma_i^2 - \sum x_i^2 \sigma_i^2}{(n-1)(\sum x_i^2)^2}$$

whereas the true variance is

$$\frac{\sum x_i^2 \sigma_i^2}{(\sum x_i^2)^2}$$

Thus the estimated variances are also biased. If σ_i^2 and x_i^2 are positively correlated, as is often the case with economic data so that $\sum x_i^2 \sigma_i^2 > (1/n) \sum x_i^2 \sum \sigma_i^2$, then the expected value of the estimated variance is smaller than the true variance. Thus we would be *underestimating* the true variance of the OLS estimator and getting shorter confidence intervals than the true ones. This also affects tests of hypotheses about β.

Estimation of the Variance of the OLS Estimator Under Heteroskedasticity

The solution to the heteroskedasticity problem depends on the assumptions we make about the sources of heteroskedasticity. When we are not sure of this, we can at least try to make corrections for the standard errors, since we have seen that the least squares estimator is unbiased but inefficient, and moreover, the standard errors are also biased.

White[7] suggests that we use the formula (5.2) with $\hat{u}_i^2$ substituted for σ_i^2. Using this formula we find that in the case of the illustrative example with data in Table 5.1, the standard error of $\hat{\beta}$, the slope coefficient, is 0.027. Earlier, we estimated it from the OLS regression as 0.0253. Thus the difference is really not very large in this example.

5.4 SOLUTIONS TO THE HETEROSKEDASTICITY PROBLEM

There are two types of solutions that have been suggested in the literature for the problem of heteroskedasticity:

1. Solutions dependent on particular assumptions about σ_i^2.
2. General solutions.

We first discuss category 1. Here we have two methods of estimation: weighted least squares and maximum likelihood (ML).

If the error variances are known up to a multiplicative constant, there is no problem at all. If $V(u_i) = \sigma^2 z_i^2$, where z_i are known, we divide the equation through by z_i and use ordinary least squares. The only thing to remember is that

---

[7] White, "A Heteroskedasticity." A similar suggestion was made earlier in C. R. Rao, "Estimation of Heteroskedastic Variances in Linear Models," Journal of the American Statistical Association, March 1970, pp. 161–172.

if the original equation contained a constant term, that is, $y_i = \alpha + \beta x_i + u_i$, the transformed equation will *not* have a constant term. It is

$$\frac{y_i}{z_i} = \alpha\frac{1}{z_i} + \beta\frac{x_i}{z_i} + v_i$$

where $v_i = u_i/z_i$. Now $V(v_i) = \sigma^2$ for all i. Thus we should be running a regression of y_i/z_i on $1/z_i$ and x_i/z_i *without* a constant term.

One interesting case is where $V(u_i) = \sigma^2 x_i$ and $\alpha = 0$. In this case the transformed equation is

$$\frac{y_i}{\sqrt{x_i}} = \beta\frac{x_i}{\sqrt{x_i}} + v_i$$

Hence

$$\beta^* = \frac{\sum(y_i x_i/x_i)}{\sum(\sqrt{x_i})^2} = \frac{\bar{y}}{\bar{x}}$$

that is, the WLS estimator is just the ratio of the means. Another case is where $\sigma_i^2 = \sigma^2 x_i^2$. In this case the transformed equation is

$$\frac{y_i}{x_i} = \alpha\frac{1}{x_i} + \beta + v_i$$

Thus the constant term in this equation is the slope coefficient in the original equation.

Prais and Houthakker[8] found in their analysis of family budget data that the errors from the equation had variance increasing with household income. They considered a model $\sigma_i^2 = \sigma^2[E(y_i)]^2$, that is, $\sigma_i^2 = \sigma^2(\alpha + \beta x_i)^2$. In this case we cannot divide the whole equation by a known constant as before. For this model we can consider a *two-step* procedure as follows. First estimate α and β by OLS. Let these estimators be $\hat{\alpha}$ and $\hat{\beta}$. Now use the WLS procedure as outlined earlier, that is, regress $y_i/(\hat{\alpha} + \hat{\beta}x_i)$ on $1/(\hat{\alpha} + \hat{\beta}x_i)$ and $x_i/(\hat{\alpha} + \hat{\beta}x_i)$ with no constant term. This procedure is called a *two-step weighted least squares* procedure. The standard errors we get for the estimates of α and β from this procedure are valid only asymptotically. They are asymptotic standard errors because the weights $1/(\alpha + \beta x_i)$ have been estimated.

One can iterate this WLS procedure further, that is, use the new estimates of α and β to construct new weights and then use the WLS procedure, and repeat this procedure until convergence. This procedure is called the *iterated weighted least squares procedure*. However, there is no gain in (asymptotic) efficiency by iteration).

If we make some specific assumptions about the errors, say that they are normal, we can use the maximum likelihood method, which is more efficient than the WLS if errors are normal.[9] Under the assumption of normality we can write the log-

[8] S. J. Prais and H. S. Houthakker, *The Analysis of Family Budgets* New York: Cambridge University Press, (1955), p. 55ff.

[9] Amemiya discusses the ML estimation for this model when the errors follow a normal, log-normal, and gamma distribution. See T. Amemiya, "Regression Analysis When Variance of the Dependent Variable Is Proportional to Square of Its Expectation," *Journal of the American Statistical Association*, December 1973, 928–934.

likelihood function as

$$\log L = -n \log \sigma - \sum \log(\alpha + \beta x_i) - \frac{1}{2\sigma^2} \sum \left(\frac{y_i - \alpha - \beta x_i}{\alpha + \beta x_i}\right)^2$$

Note that maximizing this likelihood function is not the same as the weighted least squares that minimizes the expression

$$\sum \left(\frac{y_i - \alpha - \beta x_i}{\alpha + \beta x_i}\right)^2$$

A more general model is to assume that the variance σ_i^2 is equal to $(\gamma + \delta x_i)^2$. In this case, too, we can consider a WLS procedure, that is, minimize

$$\sum_i \left(\frac{y_i - \alpha - \beta x_i}{\gamma + \delta x_i}\right)^2$$

or if the errors can be assumed to follow a known distribution, use the ML method. For instance, if the errors follow a normal distribution, we can write the log-likelihood function as

$$\log L = \text{const.} - \sum \log(\gamma + \delta x_i) - \frac{1}{2} \sum \left(\frac{y_i - \alpha - \beta x_i}{\gamma + \delta x_i}\right)^2$$

Again, note that the WLS and ML procedures are not the same.[10] A two-step WLS estimation for this model would proceed as follows. Compute the OLS estimates of α and β. Get the estimated residuals and regress the absolute values of these residuals on x to get estimates of γ and δ. Then use WLS.

Illustrative Example

As an illustration, again consider the data in Table 5.1. We saw earlier that regressing the absolute values of the residuals on x (in Glejser's tests) gave the following estimates:

$$\hat{\gamma} = -0.209 \qquad \hat{\delta} = 0.0512$$

Now we regress y_i/w_i on $1/w_i$ and x_i/w_i (with no constant term) where $w_i = \hat{\gamma} + \hat{\delta} x_i$. The resulting equation is

$$\frac{y_i}{w_i} = \underset{(0.1643)}{0.4843}(1/w_i) + \underset{(0.0157)}{0.9176}(x_i/w_i) \qquad R^2 = 0.9886$$

If we assume that $\sigma_i^2 = \gamma_0 + \gamma_1 x_i + \gamma_2 x_i^2$, the two-step WLS procedure would be as follows.

First, we regress $\hat{u}_i^2$ on x_i and x_i^2. Earlier, using this regression we obtained the estimates as

$$\hat{\gamma}_0 = 0.493 \qquad \hat{\gamma}_1 = -0.071 \qquad \hat{\gamma}_2 = 0.0037$$

---

[10] The ML estimation of this model is discussed in H. C. Rutemiller and D. A. Bowers, "Estimation in a Heteroscedastic Regression Model," *Journal of the American Statistical Association*, June 1968.

Next we compute

$$w_i^2 = 0.493 - 0.071x_i + 0.0037x_i^2$$

and regress y_i/w_i on $1/w_i$ and x_i/w_i. The results were

$$\frac{y_i}{w_i} = \underset{(0.3302)}{0.7296}(1/w_i) + \underset{(0.0199)}{0.9052}(x_i/w_i) \qquad R^2 = 0.9982$$

The R^2's in these equations are not comparable. But our interest is in estimates of the parameters in the consumption function

$$y_i = \alpha + \beta x_i$$

Comparing the results with the OLS estimates presented in Section 5.2, we notice that the estimates of β are higher than the OLS estimates, the estimates of α are lower, and the standard errors are lower.

5.5 HETEROSKEDASTICITY AND THE USE OF DEFLATORS

There are two remedies often suggested and used for solving the heteroskedasticity problem:

1. Transforming the data to logs.
2. Deflating the variables by some measure of "size."

The first method often does reduce the heteroskedasticity in the error variances, although there are other criteria by which one has to decide between the linear and the logarithmic functional forms. This problem is discussed in greater detail in Section 5.6.

Regarding the use of deflators, one should be careful in estimating the equation with the correct explanatory variables (as explained in the preceding section). For instance, if the original equation involves a constant term, one should not estimate a similar equation in the deflated variables. One should be estimating an equation with the reciprocal of the deflator added as an extra explanatory variable. As an illustration, consider the estimation of railroad cost functions by Griliches [11] where deflation was used to solve the heteroskedasticity problem. The variables are: C = total cost, M = miles of road, and X = output.

If $C = aM + bX$, dividing by M gives $C/M = a + b(X/M)$. But if the true relation is $C = aM + bX + c$, deflation leads to $C/M = a + b(X/M) + c(1/M)$. For 97 observations using 1957–1969 averages as units, the regressions were

$$\frac{C}{M} = \underset{(6218)}{13{,}016} + \underset{(0.871)}{6.431}\frac{X}{M} \qquad R^2 = 0.365$$

$$\frac{C}{M} = \underset{(5115)}{827} + \underset{(0.682)}{6.439}\frac{X}{M} + \underset{(393{,}000)}{3{,}065{,}000}\frac{1}{M} \qquad R^2 = 0.614$$

[11] Z. Griliches, "Railroad Cost Analysis," *The Bell Journal of Economics and Management Science*, Spring 1972.

$$C = -\underset{(2.906)}{1.884}M + \underset{(0.375)}{6.613}X + \underset{(4730)}{3676} \qquad R^2 = 0.945$$

The coefficient c is significant in the second equation but not in the third, and the coefficient of a is not significant in either the second or third equation. From this Griliches concludes that there is no evidence that M belongs in the equation in any form. It appears in a significant form in the second equation only because the other variables were divided by it.

Some other equations estimated with the same data are the following:

$$C = \underset{(4524)}{2811} + \underset{(0.18)}{6.39}X \qquad R^2 = 0.944$$

$$\frac{C}{\sqrt{M}} = \underset{(3713)}{3805}\frac{1}{\sqrt{M}} + \underset{(0.51)}{6.06}\frac{X}{\sqrt{M}} \qquad R^2 = 0.826$$

The last equation is the appropriate one to estimate if $C = a + bX + u$ and $V(u) = M\sigma^2$.

One important thing to note is that the purpose in all these procedures of deflation is to get more efficient estimates of the parameters. But once those estimates have been obtained, one should make all inferences—calculation of the residuals, prediction of future values, calculation of elasticities at the means, etc., from the original equation—not the equation in the deflated variables.

Another point to note is that since the purpose of deflation is to get more efficient estimates, it is tempting to argue about the merits of the different procedures by looking at the standard errors of the coefficients. However, this is not correct, because in the presence of heteroscedasticity the standard errors themselves are biased, as we showed earlier. For instance, in the five equations presented above, the second and third are comparable and so are the fourth and fifth. In both cases if we look at the standard errors of the coefficient of X, the coefficient in the undeflated equation has a smaller standard error than the corresponding coefficient in the deflated equation. However, if the standard errors are biased, we have to be careful in making too much of these differences. An examination of the residuals will give a better picture.

In the preceding example we have considered miles M as a deflator and also as an explanatory variable. In this context we should mention some discussion in the literature on "spurious correlation" between ratios.[12] The argument simply is that even if we have two variables X and Y that are uncorrelated, if we deflate both the variables by another variable Z, there could be a strong correlation between X/Z and Y/Z because of the common denominator Z. It is wrong to infer from this correlation that there exists a close relationship between X and Y. Of course, if our interest is in fact the relationship between X/Z and Y/Z, there is no reason why this correlation need be called "spurious." As Kuh and Meyer[13] point out, "The question of spurious correlation quite obviously does not arise when the hypothesis to be tested has initially been formulated in terms of ratios, for instance, in problems involving relative prices. Similarly, when a series such as money value of output is

[12] See E. Kuh and J. R. Meyer, "Correlation and Regression Estimates When the Data Are Ratios," *Econometrica*, October 1955, pp. 400–416

divided by a price index to obtain a 'constant dollar' estimate of output, no question of spurious correlation need arise. Thus, spurious correlation can only exist when a hypothesis pertains to undeflated variables and the data have been divided through by another series for reasons extraneous to but not in conflict with the hypothesis framed as an exact, i.e., nonstochastic relation."

However, even in cases where deflation is done for reasons of estimation, we should note that the problem of "spurious correlation" exists only if we start drawing inferences on the basis of correlation coefficients when we should not be doing so. For example, suppose that the relationship we derive is of the form

$$Y = \alpha Z + \beta X + u \tag{5.4}$$

and we find that the residuals u are heteroscedastic with variance roughly proportional to Z^2. Then we should not hesitate to divide (5.4) throughout by Z and estimate the regression equation

$$\frac{Y}{Z} = \alpha + \beta \frac{X}{Z} + u' \tag{5.5}$$

where $u' = u/Z$ has a constant variance σ^2. The estimates of α, β, and σ^2 should be obtained from (5.5) and not from (5.4). Whether the correlation between Y/Z and X/Z is higher or lower than the correlation between Y and X is irrelevant. The important point to note is that we cannot argue whether (5.4) or (5.5) is a better equation to consider by looking at correlations. As long as we do not base our inferences on correlations, there is nothing wrong with deflation in this case. It should also be noted that if (5.4) is not homogeneous (i.e., it involves a constant term), we end up with an equation of the form

$$\frac{Y}{Z} = \gamma \frac{1}{Z} + \alpha + \beta \frac{X}{Z} + u'$$

which is different from (5.5). The equation will also be different if the variance of u is proportional not to Z^2 but to Z or some other function of Z.

In actual practice, deflation may increase or decrease the resulting correlation. The algebra is somewhat tedious, but with some simplifying assumptions Kuh and Meyer derive the conditions under which the correlation between X/Z and Y/Z is in fact less than that between X and Y.

In summary, often in econometric work deflated or ratio variables are used to solve the heteroskedasticity problem. Deflation can sometimes be justified on pure economic grounds, as in the case of the use of "real" quantities and relative prices. In this case all the inferences from the estimated equation will be based on the equation in the deflated variables. However, if deflation is used to solve the heteroskedasticity problem, any inferences we make have to be based on the original equation, not the equation in the deflated variables. In any case, deflation may increase or decrease the resulting correlations, but this is beside the point. Since the correlations are not comparable anyway, one should not draw any inferences from them.

Illustrative Example: The Density Gradient Model

In Table 5.5 we present data on

$$y = \text{population density}$$

$$x = \text{distance from the central business district}$$

for 39 census tracts on the Baltimore area in 1970. It has been suggested (this is called the "density gradient model") that population density follows the relationship

$$y = Ae^{-\beta x} \qquad \beta > 0$$

where A is the density of the central business district. The basic hypothesis is that as you move away from the central business district population density drops off. For estimation purposes we take logs and write

$$\log y = \log A - \beta x$$

Table 5.5 Data on Population Density in Different Census Tracts in the Baltimore Area in 1970[a]

Observation	y	x	Observation	y	x
1	18,640.0	1.002	21	5,485.8	6.748
2	38,275.0	1.403	22	3,416.5	6.882
3	2,450.3	2.004	23	8,194.7	6.948
4	21,969.0	2.138	24	5,091.9	6.948
5	9,573.7	2.205	25	1,183.8	7.082
6	13,751.0	3.608	26	4,157.9	7.416
7	38,947.0	3.675	27	2,158.3	7.483
8	17,921.0	4.009	28	12,428.0	7.617
9	5,050.7	4.276	29	6,788.5	7.750
10	4,519.0	4.410	30	3,277.4	7.750
11	6,781.1	4.543	31	3,258.2	7.951
12	8,246.2	4.810	32	5,491.3	8.084
13	5,166.4	4.944	33	865.02	11.250
14	7,762.4	5.211	34	340.69	13.250
15	11,081.0	5.345	35	507.03	15.500
16	7,188.0	5.679	36	323.67	18.000
17	13,753.0	5.813	37	108.36	19.000
18	7,492.4	5.813	38	805.66	23.000
19	3,620.9	5.879	39	156.84	26.250
20	6,390.6	6.080			

[a] y, density of population in the census tract: x, distance of the census tract from the central business district.
Source: I would like to thank Kajal Lahiri for providing me with these data. These data formed the basis of the study in K. Lahiri and R. Numrich, "An Econometric Study of the Dynamics of Urban Spatial Structure," *Journal of Urban Economics*, 1983, pp. 55–79.

Adding an error term u we estimate the model

$$y^* = \alpha - \beta x + u$$

where $y^* = \log y$ and $\alpha = \log A$. Estimation of this equation by OLS gave the following results:

$$\hat{y}^* = 10.093 - 0.2395x \qquad R^2 = 0.803$$
$$\quad\;\;(54.7)\quad (-12.28)$$

(Figures in parentheses are the t-values, not standard errors.) The t-values are very high and the coefficients α and β are significantly different from zero (with a significance level of less than 1%). The sign of β is negative, as expected. With cross-sectional data like these we expect heteroskedasticity, and this could result in an underestimation of the standard errors (and thus an overestimation of the t-ratios). To check whether there is heteroskedasticity, we have to analyze the estimated residuals $\hat{u}_i$. A plot of $\hat{u}_i^2$ against x_i showed a positive relationship and hence Glejser's tests were applied.

Defining $|\hat{u}_i|$ by z_i, the following equations were estimated:

$$z_i = \gamma x_i + v_i$$

$$z_i = \gamma \sqrt{x_i} + v_i$$

$$z_i = \gamma \frac{1}{x_i} + v_i$$

$$z_i = \gamma \frac{1}{\sqrt{x_i}} + v_i$$

We choose the specification that gives the highest R^2 [or equivalently the highest t-value, since $R^2 = t^2/(t^2 + \text{d.f.})$ in the case of only one regressor]. The estimated regressions with t-values in parentheses were

$$\hat{z}_i = 0.0445 x_i$$
$$\quad\;(5.06)$$

$$\hat{z}_i = 0.1733 \sqrt{x_i}$$
$$\quad\;(6.42)$$

$$\hat{z}_i = 1.390(1/x_i)$$
$$\quad\;(4.50)$$

$$\hat{z}_i = 1.038(1/\sqrt{x_i})$$
$$\quad\;(6.42)$$

All the t-statistics are significant, indicating the presence of heteroskedasticity. Based on the highest t-ratio, we chose the second specification (although the fourth specification is equally valid). Deflating throughout by $\sqrt{x_i}$ gives the regression equations to be estimated as

$$\frac{y_i^*}{\sqrt{x_i}} = \alpha \frac{1}{\sqrt{x_i}} + \beta \sqrt{x_i} + \text{error}$$

The estimates were

$$\hat{\alpha} = 9.932 \quad \text{and} \quad \hat{\beta} = -0.2258$$
$$\underset{(47.87)}{} \qquad \qquad \underset{(-15.10)}{}$$

(Figures in parentheses are t-ratios.) The estimate of β is negative and highly significant. The estimated density of the central business district is given by $\exp(\hat{\alpha}) = \exp(9.932) = 20{,}577$. Further analysis of these data is left as an exercise. (What is the R^2 for the equation in the deflated variables? What can you conclude?)

*5.6 TESTING THE LINEAR VERSUS LOG-LINEAR FUNCTIONAL FORM

As we mentioned in the introduction, sometimes equations are estimated in log form to take care of the heteroskedasticity problem. In many cases the choice of the functional form is dictated by other considerations like convenience in interpretation and some economic reasoning. For instance, if we are estimating a production function, the linear form

$$X = \alpha + \beta_1 L + \beta_2 K$$

where X is the output, L the labor, and K the capital, implies perfect substitutability among the inputs of production. On the other hand, the logarithmic form

$$\log X = \alpha + \beta_1 \log L + \beta_2 \log K$$

implies a Cobb–Douglas production function with unit elasticity of substitution. Both these formulations are special cases of the CES (constant elasticity of substitution) production function.

For the estimation of demand functions the log form is often preferred because it is easy to interpret the coefficients as elasticities. For instance,

$$\log Q = \alpha + \beta_1 \log P + \beta_2 \log Y$$

where Q is the quantity demanded, P the price, and Y the income, implies that β_1 is the price elasticity and β_2 is the income elasticity. A linear demand function implies that these elasticities depend on the particular point along the demand curve that we are at. In this case we have to consider some methods of choosing statistically between the two functional forms.

When comparing the linear with the log-linear forms, we cannot compare the R^2's because R^2 is the ratio of explained variance to the total variance and the variances of y and $\log y$ are different. Comparing R^2's in this case is like comparing two individuals A and B, where A eats 65% of a carrot cake and B eats 70% of a strawberry cake. The comparison does not make sense because there are two different cakes.

The Box–Cox Test

One solution to this problem is to consider a more general model of which both the linear and log-linear forms are special cases. Box and Cox [14] consider the transformation

$$y(\lambda) = \begin{cases} \dfrac{y^\lambda - 1}{\lambda} & \text{for } \lambda \neq 0 \\[2mm] \log y & \text{for } \lambda = 0 \end{cases} \tag{5.6}$$

This transformation is well defined for all $y > 0$. Also, the transformation is continuous since

$$\lim_{\lambda \to 0} \frac{y^\lambda - 1}{\lambda} = \log \lambda$$

Box and Cox consider the regression model

$$y_i(\lambda) = \beta x_i + u_i \tag{5.7}$$

where $u_i \sim \text{IN}(0, \sigma^2)$. For the sake of simplicity of exposition we are considering only one explanatory variable. Also, instead of considering x_i we can consider $x_i(\lambda)$. For $\lambda = 0$ this is a log-linear model, and for $\lambda = 1$ this is a linear model.

There are two main problems with the specification in equation (5.7):

1. The assumption that the errors u_i in (5.7) are $\text{IN}(0, \sigma^2)$ for *all* values of λ is not a reasonable assumption.
2. Since $y > 0$, unless $\lambda = 0$ the definition of $y(\lambda)$ in (5.6) imposes some constraints on $y(\lambda)$ that depend on the unknown λ. Since $y > 0$, we have, from equation (5.6),

$$y(\lambda) > -\frac{1}{\lambda} \quad \text{if } \lambda > 0 \qquad \text{and} \qquad y(\lambda) < -\frac{1}{\lambda} \quad \text{if } \lambda < 0$$

However, we will ignore these problems and describe the Box–Cox method.

Based on the specification given by (5.7) Box and Cox suggest estimating λ by the maximum likelihood (ML) method. We can then test the hypotheses: $\lambda = 0$ and $\lambda = 1$. If the hypothesis $\lambda = 0$ is accepted, we use $\log y$ as the explained variable. If the hypothesis $\lambda = 1$ is accepted, we use y as the explained variable. A problem arises only if both hypotheses are rejected or both accepted. In this case we have to use the estimated λ, and work with $y(\lambda)$.

The ML method suggested by Box and Cox amounts to the following procedure: [15]

1. Divide each y by the geometric mean of the y's.
2. Now compute $y(\lambda)$ for different values of λ and regress it on x. Compute the residual sum of squares and denote it by $\hat{\sigma}^2(\lambda)$.

[14] G. E. P. Box and D. R. Cox, "An Analysis of Transformations" (with discussion), *Journal of the Royal Statistical Society, Series B*, 1962, pp. 211–243.
[15] G. S. Maddala, *Econometrics* (New York: McGraw-Hill, 1977), pp. 316–317.

3. Choose the value of λ for which $\hat{\sigma}^2(\lambda)$ is minimum. This value of λ is the ML estimator of λ.

As a special case, consider the problem of choosing between the linear and log-linear models:

$$y = \alpha + \beta x + u$$

and

$$\log y = \alpha' + \beta' x + u$$

What we do is first divide each y_i by the geometric mean of the y's. Then we estimate the two regressions and choose the one with the smaller residual sum of squares. This is the Box–Cox procedure.

We will now describe two other tests that are based on *artificial regressions*.

The BM Test

This is the test suggested by Bera and McAleer.[16] Suppose the log–linear and linear models to be tested are given by

$$H_0: \quad \log y_t = \beta_0 + \beta_1 x_t + u_{0t} \qquad u_{0t} \sim IN(\sigma_0^2)$$

and

$$H_1: \quad y_t = \beta_0 + \beta_1 x_t + u_{1t} \qquad u_{1t} \sim IN(\sigma_1^2)$$

The BM test involves three steps.

Step 1. Obtain the predicted values $\log \hat{y}_t$ and $\tilde{y}_t$ from the two equations, respectively. The predicted value of y_t from the log-linear equation is $\exp(\log \hat{y}_t)$. The predicted value of $\log y_t$ from the linear equation is $\log \tilde{y}_t$.

Step 2. Compute the artificial regressions:

$$\exp(\log \hat{y}_t) = \beta_0 + \beta_1 x_t + v_{1t}$$

and

$$\log \tilde{y}_t = \beta_0 + \beta_1 x_t + v_{0t}$$

Let the estimated residuals from these two regression equations be $\hat{v}_{1t}$ and $\hat{v}_{0t}$, respectively.

Step 3. The tests for H_0 and H_1 are based on θ_0 and θ_1 in the artificial regressions:

$$\log y_t = \beta_0 + \beta_1 x_t + \theta_0 \hat{v}_{1t} + \varepsilon_t$$

and

$$y_t = \beta_0 + \beta_1 x_t + \theta_1 \hat{v}_{0t} + \varepsilon_t$$

We use the usual t-tests to test these hypotheses. If $\theta_0 = 0$ is accepted, we choose the log-linear model. If $\theta_1 = 0$ is accepted, we choose the linear model. A problem arises if both these hypotheses are rejected or both are accepted.

[16] A. K. Bera and M. McAleer, "Further Results on Testing Linear and Log-Linear Regression Models," paper presented at the SSRC Econometric Group Conference on Model Specification and Testing, Warwick, England, 1982.

The PE Test

The PE test [17] also uses artificial regressions. It involves only two steps. Step 1 is the same as in the BM test.

Step 2. Test $\theta_0 = 0$ and $\theta_1 = 0$ in the artificial regressions:

$$\log y_t = \beta_0 + \beta_1 x_t + \theta_0 [\tilde{y}_t - \exp(\log \hat{y}_t)] + \varepsilon_t$$

and

$$y_t = \beta_0 + \beta_1 x_t + \theta_1 [\log \hat{y}_t - \log \tilde{y}_t] + \varepsilon_t.$$

There are many other tests for this problem of choosing linear versus log-linear forms. [18] The three tests mentioned here are the easiest to compute. We are not presenting an illustrative example here. The computation of the Box–Cox, BM, and PE tests for the data in Tables 4.7 and 5.5 is left as an exercise.

SUMMARY

1. If the error variance is not constant for all the observations, this is known as the heteroskedasticity problem. The problem is informally illustrated with an example in Section 5.1.

2. First, we would like to know whether the problem exists. For this purpose some tests have been suggested. We have discussed the following tests:

(a) Ramsey's test.
(b) Glejser's tests.
(c) Breusch and Pagan's test.
(d) White's test.
(e) Goldfeld and Quandt's test.
(f) Likelihood ratio test.

Some of these tests have been illustrated with examples (see Section 5.2). Others have been left as exercises. There are two data sets (Tables 4.7 and 5.5) that have been provided for use by students who can experiment with these tests.

3. The consequences of the heteroskedasticity problem are

(a) The least squares estimators are unbiased but inefficient.
(b) The estimated variances are themselves biased.

If the heteroskedasticity problem is detected, we can try to solve it by the use of weighted least squares. Otherwise, we can at least try to correct the error variances (since the estimators are unbiased). This correction (due to White) is illustrated at the end of Section 5.3.

[17] J. G. Mackinnon, H. White, and R. Davidson, "Tests for Model Specification in the Presence of Alternative Hypotheses: Some Further Results," *Journal of Econometrics*, Vol. 21, 1983, pp. 53–70.

[18] For instance, L. G. Godfrey and M. R. Wickens, "Testing Linear and Log-Linear Regressions for Functional Form," *Review of Economic Studies*, 1981, pp. 487–496 and R. Davidson and J. G. Mackinnon, "Testing Linear and Log-Linear Regressions Against Box–Cox Alternatives," *Canadian Journal of Economics*, 1985, pp. 499–517.

4. There are three solutions commonly suggested for the heteroskedasticity problem:

(a) Use of weighted least squares.

(b) Deflating the data by some measure of "size."

(c) Transforming the data to the logarithmic form.

In weighted least squares, the particular weighting scheme used will depend on the nature of heteroskedasticity. Weighted least squares methods are illustrated in Section 5.4.

5. The use of deflators is similar to the weighted least squares method, although it is done in a more ad hoc fashion. Some problems with the use of deflators are discussed in Section 5.5.

6. The question of estimation in linear versus logarithmic form has received considerable attention during recent years. Several statistical tests have been suggested for testing the linear versus logarithmic form. In Section 5.6 we discuss three of these tests: the Box–Cox test, the BM test, and the PA test. All are easy to implement with standard regression packages. We have not illustrated the use of these tests. This is left as an exercise. It would be interesting to see which functional form is chosen and whether the heteroskedasticity problem exists for the functional form chosen.

7. Note that the tests discussed in Section 5.6 start by assuming homoskedastic errors for both functional forms.

EXERCISES

1. Define the terms "heteroskedasticity" and "homoskedasticity." Explain the effects of heteroskedasticity on the estimates of the parameters and their variances in a normal regression model.

2. Explain the following tests for homoskedasticity.
   (a) Ramsey's test.
   (b) Goldfeld and Quandt's test.
   (c) Glejser's test.
   (d) Breusch and Pagan's test.

   Illustrate each of these tests with the data in Tables 4.7 and 5.5.

3. Indicate whether each of the following statements is true (T), false (F), or uncertain (V), and give a brief explanation.
   (a) Heteroskedasticity in the errors leads to biased estimates of the regression coefficients and their standard errors.
   (b) Deflating income and consumption by the same price results in a higher estimate for the marginal propensity to consume.
   (c) The correlation between two ratios which have the same denominator is always biased upward.

4. Apply the following tests to choose between the linear and log-linear regression models with the data in Tables 4.7 and 5.5.
   (a) Box–Cox test.
   (b) BM test.
   (c) PA test.

5. In the model

$$y_{1t} = a_{11}x_{1t} + a_{12}x_{2t} + u_{1t}$$
$$y_{2t} = a_{21}x_{1t} + a_{22}x_{2t} + u_{2t}$$

you are told that

$$a_{11} + a_{12} = a_{21}$$
$$a_{11} - a_{12} = a_{22}$$

$u_{1t} \sim \mathrm{IN}(0, \sigma^2)$, $u_{2t} \sim \mathrm{IN}(0, 4\sigma^2)$, and u_{1t} and u_{2t} are independent. Explain how you will estimate the parameters $a_{11}, a_{12}, a_{21}, a_{22}$, and σ^2.

6. Explain how you will choose among the following four regression models.

$$y = \alpha_1 + \beta_1 x + u_1$$
$$y = \alpha_2 + \beta_2 \log x + u_2$$
$$\log y = \alpha_3 + \beta_3 x + u_3$$
$$\log y = \alpha_4 + \beta_4 \log x + u_4$$

7. In the linear regression model

$$y_i = \alpha + \beta x_i + u_i$$

the errors u_i are presumed to have a variance depending on a variable z_i. Explain how you will choose among the following four specifications.

$$\mathrm{var}(u_i) = \sigma^2$$
$$\mathrm{var}(u_i) = \sigma^2 z_i$$
$$\mathrm{var}(u_i) = \sigma^2 z_i^2$$
$$\mathrm{var}(u_i) = \sigma^2 z_i^3$$

8. In a study of 27 industrial establishments of varying size, y = the number of supervisors and x = the number of supervised workers. y varies from 30 to 210 and x from 247 to 1650. The results obtained were as follows:

Variable	Coefficient	SE	t
x	0.115	0.011	9.30
Constant	14.448	9.562	1.51
$n = 27$	$s = 21.73$	$R^2 = 0.776$	

After the estimation of the equation and plotting the residuals against x, it was found that the variance of the residuals increased with x. Plotting the residuals against $1/x$ showed that there was no such relationship. Hence the assumption made was

$$\mathrm{var}(u_i) = \sigma^2 x_i^2$$

The estimated equation was

$$\frac{y}{x} = \underset{(0.009)}{0.121} + \underset{(4.570)}{3.803}(1/x) \qquad R^2 = 0.03$$

In terms of the original variables, we have

$$y = 3.803 + 0.121x$$

The estimation gave the following results:

Variable	Coefficient	SE	t
x	0.121	0.009	13.44
Constant	3.803	4.570	0.832

$$n = 27 \quad s = 22.577 \quad R^2 = 0.7587$$

(a) An investigator looks at the drop in R^2 and concludes that the first equation is better. Is this conclusion valid?

(b) What would the equation to be estimated be if $\text{var}(u_i) = \sigma^2 x_i$ instead of $\sigma^2 x_i^2$? How would you determine which of these alternative hypotheses is the better one?

(c) Comment on the computation of R^2 from the transformed equation and the R^2 from the equation in terms of the original variables.

9. In discussions of real estate assessment, it is often argued that the higher-priced houses get assessed at a lower proportion of value than the lower-priced houses. To determine whether such inequity exists, the following equations are estimated:

1. $A_i = \alpha + \beta S_i + u_i$
2. $A_i/S_i = \gamma + \delta S_i + u_i'$
3. $\log A_i = \theta + \lambda \log S_i + u_i''$

where A_i is the assessment for property i and S_i is the observed selling price. In a sample of 416 houses in King County, Washington during the period 1977–1979, the following results were obtained.

1. $A_i = 7505.40 + 0.3382S_i \qquad R^2 = 0.597$
   (559.2) (0.0136) standard errors
   (13.42) (24.79) t-ratios

2. $A_i/S_i = 0.7374 - 4.5714 \times 10^{-6} S_i \qquad R^2 = 0.2917$
   (0.0144) (3.5005×10^{-7}) standard errors
   51.38 -13.06 t-ratios

3. $\log A_i = 2.8312 + .6722 \log S_i \qquad R^2 = .6547$
   (.2513) (.0240)

It has been suggested that it is more appropriate to answer this question by estimating a reverse regression:

4. $S_i = \gamma_0 + \gamma_1 A_i + \eta_i$
5. $A_i/S_i = \beta_0 + \beta_1 A_i + \eta_i'$

The estimation now gave the results:

6. $S_i = 2050.07 + 1.7669A_i \qquad R^2 = 0.597$
   (1527.93) (0.0713) standard errors
   (1.3417) (24.79) t-ratios

7. $A_i/S_i = 0.5556 + 3.8288 \times 10^{-7} A_i$ $\quad R^2 = 0.0004$
       (0.0203)   (9.506 × 10⁻⁷) $\qquad$ standard errors
       (27.26)   (0.403) $\qquad\quad$ t-ratios

The average value of A/S was 5.6439.

(a) Interpret what the coefficients in each of these equations mean to answer the question of whether there is inequity in real estate assessment.

(b) Given some arguments as to why equations (4) and (5) may be more appropriate to look at than equations (1) to (3).

(c) Also, explain why equations (2) and (5) may be more appropriate than equations (1) and (4) respectively.

(The results are from: L. A. Kochin and R. W. Parks: "Testing for Assessment Uniformity: A Reappraisal", *Property Tax Journal*, March 1984, pp. 27–54.)

6

Autocorrelation

6.1 INTRODUCTION

In Chapter 5 we considered the consequences of relaxing the assumption that the variance of the error term is constant. We now come to the next assumption that the error terms in the regression model are independent. In this chapter we study the consequences of relaxing this assumption.

There are two situations under which error terms in the regression model can be correlated. In cross-section data it can arise among contiguous units. For instance, if we are studying consumption patterns of households, the error terms for households in the same neighborhood can be correlated. This is because the error term picks up the effect of omitted variables and these variables tend to be correlated for households in the same neighborhood (because of the "keeping up with the Joneses" effect). Similarly, if our data are on states, the error terms for contiguous states tend to be correlated. All these examples fall in the category of *spatial correlation*. In this chapter we will not be concerned with this type of correlation. Some of the factors that produce this type of correlation among the error terms can be taken care of by the use of dummy variables discussed in Chapter 8.

What we will be discussing in this chapter is the correlation between the error terms arising in time series data. This type of correlation is called *autocorrelation* or *serial correlation*. The error term u_t at time period t is correlated with error terms $u_{t+1}, u_{t+2}, \ldots$ and $u_{t-1}, u_{t-2}, \ldots$ and so on. Such correlation in the error terms often arises from the correlation of the omitted variables that the error term captures.

The correlation between u_t and u_{t-k} is called an autocorrelation of order k. The correlation between u_t and u_{t-1} is the first-order autocorrelation and is usually denoted by ρ_1. The correlation between u_t and u_{t-2} is called the second-order autocorrelation and is denoted by ρ_2 and so on. There are $(n-1)$ such autocorrelations if we have n observations. However, we cannot hope to estimate all of these from our data. Hence we often asssume that these $(n-1)$ autocorrelations can be represented in terms of one or two parameters.

In the following sections we discuss how to

1. Test for the presence of serial correlation.
2. Estimate the regression equation when the errors are serially correlated.

6.2 DURBIN–WATSON TEST

The simplest and most commonly used model is one where the errors u_t and u_{t-1} have a correlation ρ. For this model one can think of testing hypotheses about ρ on the basis of $\hat{\rho}$, the correlation between the least squares residuals $\hat{u}_t$ and $\hat{u}_{t-1}$. A commonly used statistic for this purpose (which is related to $\hat{\rho}$) is the Durbin–Watson (DW) statistic, which we will denote by d. It is defined as

$$d = \frac{\sum_{1}^{n-1} (\hat{u}_t - \hat{u}_{t-1})^2}{\sum_{1}^{n} \hat{u}_t^2}$$

where $\hat{u}_t$ is the estimated residual for period t. We can write d as

$$d = \frac{\sum \hat{u}_t^2 + \sum \hat{u}_{t-1}^2 - 2\sum \hat{u}_t \hat{u}_{t-1}}{\sum \hat{u}_t^2}$$

Since $\sum \hat{u}_t^2$ and $\sum \hat{u}_{t-1}^2$ are approximately equal if the sample is large, we have $d \simeq 2(1 - \hat{\rho})$. If $\hat{\rho} = +1$, then $d = 0$, and if $\hat{\rho} = -1$, then $d = 4$. We have $d = 2$ if $\hat{\rho} = 0$. If d is close to 0 or 4, the residuals are highly correlated.

The sampling distribution of d depends on the values of the explanatory variables and hence Durbin and Watson [1] derived upper (d_U) limits and lower (d_L) limits for the significance levels for d. There are tables to test the hypothesis of zero autocorrelation against the hypothesis of first-order positive autocorrelation. (For negative autocorrelation we interchange d_L and d_U)

If $d < d_L$, we reject the null hypothesis of no autocorrelation.
If $d > d_U$, we do not reject the null hypothesis.
If $d_L < d < d_U$, the test is inconclusive.

Hannan and Terrell [2] show that the upper bound of the DW statistic is a good approximation to its distribution when the regressors are slowly changing. They argue that economic time series are slowly changing and hence one can use d_U as the correct significance point.

The significance points in the DW tables at the end of the book are tabulated for testing $\rho = 0$ against $\rho > 0$. If $d > 2$ and we wish to test the hypothesis $\rho = 0$ against $\rho < 0$, we consider $4 - d$ and refer to the Durbin–Watson tables as if we are testing for positive autocorrelation.

Although we have said that $d \simeq 2(1 - \rho)$ this approximation is valid only in large samples. The mean of d when $\rho = 0$ has been shown to be given approximately by (the proof is rather complicated for our purpose)

$$E(d) \simeq 2 + \frac{2(k - 1)}{n - k}$$

where k is the number of regression parameters estimated (including the constant term) and n is the sample size. Thus, even for zero serial correlation, the statistic is biased upward from 2. If $k = 5$ and $n = 15$, the bias is as large as 0.8. We illustrate the use of the DW test with an example.

Illustrative Example

Consider the data in Table 3.11. The estimated production function is

$$\log X = -3.938 + 1.451 \log L_1 + 0.384 \log K_1$$
$$\quad\quad\quad (0.237) \quad\; (0.083) \quad\quad\quad (0.048)$$

$$R^2 = 0.9946 \qquad DW = 0.858 \qquad \hat{\rho} = 0.559$$

Referring to the DW tables with $k' = 2$ and $n = 39$ for the 5% significance level, we see that $d_L = 1.38$. Since the observed $d = 0.858 < d_L$, we reject the hypothesis $\rho = 0$ at the 5% level.

Although the DW test is the most commonly used test for serial correlations, it has several limitations.

[1] J. Durbin and G. S. Watson, "Testing for Serial Correlation in Least Squares Regression," *Biometrika*, 1950, pp. 409–428; 1951, pp. 159–178.
[2] E. J. Hannan and R. D. Terrell, "Testing for Serial Correlation After Least Squares Regression," *Econometrica*, 1966, pp. 646–660.

1. It tests for only first-order serial correlation.
2. The test is inconclusive if the computed value lies between d_L and d_U.
3. The test cannot be applied in models with lagged dependent variables.

At this point it would be distracting to answer all these criticisms. We will present answers to these points in the last sections of this chapter. First we discuss some simple solutions to the serial correlation problem.

6.3 ESTIMATION IN LEVELS VERSUS FIRST DIFFERENCES

If the DW test rejects the hypothesis of zero serial correlation, what is the next step?

In such cases one estimates a regression by transforming all the variables by ρ-*differencing*, that is, regress $y_t - \hat{\rho}y_{t-1}$ on $x_t - \hat{\rho}x_{t-1}$ where $\hat{\rho}$ is the estimated ρ. However, since $\hat{\rho}$ is subject to sampling errors, one other alternative that is followed if the DW statistic d is small is to use a *first-difference equation*. In fact, a rough rule of thumb is: *Estimate an equation in first differences whenever the DW statistic is* $< R^2$. In first difference equations, we regress $y_t - y_{t-1}$ on $x_t - x_{t-1}$ (with all the explanatory variables differenced similarly). The implicit assumption is that the first differences of the errors $(u_t - u_{t-1})$ are independent. For instance, if

$$y_t = \alpha + \beta x_t + u_t$$

is the regression equation, then

$$y_{t-1} = \alpha + \beta x_{t-1} + u_{t-1}$$

and we have by subtraction

$$(y_t - y_{t-1}) = \beta(x_t - x_{t-1}) + (u_t - u_{t-1})$$

If the errors in this equation are independent, we can estimate the equation by OLS. However, since the constant term α disappears under subtraction, we should be estimating the regression equation with no constant term. Often, we find a constant term also included in regression equations with first differences. This procedure is valid only if there is a linear trend term in the original equation. If the regression equation is

$$y_t = \alpha + \delta t + \beta x_t + u_t$$

then

$$y_{t-1} = \alpha + \delta(t - 1) + \beta x_{t-1} + u_{t-1}$$

and on subtraction we get

$$(y_t - y_{t-1}) = \delta + \beta(x_t - x_{t-1}) + (u_t - u_{t-1})$$

which is an equation with a constant term.

When comparing equations in levels and first differences, one cannot compare the

R^2's because the explained variables are different. One can compare the residual sum of squares *but only after making a rough adjustment*. Note that if $\text{var}(u_t) = \sigma^2$, then the variance of the error term in the first difference equation is

$$\text{var}(u_t - u_{t-1}) = \text{var}(u_t) + \text{var}(u_{t-1}) - 2\,\text{cov}(u_t, u_{t-1})$$
$$\simeq \sigma^2 + \sigma^2 - 2\sigma^2\rho$$
$$= 2\sigma^2(1 - \rho)$$

where ρ is the correlation coefficient between u_t and u_{t-1}. Since the residual sum of squares divided by the appropriate degrees of freedom gives a consistent estimator for the error variance, the two residual sums of squares can be made roughly comparable if we multiply the residual sum of squares from the levels equation by

$$\left(\frac{n-k-1}{n-k}\right)2(1-\rho)$$

where k is the number of regressors. If $\hat{\rho}$ is an estimates of ρ from the levels equation, since $\hat{\rho} = (2 - d)/2$ where d is the DW test statistic, we get $2(1 - \hat{\rho}) = d$. Thus, we can multiply the residual sum of squares from the levels equation by

$$\left(\frac{n-k-1}{n-k}\right)d$$

or if n is large, just by d. For instance, if the residual sum of squares is, say, 1.2 by the levels equation, and 0.8 by the first difference equation and $n = 11$, $k = 1$, DW $= 0.9$, then the adjusted residual sum of squares with the levels equation is $(9/10)(0.9)(1.2) = 0.97$ which is the number to be compared with 0.8.

All this discussion, however, assumes that there are no lagged dependent variables among the explanatory variables. If there are lagged dependent variables in the equation, then the estimators of the parameters are not consistent and the above arguments do not hold.

Since we have comparable residual sum of squares, we can get the comparable R^2's as well, using the relationship $\text{RSS} = S_{yy}(1 - R^2)$:

Let $\qquad R_1^2 = R^2$ from the first difference equation

RSS_0 = residual sum of squares from the levels equation

RSS_1 = residual sum of squares from the first difference equation.

R_D^2 = comparable R^2 from the levels equation.

Then

$$\frac{1 - R_D}{1 - R_1^2} = \left(\text{RSS}_0 \cdot \frac{n-k-1}{n-k} \cdot d\right)\Big/ \text{RSS}_1$$
$$= \frac{\text{RSS}_0}{\text{RSS}_1}\left(\frac{n-k-1}{n-k}d\right)$$

An alternative formula by Harvey which does not contain the last term will be presented after some illustrative examples.

Some Illustrative Examples

Consider the simple Keynesian model discussed by Friedman and Meiselman.[3] The equation estimated in levels is:

$$C_t = \alpha + \beta A_t + \varepsilon_t \qquad t = 1, 2, \ldots, T$$

where C_t = personal consumption expenditure (current dollars)
A_t = autonomous expenditures (current dollars)

The model fitted for the 1929–1939 period gave [4]:

1. $C_t = 58,335.9 + 2.498 A_t$
          (0.312)
   $R^2 = 0.8771$, DW $= 0.89$, RSS $= 11,943 \times 10^4$
2. $\Delta C_t = 1.993 \Delta A_t$
           (0.324)
   $R^2 = 0.8096$, DW $= 1.51$, RSS $= 8387 \times 10^4$

(Figures in parentheses are standard errors.) There is a reduction in the R^2 but the R^2 values are not comparable. The equation in first differences is better because of the larger DW statistic and lower residual sum of squares than for the equation in the levels (even after the adjustments described).

For the production function data in Table 3.11 the first difference equation is

$$\Delta \log X = 0.987 \, \Delta \log L_1 + 0.502 \, \Delta \log K_1$$
$$\quad\quad\quad (0.158) \quad\quad\quad\quad (0.134)$$

$$R^2 = 0.8405 \qquad DW = 1.177 \qquad RSS = 0.0278$$

The comparable figures for the levels equation reported earlier in Chapter 4, equation (4.25) are

$$R^2 = 0.9946 \qquad DW = 0.858 \qquad RSS = 0.0434$$

Again, even though the R^2 is larger for the equation in levels, the equation in first differences is better than the equation in levels, because it gives a lower RSS (even after the adjustments described) and a higher DW statistic. The estimate of returns to scale is $0.987 + 0.502 = 1.489$ in the first difference equation compared to $1.451 + 0.384 = 1.835$ in the levels equation.

We can also compute R_D^2, the comparable R^2 from the equation in levels and see how it compares with R_1^2, the R^2 from the equation in first differences. In the

---

[3] M. Friedman and D. Meiselman, "The Relative Stability of Monetary Velocity and the Investment Multiplier in the U.S., 1897–1958," in *Stabilization Policies* (Commission on Money and Credit) (Englewood Cliffs, N.J.: Prentice-Hall, 1963).
[4] A. C. Harvey, "On Comparing Regression Models in Levels and First Differences," *International Economic Review*, Vol. 21, No. 3, October 1980, pp. 707–720.

example with the Friedman-Meiselman data the value of R_D^2 is given by

$$R_D^2 = 1 - \frac{RSS_0}{RSS_1}\left(\frac{n-k-1}{n-k}\right)d(1 - R_1^2)$$

$$= 1 - \frac{11.943}{8.387}\left(\frac{9}{10}\right)(0.89)(1 - 0.8096)$$

$$= 1 - 0.2172 = 0.7828$$

This is to be compared with $R_1^2 = 0.8096$ from the equation in first differences. For the production function data we get

$$R_D^2 = 1 - \left(\frac{0.0434}{0.0278}\right)\left(\frac{36}{37}\right)(0.858)(1 - 0.8405)$$

$$= 1 - 0.2079 = 0.7921$$

This is to be compared with $R^2 = 0.8405$ from the equation in first differences.
Harvey[5] gives a different definition of R_D^2. He defines it as:

$$R_D^2 = 1 - \frac{RSS_0}{RSS_1}(1 - R_1^2)$$

This does not adjust for the fact that the error variances in the levels equations and the first difference equation are not the same. The arguments for his suggestion are given in his paper. In the example with the Friedman-Meiselman data his measure of R_D^2 is given by

$$R_D^2 = 1 - \frac{119,430}{83,872}(1 - 0.8096) = 0.7289$$

Although R_D^2 cannot be greater than 1, it can be negative. This would be the case when $\sum(\Delta y_t - \overline{\Delta y})^2 < RSS_0$, that is, when the levels model is giving a poorer explanation than the naive model, which says that Δy_t is a constant.

Usually, with time-series data, one gets high R^2 values if the regressions are estimated with the levels y_t and x_t but one gets low R^2 values if the regressions are estimated in first differences $(y_t - y_{t-1})$ and $(x_t - x_{t-1})$. Since a high R^2 is usually considered as proof of a strong relationship between the variables under investigation, there is a strong tendency to estimate the equations in levels rather than in first differences. This is sometimes called the "R^2 syndrome." However, if the DW statistic is very low, it often implies a misspecified equation, no matter what the value of the R^2 is. In such cases one should estimate the regression equation in first differences and if the R^2 is low, this merely indicates that the variables y and x are not related to each other. Granger and Newbold[6] present some examples with artificially generated data where y, x, and the error u are each generated

---

[5] Harvey, "On Comparing Regression Models," p. 711.
[6] C. W. J. Granger and P. Newbold, "Spurious Regressions in Econometrics," *Journal of Econometrics*, Vol. 2, No. 2, July 1976, pp. 111–120.

independently so that there is no relationship between y and x, but the correlations between y_t and y_{t-1}, x_t and x_{t-1}, and u_t and u_{t-1} are very high. Although there is no relationship between y and x the regression of y on x gives a high R^2 but a low DW statistic. When the regression is run in first differences, the R^2 is close to zero and the DW statistic is close to 2, thus demonstrating that there is indeed no relationship between y and x and that the R^2 obtained earlier is spurious. Thus regressions in first differences might often reveal the true nature of the relationship between y and x. (Further discussion of this problem is in Section 6.10).

Finally, it should be emphasized that all this discussion of the Durbin–Watson statistic, first differences, and quasi-first differences is relevant only if we believe that the correlation structure between the errors can be entirely described in terms of ρ, the correlation coefficient between u_t and u_{t-1}. This may not always be the case. We will discuss some general formulations of the correlation structure of the errors in Section 6.9 after we analyze the simple case thoroughly. Also, even if the correlation structure can be described in terms of just one parameter, this need not be the correlation between u_t and u_{t-1}. For instance, suppose that we have quarterly data; then it is possible that the errors in any quarter this year are most highly correlated with the errors in the corresponding quarter last year rather than the errors in the preceding quarter; that is, u_t could be uncorrelated with u_{t-1} but it could be highly correlated with u_{t-4}. If this is the case, the DW statistic will fail to detect it. What we should be using is a modified statistic defined as

$$d_4 = \frac{\sum (\hat{u}_t - \hat{u}_{t-4})^2}{\sum \hat{u}_t^2}$$

Also, instead of using first differences or quasi first differences in the regressions, we should be using fourth differences or quasi fourth differences, that is, $y_t - y_{t-4}$ and $x_t - x_{t-4}$ or $y_t - \hat{\rho} y_{t-4}$ and $x_t - \hat{\rho} x_{t-4}$, where $\hat{\rho}$ is the correlation coefficient between the estimated residuals $\hat{u}_t$ and $\hat{u}_{t-4}$.

6.4 ESTIMATION PROCEDURES WITH AUTOCORRELATED ERRORS

In Section 6.3 we considered estimation in first differences. We will now consider estimation with *quasi first differences*, that is, regressing $y_t - \rho y_{t-1}$ on $x_t - \rho x_{t-1}$. As we said earlier, we will be discussing the simplest case where the entire correlation structure of the errors u_t can be summarized in a single parameter ρ. This would be the case if the errors u_t are *first-order autoregressive*, that is,

$$u_t = \rho u_{t-1} + e_t \tag{6.1}$$

where e_t are serially uncorrelated, with mean zero and common variance σ_e^2. Equation (6.1) is called an autoregression because it is the usual regression model with u_t regressed on u_{t-1}. It is called first-order autoregression because u_t is regressed on its past with only one lag. If there are two lags, it is called second-order autoregression. If there are three lags, it is called third-order autoregression, and so on. If the errors u_t satisfy equation (6.1), we say u_t are AR(1) (i.e., autoregressive of first order). If the errors u_t satisfy the equation

$$u_t = \rho_1 u_{t-1} + \rho_2 u_{t-2} + e_t$$

then we say that u_t are AR(2), and so on.

Now we will derive var (u_t) and the correlations between u_t and lagged values of u_t. From (6.1) note that u_t depends on e_t and u_{t-1}, u_{t-1} depends on e_{t-1} and u_{t-2}, and so on. Thus u_t depends on $e_t, e_{t-1}, e_{t-2}, \dots$. Since e_t are serially independent, and u_{t-1} depends on e_{t-1}, e_{t-2} and so on, but *not* e_t, we have

$$E(u_{t-1} e_t) = 0$$

Since $E(e_t) = 0$, we have $E(u_t) = 0$ for all t.

If we denote var (u_t) by σ^2, we have

$$\sigma^2 = \text{var}\,(u_t) = E(u_t^2)$$
$$= E(\rho u_{t-1} + e_t)^2$$
$$= \rho^2 \sigma^2 + \sigma_e^2 \qquad \text{since cov}\,(u_{t-1}, e_t) = 0$$

Thus we have

$$\sigma^2 = \frac{\sigma_e^2}{1 - \rho^2}$$

This gives the variance of u_t in terms of variance of e_t and the parameter ρ.

Let us now derive the correlations. Denoting the correlation between u_t and u_{t-s} (which is called the correlation of lag s) by ρ_s, we get

$$E(u_t u_{t-s}) = \sigma^2 \rho_s$$

But

$$E(u_t u_{t-s}) = \rho E(u_{t-1} u_{t-s}) + E(e_t u_{t-s})$$

Hence

$$\rho_s = \rho \cdot \rho_{s-1} + 0$$

or

$$\rho_s = \rho \cdot \rho_{s-1}$$

Since $\rho_0 = 1$ we get by successive substitution

$$\rho_1 = \rho, \quad \rho_2 = \rho^2, \quad \rho_3 = \rho^3, \quad \dots$$

Thus the lag correlations are all powers of ρ and decline geometrically.

These expressions can be used to derive the covariance matrix of the errors and using what is known as generalized least squares (GLS).[7] We will not derive the expression for GLS here but will outline the minor changes that it implies. Consider the model

$$y_t = \alpha + \beta x_t + u_t \qquad t = 1, 2, \dots, T \tag{6.2}$$

$$u_t = \rho u_{t-1} + e_t \tag{6.3}$$

---

[7] The derivation involves the use of matrix algebra, which we have avoided.

Except for the treatment of the first observation in the case of AR(1) errors as in (6.3), and the treatment of the first two observations in the case of AR(2) errors, and so on, the GLS procedure amounts to the use of transformed data, which are obtained as follows[8].

Lagging (6.2) by one period and multiplying it by ρ, we get

$$\rho y_{t-1} = \alpha\rho + \beta\rho x_{t-1} + \rho u_{t-1} \tag{6.4}$$

Subtracting (6.4) from (6.2) and using (6.3), we get

$$y_t - \rho y_{t-1} = \alpha(1 - \rho) + \beta(x_t - \rho x_{t-1}) + e_t \tag{6.5}$$

Since e_t are serially independent with a constant variance σ_e^2, we can estimate the parameters in this equation by an OLS procedure. Equation (6.5) is often called the *quasi-difference* transformation of (6.4). What we do is transform the variables y_t and x_t to

$$
\begin{aligned}
y_t^* &= y_t - \rho y_{t-1} \qquad t = 2, 3, \ldots, T \\
x_t^* &= x_t - \rho x_{t-1}
\end{aligned}
\tag{6.6}
$$

and run a regression of y^* on x^*, with or without a constant term depending on whether the original equation has a constant term or not. In this method we use only $(T - 1)$ observations because we lose one observation in the process of taking differences. This procedure is not exactly the GLS procedure. The GLS procedure amounts to using all the T observations with

$$
\begin{aligned}
y_1^* &= \sqrt{1 - \rho^2}\, y_1 \\
x_1^* &= \sqrt{1 - \rho^2}\, x_1
\end{aligned}
\tag{6.6'}
$$

and regressing y^* and x^* using the T observations.

In actual practice ρ is not known. There are two types of procedures for estimating ρ:

1. Iterative procedures.
2. Grid-search procedures.

Iterative Procedures

Among the iterative procedures, the earliest was the Cochrane–Orcutt procedure.[9] In the Cochrane–Orcutt procedure we estimate equation (6.2) by OLS, get the estimated residuals $\hat{u}_t$, and estimate ρ by $\hat{\rho} = \sum \hat{u}_t \hat{u}_{t-1} / \sum \hat{u}_t^2$.

Durbin[10] suggested an alternative method of estimating ρ. In this procedure, we write equation (6.5) as

$$y_t = \alpha(1 - \rho) + \rho y_{t-1} + \beta x_t - \beta\rho x_{t-1} + e_t \tag{6.7}$$

---

[8] If the number of observations is large, the omission of these initial observations does not matter much.

[9] D. Cochrane and G. H. Orcutt, "Application of Least Squares Regressions to Relationships Containing Autocorrelated Error Terms," *Journal of the American Statistical Association*, 1949, pp. 32–61.

[10] J. Durbin, "Estimation of Parameters in Time Series Regression Models," *Journal of the Royal Statistical Society*, Series B, 1960, pp. 139–153.

We regress y_t on y_{t-1}, x_t, and x_{t-1} and take the estimated coefficient of y_{t-1} as an estimate of ρ.

Once an estimate of ρ is obtained, we construct the transformed variables y^* and x^* as defined in (6.6) and (6.6') and estimate a regression of y^* on x^*. The only thing to note is that the slope coefficient in this equation is β, but the intercept is $\alpha(1 - \rho)$. Thus after estimating the regression of y^* on x^*, we have to adjust the constant term appropriately to get estimates of the parameters of the original equation (6.2). Further, the standard errors we compute from the regression of y^* on x^* are now "asymptotic" standard errors because of the fact that ρ has been estimated. If there are lagged values of y as explanatory variables, these standard errors are not correct even asymptotically. The adjustment needed in this case is discussed in Section 6.7.

If there are many explanatory variables in the equation, Durbin's method involves a regression in too many variables (twice the number of explanatory variables plus y_{t-1}). Hence it is often customary to prefer the Cochrane–Orcutt procedure until it converges. However, there are examples[11] to show that the minimization of $\sum e_t^2$ in (6.5) can produce multiple solutions for ρ. In this case the Cochrane–Orcutt procedure, which relies on a single solution for ρ, might give a local minimum, and even when iterated might converge to a local minimum. Hence it is better to use a grid-search procedure, which we will now describe.

Grid-Search Procedures

One of the first grid-search procedures is the Hildreth and Lu procedure[12] suggested in 1960. The procedure is as follows. Calculate y_t^* and x_t^* in (6.6) for different values of ρ at intervals of 0.1 in the range $-1 \le \rho \le 1$. Estimate the regression of y_t^* and x_t^* and calculate the residual sum of squares RSS in each case. Choose the value of ρ for which the RSS is minimum. Again repeat this procedure for smaller intervals of ρ around this value. For instance, if the value of ρ for which RSS is minimum is -0.4, repeat this search procedure for values of ρ at intervals of 0.01 in the range $-0.5 < \rho < -0.3$.

This procedure is *not* the same as the maximum likelihood (ML) procedure. If the errors e_t are normally distributed, we can write the log-likelihood function as (derivation is omitted)

$$\log L = \text{const.} - \frac{T}{2}\log \sigma_e^2 + \frac{1}{2}\log(1 - \rho^2) - \frac{Q}{2\sigma_e^2} \tag{6.8}$$

where

$$Q = \sum [y_t - \rho y_{t-1} - \alpha(1 - \rho) - \beta(x_t - \rho x_{t-1})]^2$$

[11] J. M. Dufour, M. J. I. Gaudry, and T. C. Lieu, "The Cochrane–Orcutt Procedure: Numerical Examples of Multiple Admissible Minima," *Economics Letters*, 1980 (6), pp. 43–48.
[12] Clifford Hildreth and John Y. Lu, *Demand Relations with Autocorrelated Disturbances*, AES Technical Bulletin 276, Michigan State University, East Lansing, Mich., November 1960.

Thus minimizing Q is not the same as maximizing $\log L$. We can use the grid-search procedure to get the ML estimates. The only difference is that after we compute the residual sum of squares $\text{RSS}(\rho)$ for each ρ, we choose the value of ρ for which $(T/2)\log\text{RSS}(\rho) - (1/2)\log(1 - \rho^2)$ is minimum. If the number of observations is large, the latter term will be small compared to the former, and the ML procedure and the Hildreth–Lu procedure will give almost the same results.

Illustrative Example

Consider the data in Table 3.11 and the estimation of the production function

$$\log X = \alpha + \beta_1 \log L_1 + \beta_2 \log K_1 + u$$

The OLS estimation gave a DW statistic of 0.86, suggesting significant positive autocorrelation. Assuming that the errors were AR(1), two estimation procedures were used: the Hildreth–Lu grid search and the iterative Cochrane–Orcutt (C–O). The other procedures we have described can also be tried, but this is left as an exercise.

The Hildreth–Lu procedure gave $\hat\rho = 0.77$. The iterative C–0 procedure gave $\hat\rho = 0.80$. The DW test statistic implies that $\hat\rho = (1/2)(2 - 0.86) = 0.57$.

The estimates of the parameters (with the standard errors in parentheses) were as follows:

Estimate of:	OLS	Hildreth–Lu	Iterative C–O
α	-3.938 (0.237)	-2.909 (0.462)	-2.737 (0.461)
β_1	1.451 (0.083)	1.092 (0.151)	1.070 (0.153)
β_2	0.384 (0.048)	0.570 (0.104)	0.558 (0.097)
RSS	0.04338	0.02635	0.02644

In this example the parameter estimates given by the Hildreth–Lu and the iterative C–O procedures are pretty close to each other. Correcting for the autocorrelation in the errors has resulted in a significant change in the estimates of β_1 and β_2.

6.5 EFFECT OF AR(1) ERRORS ON OLS ESTIMATES

In Section 6.4 we described different procedures for the estimation of regression models with AR(1) errors. We will now answer two questions that might arise with the use of these procedures:

1. What do we gain from using these procedures?
2. When should we not use these procedures?

First, in the case we are considering (i.e., the case where the explanatory variable x_t is independent of the error u_t), the ordinary least squares (OLS) estimates are unbiased. However, they will not be efficient. Further, the tests of significance we apply, which will be based on the wrong covariance matrix, will be wrong. In the case where the explanatory variables include lagged dependent variables, we will have some further problems, which we discuss in Section 6.7. For the present, let us consider the simple regression model

$$y_t = \beta x_t + u_t \tag{6.9}$$

Let $\text{var}(u_t) = \sigma^2$, $\text{cov}(u_t, u_{t-j}) = \rho_j \sigma^2$. If u_t are AR(1), we have $\rho_j = \rho^j$.
   The OLS estimator of β is

$$\hat{\beta} = \frac{\sum x_t y_t}{\sum x_t^2}$$

Hence

$$\hat{\beta} - \beta = \frac{\sum x_t u_t}{\sum x_t^2} \quad \text{and} \quad E(\hat{\beta} - \beta) = 0$$

$$V(\hat{\beta}) = \frac{1}{(\sum x_t^2)^2} \text{var}(\sum x_t u_t)$$

$$= \frac{\sigma^2}{(\sum x_t^2)^2} \left(\sum x_t^2 + 2\rho \sum x_t x_{t-1} + 2\rho^2 \sum x_t x_{t-2} + \cdots \right)$$

since $\text{cov}(u_t, u_{t-j}) = \rho^j \sigma^2$. Thus we have

$$V(\hat{\beta}) = \frac{\sigma^2}{\sum x_t^2} \left(1 + 2\rho \frac{\sum x_t x_{t-1}}{\sum x_t^2} + 2\rho^2 \frac{\sum x_t x_{t-2}}{\sum x_t^2} + \cdots \right) \tag{6.10}$$

If we ignore the autocorrelation problem, we would be computing $V(\hat{\beta})$ as $\sigma^2 / \sum x_t^2$. Thus we would be ignoring the expression in the parentheses of (6.10). To get an idea of the magnitude of this expression, let us assume that the x_t series also follow an AR(1) process with $\text{var}(x_t) = \sigma_x^2$ and $\text{cor}(x_t, x_{t-1}) = r$. Since we are now assuming x_t to be stochastic, we will consider the asymptotic variance of β. The expression in parentheses in (6.10) is now

$$1 + 2\rho r + 2\rho^2 r^2 + \cdots = 1 + \frac{2\rho r}{1 - \rho r} = \frac{1 + \rho r}{1 - \rho r}$$

Thus

$$V(\hat{\beta}) = \frac{\sigma^2}{T\sigma_x^2} \frac{1 + r\rho}{1 - r\rho}$$

where T is the number of observations. If $r = \rho = 0.8$, then

$$\frac{1 + r\rho}{1 - r\rho} = \frac{1.64}{0.36}$$

Thus ignoring the expression in the parentheses of (6.10) results in an underestimation by close to 78% for the variance of $\hat{\beta}$.

One further error is also involved. This is that we use $\sum \hat{u}_t^2/(T-1)$ as an estimate of σ^2. If $\rho = 0$, this is an unbiased estimate of σ^2. If $\rho \neq 0$, then under the assumptions we are making, we have approximately [13]

$$E(\sum \hat{u}_t^2) = \sigma^2 \left(T - \frac{1 + r\rho}{1 - r\rho} \right)$$

Again if $\rho = r = 0.8$ and $T = 20$, we have

$$E\left(\frac{\sum \hat{u}_t^2}{T-1} \right) = \frac{15.45}{19} \sigma^2 \simeq 0.81\sigma^2$$

Thus there is a further underestimation of 19%. Both these effects result in an underestimation of the standard errors of more than 80%.

We can also derive the asymptotic variance of the ML estimator $\tilde{\beta}$ when both x and u are first order autoregressive as follows: Note that the ML estimator of β is asymptotically equivalent to the estimator obtained from a regression of $(y_t - \rho y_{t-1})$ on $(x_t - \rho x_{t-1})$. Hence

$$V(\tilde{\beta}) = \text{var} \frac{\sum (x_t - \rho x_{t-1})(u_t - \rho u_{t-1})}{\sum (x_t - \rho x_{t-1})^2}$$

$$= \text{var} \frac{\sum (x_t - \rho x_{t-1})e_t}{\sum (x_t - \rho x_{t-1})^2}$$

$$= \frac{\sigma_e^2}{\sum (x_t - \rho x_{t-1})^2}$$

where $\sigma_e^2 = \text{var}(e_t)$. When x_t is autoregressive we have

$$\lim \frac{1}{T} \sum (x_t - \rho x_{t-1})^2 = \sigma_x^2(1 + \rho^2 - 2r\rho)$$

Also,

$$\text{var}(u) = \sigma^2 = \frac{\sigma_e^2}{1 - \rho^2} \qquad \text{or} \qquad \sigma_e^2 = \sigma^2(1 - \rho^2)$$

Hence by substitution we get the asymptotic variance of $\tilde{\beta}$ as

$$V(\tilde{\beta}) = \frac{\sigma^2}{T\sigma_x^2} \frac{1 - \rho^2}{1 + \rho^2 - 2r\rho}$$

---

[13] Note that $\hat{u}_t = u_t - x_t(\hat{\beta} - \beta)^2$. Hence $E(\sum \hat{u}_t^2) = E(\sum u_t^2) + E[(\hat{\beta} - \beta)^2 \sum x_t^2] - 2E[(\hat{\beta} - \beta) \sum x_t u_t]$. The first term is $T\sigma^2$. The second term is

$$\sigma^2 \frac{1 + r\rho}{1 - r\rho}$$

The last term is

$$-2\sigma^2 \frac{1 + r\rho}{1 - r\rho}$$

In all this note that we take probability limits rather than expectations, since these results are all asymptotic.

Thus the efficiency of the OLS estimator is

$$\frac{V(\tilde{\beta})}{V(\hat{\beta})} = \frac{1 - r\rho}{1 + r\rho} \frac{1 - \rho^2}{1 + \rho^2 - 2r\rho}$$

One can compute this for different values of r and ρ. For $r = \rho = 0.8$ this efficiency is 0.21.

Thus the consequences of autocorrelated errors are:

1. The least squares estimators are unbiased but are not efficient. Sometimes they are considerably less efficient than the procedures that take account of the autocorrelation.
2. The sampling variances are biased and sometimes likely to be seriously understated. Thus R^2 as well as t and F statistics tend to be exaggerated.

The solution to these problems is to use the maximum likelihood procedure or some other procedure mentioned earlier that takes account of the autocorrelation. However, there are three important points to note:

1. If ρ is known, it is true that one can get estimators better than OLS that take account of autocorrelation. However, in practice ρ is not known and has to be estimated. In small samples it is not necessarily true that one gains (in terms of mean-square error for $\hat{\beta}$) by estimating ρ. This problem has been investigated by Rao and Griliches,[14] who suggest the rule of thumb (for samples of size 20) that one can use the methods that take account of autocorrelation if $|\hat{\rho}| \geq .3$, where $\hat{\rho}$ is the estimated first-order serial correlation from an OLS regression.[15] In samples of larger sizes it would be worthwhile using these methods for $\hat{\rho}$ smaller than 0.3.
2. The discussion above assumes that the true errors are first-order autoregressive. If they have a more complicated structure (e.g., second-order autoregressive), it might be thought that it would still be better to proceed on the assumption that the errors are first-order autoregressive rather than ignore the problem completely and use the OLS method. Engle[16] shows that this is not necessarily true (i.e., sometimes one can be worse off making the assumption of first-order autocorrelation than ignoring the problem completely).
3. In regressions with quarterly (or monthly) data, one might find that the errors exhibit fourth (or twelfth)-order autocorrelation because of not making adequate allowance for seasonal effects. In such cases if one looks for only first-order autocorrelation, one might not find any. This does not mean that autocorrelation is not a problem. In this case the appropriate specification for the error term may be $u_t = \rho u_{t-4} + e_t$ for quarterly data and $u_t = \rho u_{t-12} + e_t$ for monthly data.

---

[14] P. Rao and Z. Griliches, "Some Small Sample Properties of Several Two-Stage Regression Methods in the Context of Autocorrelated Errors," *Journal of the American Statistical Association*, March 1969.

[15] Of course, it is not sufficient to argue in favor of OLS on the basis of mean-square errors of the estimators alone. What is also relevant is how seriously the sampling variances are biased.

[16] Robert F. Engle, "Specification of the Disturbance for Efficient Estimation," *Econometrica*, 1973.

4. Finally, and most important, it is often possible to confuse misspecified dynamics with serial correlation in the errors. For instance, a static regression model with first-order autocorrelation in the errors, that is, $y_t = \beta x_t + u_t$, $u_t = \rho u_{t-1} + e_t$, can be written as

$$y_t = \rho y_{t-1} + \beta x_t - \beta \rho x_{t-1} + e_t \tag{6.11}$$

This model is the same as

$$y_t = \alpha_1 y_{t-1} + \alpha_2 x_t + \alpha_3 x_{t-1} + e_t \tag{6.11'}$$

with the restriction $\alpha_1 \alpha_2 + \alpha_3 = 0$. We can estimate the model (6.11′) and test this restriction. If it is rejected, clearly it is not valid to estimate (6.11). (The test procedure is described in Section 6.8).

The errors would be serially correlated but not because the errors follow a first-order autoregressive process but because the terms x_{t-1} and y_{t-1} have been omitted. This is what is meant by "misspecified dynamics." Thus a significant serial correlation in the estimated residuals does not necessarily imply that we should estimate a serial correlation model. Some further tests are necessary (like the restriction $\alpha_1 \alpha_2 + \alpha_3 = 0$ in the above-mentioned case). In fact, it is always best to start with an equation like (6.11′) and test this restriction before applying any tests for serial correlation.

6.6 SOME FURTHER COMMENTS ON THE DW TEST

In Section 6.2 we discussed the Durbin–Watson test for first-order autocorrelation which is based on least-squares residuals. There are two other tests that are also commonly used to test first-order autocorrelation. These are

1. The von Neumann ratio.
2. The Berenblut–Webb test.

We will briefly describe what they are:

The Von Neumann Ratio

The von Neumann ratio[17] is defined as

$$\frac{\delta^2}{s^2} = \frac{\sum\limits_{t=2}^{n} (e_t - e_{t-1})^2/(n-1)}{\sum\limits_{t=1}^{n} (e_t - \bar{e})^2/n}$$

where e_t are the residuals. The von Neumann ratio can be used only when e_t are

[17] J. von Neumann, "Distribution of the Ratio of the Mean Square Successive Difference to the Variance," *Annals of Mathematical Statistics*, 1941, pp. 367–395.

independent (under the null hypothesis) and have a common variance. The least squares residuals $\hat{u}_t$ do not satisfy these conditions and hence one cannot use the von Neumann ratio with least squares residuals.

During recent years there are a large number of alternative residuals that have been suggested for the linear regression model. Many of these residuals, particularly the "recursive residuals," satisfy the properties that they are independent and have a common variance. These different types of residuals are useful for diagnostic checking of the regression model and are discussed in Chapter 12. The recursive residuals, in particular, can easily be computed. Since they are independent and have a common variance, one can use them to compute the von Neumann ratio, as suggested by Phillips and Harvey.[18]

For large samples δ^2/s^2 can be taken as normally distributed with mean and variance given by

$$E\left(\frac{\delta^2}{s^2}\right) = \frac{2n}{n-1}$$

$$V\left(\frac{\delta^2}{s^2}\right) = \frac{4n^2(n-2)}{(n+1)(n-1)^3}$$

For finite samples one can use the tables prepared by G. I. Hart, published in *Annals of Mathematical Statistics*, 1962, pp. 207–214.

There are many other residuals suggested in the literature for the purpose of testing serial correlation. These are the Durbin residuals, Sims' residuals, and so on. But all these are more complicated to compute. The recursive residuals, which are useful for analysis of stability of the regression relationships and are easy to compute, can be used for tests for serail correlation in case the Durbin–Watson test is inconclusive.

The Berenblut–Webb Test

The Berenblut–Webb test[19] is based on the statistic

$$g = \frac{\sum\limits_{t=2}^{n} \hat{e}_t^2}{\sum\limits_{t=1}^{n} \hat{u}_t^2}$$

where $\hat{e}_t$ are the estimated residuals from a regression of first difference of y on first differences of the explanatory variables (with no constant term). If the original equation contains a constant term, we can use the Durbin–Watson tables on bounds with the g-statistic. The g-statistic is useful when values of $|\rho| \geq 1$ are possible.

[18] G. D. A. Phillips and A. C. Harvey, "A Simple Test for Serial Correlation in Regression Analysis," *Journal of the American Statistical Association*, December 1974, pp. 935–939.

[19] I. I. Berenblut and G. I. Webb, "A New Test for Autocorrelated Errors in the Linear Regression Model," *Journal of the Royal Statistical Society*, Series B, Vol. 35, 1973, pp. 33–50.

The literature on the DW test and the problem of testing for autocorrelation is enormous. We will summarize a few of the important conclusions:

A. Since the DW statistic is usually printed out from almost all computer programs, and the tables for its use are readily available, one should use this test with least squares residuals. However, with most economic data it is better to use the upper bound as the true significance point (i.e., treat the inconclusive region as a rejection region). For instance, with $n = 25$ and the number of explanatory variables 4, we have $d_L = 1.04$ and $d_U = 1.77$ as the 5% level significance points. Thus if the computed DW statistic is $d = 1.5$, we would normally say that the test is inconclusive at the 5% level. Treating d_U as the 5% significance point, we would reject the null hypothesis $\rho = 0$ at the 5% level. If more accuracy is required when d is in the inconclusive region, there are a number of alternatives suggested but all are computationally burdensome. The whole idea of testing for serial correlation is that if we do not reject the hypothesis $\rho = 0$, we can stay with OLS and avoid excessive computational burden. Thus trying to use all these other tests is more burdensome than estimating the model assuming $\rho \neq 0$. If we generate the recursive residuals for some other purposes, we can apply the von Neumann ratio test using these residuals. Also, if we are estimating the first difference equation, we can use the Berenblut–Webb test as well, without any extra computational burden.

B. There are many tables other than those reprinted at the end of this book for the DW test that have been prepared to take care of special situations. Some of these are:

1. R. W. Farebrother in *Econometrica*, Vol. 48, September 1980, pp. 1553–1563, gives tables for regression models with no intercept term.
2. N. E. Savin and K. J. White, in *Econometrica*, Vol. 45, No. 8, November 1977, pp. 1989–1996, present tables for the DW test for samples with 6 to 200 observations and for as many as 20 regressors.
3. K. F. Wallis in *Econometrica*, Vol. 40, 1972, pp. 617–636, gives tables for regression models with quarterly data. Here one would like to test for fourth-order autocorrelation rather than first-order autocorrelation. In this case the DW statistic is

$$d_4 = \frac{\sum\limits_{t=5}^{n} (\hat{u}_t - \hat{u}_{t-4})^2}{\sum\limits_{t=1}^{n} \hat{u}_t^2}$$

Wallis provides 5% critical values d_L and d_U for two situations: where the k regressors include an intercept (but not a full set of seasonal dummy variables) and another where the regressors include four quarterly seasonal dummy variables. In each case the critical values are for testing H_0: $\rho = 0$ against H_1: $\rho > 0$. For the hypothesis H_1: $\rho < 0$ Wallis suggests that the appropriate critical values are $(4 - d_U)$ and $(4 - d_L)$. M. L. King and D. E. A. Giles in *Journal of Econometrics*, Vol. 8, 1978, pp. 255–260, give further significance points for Wallis's test.
4. M. L. King in *Econometrica*, Vol. 49, November 1981, pp. 1571–1581, gives the

5% points for d_L and d_U for quarterly time-series data with trend and/or seasonal dummy variables. These tables are for testing first-order autocorrelation.

5. M. L. King in *Journal of Econometrics*, Vol. 21, 1983, pp. 357–366, gives tables for the DW test for monthly data. In the case of monthly data we would want to test for twelfth-order autocorrelation.

C. All the elaborate tables mentioned in B have been prepared for 5% level of significance (and 1% level of significance) and a question arises as to what the appropriate level of significance is for the DW test. Given that the test for serial correlation is a prelude to further estimation and not an end in itself, the theory of pretest estimation suggests that a significance level of, say, 0.35 or 0.4 is more appropriate than the conventional 0.05 significance level. [20]

D. A significant DW statistic can arise from a lot of different sources. The DW statistic can detect moving average errors, AR(2) errors, or just the effect of omitted variables that are themselves autocorrelated. This raises the question of what the appropriate strategy should be when the DW statistic is significant. It does not necessarily imply that the errors are AR(1). One can proceed in different directions. The different strategies are discussed in Section 6.9.

Finally, the DW test is not applicable if the explanatory variables contain lagged dependent variables. The appropriate tests are discussed in the next section.

6.7 TESTS FOR SERIAL CORRELATION IN MODELS WITH LAGGED DEPENDENT VARIABLES

In previous sections we considered explanatory variables that were uncorrelated with the error term. This will not be the case if we have lagged dependent variables among the explanatory variables and we have serially correlated errors. There are several situations under which we would be considering lagged dependent variables as explanatory variables. These could arise through expectations, adjustment lags, and so on. The various situations and models are explained in Chapter 10. For the present we will not be concerned with how the models arise. We will merely study the problem of testing for autocorrelation in these models.

Let us consider a simple model

$$y_t = \alpha y_{t-1} + \beta x_t + u_t \tag{6.12}$$

$$u_t = \rho u_{t-1} + e_t \tag{6.13}$$

e_t are independent with mean 0 and variance σ^2 and $|\alpha| < 1$, $|\rho| < 1$. Because u_t

---

[20] See, for instance, T. B. Fomby and D. K. Guilkey, "On Choosing the Optimal Level of Significance for the Durbin–Watson Test and a Bayesian Alternative," *Journal of Econometrics*, Vol. 8, 1978, pp. 203–214.

depends on u_{t-1} and y_{t-1} depends on u_{t-1}, the two variables y_{t-1} and u_t will be correlated. The least squares estimator $\hat{\alpha}$ will be inconsistent. It can be shown that [21]

$$\text{plim } \hat{\alpha} = \alpha + A$$

and

$$\text{plim } \hat{\rho} = \rho - A$$

where

$$A = \frac{\rho \sigma_x^2 \sigma_u^2}{(1 - \alpha\rho)D}$$

$$D = \text{var}(y_{-1})\text{var}(x) - \text{cov}^2(y_{-1}, x) > 0$$

$$\sigma_x^2 = \text{var}(x) \qquad \sigma_u^2 = \text{var}(u)$$

Thus if ρ is positive, the estimate of α is biased upward and the estimate of ρ is biased downward. Hence the DW statistic, which is $\simeq (2(1 - \hat{\rho})$, is biased toward 2 and we would not find any significant serial correlation even if the errors are serially correlated.

Durbin's h-Test

Since the DW test is not applicable in these models, Durbin suggests an alternative test, called the h-test. [22] This test uses

$$h = \hat{\rho}\sqrt{\frac{n}{1 - n\hat{V}(\hat{\alpha})}}$$

as a standard normal variable. Here the $\hat{\rho}$ is the estimated first-order serial correlation from the OLS residuals $\hat{V}(\hat{\alpha})$ is the estimated variance of the OLS estimate of α, and n is the sample size. If $n\hat{V}(\hat{\alpha}) > 1$, the test is not applicable. In this case Durbin suggests the following test:

Durbin's Alternative Test

From the OLS estimation of (6.12) compute the residuals $\hat{u}_t$. Then regress $\hat{u}_t$ on $\hat{u}_{t-1}$, y_{t-1}, and x_t. The test for $\rho = 0$ is carried out by testing the significance of the coefficient of $\hat{u}_{t-1}$ in the latter regression.

---

[21] The proofs are somewhat long and are omitted. For a first-order autoregressive x, they can be found in G. S. Maddala and A. S. Rao, "Tests for Serial Correlation in Regression Models with Lagged Dependent Variables and Serially Correlated Errors," *Econometrica*, Vol. 47, No. 4, July 1973, App. A, pp. 761–774.
[22] J. Durbin, "Testing for Serial Correlation in Least Squares Regression When Some of the Regressors Are Lagged Dependent Variables," *Econometrica*, 1970, pp. 410–421.

Illustrative Example

An equation of demand for food estimated from 50 observations gave the following results.

$$\log q_t = \text{const.} - \underset{(0.05)}{0.31} \log P_t + \underset{(0.20)}{0.45} \log y_t + \underset{(0.14)}{0.65} \log q_{t-1}$$

$$R^2 = 0.90 \qquad DW = 1.8$$

(Figures in parentheses are standard errors.)

q_t = food consumption per capita

p_t = food price (retail price deflated by the Consumer Price Index)

y_t = per capita disposable income deflated by the Consumer Price Index

We have

$$\hat{\alpha} = 0.65 \qquad \hat{V}(\hat{\alpha}) = (0.14)^2 = 0.0196$$

$$\hat{\rho} = 0.1 \qquad \text{since } DW \simeq 2(1 - \hat{\rho})$$

Hence Durbin's h-statistic is

$$h = 0.1 \sqrt{\frac{50}{1 - 50(0.0196)}} = 5.0$$

This is significant at the 1% level. Thus we reject the hypothesis $\rho = 0$, even though the DW statistic is close to 2 and the estimate $\hat{\rho}$ from the OLS residuals is only 0.1.

Let us keep all the numbers the same and just change the standard error of $\hat{\alpha}$. The following are the results:

$SE(\hat{\alpha})$	$\hat{V}(\hat{\alpha})$	$1 - n\hat{V}(\hat{\alpha})$	h	Conclusion
0.13	0.0169	0.155	1.80	Not significant at the 5% level
0.15	0.0225	−0.125		Test not defined

Thus, other things equal, the precision with which $\hat{\alpha}$ is estimated has significant effect on the outcome of the h-test.

In the case where the h-test cannot be used, we can use the alternative test suggested by Durbin. However, the Monte Carlo study by Maddala and Rao[23] suggests that this test does not have good power in those cases where the h-test cannot be used. On the other hand, in cases where the h-test can be used, Durbin's second test is almost as powerful. It is not often used because it involves more computations. However, we will show that Durbin's second test can be generalized to higher-order autoregressions, whereas the h-test cannot be.

---

[23] Maddala and Rao, "Tests for Serial Correlation."

6.8 A GENERAL TEST FOR HIGHER-ORDER SERIAL CORRELATION: THE LM TEST

The h-test we have discussed is, like the Durbin–Watson test, a test for first-order autoregression. Breusch[24] and Godfrey[25] discuss some general tests that are easy to apply and are valid for very general hypotheses about the serial correlation in the errors. These tests are derived from a general principle—called the Lagrange multiplier (LM) principle. A discussion of this principle is beyond the scope of this book. For the present we will explain what the test is. The test is similar to Durbin's second test that we have discussed.

Consider the regression model

$$y_t = \sum_{i=1}^{k} x_{it}\beta_i + u_t \qquad t = 1, 2, \ldots, n \qquad (6.14)$$

and

$$u_t = \rho_1 u_{t-1} + \rho_2 u_{t-2} + \cdots + \rho_p u_{t-p} + \varepsilon_t \qquad (6.15)$$

$$\varepsilon_t \sim \text{IN}(0, \sigma^2)$$

We are interested in testing H_0: $\rho_1 = \rho_2 = \cdots = \rho_p = 0$. The x's in equation (6.14) include lagged dependent variables as well. The LM test is as follows:

First, estimate (6.14) by OLS and obtain the least squares residuals $\hat{u}_t$. Next, estimate the regression equation

$$\hat{u}_t = \sum_{i=1}^{k} x_{it}\gamma_i + \sum_{i=1}^{p} \hat{u}_{t-i}\rho_i + \eta_t \qquad (6.16)$$

and test whether the coefficients of $\hat{u}_{t-i}$ are all zero. We take the conventional F-statistic and use $p \cdot F$ as χ^2 with degrees of freedom p. We use the χ^2-test rather than the F-test because the LM test is a large sample test.

The test can be used for different specifications of the error process. For instance, for the problem of testing for fourth-order autocorrelation

$$u_t = \rho_4 u_{t-4} + e_t \qquad (6.17)$$

we just estimate

$$\hat{u}_t = \sum_{i=1}^{k} x_{it}\gamma_i + \rho_4 \hat{u}_{t-4} + \eta_t \qquad (6.18)$$

instead of (6.16) and test $\rho_4 = 0$.

The test procedure is the same for autoregressive or moving average errors. For

---

[24] T. S. Breusch, "Testing for Autocorrelation in Dynamic Linear Models," *Australian Economic Papers*, Vol. 17, 1978, pp. 334–355.

[25] L. G. Godfrey, "Testing for Higher Order Serial Correlation in Regression Equations When the Regressors Include Lagged Dependent Variables," *Econometrica*, Vol. 46, 1978, pp. 1303–1310.

instance, if we have a moving average (MA) error

$$u_t = e_t + \rho_4 e_{t-4}$$

instead of (6.17), the test procedure is still to estimate (6.18) and test $\rho_4 = 0$.
Consider the following types of errors:

$$\text{AR(2):} \quad u_t = \rho_1 u_{t-1} + \rho_2 u_{t-2} + e_t$$

$$\text{MA(2):} \quad u_t = e_t + \rho_1 e_{t-1} + \rho_2 e_{t-2}$$

$$\text{AR(2) with interaction:} \quad u_t = \rho_1 u_{t-1} + \rho_2 u_{t-2} - \rho_1 \rho_2 u_{t-3} + e_t$$

In all these cases, we just test H_0 by estimating equation (6.16) with $p = 2$ and test
$\rho_1 = \rho_2 = 0$. What is of importance is the degree of autoregression, not the nature.
Finally, an alternative to the estimation of (6.16) is to estimate the equation

$$y_t = \sum_{i=1}^{k} x_{it} \beta_i + \sum_{i=1}^{p} \hat{u}_{t-1} \rho_i + \eta_t \tag{6.19}$$

Thus the LM test for serial correlation is:

1. Estimate equation (6.14) by OLS and get the residuals $\hat{u}_t$.
2. Estimate equation (6.16) or (6.19) by OLS and compute the F-statistic for
   testing the hypothesis H_0: $\rho_1 = \rho_0 = \cdots = \rho_p = 0$.
3. Use $p \cdot F$ as χ^2 with p degrees of freedom.

6.9 STRATEGIES WHEN THE DW TEST STATISTIC IS SIGNIFICANT

The DW test is designed as a test for the hypothesis $\rho = 0$ if the errors follow a first-
order autoregressive process $u_t = \rho u_{t-1} + e_t$. However, the test has been found to be
robust against other alternatives such as AR(2), MA(1), ARMA(1, 1), and so on.
Further, and more disturbingly, it catches specification errors like omitted variables
that are themselves autocorrelated, and misspecified dynamics (a term that we will
explain). Thus the strategy to adopt, if the DW test statistic is significant, is not clear.
We discuss three different strategies.

1. Assume that the significant DW statistic is an indication of serial correlation
   but may not be due to AR(1) errors.
2. Test whether serial correlation is due to omitted variables.
3. Test whether serial correlation is due to misspecified dynamics.

Errors Not AR(1)

In case 1, if the DW statistic is significant, since it does not necessarily mean that
the errors are AR(1), we should check for higher-order autoregressions by estimating equations of the form

$$u_t = \rho_1 u_{t-1} + \rho_2 u_{t-2} + e_t$$

Once the order has been determined, we can estimate the model with the appropriate assumptions about the error structure by the methods described in Section 6.4. Actually, there are two ways of going about this problem of determining the appropriate order of the autoregression. The first is to progressively complicate the model by testing for higher-order autoregressions. The second is to start with an autoregression of sufficiently high order and progressively simplify it. Although the former approach is the one commonly used, the latter approach is better from the theoretical point of view.

One other question that remains is that of moving average errors and ARMA errors. Estimation with moving average errors and ARMA errors is more complicated than with AR errors. Moreover, Hendry[26] and Hendry and Trivedi[27] argue that it is the order of the error process that is more important than the particular form. Thus from the practical point of view, for most economic data, it is just sufficient to determine the order of the AR process. Thus if a significant DW statistic is observed, the appropriate strategy would be to try to see whether the errors are generated by a higher-order AR process than AR(1) and then undertake estimation.

Autocorrelation Caused by Omitted Variables

Case 2, serial correlation being caused by omitted variables, is rather difficult to tackle. It is often asserted that the source of serial correlation in the errors is that some variables that should have been included in the equation are omitted and that these omitted variables are themselves autocorrelated. However, if this is the argument for serial correlation, and it is an appealing one, one should be careful in suggesting the methods that we have discussed until now.

Suppose that the true regression equation is

$$y_t = \beta_0 + \beta_1 x_t + \beta_2 x_t^2 + u_t$$

and instead we estimate

$$y_t = \beta_0 + \beta_1 x_t + v_t \tag{6.20}$$

Then since $v_t = \beta_2 x_t^2 + u_t$, if x_t is autocorrelated, this will produce autocorrelation in v_t. However, v_t is no longer independent of x_t. Thus not only are the OLS estimators of β_0 and β_1 from (6.20) inefficient, they are inconsistent as well.

As yet another example, suppose that the true relation is

$$y_t = \beta_1 x_t + \beta_2 z_t + u_t \tag{6.21}$$

and we estimate

$$y_t = \beta_1 x_t + w_t \tag{6.22}$$

[26] D. F. Hendry, "Comments on the Papers by Granger–Newbold and Sargent–Sims," in *New Methods in Business Cycle Research* (Minneapolis: Federal Reserve Bank of Minneapolis, October 1977).
[27] D. F. Hendry and P. K. Trivedi, "Maximum Likelihood Estimation of Difference Equations with Moving Average Errors: A Simulation Study," *The Review of Economic Studies*, Vol. 39, April 1972, pp. 117–145.

Again, if z_t are autocorrelated, w_t will also be. But if z_t and x_t are independent, the methods we have discussed earlier are applicable. Thus, <u>to justify the methods of estimation we have discussed, we have to argue that the autocorrelated omitted variables that are producing the autocorrelation in the errors, are uncorrelated with the included explanatory variables.</u> Further, if there are any time trends in these omitted variables, they will produce not only autocorrelated errors but also heteroskedastic errors.

In equation (6.21) let us assume that the errors u_t are independent with a common variance σ^2. However, we estimate equation (6.22) and compute the DW statistic d. What can we say about it? Note that since the least squares residuals are always uncorrelated with the included variables (by virtue of the normal equations), the DW statistic d is determined not by the autocorrelation in z_t but the autocorrelation in z_t^*, which is that part of z_t left unexplained by x_t.

Consider a regression of z_t on x_t. Let the regression coefficient be denoted by b. Then $z_t = bx_t + z_t^*$, where z_t^* is the residual from a regression of z_t on x_t. Equation (6.21) can be written as

$$y_t = \beta_1 x_t + \beta_2 (bx_t + z_t^*) + u_t$$
$$= (\beta_1 + \beta_2 b)x_t + w_t \tag{6.23}$$

where $w_t = \beta_2 z_t^* + u_t$.

If we estimate (6.22) by OLS and $\hat{\beta}_1$ is the OLS estimator of β_1, then $E(\hat{\beta}_1) = \beta_1 + \beta_2 b$ and the residual $\hat{w}_t$ would be estimating $\beta_2 z_t^* + u_t$. Let $\text{var}(z_t^*) = \sigma_*^2$ and $\text{cov}(z_t^*, z_{t-1}^*) = \rho^* \sigma_*^2$. Then since $\text{cov}(z_t^*, u_t) = 0$ we have

$$\text{cov}(\beta_2 z_t^* + u_t, \beta_2 z_{t-1}^* + u_{t-1}) = \beta_2^2 \rho^* \sigma_*^2$$

and

$$\text{var}(\beta_2 z_t^* + u_t) = \beta_2^2 \sigma_*^2 + \sigma^2$$

The first order serial correlation in w_t would be [28]

$$\rho_w = \frac{\rho^*}{1 + \sigma^2/\beta_2^2 \sigma_*^2}$$

If d is the DW statistic from a OLS estimation of (6.21), then

$$\text{plim } d = 2(1 - \rho_w)$$

Note that the observed serial correlation depends on the serial correlation in z_t^*, not z_t (the omitted variable), *and* the variance ratio $\sigma^2/\beta_2^2 \sigma_*^2$. If this variance ratio is large, then, even if ρ^* is high, ρ_w can be small.

One can test for omitted variables using the RESET test of Ramsey or White's test outlined in Section 5.3. If the DW test statistic is significant but these tests also show significance, the appropriate strategy would be to estimate the model by some general procedure like the Cragg procedure described in Section 5.4 rather than use a transformation based on the estimated first-order autocorrelation.

---

[28] This formula has been derived in a more general case in M. Chaudhuri, "Autocorrelated Disturbances in the Light of Specification Analysis," *Journal of Econometrics*, Vol. 5, 1977, pp. 301–313.

Serial Correlation Due to Misspecified Dynamics

In a seminal paper published in 1964. Sargan [29] pointed out that a significant DW statistic does not necessarily imply that we have a serial correlation problem. This point was also emphasized by Hendry and Mizon. [30] The argument goes as follows. Consider

$$y_t = \beta x_t + u_t \quad \text{with} \quad u_t = \rho u_{t-1} + e_t \tag{6.24}$$

and e_t are independent with a common variance σ^2. We can write this model as

$$y_t = \rho y_{t-1} + \beta x_t - \beta \rho x_{t-1} + e_t \tag{6.25}$$

Consider an alternative stable dynamic model:

$$y_t = \beta_1 y_{t-1} + \beta_2 x_t + \beta_3 x_{t-1} + e_t \qquad |\beta_1| < 1 \tag{6.26}$$

Equation (6.25) is the same as equation (6.26) with the restriction

$$\beta_1 \beta_2 + \beta_3 = 0 \tag{6.27}$$

A test for $\rho = 0$ is a test for $\beta_1 = 0$ (and $\beta_3 = 0$). But before we test this, what Sargan says is that we should first test the restriction (6.27) and test for $\rho = 0$ only if the hypothesis H_0: $\beta_1 \beta_2 + \beta_3 = 0$ is not rejected. If this hypothesis is rejected, we do not have a serial correlation model and the serial correlation in the errors in (6.24) is due to "misspecified dynamics," that is, the omission of the variables y_{t-1} and x_{t-1} from the equation.

The restriction (6.27) is nonlinear in the β's and hence one has to use the Wald test or the LR or LM tests. If the DW test statistic is significant, a proper approach is to test the restriction (6.27) to make sure that what we have is a serial correlation model before we undertake any autoregressive transformations of the variables. In fact, Sargan suggests starting with the general model (6.26) and testing the restriction (6.27) first, before attempting any tests for serial correlation. [31]

In this case there is, in general, no exact t-test as in the case of linear restrictions. What we do is linearize the restriction by a Taylor series expansion and use what is known as a Wald test, which is an asymptotic test (or use the LR or LM tests).

The Wald Test

Define

$$f(\beta) = \beta_1 \beta_2 + \beta_3$$

[29] J. D. Sargan, "Wages and Prices in the United Kingdom: A Study in Econometric Methodology," in P. E. Hart, G. Mills, and J. K. Whitaker (eds.), *Econometric Analysis for National Economic Planning,* Colston Papers 16 (London: Butterworth, 1964), pp. 25–54.

[30] D. F. Hendry and G. E. Mizon, "Serial Correlation as a Convenient Simplification, Not a Nuisance: A Comment on a Study of the Demand for Money by the Bank of England," *The Economic Journal,* Vol. 88, September 1978, pp. 549–563.

[31] J. G. Thursby, "A Test Strategy for Discriminating Between Autocorrelation and Misspecification in Regression Analysis," *The Review of Economics and Statistics,* Vol. 63, 1981, pp. 117–123 considers the use of the DW, Ramsey's RESET, and Sargan's test together. This is useful for warning against autoregressive transformations based on the DW statistic but does not tell what the estimation strategy should be after the tests.

Using a first-order Taylor series expansion, we get

$$f(\hat{\beta}) = f(\beta) + \sum_{i=1}^{3} g_i(\hat{\beta}_i - \beta_i)$$

where $g_i = \partial f/\partial \beta_i$. Under the null hypothesis $f(\beta) = 0$ we have

$$E[f(\hat{\beta})] = 0 \qquad \text{since} \qquad E(\hat{\beta}_i) = \beta_i$$

and

$$\text{var}[f(\hat{\beta})] = \sigma^2 \left(\sum_i \sum_j g_i g_j C_{ij} \right) = \Psi^2 \quad \text{(say)}$$

since

$$\text{cov}(\hat{\beta}_i, \hat{\beta}_j) = \sigma^2 C_{ij}$$

The Wald test statistic is obtained by substituting $\hat{g}_i$ for g_i and $\hat{\sigma}^2$ for σ^2 in Ψ^2. Denoting the resulting expression by $\hat{\Psi}^2$, we get the statistic

$$W = \frac{[f(\hat{\beta})]^2}{\hat{\Psi}^2}$$

which has (asymptotically) a χ^2-distribution with 1 degree of freedom.

In the particular case we are considering, note that $g_1 = \beta_2, g_2 = \beta_1$, and $g_3 = 1$.

However, there are some problems with the Wald test. The restriction (6.27) can as well be written as

$$f_1(\beta) = \beta_1 + \frac{\beta_3}{\beta_2} = 0 \tag{6.28}$$

or

$$f_2(\beta) = \beta_2 + \frac{\beta_3}{\beta_1} = 0 \tag{6.28'}$$

If we write it as (6.28), we have

$$g_1 = 1 \qquad g_2 = -\frac{\beta_3}{\beta_2^2} \qquad g_3 = \frac{1}{\beta_2}$$

and if we write it as (6.28') we have

$$g_1 = -\frac{\beta_3}{\beta_1^2} \qquad g_2 = 1 \qquad g_3 = \frac{1}{\beta_1}$$

Although, asymptotically, it should not matter how the Wald test is constructed, in practice it has been found that the results differ depending on how we formulate the restrictions.[32] However, formulations (6.28) and (6.28') implicitly assume that $\beta_2 \neq 0$ or $\beta_1 \neq 0$, respectively, and thus in this case it is more meaningful to use the restriction in the form (6.27) rather than (6.28) or (6.28').

---

[32] A. W. Gregory and M. R. Veall, "On Formulating Wald Tests of Non-linear Restrictions," *Econometrica*, November 1985. The authors confirm by Monte Carlo studies and an empirical example that these differences can be substantial. See also A. W. Gregory and M. R. Veall, "Wald Tests of Common Factor Restrictions," *Economics Letters* 22(1986), pp. 203–208.

Note that a hypothesis like $\beta_1/\beta_2 = C$ can be transformed into a linear hypothesis $\beta_1 - C\beta_2 = 0$. Similarly, $\beta_1/(1 - \beta_2) = C$ can be transformed to $\beta_1 + C\beta_2 - C = 0$. On the other hand, if, for some reason, an exact confidence interval was also needed for β_1/β_2, we can use Feiller's method described in Section 3.10. Noting the relationship between confidence intervals and tests of hypotheses, one can construct a test for the hypothesis $\beta_1/\beta_2 = C$.

Illustrative Example

Consider the data in Table 4.7 and the estimation of the production function (4.25). In Section 6.4 we presented estimates of the equation assuming that the errors are AR(1). This was based on a DW test statistic of 0.86.

Suppose that we estimate an equation of the form (6.26). The results are as follows (all variables in logs; figures in parentheses are standard errors):

$$X_t = -2.254 + 0.884 L_t + 0.710 K_t + 0.489 X_{t-1}$$
$$(0.530) \quad (0.139) \quad (0.152) \quad (0.120)$$

$$-0.073 L_{t-1} - 0.541 K_{t-1} \qquad \text{RSS}_0 = 0.01718$$
$$(0.252) \qquad (0.150)$$

Under the assumption that the errors are AR(1), the residual sum of squares, obtained from the Hildreth–Lu procedure we used in Section 6.4 is: $\text{RSS}_1 = 0.02635$.

Since we have two slope coefficients, we have two restrictions of the form (6.27). Note that for the general dynamic model we are estimating six parameters (α and five β's). For the serial correlation model we are estimating four parameters (α, two β's, and ρ). We will use the likelihood ratio test (LR), which is based on (see the appendix to Chapter 3)

$$\lambda = \left(\frac{\text{RSS}_0}{\text{RSS}_1}\right)^{n/2}$$

and $-2\log_e\lambda$ has a χ^2-distribution with d.f. 2 (number of restrictions). In our example

$$-2\log_e\lambda = -39\log_e\left(\frac{0.01718}{0.02635}\right) = 16.7$$

which is significant at the 1% level. Thus the hypothesis of a first-order autocorrelation is rejected. Although the DW statistic is significant, this does not mean that the errors are AR(1).

*6.10 TRENDS AND RANDOM WALKS

Throughout our discussion we have assumed that

$$E(u_t) = 0 \text{ and } \text{var}(u_t) = \sigma^2 \text{ for all } t, \text{ and}$$

$$\text{cov}(u_t, u_{t-k}) = \sigma^2 \rho_k \text{ for all } t \text{ and } k$$

where ρ_k is serial correlation of lag k (this is simply a function of the lag k and does not depend on t). If these assumptions are satisfied, the series u_t is called *covariance stationary* (covariances are constant over time) or just *stationary*. Many economic time series are clearly nonstationary in the sense that the mean and variance depend on time, and they tend to depart ever further from any given value as time goes on. If this movement is predominantly in one direction (up or down) we say that the series exhibits a *trend*.

Nonstationary time-series are frequently de-trended before further analysis is done. There are two procedures used for de-trending.

1. Estimating regressions on time.
2. Successive differencing.

In the regression approach it is assumed that the series y_t is generated by the mechanism

$$y_t = f(t) + u_t$$

where $f(t)$ is the trend and u_t is a stationary series with mean zero and variance σ_u^2. Let us suppose that $f(t)$ is linear so that we have

$$y_t = \alpha + \beta t + u_t \tag{6.29}$$

Note that the trend-eliminated series is $\hat{u}_t$ the least squares residuals, that satisfy the relationship $\sum \hat{u}_t = 0$ and $\sum t\hat{u}_t = 0$. If differencing is used to eliminate the trend we get $\Delta y_t = y_t - y_{t-1} = \beta + u_t - u_{t-1}$. We have to take a first difference again to eliminate β and we get $\Delta^2 y_t = \Delta^2 u_t = u_t - 2u_{t-1} + u_{t-2}$ as the de-trended series.

On the other hand, suppose we assume that y_t is generated by the model

$$y_t - y_{t-1} = \beta + \varepsilon_t \tag{6.30}$$

where ε_t is a stationary series with mean zero and variance σ^2. In this case the first difference of y_t is stationary with mean β. This model is also known as the *random-walk model*. Accumulating y_t starting with an initial value y_0 we get from (6.30)

$$y_t = y_0 + \beta t + \sum_{j=1}^{t} \varepsilon_j \tag{6.31}$$

which has the same form as (6.29) except for the fact that the disturbance is not stationary, it has variance $t\sigma^2$ that increases over time. Nelson and Plosser[33] call the model (6.29) *trend-stationary processes* (TSP) and model (6.30) *difference-stationary processes* (DSP). Both the models exhibit a linear trend. But the appropriate method of eliminating the trend differs. To test the hypothesis that a time-series belongs to the TSP class against the alternative that it belongs to the DSP class, Nelson and Plosser use a test developed by Dickey and Fuller.[34] This consists of estimating the model

$$y_t = \alpha + \rho y_{t-1} + \beta t + \varepsilon_t \tag{6.32}$$

which belongs to the DSP class if $\rho = 1$, $\beta = 0$ and the TSP class if $|\rho| < 1$. Thus, we

[33] C. R. Nelson and C. I. Plosser, "Trends and Random Walks in Macroeconomic Time Series: Some Evidence and Implications," *Journal of Monetary Economics*, Vol. 10, 1982, pp. 139–162.
[34] D. A. Dickey and W. A. Fuller, "Distribution of the Estimators for Autoregressive Time-Series With a Unit Root," *Journal of the American Statistical Association*, Vol. 74, 1979, pp. 427–431.

have to test the hypothesis $\rho = 1$, $\beta = 0$ against $|\rho| < 1$. The problem here is that we cannot use the usual least squares distribution theory when $\rho = 1$. Dickey and Fuller show that the least squares estimate of ρ is not distributed around unity under the DSP hypothesis (that is, the true value $\rho = 1$) but rather around a value less than one. However, the negative bias diminishes as the number of observations increases. They tabulate the significance points for testing the hypothesis $\rho = 1$ against $|\rho| < 1$. Nelson and Plosser applied the Dickey–Fuller test to a wide range of historical time series for the U.S. economy and found that the DSP hypothesis was accepted in all cases, with the exception of the unemployment rate. They conclude that for most economic time series the DSP model is more appropriate, and that the TSP model would be the relevant one only if we assume that the errors u_t in (6.29) are highly autocorrelated.

The problem of testing the hypothesis $\rho = 1$ in the first order autoregressive equation of the form

$$y_t = \alpha + \rho y_{t-1} + u_t$$

is called "testing for unit roots." There is an enormous literature on this problem but one of the most commonly used tests is the Dickey–Fuller test. The standard expression for the large sample variance of the least squares estimator $\hat{\rho}$ is $(1 - p^2)/T$ which would be zero under the null hypothesis. Hence, one needs to derive the limiting distributon of $\hat{\rho}$ under H_0, $\rho = 1$ to apply the test.

For testing the hypothesis $\rho = 1$, $\beta = 0$ in (6.32) Dickey and Fuller[35] suggest a LR test, derive the limiting distribution and present tables for the test. The F-values are much higher than those in the usual F-tables. For instance, the 5% significance values from the tables presented in Dickey and Fuller, and the corresponding F-values from the standard F-tables (when the numerator d.f. is 2 as in this test) are as follows:

Sample Size n	F-ratio from Dickey-Fuller	F-ratios from Standard F-tables[a]
25	7.24	3.42
50	6.73	3.20
100	6.49	3.10
∞	6.25	3.00

[a] d.f. for denominator $= n - 3$.

As an illustration consider the example given by Dickey and Fuller.[36] For the logarithm of the quarterly Federal Reserve Board Production Index 1950–1 through 1977–4 they assume that the time-series is adequately represented by the model:

$$y_t = \beta_0 + \beta_1 t + \alpha_1 y_{t-1} + \alpha_2 (y_{t-1} - y_{t-2}) + e_t \tag{6.33}$$

where e_t are independent identically distributed $(0, \sigma^2)$ random variables. The

[35] D. A. Dickey and W. A. Fuller, "Likelihood Ratio Statistics for Autoregressive Time Series With a Unit Root," *Econometrica*, Vol. 49, No. 4, 1981, pp. 1057–1072. See Tables on p. 1063.
[36] Dickey and Fuller (1981), op. cit., p. 1070–1071.

ordinary least squares estimates are:

$$y_t - y_{t-1} = \underset{(0.15)}{0.52} + \underset{(0.00034)}{0.00120t} - \underset{(0.033)}{0.119y_{t-1}} + \underset{(0.081)}{0.498(y_{t-1} - y_{t-2})}$$

$$\text{RSS} = 0.056448$$

$$y_t - y_{t-1} = \underset{(0.0025)}{0.0054} + \underset{(0.083)}{0.447(y_{t-1} - y_{t-2})}$$

$$\text{RSS} = 0.063211$$

where RSS denotes the residual sum of squares and the numbers in parentheses are the "standard errors" as output from the usual regression program.

The F-test for the hypothesis $\beta_1 = 0$, $\alpha_1 = 1$ is

$$F = \frac{(0.063211 - 0.056448)/2}{0.056448/106} = 6.34$$

If we use the standard F-tables this F-ratio is significant at even the 1% significance level. But the F-ratio tabulated by Dickey and Fuller is 6.49 for the 5% significance level. Thus, the hypothesis that the second order autoregressive process (6.33) has a unit root is accepted at the 5% significance level, though it is rejected at the 10% significance level.

Spurious Trends

If $\beta = 0$ in equation (6.30) the model is called a trendless random walk or a random walk with zero drift. However, from equation (6.31) note that even though there is no trend in the mean, there is a trend in the variance. Suppose that the true model is of the DSP true with $\beta = 0$. What happens if we estimated a TSP type model? That is, the type model is one with no trend in the mean but only a trend in the variance, and we estimate a model with a trend in the mean but no trend in the variance. It is intuitively clear that the trend in the variance will be transmitted to the mean and we will find a significant coefficient for t even though in reality there is no trend in the mean. How serious is this problem? Nelson and Kang [37] analyze this. They conclude that:

1. Regression of a random walk on time by least squares will produce R^2 values of around 0.44 regardless of sample size when, in fact, the mean of the variable has no relationship with time whatsoever.
2. In the case of random walks with drift, that is $\beta \neq 0$, the R^2 will be higher and will increase with the sample size, reaching one in the limit regardless of the value of β.
3. The residual from the regression on time which we take as the de-trended series, has on the average only about 14 percent of the true stochastic variance of the original series.

---

[37] C. R. Nelson and H. Kang, "Pitfalls in the Use of Time as an Explanatory Variable in Regression," *Journal of Business and Economic Statistics*, Vol. 2, January 1984, pp. 73–82.

4. The residuals from the regression on time are also autocorrelated being roughly $(1 - 10/N)$ at lag one, where N is the sample size.
5. Conventional t-tests to test the significance of some of the regressors are not valid. They tend to reject the null hypothesis of no dependence on time, with very high frequency.
6. Regression of one random walk on another, with time included for trend, is strongly subject to the spurious regression phenomenon. That is, the conventional t-test will tend to indicate a relationship between the variables when none is present.

The main conclusion is that using a regression on time has serious consequences when, in fact, the time series is of the DSP type and, hence, differencing is the appropriate procedure for trend-elimination. Plosser and Schwert [38] also argue that with most economic time series it is always best to work with differenced data rather than data in levels. The reason is that if indeed the data series are of the DSP type, the errors in the levels equation will have variances increasing over time. Under these circumstances many of the properties of least squares estimators as well as tests of significance are invalid. On the other hand, suppose that the levels equation is correctly specified. Then all differencing will do is produce a moving average error and at worst ignoring it will give inefficient estimates. For instance, suppose that we have the model

$$y_t = \alpha + \beta x_t + \gamma t + u_t$$

where u_t are independent with mean zero and common variance σ^2. If we difference this equation, we get

$$\Delta y_t = \beta \cdot \Delta x_t + \gamma + v_t$$

where the error $v_t = \Delta u_t = u_t - u_{t-1}$ is a moving average, and, hence, not serially independent. But estimating the first difference equation by least squares still gives us consistent estimates. Thus, the consequences of differencing when it is not needed are much less serious than those of failing to difference when it is appropriate (when the true model is of the DSP type).

In practice, it is best to use the Dickey-Fuller test to check whether the data are of DSP or TSP type. Otherwise, it is better to use differencing and regressions in first differences, rather than regressions in levels with time as an extra explanatory variable.

Differencing and Long-run Effects: The Concept of Co-integration

One drawback of the procedure of differencing is that it results in a loss of valuable "long-run information" in the data. Recently, the concept of co-integrated series has been suggested as one solution to this problem. [39] First, we need to define the term

[38] C. I. Plosser and G. W. Schwert, "Money, Income and Sunspots: Measuring Economic Relationships and the Effects of Differencing," *Journal of Monetary Economics*, Vol. 4, (1978) pp. 637–660.

[39] A reference which is, however, quite technical for our purpose, is: R. F. Engle and C. W. J. Granger, "Co-Integration and Error Correction: Representation, Estimation and Testing," *Econometrica*, March 1987, Vol. 55, pp. 251–276.

"co-integration." Though we do not need the assumption of normality, we will define the terms under this assumption.

If ε_t are $IN(0, \sigma^2)$ we say ε_t are I(0) that is, integrated of order zero.

If y_t follow a random walk model, that is,

$$y_t = y_{t-1} + \varepsilon_t$$

then we get by successive substitution,

$$y_t = \sum_{j=0}^{t-1} \varepsilon_{t-j} \qquad \text{if } y_0 = 0.$$

Thus, y_t is a summation of ε_j, and

$$\Delta y_t = \varepsilon_t$$

which is I(0). We say in this case that y_t is I(1) [integrated to order one]. If y_t is I(1) and we add to this z_t which is I(0), then $y_t + z_t$ will be I(1). When we specify regression models in time series, we have to make sure that the different variables are integrated to the same degree. Otherwise, the equation does not make sense. For instance, if we specify the regression model:

$$y_t = \beta x_t + u_t \tag{6.34}$$

and we say that $u_t \sim IN(0, \sigma^2)$, that is u_t is I(0), we have to make sure that y_t and x_t are integrated to the same order. For instance, if y_t is I(1) and x_t is I(0) there will not be any β that will satisfy the relationship (6.34). Suppose y_t is I(1) and x_t is I(1); then if there is a nonzero β such that $y_t - \beta x_t$ is I(0) then y_t and x_t are said to be *co-integrated*.

Suppose that y_t and x_t are both random walks, so that they are both I(1). Then an equation in first differences of the form

$$\Delta y_t = \alpha \Delta x_t + \lambda(y_t - \beta x_t) + v_t \tag{6.35}$$

is a valid equation. Since Δy_t, Δx_t, $(y_t - \beta x_t)$ and v_t are all I(0). Equation (6.34) is considered a long-run relationship between y_t and x_t and equation (6.35) describes short-run dynamics. Engle and Granger suggest estimating (6.34) by ordinary least squares, obtaining the estimator $\hat{\beta}$ of β and substituting it in equation (6.35) to estimate the parameters α and λ. This two-step estimation, procedure, however, rests on the assumption that y_t and x_t are co-integrated. It is, therefore, important to test for co-integration. Engle and Granger suggest estimating (6.34) by ordinary least squares, getting the residual $\hat{u}_t$ and then applying the Dickey-Fuller test (or some other test [40]) based on $\hat{u}_t$. What this test amounts to is testing the hypothesis $\rho = 1$ in

$$u_t = \rho u_{t-1} + e_t$$

[40] Since $\hat{u}_t$ are estimated residuals, the Dickey–Fuller tables have to be adjusted. An alternative test that is also often suggested for testing unit roots is the Sargan–Bhargava test. See J. D. Sargan and A. Bhargava, "Testing Residuals from Least Squares Regression for Being Generated by the Gaussian Random Walk," *Econometrica*, 1983, Vol. 51, pp. 153–174. This is a Durbin–Watson type test with significance levels corrected.

that is, testing the hypothesis

$$H_0: \quad u_t \text{ is I(1)}.$$

In essence, we are testing the null hypothesis that y_t and x_t are *not* co-integrated. Note that y_t is I(1) and x_t is I(1), so we are trying to see that u_t is not I(1).

Wickens and Breusch[41] argue that the two-step estimation procedure suggested by Engle and Granger of first estimating the long-run parameter β and then estimating the short-run parameters α and λ in equation (6.35) is unnecessary. They argue that one should estimate both the long-run and short-run parameters simultaneously and one would get more efficient estimates of the long-run parameter β by this procedure. Dividing (6.35) by λ and rearranging we get

$$y_t = \beta x_t + \frac{1}{\lambda}\Delta y_t - \frac{\alpha}{\lambda}\Delta x_t - \frac{u_t}{\lambda} \tag{6.36}$$

Since Δy_t will be correlated with the error u_t, equation (6.36) has to be estimated by the instrumental variable method. The coefficients of Δy_t and Δx_t describe the short-run dynamics. Note that if y_t and x_t are I(1), then Δy_t and Δx_t are like u_t, I(0), that is, they are of a lower order. Wickens and Breusch show that misspecification of the short-run dynamics does not have much of an effect on the estimation of the long-run parameters. For instance, in equation (6.36) even if Δx_t is omitted, the estimate of the parameter β will still be consistent. The intuitive reasoning behind this is that Δy_t and Δx_t are of a lower order than y_t and x_t.

*6.11 ARCH MODELS AND SERIAL CORRELATION

We saw in Section 6.9 that a significant DW statistic can arise through a number of misspecifications. We will now discuss one other source. This is the ARCH model suggested by Engle[42] which has, in recent years, been found useful in the analysis of speculative prices. ARCH stands for "Autoregressive Conditional Heteroskedasticity."

When we write the simple autoregressive model

$$y_t = \lambda y_{t-1} + \varepsilon_t \qquad \varepsilon_t \sim \text{IN}(0, \sigma^2)$$

we are saying that the conditional mean $E(y_t \mid y_{t-1}) = \lambda y_{t-1}$ depends on t but the conditional variance $\text{var}(y_t \mid y_{t-1}) = \sigma^2$ is a constant. The unconditional mean of y_t is zero and the unconditional variance is $\sigma^2/(1 - \lambda^2)$.

The ARCH model is a generalization of this, in that the conditional variance is also made a function of the past. If the conditional density $f(y_t \mid z_{t-1})$ is normal, a

[41] M. R. Wickens and T. S. Breusch, "Dynamic Specification, the Long Run and the Estimation of Transformed Regression Models," Forthcoming, *Economic Journal*, 1988 (supplement).
[42] R. F. Engle, "Autoregressive Conditional Heteroscedasticity With Estimates of the Variance of U. K. Inflation," *Econometrica*, Vol. 50, 1982, pp. 987–1007.

general expression for the ARCH model is

$$y_t \,|\, z_{t-1} \sim N(g(z_{t-1}), h(z_{t-1})).$$

To make this operational, Engle specifies the conditional mean $g(z_{t-1})$ as a linear function of the variables z_{t-1} and h as

$$h_t = \alpha_0 + \alpha_1 \varepsilon_{t-1}^2 + \alpha_2 \varepsilon_{t-2}^2 + \cdots + \alpha_p \varepsilon_{t-p}^2$$

where $\varepsilon_t = y_t - g_t$. In the simplest case we can consider the model

$$y_t = \lambda y_{t-1} + \beta x_t + \varepsilon_t \qquad \varepsilon_t \sim IN(0, h_t) \tag{6.37}$$

$$h_t = \operatorname{var} \varepsilon_t = \alpha_0 + \alpha_1 \varepsilon_{t-1}^2 \tag{6-38}$$

Note that ε_t are not autocorrelated. But the fact that the variance of ε_t depends on ε_{t-1}^2 gives a misleading impression of there being a serial correlation. For instance, suppose that in (6.37) $\lambda = 0$, that is we do not have y_{t-1} as an explanatory variable. If we estimate that equation by OLS we will find a significant DW statistic because of the ARCH effect given by (6.38). The situation is similar to the one we discussed in Section 6.10 where a trend in the variance was transmitted to a trend in the mean. In this case a simple test for the ARCH effect, that is, a test for the hypothesis $\alpha_1 = 0$ in (6.38) is to get the OLS residuals $\hat{\varepsilon}_t$ and regress $\hat{\varepsilon}_t^2$ on $\hat{\varepsilon}_{t-1}^2$ (with a constant term) and testing whether the coefficient of $\hat{\varepsilon}_{t-1}^2$ is zero. An LM (Lagrangian Multiplier test) is to use nR^2 as χ^2 with one d.f. This would enable us to see whether the significant DW test statistic is due to serial correlation in ε_t or due to the ARCH effect. Many empirical studies have found significant ARCH effects.

The estimation of the ARCH model can be carried out by an iterative procedure. First, we estimate (6.37). We then get estimates of α_0 and α_1 in (6.38) by regressing $\hat{\varepsilon}_t^2$ on $\hat{\varepsilon}_{t-1}^2$. Now we estimate (6.37) as a heteroskedastic regression model, since we have an estimate of h_t. This process can be repeated until convergence.

There are, however, problems with this simple procedure that we have ignored. We might get estimates of α_1 less than zero or greater than one. These problems as well as the computation of the asymptotic variances and covariances are discussed in Engle's paper. The purpose of our discussion is to point out one more source for a significant DW test statistic when, in fact, there is no serial correlation.

SUMMARY

1. Most economic data consist of time series and there is very often a correlation in the errors corresponding to successive time periods. This is the problem of autocorrelation.

2. The Durbin–Watson (DW) test is the most often used to test for the presence of autocorrelation. If this test detects the presence of autocorrelation, it is customary to transform the data on the basis of the estimated first-order autocorrelation and use least squares with the transformed data.

3. There are several limitations to this procedure. These limitations (discussed in Section 6.9) are:

(a) The serial correlation might be of a higher order.

(b) The serial correlation might be due to omitted variables.

(c) The serial correlation might be due to the noninclusion of lagged values of the explained and explanatory variable, that is, due to misspecification of the dynamic process.

4. Very often, simple solutions are suggested for handling the serial correlation problem, such as estimation in first differences. The issue of estimation of equations in levels versus first differences is discussed in Section 6.3 and also in Section 6.10. Other solutions are discussed in Section 6.4.

5. There have been some extensions and further tables prepared for the DW test. These extensions are outlined in Section 6.6.

6. The DW test is not applicable if there are lagged dependent variables in the model. Durbin suggested an alternative test, known as Durbin's h-test. This test is explained and illustrated in Section 6.7. Some problems with its use are also illustrated there. This test again, is for first-order autocorrelation only.

7. A general test which is, however, asymptotic, is the LM test. This test can be used for any specified order of the autocorrelation. It can be applied whether there are lagged dependent variables or not. It can be used with standard regression packages. It is based on omitted variables. This test is discussed in Section 6.8. It consists of two steps:

(a) First estimate the equation by ordinary least squares and get the residual $\hat{u}_t$.

(b) Now introduce appropriate lags of $\hat{u}_t$ in the original equation and reestimate it by least squares. Test that the coefficients of the lagged $\hat{u}_t$'s are zero using the standard tests.

The LM test has not been illustrated with an example. This is left as an exercise. Many of the data sets presented in the book are time-series data, and students can use these to apply the LM test.

8. The effect of autocorrelated errors on least squares estimators are:

(a) If there are no lagged dependent variables among the explanatory variables, the estimators are unbiased but inefficient. However, the estimated variances are biased, sometimes substantially. These problems are discussed in Section 6.5 and the biases are presented for some simple cases.

(b) If there are lagged dependent variables among the explanatory variables, the least squares estimators are not even consistent (see Section 6.7). In this case the DW test statistic is biased as well. This is the reason for the use of Durbin's h-test.

9. Obtaining a significant DW test statistic does not necessarily mean that we have a serial correlation problem. In fact, we may not have a serial correlation problem and we may be applying the wrong solution. For this purpose Sargan suggested that we first test for common factors and *then* apply tests for serial correlation if there is a common factor. This argument is explained at the end of Section 6.9 and illustrated with an example.

10. Economic time series can conveniently be classified as belonging to the DSP class or TSP class. The appropriate procedure for trend elimination (whether to use differences or regressions on time) will depend on this classification. One can apply the Dickey–Fuller test (or Sargan–Bhargava test) to test whether the time series is of the DSP type or TSP type. Most economic time series, however, are of the DSP type and, thus, estimation in first differences is appropriate. However, dif-

ferencing eliminates all information on the long-run properties of the model. One suggestion that has been made is to see whether the time series are co-integrated. If this is so, then both long-run and short-run parameters can be estimated (either separately or jointly).

11. Sometimes even though the errors in the equation are not autocorrelated, the variance of the error term can depend on the past history of errors. In such models, called ARCH models, one can find a significant DW test statistic even though there is no serial correlation in the errors. A test for the ARCH effect will enable us to judge whether the observed serial correlation is spurious.

EXERCISES

1. Explain the following.
    (a) The Durbin–Watson test.
    (b) Estimation with quasi first differences.
    (c) The Cochrane–Orcutt procedure.
    (d) Durbin's h-test.
    (e) Serial correlation due to misspecified dynamics.
    (f) Estimation in levels versus first differences.
2. Use the Durbin–Watson test to test for serial correlation in the errors in Exercises 17 and 19 at the end of Chapter 4.
3. I am estimating an equation in which y_{t-1} is also an explanatory variable. I get the following results.

$$y_t = 2.7 + \underset{(0.4)}{0.4x_t} + \underset{(0.06)}{0.9y_{t-1}} \qquad \begin{array}{l} R^2 = 0.98 \\ \text{DW} = 1.9 \end{array}$$

I find that the R^2 is very high and the Durbin–Watson statistic is close to 2, showing that there is no serial correlation in the errors. My friend tells me that even if the R^2 is high, this is a useless equation. Why is this a useless equation?
4. Examine whether the following statements are true or false. Give an explanation.
    (a) Serial correlation in the errors u lead to biased estimates and biased standard errors when the regression equation $y = \beta x + u$ is estimated by ordinary least squares.
    (b) The Durbin–Watson test for serial correlation is not applicable if the errors are heteroskedastic.
    (c) The Durbin–Watson test for serial correlation is not applicable if there are lagged dependent variables as explanatory variables.
    (d) An investigator estimating a demand function in levels and first differences obtained R^2's of 0.90 and 0.80, respectively. He chose the equation in levels because he got a higher R^2. This is a valid reason for choosing between the two models.
    (e) Least squares techniques when applied to economic time-series data usually yield biased estimates because many economic time series are autocorrelated.

(f) The Durbin–Watson test can be used to describe whether the errors in a regression equation based on time-series data are serially independent.

(g) The fact that the Durbin–Watson statistic is significant does not necessarily mean that there is serial correlation in the errors. One has to apply some other tests to come to this conclusion.

(h) Consider the model $y_t = \alpha y_{t-1} + \beta x_t + u_t$, where the errors are autoregressive. Even if the OLS method gives inconsistent estimates of the parameters, we can still use the equation for purposes of prediction if the evolution of x_t during the prediction period is the same as in the estimation period.

(i) Consider the model

$$y_t = \alpha + \beta x_t + u_t$$
$$u_t = \rho u_{t-1} + e_t \qquad 0 \le \rho \le 1$$

e_t are $IN(0, \sigma^2)$. By regressing Δy_t on Δx_t, it is possible to get more efficient estimates of β than by regressing y_t on x_t.

(j) The Durbin–Watson test is a useless test because it is inapplicable in almost every situation that we encounter in practice.

5. The phrase "since the model contains a lagged dependent variable, the DW statistic is unreliable" is frequently seen in empirical work.

  (a) What does this phrase mean?

  (b) Is there some way to get around this problem?

6. Apply the LM test to test for first-order and second-order serial correlation in errors for the estimation of some multiple regression models with the data sets presented in Chapter 4. In each case compare the results with those obtained by using the DW test and Durbin's h-test if there are lagged dependent variables in the explanatory variables.

7. Apply Sargan's common factor test to check that the significant serial correlation is not due to misspecified dynamics.

8. In the case of data with housing starts in Table 4.10 illustrate the use of fourth-order autocorrelation using the DW test and the LM test.

7

Multicollinearity

7.1 INTRODUCTION

Very often the data we use in multiple regression analysis cannot give decisive answers to the questions we pose. This is because the standard errors are very high or the t-ratios are very low. The confidence intervals for the parameters of interest are thus very wide. This sort of situation occurs when the explanatory variables display little variation and/or high intercorrelations. The situation where the explanatory variables are highly intercorrelated is referred to as *multicollinearity*. When the explanatory variables are highly intercorrelated, it becomes difficult to disentangle the separate effects of each of the explanatory variables on the explained variable. The practical questions we need to ask is how high these intercorrelations have to be to cause problems in our inference about the individual parameters and what we can do about this problem. We argue in the subsequent sections that high inter-correlations among the explanatory variables need not necessarily create a problem

223

and some solutions often suggested for the multicollinearity problem can actually lead us on a wrong track. The suggested cures are sometimes worse than the disease.

The term "multicollinearity" was first introduced in 1934 by Ragnar Frisch[1] in his book on confluence analysis and referred to a situation where the variables dealt with are subject to two or more relations. In his analysis there was no dichotomy of explained and explanatory variables. It was assumed that all variables were subject to error and given the sample variances and covariances, the problem was to estimate the different linear relationships among the true variables. The problem was thus one of errors in variables. We will, however, be discussing the multicollinearity problem as it is commonly discussed in multiple regression analysis, namely, the problem of high intercorrelations among the explanatory variables.

Multicollinearity or high intercorrelations among the explanatory variables need not necessarily be a problem. Whether or not it is a problem depends on other factors, as we will see presently. Thus the multicollinearity problem cannot be discussed entirely in terms of the intercorrelations among the variables. Further, different parametrizations of the variables will give different magnitudes of these intercorrelations. This point is explained in the next section with some examples. Most of the discussions of the multicollinearity problem and its solutions are based on criteria based on the intercorrelations between the explanatory variables. However, this is an incorrect approach, as will be clear from the examples given in the next section.

7.2 SOME ILLUSTRATIVE EXAMPLES

We first discuss some examples where the intercorrelationships between the explanatory variables are high and study the consequences.

Consider the model $y = \beta_1 x_1 + \beta_2 x_2 + u$. If $x_2 = 2x_1$, we have

$$y = \beta_1 x_1 + \beta_2(2x_1) + u = (\beta_1 + 2\beta_2)x_1 + u$$

Thus only $(\beta_1 + 2\beta_2)$ would be estimable. We cannot get estimates of β_1 and β_2 separately. In this case we say that there is "perfect multicollinearity," because x_1 and x_2 are prefectly correlated (with $r_{12}^2 = 1$). In actual practice we encounter cases where r^2 is not exactly 1 but close to 1.

As an illustration, consider the case where

$$S_{11} = 200 \qquad S_{1y} = 350$$
$$S_{12} = 150 \qquad S_{2y} = 263$$
$$S_{22} = 113$$

so that the normal equations are

$$200\hat{\beta}_1 + 150\hat{\beta}_2 = 350$$
$$150\hat{\beta}_1 + 113\hat{\beta}_2 = 263$$

[1] Ragnar Frisch, *Statistical Confluence Analysis by Means of Complete Regression Systems*, Publication 5 (Oslo: University Institute of Economics, 1934).

The solution is $\hat{\beta}_1 = 1$ and $\hat{\beta}_2 = 1$. Suppose that we drop an observation and the new values are

$$S_{11} = 199 \qquad S_{1y} = 347.5$$
$$S_{12} = 149 \qquad S_{2y} = 261.5$$
$$S_{22} = 112$$

Now when we solve the equations

$$199\hat{\beta}_1 + 149\hat{\beta}_2 = 347.5$$
$$149\hat{\beta}_1 + 112\hat{\beta}_2 = 261.5$$

we get $\hat{\beta}_1 = -\frac{1}{2}, \hat{\beta}_2 = 3$.

Thus very small changes in the variances and covariances produce drastic changes in the estimates of the regression parameters. It is easy to see that the correlation coefficient between the two explanatory variables is given by

$$r_{12}^2 = \frac{(150)^2}{200(113)} = 0.995$$

which is very high.

In practice, addition or deletion of observations would produce changes in the variances and covariances. Thus one of the consequences of high correlation between x_1 and x_2 is that the parameter estimates would be very sensitive to the addition or deletion of observations. This aspect of multicollinearity can be checked in practice by deleting or adding some observations and examining the sensitivity of the estimates to such perturbations.

One other symptom of the multicollinearity problem that is often mentioned is that the standard errors of the estimated regression coefficients will be very high. However, high values of r_{12}^2 need not necessarily imply high standard errors, and conversely, even low values of r_{12}^2 can produce high standard errors. In Section 4.3 we derived the standard errors for the case of two explanatory variables. There we derived the following formulas:

$$V(\hat{\beta}_1) = \frac{\sigma^2}{S_{11}(1 - r_{12}^2)} \tag{7.1}$$

$$V(\hat{\beta}_2) = \frac{\sigma^2}{S_{22}(1 - r_{12}^2)} \tag{7.2}$$

and

$$\text{cov}(\hat{\beta}_1, \hat{\beta}_2) = -\frac{\sigma^2 r_{12}^2}{S_{12}(1 - r_{12}^2)} \tag{7.3}$$

where σ^2 is the variance of the error term. Thus the variance of $\hat{\beta}_1$ will be high if

1. σ^2 is high.
2. S_{11} is low.
3. r_{12}^2 is high.

Even if r_{12}^2 is high, if σ^2 is low and S_{11} high, we will not have the problem of high standard errors. On the other hand, even if r_{12}^2 is low, the standard errors can be high if σ^2 is high and S_{11} is low (i.e., there is not sufficient variation in x_1). What this suggests is that high values of r_{12}^2 do not tell us anything whether we have a multicollinearity problem or not.

When we have more than two explanatory variables, the simple correlations among them become all the more meaningless. As an illustration, consider the following example with 20 observations on x_1, x_2, and x_3.

$$x_1 = (1, 1, 1, 1, 1, 0, 0, 0, 0, 0, \text{ and } 10 \text{ zeros})$$

$$x_2 = (0, 0, 0, 0, 1, 1, 1, 1, 1, 1, \text{ and } 10 \text{ zeros})$$

$$x_3 = (1, 1, 1, 1, 1, 1, 1, 1, 1, 1, \text{ and } 10 \text{ zeros})$$

Obviously, $x_3 = x_1 + x_2$ and we have perfect multicollinearity. But we can easily see that $r_{12} = -\frac{1}{3}$ and $r_{13} = r_{23} = 1/\sqrt{3} \simeq 0.59$, and thus the simple correlations are not high. In the case of more than two explanatory variables, what we have to consider are multiple correlations of each of the explanatory variables with the other explanatory variables. Note that the standard error formulas corresponding to (7.1) and (7.2) are

$$V(\hat{\beta}_i) = \frac{\sigma^2}{S_{ii}(1 - R_i^2)} \tag{7.4}$$

where σ^2 and S_{ii} are defined as before in the case of two explanatory variables and R_i^2 represents the squared multiple correlations coefficient between x_i and the other explanatory variables. Again, it is easy to see that $V(\hat{\beta}_i)$ will be high if

1. σ^2 is high.
2. S_{ii} is low.
3. R_i^2 is high.

Thus high R_i^2 is neither necessary nor sufficient to get high standard errors and thus multicollinearity by itself need not cause high standard errors.

There are several rules of thumb that have been suggested in the literature to detect when multicollinearity can be considered a serious problem. For instance, Klein says [2]: "Intercorrelation of variables is not necessarily a problem unless it is high relative to the overall degree of multiple correlation." By Klein's rule multicollinearity would be regarded as a problem only if $R_y^2 < R_i^2$ where R_y^2 is the squared multiple correlation coefficient between y and the explanatory variables, and R_i^2 is as defined earlier. However, note that even if $R_y^2 < R_i^2$ we can still have significant partial correlation coefficients (i.e., significant t-ratios for the regression coefficients). For example, suppose that the correlations between y, x_1 and x_2 are

---

[2] L. R. Klein, *An Introduction to Econometrics* (Englewood Cliffs, N.J.: Prentice-Hall, 1962), p. 101.

given by

	y	x_1	x_2
y	1.00	0.95	0.95
x_1	0.95	1.00	0.97
x_2	0.95	0.97	1.00

Then it can be verified that $R^2_{y \cdot 12} = 0.916$ and $r^2_{12} = 0.941$. Thus $R^2_y < r^2_{12}$. But $r^2_{y1 \cdot 2} = r^2_{y2 \cdot 1} \simeq 0.14$. Since the relationship between the t-ratio and partial r^2 is given by (see Section 4.5)

$$r^2 = \frac{t^2}{t^2 + \text{degrees of freedom}}$$

we will get t-values greater than 3 if the number of observations is greater than 60. We can summarize the previous discussion as follows:

1. If we have more than two explanatory variables, we should use R^2_i values to measure the degree of intercorrelations among the explanatory variables, not the simple correlations among the variables. [3]
2. However, whether multicollinearity is a problem or not for making inferences on the parameters will depend on other factors besides R^2_i's, as is clear from equation (7.4). What is relevant is the standard errors and t-ratios. Of course, if R^2_i is low, we would be better off. But this argument is only a poor consolation. It is not appropriate to make any conclusions about whether multicollinearity is a problem or not just on the basis of R^2_i's. The R^2_i's are useful only as a complaint. Moreover, the R^2_i's depend on the particular parametrization adopted, as we discuss in the next section.

7.3 SOME MEASURES OF MULTICOLLINEARITY

It is important to be familiar with two measures that are often suggested in the discussion of multicollinearity: the *variance-inflation factor* (VIF) and the *condition number*.

The VIF is defined as

$$\text{VIF}(\hat{\beta}_i) = \frac{1}{1 - R^2_i}$$

where R^2_i is the squared multiple correlation coefficient between x_i and the other

---

[3] Of course, some other measures based on the eigenvalues of the correlation matrix have been suggested in the literature, but a discussion of this is beyond our scope. Further, all these measures are only a "complaint" that the explanatory variables are highly intercorrelated; they do not tell whether the problem is serious.

explanatory variables. Looking at the formula (7.4), we can interpret VIF $(\hat{\beta}_i)$ as the ratio of the actual variance of $\hat{\beta}_i$ to what the variance of $\hat{\beta}_i$ would have been if x_i were to be uncorrelated with the remaining x's. Implicitly, an ideal situation is considered to be one where the x's are all uncorrelated with each other and the VIF_i compares the actual situation with an ideal situation. This comparison is not very useful and does not provide us guidance as to what to do with the problem. It is more a complaint that things are not ideal. Also, looking at formula (7.4), as we have discussed earlier, $1/(1 - R_i^2)$ is not the only factor determining whether multicollinearity presents a problem in making inferences.

Whereas the VIF_i is something we compute for each explanatory variable separately, the *condition number* discussed by Raduchel[4] and Belsley, Kuh, and Welsch[5] is an overall measure. The condition number is supposed to measure the sensitivity of the regression estimates to small changes in the data. Explaining the concept requires the use of matrix algebra and hence we will not attempt it here. It is defined as the square root of the largest to the smallest eigenvalue of the matrix $X'X$ of the explanatory variables. For the two-variable case in Section 7.2 it is easily computed. We solve the equation

$$(S_{11} - \lambda)(S_{22} - \lambda) - S_{12}^2 = 0$$

$$(200 - \lambda)(113 - \lambda) - (150)^2 = 0$$

or

$$\lambda^2 - 313\lambda + 100 = 0$$

which gives $\lambda_1 = 312.68$, $\lambda_2 = 0.32$ as the required eigenvalues. The condition number $= \sqrt{\lambda_1/\lambda_2} = 31.26$. The closer the condition number is to 1, the better the condition is.

Again, there are three problems with this:

1. It looks at only the correlations among the explanatory variables and formula (7.4) shows that this is not the only relevant factor.
2. The condition number can change by a reparametrization of the variables. For instance, if we define $z_1 = x_1 + x_2$ and $z_2 = x_1 - x_2$, the condition number will change. In fact, it can be made equal to 1 with suitable transformations of the variables.
3. Even if such transformations of variables are not always meaningful (what does 2 apples + 3 oranges mean?), the condition number is merely a complaint that things are not ideal.[6]

In Section 7.4 we consider an example where transformations of variables is meaningful. However, even when they are not, the VIF and condition numbers are

[4] W. J. Raduchel, "Multicollinearity Once Again," Paper No. 205, Harvard Institute of Economic Research, Cambridge, Mass., 1971.
[5] D. Belsley, E. Kuh, and R. Welsch, *Regression Diagnosis* (New York: Wiley, 1980).
[6] E. E. Leamer, "Model Choice and Specification Analysis," in Z. Griliches and M. D. Intrilligator (eds.), *Handbook of Econometrics*, Vol. 1 (Amsterdam: North-Holland, 1983), pp. 286–330.

only measures of how bad things are relative to some ideal situation, but the standard errors and t-ratios will tell a better story of how bad things are.

The VIFs and condition number will be useful for dropping some variables and imposing parameter constraints only in some very extreme cases where $R_i^2 \simeq 1.0$ or the smallest eigenvalue is very close to zero. In this case we estimate the model subject to some constraints on the parameters. This point is illustrated in Section 7.5 with an example.

The major aspect of the VIF and the condition number is that they look at only the intercorrelations among the explanatory variables. A measure that considers the correlations of the explanatory variable with the explained variable is Theil's measure,[7] which is defined as

$$m = R^2 - \sum_{i=1}^{k} (R^2 - R_{-i}^2)$$

where R^2 = squared multiple correlation from a regression of y
on $x_1, x_2, \ldots, x_k$
R_{-i}^2 = squared multiple correlation from a regression of y
on $x_1, x_2, \ldots, x_k$ with x_i omitted

The quantity $(R^2 - R_{-i}^2)$ is termed the "incremental contribution" to the squared multiple correlation by Theil. If $x_1, x_2, \ldots, x_k$ are mutually uncorrelated, then m will be 0 because the incremental contributions all add up to R^2. In other cases m can be negative as well as highly positive. This makes it difficult to use it for any guidance.

To see what this measure means and how it is related to the t-ratios, let us consider the case of two explanatory variables. Following the notation in Section 4.6, we will write R^2 as $R_{y \cdot 12}^2$. R_{-i}^2 are now just the squared simple correlations r_{y1}^2 and r_{y2}^2. Thus

$$m = R_{y \cdot 12}^2 - (R_{y \cdot 12}^2 - r_{y1}^2) - (R_{y \cdot 12}^2 - r_{y2}^2)$$

The t-ratios are related to the partial r^2's, $r_{y1 \cdot 2}^2$ and $r_{y2 \cdot 1}^2$. We also derived in Section 4.6 the relation that

$$(1 - R_{y \cdot 12}^2) = (1 - r_{y1}^2)(1 - r_{y2 \cdot 1}^2)$$
$$= 1 - r_{y1}^2 - (1 - r_{y1}^2)r_{y2 \cdot 1}^2$$

Hence

$$(R_{y \cdot 12}^2 - r_{y1}^2) = (1 - r_{y1}^2)r_{y2 \cdot 1}^2$$

Thus

$m =$ (squared multiple correlation coefficient) $-$ (weighted sum of the partial r^2's)

This weighted sum is $w_1 \cdot r_{y2 \cdot 1}^2 + w_2 \cdot r_{y1 \cdot 2}^2$, where $w_1 = 1 - r_{y1}^2$ and $w_2 = 1 - r_{y2}^2$. If the partial r^2's are all very low, m will be very close to multiple R^2.

---

[7] H. Theil, *Principles of Econometrics* (New York: Wiley, 1971), p. 179.

In the earlier example that we gave to illustrate Klein's measure of multicollinearity, we had $R^2_{y \cdot 12} = 0.916$, $r^2_{y2} = 0.9025$, and $r^2_{y1 \cdot 2} = r^2_{y2 \cdot 1} = 0.14$. Thus Theil's measure of multicollinearity is

$$m = 0.916 - 2(1 - 0.9025)(0.14)$$

$$= 0.888$$

Of course, m is not zero. But is multicollinearity serious or not? One can never tell. If the number of observations is greater than 60, we will get significant t-ratios. Thus Theil's measure is even less useful than VIF and condition number.

We have discussed several measures of multicollinearity and they are all of limited use from the practical point of view. As Leamer puts it, they are all merely complaints that things are not ideal. The standard errors and t-ratios give us more information about how serious things are. It is relevant to remember formula (7.4) while assessing any measures of multicollinearity.

Leamer suggests some measures of multicollinearity based on the sensitivity of inferences to different forms of prior information. Since a discussion of these measures involves a knowledge of bayesian statistical inference and multivariate statistics, we have to omit these measures.

7.4 PROBLEMS WITH MEASURING MULTICOLLINEARITY

In Section 7.3 we talked of measuring multicollinearity in terms of the intercorrelations among the explanatory variables. However, there is one problem with this. The intercorrelations can change with a redefinition of the explanatory variables. Some examples will illustrate this point.

Let us define

$$C = \text{real consumption per capita}$$

$$Y = \text{real per capita current income}$$

$$Y_P = \text{real per capita permanent income}$$

$$Y_T = \text{real per capita transitory income}$$

$$Y = Y_T + Y_P \text{ and } Y_P \text{ and } Y_Y \text{ are uncorrelated}$$

Suppose that we formulate the consumption function as

$$C = \alpha Y + \beta Y_P + u \tag{7.5}$$

This equation can alternatively be written as

$$C = \alpha Y_T + (\alpha + \beta) Y_P + u \tag{7.6}$$

or

$$C = (\alpha + \beta) Y - \beta Y_T + u \tag{7.7}$$

All these equations are equivalent. However, the coefficients between the explana-tory variables will be different depending on which of the three equations is con-sidered. In equation (7.5), since Y and Y_P are often highly correlated, we would say that there is high multicollinearity. In equation (7.6), since Y_T and Y_P are uncorrelated, we would say that there is no multicollinearity. However, the two equations are essentially the same. What we should be talking about is the precision with which α and β or $(\alpha + \beta)$ are estimable.

Consider, for instance, the following data. [8]

$$\text{var}(C) = 7.3 \qquad \text{cov}(C, Y) = 8.3 \qquad \text{cov}(Y, Y_P) = 9.0$$

$$\text{var}(Y) = 10.0 \qquad \text{cov}(C, Y_P) = 8.0 \qquad \text{cov}(Y, Y_T) = 1.0$$

$$\text{var}(Y_P) = 9.0 \qquad \text{cov}(C, Y_T) = 0.3 \qquad \text{cov}(Y_P, Y_T) = 0 \quad \text{by definition}$$

$$\text{var}(Y_T) = 1.0$$

For these data the estimation of equation (7.5) gives (all variables measured as deviations from their means)

$$C = \underset{(0.32)}{0.30}Y + \underset{(0.33)}{0.59}Y_P \qquad \hat{\sigma}_u^2 = 0.1$$

(The figures in parentheses are standard errors.) One reason for the imprecision in the estimates is that Y and Y_P are highly correlated (the correlation coefficient is 0.95).

For equation (7.6) the correlation between the explanatory variables is zero and for equation (7.7) it is 0.32. The least squares estimates of α and β are no more precise in equation (7.6) or (7.7).

Let us consider the estimation of equation (7.6). We get

$$C = \underset{(0.32)}{0.30}Y_T + \underset{(0.11)}{0.89}Y_P$$

The estimate at $(\alpha + \beta)$ is thus 0.89 and the standard error is 0.11. Thus $\alpha + \beta$ is indeed more precisely estimated than either α or β. As for α, it is not precisely estimated even though the explanatory variables in this equation are uncorrelated. The reason is that the variance of Y_T is very low [see formula (7.1)].

We can summarize the conclusions from this illustrative example as follows:

1. It is difficult to define multicollinearity in terms of the correlations between the explanatory variables because the explanatory variables can be redefined in a number of different ways and these can give drastically different mea-sures of intercorrelations. In some cases, these redefinitions may not make sense, but in the example above involving measured income, permanent income, and transitory income, these redefinitions make sense.

2. Just because the explanatory variables are uncorrelated does not mean that we have no problems with inference. Note that the estimate of α and its standard

---

[8] The data are those used in an illustrative example by Gary Smith, "An Example of Ridge Regression Difficulties," *Canadian Journal of Statistics*, Vol. 8, No. 2, 1980, pp. 217–225.

Table 7.1 Data on Consumption, Income, and Liquid Assets

Year, Quarter		C	Y	L	Year, Quarter		C	Y	L
1952	I	220.0	238.1	182.7	1957	I	268.9	291.1	218.2
	II	222.7	240.9	183.0		II	270.4	294.6	218.5
	III	223.8	245.8	184.4		III	273.4	296.1	219.8
	IV	230.2	248.8	187.0		IV	272.1	293.3	219.5
1953	I	234.0	253.3	189.4	1958	I	268.9	291.3	220.5
	II	236.2	256.1	192.2		II	270.9	292.6	222.7
	III	236.0	255.9	193.8		III	274.4	299.9	225.0
	IV	234.1	255.9	194.8		IV	278.7	302.1	229.4
1954	I	233.4	254.4	197.3	1959	I	283.8	305.9	232.2
	II	236.4	254.8	197.0		II	289.7	312.5	235.2
	III	239.0	257.0	200.3		III	290.8	311.3	237.2
	IV	243.2	260.9	204.2		IV	292.8	313.2	237.7
1955	I	248.7	263.0	207.6	1960	I	295.4	315.4	238.0
	II	253.7	271.5	209.4		II	299.5	320.3	238.4
	III	259.9	276.5	211.1		III	298.6	321.0	240.1
	IV	261.8	281.4	213.2		IV	299.6	320.1	243.3
1956	I	263.2	282.0	214.1	1961	I	297.0	318.4	246.1
	II	263.7	286.2	216.5		II	301.6	324.8	250.0
	III	263.4	287.7	217.3					
	IV	266.9	291.0	217.3					

error are the same in equation (7.5) (with the correlation among the explanatory variables equal to 0.95) and in equation (7.6) (with the explanatory variables uncorrelated).

3. Often, though the individual parameters are not precisely estimable, some linear combinations of the parameters are. For instance, in our example, $\alpha + \beta$ is estimable with good precision. Sometimes, these linear combinations do not make economic sense. But at other times they do.

We will present yet another example to illustrate some problems in judging whether multicollinearity is serious or not and also to illustrate the fact that even if individual parameters are not estimable with precision, some linear functions of the parameters are.

In Table 7.1 we present data on C, Y, and L for the period from the first quarter of 1952 to the second quarter of 1961. C is consumption expenditures, Y is disposable income, and L is liquid assets at the end of the previous quarter. All figures are in billions of 1954 dollars.[9] Using the 38 observations we get the following

[9] The data are from Z. Griliches, et al., "Notes on Estimated Aggregate Quarterly Consumption Functions," *Econometrica*, July 1962.

regression equations:

$$C = -7.160 + 0.95213Y \qquad r^2 = 0.9933 \qquad (7.8)$$
$$ \underset{(-1.93)}{} \quad \underset{(73.25)}{}$$

$$C = -10.627 + 0.68166Y + 0.37252L \qquad R^2 = 0.9953 \qquad (7.9)$$
$$ \underset{(-3.25)}{} \quad \underset{(9.60)}{} \quad \underset{(3.96)}{}$$

$$L = 9.307 + 0.76207Y \qquad r^2_{LY} = 0.9758 \qquad (7.10)$$
$$ \underset{(1.80)}{} \quad \underset{(37.20)}{}$$

(Figures in parentheses are t-ratios, not standard errors.)

Equation (7.10) shows that L and Y are very highly correlated. In fact, substituting the value of L in terms of Y from (7.10) into equation (7.9) and simplifying, we get equation (7.8) correct to four decimal places! However, looking at the t-ratios in equation (7.9) we might conclude that multicollinearity is not a problem.

Are we justified in this conclusion? Let us consider the stability of the coefficients with deletion of some observations. Using only the first 36 observations we get the following results:

$$C = -6.980 + 0.95145Y \qquad r^2 = 0.9925 \qquad (7.11)$$
$$ \underset{(-1.74)}{} \quad \underset{(67.04)}{}$$

$$C = -13.391 + 0.63258Y + 0.450651 \qquad R^2 = 0.9951 \qquad (7.12)$$
$$ \underset{(-3.71)}{} \quad \underset{(8.32)}{} \quad \underset{(4.24)}{}$$

$$L = 14.255 + 0.70758Y \qquad r^2_{LY} = 0.9768 \qquad (7.13)$$
$$ \underset{(2.69)}{} \quad \underset{(37.80)}{}$$

Comparing (7.11) with (7.8) and (7.12) with (7.9) we see that the coefficients in the latter equation show far greater changes than in the former equation. Of course, if one applies the tests for stability discussed in Section 4.11, one might conclude that the results are not statistically significant at the 5% level. Note that the test for stability that we use is the "predictive" test for stability.

Finally, we might consider predicting C for the first two quarters of 1961 using equations (7.11) and (7.12). The predictions are:

		Equation (7.11)	Equation (7.12)
1961	I	295.96	298.93
	II	302.05	304.73

Thus the prediction from the equation including L are further off from the true values than the predictions from the equations excluding L. Thus if prediction was the sole criterion, one might as well drop the variable L.

The example above illustrates four different ways of looking at the multicollinearity problem:

1. Correlation between the explanatory variables L and Y, which is high. This suggests that the multicollinearity may be serious. However, we explained earlier the fallacy in looking at just the correlation coefficients between the explanatory variables.

2. Standard errors or t-ratios for the estimated coefficients: In this example the t-ratios are significant, suggesting that multicollinearity might not be serious.
3. Stability of the estimated coefficients when some observations are deleted. Again one might conclude that multicollinearity is not serious, if one uses a 5% level of significance for this test.
4. Examining the predictions from the model: If multicollinearity is a serious problem, the predictions from the model would be worse than those from a model that includes only a subset of the set of explanatory variables.

The last criterion should be applied if prediction is the object of the analysis. Otherwise, it would be advisable to consider the second and third criteria. The first criterion is not useful, as we have so frequently emphasized.

7.5 SOLUTIONS TO THE MULTICOLLINEARITY PROBLEM: RIDGE REGRESSION

One of the solutions often suggested for the multicollinearity problem is to use what is known as ridge regression first introduced by Hoerl and Kennard.[10] Simply stated, the idea is to add a constant λ to the variances of the explanatory variables before solving the normal equations. For instance, in the example in Section 7.2, we add 5 to S_{11} and S_{22}. It is easy to see that the squared correlation now drops to

$$r_{12}^2 = \frac{(150)}{205(118)} = 0.930$$

Thus the intercorrelations are decreased. One can easily see what a mechanical solution this is. However, there is an enormous literature on ridge regression.

The addition of λ to the variances produces biased estimators but the argument is that if the variance can be decreased, the mean-squared error will decline. Hoerl and Kennard show that there always exists a constant $\lambda > 0$ such that

$$\sum_{i=1}^{k} \text{MSE}(\tilde{\beta}_i) < \sum_{i=1}^{k} \text{MSE}(\hat{\beta}_i)$$

where $\tilde{\beta}_i$ are the estimators of β_i from the ridge regression and $\hat{\beta}_i$ are the least squares estimators and k is the number of regressors. Unfortunately, λ is a function of the regression parameters β_i and error variance σ^2, which are unknown. Hoerl and Kennard suggest trying different values of λ and picking the value of λ so that "the system will stabilize" or the "coefficients do not have unreasonable values." Thus subjective arguments are used. Some others have suggested obtaining initial estimates of β_i and σ^2 and then using the estimated λ. This procedure can be iterated

---

[10] A. E. Hoerl and R. W. Kennard, "Ridge Regression: Biased Estimation for Non-orthogonal Problems," and "Ridge Regression: Applications to Non-orthogonal Problems," *Technometrics*, Vol. 12, 1977, pp. 55–67 and 69–82.

and we get the iterated ridge estimator. The usefulness of these procedures has also been questioned. [11]

One other problem about ridge regression is the fact that it is not invariant to units of measurement of the explanatory variables and to linear transformations of variables. If we have two explanatory variables x_1 and x_2 and we measure x_1 in tens and x_2 in thousands, it does not make sense to add the same value of λ to the variances of both. This problem can be avoided by normalizing each variable by dividing it by its standard deviation. Even if x_1 and x_2 are measured in the same units, in some cases there are different linear transformations of x_1 and x_2 that are equally sensible. For instance, as discussed in Section 7.4, equations (7.5), (7.6), (7.7) are all equivalent and they are all sensible. The ridge estimators, however, will differ depending on which of these forms is used.

There are different situations under which the ridge regression arises naturally. These will throw light on the matter of the circumstances under which the method will be useful. We mention three of them.

1. *Constrained least squares.* Suppose that we estimated the regression coefficients subject to the condition that

$$\sum_{i=1}^{k} \beta_i^2 = c \tag{7.14}$$

Then we would get something like the ridge regression. The λ that we use is the Lagrangian multiplier in the minimization. To see this, suppose that we have two explanatory variables.

We get the constrained least squares estimator by minimizing

$$\sum (y - \beta_1 x_1 - \beta_2 x_2)^2 + \lambda(\beta_1^2 + \beta_2^2 - c)$$

where λ is the Lagrangian multiplier. Differentiating this expression with respect to β_1 and β_2 and equating the derivatives to zero, we get the normal equations

$$2\sum (y - \beta_1 x_1 - \beta_2 x_2)(-x_1) + 2\lambda\beta_1 = 0$$
$$2\sum (y - \beta_1 x_1 - \beta_2 x_2)(-x_2) + 2\lambda\beta_2 = 0$$

These equations can be written as

$$(S_{11} + \lambda)\beta_1 + S_{12}\beta_2 = S_{1y}$$
$$S_{12}\beta_1 + (S_{22} + \lambda)\beta_2 = S_{2y}$$

where $S_{11} = \sum x_1^2$, $S_{12} = \sum x_1 x_2$, and so on. Thus we get the ridge regression and λ is the Lagrangian multiplier. The value of λ is decided by the criterion $\beta_1^2 + \beta_2^2 = c$. In this case there is a clear-cut procedure for choosing λ.

It is rarely the case that we would have prior knowledge about the β_i that is in the form $\sum \beta_i^2 = c$. But some other less concrete information can also be used to choose

---

[11] These methods are all reviewed in N. R. Draper and R. Craig Van Nostrand, "Ridge Regression and James–Stein Estimation: Review and Comments," *Technometrics*, Vol. 21, No. 4, November 1979, pp. 451–466. The authors do not approve of these methods and discuss the shortcomings of each.

the value of λ in ridge regression. Brown and Beattie's [12] ridge regression on production function data used their prior knowledge on the relationship between the signs of the β_i''s.

2. *Bayesian interpretation.* We have not discussed the Bayesian approach to statistics in this book. However, roughly speaking, what the approach does is to combine systematically some prior information on the regression parameters with sample information. Under this approach we get the ridge regression estimates of the β_i's if we assume that the prior information is of the form that $\beta_i \sim \text{IN}(0, \sigma_\beta^2)$. In this case the ridge constant λ is equal to σ^2/σ_β^2. Again, σ^2 is not known but has to be estimated. However, in almost all economic problems, this sort of prior information (that the means of the β_i's are zero) is very unreasonable. This suggests that the simple ridge estimator does not make sense in econometrics (with the Bayesian interpretation). Of course, the assumption that β_i has mean zero can be relaxed. But then we will get more complicated estimators (generalized ridge estimators).

3. *Measurement error interpretation.* Consider the two-variable model we discussed under constrained least squares. Suppose that we add random errors with zero mean and variance λ to both x_1 and x_2. Since these errors are random, the covariance between x_1 and x_2 will be unaffected. The variances of x_1 and x_2 will both increase by λ. Thus we get the ridge regression estimator. This interpretation makes the ridge estimator somewhat suspicious. Smith and Campbell [13] say that a one-liner summary of this is: "Use less precise data to get more precise estimates."

These are situations in which the ridge regression can be easily justified. In almost all other cases, there is subjective judgment involved. This subjective judgment is sometimes equated to "vague prior information." The Bayesian methods allow a systematic analysis of the data with "vague prior information" but a discussion of these methods is beyond the scope of this book.

Because of the deficiencies of ridge regression discussed above, the method is not recommended as a general solution to the multicollinearity problem. Particularly the simplest form of the method (where a constant λ is added to each variance) is not very useful. Nevertheless, for the sake of curiosity, we will present some results on the method. For the consumption function data in Table 7.1 we estimated the regression equation

$$c_t = \beta_0 y_t + \beta_1 y_{t-1} + \beta_2 y_{t-2} + \cdots + \beta_8 y_{t-8} + u_t$$

Needless to say, the y_t's are highly intercorrelated. The results are presented in Table 7.2. Note that as λ increases, there is a smoothing of the coefficients and the estimate of β_0 declines. The OLS coefficients, of course, are very erratic. But the estimates of β_0 (portion of current income going into current consumption) are implausibly low with the ridge regression method. The sudden pick up of coefficients after the fifth quarter is also something very implausible. Maybe we can just

[12] W. G. Brown and B. R. Beattie, "Improving Estimates of Economic Parameters by the Use of Ridge Regression with Production Function Applications," *American Journal of Agricultural Economics*, Vol. 57, 1975, pp. 21–32.

[13] Gary Smith and Frank Campbell, "A Critique of Some Ridge Regression Methods" (with discussion), *Journal of the American Statistical Association*, Vol. 75, March 1980, pp. 74–103.

Table 7.2 Ridge Estimates for Consumption Function Data

Lag	0.0	0.0002	0.0006	0.0010	0.0014	0.0020
			Value of λ			
0	0.70974	0.42246	0.29302	0.24038	0.21096	0.18489
1	0.20808	0.28187	0.22554	0.19578	0.17773	0.16096
2	0.27463	0.15615	0.14612	0.13865	0.13324	0.12764
3	−0.48068	−0.06079	0.03052	0.05761	0.07060	0.08088
4	0.25129	−0.00301	0.02429	0.04473	0.05736	0.06902
5	−0.23845	−0.06461	−0.00562	0.02304	0.04010	0.05578
6	0.12432	0.01705	0.03600	0.05116	0.06135	0.07138
7	−0.11278	0.06733	0.07964	0.08491	0.08862	0.09254
8	0.19838	0.12632	0.11941	0.11563	0.11367	0.11220
Sum	0.93453	0.94277	0.94892	0.95189	0.95363	0.95529

estimate the effects only up to four lags. The OLS estimates are erratic even with four lags. The computation of the ridge regression estimates with four lags is left as an exercise.

7.6 PRINCIPAL COMPONENT REGRESSION

Another solution that is often suggested for the multicollinearity problem is the *principal component regression*, which is as follows. Suppose that we have k explanatory variables. Then we can consider linear functions of these variables:

$$z_1 = a_1 x_1 + a_2 x_2 + \cdots + a_k x_k$$
$$z_2 = b_1 x_1 + b_2 x_2 + \cdots + b_k x_k \qquad \text{etc.}$$

Suppose we choose the a's so that the variance of z_1 is maximized subject to the condition that

$$a_1^2 + a_2^2 + \cdots + a_k^2 = 1$$

This is called the normalization condition. (It is required or else the variance of z_1 can be increased indefinitely.) z_1 is then said to be the first principal component. It is the linear function of the x's that has the higher variance (subject to the normalization rule).

The detailed derivation of the principal components is beyond the scope of this book, but we will discuss the main features and uses of the method which are easy to understand. Further, for using the method there are computer programs available that give the principal components (z's) given any set of variables $x_1, x_2, \ldots, x_k$.

The process of maximizing the variance of the linear function z subject to the condition that the sum of squares of the coefficients of the x's is equal to 1, produces

k solutions. Corresponding to these we construct k linear functions $z_1, z_2, \ldots, z_k$. These are called the principal components of the x's. They can be ordered so that

$$\text{var}(z_1) > \text{var}(z_2) > \cdots > \text{var}(z_k)$$

z_1, the one with the highest variance is called the first principal component, z_2 with the next highest variance is called the second principal component, and so on. These principal components have the following properties:

1. $\text{var}(z_1) + \text{var}(z_2) + \cdots + \text{var}(z_k) = \text{var}(x_1) + \text{var}(x_2) + \cdots + \text{var}(x_k)$.
2. Unlike the x's, which are correlated, the z's are orthogonal or uncorrelated. Thus there is zero multicollinearity among the z's.

Sometimes it is suggested that instead of regressing y on $x_1, x_2, \ldots, x_k$, we should regress y on $z_1, z_2, \ldots, z_k$. But this is *not* a solution to the multicollinearity problem. If we regress y on the z's and then substitute the values of z's in terms of x's, we finally get the same answers as before. This is similar to the example we considered in Section 7.4. The fact that the z's are uncorrelated does not mean that we will get better estimates of the coefficients in the original regression equation. So there is a point in using the principal components *only* if we regress y on a subset of the z's. But there are some problems with this procedure as well. They are:

1. The first principal component z_1, although it has the highest variance need not be the one that is most highly correlated with y. In fact, there is no necessary relationship between the order of the principal components and the degree of correlation with the dependent variable y.
2. One can think of choosing only those principal components that have high correlation with y and discard the rest, but the same sort of procedure can be used with the original set of variables $x_1, x_2, \ldots, x_k$ by first choosing the variable with the highest correlation with y, then the one with the highest partial correlation, and so on. This is what "stepwise regression programs" do.
3. The linear combinations z's often do not have economic meaning. For example, what does 2(income) + 3(price) mean? This is one of the most important drawbacks of the method.
4. Changing the units of measurement of the x's will change the principal components. This problem can be avoided if all variables are standardized to have unit variance.

However, there are some uses for the principal component method in exploratory stages of the investigation. For instance, suppose that there are many interest rates in the model (since all are measured in the same units, there is no problem of choice of units of measurement). If the principal component analysis shows that two principal components account for 99% of the variation in the interest rates and if by looking at the coefficients, we can identify them as short-term component and long-term component, we can argue that there are only two "latent" variables that account for all variations in the interest rates. Thus the principal component method will give us some guidance as to the question: "How many independent sources of variation are there?" In addition, if we can give an economic interpretation to the principal components, this is useful.

Table 7.3 Imports, Production, Stock Formation, and Consumption in France (Millions of New Francs at 1959 Prices)

Years	Imports, y	Gross Domestic Production, x_1	Stock Formation, x_2	Consumption, x_3
1949	15.9	149.3	4.2	108.1
1950	16.4	161.2	4.1	114.8
1951	19.0	171.5	3.1	123.2
1952	19.1	175.5	3.1	126.9
1953	18.8	180.8	1.1	132.1
1954	20.4	190.7	2.2	137.7
1955	22.7	202.1	2.1	146.0
1956	26.5	212.4	5.6	154.1
1957	28.1	226.1	5.0	162.3
1958	27.6	231.9	5.1	164.3
1959	26.3	239.0	0.7	167.6
1960	31.1	258.0	5.6	176.8
1961	33.3	269.8	3.9	186.6
1962	37.0	288.4	3.1	199.7
1963	43.3	304.5	4.6	213.9
1964	49.0	323.4	7.0	223.8
1965	50.3	336.8	1.2	232.0
1966	56.6	353.9	4.5	242.9

Source: E. Mallinvaud, *Statistical Methods of Econometrics*, 2nd ed., North-Holland, Amsterdam, 1970, p. 19.

We illustrate the method with reference to a data set from Malinvaud.[14] We have chosen this data set because it has been used by Chatterjee and Price[15] to illustrate the principal component method. We will also be using this same data set in Chapter 11 to illustrate the errors in variables methods.

The data are presented in Table 7.3. First let us estimate an import demand function. The regression of y on x_1, x_2, x_3 gives the following results.

Variable	Coefficient	SE	t
x_1	0.032	0.187	.17
x_2	0.414	0.322	1.29
x_3	0.243	0.285	0.85
Constant	−19.73	4.125	−4.78

$$n = 18 \qquad R^2 = 0.973 \qquad F_{3,14} = 168.4$$

[14] E. Malinvaud, *Statistical Methods of Econometrics*, 2nd ed. (Amsterdam: North-Holland, 1970).

[15] S. Chatterjee and B. Price, *Regression Analysis by Example* (New York: Wiley, 1977).

The R^2 is very high and the F-ratio is highly significant but the individual t-ratios are all insignificant. This is evidence of the multicollinearity problem. Chatterjee and Price argue that before any further analysis is made, we should look at the residuals from this equation. They find (we are omitting the residual plot here) a distinctive pattern — the residuals declining until 1960 and then rising. Chatterjee and Price argue that the difficulty with the model is that the European Common Market began operations in 1960, causing changes in import–export relationships. Hence they drop the years after 1959 and consider only the 11 years 1949–59. The regression results now are as follows:

Variable	Coefficient	SE	t
x_1	−0.051	0.070	−0.731
x_2	0.587	0.095	6.203
x_3	0.287	0.102	2.807
Constant	−10.13	1.212	−8.355

$$n = 11 \qquad R^2 = 0.992$$

The residual plot (not shown here) is now satisfactory (there are no systematic patterns), so we can proceed. Even though the R^2 is very high, the coefficient of x_1 is not significant. There is thus a multicollinearity problem.

To see what should be done about it, we first look at the simple correlations among the explanatory variables. These are $r_{12}^2 = 0.026$, $r_{13}^2 = 0.99$, and $r_{23}^2 = 0.036$. We suspect that the high correlation between x_1 and x_3 could be the source of the trouble.

Does principal component analysis help us? First, the principal components (obtained from a principal components program)[16] are:

$$z_1 = 0.7063X_1 + 0.0435X_2 + 0.7065X_3$$

$$z_2 = -0.0357X_1 + 0.9990X_2 - 0.0258X_3$$

$$z_3 = -0.7070X_1 - 0.0070X_2 + 0.7072X_3$$

X_1, X_2, X_3 are the normalized values of x_1, x_2, x_3. That is, $X_1 = (x_1 - m_1)/\sigma_1$, $X_2 = (x_2 - m_2)/\sigma_2$, and $X_3 - (x_3 - m_3)/\sigma_3$, where m_1, m_2, m_3 are the means and $\sigma_1, \sigma_2, \sigma_3$ are the standard deviations of x_1, x_2, x_3, respectively. Hence

$$\text{var}(X_1) = \text{var}(X_2) = \text{var}(X_3) = 1$$

The variances of the principal components are

$$\text{var}(z_1) = 1.999 \qquad \text{var}(z_2) = 0.998 \qquad \text{var}(z_3) = 0.003$$

---

[16] These are from Chatterjee and Price, *Regression Analysis*, p. 161. The details of how the principal components are computed need not concern us here.

Note that $\sum \mathrm{var}(z_i) = \sum \mathrm{var}(X_i) = 3$. The fact that $\mathrm{var}(z_3) = 0$ identifies that linear function as the source of multicollinearity. In this example there is only one such linear function. In some examples there could be more. Since $E(X_1) = E(X_2) = E(X_3) = 0$ because of normalization, the z's have mean zero. Thus z_3 has mean zero and its variance is also close to zero. Thus we can say that $z_3 \simeq 0$. Looking at the coefficients of the X's, we can say that (ignoring the coefficients that are very small)

$$z_1 \simeq 0.706(X_1 + X_3)$$

$$z_2 \simeq X_2$$

$$z_3 \simeq 0.707(X_3 - X_1)$$

$$z_3 \simeq 0 \text{ gives us } X_1 \simeq X_3$$

Actually, we would have gotten the same result from a regression of X_3 on X_1. The regression coefficient is $r_{13} = 0.9984$. (Note that X_1 and X_3 are in standardized form. Hence the regression coefficient is r_{13}.)

In terms of the original (nonnormalized) variables the regression of x_3 on x_1 is

$$x_3 = 6.258 + \underset{(0.0077)}{0.686 x_1} \qquad r^2 = 0.998$$

(The figure in parentheses is the SE.)

In a way we have got no more information from the principal component analysis than from a study of the simple correlations in this example. Anyway, what is the solution now? Given that there is an almost exact relationship between x_3 and x_1, we cannot hope to estimate the coefficients of x_1 and x_3 separately. If the original equation is

$$y = \beta_0 + \beta_1 x_1 + \beta_2 x_2 + \beta_3 x_3 + u$$

then substituting for x_3 in terms of x_1 we get

$$y = (\beta_0 + 6.258\beta_3) + (\beta_1 + 0.686\beta_3)x_1 + \beta_2 x_2 + u$$

This gives the linear functions of the β's that are estimable. They are $\beta_0 + 6.258\beta_3$, $\beta_1 + 0.686\beta_3$, and β_2. The regression of y on x_1 and x_2 gave the following results.

Variable	Coefficient	SE	t
x_1	0.145	0.007	20.67
x_2	0.622	0.128	4.87
Constant	−8.440	1.435	−5.88

$$R^2 = 0.983$$

Of course, we can estimate a regression of x_1 and x_3. The regression coefficient is 1.451. We now substitute for x_1 and estimate a regression of y on x_1 and x_3. The results we get are slightly better (we get a higher R^2). The results are:

Variable	Coefficient	SE	t
x_2	0.596	0.091	6.55
x_3	0.212	0.007	29.18
Constant	-9.743	1.059	-9.20
	$R^2 = 0.991$		

The coefficient of x_3 now is $(\beta_3 + 1.451\beta_1)$.

We can get separate estimates of β_1 and β_3 only if we have some prior information. As this example as well as the example in Section 7.3 indicate, what multicollinearity implies is that we cannot estimate individual coefficients with good precision but can estimate some linear functions of the parameters with good precision. If we want to estimate the individual parameters, we would need some prior information. We will show that the use of principal components implies the use of some prior information about the restrictions on the parameters.

Suppose that we consider regressing y on the principal components z_1 and z_2 (z_3 is omitted because it is almost zero). We saw that $z_1 = 0.7(X_1 + X_3)$ and $z_2 = X_2$. We have to transform these to the original variables. We get

$$z_1 = 0.7\left(\frac{x_1 - m_1}{\sigma_1} + \frac{x_3 - m_2}{\sigma_3}\right)$$

$$= \frac{0.7}{\sigma_1}\left(x_1 + \frac{\sigma_1}{\sigma_3}x_3\right) + \text{a constant}$$

$$z_2 = \frac{1}{\sigma_2}(x_2 - m_2)$$

Thus, using z_2 as a regressor is equivalent to using x_2, and using z_1 is equivalent to using $x_1 + (\sigma_1/\sigma_3)x_3$. Thus the principal component regression amounts to regressing y on $(x_1 + (\sigma_1/\sigma_3)(x_3)$ and x_2. In our example $\sigma_1/\sigma_3 = 1.4536$. The results are:

Variable	Coefficient	SE	t
$x_1 + 1.4536x_3$	0.073	0.003	25.12
x_2	0.609	0.106	5.77
Constant	-9.129	1.207	-7.56
	$R^2 = 0.988$		

This is the regression equation *we would have* estimated if we assumed that $\beta_3 = (\sigma_1/\sigma_3)\beta_1 = 1.4536\beta_1$. Thus the principal component regression amounts, in this example, to the use of the prior information $\beta_3 = 1.4536\beta_1$.

If all principal components are used, it is exactly equivalent to using all the original set of explanatory variables. If some principal components are omitted, this amounts to using some prior information on the β's. In our example the question is whether the assumption $\beta_3 = 1.45\beta_1$ makes economic sense. Without having more disaggregated data that break down imports into consumption and production goods we cannot say anything. Anyway, with 11 observations we cannot hope to answer many questions. The purpose of our analysis has been merely to show what principal component regression is and to show that it implies some prior information.

7.7 DROPPING VARIABLES

The problem with multicollinearity is essentially lack of sufficient information in the sample to permit accurate estimation of the individual parameters. In some cases it may be the case that we are not interested in all the parameters. In such cases we can get estimators for the parameters we are interested in that have smaller mean square errors than the OLS estimators, by dropping some variables.

Consider the model

$$y = \beta_1 x_1 + \beta_2 x_2 + u \tag{7.15}$$

and the problem is that x_1 and x_2 are very highly correlated. Suppose that our main interest is in β_1. Then we drop x_2 and estimate the equation

$$y = \beta_1 x_1 + v \tag{7.16}$$

Let the estimator of β_1 from the complete model (7.15) be denoted by $\hat{\beta}_1$ and the estimator of β_1 from the omitted variable model be denoted by β_1^*. $\hat{\beta}_1$ is the OLS estimator and β_1^* is the OV (omitted variable) estimator. For the OLS estimator we know that

$$E(\hat{\beta}_1) = 0 \quad \text{and} \quad \text{var}(\hat{\beta}_1) = \frac{\sigma^2}{S_{11}(1 - r_{12}^2)}$$

[see formula (7.1)]. For the OV estimator we have to compute $E(\beta_1^*)$ and $\text{var}(\beta_1^*)$. Now

$$\beta_1^* = \frac{\sum x_1 y}{\sum x_1^2}$$

substituting for y from (7.15) we get

$$\beta_1^* = \frac{\sum x_1(\beta_1 x_1 + \beta_2 x_2 + u)}{\sum x_1^2}$$

$$= \beta_1 + \frac{S_{12}}{S_{11}}\beta_2 + \frac{\sum x_1 u}{S_{11}}$$

(Note that we used $S_{11} = \sum x_1^2$ and $S_{12} = \sum x_1 x_2$.) Hence

$$E(\beta_1^*) = \beta_1 + \beta_2 \frac{S_{12}}{S_{11}}$$

and

$$\text{var}(\beta_1^*) = \text{var}\left(\frac{\sum x_1 u}{S_{11}}\right) = \frac{\sigma^2 S_{11}}{S_{11}^2} = \frac{\sigma^2}{S_{11}}$$

Thus β_1^* is biased but has a smaller variance than $\hat{\beta}_1$. We have

$$\frac{\text{var}(\beta_1^*)}{\text{var}(\hat{\beta}_1)} = 1 - r_{12}^2$$

and if r_{12} is very high, then $\text{var}(\beta_1^*)$ will be considerably less than $\text{var}(\hat{\beta}_1)$. Now

$$\frac{(\text{Bias in }\beta_1^*)^2}{\text{var}(\hat{\beta}_1)} = \left(\frac{\beta_2 S_{12}}{S_{11}}\right)^2 \frac{S_{11}(1 - r_{12}^2)}{\sigma^2}$$

$$= \frac{S_{12}^2}{S_{11}S_{22}} \beta_2^2 \frac{S_{22}(1 - r_{12}^2)}{\sigma^2}$$

The first term in this expression is r_{12}^2. The last term is the reciprocal of $\text{var}(\hat{\beta}_2)$ [see formula (7.2)]. Thus the whole expression can be written as $r_{12}^2 t_2^2$, where

$$t_2^2 = \frac{\beta_2^2}{\text{var}(\hat{\beta}_2)}$$

t_2 is the "true" t-ratio for x_2 in equation (7.15), not the "estimated" t-ratio.

Noting that mean-square error $\text{MSE} = (\text{bias})^2 + \text{variance}$, and that for $\hat{\beta}_1$, $\text{MSE} = \text{variance}$, we get

$$\frac{\text{MSE}(\beta_1^*)}{\text{MSE}(\hat{\beta}_1)} = \frac{(\text{bias in }\beta_1^*)^2}{\text{var}(\hat{\beta}_1)} + \frac{\text{var}(\beta_1^*)}{\text{var}(\hat{\beta}_1)}$$

$$= r_{12}^2 t_2^2 + (1 - r_{12}^2)$$

$$= 1 + r_{12}^2(t_2^2 - 1) \tag{7.17}$$

Thus if $|t_2| < 1$, then $\text{MSE}(\beta_1^*) < \text{MSE}(\hat{\beta}_1)$. Since t_2 is not known, what is usually done is to use the estimated t-value $\hat{t}_2$ from equation (7.15). As an estimator of β_1, we use the conditional-omitted-variable (COV) estimator, defined as

$$\tilde{\beta}_1 = \begin{cases} \hat{\beta}_1 & \text{the OLS estimator if } |\hat{t}_2| \geq 1 \\ \beta_1^* & \text{the OV estimator if } |\hat{t}_2| < 1 \end{cases}$$

Also, instead of using $\hat{\beta}_1$ or β_1^*, depending on $\hat{t}_2$ we can consider a linear combination of both, namely

$$\lambda \hat{\beta}_1 + (1 - \lambda)\beta_1^*$$

This is called the weighted (WTD) estimator and it has minimum mean square error if $\lambda = t_2^2/(1 + t_2^2)$. Again t_2 is not known and we have to use its estimated value $\hat{t}_2$. This weighted estimator was first suggested by Huntsberger. The COV estimator was first suggested by Bancroft. Feldstein[17] studied the mean-squared error of these

---

[17] M. S. Feldstein, "Multicollinearity and the Mean Square Error of Alternative Estimators," *Econometrica*, Vol. 41, March 1973, pp. 337–345. References to the papers by Bancroft, Huntsberger, and others can be found in that paper.

two estimators for different values of t_2 and $\hat{t}_2$. He argues that:

1. Omitting a collinear nuisance variable on the basis of its sample t-statistic $\hat{t}_2$ is generally not advisable. OLS is preferable to any COV estimator unless one has a strong prior notion that $|t_2|$ is < 1.
2. The WTD estimator is generally better than the COV estimator.
3. The WTD estimator is superior to OLS for $|t_2| \leq 1.25$ and only slightly inferior for $1.5 \leq |t_2| \leq 3.0$.
4. The inadequacy of collinear data should not be disguised by reporting results from the omitted variable regressions. Even if a WTD estimator is used, one should report the OLS estimates and their standard errors to let readers judge the extent of multicollinearity.

What all this discussion shows is that even in the use of the COV or WTD estimators prior information on t_2 is very important. This brings us back to the same story as our discussion of the ridge regression and principal components regression, namely, the importance of prior information. The prior information regarding the omission of nuisance variables pertains to the *true* t-values for the coefficients of these variables.

Leamer[18] suggests studying the sensitivity of estimates of the coefficients to different specifications about prior information on the coefficients. Although his approach is Bayesian and is beyond the scope of this book, one can do a simple sensitivity analysis in each problem to assess the impact on the estimates of the coefficients of interest of changes in the assumptions about the coefficients of the nuisance parameters. Such sensitivity analysis would be more useful than using one solution like ridge regression, principal component regression, omitting variables, and so on, each of which implies some particular prior information in a concealed way. Very often, this may not be the prior information you would want to consider.

7.8 MISCELLANEOUS OTHER SOLUTIONS

There have been several other solutions to the multicollinearity problem that one finds in the literature. All these, however, should be used only if there are other reasons to use them—not for solving the collinearity problem as such. We will discuss them briefly.

Using Ratios or First Differences

We have discussed the method of using ratios in our discussion of heteroskedasticity (Chapter 5) and first differences in our discussion of autocorrelation (Chapter 6). Although these procedures might reduce the intercorrelations among the explanatory variables, they should be used on the basis of the considerations discussed in those chapters, not as a solution to the collinearity problem.

[18] E. E. Leamer, "Multicollinearity: A Bayesian Interpretation," *Review of Economics and Statistics*, Vol. 55, 1973, pp. 371–380; "Regression Selection Strategies and Revealed Priors," *Journal of the American Statistical Association*. Vol. 73, 1978, 580–587.

Using Extraneous Estimates

This method was followed in early demand studies. It was found that in time-series data income and price were both highly correlated. Hence neither the price nor income elasticity could be estimated with precision. What was done was to get an estimate of the income elasticity from budget studies (where prices do not vary much) use this estimate to "correct" the quantity series for income variation and then estimate the price elasticity.[19] For example, if the equation to be estimated is

$$\log Q = \alpha + \beta_1 \log p + \beta_2 \log y + u$$

we first get $\hat{\beta}_2$ from budget studies and then regress $(\log Q - \hat{\beta}_2 \log y)$ on $\log p$ to get estimates of α and β_1. Here $\hat{\beta}_2$ is known as the "extraneous estimate." There are two main problems with this procedure. First, the fact that β_2 is estimated should be taken into account in computing the variances of $\hat{\alpha}$ and $\hat{\beta}_1$. This is not usually done, but it can be. Second, and this is the more important problem, the cross-section estimate of β_2 may be measuring something entirely different from what the time-series estimate is supposed to measure. As Meyer and Kuh[20] argue, the "extraneous" estimate can be really extraneous.

Suppose that we want to use an estimate for a parameter from another data set. What is the best procedure for doing this? Consider the equation

$$y_1 = \beta_1 x_1 + \beta_2 x_2 + u \tag{7.18}$$

Suppose that because of the high correlation between x_1 and x_2, we cannot get good estimates of β_1 and β_2. We try to get an estimate of β_1 from another data set and another equation

$$y_2 = \beta_1 x_1 + \gamma z + v \tag{7.19}$$

In this equation x_1 and z are not highly correlated and we get a good estimate of β_1, say $\hat{\beta}_1$. Now we substitute this in (7.18) and regress $(y_1 - \hat{\beta}_1 x_1)$ on x_2 to get an estimate $\hat{\beta}_2$ of β_2. This is the procedure we mentioned earlier. The estimate of $\hat{\beta}_2$ is a *conditional estimate*, conditional on $\beta_1 = \hat{\beta}_1$. Also, we have to make corrections for the estimated variance of $\hat{\beta}_2$ because the error in the equation now is

$$(y - \hat{\beta}_1 x_1) = \beta_2 x_2 + W$$

where $W = u + (\beta_1 - \hat{\beta}_1)x_1$ is not the same as u. This procedure is advisable only when the data behind the estimation of (7.19) are not available to us (the study is done by somebody else).

On the other hand, if the two sets of data are available to us, there is no reason to use this conditional estimation procedure. A better procedure would be to estimate equations (7.18) and (7.19) jointly. This is what was done by Maddala[21] for the data

---

[19] An example of this is J. Tobin, "A Statistical Demand Function for Food in the U.S.A.," *Journal of the Royal Statistical Society, Series A*, 1950, pp. 113–141.

[20] John Meyer and Edwin Kuh, "How Extraneous Are Extraneous Estimates?" *Review of Economics and Statistics*, November 1957.

[21] G. S. Maddala, "The Likelihood Approach to Pooling Cross-Section and Time-Series Data," *Econometrica*, Vol. 39, November 1971, 939–953.

used by Tobin in his study on demand for food. It is also possible to test, by using the joint estimation of equations (7.18) and (7.19) and separate estimation of the equations, whether the coefficient of x_1 is the same in the two equations.[22]

In summary, as a solution to the multicollinearity problem, it is not advisable to substitute extraneous parameter estimates in the equation. One can, of course, pool the different data sets to get more efficient estimates of the parameters, but one should also perform some tests to see whether the parameters in the different equations are indeed the same.

Getting More Data

One solution to the multicollinearity problem that is often suggested is to "go and get more data." Actually, the extraneous estimators case we have discussed also falls in this category (we look for another model with common parameters and the associated data set). Sometimes using quarterly or monthly data instead of annual data helps us in getting better estimates. However, we might be adding more sources of variation like seasonality. In any case, since weak data and inadequate information are the sources of our problem, getting more data will help matters.

SUMMARY

1. In multiple regression analysis it is usually difficult to interpret the estimates of the individual coefficients if the variables are highly intercorrelated. This problem is often referred to as the multicollinearity problem.

2. However, high intercorrelations among the explanatory variables by themselves need not necessarily cause any problems in inference. Whether or not this is a problem will depend on the magnitude of the error variance and the variances of the explanatory variables. If there is enough variation in the explanatory variables and the variance of the error term is sufficiently small, high intercorrelations among the explanatory variables need not cause a problem. This is illustrated by using formulas (7.1)–(7.4) in Section 7.2.

3. Measures of multicollinearity based solely on high intercorrelations among the explanatory variables are useless. These are discussed in Section 7.3. Also, as shown in Section 7.4, these correlations can change with simple transformations of the explanatory variables. This does not mean that the problem has been solved.

4. There have been several solutions to the multicollinearity problem. These are:
(a) Ridge regression, on which an enormous amount of literature exists.
(b) Principal component regression—this amounts to transforming the explanatory variables to an uncorrelated set, but mere transformation does not solve the problem. (It appears through the back door.)
(c) Dropping variables.
All of these so-called solutions are really ad hoc procedures. Each implies the use of

---

[22] In the case of Tobin's demand for food example, this test done by Maddala showed that there were significant differences between the two parameters.

some prior information and it is better to examine this before undertaking a mechanical solution that has been suggested by others.

5. The basic problem is lack of enough information to answer the questions posed. The only solutions are:

(a) To get more data.

(b) To ask what questions are answerable with the data at hand.

(c) To examine what prior information will be most helpful [in fact, this should precede solution (a)].

EXERCISES

1. Define the term "multicollinearity." Explain how you would detect its presence in a multiple regression equation you have estimated. What are the consequences of multicollinearity, and what are the solutions?

2. Explain the following methods.
   (a) Ridge regression.
   (b) Omitted-variable regression.
   (c) Principle component regression.
   What are the problems these methods are supposed to solve?

3. Examine whether the following statements are true or false. Give an explanation.
   (a) In multiple regression, a high correlation in the sample among the regressors (multicollinearity) implies that the least squares estimators of the coefficients are biased.
   (b) Whether or not multicollinearity is a problem cannot be decided by just looking at the intercorrelations between the explanatory variables.
   (c) If the coefficient estimates in an equation have high standard errors, this is evidence of high multicollinearity.
   (d) The relevant question to ask if there is high multicollinearity is not what variables to drop but what other information will help.

4. In a study analyzing the determinants of faculty salaries, the results shown on p. 249 were obtained.[23] The dependent variable is 1969–1970 academic year salary.
   We have omitted eight more other explanatory variables.
   (a) Do any of the coefficients have unexpected signs?
   (b) Is there a multicollinearity problem? What variable do you expect to be highly correlated?
   (c) Teacher rating is the only nonsignificant variable among the variables presented. Can you explain why? Note that T is a dummy variable indicating whether or not the professor ranked in the top 50% of all instructors by a vote of the students.
   (d) Would dropping the variable T from the equation change the signs of any of the other variables?

---

[23] David A. Katz, "Faculty Salaries, Promotions and Productivity at a Large University," *The American Economic Review*, June 1973, pp. 469–477.

Explanatory Variable	Coefficient	Standard Error	F
Books, B	230	86	7.21
Articles, A	18	8	5.37
Excellent articles, E	102	28	13.43
Dissertations, F	489	60	66.85
Public service, P	89	38	5.65
Committees, C	156	49	10.02
Experience, Y	189	17	126.92
Teacher rating, T	53	370	0.01
English professors, D_4	−2293	529	18.75
Female, X	−2410	528	20.80
Ph.D. degree, R	1919	607	10.01

Constant $= 11,155$; $R^2 = 0.68$; $n = 596$
Standard error of regression $= 2946$
Mean of the dependent variable $= 15,679$
SD of the dependent variable $= 5093$

(e) The variable F is the number of dissertations supervised since 1964. B is the number of books published. How do you explain the high coefficient for F relative to that of B?

(f) Would you conclude from the coefficient of X that there is sex discrimination?

(g) Compute the partial r^2 for experience.

5. Estimate demand for food functions on the basis of the data in Table 4.9. Discuss if there is a multicollinearity problem and what you are going to do about it.

6. Estimate demand for gasoline on the basis of the data Table 4.8. Are the wrong signs for Pg a consequence of multicollinearity?

8

Dummy Variables and Truncated Variables

Let us remember the unfortunate econometrician who, in one of the major functions of his system, had to use a proxy for risk and a dummy for sex.

Fritz Machlup
Journal of Political Economy
July/August 1974

8.1 INTRODUCTION

In the preceding chapters we discussed the estimation of multiple regression equations and several associated problems such as tests of significance, R^2, heteroskedasticity, autocorrelation, and multicollinearity. In this chapter we discuss some special kinds of variables occurring in multiple regression equations and the problems caused by them. The variables we will be considering are:

1. Dummy variables.
2. Truncated variables.

We start with dummy explanatory variables and then discuss dummy dependent variables and truncated variables. Proxy variables referred to in Machlup's quotation are discussed in Chapter 11.

Dummy explanatory variables can be used for several purposes. They can be used to

1. Allow for differences in intercept terms.
2. Allow for differences in slopes.
3. Estimate equations with cross-equation restrictions.
4. Test for stability of regression coefficients.

We discuss each of these uses in turn.

8.2 DUMMY VARIABLES FOR CHANGES IN THE INTERCEPT TERM

Sometimes there will be some explanatory variables in our regression equation that are only qualitative (e.g., presence or absence of college education and racial, sex, or age differences). In such cases one often takes account of these effects by a dummy variable. The implicit assumption is that the regression lines for the different groups differ only in the intercept term but have the same slope coefficients. For example, suppose that the relationship between income y and years of schooling x for two groups is as shown in Figure 8.1. The dots are for group 1 and circles for group 2.

Note that the slopes of the regression lines for both groups are roughly the same but the intercepts are different. Hence the regression equations we fit will be

$$y = \begin{cases} \alpha_1 + \beta x + u & \text{for the first group} \\ \alpha_2 + \beta x + u & \text{for the second group} \end{cases} \tag{8.1}$$

These equations can be combined into a single equation,

$$y = \alpha_1 + (\alpha_2 - \alpha_1)D + \beta x + u \tag{8.2}$$

where

$$D = \begin{cases} 1 & \text{for group 2} \\ 0 & \text{for group 1} \end{cases}$$

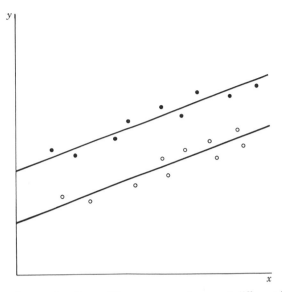

Figure 8.1. Regression lines with a common slope and different intercepts.

The variable D is the dummy variable. The coefficient of the dummy variable measures the differences in the two intercept terms.

If there are more groups, we have to introduce more dummies. For three groups we have

$$y = \begin{cases} \alpha_1 + \beta x + u & \text{for group 1} \\ \alpha_2 + \beta x + u & \text{for group 2} \\ \alpha_3 + \beta x + u & \text{for group 3} \end{cases}$$

These can be written as

$$y = \alpha_1 + (\alpha_2 - \alpha_1)D_1 + (\alpha_3 - \alpha_1)D_2 + \beta x + u \qquad (8.3)$$

where

$$D_1 = \begin{cases} 1 & \text{for group 2} \\ 0 & \text{for groups 1 and 3} \end{cases}$$

$$D_2 = \begin{cases} 1 & \text{for group 3} \\ 0 & \text{for groups 1 and 2} \end{cases}$$

It can be easily checked that by substituting the values for D_1 and D_2 in (8.3), we get the intercepts $\alpha_1, \alpha_2, \alpha_3$, respectively for the three groups. Note that in combining the three equations, we are assuming that the slope coefficient β is the same for all groups *and* that the error term u has the same distribution for the three groups.

If there is a constant term in the regression equation, the number of dummies defined should always be one less than the number of groupings by that category because the constant term is the intercept for the base group and the coefficients of the dummy variables measure differences in intercepts, as can be seen from equation (8.3). In that equation the constant term measures the intercept for the first group, the constant term plus the coefficient of D_1 measures the intercept for the second group, and the constant term plus the coefficient of D_2 measures the intercept for the third group. We have chosen group 1 as the base group, but any one group may be chosen. The coefficients of the dummy variables measure the differences in the intercepts from that of the base group. If we do not introduce a constant term in the regression equation, we can define a dummy variable for each group, and in this case the coefficients of the dummy variables measure the intercepts for the respective groups. If we include both the constant term and three dummies, we will be introducing perfect multicollinearity and the regression program will not run (or will omit one of the dummies automatically).

As yet another example, suppose that we have data on consumption C and income Y for a number of households. In addition, we have data on:

1. S: the sex of the head of the household.
2. A: age of the head of the household, which is given in three categories: <25 years, 25 to 50 years, and >50 years.
3. E: education of the head of household, also in three categories: $<$high school, $\geq$ high school but $<$college degree, $\geq$ college degree.

We include these qualitative variables in the form of dummy variables:

$$D_1 = \begin{cases} 1 & \text{if sex is male} \\ 0 & \text{if female} \end{cases}$$

$$D_2 = \begin{cases} 1 & \text{if age} < 25 \text{ years} \\ 0 & \text{otherwise} \end{cases}$$

$$D_3 = \begin{cases} 1 & \text{if age between 25 } and \text{ 50 years} \\ 0 & \text{otherwise} \end{cases}$$

$$D_4 = \begin{cases} 1 & \text{if} < \text{high school degree} \\ 0 & \text{otherwise} \end{cases}$$

$$D_5 = \begin{cases} 1 & \text{if} \geq \text{high school degree but} < \text{college degree} \\ 0 & \text{otherwise} \end{cases}$$

For each category the number of dummy variables is one less than the number of classifications.

Then we run the regression equation

$$C = \alpha + \beta Y + \gamma_1 D_1 + \gamma_2 D_2 + \gamma_3 D_3 + \gamma_4 D_4 + \gamma_5 D_5 + u$$

The assumption made in the dummy-variable method is that it is only the intercept that changes for each group but not the slope coefficients (i.e., coefficients of Y).

The intercept term for each individual is obtained by substituting the appropriate values for D_1 through D_5. For instance, for a male, age < 25, with college degree, we have $D_1 = 1$, $D_2 = 1$, $D_3 = 0$, $D_4 = 0$, $D_5 = 0$ and hence the intercept is $\alpha + \gamma_1 + \gamma_2$. For a female, age > 50 years, with a college degree, we have $D_1 = 0$, $D_2 = 0$, $D_3 = 0$, $D_4 = 0$, $D_5 = 0$ and hence the intercept terms is just α.

The dummy-variable method is also used if one has to take care of seasonal factors. For example, if we have quarterly data on C and Y, we fit the regression equation

$$C = \alpha + \beta Y + \lambda_1 D_1 + \lambda_2 D_2 + \lambda_3 D_3 + u$$

where D_1, D_2, and D_3 are seasonal dummies defined by

$$D_1 = \begin{cases} 1 & \text{for the first quarter} \\ 0 & \text{for others} \end{cases}$$

$$D_2 = \begin{cases} 1 & \text{for the second quarter} \\ 0 & \text{for others} \end{cases}$$

$$D_3 = \begin{cases} 1 & \text{for the third quarter} \\ 0 & \text{for others} \end{cases}$$

If we have monthly data, we use 11 seasonal dummies:

$$D_1 = \begin{cases} 1 & \text{for January} \\ 0 & \text{for others} \end{cases}$$

$$D_2 = \begin{cases} 1 & \text{for February} \\ 0 & \text{for others} \end{cases} \quad \text{etc.}$$

If we feel that, say, December (because of Christmas shopping) is the only month with strong seasonal effect, we use only one dummy variable:

$$D = \begin{cases} 1 & \text{for December} \\ 0 & \text{for other months} \end{cases}$$

Illustrative Example

The Environmental Protection Agency (EPA) publishes auto mileage estimates that are designed to help car buyers compare the relative fuel efficiency of different models. Does the EPA estimate provide all the information necessary for comparing the relative fuel efficiency of the different models? To investigate this problem Lovell[1] estimated the following regressions.

$$\hat{y} = 7.952 + 0.693 \text{EPA} \qquad \bar{R}^2 = 0.74$$
$$\quad\;\; (1.753) \;\;\; (0.061)$$

(Figures in parentheses are standard errors.)

$$\hat{y} = 22.008 - 0.002W - 2.760S/A + 3.280G/D + 0.415\text{EPA} \qquad \bar{R}^2 = 0.82$$
$$\quad\;\;\; (5.349) \quad\;\; (0.001) \quad\;\;\; (0.708) \qquad\;\; (1.413) \qquad\; (0.097)$$

[1] M. C. Lovell, "Tests of the Rational Expectations Hypothesis," *The American Economic Review*, March 1986, p. 120.

where y = miles per gallon as reported by Consumer Union based on
                road tests
        W = weight of the vehicle (pounds)
      S/A = dummy variable equal to 0 for standard transmission
                and 1.0 for automatic transmission
      G/D = dummy variable equal to 0 for gas and 1.0 for diesel power
       EPA = mileage estimate by the EPA

The variables W, S/A, G/D all have correct signs and are significant, showing that the EPA did not use all the information available in giving its estimates on fuel efficiency.

Two More Illustrative Examples

We will discuss two more examples using dummy variables. They are meant to illustrate two points worth noting, which are as follows:

1. In some studies with a large number of dummy variables it becomes somewhat difficult to interpret the signs of the coefficients because they seem to have the wrong signs. The first example illustrates this problem.
2. Sometimes the introduction of dummy variables produces a drastic change in the slope coefficient. The second example illustrates this point.

The examples are rather old and outdated but they establish the points we wish to make.

The first example is a study of the determinants of automobile prices. Griliches[2] regressed the logarithm of new passenger car prices on various specificatons. The results are shown in Table 8.1. Since the dependent variable is the logarithm of price, the regression coefficients can be interpreted as the estimated percentage change in the price for a unit change in a particular quality, *holding other qualities constant*. For example, the coefficient of H indicates that an increase in 10 units of horse-power, ceteris paribus, results in a 1.2% increase in price. However, some of the coefficients have to be interpreted with caution. For example, the coefficient of P in the equation for 1960 says that the presence of power steering as "standard equipment" led to a 22.5% higher price in 1960. In this case the variable P is obviously not measuring the effect of power steering alone but is measuring the effect of "luxuriousness" of the car. It is also picking up the effects of A and B. This explains why the coefficient of A is so low in 1960. In fact, A, P, and B together can perhaps be replaced by a single dummy that measures "luxuriousness." These variables appear to be highly intercorrelated. Another coefficient, at first sight puzzling, is the coefficient of V, which, though not significant, is consistently negative. Though a V-8 costs more than a six-cylinder engine on a "comparable" car,

[2] Z. Griliches, "Hedonic Price Indexes for Automobiles: An Econometric Analysis of Quality Change," *Government Price Statistics*, Hearings, U.S. Congress, Joint Economic Committee (Washington, D.C.: U.S. Government Printing Office, 1961). Further results on this problem can be found in M. Ohta and Z. Griliches, "Automobile Prices Revisited: Extensions of the Hedonic Hypothesis," in N. Terleckyj (ed.), *Household Behavior and Consumption* (New York: National Bureau of Economic Research, 1975).

Table 8.1 Determinants of Prices of Automobiles[a]

Coefficient of:[b]	1960	1959	1957
H	0.119 (0.029)	.118 (0.029)	0.117 (0.030)
W	0.136 (0.046)	0.238 (0.034)	0.135 (0.010)
L	0.015 (0.017)	−0.016 (0.015)	0.039 (0.013)
V	−0.039 (0.025)	−0.070 (0.039)	−0.025 (0.023)
T	0.058 (0.016)	0.027 (0.019)	0.028 (0.012)
A	0.003 (0.040)	0.063 (0.038)	0.114 (0.025)
P	0.225 (0.037)	0.188 (0.041)	0.078 (0.030)
B			0.159 (0.026)
C	0.048 (0.039)		
R^2	0.951	0.934	0.966

[a] Figures in parentheses are standard errors.
[b] H, advertised brake horsepower (hundreds); W, shipping weight (thousand of pounds); L, overall length in (tens of inches); V, 1 if the car has a V-8 engine, = 0 if it has a six-cylinder engine; T, 1 if the car is hard top, = 0 if not; A, 1 if automatic transmission is "standard" (i.e., included in price), = 0 if not; P, 1 if power steering is "standard," = 0 if not; B, 1 if power brakes are "standard," = 0 if not; C, 1 if car is designated as a "compact," = 0 if not.

what this coefficient says is that, holding horsepower and other variables constant, a V-8 is cheaper by about 4%. Since the V-8's have higher horsepower, what this coefficient is saying is that higher horsepower can be achieved more cheaply if one shifts to V-8 than by using the six-cylinder engine. It measures the decline in price per horsepower as one shifts to V-8's even though the total expenditure on horsepower goes up. This example illustrates the use of dummy variables and the interpretation of seemingly wrong coefficients.

As another example consider the estimates of liquid-asset demand by manufacturing corporations. Vogel and Maddala[3] computed regressions of the form $\log C = \alpha + \beta \log S$, where C is the cash and S the sales, on the basis of data from the

[3] R. C. Vogel and G. S. Maddala, "Cross-Section Estimates of Liquid Asset Demand by Manufacturing Corporations," The Journal of Finance, December 1967.

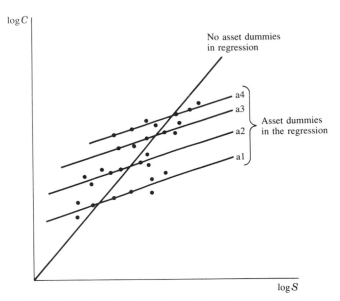

Figure 8.2.   Bias due to omission of dummy variables.

Internal Revenue Service, "Statistics of Income," for the year 1960–1961. The data consisted of 16 industry subgroups and 14 sizes classes, size being measured by total assets. When the regression equations were estimated separately for each industry, the estimates of β ranged from 0.929 to 1.077. The R^2's were uniformly high, ranging from 0.985 to 0.998. Thus one might conclude that the sales elasticity of demand for cash is close to 1. Also, when the data were pooled and a single equation estimated for the entire set of 224 observations, the estimate of β was 0.992 and $R^2 = 0.987$. When industry dummies were added, the estimate of β was 0.995 and $R^2 = 0.992$. From the high R^2's and relatively constant estimate of β one might be reassured that the sales elasticity is very close to 1. However, when asset-size dummies were introduced, the estimate of β fell to 0.334 with R^2 of 0.996. Also, all asset-size dummies were highly significant. The situation is described in Figure 8.2. That the sales elasticity is significantly less than 1 is also confirmed by other evidence. This example illustrates how one can be very easily misled by high R^2's and apparent constancy of the coefficients.

8.3 DUMMY VARIABLES FOR CHANGES IN SLOPE COEFFICIENTS

In Section 8.2 we considered dummy variables to allow for differences in the intercept term. These dummy variables assume the values zero or 1. Not all dummy variables are of this form. We can use dummy variables to allow for differences in slope coefficients as well. For example, if the regression equations are:

$$y_1 = \alpha_1 + \beta_1 x_1 + u_1 \qquad \text{for the first group}$$

and

$$y_2 = \alpha_2 + \beta_2 x_2 + u_2 \qquad \text{for the second group}$$

we can write these equations together as

$$y_1 = \alpha_1 + (\alpha_2 - \alpha_1) \cdot 0 + \beta_1 x_1 + (\beta_2 - \beta_1) \cdot 0 + u_1$$

$$y_2 = \alpha_1 + (\alpha_2 - \alpha_1) \cdot 1 + \beta_1 x_2 + (\beta_2 - \beta_1) \cdot x_2 + u_2$$

or

$$y = \alpha_1 + (\alpha_2 - \alpha_1)D_1 + \beta_1 x + (\beta_2 - \beta_1)D_2 + u \qquad (8.4)$$

where $D_1 = \begin{cases} 0 & \text{for all observations in the first group} \\ 1 & \text{for all observations in the second group} \end{cases}$

$\quad\quad\quad D_2 = \begin{cases} 0 & \text{for all observations in the first group} \\ x_2 & \text{i.e., the respective value of } x \text{ for the second group} \end{cases}$

The coefficient of D_1 measures the difference in the intercept terms and the coefficient of D_2 measures the difference in the slope. Estimation of equation (8.4) amounts to estimating the two equations separately if we assume that the errors have an identical distribution. If we delete D_2 from equation (8.4), this amounts to allowing for different intercepts but not different slopes, and if we delete D_1, it amounts to allowing for different slopes but not different intercepts.

Suitable dummy variables can be defined when there are changes in slopes and intercepts at different times. Suppose that we have data for three periods and in the second period only the intercept changed (there was a parallel shift). In the third period the intercept and the slope have changed. Then we write

$$y_1 = \alpha_1 + \beta_1 x_1 + u_1 \qquad \text{for period 1}$$

$$y_2 = \alpha_2 + \beta_1 x_2 + u_2 \qquad \text{for period 2} \qquad (8.5)$$

$$y_3 = \alpha_3 + \beta_2 x_3 + u_3 \qquad \text{for period 3}$$

Then we can combine these equations and write the model as

$$y = \alpha_1 + (\alpha_2 - \alpha_1)D_1 + (\alpha_3 - \alpha_1)D_2 + \beta_1 x + (\beta_2 - \beta_1)D_3 + u \qquad (8.6)$$

where $D_1 = \begin{cases} 1 & \text{for observations in period 2} \\ 0 & \text{for other periods} \end{cases}$

$\quad\quad\quad D_2 = \begin{cases} 1 & \text{for observations in period 3} \\ 0 & \text{for other periods} \end{cases}$

$\quad\quad\quad D_3 = \begin{cases} 0 & \text{for observations in periods 1 and 2} \\ x_3 & \text{or the respective vaoue of } x \text{ for all observations in period 3} \end{cases}$

Note that in all these examples we are assuming that the error terms in the different groups have all the same distribution. That is why we combine the data from the different groups and write an error term u as in (8.4) or (8.6) and estimate the equation by least squares.

An alternative way of writing the equations (8.5), which is very general, is to stack the y-variables and the error terms in columns. Then write all the parameters

$\alpha_1, \alpha_2, \alpha_3, \beta_1, \beta_2$ down with their multiplicative factors stacked in columns as follows:

$$\begin{pmatrix} y_1 \\ y_2 \\ y_3 \end{pmatrix} = \alpha_1 \begin{pmatrix} 1 \\ 0 \\ 0 \end{pmatrix} + \alpha_2 \begin{pmatrix} 0 \\ 1 \\ 0 \end{pmatrix} + \alpha_3 \begin{pmatrix} 0 \\ 0 \\ 1 \end{pmatrix} + \beta_1 \begin{pmatrix} x_1 \\ x_2 \\ 0 \end{pmatrix} + \beta_2 \begin{pmatrix} 0 \\ 0 \\ x_3 \end{pmatrix} + \begin{pmatrix} u_1 \\ u_2 \\ u_3 \end{pmatrix} \qquad (8.7)$$

What this says is

$$y_1 = \alpha_1(1) + \alpha_2(0) + \alpha_3(0) + \beta_1(x_1) + \beta_2(0) + u_1$$

$$y_2 = \alpha_1(0) + \alpha_2(1) + \alpha_3(0) + \beta_1(x_2) + \beta_2(0) + u_2$$

$$y_3 = \alpha_1(0) + \alpha_2(0) + \alpha_3(1) + \beta_1(0) + \beta_2(x_3) + u_3$$

where ( ) is used for multiplication, e.g., $\alpha_3(0) = \alpha_3 \times 0$.

Now we can write these equations as

$$y = \alpha_1 D_1 + \alpha_2 D_2 + \alpha_3 D_3 + \beta_1 D_4 + \beta_2 D_5 + u \qquad (8.8)$$

where the definitions of D_1, D_2, D_3, D_4, D_5 are clear from (8.7). For instance,

$$D_2 = \begin{cases} 1 & \text{for observations in the second group} \\ 0 & \text{for all others} \end{cases}$$

$$D_4 = \begin{cases} & \text{corresponding values of } x \text{ for observations in groups 1 and 2} \\ 0 & \text{for all observations in group 3} \end{cases}$$

Note that equation (8.8) has to be estimated without a constant term.

In this method we define as many dummy variables as there are parameters to estimate and we estimate the regression equation with no constant term. We will give an illustrative example in the next section, where this method is extended to take care of cross-equation constraints.

Note that equations (8.6) and (8.8) are equivalent. The method of writing the equation in terms of differences in the parameters is useful in tests for stability discussed in Section 8.5.

8.4 DUMMY VARIABLES FOR CROSS-EQUATION CONSTRAINTS

The method described in Section 8.3 can be extended to the case where some parameters across equations are equal. As an illustration, consider the joint estimation of the demand for beef, pork, and chicken on the basis of data presented in Table 8.2.[4] Waugh estimates a set of demand equations of the form

$$p_1 = \alpha_1 + \beta_{11}x_1 + \beta_{12}x_2 + \beta_{13}x_3 + \gamma_1 y + u_1$$

$$p_2 = \alpha_2 + \beta_{12}x_1 + \beta_{22}x_2 + \beta_{23}x_3 + \gamma_2 y + u_2 \qquad (8.9)$$

$$p_3 = \alpha_3 + \beta_{13}x_1 + \beta_{23}x_2 + \beta_{33}x_3 + \gamma_3 y + u_3$$

[4] The data are from F. V. Waugh, *Demand and Price Analysis: Some Example from Agriculture*, U.S.D.A. Technical Bulletin 1316, November 1964, Table 5-1, p. 39.

Table 8.2 Per Capita Consumption and Deflated Prices of Selected Meats, 1948–1963

Year	Beef Consumption per Capita[a] (lb)	Beef Price per Pound,[b] (cents)	Pork Consumption per Capita[a] (lb)	Pork Price per Pound,[b] (cents)	Lamb Consumption per Capita[a] (lb)	Lamb Price per Pound,[b] (cents)	Veal Consumption per Capita[a] (lb)	Veal Price per Pound,[b] (cents)	Chicken Consumption per Capita[a] (lb)	Chicken Price per Pound,[b] (cents)
1948	63.1	82.9	67.8	67.6	5.1	77.8	9.5	77.1	18.3	75.4
1949	63.9	76.3	67.7	61.5	4.1	82.4	8.9	75.7	19.6	71.8
1950	63.4	88.3	69.2	60.4	4.0	84.2	8.0	81.1	20.6	68.0
1951	56.1	90.0	71.9	60.6	3.4	86.7	6.6	87.6	21.7	66.0
1952	62.2	85.4	72.4	57.3	4.2	86.2	7.2	86.3	22.1	65.0
1953	77.6	66.2	63.5	62.9	4.7	70.0	9.5	68.7	21.9	62.8
1954	80.1	64.1	60.0	63.7	4.6	71.0	10.0	65.8	22.8	56.4
1955	82.0	63.2	66.8	54.6	4.6	69.0	9.4	65.8	21.3	58.7
1956	85.4	60.9	67.3	51.4	4.5	68.3	9.5	63.6	24.4	50.4
1957	84.6	63.1	61.1	57.6	4.2	69.9	8.8	65.5	25.5	47.6
1958	80.5	72.0	60.2	60.5	4.2	74.1	6.7	76.1	28.2	45.8
1959	81.4	73.3	67.6	52.8	4.8	69.6	5.7	79.8	28.9	41.4
1960	85.2	70.4	65.2	51.6	4.8	67.6	6.2	77.8	28.2	41.4
1961	88.0	68.3	62.2	53.3	5.1	63.3	5.7	77.3	30.3	37.0
1962	89.1	69.8	64.0	52.9	5.1	67.1	5.5	79.5	30.2	38.6
1963[c]	95.2	67.8	64.9	50.5	4.9	68.0	5.0	79.2	30.6	37.6

[a] Carcass weight equivalent.
[b] Divided by consumer price index (1957–1959 = 100).
[c] 1963 data are preliminary and were not used in the analysis.

where p_1 = retail price of beef
p_2 = retail price of pork
p_3 = retail price of chicken
x_1 = consumption of beef per capita
x_2 = consumption of pork per capita
x_3 = consumption of chicken per capita
y = disposable income per capita

x_1, x_2, and x_3 are given in Table 8.2. The prices in Table 8.2 are, however, retail prices divided by a consumer price index. Hence we multiplied them by the consumer price index p to get p_1, p_2, p_3. This index p and disposable income y are as follows:

	p	y		p	y		p	y
1948	0.838	1291	1953	0.932	1582	1958	1.007	1826
1949	0.830	1271	1954	0.936	1582	1959	1.015	1904
1950	0.838	1369	1955	0.934	1660	1960	1.031	1934
1951	0.906	1473	1956	0.947	1742	1961	1.041	1980
1952	0.925	1520	1957	0.981	1804	1962	1.054	2052

The special thing about the system of equations (8.9) is the symmetry in the β coefficients. We have

$$\frac{dp_1}{dx_2} = \frac{dp_2}{dx_1} = \beta_{12} \qquad \frac{dp_1}{dx_3} = \frac{dp_3}{dx_1} = \beta_{13} \qquad \frac{dp_2}{dx_3} = \frac{dp_3}{dx_2} = \beta_{23}$$

Thus there are cross-equation restrictions on the coefficients. If we assume that $V(u_1) = V(u_2) = V(u_3)$, we can minimize $\left(\sum u_1^2 + \sum u_2^2 + \sum u_3^2\right)$, obtain the normal equations, and estimate the regression coefficients. This is the method used by Waugh. This method involves working out the necessary algebraic expressions and programming things afresh. Instead, we can use the standard regression programs by using the dummy variable method. We can write equations (8.9) as a single equation:

$$\begin{pmatrix} p_1 \\ p_2 \\ p_3 \end{pmatrix} = \alpha_1 \begin{pmatrix} 1 \\ 0 \\ 0 \end{pmatrix} + \alpha_2 \begin{pmatrix} 0 \\ 1 \\ 0 \end{pmatrix} + \alpha_3 \begin{pmatrix} 0 \\ 0 \\ 1 \end{pmatrix} + \beta_{11} \begin{pmatrix} x_1 \\ 0 \\ 0 \end{pmatrix} + \beta_{12} \begin{pmatrix} x_2 \\ x_1 \\ 0 \end{pmatrix}$$

$$+ \beta_{13} \begin{pmatrix} x_3 \\ 0 \\ x_1 \end{pmatrix} + \beta_{22} \begin{pmatrix} 0 \\ x_2 \\ 0 \end{pmatrix} + \beta_{23} \begin{pmatrix} 0 \\ x_3 \\ x_2 \end{pmatrix} + \beta_{33} \begin{pmatrix} 0 \\ 0 \\ x_3 \end{pmatrix}$$

$$+ \gamma_1 \begin{pmatrix} y \\ 0 \\ 0 \end{pmatrix} + \gamma_2 \begin{pmatrix} 0 \\ y \\ 0 \end{pmatrix} + \gamma_3 \begin{pmatrix} 0 \\ 0 \\ y \end{pmatrix} + \begin{pmatrix} u_1 \\ u_2 \\ u_3 \end{pmatrix}$$

We ran this equation with 45 observations and the 12 dummies (no constant term). The values of the dummy variables are easily generated; for example, the set of observations for β_{12} consists of the 15 observations of x_2 followed by the 15 observations of x_1 and 15 zeros. The results (with t ratios in the parentheses) are [5]

$$\hat{p}_1 = 118.98 - \underset{(12.00)}{1.534}x_1 - \underset{(14.55)}{0.474}x_2 - \underset{(4.31)}{0.445}x_3 + \underset{(3.01)}{0.0650}y$$
$$\hspace{2.5cm}{\scriptstyle(12.61)}$$

$$\hat{p}_1 = 118.98 - 1.534x_1 - 0.474x_2 - 0.445x_3 + 0.0650y$$
$$\phantom{\hat{p}_1 = 118.98}\ {(12.00)}\ \ {(14.55)}\ \ \ \ {(4.31)}\ \ \ \ \ {(3.01)}\ \ \ \ \ {(12.61)}$$

$$\hat{p}_2 = 149.79 - 0.474x_1 - 1.189x_2 - 0.319x_3 + 0.0162y$$
$$\phantom{\hat{p}_2 = 149.79}\ {(9.18)}\ \ \ {(4.31)}\ \ \ \ {(6.20)}\ \ \ \ {(1.54)}\ \ \ \ \ {(2.83)}$$

$$\hat{p}_3 = 131.06 - 0.445x_1 - 0.319x_2 - 2.389x_3 + 0.0199y$$
$$\phantom{\hat{p}_3 = 131.06}\ {(7.36)}\ \ \ {(3.01)}\ \ \ \ {(1.54)}\ \ \ \ {(4.32)}\ \ \ \ \ {(1.66)}$$

One can raise questions about the appropriateness of the specification of the system of demand functions (8.9). Our purpose here has been merely to illustrate the use of dummy variable methods to estimate equations where some parameters in different equations are the same.

8.5 DUMMY VARIABLES FOR TESTING STABILITY OF REGRESSION COEFFICIENTS

Dummy variables can also be used to test for stability of regression coefficients as discussed in Section 4.11. The definition of the appropriate dummy variables depends on whether we are using the analysis of covariance test or the predictive test for stability. We will first discuss the analysis-of-covariance test.

Consider, for instance, the two equations

$$y_1 = \alpha_1 + \beta_1 x_1 + \gamma_1 z_1 + u_1 \qquad \text{for the first period}$$
$$y_2 = \alpha_2 + \beta_2 x_2 + \gamma_2 z_2 + u_2 \qquad \text{for the second period}$$

We may be interested in testing the hypothesis that none of the coefficients changed between the two time periods; only the intercept coefficients changed, or only the intercept and the coefficient of the x-variable changed, and so on. As discussed in Section 4.11, the analysis-of-variance test depends on obtaining the unrestricted and restricted residual sums of squares. Both these residual sums of squares can be obtained from the same dummy variable regression if we define enough dummy variables.

For instance, we can write the equations for the two periods as

$$y = \alpha_1 + (\alpha_2 - \alpha_1)D_1 + \beta_1 x + (\beta_2 - \beta_1)D_2 + \gamma_1 z + (\gamma_2 - \gamma_1)D_3 + u \quad (8.10)$$

Note that we write the equation in terms of differences in the parameters and define the dummy variables accordingly.

$$D_1 = \begin{cases} 1 & \text{for period 2} \\ 0 & \text{for period 1} \end{cases}$$

$$D_2 = \begin{cases} x_2 & \text{i.e., the corresponding value of } x \text{ for observations in period 2} \\ 0 & \text{for all observations in period 1} \end{cases}$$

[5] The results are almost the same as those obtained by Waugh. Part of the difference could be that our program is in double precision.

$$D_3 = \begin{cases} z_2 \\ 0 \end{cases}$$ i.e., the corresponding value of z for all observations in period 2
for all observations in period 1

The unrestricted residual sum of squares is the one from estimating (8.10). As for the restricted residual sum of squares, it is obtained by deleting the dummy variables corresponding to that hypothesis.

Hypothesis	Variables Deleted
(1) All coefficients same	D_1, D_2, D_3
$\alpha_1 = \alpha_2, \beta_1 = \beta_2, \gamma_1 = \gamma_2$	
(2) Only intercepts change	D_2, D_3
$\beta_1 = \beta_2, \gamma_1 = \gamma_2$	
(3) Only intercepts and	D_2
coefficients of z change	
$\beta_1 = \beta_2$	

There are some who argue in favor of estimating equations like (8.10) and checking which of the dummy variables is significant in preference to the Chow test discussed in Chapter 4.[6] However, we should be cautious in making inferences about stability and instability of the coefficients by looking at the t-ratios of the dummy variables alone. As we pointed out in our discussion of R^2 (Section 4.10) it can happen that the t-ratios for each of a set of coefficients are all insignificant and still the F-ratio for the entire set of coefficients is significant. What one should do in any particular example is to use the F-tests and then use the t-tests on individual dummy variables only if they correspond to economically meaningful hypotheses.

As discussed in Section 4.11, the analysis-of-covariance test cannot be used if $n_2 < k$. In this case the predictive test suggested by Chow is to use

$$F = \frac{(\text{RSS} - \text{RSS}_1)/n_2}{\text{RSS}_1/(n_1 - k - 1)}$$

as an F-variate with degrees of freedom n_2 and $n_1 - k - 1$. Here RSS is the residual sum of squares with $(n_1 + n_2)$ observations and RSS_1 is the residual sum of squares with n_1 observations.

The F-test, however, does not tell which of the n_2 observations contribute to the instability of the coefficients or are outliers. To do this, we can define a set of n_2 dummy variables defined as[7]

$$D_i = \begin{cases} 1 \\ 0 \end{cases} \quad \begin{array}{l} \text{for observation } n_1 + i \\ \text{for other observations} \end{array} \quad i = 1, 2, \ldots, n_2$$

[6] D. Gujarathi, "Use of Dummy Variables in Testing for Equality of Sets of Coefficients in Two Linear Regressions: A Note," *American Statistician*, February 1970. Gujarathi argues that the Chow test might reject the hypothesis of stability but not tell us which particular coefficients are unstable, whereas the dummy variable method gives this information.

[7] D. S. Salkever, "The Use of Dummy Variables to Compute Predictions, Prediction Errors and Confidence Intervals," *Journal of Econometrics*, Vol. 4, 1976, pp. 393–397.

and test whether the coefficients of the dummy variables are zero. Since one can get the standard error for each of these dummy variables separately from the standard regression packages, one can easily check for outliers and see which of the observations are significantly outside the regression line estimated from the first n_1 observations.

The common regression parameters will be estimated from the first n_1 observations, the coefficient of the ith dummy variable for $i = n_1 + 1, \ldots, n_2$ will measure the prediction error for the prediction of this observation based on the coefficients estimated from the first n_1 observations, and the standard error of this coefficient will measure the standard error of this prediction error.

Consider, for instance,

$$Y = \begin{cases} \alpha + \beta_1 x_1 + \beta_2 x_2 + u & \text{for the first } n_1 \text{ observation} \\ \alpha + \beta_1 x_1 + \beta_2 x_2 + \gamma_1 + u & \text{for the } (n_1 + 1)\text{th observation} \\ \alpha + \beta_1 x_1 + \beta_2 x_2 + \gamma_2 + u & \text{for the } (n_1 + 2)\text{th observation} \end{cases}$$

Then minimizing the sum of squares

$$\sum_{i=1}^{n_1} u_i^2 + u_{n_1+1}^2 + u_{n_2+1}^2$$

we get $\hat{\alpha}$, $\hat{\beta}_1$, and $\hat{\beta}_2$ from the minimization of $\sum_{i=1}^{n_1} u_i^2$ and

$$\hat{\gamma}_j = Y_j - \hat{\alpha} - \hat{\beta}_1 x_{1j} - \hat{\beta}_2 x_{2j} \qquad \text{for } j = n_1 + 1 \text{ and } n_1 + 2$$

What we have considered here for tests for stability is the use of dummy variables to get within sample predictions. We can use the dummy variable method to generate out of sample predictions and their standard errors as well (a problem we discussed in Section 4.7). Suppose we have n observations on Y, x_1 and x_2. We are given the $(n + 1)$th observation on x_1 and x_2 and asked to get the predicted value of Y and a standard error for the prediction. The way we proceed is as follows.

Set the value of Y for the $(n + 1)$th observation at zero. Define a dummy variable D as

$$D = 0 \text{ for the first } n \text{ observations}$$

$$= -1 \text{ for the } (n + 1)\text{th observation.}$$

Now run a regression of Y on x_1, x_2 and D using the $(n + 1)$ observations. The coefficient of D is the prediction $\bar{Y}_{n+1}$ needed and its standard error is the standard error of the prediction. To see this is so, note that the model says:

$$Y = \alpha + \beta_1 x_1 + \beta_2 x_2 + u \qquad \text{for the } n \text{ observations}$$

$$0 = \alpha + \beta_1 x_1 + \beta_2 x_2 - \gamma + u \qquad \text{for the } (n + 1)\text{th observation.}$$

Minimizing the residual sum of squares amounts to obtaining the least squares estimators $\hat{\alpha}$, $\hat{\beta}_1$, $\hat{\beta}_2$ from the first n observations, and

$$\hat{\gamma} = \hat{\alpha} + \hat{\beta}_1 x_1 + \hat{\beta}_2 x_2 \text{ for the } (n + 1)\text{th observation.}$$

Thus, $\hat{\gamma} = \hat{Y}_{n+1}$ and its standard error gives us the required standard error of $\hat{Y}_{n+1}$.

This method has been extended by Pagan and Nicholls [8] to the case of nonlinear models and simultaneous equations models.

8.6 DUMMY VARIABLES UNDER HETEROSKEDASTICITY AND AUTOCORRELATION

In the preceding sections we discussed the use of dummy variables but we need to exercise some caution in the use of these variables when we have heteroskedasticity or autocorrelation.

Consider first the case of heteroskedasticity. Suppose that we have the two equations

$$y = \begin{cases} \alpha_1 + \beta_1 x + u_1 & \text{for the first group} \\ \alpha_2 + \beta_2 x + u_2 & \text{for the second group} \end{cases}$$

Let $\text{var}(u_1) = \sigma_1^2$ and $\text{var}(u_2) = \sigma_2^2$. When we pool the data and estimate an equation like (8.4), we are implicitly assuming that $\sigma_1^2 = \sigma_2^2$. If σ_1^2 and σ_2^2 are widely different, then, even if α_2 is not significantly different from α_1 and β_2 is not significantly different from β_1, the coefficients of the dummy variables in (8.4) can turn out to be significant. One can easily demonstrate this by generating data for the two groups imposing $\alpha_1 = \alpha_2$ and $\beta_1 = \beta_2$ but $\sigma_1^2 = 16\sigma_2^2$ (σ_1^2 being chosen suitably), and estimating equation (8.4). The reverse situation can also arise; that is, ignoring heteroskedasticity can make significant differences appear to be insignificant. Suppose that we take $\alpha_1 = 2\alpha_2$ and $\beta_1 = 2\beta_2$. Then by taking $\sigma_1^2 = 16\sigma_2^2$ (or a multiple around that) we can make the dummy variables appear nonsignificant. The problem is just the same as that of applying tests for stability under heteroskedasticity.

Regarding autocorrelation, suppose that the errors in the equations for the two groups are first-order autoregressive so that we use a first-order autoregressive transformation, that is, write

$$y_t^* = y_t - \rho y_{t-1} \quad \text{for } y_t$$

$$x_t^* = x_t - \rho x_{t-1} \quad \text{for } x_t$$

The question is: What happens to the dummy variables in equation (8.4)? These variables *should not* be subject to the autoregressive transformation and care should be taken if the computer program we use does this automatically. [9] We can easily derive the appropriate dummy variables in this case.

Consider the case with n_1 observations in the first group and n_2 observations in the second group. We will introduce the time subscript t for each observation later when needed.

---

[8] A. R. Pagan and D. F. Nicholls, "Estimating Predictions, Prediction Errors and Their Standard Deviations Using Constructed Variables," *Journal of Econometrics*, Vol. 24, 1984, pp. 293–310.

[9] This point was brought to my attention by Ben-Zion Zilberfarb through a manuscript "On the Use of Autoregressive Transformation in Equations Containing Dummy Variables."

Define

$$\alpha_2^* = \alpha_1(1 - \rho)$$
$$\alpha_2^* = \alpha_2(1 - \rho)$$

Then equation (8.4) can be rewritten as

$$y^* = \alpha_1^* + (\alpha_2^* - \alpha_1^*)D_1 + \beta_1 x^* + (\beta_2 - \beta_1)D_2 + e$$

where D_2 will be defined as before with x_2^* in place of x_2 and the random errors e_t are defined by

$$u_t - \rho u_{t-1} = e_t$$

This equation, however, is all right for the observations in the first group and the last $(n_2 - 1)$ observations in the second group. However, the problem is with the first observation in the second group. For this observation, the ρ-differenced equation turns out to be

$$y_t - \rho y_{t-1} = \alpha_2 - \rho \alpha_1 + (\beta_2 x_t - \rho \beta_1 x_{t-1}) + e_t$$

or

$$y_t^* = \alpha_1^* + \frac{1}{1 - \rho}(\alpha_2^* - \alpha_1^*) + \beta_1 x_t^* + (\beta_2 - \beta_1)x_t + e_t$$

This means that the dummy variables D_1 and D_2 have to be defined as follows:

$$D_1 = \begin{cases} 0 & \text{for all observations in the first group} \\ \dfrac{1}{1-\rho} & \text{for the first observation in the second group} \\ 1 & \text{for all the other observations in the second group} \end{cases}$$

$$D_2 = \begin{cases} 0 & \text{for all observations in the first group} \\ x_t & \text{for the first observation in the second group} \\ x_t^* & \text{for all the other observations in the second group} \end{cases}$$

8.7 DUMMY DEPENDENT VARIABLES

Until now we have been considering models where the explanatory variables are dummy variables. We now discuss models where the explained variable is a dummy variable. This dummy variable can take on two or more values but we consider here the case where it takes on only two values, zero or 1. Considering the other cases is beyond the scope of this book. [10] Since the dummy variable takes on two values,

---

[10] This is a complete area by itself, so we give only an elementary introduction. A more detailed discussion of this topic can be found in G. S. Maddala, *Limited-Dependent and Qualitative Variables in Econometrics* (Cambridge: Cambridge University Press, 1983) Chap. 2, "Discrete Regression Models;" T. Amemiya, "Qualitative Response Models: A Survey," *Journal of Economic Literature*, December 1981, pp. 483–536; and D. R. Cox, *Analysis of Binary Data* (London: Metheun, 1970).

it is called a dichotomous variable. There are numerous examples of dichotomous explained variables. For instance,

$$y = \begin{cases} 1 & \text{if a person is in the labor force} \\ 0 & \text{otherwise} \end{cases}$$

or

$$y = \begin{cases} 1 & \text{if a person owns a home} \\ 0 & \text{otherwise} \end{cases}$$

There are several methods to analyze regression models where the dependent variable is a zero or 1 variable. The simplest procedure is to just use the usual least squares method. In this case the model is called the *linear probability* model. Another method, called the "linear discriminant function," is related to the linear probability model. The other alternative is to say that there is an underlying or latent variable y^* which we do not observe. What we observe is

$$y = \begin{cases} 1 & \text{if } y^* > 0 \\ 0 & \text{otherwise} \end{cases}$$

This is the idea behind the *logit* and *probit* models. First we discuss these methods and then give an illustrative example.

8.8 THE LINEAR PROBABILITY MODEL AND THE LINEAR DISCRIMINANT FUNCTION

The Linear Probability Model

The term *linear probability model* is used to denote a regression model in which the dependent variable y is a dichotomous variable taking the value 1 or zero. For the sake of simplicity we consider only one explanatory variable, x.

The variable y is an indicator variable that denotes the occurrence or non-occurrence of an event. For instance, in an analysis of the determinants of unemployment, we have data on each person that shows whether or not the person is employed, and we have some explanatory variables that determine the state of employment. Here the event under consideration is employment. We define the dichotomous variable

$$y = \begin{cases} 1 & \text{if the person is employed} \\ 0 & \text{otherwise} \end{cases}$$

Similarly, in an analysis of bankruptcy of firms, we define

$$y = \begin{cases} 1 & \text{if the firm is bankrupt} \\ 0 & \text{otherwise} \end{cases}$$

We write the model in the usual regression framework as

$$y_i = \beta x_i + u_i \tag{8.11}$$

with $E(u_i) = 0$. The conditional expectation $E(y_i \mid x_i)$ is equal to βx_i. This has to be interpreted in this case as the probability that the event will occur given the x_i. The calculated value of y from the regression equation (i.e., $\hat{y}_i = \hat{\beta}x_i$) will then give the estimated probability that the event will occur given the particular value of x. In practice these estimated probabilities can lie outside the admissible range $(0, 1)$.

Since y_i takes the value 1 or zero, the errors in equation (8.11) can take only two values, $(1 - \beta x_i)$ and $(-\beta x_i)$. Also, with the interpretation we have given equation (8.11), and the requirement that $E(u_i) = 0$, the respective probabilities of these events are βx_i and $(1 - \beta x_i)$. Thus we have

u_i	$f(u_i)$
$1 - \beta x_i$	βx_i
$-\beta x_i$	$(1 - \beta x_i)$

Hence

$$\text{var}(u_i) = \beta x_i(1 - \beta x_i)^2 + (1 - \beta x_i)(-\beta x_i)^2$$
$$= \beta x_i(1 - \beta x_i)$$
$$= E(y_i)[1 - E(y_i)]$$

Because of this heteroskedasticity problem the ordinary least squares (OLS) estimates of β from equation (8.11) will not be efficient. We can use the following two-step procedure. [11]

First estimate (8.11) by least squares.

Next compute $\hat{y}_i(1 - \hat{y}_i)$ and use weighted least squares, that is, defining

$$w_i = \sqrt{\hat{y}_i(1 - \hat{y}_i)}$$

we regress y_i/w_i on x_i/w_i. The problems with this procedure are:

1. $\hat{y}_i(1 - \hat{y}_i)$ in practice may be negative, although in large samples this will be so with a very small probability [12] since $\hat{y}_i(1 - \hat{y}_i)$ is a consistent estimator for $E(y_i)([1 - E(y_i)])$.
2. Since the errors u_i are obviously not normally distributed, there is a problem with the application of the usual tests of significance. As we will see in the next section, on the linear discriminant function, they can be justified only under the assumption that the explanatory variables have a multivariate normal distribution.
3. The most important criticism is with the formulation itself: that the conditional expectation $E(y_i|x_i)$ be interpreted as the probability that the event will occur. In many cases $E(y_i|x_i)$ can lie outside the limits $(0, 1)$.

The limitations of the linear probability model are shown in Figure 8.3, which shows the bunching up of points [13] along $y = 0$ and $y = 1$. The predicted values can easily lie outside the interval $(0, 1)$ and the prediction errors can be very large.

---

[11] A. S. Goldberger, *Econometric Theory* (New York: Wiley, 1964), p. 250.
[12] R. G. McGilvray, "Estimating the Linear Probability Function," *Econometrica*, 1970, pp. 775–776.
[13] This bunching of points is described in M. Nerlove and S. J. Press, "Univariate and Multivariate Log-Linear and Logistic Models," Report R-1306-EDA/NIH, Rand Corporation, Santa Monica, Calif., December 1973.

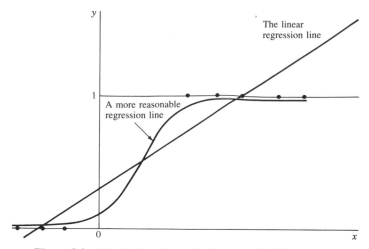

Figure 8.3. Predictions from the linear probability model.

In the 1960s and early 1970s the linear probability model was widely used mainly because it is a model that can be easily estimated using multiple regression analysis. Some others used discriminant analysis, not noting that this method is very similar to the linear probability model. For instance, Meyer and Pifer [14] analyzed bank failures using the linear probability model and Altman [15] analyzed bankruptcy of manufacturing corporations using discriminant analysis. In both studies the bankrupt banks or corporations were taken and a paired sample of nonbankrupt banks or corporations were chosen (i.e., for each bankrupt bank or corporation, a similarly situated nonbankrupt bank or corporation was found). Then the linear probability model or linear discriminant function was estimated.

Since the linear probability model and linear discriminant function are closely related, we will discuss the latter here.

The Linear Discriminant Function

Suppose that we have n individuals for whom we have observations on k explanatory variables and we observe that n_1 of them belong to a group π_1 and n_2 of them belong to a second group $\pi_2(n_1 + n_2 = n)$. We want to construct a linear function of the k variables that we can use to predict that a new observation belongs to one of the two groups. This linear function is called the *linear discriminant function*.

As an example suppose that we have data on a number of loan applicants and we observe that n_1 of them were granted loans and n_2 of them were denied loans. We

[14] Paul A. Meyer and Howard W. Pifer, "Prediction of Bank Failures," *Journal of Finance*, 1970, pp. 853–868.
[15] Edward I. Altman, "Financial Ratios, Discriminant Analysis and the Prediction of Corporate Bankruptcy," *Journal of Finance*, September 1968.

also have the socioeconomic characteristics on the applicants. Now given a new applicant with specified socioeconomic characteristics, we would want to predict whether the applicant will get a loan or not.

Let us define a linear function

$$Z = \lambda_0 + \sum_{i=1}^{k} \lambda_i x_i$$

Then it is intuitively clear that to get the best discrimination between the two groups, we would want to choose the λ_i so that the ratio

$$\frac{\text{between-group variance of } Z}{\text{within-group variance of } Z} \quad \text{is minimum}$$

Fisher[16] suggested an analogy between this problem and multiple regression analysis. He suggested that we define a dummy variable

$$y = \begin{cases} \dfrac{n_2}{n_1 + n_2} & \text{if the individual belongs to } \pi_1 \text{ (first group)} \\[2ex] -\dfrac{n_1}{n_1 + n_2} & \text{if the individual belongs to } \pi_2 \text{ (second group)} \end{cases}$$

Now estimate the multiple regression equation

$$y = \beta_0 + \beta_1 x_1 + \beta_2 x_2 + \cdots + \beta_k x_k + u$$

Get the residual sum of squares RSS. Then

$$\hat{\beta}_i = \hat{\lambda}_i \frac{\text{RSS}}{n_1 + n_2 - 2}$$

Thus, once we have the regression coefficients and the residual sum of squares from the dummy dependent variable regression, we can very easily obtain the discriminant function coefficients.[17]

The linear probability model is only slightly different from the formulation of Fisher. In the linear probability model we define

$$y = \begin{cases} 1 & \text{if the individual belongs to } \pi_1 \\ 0 & \text{if the individual belongs to } \pi_2 \end{cases}$$

This merely amounts to adding $n_1/(n_1 + n_2)$ to each observation of y as defined by Fisher. Thus only the estimate of the constant term changes.

---

[16] R. A. Fisher, "The Use of Multiple Measurements in Taxonomic Problems," *Annals of Eugenics*, 1936, pp. 179–188.

[17] We are omitting the algebraic details here. They can be found in Maddala, *Limited-Dependent*, pp. 18–21. Also, the tests of significance for the coefficients of the linear discriminant function or the linear probability model discussed later are described there.

8.9 THE PROBIT AND LOGIT MODELS

An alternative approach is to assume that we have a regression model

$$y_i^* = \beta_0 + \sum_{j=1}^{k} \beta_j x_{ij} + u_i \tag{8.12}$$

where y_i^* is not observed. It is commonly called a "latent" variable. What we observe is a dummy variable y_i defined by

$$y_i = \begin{cases} 1 & \text{if } y^* > 0 \\ 0 & \text{otherwise} \end{cases} \tag{8.13}$$

The probit and logit models differ in the specification of the distribution of the error term u in (8.12). The difference between the specification (8.12) and the linear probability model is that in the linear probability model we analyze the dichotomous variables as they are, whereas in (8.12) we assume the existence of an underlying latent variable for which we observe a dichotomous realization. For instance, if the observed dummy variable is whether or not the person is employed, y_i^* would be defined as "propensity or ability to find employment." Similarly, if the observed dummy variable is whether or not the person has bought a car, then y_i^* would be defined as "desire or ability to buy a car." Note that in both the examples we have given, there is "desire" and "ability" involved. Thus the explantory variables in (8.12) would contain variables that explain both these elements.

Note from (8.13) that multiplying y_i^* by any positive constant does not change y_i. Hence if we observe y_i, we can estimate the β's in (8.12) only up to a positive multiple. Hence it is customary to assume $\text{var}(u_i) = 1$. This fixes the scale of y_i^*. From the relationships (8.12) and (8.13) we get

$$P_i = \text{Prob}(y_i = 1) = \text{Prob}\left[u_i > -\left(\beta_0 + \sum_{j=1}^{k} \beta_j x_{ij} \right) \right]$$

$$= 1 - F\left[-\left(\beta_0 + \sum_{j=1}^{k} \beta_j x_{ij} \right) \right]$$

where F is the cumulative distribution of u.

If the distribution of u is symmetric, since $1 - F(-Z) = F(Z)$, we can write

$$P_i = F\left(\beta_0 + \sum_{j=1}^{k} \beta_j x_{ij} \right) \tag{8.14}$$

Since the observed y_i are just realizations of a binomial process with probabilities given by (8.14) and varying from trial to trial (depending on x_{ij}), we can write the likelihood function as

$$L = \prod_{y_i = 1} P_i \prod_{y_i = 0} (1 - P_i) \tag{8.15}$$

The functional form for F in (8.14) will depend on the assumption made about the error term u. If the cumulative distribution of u_i is logistic we have what is known as the *logit* model. In this case

$$F(Z_i) = \frac{\exp(Z_i)}{1 + \exp(Z_i)} \tag{8.16}$$

Hence

$$\log \frac{F(Z_i)}{1 - F(Z_i)} = Z_i$$

Note that for the logit model

$$\log \frac{P_i}{1 - P_i} = \beta_0 + \sum_{j=1}^{k} \beta_j x_{ij}$$

The left-hand side of this equation is called the *log-odds ratio*. Thus the log-odds ratio is a linear function of the explanatory variables. For the linear probability model it is P_i that is assumed to be a linear function of the explanatory variables.

If the errors u_i in (8.12) follow a normal distribution, we have the *probit* model (it should more appropriately be called the *normit* model, but the word *probit* was used in the biometrics literature). In this case

$$F(Z_i) = \int_{-\infty}^{Z_i/\sigma} \frac{1}{\sqrt{2\pi}} \exp\left(-\frac{t^2}{2}\right) dt \tag{8.17}$$

Maximization of the likelihood function (8.15) for either the probit or the logit model is accomplished by nonlinear estimation methods. There are now several computer programs available for probit and logit analysis, and these programs are very inexpensive to run.

The likelihood function (8.15) is concave [18] (does not have multiple maxima), and hence any starting values of the parameters would do. It is customary to start the iterations for the logit and probit models with the estimates from the linear probability model.

Since the cumulative and the logistic distributions are very close to each other except at the tails, we are not likely to get very different results using (8.16) or (8.17), that is, the logit or the probit method, unless the samples are large (so that we have enough observations at the tails). However, the estimates of the parameters β_i from the two methods are not directly comparable. Since the logistic distribution has a variance $\pi^2/3$, the estimates of β_i obtained from the logit model have to be multiplied by $\sqrt{3}/\pi$ to be comparable to the estimates obtained from the probit model (where we normalize σ to be equal to 1).

Amemiya [19] suggests that the logit estimates be multiplied by $1/1.6 = 0.625$ instead of $\sqrt{3}/\pi$, saying that this transformation produces a closer approximation between the logistic distribution and the distribution function of the standard

---

[18] This is proved for a general model in J. W. Pratt, "Concavity of the Log-Likelihood," *Journal of the American Statistical Association*, 1981, pp. 137–159.
[19] T. Amemiya, "Qualitative Response Model: A Survey," *Journal of Economic Literature*, 1981, p. 1488.

normal. He also suggests that the coefficients of the linear probability model $\hat{\beta}_{Lp}$ and the coefficients of the logit model $\hat{\beta}_L$ are related by the relations:

$$\hat{\beta}_{Lp} \simeq 0.25\hat{\beta}_L \text{ except for the constant term}$$

$$\hat{\beta}_{Lp} \simeq 0.25\hat{\beta}_L + 0.5 \text{ for the constant term}$$

Thus if we need to make $\hat{\beta}_{Lp}$ comparable to the probit coefficients, we need to multiply them by 2.5 and subtract 1.25 from the constant term.

Alternative ways of comparing the models would be:

1. To calculate the sum of squared deviations from predicted probabilities.
2. To compare the percentages correctly predicted.
3. To look at the derivatives of the probabilities with respect to a particular independent variable.

Illustrative Example

As an illustration, we consider data on a sample of 750 mortgage applications in the Columbia, South Carolina, metropolitan area.[20] There were 500 loan applications accepted and 250 loan applications rejected. We define

$$y = \begin{cases} 1 & \text{if the loan application was accepted} \\ 0 & \text{if the loan application was rejected} \end{cases}$$

Three models were estimated: the linear probability model, the logit model, and the probit model. The explanatory variables were:

$$AI = \text{applicant's and coapplicant's income } (10^3 \text{ dollars})$$

$$XMD = \text{debt minus mortgage payment } (10^3 \text{ dollars})$$

$$DF = \text{dummy variable, 1 for female, 0 for male}$$

$$DR = \text{dummy variable, 1 for nonwhite, 0 for white}$$

$$DS = \text{dummy variable, 1 for single, 0 otherwise}$$

$$DA = \text{age of house } (10^2 \text{ years})$$

$$NNWP = \text{percent nonwhite in the neighborhood } (\times 10^3)$$

$$NMFI = \text{neighborhood mean family income } (10^5 \text{ dollars})$$

$$NA = \text{neighborhood average age of homes } (10^2 \text{ years})$$

The results are presented in Table 8.3.

The coefficients of the probit model were left as they were computed. The other

---

[20] This example is from G. S. Maddala and R. P. Trost, "On Measuring Discrimination in Loan Markets," *Housing Finance Review*, 1982, pp. 245–268.

Table 8.3 Comparison of the Probit, Logit, and Linear Probability Models: Loan Data from South Carolina[a]

Variable	Linear Probability Model	Logit Model	Probit Model
AI	1.489 (4.69)	2.254 (4.60)	2.030 (4.73)
XMD	−1.509 (5.74)	−1.170 (5.57)	−1.773 (5.67)
DF	0.140 (0.78)	0.563 (0.87)	0.206 (0.95)
DR	−0.266 (1.84)	−0.240 (1.60)	−0.279 (1.66)
DS	−0.238 (1.75)	−0.222 (1.51)	−0.274 (1.70)
DA	−1.426 (3.52)	−1.463 (3.34)	−1.570 (3.29)
NNWP	−1.762 (0.74)	−2.028 (0.80)	−2.360 (0.85)
NMFI	0.150 (0.23)	0.149 (0.20)	0.194 (0.25)
NA	−0.393 (1.34)	−0.386 (1.25)	−0.425 (1.26)
Constant	0.501	0.363	0.488

[a] Figures in parentheses are t-ratios not standard errors.

coefficients were adjusted as follows:[21]

1. The coefficients of the logit model were multiplied by 0.625.
2. The coefficients of the linear probability model were multiplied by 2.5 throughout and then 1.25 was subtracted from the constant term.

These are the adjustments described in the text. The three sets of coefficients reported in Table 8.3 are not much different from each other (particularly those of the logit and the probit models).

One can compare the three models by comparing the R^2's. We will illustrate this with another example in the next section after defining the different measures of R^2's for the qualitative dependent variable models.

The Problem of Disproportionate Sampling

In many applications of the logit, probit, or linear probability models it happens that the number of observations in one of the groups is much smaller than the number in the other group. For instance, in an analysis of bank failures, the number of failed banks would be much smaller than the number of solvent banks. In a study of unemployment, the number of unemployed persons is much smaller than the number of employed persons. Thus either we have to get a very large data set (which is what is done in the studies of unemployment based on census tapes)

---

[21] After getting the estimates from the three models, it is always desirable to adjust the coefficients so that they are all on a comparable level. The linear probability model can be estimated by any multiple regression program. As for the logit and probit models, there are many computer programs available now (TSP, RATS, LIMDEP etc.)

or we have to sample the two groups at different sampling rates. For instance, in an analysis of bank failures, all the failed banks are considered in the analysis, but only a small percentage of the solvent banks are sampled. Thus the two groups are sampled at different rates. In the example of loan applications in Columbia, South Carolina, (we have presented estimates in Table 8.3) the sampling was actually at different rates. There were 4600 applications in the accepted category and 250 applications in the rejected category. To have enough observations on females and blacks in the rejected category, it was decided to include all the 250 observations from the rejected category and get a random sample of 500 observations from the accepted category. Thus the sampling rate was 100% for the rejected group and 10.87% for the accepted group.

In such cases a question arises as to how one should analyze the data. It has been commonly suggested that one should use a weighted logit (or probit or linear probability) model similar to the weighted least squares method we discussed under heteroscedasticity in Chapter 5. For instance, Avery and Hanweck argue: [22] "In addition, because failed and non-failed banks were sampled at different rates, it was also necessary to weight observations in estimation" (p. 387). However, this is not a correct procedure. The usual logit model can be used without any change even with unequal sampling rates. Thus the results presented in Table 8.3 are based on the usual estimation procedures with no weighting used.

Regarding the estimation of the coefficients of the explanatory variables, if we use the logit model, the coefficients are not affected by the unequal sampling rates for the two groups. It is only the constant term that is affected. [23] In Table 8.3 the logit coefficients are all correct, except for the constant term which needs to be increased by $\log p_1 - \log p_2$, where p_1 and p_2 are the proportions of observations chosen from the two groups for which $y = 1$ and 0, respectively, and the logarithm is the natural logarithm. In the example in Table 8.3, the constant term for the logit model has to be increased by $\log(0.1087) - \log(1.0) \simeq -2.22$. Since the coefficients in Table 8.3 have been adjusted (as described earlier), we have to multiply this by 0.625. Thus the increase in the constant terms is -1.39.

Note the this result is valid for the logit model, not for the probit model or the linear probability model. However, even for these models, although one cannot derive the results analytically, it appears that the slope coefficients are not much affected by unequal sampling rates.

Weighting the observations is the correct procedure if there is a heteroskedasticity problem. There is no reason why the unequal sampling proportions should cause a heteroskedasticity problem. Thus weighting the observations is clearly not a correct solution. If our interest is mainly in examining which variables are significant, we need not make any changes in the estimated coefficients for the logit model. On the other hand, if the estimated model is going to be used for prediction purposes, an adjustment in the constant term, as suggested earlier, is necessary.

[22] Robert B. Avery and Gerald A. Hanweck, "A Dynamic Analysis of Bank Failures," *Bank Structure and Competition* (Chicago: Federal Reserve Bank of Chicago, 1984), pp. 380–395.
[23] For a discussion of this point, see Maddala, *Limited-Dependent*, pp. 90–91.

Prediction of Effects of Changes in the Explanatory Variables

After estimating the parameters β_i, we would like to know the effects of changes in any of the explantory variables on the probabilities of any observation belonging to either of the two groups. These effects are given by

$$\frac{\partial P_i}{\partial x_{ij}} = \begin{cases} \beta_j & \text{for the linear probability model} \\ \beta_j P_i(1 - P_i) & \text{for the logit model} \\ \beta_j \phi(Z_i) & \text{for the probit model} \end{cases}$$

where

$$Z_i = \beta_0 + \sum_{i=1}^{k} \beta_i x_{ij}$$

and $\phi(\cdot)$ is the density function of the standard normal.

In the case of the linear probability model these derivatives are constant. In the case of the logit and probit models, we need to calculate them at different levels of the explanatory variables to get an idea of the range of variation of the resulting changes in probabilities. If one is interested in the prediction of the effect on the log-odds ratio, then for the logit model, this effect is constant since

$$\frac{\partial}{\partial x_{ij}} \left(\log \frac{P_i}{1 - P_i} \right) = \beta_j$$

Measuring Goodness of Fit

There is a problem with the use of conventional R^2-type measures when the explained variable y takes on only two values.[24] The predicted values $\hat{y}$ are probabilities and the actual values y are either 0 or 1. For the linear probability model and the logit model we have $\sum y = \sum \hat{y}$, as with the linear regression model, if a constant term is also estimated. For the probit model there is no such exact relationship although it is approximately valid. We will see this in the illustrative example presented later.

There are several R^2-type measures that have been suggested for models with qualitative dependent variables. The following are some of them. In the case of the linear regression model, they are all equivalent. However, they are not equivalent in the case of models with qualitative dependent variables.

1. R^2 = squared correlation between y and $\hat{y}$.

2. *Measures based on residual sum of squares.* For the linear regression model we have

$$R^2 = 1 - \left[\frac{\sum_{i=1}^{n} (y_i - \hat{y}_i)^2}{\sum_{i=1}^{n} (y_i - \bar{y})^2} \right]$$

[24] These are summarized in Maddala, *Limited-Dependent*, pp. 37–41.

We can use this same measure if we can use $\sum_{i=1}^{n}(y_i - \hat{y}_i)^2$ as the measure of residual sum of squares. Effron[25] argued that we can use it.

Note that in the case of a binary dependent variable

$$\sum(y_i - \bar{y})^2 = \sum y_i^2 - n\bar{y}^2 = n_1 - n\left(\frac{n_1}{n}\right)^2 = \frac{n_1 n_2}{n}$$

Hence Effron's measure of R^2 is

$$R^2 = 1 - \frac{n}{n_1 n_2} \sum_{i=1}^{n} (y_i - \hat{y}_i)^2$$

Amemiya[26] argues that it makes more sense to define the residual sum of squares as

$$\sum_{i=1}^{n} \frac{(y_i - \hat{y}_i)^2}{\hat{y}_i(1 - \hat{y}_i)}$$

that is, to weight the squared error $(y_i - \hat{y}_i)^2$ by a weight that is inversely proportional to its variance.

3. *Measures based on likelihood ratios.* For the standard linear regression model,

$$y = \beta_0 + \sum_{i=1}^{k} \beta_i x_i + u \qquad u \sim IN(0, \sigma^2)$$

let L_{UR} be the maximum of the likelihood function when maximized with respect to all the parameters and L_R be the maximum when maximized with the restriction $\beta_i = 0$ for $i = 1, 2, \ldots, k$. Then

$$R^2 = 1 - \left(\frac{L_R}{L_{UR}}\right)^{2/n}$$

One can use an analogous measure for the logit and probit model as well. However, for the qualitative dependent variable model, the likelihood function (8.15) attains an absolute maximum of 1. This means that

$$L_R \le L_{UR} \le 1$$

or

$$L_R \le \frac{L_R}{L_{UR}} \le 1$$

or

$$L_R^{2/n} \le 1 - R^2 \le 1$$

or

$$0 \le R^2 \le 1 - L_R^{2/n}$$

[25] B. Effron, "Regression and ANOVA with Zero–One Data: Measures of Residual Variation," *Journal of the American Statistical Association*, May 1978, pp. 113–121.
[26] T. Amemiya, "Qualitative Response Models," p. 1504.

Hence Cragg and Uhler[27] suggest a pseudo R^2: (It lies in $[0, 1]$)

$$\text{pseudo } R^2 = \frac{L_{UR}^{2/n} - L_R^{2/n}}{1 - L_R^{2/n}}$$

Another measure of R^2 is that of McFadden,[28] who defines it as

$$\text{McFadden's } R^2 = 1 - \frac{\log L_{UR}}{\log L_R}$$

However, this measure does not correspond to any R^2 measure in the linear regression model.

4. Finally, we can also think of R^2 in terms of the *porportion* of correct predictions. Since the dependent variable is a zero or 1 variable, after we compute the $\hat{y}_i$ we classify the ith observation as belonging to group 1 if $\hat{y}_i > 0.5$ and classify it as belonging to group 2 if $\hat{y}_i < 0.5$. We can then count the number of correct predictions. We can define a predicted value $\hat{y}_i^*$, which is also a zero-one variable such that

$$\hat{y}_i^* = \begin{cases} 1 & \text{if } \hat{y}_i > 0.5 \\ 0 & \text{if } \hat{y}_i < 0.5 \end{cases}$$

(Provided that we calculate y_i to enough decimals, ties will be very unlikely.) Now define

$$\text{count } R^2 = \frac{\text{number of correct predictions}}{\text{total number of observations}}$$

Although this is a useful measure worth reporting in all problems, it might not have enough discriminatory power. In the illustrative example in the next section, we found that the logit model predicted 41 of the total 44 cases correctly, whereas the probit and linear probability model each predicted 40 of the 44 correctly. However, looking at $\hat{y}_i$, the linear probability model had five observations with $\hat{y}_i$ substantially greater than 1, thus outside the range of $(0, 1)$. Also, this measure did not appear to help us much in discriminating between the three models as the other measures of R^2's did. It is, however, possible that this measure has better discriminatory power in other problems. In any case, it is a measure worth reporting in every problem.

8.10 Illustrative Example

Consider the data in Table 8.4. The data refer to a study on deterrent effect of capital punishment by McManus.[29] The data are cross-sectional data for 44 states in the United States in 1950. There are two dummy variables in the data. D_2, which is

[27] J. G. Cragg and R. Uhler, "The Demand for Automobiles," *Canadian Journal of Economics*, 1970, pp. 386–406. See also Maddala, *Limited-Dependent*, pp. 39–40 for a discussion of this Pseudo-R^2.

[28] D. McFadden, "The Measurement of Urban Travel Demand," *Journal of Public Economics*, 1974, pp. 303–328.

[29] Walter S. McManus, "Estimates of the Deterrent Effect of Capital Punishment: The Importance of the Researcher's Prior Beliefs," *Journal of Political Economy*, Vol. 93, April 1985, pp. 417–425.

Table 8.4 Determinants of Murder Rates in the United States (Cross-Section Data on States in 1950)[a]

N	M	PC	PX	D_1	T	Y	LF	NW	D_2
1	19.25	0.204	0.035	1	47	1.10	51.2	0.321	1
2	7.53	0.327	0.081	1	58	0.92	48.5	0.224	1
3	5.66	0.401	0.012	1	82	1.72	50.8	0.127	0
4	3.21	0.318	0.070	1	100	2.18	54.4	0.063	0
5	2.80	0.350	0.062	1	222	1.75	52.4	0.021	0
6	1.41	0.283	0.100	1	164	2.26	56.7	0.027	0
7	6.18	0.204	0.050	1	161	2.07	54.6	0.139	1
8	12.15	0.232	0.054	1	70	1.43	52.7	0.218	1
9	1.34	0.199	0.086	1	219	1.92	52.3	0.008	0
10	3.71	0.138	0	0	81	1.82	53.0	0.012	0
11	5.35	0.142	0.018	1	209	2.34	55.4	0.076	0
12	4.72	0.118	0.045	1	182	2.12	53.5	0.299	0
13	3.81	0.207	0.040	1	185	1.81	51.6	0.040	0
14	10.44	0.189	0.045	1	104	1.35	48.5	0.069	1
15	9.58	0.124	0.125	1	126	1.26	49.3	0.330	1
16	1.02	0.210	0.060	1	192	2.07	53.9	0.017	0
17	7.52	0.227	0.055	1	95	2.04	55.7	0.166	1
18	1.31	0.167	0	0	245	1.55	51.2	0.003	0
19	1.67	0.120	0	0	97	1.89	54.0	0.010	0
20	7.07	0.139	0.041	1	177	1.68	52.2	0.076	0
21	11.79	0.272	0.063	1	125	0.76	51.1	0.454	1
22	2.71	0.125	0	0	56	1.96	54.0	0.032	0
23	13.21	0.235	0.086	1	85	1.29	55.0	0.266	1
24	3.48	0.108	0.040	1	199	1.81	52.9	0.018	0
25	0.81	0.672	0	0	298	1.72	53.7	0.038	0
26	2.32	0.357	0.030	1	145	2.39	55.8	0.067	0
27	3.47	0.592	0.029	1	78	1.68	50.4	0.075	0
28	8.31	0.225	0.400	1	144	2.29	58.8	0.064	0
29	1.57	0.267	0.126	1	178	2.34	54.5	0.065	0
30	4.13	0.164	0.122	1	146	2.21	53.5	0.065	0
31	3.84	0.128	0.091	1	132	1.42	48.8	0.090	1
32	1.83	0.287	0.075	1	98	1.97	54.5	0.016	0
33	3.54	0.210	0.069	1	120	2.12	52.1	0.061	0
34	1.11	0.342	0	0	148	1.90	56.0	0.019	0
35	8.90	0.133	0.216	1	123	1.15	56.2	0.389	1

[a] N, observation number; M, murder rate per 100,000, FBI estimate 1950; PC, (number of convictions/number of murders) in 1950; PX, average number of executions during 1946–1950 divided by convictions in 1950; Y, median family income of families in 1949 (thousands of dollars); LF, labor force participation rate 1950 (expressed as a percent); NW, proportion of population that is nonwhite in 1950; D_2, dummy variable, 1 for southern states, 0 for others; D_1, dummy variable which is 1 if the state has capital punishment, 0 otherwise ($D_1 = 1$ if $PX > 0$, 0 otherwise); T, median time served in months of convicted murderers released in 1951.

Table 8.4 (*Continued*)

N	M	PC	PX	D_1	T	Y	LF	NW	D_2
36	1.27	0.241	0.100	1	282	1.70	53.3	0.037	0
37	15.26	0.167	0.038	1	79	1.24	50.9	0.161	1
38	11.15	0.252	0.040	1	34	1.55	53.2	0.127	1
39	1.74	0.418	0	0	104	2.04	51.7	0.017	0
40	11.98	0.282	0.032	1	91	1.59	54.3	0.222	1
41	3.04	0.194	0.086	1	199	2.07	53.7	0.026	0
42	0.85	0.378	0	0	101	2.00	54.7	0.012	0
43	2.83	0.757	0.033	1	109	1.84	47.0	0.057	1
44	2.89	0.357	0	0	117	2.04	56.9	0.022	0

a South–North dummy, is clearly an explanatory variable. But D_1 can be both an explained and explanatory variable. If it is an explained variable we would consider it as "a propensity to have capital punishment."

Let us first consider the regression of M on all the other variables. The results are as follows: (Figures in parentheses are *t-ratios*, not standard errors.)

$$\hat{M} = -8.50 - 3.696PC - 3.568PX + 2.598D_1$$
$$\phantom{\hat{M} =} (-0.82) \quad (-1.38) \qquad (-0.54) \qquad (2.11)$$

$$- 0.018T - 4.095Y + 0.400LF$$
$$ (2.62) \qquad (-2.3) \qquad (1.82)$$

$$+ 6.444NW + 2.541D_2 \qquad R^2 = 0.7746$$
$$ (1.17) \qquad (1.93)$$

Some of the coefficients have signs opposite to those we would expect.

Let us now consider treating D_1 as an explained variable. We will consider T, Y, LF, NW, and D_2 as the explanatory variables.

The linear probability model gave the following results (figures in parentheses are *t*-ratios obtained from an ordinary regression program that ignores the zero-1 characteristic of the dependent variable):

$$\hat{D}_1 = 1.993 + 0.00146T + 0.658Y - 0.055LF$$
$$\phantom{\hat{D}_1 =} (1.50) \quad (1.46) \qquad (2.74) \qquad (-1.93)$$

$$+ 1.988NW + 0.343D_2 \qquad R^2 = 0.3376$$
$$ (2.62) \qquad (1.81)$$

What these results indicate is that southern states and states with higher percentages of nonwhites have a positive effect on the probability of having capital punishment. The percentage of labor force employed has a negative effect on the probability of having capital punishment. What is perplexing is the coefficient of Y (median family income), which is significantly positive. One possible explanation for this is that states with high incomes (New York, California, etc.) also have big cities where crime rates are high.

Table 8.5 Different R^2 Measures for the Logit, Probit, and Linear Probability Models

	Logit	Probit	Linear Probability
Squared correlation between D_1 and $\hat{D}_1$	0.6117	0.6099	0.3376
Effron's R^2	0.6116	0.6095	0.3376
Cragg–Uhler's R^2	0.4857	0.4901	0.2742
McFadden's R^2	0.6083	0.6124	0.3876

Let us now look at the logit and probit estimates.[30] The logit model gave (figures in parentheses are asymptotic t-ratios)

$$\hat{D}_1 = 10.99 + 0.0194T + 10.61Y - 0.668LF + 70.99NW + 13.33D_2$$
$$\quad\;\;(0.53)\quad\;(1.87)\qquad\;(1.88)\quad\;(-1.40)\qquad(1.95)\qquad\;(0.02)$$

The results of the probit model were (figures in parentheses are asymptotic t-ratios)

$$\hat{D}_1 = 6.92 + 0.0113T + 6.46Y - 0.409LF + 42.50NW + 4.63D_2$$
$$\quad\;(0.61)\quad\;(2.00)\qquad(2.05)\quad\;(-1.59)\qquad(2.05)\qquad\;(0.04)$$

As mentioned earlier, the logit coefficients have to be divided by 1.6 to be comparable to the probit coefficients. Such division produces the coefficients 6.81, 0.0121, 6.63, -0.418, 43.86, and 8.33, respectively which are close to the probit coefficients. Surprisingly, D_2 is not significant, but all the other coefficients have the same signs as in the linear probability model. The coefficient of Y is still positive and is significant.

One other problem is that, as mentioned in Section 8.9, the coefficients of the logit model should be approximately four times the coefficients of the linear probability model, but the coefficients we have obtained are much higher than that. One possible reason for this is the poor fit given by the linear probability model. To investigate this we computed the different measures of R^2's discussed in the preceding section, and the R^2's for the linear probability model are significantly lower than those for the logit and probit models.

In Table 8.5 we present four different measures of R^2's.[31] The first two are easy to compute and are reasonable measures of R^2's. The measures suggested by Cragg and Uhler and by McFadden both depend on the computation of L_R and L_{UR}. The results indicate that there is not much to choose between the logit and probit models and that both are better than the linear probability model. From the practical point of view it appears that the square correlation between D_1 and $\hat{D}_1$ and Effron's R^2 are sufficient for many problems.

---

[30] The logit and probit estimates were computed using William Greene's LIMDEP program.
[31] We did not compute Amemiya's R^2's. Although he has given an expression for the residual sum of squares, he has not given an expression for the total sum of squares (which should also be appropriately weighted). Using the unweighted total sum of squares $\sum (y_i - \bar{y})^2$ produces a negative R^2.

Since we decided on the probit and logit models and D_2 was not significant in these models, we decided to drop that variable and reestimate the probit and logit models. The revised estimates were (figures in parentheses are asymptotic t-ratios)

Logit

$$\hat{D}_1 = 16.57 + 0.0165T + 9.13Y - 0.715LF + 85.36NW$$
$$\quad\ \ (0.84)\ \ \ (1.72)\qquad (1.81)\quad\ (-1.49)\qquad (2.38)$$

$R^2(D_1, \hat{D}_1) = 0.5982$ Effron's $R^2 = 0.5982$

Cragg–Uhler's $R^2 = 0.4678$ McFadden's $R^2 = 0.5914$

Probit

$$\hat{D}_1 = 10.27 + 0.0094T + 5.55Y - 0.437LF + 50.25NW$$
$$\quad\ \ (0.98)\ \ \ (1.86)\qquad (1.97)\quad\ (-1.7)\qquad (2.50)$$

$R^2(D_1, \hat{D}_1) = 0.5950$ Effron's $R^2 = 0.5947$

Cragg–Uhler's $R^2 = 0.4721$ McFadden's $R^2 = 0.5955$

Again, to make the logit coefficients comparable to the probit coefficients, we have to divide the former by 1.6. This gives 10.36, 0.0103, 5.71, -0.447, and 53.35, respectively, which are close to the probit coefficients.

8.11 TRUNCATED VARIABLES: THE TOBIT MODEL

In our discussion of the logit and probit models we talked about a latent variable y_i^* which was not observed, for which we could specify the regression model:

$$y_i^* = \beta x_i + u_i \tag{8.18}$$

For simplicity of exposition we are assuming that there is only one explanatory variable. In the logit and probit models, what we observe is a dummy variable

$$y_i = \begin{cases} 1 & \text{if } y_i^* > 0 \\ 0 & \text{if } y_i^* \le 0 \end{cases}$$

Suppose, however, that y_i^* is observed if $y_i^* > 0$ and is not observed if $y_i^* \le 0$. Then the observed y_i will be defined as

$$y_i = \begin{cases} y_i^* = \beta x_i + u_i & \text{if } y_i^* > 0 \\ 0 & \text{if } y_i^* \le 0 \end{cases} \tag{8.19}$$

$$u_i \sim \text{IN}(0, \sigma^2)$$

This is known as the *tobit model* (Tobin's probit) and was first analyzed in the econometrics literature by Tobin.[32] It is also known as a *censored normal regression*

[32] J. Tobin, "Estimation of Relationships for Limited Dependent Variables," *Econometrica*, Vol. 26, 1958, pp. 24–36.

model because some observations on y^* (those for which $y^* \leq 0$) are censored (we are not allowed to see them). Our objective is to estimate the parameters β and σ.

Some Examples

The example that Tobin considered was that of automobile expenditures. Suppose that we have data on a sample of households. We wish to estimate, say, the income elasticity of demand for automobiles. Let y^* denote expenditures on automobiles and x denote income, and we postulate the regression equation

$$y_i^* = \beta x_i + u_i \qquad u_i \sim \text{IN}(0, \sigma^2)$$

However, in the sample we would have a large number of observations for which the expenditures on automobiles is zero. Tobin argued that we should use the censored regression model. We can specify the model as

$$y_i = \begin{cases} \beta x_i + u_i & \text{for those with positive automobile expenditures} \\ 0 & \text{for those with no expenditures} \end{cases} \qquad (8.20)$$

The structure of this model thus appears to be the same as that in (8.19).

There have been a very large number of applications of the tobit model.[33] Take, for instance, hours worked (H) or wages (W). If we have observations on a number of individuals, some of whom are employed and others not, we can specify the model for hours worked as

$$H_i = \begin{cases} \beta x_i + u_i & \text{for those working} \\ 0 & \text{for those who are not working} \end{cases} \qquad (8.21)$$

Similarly, for wages we can specify the model

$$W_i = \begin{cases} \gamma z_i + v_i & \text{for those working} \\ 0 & \text{for those who are not working} \end{cases} \qquad (8.22)$$

The structure of these models again appears to be the same as in (8.19). However, there are some limitations in the formulation of the models in (8.20)–(8.22) that we will presently outline after discussing the estimation of the model in (8.19).

Method of Estimation

Let us consider the estimation of β and σ by the use of ordinary least squares (OLS). We cannot use OLS using the positive observations y_i because when we write the model

$$y_i = \beta x_i + u_i$$

---

[33] See T. Amemiya, "Tobit Models: A Survey," *Journal of Econometrics*, Vol. 24 1984, pp. 3–61, which lists a large number of applications of the tobit model.

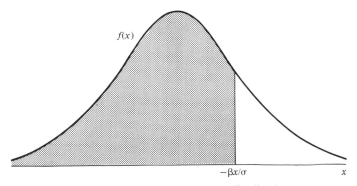

Figure 8.4. Truncated normal distribution.

the error term u_i does not have a zero mean. Since observations with $y_i^* \leq 0$ are omitted, it implies that only observations for which $u_i > -\beta x_i$ are included in the sample. Thus the distribution of u_i is a *truncated normal distribution* shown in Figure 8.4 and its mean is not zero. In fact, it depends on β, σ, and x_i and is thus different for each observation. A method of estimation commonly suggested is the maximum likelihood (ML) method, which is as follows:

Note that we have two sets of observations:

1. The positive values of y, for which we can write down the normal density function as usual. We note that $(y_i - \beta x_i)/\sigma$ has a standard normal distribution.
2. The zero observations of y for which all we know is that $y_i^* \leq 0$ or $\beta x_i + u_i \leq 0$. Since u_i/σ has a standard normal distribution, we will write this as $u_i/\sigma \leq -(\beta x_i)/\sigma$. The probability of this can be written as $F(-(\beta x_i)/\sigma)$, where $F(z)$ is the cumulative distribution function of the standard normal.

Let us denote the density function of the standard normal by $f(\cdot)$ and the cumulative distribution function by $F(\cdot)$. Thus

$$f(t) = \frac{1}{\sqrt{2\pi}} \exp\left(-\frac{t^2}{2}\right)$$

and

$$F(z) = \int_{-\infty}^{z} f(t)\, dt$$

Using this notation we can write the likelihood function for the tobit model as

$$L = \prod_{y_i > 0} \frac{1}{\sigma} f\left(\frac{y_i - \beta x_i}{\sigma}\right) \prod_{y_i \leq 0} F\left(-\frac{\beta x_i}{\sigma}\right)$$

Maximizing this likelihood function with respect to β and σ, we get the maximum likelihood (ML) estimates of these parameters. We will not go through the algebraic details of the ML method here. [34] Instead, we discuss the situations under which the tobit model is applicable and its relationship to other models with truncated variables.

Limitations of the Tobit Model

Consider the models of automobile expenditures in (8.20), of hours worked in (8.21), and of wages in (8.22). In each case there are zero observations on some individuals in the sample and thus the structure of the model looks very similar to that in (8.19). But is it really? Every time we have some zero observations in the sample, it is tempting to use the tobit model. However, it is important to understand what the model in (8.19) really says. What we have in model (8.19) is a situation where y_i^* can, *in principle*, take on negative values. However, we do not observe them because of censoring. Thus the zero values are due to nonobservability. This is *not* the case with automobile expenditures, hours worked, or wages. These variables cannot, in principle, assume negative values. The observed zero values are due not to censoring, but due to the decisions of individuals. In this case the appropriate procedure would be to model the decisions that produce the zero observations rather than use the tobit model mechanically.

Consider, for instance, the model of wages in (8.22). We can argue that each person has a reservation wage W_1 below which the person would not want to work. If W_2 is the market wage for this person (i.e., the wage that employers are willing to pay) and $W_2 \geq W_1$, then we will observe the person as working and the observed wage W is equal to W_2. On the other hand, if $W_1 < W_2$, we observe the person as not working and the observed wage is zero.

If this is the story behind the observed zero wages (one can construct other similar stories), we can formulate the model as follows. Let the reservation wages W_{1i} and market wages W_{2i} be given by

$$W_{1i} = \beta_1 x_{1i} + u_{1i}$$
$$W_{2i} = \beta_2 x_{2i} + u_{2i}$$

The observed W_i is given by

$$W_i = \begin{cases} W_{2i} & \text{if } W_{2i} \geq W_{1i} \\ 0 & \text{otherwise} \end{cases}$$

We can write this as

$$W_i = \begin{cases} \beta_2 x_{2i} + u_{2i} & \text{if } u_{2i} - u_{1i} \geq \beta_i x_{1i} - \beta_2 x_{2i} \\ 0 & \text{otherwise} \end{cases} \tag{8.23}$$

Note the difference between this formulation and the one in equation (8.19). The criterion that $W_i = 0$ is not given by $u_{2i} \leq -\beta_2 x_{2i}$ as in the simple tobit model but by

---

[34] For details see Maddala, *Limited-Dependent*, Chap. 6. A convenient computer program is the LIMDEP program by William Greene at New York University. This program can also be used to estimate the other models discussed later.

$u_{2i} - u_{1i} < \beta_1 x_{1i} - \beta_2 x_{2i}$. Hence estimation of a simple tobit model in this case produces inconsistent estimates of the parameters.

Estimation of the model given by (8.23) is somewhat complicated to be discussed here.[35] However, the purpose of the example is to show that every time we have some zero observations, we should not use the tobit model. In fact, we can construct similar models for automobile expenditures and hours worked wherein the zero observations are a consequence of decisions by individuals. The simple censored regression model (or the tobit model) is applicable only in those cases where the latent variable can, in principle, take negative values and the observed zero values are a consequence of censoring and nonobservability.

The Truncated Regression Model

The term *truncated regression model* refers to a situation where samples are drawn from a truncated distribution. It is important to keep in mind the distinction between this model and the tobit model. In the censored regression model (tobit model) we have observations on the explanatory variable x_i for all individuals. It is only the dependent variable y_i^* that is missing for some individuals. In the truncated regression model, we have no data on either y_i^* or x_i for some individuals because no samples are drawn if y_i^* is below or above a certain level. The New Jersey negative-income-tax experiment was an example in which high-income families were not sampled at all. Families were selected at random but those with incomes higher than 1.5 times the 1967 poverty line were eliminated from the study. If we are estimating earnings functions from these data, we cannot use the OLS method. We have to take account of the fact that the sample is from a truncated distribution. Figure 8.5

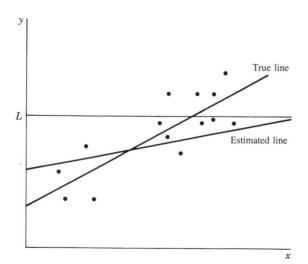

Figure 8.5. Truncated regression model.

[35] It is discussed in Maddala, *Limited-Dependent*, (Sec. 6.11.)

illustrates this point. The observations above $y = L$ are omitted from the sample. If we use OLS, the estimated line gives a biased estimate of the true slope. A method of estimation often suggested is, again, the maximum likelihood method.[36]

Suppose that the untruncated regression model is

$$y_i^* = \beta x_i + u_i \qquad u_i \sim \text{IN}(0, \sigma^2)$$

Now, only observations with $y_i^* \le L$ are included in the sample. The total area under the normal curve up to $y_i^* < L$, that is, $u_i/\sigma < (L - \beta x_i)/\sigma$ is $F[(L - \beta x_i)/\sigma]$, where $F(\cdot)$ is the cumulative distribution function of the standard normal. The density function of the observed y_i is the standard normal density except that its total area is $F[(L - \beta x_i)/\sigma]$. Since the total area under a probability density function should be equal to 1, we have to normalize by this factor. Thus the density function of the observations y_i from the truncated normal is

$$g(y_i) = \begin{cases} \dfrac{1}{\sigma} f\left(\dfrac{y_i - \beta x_i}{\sigma}\right) \Big/ F\left(\dfrac{L - \beta x_i}{\sigma}\right) & \text{if } y_i \le L \\ 0 & \text{otherwise} \end{cases}$$

The log-likelihood is, therefore,

$$\log L = -n \log \sigma - \frac{1}{2\sigma^2} \sum (y_i - \beta x_i)^2 - \sum \log F\left(\frac{L - \beta x_i}{\sigma}\right)$$

Table 8.6 Earnings Equations Estimated from the New Jersey Negative Income-Tax Experiment[a]

Variable	OLS	ML
Constant	8.203 (0.091)	9.102 (0.026)
Education	0.010 (0.006)	0.015 (0.007)
IQ	0.002 (0.002)	0.006 (0.005)
Training	0.002 (0.001)	0.006 (0.003)
Union	0.090 (0.030)	0.246 (0.089)
Illness	−0.076 (0.038)	−0.226 (0.107)
Age (linear)	−0.003 (0.002)	−0.016 (0.005)

[a] Figures in parentheses are standard errors.

[36] Maddala, *Limited-Dependent*, Chap. 6.

Maximizing this with respect to β and σ, we get the ML estimates of β and σ. Again, we need not be concerned with the details of the ML estimation method. As an illustration of how different the OLS and ML estimates can be, we present the estimates obtained by Hausman and Wise [37] in Table 8.6. The dependent variable was log earnings. The results show how the OLS estimates are biased. In this particular case they are all biased toward zero.

SUMMARY

1. In this chapter we discussed
   (a) Dummy explanatory variables.
   (b) Dummy dependent variables.
   (c) Truncated dependent variables.

2. Dummy explanatory variables can be used in tests for coefficient stability in the linear regression models, for obtaining predictions in the linear regression models, and for imposing cross-equation constraints. These uses have been illustrated with examples.

3. One should exercise caution in using the dummy variables when there is heteroskedasticity or autocorrelation. In the presence of autocorrelated errors, the dummy variables for testing stability have to be defined suitably. The proper definitions are given in Section 8.6.

4. Regarding the dummy dependent variables, there are three different models that one can use: the linear probability model, the logit model, and the probit model. The linear discriminant function is closely related to the linear probability model. The coefficients of the discriminant function are just proportional to those of the linear probability model (see Section 8.8). Thus there is nothing new in linear discriminant analysis. The linear probability model has the drawback that the predicted values can be outside the permissible interval $(0, 1)$.

5. In the analysis of models with dummy dependent variables, we assume the existence of a latent (unobserved) continuous variable which is specified as the usual regression model. However, the latent variable can be observed only as a dichotomous variable. The difference between the logit and probit models is in the assumptions made about the error term. If the error term has a logistic distribution, we have the logit model. If it has a normal distribution, we have the probit model. From the practical point of view, there is not much to choose between the two. The results are usually very similar. If both the models are computed, one should make some adjustments in the coefficients to make them comparable. These adjustments have been outlined in Section 8.9.

6. For comparing the linear probability, logit, and probit models, one can look at the number of cases correctly predicted. However, this is not enough. It is better to look at some measures of R^2's. In Section 8.9 we discuss several measures of R^2: squared correlation between y and $\hat{y}$, Effron's R^2, Cragg and Uhler's R^2, and

---

[37] J. A. Hausman and D. A. Wise, "Social Experimentation, Truncated Distributions, and Efficient Estimation," *Econometrica*, Vol. 45 1977, pp. 319–339.

McFadden's R^2. For practical purposes the first two are descriptive enough. The computation of the different R^2's is illustrated with an example in Section 8.10.

7. The tobit model is a censored regression model. Observations on the latent variable y^* are missing (or censored) if y^* is below (or above) a certain threshold level. This model has been used in a large number of applications where the dependent variable is observed to be zero for some individuals in the sample (automobile expenditures, medical expenditures, hours worked, wages, etc.). However, on careful scrutiny we find that the censored regression model (tobit model) is inappropriate for the analysis of these problems. The tobit model is, strictly speaking, applicable in only those situations where the latent variable can, in principle, take negative values, but these negative values are not observed because of censoring. Where the zero observations are a consequence of individual decisions, these decisions should be modeled appropriately and the tobit model should not be used mechanically.

8. Sometimes samples are drawn from truncated distributions. In this case the truncated regression model should be used. This model is different from the censored regression model (tobit model).

9. The LIMDEP program can be used to compute the logit, probit, tobit, truncated regression, and related models discussed here.

EXERCISES

1. Explain the meaning of each of the following terms.
    (a) Seasonal dummy variables.
    (b) Dummy dependent variables.
    (c) Linear probability model.
    (d) Linear discriminant function.
    (e) Logit model.
    (f) Probit model.
    (g) Tobit model.
    (h) Truncated regression model.
2. What would be your answer to the following queries?
    (a) My regression program refuses to estimate four seasonal coefficients when I enter the quarterly data including a zero–one dummy for each quarter. What am I supposed to do?
    (b) I estimated a model with a zero–one dependent variable using the logit and probit programs. The coefficients I got from the probit program were all smaller than the corresponding coefficients estimated by the logit program. Is there something wrong with my programs?
    (c) I have data on medical expenditures on a sample of individuals. Some of them, who did not have any ailments, or did not bother to go to the doctor even if they had ailments, had no expenditures. I wish to estimate the income elasticity of medical expenditures. I am thinking of dropping the individuals with zero expenditures and estimating the model by OLS. My

friend says that I would be overestimating the income elasticity by doing this. Is she correct?

3. Explain how you would use dummy variables for generating predictions from a regression model.

4. In the model

$$Y_t = \beta_1 x_{1t} + \beta_2 x_{2t} + \beta_3 x_{3t} + u_t$$

the coefficients are known to be related to a more basic economic parameter α according to the equations

$$\beta_1 + \beta_2 = \alpha$$
$$\beta_1 + \beta_3 = -\alpha$$

Explain how you would estimate α and the variance of $\hat{\alpha}$.

5. In the model

$$Y_{1t} = \alpha x_{1t} + \beta x_{2t} + u_{1t}$$
$$Y_{2t} = \alpha x_{2t} + u_{2t}$$
$$Y_{3t} = \beta x_{1t} + u_{3t}$$

where $u_{1t} \sim IN(0, 2\sigma^2)$, $u_{2t} \sim IN(0, \sigma^2)$, $u_{3t} \sim IN(0, \sigma^2)$ and u_{1t}, u_{2t}, u_{3t} are mutually independent, explain how you will estimate α, β, and σ^2.

6. The following equation was estimated to explain a short-term interest rate: (Figures in parentheses are standard errors).

$$Y_t = 5.5 + 0.93x_t - 0.38x_{t-1} - 5.2(P_t/P_{t-4}) + 0.50Y_{t-1}$$
$$\quad (1.3) \quad (0.04) \qquad (0.09) \qquad (1.3) \qquad\qquad (0.07)$$

$$\quad - 0.05(D_1 - D_4) + 0.08(D_2 - D_4) + 0.06(D_3 - D_4)$$
$$\qquad (0.04) \qquad\qquad (0.04) \qquad\qquad (0.04)$$

$$R^2 = 0.90 \qquad \bar{R}^2 = 0.89 \qquad SEE = 0.19 \qquad DW = 1.3 \qquad T = 92$$

where Y = interest rate on 4 to 6-month commercial paper (percent)
x = interest rate on 90-day Treasury bills (percent)
P_t = price index

$$D_1 = \text{seasonal dummy} = \begin{cases} 1 & \text{for first quarter} \\ 0 & \text{otherwise} \end{cases}$$

$$D_2 = \text{seasonal dummy} = \begin{cases} 1 & \text{for second quarter} \quad \text{etc.} \\ 0 & \text{otherwise} \end{cases}$$

$SEE = \hat{\sigma}$

(a) What is the estimated seasonal pattern in the commercial paper rate?
(b) About how much would R^2 drop if P_t/P_{t-4} were dropped from the equation?
(c) Will $\bar{R}^2$ increase or decrease if P_t/P_{t-4} is dropped?
(d) Instead of using P_t/P_{t-4}, suppose that we use the percentage rate of inflation Π_t defined by

$$\Pi_t = 100\left(\frac{P_t - P_{t-4}}{P_{t-4}}\right)$$

What will be the new coefficients and their standard errors?

7. You are asked to estimate the coefficients in a linear discriminant function. You do not have a computer program for this. All you have is a program for multiple regression analysis. How will you compute the linear discriminant function?

8. Consider a model with a zero–one dependent variable. You have a multiple regression program and a program for the logit and probit models. You have computed the coefficients of the linear probability model and the logit and probit models:

   (a) How will you transform the coefficients of the three models so that they are comparable?

   (b) How will you compute the R^2's for the three models?

   (c) By what criteria will you choose the best model?

9. Explain how you will formulate a model explaining the following. In each case the sample consists of some observations for which the dependent variable is zero. Suggest a list of explanatory variables in each case.

   (a) Automobile expenditures (in a year) of a number of families.

   (b) Hours worked by a group of married women.

   (c) Amount of child support received by a number of working wives.

   (d) Medical expenditures of a number of families.

   (e) Amount of loan granted by a bank to a number of applicants.

   (f) Amount of financial aid received by a group of students at a college.

9

Simultaneous Equations Models

9.1 INTRODUCTION

In the usual regression model y is the dependent or determined variable and x_1, $x_2, \ldots$, are the independent or determining variables. The crucial assumption we make is that the x's are independent of the error term u. Sometimes, this assumption is violated: for example, in demand and supply models. It is also violated in the case where the x's are measured with error, but we postpone discussion of this case to Chapter 11. We illustrate here the case of a demand and supply model.

Suppose that we write the demand function as

$$q = \alpha + \beta p + u \tag{9.1}$$

where q is the quantity demanded, p the price, and u the disturbance term, which denotes random shifts in the demand function. In Figure 9.1 we see that a shift in the demand function produces a change in *both* price and quantity if the supply curve has an upward slope. If the supply curve is horizontal (i.e., completely price in-elastic), a shift in the demand curve produces a change in price only, and if the supply curve is vertical (infinite price elasticity), a shift in the demand curve produces a change in quantity only.

Thus in equation (9.1) the error term u is correlated with p when the supply curve is upward sloping or perfectly horizontal. Hence an estimation of the equation by ordinary least squares produces inconsistent estimates of the parameters.

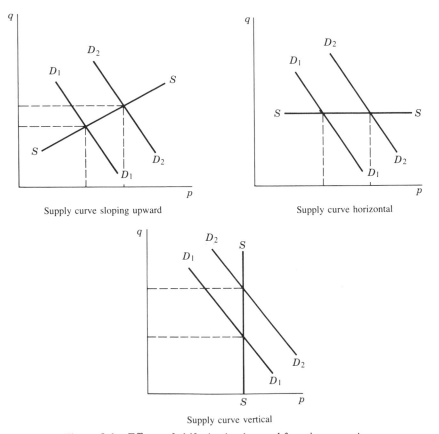

Supply curve sloping upward

Supply curve horizontal

Supply curve vertical

Figure 9.1   Effects of shifts in the demand function on price.

We could have written the demand function as

$$p = \alpha' + \beta' q + u' \tag{9.1'}$$

But, again, u' will be correlated with q if the supply function is upward sloping or perfectly vertical. There is the question of whether the demand function should be written as in equation (9.1) or (9.1'). If it is written as in (9.1), we say that the equation is *normalized with respect to q* (i.e., the coefficient of q is unity). If it is written as in (9.1'), we say that the equation is *normalized with respect to p*. Since price and quantity are determined by the interaction of demand and supply, it should not matter whether we normalize the equations with respect to p or with respect to q.

The estimation methods we use should produce identical estimates whatever normalization we adopt. However, the preceding discussion and Figure 9.1 suggest that if quantity supplied is not responsive to price, the demand function should be normalized with respect to p, that is, it should be written as in (9.1'). On the other hand, if quantity supplied is highly responsive to price, the demand function should be normalized with respect to q as in (9.1). An empirical example will be given in Section 9.3 to illustrate this point. The question of normalization is discussed in greater detail in Section 9.7.

Returning to the demand and supply model, the problem is that we cannot consider the demand function in isolation when we are studying the relationship between quantity and price as in (9.1). The solution is to bring the supply function into the picture, and estimate the demand and supply functions together. Such models are known as *simultaneous equations models*.

9.2 ENDOGENOUS AND EXOGENOUS VARIABLES

In simultaneous equations models variables are classified as endogenous and exogenous. The traditional definition of these terms is that endogenous variables are variables that are determined by the economic model and exogenous variables are those determined from outside.

Endogenous variables are also called *jointly determined* and exogenous variables are called *predetermined*. (It is customary to include past values of endogenous variables in the predetermined group.) Since the exogenous variables are predetermined, they are independent of the error terms in the model. They thus satisfy the assumptions that the x's satisfy in the usual regression model of y on x's.

The foregoing definition of exogeneity has recently been questioned in recent econometric literature, but we have to postpone this discussion to a later section (Section 9.10). We will discuss this criticism and its implications after going through the conventional methods of estimation for simultaneous equation models.

Consider now the demand and supply model

$$
\begin{aligned}
q &= a_1 + b_1 p + c_1 y + u_1 \qquad \text{demand function} \\
q &= a_2 + b_2 p + c_2 R + u_2 \qquad \text{supply function}
\end{aligned}
\tag{9.2}
$$

q is the quantity, p the price, y the income, R the rainfall, and u_1 and u_2 are the error terms. Here p and q are the endogenous variables and y and R are the exogenous variables. Since the exogenous variables are independent of the error terms u_1 and u_2 and satisfy the usual requirements for ordinary least squares estimation, we can estimate regressions of p and q on y and R by ordinary least squares, although we cannot estimate equations (9.2) by ordinary least squares. We will show presently that from these regressions of p and q on y and R we can recover the parameters in the original demand and supply equations (9.2). This method is called *indirect least squares*—it is indirect because we do not apply least squares to equations (9.2). The indirect least squares method does not always work, so we will first discuss the conditions under which it works and how the method can be simplified. To discuss this issue, we first have to clarify the concept of identification.

9.3 THE IDENTIFICATION PROBLEM: IDENTIFICATION THROUGH REDUCED FORM

We have argued that the error terms u_1 and u_2 are correlated with p in equations (9.2), and hence if we estimate the equation by ordinary least squares, the parameter estimates are inconsistent. Roughly speaking, the concept of identification is related to consistent estimation of the parameters. Thus if we can somehow obtain consistent estimates of the parameters in the demand function, we say that the demand function is *identified*. Similarly, if we can somehow get consistent estimates of the parameters in the supply function, we say that the supply function is *identified*. Getting consistent estimates is just a necessary condition for identification, not a sufficient condition, as we show in the next section.

If we solve the two equations in (9.2) for q and p in terms of y and R, we get

$$q = \frac{a_1 b_2 - a_2 b_1}{b_2 - b_1} + \frac{c_1 b_2}{b_2 - b_1} y - \frac{c_2 b_1}{b_2 - b_1} R + \text{an error}$$

$$p = \frac{a_1 - a_2}{b_2 - b_1} + \frac{c_1}{b_2 - b_1} y - \frac{c_2}{b_2 - b_1} R + \text{an error}$$

(9.3)

These equations are called the *reduced-form equations*. Equations (9.2) are called the *structural equations* because they describe the structure of the economic system. We can write equations (9.3) as

$$q = \pi_1 + \pi_2 y + \pi_3 R + v_1$$

$$p = \pi_4 + \pi_5 y + \pi_6 R + v_2$$

(9.4)

where v_1 and v_2 are error terms and

$$\pi_1 = \frac{a_1 b_2 - a_2 b_1}{b_2 - b_1}, \quad \pi_2 = \frac{c_1 b_2}{b_2 - b_1},$$

The π's are called *reduced-form parameters*. The estimation of the equations (9.4) by ordinary least squares gives us consistent estimates of the reduced form parameters. From these we have to obtain consistent estimates of the parameters in equations (9.2). These parameters are called *structural parameters*. Comparing (9.3) with (9.4) we get

$$\hat{b}_1 = \frac{\hat{\pi}_3}{\hat{\pi}_6} \qquad \hat{b}_2 = \frac{\hat{\pi}_2}{\hat{\pi}_5},$$

$$\hat{c}_2 = \hat{\pi}_6(\hat{b}_1 - \hat{b}_2) \qquad \hat{c}_1 = -\hat{\pi}_5(\hat{b}_1 - \hat{b}_2)$$

$$\hat{a}_1 = \hat{\pi}_1 - \hat{b}_1\hat{\pi}_4 \qquad \hat{a}_2 = \hat{\pi}_1 - \hat{b}_2\hat{\pi}_4$$

Since $\hat{a}_1, \hat{a}_2, \hat{b}_1, \hat{b}_2, \hat{c}_1, \hat{c}_2$ are all single-valued function of the $\hat{\pi}$, they are consistent estimates of the corresponding structural parameters. As mentioned earlier, this method is known as the *indirect least squares method*.

It may not be always possible to get estimates of the structural coefficients from the estimates of the reduced-form coefficients, and sometimes we get multiple estimates and we have the problem of choosing between them. For example, suppose that the demand and supply model is written as

$$q = a_1 + b_1 p + c_1 y + u_1 \qquad \text{demand function}$$
$$q = a_2 + b_2 p + u_2 \qquad \text{supply function}$$

(9.5)

Then the reduced form is

$$q = \frac{a_1 b_2 - a_2 b_1}{b_2 - b_1} + \frac{c_1 b_2}{b_2 - b_1} y + v_1$$

$$p = \frac{a_1 - a_2}{b_2 - b_1} + \frac{c_1}{b_2 - b_1} y + v_2$$

or

$$q = \pi_1 + \pi_2 y + v_1$$
$$p = \pi_3 + \pi_4 y + v_2$$

In this case $\hat{b}_2 = \hat{\pi}_2/\hat{\pi}_4$ and $\hat{a}_2 = \hat{\pi}_1 - \hat{b}_2\hat{\pi}_3$. But there is no way of getting estimates of a_1, b_1, and c_1. Thus the supply function is identified but the demand function is not. On the other hand, suppose that we have the model

$$q = a_1 + b_1 p + u_1 \qquad \text{demand function}$$
$$q = a_2 + b_2 p + c_2 R + u_2 \qquad \text{supply function}$$

Now we can check that the demand function is identified but the supply function is not.

Finally, suppose that we have the system

$$q = a_1 + b_1 p + c_1 y + d_1 R + u_1 \qquad \text{demand function}$$
$$q = a_2 + b_2 p + u_2 \qquad \text{supply function}$$

(9.6)

Rainfall affects demand (if there is rain, people do not go shopping), but not supply. The reduced-form equations are

$$q = \frac{a_1 b_2 - a_2 b_1}{b_2 - b_1} + \frac{c_1 b_2}{b_2 - b_1} y + \frac{d_1 b_2}{b_2 - b_1} R + v_1$$

$$p = \frac{a_1 - a_2}{b_2 - b_1} + \frac{c_1}{b_2 - b_1} y + \frac{d_1}{b_2 - b_1} R + v_2$$

or

$$q = \pi_1 + \pi_2 y + \pi_3 R + v_1$$

$$p = \pi_4 + \pi_5 y + \pi_6 R + v_2$$

Now we get two estimates of b_2. One is $\hat{b}_2 = \hat{\pi}_2/\hat{\pi}_5$ and the other is $\hat{b}_2 = \hat{\pi}_3/\hat{\pi}_6$, and these need not be equal. For each of these we get an estimate of a_2, which is $\hat{a}_2 = \hat{\pi}_1 - \hat{b}_2 \hat{\pi}_4$.

On the other hand, we get no estimates for the parameters a_1, b_1, c_1, and d_1 of the demand function. Here we say that the supply function is *over-identified* and the demand function is *under-identified*. When we get unique estimates for the structural parameters of an equation from the reduced-form parameters, we say that the equation is *exactly identified*. When we get multiple estimates, we say that the equation is *over-identified*, and when we get no estimates, we say that the equation is *under-identified* (or *not identified*).

There is a simple counting rule available in the linear systems that we have been considering. This counting rule is also known as the *order condition* for identification. This rule is as follows: Let g be the number of endogenous variables in the system and k the total number of variables (endogenous and exogenous) missing from the equation under consideration. Then:

1. If $k = g - 1$, the equation is exactly identified.
2. If $k > g - 1$, the equation is over-identified.
3. If $k < g - 1$, the equation is under-identified.

This condition is *only necessary but not sufficient*. In Section 9.4 we will give a necessary and sufficient condition.

Let us apply this rule to the equation systems we are considering. In equations (9.2), g, the number of endogenous variables, is 2, and there is only one variable missing from each equation. Hence both equations are identified exactly. In equations (9.5), again $g = 2$. There is no variable missing from the first equation; hence it is under-identified. There is one variable missing in the second equation; hence it is exactly identified. In equation (9.6), there is no variable missing in the first equation; hence it is not identified. In the second equation there are two variables missing; thus $k > g - 1$ and the equation is over-identified.

Illustrative Example

The indirect least squares method we have described is rarely used. In the following sections we describe a more popular method of estimating simultaneous equation models. This is the method of two-stage least squares (2SLS). However, if some

Table 9.1 Demand and Supply of Pork, United States, 1922–1941[a]

Year	P_t	Q_t	Y_t	Z_t
1922	26.8	65.7	541	74.0
1923	25.3	74.2	616	84.7
1924	25.3	74.0	610	80.2
1925	31.1	66.8	636	69.9
1926	33.3	64.1	651	66.8
1927	31.2	67.7	645	71.6
1928	29.5	70.9	653	73.6
1929	30.3	69.6	682	71.2
1930	29.1	67.0	604	69.6
1931	23.7	68.4	515	68.0
1932	15.6	70.7	390	74.8
1933	13.9	69.6	364	73.6
1934	18.8	63.1	411	70.2
1935	27.4	48.4	459	46.5
1936	26.9	55.1	517	57.6
1937	27.7	55.8	551	58.7
1938	24.5	58.2	506	58.0
1939	22.2	64.7	538	67.2
1940	19.3	73.5	576	73.7
1941	24.7	68.4	697	66.5

[a] P_t, retail price of pork (cents per pound); Q_t, consumption of pork (pounds per capita); Y_t, disposable personal income (dollars per capita): Z_t, "predetermined elements in pork production."
Source: William C. Merrill and Karl A. Fox, *Introduction to Economic Statistics*, New York, Wiley, 1971, p. 539.

coefficients in the reduced-form equations are close to zero, this gives us some information about what variables to omit in the structural equations. We will provide a simple example of a two-equation demand and supply model where the estimates from OLS, reduced-form least squares, and indirect least squares provide information on how to formulate the model. The example also illustrates some points we have raised in Section 9.1 regarding normalization.

The model is from Merrill and Fox.[1] In Table 9.1 data are presented for demand and supply of pork in the United States for 1922–1941. The model estimated by Merrill and Fox is

$$Q = a_1 + b_1 P + c_1 Y + u \qquad \text{demand function}$$

$$Q = a_2 + b_2 P + c_2 Z + v \qquad \text{supply function}$$

[1] William C. Merrill and Karl A. Fox, *Introduction to Economic Statistics* (New York: Wiley, 1971).

The equations were fitted for 1922–1941. The reduced-form equations were (standard errors in parentheses)

$$\hat{P} = -0.0101 + \underset{(0.1339)}{1.0813}Y - \underset{(0.1159)}{0.8320}Z \qquad R^2 = 0.893$$

$$\hat{Q} = 0.0026 - \underset{(0.0673)}{0.0018}Y + \underset{(0.0582)}{0.6839}Z \qquad R^2 = 0.898$$

The coefficient of Y in the second equation is very close to zero and the variable Y can be dropped from this equation. This would imply that $b_2 = 0$, or supply is not responsive to price. In any case, solving from the reduced form to the structural form, we get the estimates of the structural equations as

$$Q = -0.0063 - 0.8220P + 0.8870Y \qquad \text{demand function}$$

$$Q = 0.0026 - 0.0017P + 0.6825Z \qquad \text{supply function}$$

The least squares estimates of the demand function are: Normalized with respect to Q:

$$\hat{Q} = -0.0049 - \underset{(0.0594)}{0.7205}P + \underset{(0.0967)}{0.7646}Y \qquad R^2 = 0.903$$

Normalized with respect to P:

$$\hat{P} = -0.0070 - \underset{(0.1032)}{1.2518}Q + \underset{(0.0861)}{1.0754}Y \qquad R^2 = 0.956$$

The structural demand function can also be written in the two forms: Normalized with respect to Q:

$$\hat{Q} = 0.0063 - 0.8220P + 0.8870Y$$

Normalized with respect to P:

$$\hat{P} = -0.0077 - 1.2165Q + 1.0791Y$$

The estimates of the parameters in the demand function are almost the same with the direct least squares method as with the indirect least squares method when the demand function is normalized with respect to P.

Which is the correct normalization? We argued in Section 9.1 that if quantity supplied is not responsive to price, the demand function should be normalized with respect to P. We saw that the fact that the coefficient of Y in the reduced-form equation for Q was close to zero implied that $b_2 = 0$ or quantity supplied is not responsive to price. This is also confirmed by the structural estimate of b_2, which shows a wrong sign for b_2 as well but a coefficient close to zero.

Dropping P from the supply function and using OLS, we get the supply function as

$$\hat{Q} = 0.0025 + \underset{(0.0857)}{0.6841}Z \qquad R^2 = 0.898$$

Thus we normalize the demand function with respect to P, drop the variable P from the supply function, and estimate both equations by OLS.

9.4 NECESSARY AND SUFFICIENT CONDITIONS FOR IDENTIFICATION

In Section 9.3 our discussion was in terms of obtaining estimates for the structural parameters from estimates of the reduced-form parameters. An alternative way of looking at the identification problem is to see whether the equation under consideration can be obtained as a linear combination of the other equations.

Consider, for instance, equations (9.5). Take a weighted average of the two equations with weights w and $(1 - w)$. Then we get

$$q = w(a_1 + b_1 p + c_1 y) + (1 - w)(a_2 + b_2 p)$$
$$= a_1^* + b_1^* p + c_1^* y \tag{9.7}$$

where $a_1^* = wa_1 + (1 - w)a_2$
$b_1^* = wb_1 + (1 - w)b_2$
$c_1^* = wc_1$

Equation (9.7) looks like the first equation in (9.5). Thus when we estimate the parameters of the demand function, we do not know whether we are getting estimates of the parameters in the demand function or in some weighted average of the demand and supply functions. Thus the parameters in the demand function are not identified. The same cannot be said about the supply function because the only way that equation (9.7) can look like the supply function in (9.5) is if $c_1^* = 0$ (i.e., $wc_1 = 0$). But since $c_1 \neq 0$, we must have $w = 0$. That is, the weighted average gives zero weight to the demand function. Hence when we estimate the supply function, we are sure that the estimates we have are of the supply function. Thus the parameters of the supply function are identified.

Checking this condition has been easy with two equations. But when we have many equations, we need a more systematic way of checking this condition. For illustrative purposes consider the case of three endogenous variables y_1, y_2, y_3 and three exogenous variables z_1, z_2, z_3. We will mark with a cross $\times$ if a variable occurs in an equation, and a 0 if not. Suppose that the equation system is the following:

Equation	y_1	y_2	y_3	z_1	z_2	z_3
1	$\times$	0	$\times$	$\times$	0	$\times$
2	$\times$	0	0	$\times$	0	$\times$
3	0	$\times$	$\times$	$\times$	$\times$	0

The rule for identification of any equation is as follows

1. Delete the particular row.
2. Pick up the columns corresponding to the elements that have zeros in that row.
3. If from this array of columns we can find $(g - 1)$ rows and columns that are not all zeros, where g is the number of endogenous variables, then the equation is identified. Otherwise, not.

This condition is called the *rank condition* for identification and is a necessary and sufficient condition. [2]

We will now apply the order and rank conditions to the illustrative example we have. The number of equations is $g = 3$. Hence the number of missing variables is 2 for the first equation, 3 for the second, and 2 for the third. Thus, by the order condition, the first and third equations are exactly identified and the second equation is over-identified. We will see that the rank condition gives us a different answer.

To check the rank condition for equation 1, we delete the first row and pick up the columns corresponding to the missing variables y_2 and z_2. The columns are

$$
\begin{array}{cc}
0 & 0 \\
\times & \times
\end{array}
$$

Note that we have only one row with not all elements zero. Thus, by the rank condition the equation is not identified. For equation 2, we delete row 2, and pick up the columns corresponding to y_2, y_3 and z_2. We get

$$
\begin{array}{ccc}
0 & \times & 0 \\
\times & \times & \times
\end{array}
$$

We now have two rows (and two columns) with not all elements zero. Thus the equation is identified. Similarly, for the third equation deleting the third row, the columns for y_1 and z_3 give

$$
\begin{array}{cc}
\times & \times \\
\times & \times
\end{array}
$$

Again we have two rows (and two columns) with not all elements zero. Hence the equation is identified. Note that the rank condition states whether the equation is identified or not. From the order condition we know whether it is exactly identified or over-identified.

In summary the second and third equations are estimable. The first one is not, and the order condition misleads us into thinking that it is so. There are many estimation methods for simultaneous equations models that break down if the order condition is not satisfied but do give us estimates of the parameters if the order condition is satisfied even if the rank condition is not. In such cases these estimates are meaningless. Thus it is desirable to check the rank condition. In our example, for equation 1, the rank condition is not satisfied. What this means is that the estimates we obtain for the parameters in equation 1 are actually estimates of some linear combinations of the parameters in all the equations and thus have no special economic interpretation. This is what we mean when we say that equation 1 is not estimable.

---

[2] The array of columns is called a *matrix* and the condition that we have stated is that the rank of this matrix be $(g - 1)$: hence the use of the term *rank condition*. We have avoided the use of matrix notation and stated the condition in an alternative fashion.

Illustrative Example

As an illustration, consider the following macroeconomic model with seven endogenous variables and three exogenous variables. The endogenous and exogenous variables are:

Endogenous	Exogenous
C = real consumption	G = real government purchases
I = real investment	T = real tax receipts
N = employment	M = nominal money stock
P = price level	
R = interest rate	
Y = real income	
W = money wage rate	

The equations are:

(1) $C = a_1 + b_1 Y - c_1 T + d_1 R + u_1$ (consumption function)

(2) $I = a_2 + b_2 Y + c_2 R + u_2$ (investment function)

(3) $Y = C + I + G$ (identity)

(4) $M = a_3 + b_3 Y + c_3 R + d_3 P + u_3$ (liquidity preference function)

(5) $Y = a_4 + b_4 N + u_4$ (production function)

(6) $N = a_5 + b_5 W + c_5 P + u_5$ (labor demand)

(7) $N = a_6 + b_6 W + c_6 P + u_6$ (labor supply)

The question is which of these equations is under-identified, exactly identified, and over-identified. To answer this question, we prepare the following table. A 1 denotes that the variable is present, a 0 denotes that it is missing.

Equation	C	I	N	P	R	Y	W	G	T	M
1	1	0	0	0	1	1	0	0	1	0
2	0	1	0	0	1	1	0	0	0	0
3	1	1	0	0	0	1	0	1	0	0
4	0	0	0	1	1	1	0	0	0	1
5	0	0	1	0	0	1	0	0	0	0
6	0	0	1	1	0	0	1	0	0	0
7	0	0	1	1	0	0	1	0	0	0

Note that equation 3 is an identity and does not have any parameters to be estimated. Hence we do not need to discuss its identification. The number of endogenous variables minus one is 6 in this model. By the order condition we get the result that equations 1 and 4 are exactly identified and equations 2, 5, 6, and 7 are over-identified.

Let us look at the rank condition for equation 1. The procedure is similar for other equations. Delete the first row and gather the columns for the missing variables I, N, P, W, G, M. We get

$$
\begin{array}{cccccc}
1 & 0 & 0 & 0 & 0 & 0 \\
1 & 0 & 0 & 0 & 1 & 0 \\
0 & 0 & 1 & 0 & 0 & 1 \\
0 & 1 & 0 & 0 & 0 & 0 \\
0 & 1 & 1 & 1 & 0 & 0 \\
0 & 1 & 1 & 1 & 0 & 0
\end{array}
$$

Since we have six rows (and six columns) whose elements are not all zero, the equation is identified. It can be checked that the same is true for equations 2, 4 and 5. However, for equations 6 and 7, we cannot find six rows whose elements are not all zero. Thus, equations 6 and 7 are not identified by the rank condition even though they are over-identified by the order condition.

9.5 METHODS OF ESTIMATION: THE INSTRUMENTAL VARIABLE METHOD

In previous sections we discussed the identification problem. Now we discuss some methods of estimation for simultaneous equations models. Actually, we have already discussed one method of estimation: the indirect least squares method. However, this method is very cumbersome if there are many equations and hence it is not often used. Here we discuss some methods that are more generally applicable. These methods of estimation can be classified into two categories:

1. Single-equation methods (also called "limited-information methods").
2. System methods (also called "full-information methods").

We will not discuss the full-information methods here because they involve algebraic detail beyond the scope of this book. We discuss single-equation methods only. In these methods we estimate each equation separately using only the information about the restrictions on the coefficients of that particular equation. For instance, in the illustrative example in Section 9.4 when we estimate the consumption function (the first equation), we just make use of the fact that the variables I, N, P, W, G, M are missing and that the last two variables are exogenous. We are not concerned about what variables are missing from the other equations. The restrictions on the other equations are used only to check identification, not for estimation. This is the reason these methods are called limited-information methods. In full-information methods we use information on the restrictions on all equation, as well as information on the variances and covariances in all the equations.

A general method of obtaining consistent estimates of the parameters in simultaneous-equations models is the *instrumental variable method*. Broadly speaking, an instrumental variable is a variable that is uncorrelated with the error term but correlated with the explanatory variables in the equation.

For instance, suppose that we have the equation

$$y = \beta x + u$$

where x is correlated with u. Then we cannot estimate this equation by ordinary least squares. The estimate of β is inconsistent because of the correlation between x and u. If we can find a variable z that is uncorrelated with u, we can get a consistent estimator for β. We replace the condition $\text{cov}(z, u) = 0$ by its sample counterpart

$$\frac{1}{n}\sum z(y - \beta x) = 0$$

This gives

$$\hat{\beta} = \frac{\sum zy}{\sum zx} = \frac{\sum z(\beta x + u)}{\sum zx} = \beta + \frac{\sum zu}{\sum zx}$$

But $\sum zu / \sum zx$ can be written as $1/n \sum zu \big/ 1/n \sum zx$. The probability limit of this expression is

$$\frac{\text{cov}(z, u)}{\text{cov}(z, x)} = 0$$

since $\text{cov}(z, x) \neq 0$. Hence plim $\hat{\beta} = \beta$, thus proving that $\hat{\beta}$ is a consistent estimator for β. Note that we require z to be correlated with x so that $\text{cov}(z, x) \neq 0$.

Now consider the simultaneous-equations model

$$\begin{aligned} y_1 &= b_1 y_2 + c_1 z_1 + c_2 z_2 + u_1 \\ y_2 &= b_2 y_1 + c_3 z_3 + u_2 \end{aligned} \tag{9.8}$$

where y_1, y_2 are endogenous variables, z_1, z_2, z_3 are exogenous variables, and u_1, u_2 are error terms. Consider the estimation of the first equation. Since z_1 and z_2 are independent of u_1, we have $\text{cov}(z_1, u_1) = 0$ and $\text{cov}(z_2, u_1) = 0$. However, y_2 is not independent of u_1. Hence $\text{cov}(y_2, u_1) \neq 0$. Since we have three coefficients to estimate, we have to find a variable that is independent of u_1. Fortunately, in this case we have z_3 and $\text{cov}(z_3, u_1) = 0$. z_3 is the instrumental variable for y_2. Thus, writing the sample counterparts of these three covariances, we have the three equations

$$\frac{1}{n}\sum z_1(y_1 - b_1 y_2 - c_1 z_1 - c_2 z_2) = 0$$

$$\frac{1}{n}\sum z_2(y_1 - b_1 y_2 - c_1 z_1 - c_2 z_2) = 0 \tag{9.8'}$$

$$\frac{1}{n}\sum z_3(y_1 - b_1 y_2 - c_1 z_1 - c_2 z_2) = 0$$

The difference between the normal equations for the ordinary least squares method and the instrumental variable method is only in the last equation.

Consider the second equation of our model. Now we have to find an instrumental variable for y_1 but we have a choice of z_1 and z_2. This is because this equation is over-identified (by the order condition).

Note that the order condition (counting rule) is related to the question of whether or not we have enough exogenous variables elsewhere in the system to use as instruments for the endogenous variables in the equation with unknown coefficients. If the equation is under-identified we do not have enough instrumental variables. If it is exactly identified, we have just enough instrumental variables. If it is over-identified, we have more than enough instrumental variables. In this case we have to use weighted averages of the instrumental variables available. We compute these weighted averages so that we get the most efficient (minimum asymptotic variance) estimators.

It has been shown (proving this is beyond the scope of this book) that the efficient instrumental variables are constructed by regressing the endogenous variables on *all* the exogenous variables in the system (i.e., estimating the reduced-form equations). In the case of the model given by equations (9.8), we first estimate the reduced-form equations by regressing y_1 and y_2 on z_1, z_2, z_3. We obtain the predicted values $\hat{y}_1$ and $\hat{y}_2$ and use these as instrumental variables. For the estimation of the first equation we use $\hat{y}_2$, and for the estimation of the second equation we use $\hat{y}_1$. We can write $\hat{y}_1$ and $\hat{y}_2$ as linear functions of z_1, z_2, z_3. Let us write

$$\hat{y}_1 = a_{11}z_1 + a_{12}z_2 + a_{13}z_3$$

$$\hat{y}_2 = a_{21}z_1 + a_{22}z_2 + a_{23}z_3$$

where the a's are obtained from the estimation of the reduced-form equations by OLS. In the estimation of the first equation in (9.8) we use $\hat{y}_2, z_1$, and z_2 as instruments. This is the same as using z_1, z_2, and z_3 as instruments because

$$\sum \hat{y}_2 u_1 = 0 \Rightarrow \sum (a_{21}z_1 + a_{22}z_2 + a_{23}z_3)u_1 = 0$$

$$\Rightarrow a_{21} \sum z_1 u_1 + a_{22} \sum z_2 u_1 + a_{23} \sum z_3 u_1 = 0$$

But the first two terms are zero by virtue of the first two equations in (9.8'). Thus $\sum \hat{y}_2 u_1 = 0 \Rightarrow \sum z_3 u_1 = 0$. Hence using $\hat{y}_2$ as an instrumental variable is the same as using z_3 as an instrumental variable. This is the case with exactly identified equations where there is no choice in the instruments.

The case with the second equation in (9.8) is different. Earlier, we said that we have a choice between z_1 and z_2 as instruments for y_1. The use of $\hat{y}_1$ gives the optimum weighing. The normal equations now are

$$\sum \hat{y}_1 u_2 = 0 \quad \text{and} \quad \sum z_3 u_2 = 0$$

$$\sum \hat{y}_1 u_2 = 0 \Rightarrow \sum (a_{11}z_1 + a_{12}z_2 + a_{13}z_3)u_2 = 0$$

$$\Rightarrow \sum (a_{11}z_1 + a_{12}z_2)u_2 = 0$$

since $\sum z_3 u_2 = 0$. Thus the optimal weights for z_1 and z_2 are a_{11} and a_{12}.

Measuring R^2

When we are estimating an equation with instrumental variables, a question arises as to how to report the goodness-of-fit measure R^2. This question also arises with the two-stage-least squares (2SLS) method described in Section 9.6. We can think of two measures.

1. R^2 = squared correlation between y and $\hat{y}$.
2. Measures based on residual sum of squares:

$$R^2 = 1 - \frac{\sum\limits_{i=1}^{n} (y_i - \hat{y}_i)^2}{\sum (y_i - \bar{y})^2}$$

In the results we present we will be reporting the second measure.

Note that the R^2 from the instrumental variable method will be lower than the R^2 from the OLS method. It is also conceivable that the R^2 would be negative, but this is an indication that something is wrong with the specification—perhaps the equation is not identified. We illustrate this point with an example.

Many computer programs present an R^2 for simultaneous-equations models. But since there is no unique measure of R^2 in such models, it is important to check the formula that the program uses. For instance, the SAS program gives an R^2, but it appears to be neither one of the above-mentioned measures.

Illustrative Example[3]

Table 9.2 provides data on some characteristics of the wine industry in Australia for 1955–1956 to 1974–1975. It is assumed that a reasonable demand–supply model for the industry would be (where all variables are in *logs*)

$$Q_t = a_0 + a_1 p_t^w + a_2 p_t^b + a_3 y_t + a_4 A_t + u_t \qquad \text{demand}$$

$$Q_t = b_0 + b_1 p_t^w + b_2 s_t + v_t \qquad \text{supply}$$

where Q_t = real per capita consumption of wine
p_t^w = price of wine relative to CPI
p_t^b = price of beer relative to CPI
y_t = real per capita disposable income
A_t = real per capita advertising expenditure
s_t = index of storage costs

Q_t and p_t^w are the two endogenous variables. The other variables are exogenous. For the estimation of the demand function we have only one instrumental variable s_t. But for the estimation of the supply function we have available three instrumental variables: p_t^b, y_t, and A_t.

---

[3] I would like to thank Kim Sawyer for providing me with these data and the example.

Table 9.2 Data for Wine Industry in Australia[a]

Year	Q	S	p^w	p^b	A	Y
1955–1956	0.91	85.4	77.5	35.7	89.1	1056
1956–1957	1.05	88.4	80.2	37.4	83.3	1037
1957–1958	1.18	89.1	79.5	37.7	84.4	1006
1958–1959	1.27	90.5	84.9	37.1	90.1	1047
1959–1960	1.27	93.1	94.9	36.2	89.4	1091
1960–1961	1.37	97.2	92.7	35.0	89.3	1093
1961–1962	1.46	100.3	92.5	37.6	89.8	1102
1962–1963	1.59	100.3	92.7	40.1	96.7	1154
1963–1964	1.86	101.5	97.1	39.7	99.9	1234
1964–1965	1.96	104.8	93.9	38.3	103.2	1254
1965–1966	2.32	107.5	102.7	37.0	102.2	1241
1966–1967	2.86	111.8	100.0	36.1	100.0	1299
1967–1968	3.50	114.9	119.5	35.4	103.0	1287
1968–1969	3.96	117.9	119.7	35.1	104.2	1369
1969–1970	4.21	122.3	125.2	34.5	113.0	1443
1970–1971	4.54	128.2	134.1	34.5	132.5	1517
1971–1972	4.93	134.1	124.3	34.3	143.6	1562
1972–1973	5.40	145.1	119.0	34.3	176.2	1678
1973–1974	6.13	174.9	108.5	31.9	159.9	1769
1974–1975	6.29	237.2	107.9	31.0	182.1	1847

[a] Data are not in logs.

The OLS estimation of the demand function gave the following results (all variables are in logs and figures in parentheses are t-ratios):

$$\hat{Q} = -23.651 + 1.158P_w - 0.275P_B - 0.603A + 3.212Y \qquad R^2 = 0.9772$$
$$\quad\;\; (-6.04) \quad\;\; (4.0) \qquad (-0.45) \quad\;\; (-1.3) \qquad (4.50)$$

All the coefficients except that of Y have the wrong signs. The coefficient of P_w not only has the wrong sign but is also significant.

Treating P_w as endogenous and using S as an instrument, we get the following results:

$$Q = -26.195 + 0.643P_w - 0.140P_B - 0.985A + 4.082Y \qquad R^2 = 0.9724$$
$$\quad\; (-5.09) \quad\;\; (0.98) \qquad (-0.20) \quad\;\; (-1.51) \qquad (3.28)$$

The coefficient of P_w still has a wrong sign but it is at least not significant. In any case the conclusion we arrive at is that the quantity demanded is not responsive to prices and advertising expenditures but is responsive to income. The income elasticity of demand for wine is about 4.0 (significantly greater than unity).

Turning next to the supply function, there are three instrumental variables available for P_w: P_B, A, and Y. Also, the efficient instrumental variable is obtained by regressing P_w on P_B, A, Y, and S. The results obtained by using the OLS method and the different instrumental variables are as follows (figures in parentheses are asymptotic t-ratios for the instrumental variable methods; the R^2's for the IV methods are computed as explained earlier):

Method	OLS	Instrumental Variables			
		P_B	A	Y	$\hat{P}_w$
Constant	−15.57	−10.76	−17.65	−16.98	−16.82
	(−18.36)	(−0.28)	(−6.6)	(−14.56)	(−15.57)
P_w	2.145	0.336	2.928	2.676	2.616
	(8.99)	(0.02)	(3.02)	(7.30)	(7.89)
S	1.383	2.131	1.058	1.163	1.188
	(8.95)	(0.36)	(2.47)	(5.72)	(6.24)
R^2	0.9632	0.8390	0.9400	0.9525	0.9548

There are considerable differences between the estimates obtained by the different instrumental variables methods. Particularly, the use of P_B seems to produce very different results. Y appears to be the best of all the instrumental variables.

The IV estimates can be obtained by the procedures outlined earlier. But an easier way is to note that the IV estimator and the two-stage least squares (2SLS) estimator (which we will describe in Section 9.6) are the same if the equation is exactly identified. This implies that we can get the IV estimator by the 2SLS method by changing the model so that the supply function is exactly identified. In this case, a standard computer program like the SAS can be used to get the estimates as well as their standard errors. In fact, this is the procedure we have followed.

For instance, to get the IV estimator of the supply function using Y as the instrumental variable, we can specify the model as

$$Q = \beta_0 + \beta_1 P_w + \beta_2 Y + u \quad \text{demand function}$$

$$Q = \alpha_0 + \alpha_1 P_w + \alpha_2 S + v \quad \text{supply function}$$

Now the supply function is identified exactly.

In this particular case, this does not seem to be an unreasonable model.

Before we leave this example, we will present a case where the R^2 from the IV method is negative. Consider the model

$$Q = \beta_0 + \beta_1 P_w + \beta_2 A + u \quad \text{demand function}$$

$$Q = \alpha_0 + \alpha_1 P_w + \alpha_2 S + u \quad \text{supply function}$$

The first equation is exactly identified. We will use S as the instrumental variable for P_w. (The IV estimator is the same as the 2SLS estimator.) The OLS estimation of the demand function gave the following results (figures in parentheses are t-ratios):

$$\hat{Q} = -15.30 + 2.064 P_w + 1.418 A \quad R^2 = 0.9431$$
$$\quad (-14.50) \quad (6.60) \quad (6.76)$$

The IV estimation gave the following results:

$$\hat{Q} = -304.13 + 119.035 P_w - 52.177 A \quad R^2 = -467.3$$
$$\quad (-0.03) \quad (0.03) \quad (-0.03)$$

What is the problem? To see what the problem is, let us look at the reduced-form equations:

$$\hat{Q} = -10.42 + 1.316A + 1.085S \qquad R^2 = 0.8208$$
$$\phantom{\hat{Q} = } (-8.12) \quad\;\; (1.75) \quad\;\; (1.50)$$

$$\hat{P}_w = 2.47 + 0.449A + 0.00912S \qquad R^2 = 0.4668$$
$$\phantom{\hat{P}_w = } (4.40) \quad\; (1.37) \quad\;\; (0.03)$$

The coefficient of S in the equation for P_w is almost zero. From the relationships (9.3) and (9.4) between the parameters in the reduced form and structural form discussed in Section 9.3, we note that this implies that $\beta_1 \to \infty$ and α_2 is indeterminate. Thus the demand function is not identified. Whenever, the R^2 from the IV estimator (or the 2SLS estimator) is negative or very low and the R^2 from the OLS estimation is high, it should be concluded that something is wrong with the specification of the model or the identification of that particular equation.

9.6 METHODS OF ESTIMATION: THE TWO-STAGE LEAST SQUARES METHOD

The two-stage least squares (2SLS) method differs from the instrumental variable (IV) method described in Section 9.5 in that the $\hat{y}$'s are used as regressors rather than as instruments, but the two methods give identical estimates.

Consider the equation to be estimated:

$$y_1 = b_1 y_2 + c_1 z_1 + u_1 \tag{9.9}$$

The other exogenous variables in the system are z_2, z_3, and z_4.

Let $\hat{y}_2$ be the predicted value of y_2 from a regression of y_2 on z_1, z_2, z_3, z_4 (the reduced-form equation). Then

$$y_2 = \hat{y}_2 + v_2$$

where v_2, the residual is uncorrelated with each of the regressors z_1, z_2, z_3, z_4 and hence with $\hat{y}_2$ as well. (This is the property of least squares regression that we discussed in Chapter 4.)

The normal equations for the efficient IV method are

$$\sum \hat{y}_2(y_1 - b_1 y_2 - c_1 z_1) = 0$$
$$\sum z_1(y_1 - b_1 y_2 - c_1 z_1) = 0 \tag{9.10}$$

Substituting $y_2 = \hat{y}_2 + v_2$ we get

$$\sum \hat{y}_2(y_1 - b_1 \hat{y}_2 - c_1 z_1) - b_1 \sum \hat{y}_2 v_2 = 0$$
$$\sum z_1(y_1 - b_1 \hat{y}_2 - c_1 z_1) - b_1 \sum z_1 v_2 = 0 \tag{9.11}$$

But $\sum z_1 v_2 = 0$ and $\sum \hat{y}_2 v_2 = 0$ since z_1 and $\hat{y}_2$ are uncorrelated with v_2. Thus equations (9.11) give

$$\sum \hat{y}_2(y_1 - b_1 \hat{y}_2 - c_1 z_1) = 0$$
$$\sum z_1(y_1 - b_1 \hat{y}_2 - c_1 z_1) = 0 \tag{9.12}$$

But these are the normal equations if we replace y_2 by $\hat{y}_2$ in (9.9) and estimate the equation by OLS. This method of replacing the endogenous variables on the right-hand side by their predicted values from the reduced form and estimating the equation by OLS is called the *two-stage least squares* (2SLS) method. The name arises from the fact that OLS is used in two stages:

Stage 1. Estimate the reduced-form equations by OLS and obtain the predicted $\hat{y}$'s.

Stage 2. Replace the right-hand-side endogenous variables by $\hat{y}$'s and estimate the equation by OLS.

Note that the estimates do not change even if we replace y_1 by $\hat{y}_1$ in equation (9.9). Take the normal equations (9.12). Write

$$y_1 = \hat{y}_1 + v_1$$

where v_1 is again uncorrelated with each of z_1, z_2, z_3, z_4. Thus it is also uncorrelated with $\hat{y}_1$ and $\hat{y}_2$, which are both linear functions of the z's. Now substitute $y_1 = \hat{y}_1 + v_1$ in equations (9.12). We get

$$\sum \hat{y}_2(\hat{y}_1 - b_1\hat{y}_2 - c_1 z_1) + \sum \hat{y}_2 v_1 = 0$$
$$\sum z_1(\hat{y}_1 - b_1\hat{y}_2 - c_1 z_1) + \sum z_1 v_1 = 0$$

The last terms of these two equations are zero and the equations that remain are the normal equations from the OLS estimation of the equation

$$\hat{y}_1 = b_1\hat{y}_2 + c_1\hat{z}_1 + w$$

Thus in stage 2 of the 2SLS method we can replace *all* the endogenous variables in the equation by their predicted values from the reduced forms and then estimate the equation by OLS.

What difference does it make? The answer is that the estimated standard errors from the second stage will be different because the dependent variables is $\hat{y}_1$ instead of y_1. However, the estimated standard errors from the second stage are the wrong ones anyway, as we will show presently. Thus it does not matter whether we replace the endogenous variables on the right-hand side or all the endogenous variables by $\hat{y}$'s in the second stage of the 2SLS method.

The preceding discussion has been in terms of a simple model, but the arguments are general because all the $\hat{y}$'s are uncorrelated with the reduced form residuals $\hat{v}$'s. Since our discussion has been based on replacing y by $\hat{y} + \hat{v}$, the arguments all go through for the general models.

Computing Standard Errors

We will now show how the standard errors we obtain from the second stage of the 2SLS method are not the correct ones and how we can obtain the correct standard errors. Consider the very simple model

$$y_1 = \beta y_2 + u \tag{9.13}$$

where y_1 and y_2 are endogenous variables. There are some (more than one exogenous variables in the system. We first estimate the reduced-form equation for y_2 and write

$$y_2 = \hat{y}_2 + v_2$$

The IV estimator of β is obtained by solving $\sum \hat{y}_2(y_1 - \beta y_2) = 0$, or

$$\hat{\beta}_{IV} = \frac{\sum \hat{y}_2 y_1}{\sum \hat{y}_2 y_2}$$

The 2SLS estimator of β is obtained by solving $\sum \hat{y}_2(y_1 - \beta \hat{y}_2) = 0$, or

$$\hat{\beta}_{2SLS} = \frac{\sum \hat{y}_2 y_1}{\sum \hat{y}_2^2}$$

Since $\sum \hat{y}_2 y_2 = \sum \hat{y}_2(\hat{y}_2 + v_2) = \sum \hat{y}_2^2$ the two estimators are identical and we will drop the subscripts IV and 2SLS and just write $\hat{\beta}$.

$$\hat{\beta} = \frac{\sum \hat{y}_2 y_1}{\sum \hat{y}_2^2} = \frac{\sum \hat{y}_2(\beta y_2 + u)}{\sum \hat{y}_2^2}$$

$$= \beta + \frac{\sum \hat{y}_2 u}{\sum \hat{y}_2^2}$$

(Note: $\sum \hat{y}_2 y_2 = \sum \hat{y}_2^2$). Hence

$$\hat{\beta} - \beta = \frac{(1/n) \sum \hat{y}_2 u}{(1/n) \sum \hat{y}_2^2}$$

where n is the sample size. Since u is independent of the exogenous variables in the system and $\hat{y}_2$ is a linear function of the exogenous variables, we have

$$\text{plim} \frac{1}{n} \sum \hat{y}_2 u = 0$$

If we assume that

$$\text{plim} \frac{1}{n} \sum \hat{y}_2^2 \neq 0$$

we see that plim $\hat{\beta} = \beta$ and thus $\hat{\beta}$ is a consistent estimator for β.

To compute the asymptotic variance of $\hat{\beta}$, note that as $n \to \infty$, var $(\hat{\beta}) \to 0$. Hence it is customary to consider n var $(\hat{\beta})$. We have

$$n \text{ var}(\hat{\beta}) = n \text{ plim}(\hat{\beta} - \beta)^2$$

$$= n \text{ plim} \frac{[(1/n) \sum \hat{y}_2 u][(1/n) \sum \hat{y}_2 u]}{[(1/n) \sum \hat{y}_2^2]^2}$$

$$= \sigma_u^2 / \text{plim} \left(\frac{1}{n} \sum \hat{y}_2^2 \right) \tag{9.14}$$

where $\sigma_u^2 = \text{var}(u)$. In practice, we get an estimate of var $(\hat{\beta})$ as $\hat{\sigma}_u^2 / \sum \hat{y}_2^2$, where $\hat{\sigma}_u^2$ is a consistent estimator of σ_u^2. This is obtained by plugging in the consistent estimator $\hat{\beta}$ of β in (9.13) and computing the sum of squares of residuals. Thus

$$\hat{\sigma}_u^2 = \frac{1}{n}\sum(y_1 - \hat{\beta}y_2)^2$$

There is the question of whether we should use n as divisor on $(n - 1)$. Since the expression is asymptotic, the choice does not matter. Note that if we ignored the fact that $\hat{y}_2$ is a random variable, then using (9.14) we would have written

$$\text{var}(\hat{\beta}) = \text{var}\left(\frac{\sum \hat{y}_2 u}{\sum \hat{y}_2^2}\right) = \frac{\sigma_u^2}{\sum \hat{y}_2^2} \tag{9.15}$$

as in a simple regression model. In effect, this is the expression we use in getting the asymptotic standard errors (after substituting $\hat{\sigma}_u^2$ for σ_u^2), but the correct derivation will have to use probability limits.

Now what is wrong with the standard errors obtained at the second stage of the 2SLS method? To see what is wrong, let us write equation (9.13) as

$$y_1 = \beta\hat{y}_2 - (u + \beta v_2)$$
$$= \beta\hat{y}_2 + w \tag{9.16}$$

When we estimate this equation by OLS, the standard error of $\hat{\beta}$ is obtained as

$$\left(\frac{\hat{\sigma}_w^2}{\sum \hat{y}_2^2}\right)^{1/2}$$

Comparing this with (9.15), we note that what we need is $\hat{\sigma}_u^2$ and what we get from the second stage of 2SLS is $\hat{\sigma}_w^2$. The denominator is correct. It is the estimate of the error variance that is wrong. We can correct this by multiplying the standard errors obtained by $\hat{\sigma}_u/\hat{\sigma}_w$, where

$$\hat{\sigma}_u^2 = \frac{1}{n}\sum(y_1 - \hat{\beta}y_2)^2$$

$$\hat{\sigma}_w^2 = \frac{1}{n}\sum(y_1 - \hat{\beta}\hat{y}_2)^2$$

The latter is the expression we get from the OLS program at the second stage. Most computer programs make this correction anyway, so when using the standard programs we do not have to worry about this problem. The discussion above is meant to show how the correct standard errors are obtained.

The preceding results are also valid when there are exogenous variables in equation (9.13). We have considered a simple model for ease of exposition.

Illustrative Example

In Table 9.3 data are provided on commercial banks' loans to business firms in the United States for 1979–1984. The following demand–supply model has been

Table 9.3 Data for U.S. Commercial Loan Market January 1979–December 1984 (Monthly)

N	Q	R	RD	X	RS	y
1	251.8	11.75	9.25	150.8	9.35	994.3
2	255.6	11.75	9.26	151.5	9.32	1002.5
3	259.8	11.75	9.37	152.0	9.48	994.0
4	264.7	11.75	9.38	153.0	9.46	997.4
5	268.8	11.75	9.50	150.8	9.61	1013.2
6	274.6	11.65	9.29	152.4	9.06	1015.6
7	276.9	11.54	9.20	152.6	9.24	1012.3
8	280.5	11.91	9.23	152.8	9.52	1020.9
9	288.1	12.90	9.44	151.6	10.26	1043.6
10	288.3	14.39	10.13	152.4	11.70	1062.6
11	287.9	15.55	10.76	152.4	11.79	1058.5
12	295.0	15.30	11.31	152.1	12.64	1076.3
13	295.1	15.25	11.86	152.2	13.50	1063.1
14	298.5	15.63	12.36	152.7	14.35	1070.0
15	301.7	18.31	12.96	152.6	15.20	1073.5
16	302.0	19.77	12.04	152.1	13.20	1101.1
17	298.1	16.57	10.99	148.3	8.58	1097.1
18	297.8	12.63	10.58	144.0	7.07	1088.7
19	301.2	11.48	11.07	141.5	8.06	1099.9
20	304.7	11.12	11.64	140.4	9.13	1111.1
21	308.1	12.23	12.02	141.8	10.27	1122.2
22	315.6	13.79	12.31	144.1	11.62	1161.4
23	323.1	16.06	11.94	146.9	13.73	1200.6
24	330.6	20.35	13.21	149.4	15.49	1239.9
25	330.9	20.16	12.81	151.0	15.02	1223.5
26	331.3	19.43	13.35	151.7	14.79	1207.1
27	331.6	18.04	13.33	151.5	13.36	1190.6
28	336.2	17.15	13.88	152.1	13.69	1206.0
29	340.9	19.61	14.32	151.9	16.30	1221.4
30	345.5	20.03	13.75	152.7	14.73	1236.7
31	350.3	20.39	14.38	152.9	14.95	1221.5
32	354.2	20.50	14.89	153.9	15.51	1250.3
33	366.3	20.08	15.49	153.6	14.70	1293.7
34	361.7	18.45	15.40	151.6	13.54	1224.6
35	365.5	16.84	14.22	149.1	10.86	1254.1
36	361.4	15.75	14.23	146.3	10.85	1288.7
37	359.8	15.75	15.18	143.4	12.28	1251.5
38	364.6	16.56	15.27	140.7	13.48	1258.3
39	372.4	16.50	14.58	142.7	12.68	1295.0
40	374.7	16.50	14.46	141.5	12.70	1272.1
41	379.3	16.50	14.26	140.2	12.09	1286.1
42	386.7	16.50	14.81	139.2	12.47	1325.8

Table 9.3 *(Continued)*

N	Q	R	RD	X	RS	y
43	384.4	16.26	14.61	138.7	11.35	1307.3
44	384.5	14.39	13.71	138.8	8.68	1321.7
45	395.0	13.50	12.94	138.4	7.92	1335.5
46	393.7	12.52	12.12	137.3	7.71	1345.2
47	398.9	11.85	11.68	135.7	8.07	1358.1
48	395.3	11.50	11.83	134.9	7.94	1409.7
49	392.4	11.16	11.79	135.2	7.86	1385.4
50	392.3	10.98	12.01	137.4	8.11	1412.6
51	395.9	10.50	11.73	138.1	8.35	1419.5
52	393.5	10.50	11.51	140.0	8.21	1411.0
53	391.7	10.50	11.46	142.6	8.19	1413.1
54	395.3	10.50	11.74	144.4	8.79	1443.8
55	397.7	10.50	12.15	146.4	9.08	1438.1
56	400.6	10.89	12.51	149.7	9.34	1461.4
57	402.7	11.00	12.37	151.8	9.00	1448.9
58	405.3	11.00	12.25	153.8	8.64	1459.0
59	412.0	11.00	12.41	155.0	8.76	1499.4
60	420.1	11.00	12.57	155.3	9.00	1508.9
61	424.4	11.00	12.20	156.2	8.90	1504.1
62	428.8	11.00	12.08	158.5	9.09	1499.3
63	433.1	11.21	12.57	160.0	9.52	1494.5
64	439.7	11.93	12.81	160.8	9.69	1501.5
65	447.3	12.39	13.28	162.1	9.83	1541.3
66	452.9	12.60	13.55	162.8	9.87	1532.9
67	454.4	13.00	13.44	164.4	10.12	1535.5
68	455.2	13.00	12.87	165.9	10.47	1539.0
69	459.9	12.97	12.66	166.0	10.37	1549.9
70	467.7	12.58	12.63	165.0	9.74	1578.9
71	468.7	11.77	12.29	164.4	8.61	1578.2
72	476.8	11.06	12.13	164.8	8.06	1631.2

Source: Several issues of the *Federal Reserve Bulletin.* I would like to thank Walter Mayer for providing me with the data.

estimated:[4] Demand for loans by business firms:

$$Q_t = \beta_0 + \beta_1 R_t + \beta_2 RD_t + \beta_3 X_t + u_t$$

and supply by banks of commercial loans

$$Q_t = \alpha_0 + \alpha_1 R_t + \alpha_2 RS_t + \alpha_3 y_t + v_t$$

[4] The model postulated here is not necessarily the right model for the problem of analyzing the commercial loan market. It is adequate for our purpose of a two-equation model with both equations over-identified.

where Q_t = total commercial loans (billions of dollars)
$\quad R_t$ = average prime rate charged by banks
$\quad RS_t$ = 3-month Treasury bill rate (represents an alternative
$\qquad$ rate of return for banks)
$\quad RD_t$ = Aaa corporate bond rate (represents the price of
$\qquad$ alternative financing to firms)
$\quad X_t$ = industrial production index and represents firms' expectation
$\qquad$ about future economic activity
$\quad y_t$ = total bank deposits (represents a scale variable)
$\qquad$ (billions of dollars)

Both the equations are over-identified. So we chose to estimate them by 2SLS. R_t is expected to have a negative sign in the demand function and a positive sign in the supply function. The coefficient of RS_t is expected to be negative. The coefficients of RD_t, X_t, and y_t are expected to be positive. Both the OLS and 2SLS estimates of the parameters had the expected signs. These estimates are presented in Table 9.4. Note that the R^2 might increase or decrease when we use 2SLS as compared to OLS.

There are only minor changes in the 2SLS estimates compared to the OLS estimates for the demand function. As for the supply function, the only changes we see are in the parameters α_1 and α_2 (coefficients of R_t and RS_t). In this example this is quite important because what this shows is that quantity supplied is more responsive to changes in interest rates than is evidenced from the OLS estimates.

If the R^2 values from the reduced-form equations are very high, the 2SLS and OLS estimates will be almost identical. This is because the $\hat{y}$'s that we substitute in the 2SLS estimation procedure are very close to the corresponding y's in case the

Table 9.4 OLS and 2SLS Estimates for the Demand–Supply Model of the Commercial Loan Market

	OLS		2SLS[a]	
	Coefficient	t-Ratio	Coefficient	t-Ratio
	Demand function			
β_0	− 203.70	− 2.9	− 210.53	− 2.8
β_1	− 15.99	− 12.0	− 20.19	− 12.6
β_2	− 2.29	5.4	2.34	5.2
β_3	36.07	14.2	40.76	14.4
R^2	0.7804		0.7485	
	Supply function			
α_0	− 77.41	− 6.9	− 87.97	− 6.3
α_1	2.41	2.9	6.90	3.6
α_2	− 1.89	− 1.8	− 7.08	− 3.1
α_3	0.33	51.3	0.33	42.9
R^2	0.9768		0.9666	

[a] For the 2SLS, the "t-ratio" is coefficient/asymptotic SE.

R^2's are very high. This is often the case in large econometric models with a very large number of exogenous variables. An example of this is the quarterly model of T. C. Liu.[5] Liu presents 2SLS and OLS estimates side by side and for some equations they are identical to three decimals. Many studies, however, do not report OLS and 2SLS estimates at the same time.

9.7 THE QUESTION OF NORMALIZATION

Going back to equations (9.8), we notice that the coefficient of y_1 in the first equation and that of y_2 in the second equation are both unity. This is expressed by saying that the first equations is normalized with respect to y_1 and the second equation with respect to y_2. Sometimes this is taken to mean that y_1 is the "dependent" variable in the first equation and y_2 is the "dependent" variable in the second equation. This is particularly so in the 2SLS method. Strictly speaking, this goes contrary to the spirit of simultaneous equation models because by definition y_1 and y_2 are jointly determined and we cannot label any single variable as the dependent variable in any equation. Of course, we have to assume the coefficient of one of the variables as 1 (i.e., normalize with respect to one variable). But the method of estimation should be such that it should not matter which variable we choose for normalization. The early methods of estimation like full-information maximum likelihood (FIML) and limited-information maximum likelihood (LIML) satisfied this requirement. But the more popular method like 2SLS does not and is, strictly speaking, not in the spirit of simultaneous equations estimation. A discussion of FIML is beyond the scope of this book, but we discuss LIML in Section 9.8.

In practice, normalization is determined by the way the economic theories are formulated. For instance, in a macro model of income determination, although consumption C and income y are considered as jointly determined, we write the consumption function as

$$C = \alpha + \beta y + u$$

and not as

$$y = \alpha' + \beta' C + u'$$

This is because, at the level of individuals, consumption C is determined by income y. At the back of our minds there is a causal relationship from y to C at the micro level, and we carry this to the macro level as well.

In an exactly identified system normalization does not matter. To see this, consider the first equation in (9.8). We saw earlier that we use z_1, z_2, z_3 as instrumental variables. Since there is no problem of weighting these instrumental variables, it does not matter how the equation is normalized. On the other hand, for the second equation in (9.8) we have the choice between z_1 and z_2 as instruments and the optimum instrumental variable is a weighted average of z_1 and z_2. We saw that

[5] T. C. Liu, "An Exploratory Quarterly Model of Effective Demand in the Post-war U.S. Economy," *Econometrica*, Vol. 31, July 1963.

these weights were obtained from the reduced-form equation for y_1. On the other hand, if the equation is normalized with respect to y_1 and written as

$$y_1 = b_2' y_2 + c_3' z_3 + u_2'$$

then the weights for z_1 and z_2 are obtained from the reduced-form equations for y_2. Thus 2SLS and IV estimators are different for different normalizations in over-identified systems.

*9.8 THE LIMITED-INFORMATION MAXIMUM LIKELIHOOD METHOD

The LIML method, also known as the least variance ratio (LVR) method is the first of the single-equation methods suggested for simultaneous-equations models. It was suggested by Anderson and Rubin [6] in 1949 and was popular until the advent of the 2SLS introduced by Theil [7] in the late 1950s. The LIML method is computationally more cumbersome, but for the simple models we are considering, it is easy to use.

Consider again the equations in (9.8). We can write the first equation as

$$y_1^* = y_1 - b_1 y_2 = c_1 z_1 + c_2 z_2 + u_1 \tag{9.17}$$

For each b_1 we can construct a y_1^*. Consider a regression of y_1^* on z_1 and z_2 only and compute the residual sum of squares (which will be a function of b_1). Call it RSS_1. Now consider a regression of y_1^* on all the exogenous variables z_1, z_2, z_3 and compute the residual sum of squares. Call it RSS_2. What equation (9.17) says is that z_3 is not important in determining y_1^*. Thus the extra reduction in RSS by adding z_3 should be minimal. The LIML or LVR method says that we should choose b_1 so that $(RSS_1 - RSS_2)/RSS_1$ or RSS_1/RSS_2 is minimized. After b_1 is determined, the estimates of c_1 and c_2 are obtained by regressing y_1^* on z_1 and z_2. The procedure is similar for the second equation in (9.8).

There are some important relationships between the LIML and 2SLS methods. (We will omit the proofs, which are beyond the scope of this book.)

1. The 2SLS method can be shown to minimize the *difference* $(RSS_1 - RSS_2)$, whereas the LIML minimizes the *ratio* (RSS_1/RSS_2).
2. If the equation under consideration is exactly identified, then 2SLS and LIML give identical estimates.
3. The LIML estimates are invariant to normalization.
4. The asymptotic variances and covariances of the LIML estimates are the same as those of the 2SLS estimates. However, the standard errors will differ because the error variance σ_u^2 is estimated from different estimates of the structural parameters.

---

[6] T. W. Anderson and H. Rubin, "Estimation of the Parameters of a Single Equation in a Complete System of Stochastic Equations," *Annals of Mathematical Statistics*, Vol. 20, No. 1, March 1949.
[7] H. Theil, *Economic Forecasts and Policy* (Amsterdam: North-Holland, 1958).

5. In the computation of LIML estimates we use the variances and covariances among the endogenous variables as well. But the 2SLS estimates do not depend on this information. For instance, in the 2SLS estimation of the first equation in (9.8), we regress y_1 on $\hat{y}_2$, z_1, and z_2. Since $\hat{y}_2$ is a linear function of the z's we do not make any use of $\text{cov}(y_1, y_2)$. This covariance is used only in the computation of $\hat{\sigma}_u^2$.

Illustrative Example

Consider the demand and supply model of the Australian wine industry discussed in Section 9.5. Since the demand function is exactly identified, the 2SLS and LIML estimates would be identical and they are also identical to the instrumental variable estimates (using S as an instrument) presented earlier in Section 9.5.

As for the supply function, since it is over-identified, the 2SLS and LIML estimates will be different. The following are the 2SLS and LIML estimates of the parameters of the supply function (as computed from the SAS program). All variables are in logs:

Variable	2SLS			LIML		
	Coefficient	SE	t-Ratio	Coefficient	SE	t-Ratio
Intercept	− 16.820	1.080	− 15.57	− 16.849	1.087	− 15.49
P_w	2.616	0.331	7.89	2.627	0.334	7.86
S	1.188	0.190	6.24	1.183	0.191	6.18
R^2 (as computed by the SAS program		0.9548			0.9544	

Actually, in this particular example, the LIML and 2SLS estimates are not much different. But this is not usually the experience in many studies of over-identified models.

*9.9   ON THE USE OF OLS IN THE ESTIMATION OF SIMULTANEOUS-EQUATIONS MODELS

Although we know that the simultaneity problem results in inconsistent estimators of the parameters, when the structural equations are estimated by ordinary least squares (OLS), this does not mean that OLS estimation of simultaneous-equations models is useless. In some instances we may be able to say something about the direction of the (large-sample) bias, and this would be useful information. Also, if an equation is under-identified, it does not necessarily mean that nothing can be said about the parameters in that equation.

Consider the demand and supply model:

$$q_t = \beta p_t + u_t \qquad \text{demand function}$$

$$q_t = \alpha p_t + v_t \qquad \text{supply function}$$

q_t and p_t are in log form and are measured in deviations from their means. Thus β is the demand elasticity and α the price elasticity. Let $\text{var}(u_t) = \sigma_u^2$, $\text{var}(v_t) = \sigma_v^2$, and $\text{cov}(u_t, v_t) = \sigma_{uv}$. The OLS estimator of β is

$$\hat{\beta} = \frac{\sum p_t q_t}{\sum p_t^2} = \beta + \frac{\sum p_t u_t}{\sum p_t^2}$$

$$= \beta + \frac{(1/n)\sum p_t u_t}{(1/n)\sum p_t^2}$$

where n is the sample size. Now

$$\beta p_t + u_t = \alpha p_t + v_t$$

or

$$p_t = \frac{v_t - u_t}{\beta - \alpha}$$

Hence we have

$$\text{plim}\left(\frac{1}{n}\sum p_t u_t\right) = \text{cov}(p_t, u_t) = \frac{\sigma_{uv} - \sigma_u^2}{\beta - \alpha}$$

and

$$\text{plim}\left(\frac{1}{n}\sum p_t^2\right) = \text{var}(p_t) = \frac{\sigma_v^2 + \sigma_u^2 - 2\sigma_{uv}}{(\beta - \alpha)^2}$$

Thus

$$\text{plim}\,\hat{\beta} = \beta + (\beta - \alpha)\frac{\sigma_{uv} - \sigma_u^2}{\sigma_v^2 + \sigma_u^2 - 2\sigma_{uv}}$$

This expression is not very useful, but if $\sigma_{uv} = 0$ (i.e., the shifts in the demand and supply functions are unrelated), we get

$$\text{plim}\,\hat{\beta} = \beta + (\beta - \alpha)\left(-\frac{\sigma_u^2}{\sigma_v^2 + \sigma_u^2}\right)$$

Now β is expected to be negative and α positive. Thus the bias term is expected to be positive. Hence if we find a price elasticity of demand of -0.8, the true price elasticity is < -0.8.

We can show by a similar reasoning that if we estimate the supply function by OLS we get

$$\hat{\alpha} = \frac{\sum p_t q_t}{\sum p_t^2}$$

and if $\sigma_{uv} = 0$, then

$$\text{plim } \hat{\alpha} = \alpha + (\beta - \alpha)\frac{\sigma_v^2}{\sigma_v^2 + \sigma_u^2}$$

The bias is now negative since $(\beta - \alpha)$ is expected to be negative. Again, suppose that the supply elasticity is estimated to be 0.6; then we know that the true price elasticity is > 0.6.

In practice, when we regress q on p we do not know whether we are estimating the demand function or the supply function. However, if the regression coefficient is, say, $+0.3$, we know that the supply elasticity is $0.3 +$ a positive number and the demand elasticity is $0.3 +$ a negative number. Thus the practically useful conclusion is that the supply elasticity is > 0.3. On the other hand, if the regression coefficient is -0.9, we know that the supply elasticity is $-0.9 +$ a positive number and the demand elasticity is $-0.9 +$ a negative number. Thus the practically useful conclusion is that the demand elasticity < -0.9 (or greater than 0.9 in absolute value).

In the example above we also note that

$$\text{plim }\left(\frac{\sum p_t q_t}{\sum p_t^2}\right) \to \beta \text{ as } \sigma_u^2 \to 0$$

$$= \alpha \text{ as } \sigma_v^2 \to 0$$

Since σ_u^2 is the variance of the random shift in the demand function, $\sigma_u^2 \to 0$ means that the demand function does not shift or is stable. Thus the regression of q on p will estimate the demand elasticity if the demand function is stable and the supply elasticity if the supply function is stable.

Figure 9.2 gives the case of a supply curve shifting and the demand curve not shifting. What we observe in practice are the points of intersection of the demand

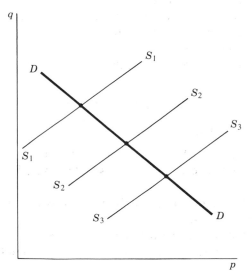

Figure 9.2.   Stable demand and shifting supply.

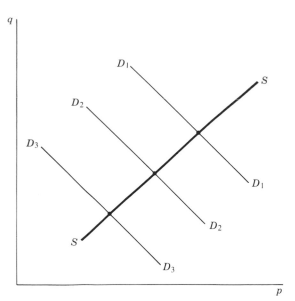

Figure 9.3.   Stable supply and shifting demand.

curve and the supply curve. As can be seen, the locus of these points of intersection traces out the demand curve. In Figure 9.3, where the demand curve shifts and the supply curve does not, this locus determines the supply curve.[8]

Working's Concept of Identification

After concluding that if the demand curve did not shift much, but the supply curve did, then the locus of the points of intersection would come close to tracing a demand curve, Working added that by "correcting" for the influence of an additional important determining variable (such as income) in the demand curve, we could reduce its shifts and hence get a better approximation of the price elasticity of demand. If we add income to the demand function, we get the equation system

$$q_t = \beta p_t + \gamma y_t + u_t \qquad \text{demand function}$$

$$q_t = \alpha p_t + v_t \qquad \text{supply function}$$

What Working said was that by introducing y_t in the demand function, we can get a better estimate of β. What he had in mind was that the introduction of y_t reduced the variance of u_t.

If we use the results on identification discussed earlier in Sections 9.3 and 9.4, we come to the conclusion that the supply equation is identified (it has one missing variable) but the demand function is not. This is exactly the opposite of what Working said. The problem here is that the concept of identification we have

---

[8] This was the main conclusion of the article by E. J. Working, "What Do Statistical Demand Curves Show?" *Quarterly Journal of Economics*, February 1927.

discussed is in terms of our ability to get consistent estimates. What Working was concerned about is the least squares bias. His argument is that if σ_u^2 is somehow reduced, we get good estimates by OLS (i.e., the bias would be negligible). Consider two estimates $\hat{\beta}_1$ and $\hat{\beta}_2$ for β. Suppose that

$$\text{plim } \hat{\beta}_1 = \beta \qquad \text{and} \qquad \text{plim } \hat{\beta}_2 = 0.999\beta$$

then $\hat{\beta}_1$ is consistent but $\hat{\beta}_2$ is not. But for all practical purposes $\hat{\beta}_2$ is also consistent.

Suppose that we include all the relevant explanatory variables in the demand function so that σ_u^2 is very small, whereas the supply function includes only price as the "explanatory" variable. Then, even if the demand equation is not identified by the rules we discussed earlier, we are still justified in estimating the equation by OLS. On the other hand, even if the supply function is over-identified, if σ_v^2 is very large, we get a poor estimate of the supply elasticity α. We can get a consistent estimator for α, but its variance will be very high.

In summary, it is not true that if an equation is under-identified, we have to give up all hopes of estimating it. Nor does it follow that an equation that is over-identified can be better estimated than one that is exactly-identified or under-identified. Further discussion of the demand supply model considered here can be found in Maddala [9] and Leamer. [10]

In simultaneous equations models the classification of variables as endogenous and exogenous is quite arbitrary. Often, current values of some variables are treated as endogenous and lagged values of these same variables are treated as exogenous even when the current and lagged values are very highly correlated. In addition, some equations are regarded as identified (over- or exactly-) and others are not identified by merely looking at how many variables are missing from the equation, and the under-identified equations are regarded as nonestimable. The discussion above illustrates that least squares estimation of under-identified equations can still be worthwhile. Also, instead of simply counting the number of exogenous variables, one should also look at how high their inter-correlations are.

Recursive Systems

Not all simultaneous equations models give biased estimates when estimated by OLS. An important class of models for which OLS estimation is valid is that of recursive models. These are models in which the errors from the different equations are independent and the coefficients of the endogenous variables show a triangular pattern. For example, consider a model with three endogenous variables: $y_1, y_2,$ and y_3, and three exogenous variables, $z_1, z_2,$ and z_3, which has the following structure:

$$y_1 + \beta_{12}y_2 + \beta_{13}y_3 + \alpha_1 z_1 = u_1$$

$$y_2 + \beta_{23}y_3 + \alpha_2 z_2 = u_2$$

$$y_3 + \alpha_3 z_3 = u_3$$

[9] G. S. Maddala, *Econometrics* (New York; McGraw-Hill, 1977), pp. 244–249.
[10] E. E. Leamer, "Is It a Demand Curve or Is It a Supply Curve: Partial Identification Through Inequality Constraints," *The Review of Economics and Statistics*, Vol. 63, No. 3, August 1981, pp. 319–327.

where u_1, u_2, u_3 are independent. The coefficients of the endogenous variables are

$$
\begin{array}{ccc}
1 & \beta_{12} & \beta_{13} \\
 & 1 & \beta_{23} \\
 & & 1
\end{array}
$$

which form a triangular structure. In such systems, each equation can be estimated by ordinary least squares. Suppose that in the example above u_2 and u_3 are correlated but they are independent of u_1; then the model is said to be *block-recursive*. The second and third equations have to be estimated jointly, but the first equation can be estimated by OLS. Note that y_2 and y_3 depend on u_2 and u_3 only and hence are independent of the error term u_1.

Estimation of Cobb–Douglas Production Functions

In the estimation of production functions, output, labor input, and capital input are usually considered the endogenous variables and wage rate and price of capital as the exogenous variables.

Suppose that we use the Cobb–Douglas production function

$$
X_i = AL_i^{\alpha} K_i^{\beta} e^{u_{1i}} \tag{9.18}
$$

where u_{1i} is the error term; then taking logs we can write it as

$$
y_{1i} - \alpha y_{2i} - \beta y_{3i} = c_1 + u_{1i} \tag{9.19}
$$

where $y_{1i} = \log X_i$, $y_{2i} = \log L_i$, $y_{3i} = \log K_i$ and $c_1 = \log A$.

Since y_{2i} and y_{3i} are endogenous variables, we cannot estimate this equation by OLS. We have to add the equations for y_{2i} and y_{3i} and these are obtained from the marginal productivity conditions. However, Zellner, Kmenta, and Dreze[11] argue that in this case we can estimate equation (9.19) by OLS. Their argument is that since output given by (9.18) is stochastic, the firm should be maximizing expected profits (not profits). If $u_{1i} \sim IN(0, \sigma^2)$, then

$$
E(e^{u_{1i}}) = \exp\left(\tfrac{1}{2}\sigma^2\right)
$$

Hence

$$
E(X_i) = AL_i^{\alpha} K_i^{\beta} \exp\left(\tfrac{1}{2}\sigma^2\right)
$$

Expected profits $= R_i = p_i E(X_i) - W_i L_i - r_i K_i$, where p is the price of output, w the price of labor input, and r the price of capital input. Maximization of expected profits gives us the following conditions:

$$
\frac{\partial R_i}{\partial L_i} = 0 \Rightarrow \frac{X_i}{L_i} = \frac{w_i}{\alpha p_i} \exp\left(u_{1i} - \tfrac{1}{2}\sigma^2\right)
$$

$$
\frac{\partial R_i}{\partial K_i} = 0 \Rightarrow \frac{X_i}{K_i} = \frac{r_i}{\beta p_i} \exp\left(u_{1i} - \tfrac{1}{2}\sigma^2\right)
$$

[11] A. Zellner, J. Kmenta, and J. Dreze, "Specification and Estimation of Cobb–Douglas Production Function Models," *Econometrica*, October 1966, pp. 786–795.

Taking logs and adding error terms u_{2i} and u_{3i} to these equations, we get (the errors depict errors in maximization of expected profits)

$$y_{1i} - y_{2i} = c_{2i} + u_{1i} + u_{2i}$$

$$y_{1i} - y_{3i} = c_{3i} + u_{1i} + u_{3i}$$

$$\text{where } c_{2i} = \log\left(\frac{w_i}{\alpha p_i}\right) - \frac{1}{2}\sigma^2 \tag{9.20}$$

$$c_{3i} = \log\left(\frac{r_i}{\beta p_i}\right) - \frac{1}{2}\sigma^2$$

Now we can solve equations (9.19) and (9.20) to get the reduced forms for y_{1i}, y_{2i}, y_{3i}. We can easily see that when we substitute for y_{1i} from equation (9.19) into equations (9.20), the u_{1i} term cancels. Thus y_{2i} and y_{3i} involve only the error terms u_{2i} and u_{3i}.

It is reasonable to assume that u_{1i} are independent of u_{2i} and u_{3i} because u_{1i} are errors due to "acts of nature" like weather and u_{2i} and u_{3i} are "human errors." Under these assumptions y_{2i} and y_{3i} (which depend on u_{2i} and u_{3i} only) are independent of u_{1i}. Hence OLS estimation of the production function (9.19) yields consistent estimates of the parameters α and β. We thus regress y_{1i} on y_{2i} and y_{3i}.

Here is an example where there is no simultaneity bias by using the OLS method. The model is not recursive either, but from the peculiar way the error terms entered the equations we could show that in the first equation the included endogenous variables are independent of the error term in that equation.

*9.10 EXOGENEITY AND CAUSALITY

The approach to simultaneous equations models that we have discussed until now is called the *Cowles Foundation approach*. Its name derives from the fact that it was developed during the late 1940s and early 1950s by the econometricians at the Cowles Foundation at the University of Chicago. The basic premise of this approach is that the data are assumed to have been generated by a system of simultaneous equations. The classification of variables into "endogenous" and "exogenous," and the causal structure of the model are both given a priori and are untestable. The main emphasis is on the estimation of the unknown parameters for which the Cowles Foundation devised several methods (limited-information and full-information methods).

This approach has, in recent years, been criticized on several grounds:

1. The classification of variables into endogenous and exogenous is sometimes arbitrary.
2. There are usually many variables that should be included in the equation that are excluded to achieve identification. This argument was made by

T. C. Liu[12] in 1960 but did not receive much attention. It is known as the *Liu critique.*

3. One of the main purposes of simultaneous equations estimation is to forecast the effect of changes in the exogenous variables on the endogenous variables. However, if the exogenous variables are changed and profit-maximizing agents see the change coming, they would modify their behavior accordingly. Thus the coefficients in the simultaneous equations models cannot be assumed to be independent of changes in the exogenous variables. This is now called the *Lucas critique.*[13]

One solution to the Lucas critique is to make the coefficients of the simultaneous equations system depend on the exogenous policy variables. Since this makes the model a varying parameter model, which is beyond the scope of this book, we will not pursue it here.[14]

Leamer[15] suggests redefining the concept of exogeneity. He suggests defining the variable x as exogenous if the conditional distribution of y given x is invariant to modifications that alter the process generating x. What this says is that a variable is defined as exogenous if the Lucas critique does not apply to it. It is, however, not clear whether such a redefinition solves the problem raised by Lucas.

There are two concepts of exogeneity that are usually distinguished:

1. *Predeterminedness.* A variable is predetermined in a particular equation if it is independent of the *contemporaneous and future* errors in that equation.
2. *Strict exogeneity.* A variable is strictly exogenous if it is independent of the *contemporaneous, future, and past* errors in the relevant equation.

To explain these concepts we have to consider a model with lagged variables. Consider[16]

$$y_t = \alpha_1 x_t + \beta_{11} y_{t-1} + \beta_{12} x_{t-1} + u_{1t}$$
$$x_t = \alpha_2 y_t + \beta_{21} y_{t-1} + \beta_{22} x_{t-1} + u_{2t}$$

(9.21)

with u_{1t} and u_{2t} mutually and serially independent. If $\alpha_2 = 0$, x_t is predetermined for y_t in the first equation. On the other hand, x_t is strictly exogenous for y_t only if $\alpha_2 = 0$ and $\beta_{21} = 0$. Because if $\beta_{21} \neq 0$, x_t depends on $u_{1,t-1}$ through y_{t-1}. That is, in the first equation x_t is not independent of past errors.

In nondynamic models, and models with no serial correlation in the errors, we do not have to make this distinction. For instance, in Section 9.9 we considered an example of estimation of the Cobb–Douglas production function under the hypothesis of maximization of expected profit. We saw that y_2 and y_3 were

---

[12] T. C. Liu, "Under-Identification, Structural Estimation, and Forecasting," *Econometrica*, Vol. 28, 1960, pp. 855–865.

[13] R. E. Lucas, "Econometric Policy Evaluation: A Critique," in Karl L. Brunner (ed.), *The Phillips Curve and Labor Markets* (supplement to the *Journal of Monetary Economics*), 1976, pp. 19–46.

[14] This is the solution suggested in G. S. Maddala, *Econometrics* (New York: McGraw-Hill, 1977), Chap. 17, "Varying Parameter Models,"

[15] E. E. Leamer, "Vector Autoregressions for Causal Inference," in K. Brunner and A. Meltzer (eds.), *Understanding Monetary Regimes* (supplement to *Journal of Monetary Economics*), 1985, pp. 255–304.

[16] This example and the discussion that follows is from R. L. Jacobs, E. E. Leamer, and M. P. Ward, "Difficulties with Testing for Causation," *Economic Inquiry*, 1979, pp. 401–413.

independent of the error term u_1. Thus these variables are exogenous for the estimation of the parameters in the production function. Similarly, in a recursive system, the (nonnormalized) endogenous variables in each equation can be treated as exogenous for the purpose of estimation of the parameters in that equation.

Engle, Hendry, and Richard [17] are not satisfied with the foregoing definitions of exogeneity and suggest three more concepts:

1. Weak exogeneity.
2. Strong exogeneity.
3. Super exogeneity.

Since these concepts are often used and they are not difficult to understand anyway, we will discuss them briefly. The concept of strong exogeneity is linked to another concept: "Granger causality." There is a proliferation of terms here but since they occur frequently in recent econometric literature and are not difficult to understand, we will go through them.

One important point to note is that whether a variable is exogenous or not depends on the parameter under consideration. Consider the equation [18]

$$y = bx + u$$

where b is the unknown parameter and u is a variable that is unknown and unnamed. This equation can also be written as

$$y = b^*x + v$$

where $b^* = b + 1$ and $v = u - x$. Again, b^* is an unknown parameter and v is an unknown variable. If $E(u|x) = 0$, it cannot be true that $E(v|x) = 0$. So is x exogenous or not? It clearly depends on the parameter value. This points to the importance of the question: "Exogenous for what?"

As yet another example, consider the case where y_t and x_t have a bivariate normal distribution with means $E(y_t) = \mu_1$, $E(x_t) = \mu_2$ and variances and covariance given by $\text{var}(y_t) = \sigma_{11}$, $\text{var}(x_t) = \sigma_{22}$, and $\text{cov}(y_t, x_t) = \sigma_{12}$. The conditional distribution of y_t given x_t is

$$y_t | x_t \sim \text{IN}(\alpha + \beta x_t, \sigma^2)$$

where $\beta = \sigma_{12}/\sigma_{22}$, $\alpha = \mu_1 - \beta\mu_2$, and $\sigma^2 = \sigma_{11} - \sigma_{12}^2/\sigma_{22}$.

We can write the joint distribution of y_t and x_t as

$$f(y_t, x_t) = g(y_t | x_t)h(x_t)$$

and we can write the model as

$$\begin{aligned} y_t &= \alpha + \beta x_t + u_{1t} & u_{1t} &\sim \text{IN}(0, \sigma^2) \\ x_t &= \mu_2 + v_{2t} & v_{2t} &\sim \text{IN}(0, \sigma_{22}) \end{aligned} \tag{9.22}$$

[17] R. F. Engle, D. F. Hendry, and J. F. Richard, "Exogeneity," *Econometrica*, Vol. 51, March 1983, pp. 277–304.

[18] The example is from J. W. Pratt and R. Schlaifer, "On the Nature and Discovery of Structure," *Journal of the American Statistical Association*, Vol. 79, March 1984, pp. 9–21. It is also discussed in Leamer, "Vector Autoregressions."

where $\text{cov}(x_t, u_{1t}) = 0$ and $\text{cov}(u_{1t}, v_{2t}) = 0$ by construction. If we consider this set of equations, x_t is "exogenous."

On the other hand, we can similarly write

$$f(y_t, x_t) = h(x_t \mid y_t)g(y_t)$$

and write the model as

$$
\begin{aligned}
x_t &= \gamma + \delta y_t + u_{2t} & u_{2t} &\sim \text{IN}(0, \omega^2) \\
y_t &= \mu_1 + v_{1t} & v_{1t} &\sim \text{IN}(0, \sigma_{11})
\end{aligned}
\tag{9.23}
$$

where $\text{cov}(y_t, u_{2t}) = \text{cov}(u_{2t}, v_{1t}) = 0$ by construction and $\delta = \sigma_{12}/\sigma_{11}$, $\gamma = \mu_2 - \delta\mu_1$, $\omega^2 = \sigma_{22} - \sigma_{12}^2/\sigma_{11}$. Now y_t is "exogenous" in this model. So which of x_t and y_t is exogenous, if at all? The answer depends on the parameters of interest. If we are interested in the parameters α, β, σ^2, then x_t is exogenous and equations (9.22) are the ones to estimate. If we are interested in the parameters γ, δ, ω^2, then y_t is exogenous and equations (9.23) are the ones to estimate.

The considerations above led to the following definition of weak exogeneity by Engle, Hendry, and Richard:

Weak Exogeneity

A variable x_t is said to be weakly exogenous for estimating a set of parameters λ if inference on λ conditional on x_t involves no loss of information. That is, if we write

$$f(y_t, x_t) = g(y_t \mid x_t)h(x_t)$$

where $g(y_t \mid x_t)$ involves the parameters λ, weak exogeneity implies that the marginal distribution $h(x_t)$ does not involve the parameters λ. Essentially, the parameters in $h(x_t)$ are nuisance parameters.

In the example where y_t and x_t have a bivariate normal distribution, there are five parameters: $\mu_1, \mu_2, \sigma_{11}, \sigma_{22}, \sigma_{12}$. These can be transformed by a one-to-one transformation into $(\alpha, \beta, \sigma^2)$ and (μ_2, σ_{22}). The two sets are separate. Thus for the estimation of $(\alpha, \beta, \sigma^2)$ we do not need information on (μ_2, σ_{22}). Hence x_t is weakly exogenous for the estimation of $(\alpha, \beta, \sigma^2)$.

Superexogeneity

The concept of superexogeneity is related to the Lucas critique. If x_t is weakly exogenous and the parameters in $f(y_t \mid x_t)$ remain invariant to changes in the marginal distribution of x_t, then x_t is said to be *superexogenous*. In the example we have been considering, namely that of y_t and x_t having a bivariate normal distribution, x_t is weakly exogenous for the estimation of $(\alpha, \beta, \sigma^2)$ in (9.22). But it is *not* superexogenous because if we change μ_2 and σ_{22} the parameters in the marginal distribution of x_t, this will produce changes in $(\alpha, \beta, \sigma^2)$. Note that weak exogeneity is a condition required for efficient estimation. Superexogeneity is a condition required for policy purposes.

Leamer finds it unnecessary to require weak exogeneity as a condition for superexogeneity. He argues that this confounds the problem of efficient estimation with that of policy analysis. His definition of exogeneity is the same as the definition of superexogeneity by Engle, Hendry, and Richard without the requirement of weak exogeneity.

Strong Exogeneity

If x_t is weakly exogenous and x_t is *not preceded* by any of the endogenous variables in the system, x_t is defined to be strongly exogenous. As an example, consider the model

$$y_t = \beta x_t + u_{1t}$$

$$x_t = \alpha_1 x_{t-1} + \alpha_2 y_{t-1} + u_{2t}$$

(u_{1t}, u_{2t}) have a bivariate normal distribution and are serially independent; $\text{var}(u_{1t}) = \sigma_{11}$, $\text{var}(u_{2t}) = \sigma_{22}$, and $\text{cov}(u_{1t}, u_{2t}) = \sigma_{12}$. If $\sigma_{12} = 0$, then x_t is weakly exogenous because the marginal distribution of x_t does not involve β and σ_{11}. However, the second equation shows that y_t precedes x_t. (x_t depends on y_{t-1}.) Hence x_t is not strongly exogenous.

We have used the word "precedence" following Leamer but the definition by Engle, Hendry, and Richard is in terms of a concept called *Granger causality* and is as follows. If x_t is weakly exogenous and x_t is *not caused* in the sense of Granger by any of the endogenous variables in the system, then x_t is defined to be *strongly exogenous*. Simply stated the term "Granger causality" means "precedence" but we will discuss it in greater detail.

Granger Causality

Granger starts from the premise that the future cannot cause the present or the past. If event A occurs after event B, we know that A cannot cause B. At the same time, if A occurs before B, it does not necessarily imply that A causes B. For instance, the weatherman's prediction occurs before the rain. This does not mean that the weatherman causes the rain. In practice, we observe A and B as time series and we would like to know whether A precedes B, or B precedes A, or they are contemporaneous. For instance, do movements in prices precede movements in interest rates, or is it the opposite, or are the movements contemporaneous? This is the purpose of Granger causality. It is not causality as it is usually understood.

Granger [19] devised some tests for causality (in the limited sense discussed above) which proceed as follows. Consider two time series, $\{y_t\}$ and $\{x_t\}$. The series x_t *fails to Granger cause* y_t if in a regression of y_t on lagged y's and lagged x's, the coefficients of the latter are zero. That is, consider

$$y_t = \sum_{i=1}^{k} \alpha_i y_{t-i} + \sum_{i=1}^{k} \beta_i x_{t-i} + u_t$$

[19] C. W. J. Granger, "Investigating Causal Relations by Econometric Models and Cross-Spectral Methods," *Econometrica*, Vol. 37, January 1969, pp. 24–36.

Then if $\beta_i = 0$ $(i = 1, 2, \ldots, k)$, x_t fails to cause y_t. The lag length k is, to some extent, arbitrary.

An alternative test provided by Sims[20] is as follows: x_t fails to cause y_t in the Granger sense if in a regression of y_t on lagged, current, and future x's, the latter coefficients are zero. Consider the regression

$$y_t = \sum_{j=-k_1}^{k_2} \beta_j x_{t-j} + u_t$$

Test $\beta_{-j} = 0 (j = 1, 2, \ldots, k_1)$. What this says is that the prediction of y from current and past x's would not be improved if future values of x are included. There are some econometric differences between the two tests, but the two tests basically test the same hypothesis.[21]

As mentioned earlier, Leamer suggests using the simple word "precedence" instead of the complicated word Granger causality since all we are testing is whether a certain variable precedes another and we are not testing causality as it is usually understood. However, it is too late to complain about the term since it has already been well established in the econometrics literature. Hence it is important to understand what it means.

Granger Causality and Exogeneity

As we defined earlier, Granger noncausality is necessary for strong exogeneity as defined by Engle, Hendry, and Richard. Sims also regards tests for Granger causality as tests for exogeneity.[22] However, Granger noncausality is neither necessary nor sufficient for exogeneity as understood in the usual simultaneous equations literature.[23] This point can be illustrated with the example in equations (9.21). We said that x_t is predetermined for y_t in the first equation if $\alpha_2 = 0$, and x_t is strictly exogenous for y_t if $\alpha_2 = 0$ and $\beta_{12} = 0$.

Now to see what the Granger test does, write the reduced forms for y_t and x_t:

$$y_t = \pi_{11} y_{t-1} + \pi_{12} x_{t-1} + v_{1t}$$

$$x_t = \pi_{21} y_{t-1} + \pi_{22} x_{t-1} + v_{2t}$$

For Granger noncausality, we have to have $\pi_{21} = 0$. But

$$\pi_{21} = \frac{\alpha_2 \beta_{11} + \beta_{21}}{1 - \alpha_1 \alpha_2}$$

Thus $\pi_{21} = 0$ implies that $\alpha_2 \beta_{11} + \beta_{21} = 0$. From this it does not follow that $\alpha_2 = 0$. Thus Granger noncausality does not necessarily imply that x_t is predetermined.

[20] C. A. Sims, "Money, Income and Causality," *American Economic Review*, Vol. 62, 1972, pp. 540–552.
[21] G. Chamberlain, "The General Equivalence of Granger and Sims Causality," *Econometrica*, Vol. 50, 1982, pp. 569–582.
[22] Sims, "Money," p. 550.
[23] T. F. Cooley and S. F. LeRoy, "A-theoretical Macroeconometrics," *Journal of Monetary Economics*, Vol. 16, No. 3, November 1985, pp. 283–308, see Sect. 5 on Granger causality and Cowles causality.

Conversely, $\alpha_2 = 0$ does not imply that $\pi_{21} = 0$. However, $\alpha_2 = 0$ and $\beta_{21} = 0$ implies that $\pi_{21} = 0$, although the converse is not true.

Thus a test for Granger noncausality is not useful as a test for exogeneity. Some argue that it is, nevertheless, useful as a descriptive device for time-series data.

Tests for Exogeneity

The Cowles Foundation approach to simultaneous equations held the view that causality and exogeneity cannot be tested. These are things that have to be specified a priori. In recent years it has been argued that if some variables are specified as exogenous and the equation is over-identified, one can test whether some other variables considered exogenous are indeed exogenous or not.

As an illustration, consider the following. We have a simultaneous equations model with three endogenous variables y_1, y_2, and y_3, and three exogenous variables z_1, z_2, and z_3. Suppose that the first equation of the model is

$$y_1 = \beta_2 y_2 + \beta_3 y_3 + \alpha_1 z_1 + u_1$$

We want to test whether y_2 and y_3 can be treated as exogenous for the estimation of this equation. To test this hypothesis, we obtain the predicted values $\hat{y}_2$ and $\hat{y}_3$ of y_2 and y_3, respectively, from the reduced form equations for y_2 and y_3. We then estimate the model

$$y_1 = \beta_2 y_2 + \beta_3 y_3 + \alpha_1 z_1 + \gamma_2 \hat{y}_2 + \gamma_3 \hat{y}_3 + u_1$$

by OLS and test the hypothesis: $\gamma_2 = \gamma_3 = 0$ (using the F-test described in Chapter 4). If the hypothesis is rejected, y_2 and y_3 cannot be treated as exogenous. If it is not rejected, y_2 and y_3 can be treated as exogenous.[24]

SUMMARY

1. In simultaneous equations models, each equation is normalized with respect to one endogenous variable. Strictly speaking, since the endogenous variables are all jointly determined, it should not matter which variable is chosen for normalization. However, some commonly used methods of estimation (like the two-stage least squares) do depend on the normalization rule adopted. In practice, normalization is determined by the way economic theories are formulated.

2. In a demand and supply model, if quantity supplied is not responsive to price, the demand function should be normalized with respect to price. On the other hand, if quantity supplied is highly responsive to price, the demand function should be normalized with respect to quantity. (See Section 9.1 for a graphical discussion and Section 9.3 for an empirical illustration.)

---

[24] The test procedure described here is Hausman's test discussed in greater detail in Section 12.10. It is equivalent to some other tests suggested in the literature. Two references are: D. Wu, "Alternative Tests of Independence Between Stochastic Regressors and Disturbances," *Econometrica*, Vol. 41, 1973, pp. 733–750 and N. S. Revankar, "Asymptotic Relative Efficiency Analysis of Certain Tests of Independence in Structural Systems," *International Economic Review*, Vol. 19, 1978, pp. 165–179.

3. Before a simultaneous equations model is estimated, one should check whether each equation is identified or not. In linear simultaneous equations systems, a necessary condition for the identification of an equation is the order condition which says that the number of variables missing from the equation should be greater than or equal to the number of endogenous variables in the equation minus one. This counting rule is only a necessary condition. One also has to check the rank condition which is based on the structure of the missing variables in the other equations. This is illustrated with some examples in Section 9.4.

4. It is customary to classify an equation into the over-identified, exactly identified, and under-identified categories according as the number of variables missing from the equation is, respectively, greater than, equal to, or less than the number of endogenous variables minus one. It is not possible to get consistent estimates of the parameters in the under-identified equations. The difference between over-identified and exactly identified equations is simply that the latter are easier to estimate than the former.

5. We have discussed only single-equation methods, that is, estimation of each equation at a time. The methods we have discussed are:
(a) The instrumental variable (IV) methods (Section 9.5).
(b) The two-stage least squares (2SLS) method (Section 9.6).
(c) The limited-information maximum likelihood (LIML) method (Section 9.8).
For an exactly identified equation, all the methods are equivalent and give the same answers. For an over-identified equation the IV method gives different estimates depending on which of the missing exogenous variables are chosen as instruments. The 2SLS method is a weighted instrumental variable method.

6. In over-identified equations, the 2SLS estimates depend on the normalization rule adopted. The LIML estimates do not depend on the choice of normalization. The LIML method is thus a truly simultaneous estimation method, but the 2SLS is not because, strictly speaking, since the endogenous variable are jointly determined, normalization should not matter.

7. It is not always true that we can say nothing about the parameters of an under-identified equation. In some cases the ordinary least squares (OLS) estimates, even if they are not consistent, do give us some information about the parameters. Some examples are given in Section 9.9. It is also interesting to note that the concept of identification as discussed by Working in 1927 is quite different from the current discussion which is concentrated on getting consistent estimators for the parameters (see Section 9.9).

8. There are some cases where the simultaneous equations model can be estimated by using the OLS method. One such example is the recursive model. We also give another example—that of estimation of the Cobb–Douglas production function under uncertainty where the OLS method is the appropriate one (see Section 9.9).

9. In recent years, the usual definition of exogeneity has been questioned. Some new terms have been introduced, such as weak exogeneity, strong exogeneity, and super exogeneity. One important question that has been raised is: "Exogenous for what?" If it is for efficient estimation of the parameters (this is the concept of weak exogeneity), a variable can be treated as endogenous in one equation and exogenous

in another (as in a recursive system). Also, whether a variable is exogenous or not depends on the parameter to be estimated (see Pratt's example).

10. Strong exogeneity is weak exogeneity plus Granger causality. The term "Granger causality" has nothing to do with causality as it is usually understood. A better term for it is "precedence." Some econometricians have equated the concept of exogeneity with Granger causality. The example in Section 9.10 shows that linking Granger causality to exogeneity has some pitfalls. It is better to keep the two concepts separate.

11. A variable is considered superexogenous if interventions in that variable leave the parameters in the system unaltered. It is a concept that has to do with Lucas's critique of econometric policy evaluation. As a definition, the concept is all right. But from the practical point of view its use is questionable.

12. There have been some tests of exogeneity suggested in the context of simultaneous equations systems. These tests depend on the availability of extra instrumental variables. The tests are easy to apply because they depend on the addition of some constructed variables to the usual models, and testing that the coefficients of these added variables are zero.

EXERCISES

1. Explain the meaning of each of the following terms.
    (a) Endogenous variables.
    (b) Exogenous variables.
    (c) Structural equations.
    (d) Reduced-form equations.
    (e) Order condition for identification.
    (f) Rank condition for identification.
    (g) Indirect least squares.
    (h) Two-stage least squares.
    (i) Instrumental variable methods.
    (j) Normalization.
    (k) Simultaneity bias.
    (l) Recursive systems.
2. Explain concisely what is meant by "the identification problem" in the context of the linear simultaneous equations model.
3. Consider the three-equation model

$$y_1 = \beta_{13}y_3 + \gamma_{12}x_2 + u_1$$
$$y_2 = \beta_{21}y_1 + \beta_{23}y_3 + \gamma_{21}x_1 + \gamma_{22}x_2 + u_2$$
$$y_3 = \beta_{31}x_3 + u_3$$

where y_1, y_2, and y_3 are endogenous, and x_1, x_2, and x_3 are exogenous. Discuss the identification of each of the equations of the model, based on the order and rank conditions.

Now suppose that you want to estimate the first equation by two-stage least squares, but you have only an ordinary least squares program available. Explain carefully, step by step, how you would estimate β_{13}, γ_{12}, and var (u_1).

4. Consider the model

$$y_1 = \alpha y_2 + \delta x + u_1$$
$$y_2 = \beta y_1 + \gamma x + u_2$$

where x is exogenous, and the error terms u_1 and u_2 have mean zero and are serially uncorrelated.

   (a) Write down the equations expressing the reduced-form coefficients in terms of the structural parameters.
   (b) Show that if $\gamma = 0$, then β can be identified. Are the parameters α and δ identified in this case? Why or why not?
   (c) In the case of $\gamma = 0$, what formula would you use to estimate β? What is the asymptotic variance of your estimator of β?

5. What is meant by the phrase: "The estimator is invariant to normalization"? Do any problems arise if an estimator is not invariant to normalization? Which of the following estimation methods give estimators that are invariant to normalization?

   (a) Indirect least squares.
   (b) 2SLS.
   (c) Instrumental variable methods.
   (d) LIML

Explain how you would choose the appropriate normalization (with respect to quantity or price) in a demand and supply model.

6. The structure of a model with four endogenous and three exogenous variables is as follows: (1 indicates presence and 0 absence of the variable in the equation)

$$
\begin{array}{ccccccc}
1 & 0 & 1 & 1 & 1 & 0 & 0 \\
1 & 1 & 1 & 0 & 0 & 1 & 1 \\
0 & 0 & 1 & 0 & 1 & 0 & 0 \\
1 & 0 & 1 & 1 & 0 & 1 & 0 \\
\end{array}
$$

Which of the four equations are identified?

7. Explain how you would compute R^2 in simultaneous equations estimation methods.

8. Examine whether each of the following statements is true (T), false (F), or uncertain (U), and give a short explanation.

   (a) In a simultaneous equation system, the more the number of exogenous variables the better.
   (b) If the multiple correlations of the reduced-form equations are nearly 1, the OLS and 2SLS estimates of the parameters will be very close to each other.
   (c) In the 2SLS method we should replace only the endogenous variables on the right-hand side of the equation by their fitted values from the reduced form. We should not replace the endogenous variable on the left-hand side by its fitted value.
   (d) Which variables should be tested as exogenous and which as endogenous cannot be determined from the data.

(e) An estimation of the demand function for steel gave the price elasticity of steel as $+0.3$. This finding should be interpreted to mean that the price elasticity of supply is at least $+0.3$.

(f) Any equation can be made identified by deleting enough exogenous variables from the equation or adding enough exogenous variables to the other equations.

(g) Any variable can be endogenous in one equation and exogenous in another equation.

(h) Some simultaneous equation systems can be estimated by ordinary least squares.

(i) If the R^2 from the 2SLS method is negative or very low and the R^2 from the OLS method is high, it should be concluded that something is wrong with the specification of the model or the identification of that particular equation.

(j) The R^2 from the OLS method will always be less than the R^2 from the 2SLS method, but this does not mean that the OLS method is better.

(k) In exactly identified equations, the choice of which variable to normalize does not matter.

(l) In exactly identified equations, we can normalize the equation with respect to an exogenous variable as well.

9. Consider the model

$$Q = \beta_0 + \beta_1 P_w + \beta_2 Y + u \qquad \text{demand function}$$
$$Q = \alpha_0 + \alpha_1 P_w + \alpha_2 S + v \qquad \text{supply function}$$

Estimate this model by 2SLS, instrumental variable, and indirect least squares methods using the data in Table 9.2 (all variables are in logs). Would you get different results using the three methods?

How would you choose the appropriate normalization (with respect to Q or P_w)? Does normalization matter in this model?

10. Estimate the supply equation in the model of the Australian wine industry in Section 9.5 if it is normalized with respect to P_w.

10

Models of Expectations

10.1 INTRODUCTION

Expectations play a crucial role in almost every economic activity. Production depends on expected sales, investment depends on expected profits, long term interest rates depend on expected short-term rates, expected inflation rates, and so on. It is, therefore, important to study models of expectations and how these models are estimated.

In the following sections we study three different models of expectation formation:

1. Naive models of expectation.
2. Adaptive models of expectation.
3. Rational expectations models.

In each case we concentrate on the econometric problems involved.

Since expectations play an important role in economic activity, there are many surveys conducted by different organizations to find out what consumers' expectations are regarding different economic variables. For instance, the Survey Research Center at the University of Michigan conducts surveys regarding consumers' attitudes toward purchases of different durable goods and their forecasts about future inflation rates. There are now survey data available on forecasts of a number of economic variables: wages, interest rates, exchange rates, and so on. An important question that arises regards how we can make use of these survey data. Many econometricians have also investigated the question of how well these survey data forecast the relevant economic variables. After discussing the three models of expectations mentioned above, we discuss the usefulness of survey data on expectations.

10.2 NAIVE MODELS OF EXPECTATIONS

The earliest models of expectations involved using past values of the relevant variables or simple extrapolations of the past values, as measures of the expected variables. Consider, for instance, an investment equation

$$y_t = a + bx^*_{t+1} + u_t \tag{10.1}$$

where y_t = investment in period t

x^*_{t+1} = expected profits during period $t + 1$

and u_t = error term

Unless otherwise noted, expectations are formed in the previous time period. Thus x^*_t denotes expectations of profits for period t as formed at period $t - 1$. Let x_t be the actual profits for period t. Then a naive model for x^*_{t+1} is

$$x^*_{t+1} = x_t \tag{10.2}$$

That is, the firm believes that the profits next period will be the same as profits this period. A simple extrapolative model would be to say that profits next period will increase by the same amount as the latest increase. This gives

$$x^*_{t+1} - x_t = x_t - x_{t-1}$$

or

$$x^*_{t+1} = 2x_t - x_{t-1} \tag{10.3}$$

Another extrapolative model would be to say that profits will increase by the same percentage as the latest rate of increase. This gives

$$\frac{x_{t+1}^*}{x_t} = \frac{x_t}{x_{t-1}}$$

or

$$x_{t+1}^* = \frac{x_t^2}{x_{t-1}} \tag{10.4}$$

In all these cases we estimate equation (10.1) after substituting the relevant formula for x_t^* from (10.2), (10.3), or (10.4). Since the formula for x_t^* is derived from outside and does not consider the equation (10.1) to be estimated, these expectations are considered *exogenous* (derived from outside the economic model under consideration). We will, in the following sections, discuss cases where expectations are *endogenous* (i.e., derived by taking account of the economic model we are considering).

The previous formulas for x_t^* need to be changed suitably if we have quarterly data or monthly data. In these cases there are quarterly or monthly fluctuations, called seasonal fluctuations. For instance, December sales this year would be comparable to December sales last year because of the Christmas season. Hence formula (10.4) would be written as

$$\frac{x_{t+1}^*}{x_{t-3}} = \frac{x_t}{x_{t-4}} \qquad \text{for quarterly data}$$
$$\tag{10.5}$$
$$\frac{x_{t+1}^*}{x_{t-11}} = \frac{x_t}{x_{t-12}} \qquad \text{for monthly data}$$

where, again, x_t^* denotes expected profits and x_t actual profits. Note that we compare the corresponding quarters or months and take the most recent percentage gain as the benchmark.

Formulas like (10.5) were used by Ferber[1] to check the predictive accuracy of railroad shippers' forecasts with actual values. He compared the shipper's forecasts with actual values and also forecasts given by formula (10.5) with the actual values and found that the railroad shippers' forecasts were worse than those given by the naive formula. For the comparison he used average absolute error AAE given by

$$\text{AAE} = \frac{1}{n} \sum |\text{actual} - \text{predicted}|$$

Hirsch and Lovell[2] did a similar study based on Manufacturers' Inventory and Sales Expectations Survey of the Office of Business Economics, U.S. Department of Commerce. However, they found that the anticipants data were more accurate than predictions from naive models.

---

[1] Robert Ferber, *The Railroad Shipper's Forecasts* (Urbana: Bureau of Economic Research, University of Illinois, 1953).
[2] A. A. Hirsch and M. C. Lovell, *Sales Anticipations and Inventory Behavior* (New York: Wiley, 1969).

Yet another naive formula that is often used, and used by Ferber, is that of *regressive expectations*. In this formula there are two components:

1. A growth component based on recent growth rates as in (10.5).
2. A return-to-normal component, also called the regressivity component.

Formula (10.5) would now be written as

$$x^*_{t+1} = x_{t-3}\left[\beta \frac{x_t}{x_{t-1}} - \alpha\left(\frac{x_t}{x_{t-1}} - 1\right)\right] \qquad (10.6)$$

α is the "reversal coefficient." Ferber estimated an equation like (10.6) using the railroad shippers' forecasts for x^*_t and the actual values for x_t. He found an estimate of $\beta = 0.986$ and $\alpha = 0.556$ and concluded that expectations were regressive. Hirsch and Lovell also found that the data they considered also showed regressivity in expectations, but they argue that this is because the actual data are also regressive.

The naive models that we have considered are by no means recommended. However, they are often used as benchmarks by which we judge any survery data on expectations.

10.3 THE ADAPTIVE EXPECTATIONS MODEL

The models considered in Section 10.2 use only a few of the past values in forming expectations. Some other models use the entire past history, with the past values receiving declining weights as we go farther into the distant past. These models are called *distributed lag models* of expectations. Consider

$$x^*_{t+1} = \beta_0 x_t + \beta_1 x_{t-1} + \cdots + \beta_k x_{t-k} \qquad (10.7)$$

This is called a *finite* distributed lag since the number of lagged (past) values is finite. $\beta_0, \beta_1, \ldots, \beta_k$ are the weights that we give to these past values. The naive model (10.2) corresponds to $\beta_0 = 1$ and $\beta_1 = \beta_2 = \cdots = \beta_k = 0$. Distributed lags like (10.7) have a long history. Irving Fisher [3] was perhaps the first one to use them. He suggested arithmetically declining weights

$$\beta_i = \begin{cases} (k + 1 - i)\beta & \text{for } 0 \le i \le k \\ 0 & \text{for } i > k \end{cases}$$

Thus the weights are $(k + 1)\beta$, $k\beta$, $(k - 1)\beta$, $(k - 2)\beta$, and so on. The sum of the weights is

$$\beta \frac{(k + 1)(k + 2)}{2}$$

We might want to restrict this sum to 1. The only problem with this is that if there is a trend in x_t, say x_t is increasing over time, then x^*_{t+1} given by (10.7) will continuously

---

[3] I. Fisher, "Our Unstable Dollar and the So-Called Business Cycle," *Journal of the American Statistical Association*, Vol. 20, 1925; also I. Fisher, "Note on a Short-Cut Method for Calculating Distributed Lags," *Bulletin of the International Statistical Institute*, Vol. 29, 1937, pp. 323–327.

underpredict the actual values. We can make adjustment for this by multiplying x^*_{t+1} by $(1 + g)$, where g is the average growth rate of x_t. Thus in using distributed lag models we make adjustments for the growth rate observed in the past (which is actually the idea in formulas like (10.4)).

The distributed lag models received greater attention in the 1950s when Koyck,[4] Cagan,[5] and Nerlove[6] suggested using an infinite lag distribution with geometrically declining weights. Equation (10.7) will now be written as

$$x^*_{t+1} = \sum_{i=0}^{\infty} \beta_i x_{t-1} \tag{10.8}$$

If β_i are geometrically decreasing we can write

$$\beta_i = \beta_0 \lambda^i \qquad 0 < \lambda < 1$$

The sum of the infinite series is $\beta_0/1 - \lambda$, and if this sum is equal to 1 we should have $\beta_0 = 1 - \lambda$. Thus we get

$$x^*_{t+1} = \sum_{i=0}^{\infty} (1 - \lambda)\lambda^i x_{t-1} \tag{10.9}$$

Figure 10.1 shows the graph of successive values of β_i. There is one interesting property with this relationship. Lag equation (10.9) by one time period and multiply by λ. We get

$$\lambda x^*_t = \lambda \sum_{i=0}^{\infty} (1 - \lambda)\lambda^i x_{t-i-1} = \sum_{i=0}^{\infty} (1 - \lambda)\lambda^{i+1} x_{t-i-1}$$

Substituting $j = i + 1$, we get

$$x^*_t = \sum_{j=1}^{\infty} (1 - \lambda)\lambda^j x_{t-j} \tag{10.10}$$

Subtracting (10.10) from (10.9) we are left with only the first term on the right-hand side of (10.9). We thus get

$$x^*_{t+1} - \lambda x^*_t = (1 - \lambda)x_t \tag{10.11}$$

or

$$\underbrace{x^*_{t+1} - x^*_t}_{\substack{\text{revision in} \\ \text{expectation}}} = (1 - \lambda)\underbrace{(x_t - x^*_t)}_{\substack{\text{last period's} \\ \text{error}}} \tag{10.12}$$

Equation (10.12) says that expectations are revised (upward or downward) based on the most recent error. Suppose that x^*_t was 100 but x_t was 120. The error in

[4] L. M. Koyck, *Distributed Lags and Investment Analysis* (Amsterdam: North-Holland, 1954). A thorough discussion of the Koyck model can be found in M. Nerlove, *Distributed Lags and Demand Analysis*, U.S.D.A. Handbook 141 (Washington, D.C.: U.S. Government Printing Office, 1958).

[5] Phillip D. Cagan, "The Monetary Dynamics of Hyperinflations," in M. Friedman (ed.), *Studies in the Quantity Theory of Money* (Chicago: University of Chicago Press, 1956), pp. 25–117.

[6] Marc Nerlove, *The Dynamics of Supply: Estimation of Farmers' Response to Price* (Baltimore: The Johns Hopkins Press, 1958).

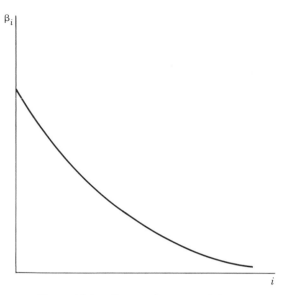

Figure 10.1. Geometric or Koyck Lag.

prediction or expectation is 20. The prediction for $(t + 1)$ will be revised upward but by less than the last period's error. The prediction will, therefore, be > 100 but < 120 (since $0 < \lambda < 1$). This is the reason why the model given by (10.9) is called the *adaptive expectations* model (adaptive based on the most recent error).

Again, since the coefficients in (10.9) sum to 1, if there is a trend in x_t, the formula for x^*_{t+1} has to be adjusted so that x^*_{t+1} is multiplied by $(1 + g)$, where g is the average growth rate in x_t. Otherwise, the adaptive expectations model can continuously underpredict the true value.

10.4 ESTIMATION WITH THE ADAPTIVE EXPECTATIONS MODEL

Consider now the estimation of the investment equation (10.1) where the expected profits x^*_{t+1} are given by the adaptive expectations model (10.9). We can either substitute (10.9) in (10.1) and try to estimate the equation in that form. This is called *estimation in the distributed lag form*.

Alternatively, we can try to use equation (10.11) to eliminate the unobserved x^*_{t+1} and estimate the resulting equation. This is called estimation in *the autoregressive form*. Since this is easier, we will discuss this first.

Estimation in the Autoregressive Form

Consider equation (10.1), which we want to estimate.

$$y_t = a + bx^*_{t+1} + u_t \tag{10.1}$$

Lag this equation by one time period and multiply throughout by λ. We get

$$\lambda y_{t-1} = a\lambda + b\lambda x_t^* + \lambda u_{t-1} \tag{10.13}$$

Subtracting (10.13) from (10.1) and using the definition of the adaptive expectations model as given in (10.11), we get

$$y_t - \lambda y_{t-1} = a(1 - \lambda) + b(x_{t+1}^* - \lambda x_t^*) + u_t - \lambda u_{t-1}$$
$$= a(1 - \lambda) + b(1 - \lambda)x_t + u_t - \lambda u_{t-1}$$

or

$$y_t = a' + \lambda y_{t-1} + b'x_t + v_t \tag{10.14}$$

where $a' = a(1 - \lambda)$, $b' = b(1 - \lambda)$, and $v_t = u_t - \lambda u_{t-1}$. We have eliminated the unobserved x_{t+1}^* and obtained an equation in the observed variable x_t.

Since equation (10.14) involves a regression of y_t on y_{t-1}, we call this the autoregressive form. One can think of estimating equation (10.14) by ordinary least squares and, in fact, this is what was done in the 1950s and that accounted for the popularity of the adaptive expectations model. However, notice that the error term v_t is equal to $u_t - \lambda u_{t-1}$ and is thus autocorrelated. Since y_{t-1} involves u_{t-1}, we see that y_{t-1} is correlated with the error term v_t. Thus estimation of equation (10.14) by ordinary least squares gives us inconsistent estimates of the parameters.

What is the solution? We can use the instrumental variable method. Use x_{t-1} as an instrument for y_{t-1}. Thus the normal equations will be

$$\sum x_t v_t = 0 \quad \text{and} \quad \sum x_{t-1} v_t = 0$$

The other alternative is to take the error structure of v_t explicitly into account (note that it depends on λ). But this amounts to not making the transformation we have made and thus is exactly the same as estimation in the distributed lag form, which is as follows.

Estimation in Distributed Lag Form

Substituting the expression (10.9) in (10.1), we get

$$y_t = a + b\left[\sum_{i=0}^{\infty} (1 - \lambda)\lambda^i x_{t-i}\right] + u_t$$

Since this involves an infinite series and we do not observe the infinite past values of x_t, we have to tackle this problem somehow. What we do is to break up the series into the observed and unobserved past. We will write the infinite series as

$$\sum_{i=0}^{t-1} (1 - \lambda)\lambda^i x_{t-i} + \sum_{i=t}^{\infty} (1 - \lambda)\lambda^i x_{t-i}$$

The first part is observed and we will denote it by $z_{1t}(\lambda)$. We use λ since it depends on λ. The second part can be written as

$$\lambda^t \sum_{i=t}^{\infty} (1 - \lambda)\lambda^{i-t} x_{t-i} = \lambda^t \sum_{j=0}^{\infty} (1 - \lambda)\lambda^j x_{-j} \quad \text{(writing } j = i - t)$$

Notice that the second part of this expression is nothing but (10.9) with $t = 0$, that is

x_1^* (the expected price for the first period). If we treat this as an unknown parameter c and define $z_{2t} = \lambda^t$, we can write

$$x_{t+1}^* = z_{1t} + cz_{2t}$$

Thus equation (10.1) that we wish to estimate can be written as

$$y_t = a + bx_{t+1}^* + u_t$$
$$= a + b(z_{1t} + cz_{2t}) + u_t$$
$$= a + bz_{1t} + c'z_{2t} + u_t \qquad (10.15)$$

with $c' = bc$. Note that z_{1t} and z_{2t} depend on λ. Actually, we are not interested in the parameter c'. The estimation proceeds as follows.

For each value of λ in the range $(0, 1)$ we construct the variables

$$z_{1t} = \sum_{i=0}^{t-1} (1 - \lambda)\lambda^i x_{t-i}$$

and $z_{2t} = \lambda^t$. Thus

$$z_{11} = (1 - \lambda)x_1$$
$$z_{12} = (1 - \lambda)(x_2 + \lambda x_1)$$
$$z_{13} = (1 - \lambda)(x_3 + \lambda x_2 + \lambda^2 x_1)$$

and so on. We estimate equation (10.15) by ordinary least squares and obtain the residual sum of squares. Call this $RSS(\lambda)$. We choose the value of λ for which $RSS(\lambda)$ is minimum and obtain the corresponding estimates of a and b as the desired least squares estimates.

Note that since z_{1t} and z_{2t} are nonlinear functions of λ, the estimation of (10.15) involves nonlinear least squares. What we have done is to note that *for given* λ we have a linear least squares model. Thus we are using a *search procedure* over λ. In practice one can choose λ in intervals of 0.1 in the first stage and then intervals of 0.01 in the second stage.

10.5   TWO ILLUSTRATIVE EXAMPLES

As mentioned earlier, the adaptive expectations model was used by (among others) Nerlove for the analysis of agricultural supply functions, and by Cagan for the analysis of hyperinflations. The hyperinflation model involves more problems than have been noted in the literature, and hence we will discuss it in greater detail. In the analysis of agricultural supply functions, we have to deal with the expectation of a current endogenous variable p_t, whereas in the hyperinflation model, we have to deal with the expectation of a future endogenous variable p_{t+1}.

Consider the supply function

$$Q_t = \alpha + \beta p_t^* + \gamma z_t + u_t$$

where p_t^* is the price expected to prevail at time t (as expected in the preceding period), Q_t the quantity supplied, z_t an exogenous variable, and u_t a disturbance term. The adaptive expectations model implies that

$$p_t^* - \lambda p_{t-1}^* = (1 - \lambda)p_{t-1}$$

Thus

$$Q_t - \lambda Q_{t-1} = \alpha - \alpha\lambda + \beta(p_t^* - \lambda p_{t-1}^*) + \gamma(z_t - \lambda z_{t-1}) + u_t - \lambda u_{t-1}$$

Eliminating p_t^*, we get

$$Q_t = \alpha(1 - \lambda) + \lambda Q_{t-1} + \beta(1 - \lambda)P_{t-1} + \gamma z_t - \lambda\gamma z_{t-1} + u_t - \lambda u_{t-1}$$

This equation can be estimated by the methods described in Section 10.4. Computation of the estimates for this model using the data in Table 9.1 is left as an exercise. We will consider Cagan's hyperinflation model in greater detail because it involves more problems than the agricultural supply model.

The hyperinflation model says that the demand for real cash balances is inversely related to the expected rate of inflation. That is, the higher the expected rate of inflation, the lower the real cash balances that individuals would want to hold. Of course, the demand for real cash balances depends on other variables like income, but during a hyperinflation the expected inflation rate is the more dominant variable. We specify the demand for money function as

$$m_t - p_t = a + b(p_{t+1}^* - p_t) + u_t \qquad b < 0$$

where m_t is the log of the money supply, p_t the log of the price level, p_{t+1}^* the expectation of p_{t+1} as expected at time t, and u_t the error term. Since the variables are in logs, $p_{t+1}^* - p_t$ is the expected inflation rate. We will denote it by π_{t+1}^*. The actual rate of inflation is $\pi_{t+1} = p_{t+1} - p_t$. Let us define $y_t = m_t - p_t$. Then the demand for money model can be written as

$$y_t = a + b\pi_{t+1}^* + u_t$$

This is similar to equation (10.1) and the estimable equation we derived in Section 10.4 is equation (10.14). This equation applies here with π_t in place of x_t. The equation we get is

$$y_t = a(1 - \lambda) + \lambda y_{t-1} + b(1 - \lambda)\pi_t + v_t \tag{10.14'}$$

where $v_t = u_t - \lambda u_{t-1}$. Cagan estimated this equation by OLS but the problem with the OLS estimation of this equation is that it gives inconsistent estimators because the equation involves the lagged dependent variable y_{t-1} and the errors are serially correlated. One can use Klein's method or estimation in the distributed lag form to avoid this problem. The equation we estimate is similar to equation (10.15) and is

$$y_t = a + bz_{1t} + cz_{2t} + u_t \tag{10.15'}$$

where

$$z_{1t} = \sum_{i=0}^{t-1} (1 - \lambda)\lambda^i \pi_{t-i}$$

and $z_{2t} = \lambda^t$. Thus for each value of λ we generate z_{1t} and z_{2t} and estimate (10.15') by

OLS. We choose the value of λ for which the residual sum of squares is minimum, and the corresponding estimates of a, b, and c.

However, even though this is the correct method of estimation for the agricultural supply functions, it is *not* the correct method for the hyperinflation model. The reason is that the model is one where money supply m_t is the exogenous variable and price level p_t is the endogenous variable. By defining the variable $y_t = m_t - p_t$ and writing the equation in a form similar to (10.1) we have missed this point. Equation (10.15') cannot be estimated by OLS because $\pi_t = p_t - p_{t-1}$ in z_{1t} is correlated with the error term u_t.

We can solve this problem by moving the variable p_t to the left-hand side. Let us define $W_t = z_{1t} - (1 - \lambda)p_t$. Now W_t involves p_{t-1} and higher-order lagged values of p_t and does not involve current p_t. We can write equation (10.15') as

$$m_t - p_t = a + b(1 - \lambda)p_t + bW_t + cz_{2t} + u_t$$

Collecting the coefficients of p_t and simplifying, we can write this equation as

$$p_t = \theta_0 + \theta_1 m_t + \theta_2 W_t + \theta_3 z_{2t} + v_t \qquad (10.15'')$$

where

$$\theta_0 = \frac{-a}{1 + b(1 - \lambda)} \qquad \theta_1 = \frac{1}{1 + b(1 - \lambda)} \qquad \theta_2 = \frac{-b}{1 + b(1 - \lambda)}$$

$$\theta_3 = \frac{-c}{1 + b(1 - \lambda)} \qquad v_t = \frac{-u_t}{1 + b(1 - \lambda)}$$

Thus the appropriate equation to estimate for the estimation of the hyperinflation model under adaptive expectations is equation (10.15'') and not equation (10.15') or the simple OLS estimation of the autoregressive form (10.14'). Both equations (10.14') and (10.15') ignore the fact that the same endogenous variable p_t occurs on both the left-hand side and the right-hand side of the equation. Equation (10.14') can also be rearranged similarly. We rewrite it as

$$m_t - p_t = a(1 - \lambda) + \lambda(m_{t-1} - p_{t-1}) + b(1 - \lambda)(p_t - p_{t-1}) + v_t$$

We have to gather the coefficients of p_t, normalize the equation with respect to p_t, and estimate it using p_t as the dependent variable and m_t, m_{t-1}, and p_{t-1} as the explanatory variables. The problem of lagged dependent variables and serially correlated errors still remains and we have to estimate the equation by instrumental variables using, say, m_{t-2} as an instrument.

In summary, the estimation of the hyperinflation model under adaptive expectations is not as straightforward as it appears at first sight looking at equation (10.14') or (10.15'). An important aspect of the model under adaptive expectations (and also some naive expectations) that has not been noticed often is the occurrence of the endogenous variable p_t on the right-hand side of the equation, which makes OLS estimation inapplicable unless some rearranging of the variables is made. The appropriate dependent variable should be p_t, and the explanatory variables are m_t and lagged values of m_t and p_t.

Since the estimation of the hyperinflation model under adaptive expectations is only of historic interest, we will not present the results here. The estimation of equations (10.14′), (10.14″), (10.15′), and (10.15″) is left as an exercise for students. Tables 10.1 and 10.2 on the following pages present the data for Hungary and Germany, respectively. The last periods (particularly since June 1924) can be omitted in the analysis. The data have been provided here because the same data can be used for the estimation of the rational expectations model discussed in Section 10.10.

10.6 EXPECTATIONAL VARIABLES AND ADJUSTMENT LAGS

In previous sections we discussed models in which the expectational variables were functions of lagged values of the relevant variables for which expectations were formed. There is another source of lagged relationships. This is lags in adjustment to desired levels. In practice both these lags will be present and there is an econometric problem of isolating (or identifying) the separate effects of these two sources.

A simple model incorporating adjustment lags is the *partial adjustment model,* which says that firms adjust their variables (say, capital stock) only partially toward their desired levels. Suppose that a firm anticipates some change in the demand for its product. In anticipation of that, it has to adjust its productive capacity or capital stock denoted by y_t. But it cannot do this immediately. Let y_t^d be the "desired" capital stock. Then $y_t^d - y_{t-1}$ is the desired change. The partial adjustment model says that the actual change is only a fraction of the desired change, that is,

$$y_t - y_{t-1} = \delta(y_t^d - y_{t-1}) \qquad \text{where} \quad 0 < \delta < 1 \qquad (10.16)$$

Note that this equation is similar to the adaptive expectations model (10.12) with $y_t = x_{t+1}^*$ and $y_t^d = x_t$. Thus y_t will be a distributed lag of y_t^d with geometrically declining weights. Now suppose that y_t is a function of anticipated sales x_t; then we can write

$$y_t^d = \alpha x_t + \varepsilon_t \qquad \text{where} \quad \varepsilon_t \sim \text{IID}(0, \sigma_0^2)$$

and combining the two equations we get

$$y_t - y_{t-1} = \delta(\alpha x_t + \varepsilon_t - y_{t-1})$$

or

$$y_t = (1 - \delta)y_{t-1} + \alpha\delta x_t + \delta\varepsilon_t$$

which can be written as

$$y_t = \beta_1 y_{t-1} + \beta_2 x_t + u_t$$

with $\beta_1 = 1 - \delta$, $\beta_2 = \alpha\delta$, and $u_t = \delta\varepsilon_t$. Note that $0 < \beta_1 < 1$ and we need this extra condition for a partial adjustment model. Also note that the properties of the error term u_t are the same as those of ε_t. Thus the partial adjustment model does not change the properties of the error term.

Table 10.1 Price Index and Money Supply for Hungary, 1921–1925[a]

	Notes in Circulation	Current Accounts and Deposits	Price Index
1921			
Jan.	15.21	3.85	—
Feb.	15.57	5.53	—
Mar.	15.65	5.25	—
Apr.	13.12	6.80	—
May	13.69	5.76	—
June	18.10	1.16	—
July	15.80	3.53	4.20
Aug.	17.33	2.98	5.40
Sept.	20.84	2.41	6.25
Oct.	23.64	2.15	6.75
Nov.	24.74	2.35	8.30
Dec.	25.18	2.24	8.25
1922			
Jan.	25.68	2.49	8.10
Feb.	26.76	2.35	8.50
Mar.	29.33	2.22	9.90
Apr.	30.58	2.90	10.75
May	31.93	3.29	11.00
June	33.60	3.74	12.90
July	38.36	3.93	17.40
Aug.	46.24	5.42	21.40
Sept.	58.46	5.93	26.60
Oct.	70.00	5.19	32.90
Nov.	72.02	6.41	32.60
Dec.	75.89	4.76	33.40
1923			
Jan.	73.72	5.89	38.50
Feb.	75.14	6.60	41.80
Mar.	82.21	11.15	66.00
Apr.	100.10	9.79	83.50
May	119.29	10.61	94.00
June	155.00	12.74	144.50
July	226.29	21.98	286.00
Aug.	399.49	23.63	462.50
Sept.	588.81	60.25	554.00
Oct.	744.93	60.18	587.00
Nov.	853.99	74.97	635.00
Dec.	931.34	84.79	714.00

[a] Money supply in 10^9 kronen.

Source: John Parke Young, *European Currency and Finance*, Commission of Gold and Silver Inquiry, U.S. Senate, Serial 9, Vol. 2, U.S. Government Printing Office, Washington, D.C., 1925.

Table 10.1 (*continued*)

	Notes in Circulation	Current Accounts and Deposits	Price Index
1924			
Jan.	1084.70	105.48	1026.00
Feb.	1278.40	164.84	1839.10
Mar.	1606.90	253.90	2076.70
Apr.	2098.10	308.10	2134.60
May	2486.30	527.10	2269.60
June	2893.70	1135.70	2207.80
July	3277.90	1424.60	2294.50
Aug.	3659.80	1473.20	2242.00
Sept.	4115.90	1416.40	2236.60
Oct.	4635.10	1465.30	2285.20
Nov.	4442.60	1929.80	2309.50
Dec.	4514.00	2069.50	2346.60
1925			
Jan.	4449.60	2138.60	2307.50
Feb.	4238.00	2542.30	2218.70
Mar.	4270.10	2552.80	2177.80
Apr.	4526.20	2470.50	—

A simple explanation as to why firms make only a partial adjustment to the desired level is as follows. The firm faces two costs: costs of making the adjustment and costs of being in disequilibrium. If the two costs are quadratic and additive, we can write total cost C_t as

$$C_t = a_1(y_t - y_{t-1})^2 + a_2(y_t^d - y_t)^2$$

Given y_{t-1} and y_t^d we have to choose y_t so that total cost C_t is minimum.

$$\frac{dC_t}{dy_t} = 0 \quad \text{gives} \quad 2a_1(y_t - y_{t-1}) = 2a_2(y_t^d - y_t)$$

$$= 2a_2[y_t^d - y_{t-1} - (y_t - y_{t-1})]$$

Thus we get

$$(y_t - y_{t-1}) = \delta(y_t^d - y_{t-1})$$

where

$$\delta = \frac{a_2}{a_1 + a_2}$$

Note that $0 < \delta < 1$ and δ is close to 1 if the costs of being in disequilibrium are much higher than the costs of adjustments. δ is close to zero if the costs of adjustment are much higher than the costs of disequilibrium.

Table 10.2   Prices and Money Supply in Germany, 1921–1924[a]

	Notes in Circulation	Total Demand Deposits	Wholesale Price-Index
1921			
Jan.	66.62	15.83	1.44
Feb.	67.43	17.36	1.38
Mar.	69.42	28.04	1.34
Apr.	70.84	20.86	1.33
May	71.84	14.09	1.31
June	75.32	20.39	1.37
July	77.39	15.82	1.43
Aug.	80.07	13.65	1.92
Sept.	86.38	19.98	2.07
Oct.	91.53	18.30	2.46
Nov.	100.90	25.31	3.42
Dec.	113.60	32.91	3.49
1922			
Jan.	115.40	23.42	3.67
Feb.	120.00	26.53	4.10
Mar.	130.70	33.36	5.43
Apr.	140.40	31.62	6.36
May	151.90	33.13	6.46
June	169.20	37.17	7.03
July	189.80	39.98	10.16
Aug.	238.10	56.12	19.20
Sept.	316.90	110.00	28.70
Oct.	469.50	140.80	56.60
Nov.	754.10	241.00	115.10
Dec.	1,280.00	530.50	147.50
1923			
Jan.	1,984.00	763.30	278.50
Feb.	3,513.00	1,583.00	588.50
Mar.	5,518.00	2,272.00	488.80
Apr.	6,546.00	3,854.00	521.20
May	8,564.00	5,063.00	817.00
June	17,290.00	9,953.00	1,938.50
July	43,600.00	27,857.00	7,478.70
Aug.	663,200.00	591,080.00	94,404.00

[a] Money supply is for end of the month and in 10^9 marks. Since Jan. 1924 the Reischsbank reported money supply in reischmarks. 1 reischmark = 10^{12} old marks. All figures have been converted to old marks and rounded to four significant digits. Thus the money supply is all on a comparable basis for the whole period.

Source: John Parke Young, *European Currency and Finance*, Commission of Gold and Silver Inquiry, U.S. Senate, Serial 9, Vol. 1, U.S. Government Printing Office, Washington, D.C., 1925.

Table 10.2 *(continued)*

	Notes in Circulation	Total Demand Deposits	Wholesale Price-index
Sept.	$2,823 \times 10^4$	$1,697 \times 10^4$	$2,395 \times 10^3$
Oct.	$2,497 \times 10^6$	$3,868 \times 10^6$	709.5×10^6
Nov.	$4,003 \times 10^8$	$3,740 \times 10^8$	72.6×10^9
Dec.	$4,965 \times 10^8$	$5,480 \times 10^8$	126×10^9
1924			
Jan.	$4,837 \times 10^8$	$2,813 \times 10^8$	117×10^9
Feb.	$5,879 \times 10^8$	$6,505 \times 10^8$	116×10^9
Mar.	$6,899 \times 10^8$	$7,047 \times 10^8$	121×10^9
Apr.	$7,769 \times 10^8$	$8,050 \times 10^8$	124×10^9
May	$9,269 \times 10^8$	$8,046 \times 10^8$	122×10^9
June	$10,970 \times 10^8$	$7,739 \times 10^8$	116×10^9
July	$12,110 \times 10^8$	$7,430 \times 10^8$	115×10^9
Aug.	$13,920 \times 10^8$	$5,619 \times 10^8$	120×10^9
Sept.	$15,210 \times 10^8$	$6,701 \times 10^8$	127×10^9
Oct.	$17,810 \times 10^8$	$7,087 \times 10^8$	131×10^9
Nov.	$18,630 \times 10^8$	$7,039 \times 10^8$	129×10^9
Dec.	$19,410 \times 10^8$	$8,209 \times 10^8$	131×10^9

Partial adjustment models were popular in the 1950s and 1960s but were criticized as being ad hoc. [7] The desired level y_t^* is derived independently by some optimization rule and then the adjustment equation is tagged on to it. However, the costs of adjustment and the costs of being in disequilibrium should be incorporated in the optimization rule. There have been many attempts along these lines but they have not resulted in any tractable estimable equations. [8]

One refinement that can easily be done is to make the partial adjustment parameter δ a function of some explanatory variables that are considered important in determining the speed of adjustment (e.g., interest rates). Denoting the interest rate by r_t, since δ_t is supposed to be between 0 and 1 we can write

$$\delta_t = \frac{\exp(\alpha_0 + \alpha_1 r_t)}{1 + \exp(\alpha_0 + \alpha_1 r_t)}$$

(we use a subscript t for δ since it changes over time).

However, there is no reason that the adjustment parameter be between 0 and 1 at all times. In this case we can make δ_t a linear function of r_t. There are many empirical

---

[7] Z. Griliches, "Distributed Lags: A survey," *Econometrica*, January 1967, pp. 16–49, Sec. 5, "Theoretical Ad-Hockery."

[8] See M. Nerlove, "Lags in Economic Behavior," *Econometrica*, March 1972, pp. 221–251, for a survey of the work on adjustment costs and the development of a model with adjustment costs. There are, however, no empirical results in the paper. Nerlove says, "current research on lags in economic behavior is not 'good' because neither is the empirical research soundly based in economic theory nor is the theoretical research very strongly empirically oriented" (p. 246).

studies that use partial adjustment models with varying coefficients. Since we have explained the basic idea we will not review them here.[9]

A more generalized version of the partial adjustment model is the *error correction model*. This model says that

$$y_t - y_{t-1} = \delta(\underbrace{y_t^d - y_t^{d-1}}_{\substack{\text{change in the} \\ \text{desired values}}}) + \gamma(\underbrace{y_{t-1}^d - y_{t-1}}_{\substack{\text{past period's} \\ \text{disequilibrium}}}) \tag{10.17}$$

where $0 < \delta < 1$ and $0 < \gamma < 1$. If $\delta = \gamma$, we have the partial adjustment model. Unlike the partial adjustment model, however, this model generates serially correlated errors in the final equation we estimate. Suppose that, as before, we write

$$y_t^d = \alpha x_t + \varepsilon_t$$

where x_t is anticipated sales. Then substituting this in (10.17), we get

$$(y_t - y_{t-1}) = \alpha\delta(x_t - x_{t-1}) + \alpha\gamma x_{t-1} - \gamma y_{t-1} + \delta\varepsilon_t - (\delta - \gamma)\varepsilon_{t-1} \tag{10.18}$$

The error term is now correlated with y_{t-1} and we cannot estimate this equation by ordinary least squares. Again, we can think of using an instrumental variable (say, x_{t-2} for y_{t-1}) and estimate this equation by instrumental variable methods.

During recent years error correction models have been more popular in empirical work than partial adjustment models.[10] The empirical evidence and economic interpretation is in favor of the former model. Also, one can have a test for the partial adjustment model by testing $\delta = \gamma$ in (10.18).

10.7 PARTIAL ADJUSTMENT WITH ADAPTIVE EXPECTATIONS

When adjustment and expectational lags are combined we may have some problems of identifying their separate effects. We can see the problem by considering the partial adjustment model with adaptive expectations. We can consider the error correction model as well but the partial adjustment model is simpler.

Suppose that

K_t^d = desired capital stock at the beginning of period t

S_t^* = expected sales in period t

$$K_t^d = \beta_0 + \beta_1 S_t^* + u_t \tag{10.19}$$

The partial adjustment model states:

$$K_t - K_{t-1} = \delta(K_t^d - K_{t-1}) \qquad 0 < \delta < 1.$$

[9] For a review of the model up to the early 1970s, see J. C. R. Rowley and P. K. Trivedi, *Econometrics of Investment* (New York: Wiley, 1975), pp. 86–89 on "variable lags."

[10] An example of this is D. F. Hendry and T. von Ungern-Sternberg, "Liquidity and Inflation Effects on Consumers' Expenditure," in A. S. Deaton (ed.), *Essays in the Theory of Measurement of Consumers' Behavior*, (Cambridge: Cambridge University Press, 1981).

and substituting for K_t^d, we get

$$K_t = \beta_0 \delta + (1 - \delta)K_{t-1} + \beta_1 \delta S_t^* + \delta u_t \qquad (10.20)$$

If we use the adaptive expectations model

$$S_t^* - S_{t-1}^* = \lambda(S_{t-1} - S_{t-1}^*) \qquad 0 < \lambda < 1$$

then, lagging equation (10.20) by one period, multiplying it by $(1 - \lambda)$ subtracting this from (10.20), and simplifying, we get

$$K_t = \delta\lambda\beta_0 + (1 - \delta + 1 - \lambda)K_{t-1} - (1 - \delta)(1 - \lambda)K_{t-2} + \lambda\beta_1\delta S_{t-1} + v_t \qquad (10.21)$$

where

$$v_t = \delta[u_t - (1 - \lambda)u_{t-1}]$$

Now if we had added the error term to the final simplified equation (10.21) rather than (10.20), it is easy to see from (10.21) that δ and λ occur symmetrically and hence there is some ambiguity in their estimates, which have to be obtained from the coefficients of K_{t-1} and K_{t-2}.

Note that this ambiguity arises only if an error term is superimposed on the final simplified equation (10.21), and the equation is estimated by ordinary least squares assuming that the error terms to be serially uncorrelated. On the other hand, we can estimate equation (10.20) in its distributed lag version.[11] For this we use the procedures for the estimation of adaptive expectations models in the distributed lag form as described in Section 10.4. Thus if the model is estimated in the distributed lag form, there is no ambiguity in the estimates of δ and λ.

The preceding discussion on partial adjustment models with adaptive expectations illustrates the point that specification of the error term cannot be done in a cavalier fashion. The estimation procedures and whether any parameters (like δ and λ in our example) are unambiguously estimable or not, depend on the specification of the error term at different stages of the modeling process.

Of course, one can argue that there is no reason why the errors u_t in (10.19) should be assumed serially independent. If for some reason one starts with (10.21) and a general specification for the error term v_t, the ambiguity in the estimation of δ, the speed of adjustment, and λ, the reaction of expectations, remains. However, in this case, if the equation (10.19) has some other explanatory variables, the parameters λ and δ are identified, for example, suppose that (ignoring the error term which we will introduce at the end after all simplifications)

$$K_t^d = \beta_0 + \beta_1 S_t^* + \beta_2 L_t$$

where L_t is the amount of labor hired. Then, on simplification, and adding an error term v_t at the end, we get

$$K_t = \beta_0 \delta\lambda + (1 - \delta + 1 - \lambda)K_{t-1} - (1 - \delta)(1 - \lambda)K_{t-2} + \beta_1 \delta\lambda S_{t-1}$$
$$+ \delta\beta_2 L_t - \delta\beta_2(1 - \lambda)L_{t-1} + v_t \qquad (10.22)$$

In this equation δ and λ do not occur symmetrically.

---

[11] This is equivalent to estimating (10.21) with a moving average error that depends on λ, as specified in the equation for v_t.

Suppose that we write the equation as

$$K_t = \alpha_1 + \alpha_2 K_{t-1} + \alpha_3 K_{t-2} + \alpha_4 S_{t-1} + \alpha_5 L_t + \alpha_6 L_{t-1} + v_t \qquad (10.23)$$

Then

$$\lambda = 1 + \frac{\alpha_6}{\alpha_5}$$

But the problem is that we get two estimates of δ. From the coefficients of K_{t-1} we get

$$\delta = 2 - \alpha_2 - \lambda$$

and from the coefficient of K_{t-2} we get

$$\delta = 1 + \frac{\alpha_3}{1 - \lambda}$$

The problem is that equation (10.23) has six parameters and our model has only five parameters $\beta_0, \beta_1, \beta_2, \lambda$, and δ. Note, however, that *given* λ, equation (10.22) can be written as

$$\bar{K}_t = \beta_0 \delta \lambda + (1 - \delta)\bar{K}_{t-1} + \beta_1 \delta \lambda S_{t-1} + \beta_2 \delta \bar{L}_t + v_t \qquad (10.24)$$

where

$$\bar{K}_t = K_t - (1 - \lambda)K_{t-1}$$
$$\bar{L}_t = L_t - (1 - \lambda)L_{t-1}$$

The estimation of (10.24) gives us unique estimates of δ, β_0, β_1, and β_2. Thus we can use the following *two-step procedure*:

1. Estimate (10.23) and get an estimate of λ.
2. Use this to construct $\bar{K}_t$ and $\bar{L}_t$ and then estimate equation (10.24) to get unique estimates of δ, β_0, β_1, and β_2.

An alternative *search method* is the following. Choose different values of λ in the interval $(0, 1)$. For each value of λ run the regression of $\bar{K}_t$ on $\bar{K}_{t-1}, S_{t-1}$, and $\bar{L}_t$. Then the value of λ for which the residual sum of squares is minimum is the best estimate of λ and the corresponding estimates of δ, β_0, β_1, and β_2 are the desired estimates of the parameters. Actually, we can conduct the search in two steps, first at steps of 0.1 and then at steps of 0.01 around the minimum given in the first step. We have discussed a similar procedure in Section 10.4. These are all examples where an equation that is nonlinear in the parameters can be reduced to an equation linear in the parameters conditional on one of the parameters being given.

10.8 ALTERNATIVE DISTRIBUTED LAG MODELS: POLYNOMIAL LAGS

We saw in previous sections that the adaptive expectations model (10.11) implies that the expectation x_{t+1}^* is a weighted average of x_t and past values of x_t, with geometrically declining weights. We also saw that the partial adjustment model

(10.16) implies that y_t is a weighted average of y_t^d and past values of y_t^d again with geometrically declining weights. Since the weights of the lagged variables all sum to 1, and they are usually all positive, it is customary to compare these weights to the successive terms in a probability distribution. The weights β_i in equations like (10.7) and (10.8) are said to form a *lag distribution*. The geometrically declining weights correspond to the geometric distribution. As we mentioned in Section 10.3, this type of lag is also called the *Koyck lag*, named after L. M. Koyck, who first used it.

In addition to the geometric lag distribution, there are some alternative forms of lag distributions that have been suggested in the literature. We will discuss these with reference to:

1. The finite lag distribution (10.7).
2. The infinite lag distribution (10.8).

Finite Lags: The Polynomial Lag

Consider the estimation of the equation

$$y_t = \beta_0 x_t + \beta_1 x_{t-1} + \cdots + \beta_k x_{t-k} + u_t \tag{10.25}$$

The problem with the estimation of this equation is that because of the high correlations between x_t and its lagged values (multicollinearity), we do not get reliable estimates of the parameters β_i. As we discussed in Section 10.3, Irving Fisher assumed the β_i to be declining arithmetically. Almon [12] generalized this to the case where the β_i follow a polynomical of degree r in i. This is known as the Almon lag or the polynomial lag. We denote this by PDL (k, r), where PDL denotes polynomial distributed lag, k is the length of the lag, and r the degree of the polynomial. For instance, if $r = 2$, we write

$$\beta_i = \alpha_0 + \alpha_1 i + \alpha_2 i^2 \tag{10.26}$$

Substituting this in (10.25), we get

$$\begin{aligned} y_t &= \sum_{i=0}^{k} (\alpha_0 + \alpha_1 i + \alpha_2 i^2) x_{t-i} + u_t \\ &= \alpha_0 z_{0t} + \alpha_1 z_{1t} + \alpha_2 z_{2t} + u_t \end{aligned} \tag{10.27}$$

where

$$z_{0t} = \sum_{i=0}^{k} x_{t-i} \qquad z_t = \sum_{i=0}^{k} i x_{t-i} \qquad z_{2t} = \sum_{i=0}^{k} i^2 x_{t-i}$$

Thus we regress y_t on the constructed variables z_{0t}, z_{1t}, and z_{2t}. After we get the estimates of the α's we use equation (10.26) to get estimates of the β_i.

Following the suggestion of Almon, often some "endpoint constraints" are used. For instance, if we use the constraints $\beta_{-1} = 0$ and $\beta_{k+1} = 0$ in (10.26), we have the following two linear relationships between the α's [substituting $i = -1$ and $i = k + 1$ in (10.26)].

$$\alpha_0 - \alpha_1 + \alpha_2 = 0 \qquad \text{and} \qquad \alpha_0 + \alpha_1(k + 1) + \alpha_2(k + 1)^2 = 0 \tag{10.28}$$

---

[12] S. Almon, "The Distributed Lag Between Capital Appropriations and Net Expenditures," *Econometrica*, January 1965, pp. 178–196.

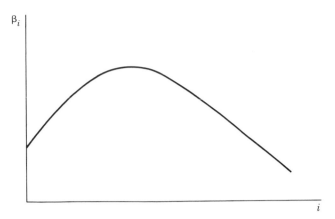

Figure 10.2.   Polynomial distributed lag.

These give the conditions

$$\alpha_0 = -\alpha_2(k + 1) \qquad \text{and} \qquad \alpha_1 = -\alpha_2 k \qquad\qquad (10.29)$$

Thus we can simplify (10.27) to

$$y_t = \alpha_2 z_t + u_t$$

where

$$z_t = \sum (i^2 - ki - k - 1)x_{t-i}$$

We get an estimates of α_2 by regressing y_t on z_t and we get estimates of α_0 and α_1 from (10.29). Using these we get estimates of β_i from (10.26).

Figure 10.2 shows a polynomial distributed lag. The curve shown is that where β_i is a quadratic function of i. A quadratic function can take many shapes and it has been argued that the imposition of the endpoint restrictions (10.29) is often responsible for the "plausible" shapes of the lag distribution fitted by the Almon method.[13] Instead of imposing endpoint constraints a priori, one can actually test them because once equation (10.27) has been estimated, tests of the hypotheses like (10.28) are standard tests of linear hypotheses (discussed in Section 4.8).

Many of the problems related to polynomial lags can be analyzed in terms of the number of restrictions that it imposes on β_i in (10.25). For instance, with a quadratic polynomial we estimate three α's, whereas we have $(k + 1)$ β's in (10.27). Thus there are $k + 1 - 3 = k - 2$ restrictions on the β's. With an rth-degree polynomial, we have $(k - r)$ restrictions.

Suppose that we fit a quadratic polynomial for lag length k and lag length $(k + 1)$. The residual sum of squares may increase or decrease.[14] The reason is that linear

[13] P. Schmidt and R. N. Waud, "The Almon Lag Technique and the Monetary Versus Fiscal Policy Debate," *Journal of the American Statistical Association*, March 1973, pp. 11–19.

[14] This is demonstrated with an empirical example in J. J. Thomas, "Some Problems in the Use of Almon's Technique in the Estimation of Distributed Lags," *Empirical Economics*, Vol. 2, 1977, pp. 175–193.

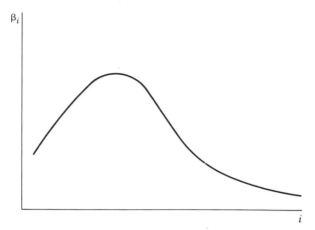

Figure 10.3. Long-tailed lag distribution.

restrictions are being imposed on two different parameter sets: $(\beta_1, \beta_2, \ldots, \beta_k)$ and $(\beta_1, \beta_2, \ldots, \beta_k, \beta_{k+1})$.

Apart from the problem of endpoint restrictions, there are three other problems with polynomial lags:

1. *Problems of long-tailed distributions.* It is difficult to capture long-tailed lag distributions like the one shown in Figure 10.3. This problem can be solved by using a piecewise polynomial. Another procedure is to have a polynomial for the initial β_i and a Koyck or geometric lag for the latter part.

2. *Problem of choosing the lag length k.* Schmidt and Waud suggest choosing k on the basis of maximum $\bar{R}^2$: Frost[15] did a simulation experiment using this criterion and found that a substantial upward bias in the lag length occurs. As we discussed in Chapter 4, the $\bar{R}^2$ criterion implies that a regressor is retained if the F-ratio is > 1. The bias that Frost suggests can be corrected by using F-ratios greater than 1, says $F = 2$.

3. *Problem of choosing r, the degree of the polynomial.* If the lag length k is correctly specified, then choosing the degree of the polynomial r is straightforward. What we do is start with a sufficiently high-degree polynomial as in (10.27). Construct $z_{0t}, z_{1t}, z_{2t}, z_{3t}, \ldots$ as defined in (10.27) and start dropping the higher terms sequentially. Note that the proper way of testing is to start with the highest-degree polynomial possible and then go backward, until one of the hypotheses is rejected. This sequential test was suggested by Anderson,[16] who showed that the resulting sequence of tests are independent

[15] P. A. Frost, "Some Properties of the Almon Lag Technique When One Searches for Degree of Polynomial and Lag," *Journal of the American Statistical Association*, Vol. 70, 1975, pp. 606–612.

[16] T. W. Anderson, "The Choice of the Degree of a Polynomial Regression as a Multiple Decision Problem," *Annals of Mathematical Statistics*, Vol. 33, No. 1, 1966, pp. 255–265. This test is also discussed in T. W. Anderson, *The Statistical Analysis of Time Series* (New York; Wiley, 1971), pp. 34–43.

and that the significance level for the jth test is

$$1 - \prod_{i=1}^{j} (1 - \gamma_i)$$

where γ_i is the significance level chosen at the ith step in the sequence. If $\gamma_i = 0.05$ for all i, the significance levels for four successive tests are 0.05, 0.0975, 0.1426, and 0.1855, respectively. Godfrey and Poskitt [17] use this procedure suggested by Anderson to choose the degree of the polynomial for the Almon lag.

We will now illustrate this procedure with an example.

Illustrative Example

Consider the data in Table 10.3. The data are on capital expenditures (y) and appropriations (x) for the years 1953–1967 on a quarterly basis. These data are from the National Industrial Conference Board. Since they have been used very often (in

Table 10.3 Capital Expenditures (Y) and Appropriations (X) for 1953–1967 (Quarterly Data)

N	Y	X	N	Y	X	N	Y	X
1	2072	1660	21	2697	1511	41	2601	2629
2	2077	1926	22	2338	1631	42	2648	3133
3	2078	2181	23	2140	1990	43	2840	3449
4	2043	1897	24	2012	1993	44	2937	3764
5	2062	1695	25	2071	2520	45	3136	3983
6	2067	1705	26	2192	2804	46	3299	4381
7	1964	1731	27	2240	2919	47	3514	4786
8	1981	2151	28	2421	3024	48	3815	4094
9	1914	2556	29	2639	2725	49	4093	4870
10	1991	3152	30	2733	2321	50	4262	5344
11	2129	3763	31	2721	2131	51	4531	5433
12	2309	3903	32	2640	2552	52	4825	5911
13	2614	3912	33	2513	2234	53	5160	6109
14	2896	3571	34	2448	2282	54	5319	6542
15	3058	3199	35	2429	2533	55	5574	5785
16	3309	3262	36	2516	2517	56	5749	5707
17	3446	3476	37	2534	2772	57	5715	5412
18	3466	2993	38	2494	2380	58	5637	5465
19	3435	2262	39	2596	2568	59	5383	5550
20	3183	2011	40	2572	2944	60	5467	5465

[17] L. G. Godfrey and D. S. Poskitt, "Testing the Restrictions of the Almon Lag Technique," *Journal of the American Statistical Association*, Vol. 70, March 1975, pp. 105–108.

fact, too often) in the illustration of different distributed lag models, they are being reproduced here. It is a good data set for some beginning exercises in distributed lag estimation.

Before we impose any functional forms on the data, it would be interesting to see what some OLS estimates of unrestricted distributed lag equations look like. There are a total of 60 observations and it was decided to estimate 12 lagged coefficients. The implicit assumptions is that the maximum time lag between appropriations and expenditures is 3 years. To make the estimated σ^2 comparable, the equations were all estimated using the last 48 observations of the dependent variable Y. The results are presented in Table 10.4.

There are several features of the lag distributions in Table 10.4 that are interesting. The $\bar{R}^2$ steadily increases until we use seven lags. The sum of the coefficients also

Table 10.4 Unrestricted Least Squares Estimates of Distributed Lags[a]

Coefficient of:	Equation				
	1	2	3	4	5
x_t	0.081 (1.3)	0.093 (1.6)	0.088 (1.6)	0.067 (1.3)	0.106 (1.9)
x_{t-1}	0.092 (0.9)	0.090 (1.0)	0.094 (1.2)	0.137 (1.8)	0.100 (1.2)
x_{t-2}	0.236 (2.2)	0.228 (2.5)	0.229 (3.1)	0.210 (2.8)	0.229 (2.8)
x_{t-3}	0.183 (1.7)	0.183 (2.1)	0.172 (2.3)	0.186 (2.5)	0.139 (1.8)
x_{t-4}	0.142 (1.2)	0.130 (1.6)	0.133 (1.7)	0.100 (1.3)	0.118 (1.5)
x_{t-5}	-0.042 (0.4)	-0.006 (0.1)	-0.002 (0.0)	0.011 (0.1)	0.003 (0.0)
x_{t-6}	0.137 (1.3)	0.123 (1.4)	0.133 (1.7)	0.119 (1.5)	0.285 (5.2)
x_{t-7}	0.058 (0.4)	0.059 (0.6)	0.057 (0.6)	0.156 (2.8)	
x_{t-8}	0.147 (1.1)	0.110 (1.1)	0.084 (1.4)		
x_{t-9}	-0.010 (0.1)	0.010 (0.1)			
x_{t-10}	-0.069 (0.5)	-0.032 (0.5)			
x_{t-11}	-0.045 (0.3)				
x_{t-12}	0.081 (1.1)				
Sum of coefficients	0.991	0.988	0.988	0.986	0.980
$\bar{R}^2$	0.9988	0.9988	0.9988	0.9988	0.9985

Coefficient of:	Equation				
	6	7	8	9	10
x_t	0.163 (1.9)	0.113 (1.0)	0.050 (0.3)	-0.011 (0.1)	0.915 (42.1)
x_{t-1}	0.056 (0.5)	0.063 (0.4)	0.075 (0.3)	0.940 (5.0)	
x_{t-2}	0.139 (1.1)	0.131 (0.8)	0.817 (5.5)		
x_{t-3}	0.131 (1.1)	0.648 (5.9)			
x_{t-4}	0.476 (5.8)				
Sum of coefficients	0.965	0.955	0.942	0.929	0.915
$\bar{R}^2$	0.9965	0.9941	0.9896	0.9829	0.9742

increases steadily. Overall, from the results presented there, it appears that a lag distribution using seven lags is appropriate. This corresponds to a maximum of 1.75-year lag between capital appropriations and expenditures. Further, about 98.6% of all appropriations are eventually spent.

One disturbing feature of the OLS estimates is that no matter how many lags we include, the DW test statistic shows significant positive correlation. For instance, the following are the DW test statistics for different lengths of the lag distribution.

Length of Lag	DW
0	0.38
4	0.58
8	0.35
12	0.44

This suggests that we should be estimating some more general dynamic models, allowing for autocorrelated errors.

Choosing the Degree of the Polynomial

Consider the data in Table 10.3. We will consider a lag length of 12 and consider the choice of the degrees of the polynomial by the sequential testing method outlined here. We start with a fourth-degree polynomial.

The results are as follows (figures in parentheses are *t-ratios*, not standard errors):

Coefficient of:	Equation			
	1	2	3	4
z_{0t}	0.1150 (5.78)	0.1108 (5.80)	0.1468 (14.20)	0.1637 (33.06)
$10^{-1} \times z_{1t}$	0.2003 (0.82)	0.3305 (1.83)	-0.0507 (-0.97)	-0.1463 (-16.70)
$10^{-2} \times z_{2t}$	-0.2681 (-0.33)	-0.8549 (-2.42)	-0.0824 (-1.86)	
$10^{-3} \times z_{3t}$	-0.4517 (-0.41)	0.4011 (2.20)	.	
$10^{-4} \times z_{4t}$	0.3951 (0.79)			
$\hat{\sigma}^2$	15,520	15,389	16,702	17,590
DW	0.514	0.465	0.518	0.536
$\bar{R}^2$	0.9988	0.9988	0.9987	0.9986

First we test the coefficient of z_{4t} at the 5% level and do not reject the hypothesis that it is zero. Next we test the coefficient of z_{3t}, and we reject the hypothesis that its coefficient is zero. Since this is the first hypothesis rejected, we use a polynomial of the third degree. The results of the other lower-degree polynomials are not needed and are just presented for the sake of curiosity. Actually, for the fourth-degree polynomial, the high R^2 and the low t-ratios indicates that there is high multicollinearity among the variables.

We now estimate the coefficients of the lag distribution using the formula

$$\beta_i = 0.1108 + 0.3305 \times 10^{-1}i - 0.8549 \times 10^{-2}i^2 + 0.4011 \times 10^{-3}i^3$$

The coefficients are:

Lag	Coefficient	Lag	Coefficient	Lag	Coefficient
0	0.1108				
1	0.1357	5	0.1125	9	0.0082
2	0.1459	6	0.0880	10	−0.0125
3	0.1438	7	0.0608	11	−0.0262
4	0.1319	8	0.0334	12	−0.0306

The sum of the coefficients is 0.9117, and furthermore, the last three coefficients are negative. This is the reason that, as mentioned earlier, some endpoint restrictions are often imposed in estimating the polynomial distributed lags. Comparing these results with the unrestricted OLS estimates in Table 10.4, it appears that not much is to be gained (in this particular example) by using the polynomial lag.

In any case, the example illustrates the procedure of choice of the degree of the polynomial for given lag length.

10.9 RATIONAL LAGS

In Section 10.8 we discussed finite lag distributions. We will now discuss infinite lag distributions. Actually, we considered one earlier: the geometric or Koyck lag. A straightforward generalization of this is the rational lag distribution.[18]

Consider equation (10.11). One way of generalizing it is to add more lags on the left-hand side and right-hand side of the equation, and have the parameters different. If p is the number of lags on the right hand side and q the number of lags on the left-hand side, we have a rational distributed lag model which we denote by RDL(p, q). For instance, the RDL$(3, 2)$ model corresponding to (10.11) is

$$x_{t+1}^* + \beta_0 x_t^* + \beta_1 x_{t-1}^* = \alpha_0 x_t + \alpha_1 x_{t-1} + \alpha_2 x_{t-2} + \alpha_3 x_{t-3}$$

A similar generalization can be given for the partial adjustment model (10.16). We have

$$y_t + \beta_1 y_{t-1} + \beta_2 y_{t-2} = \alpha_0 y_t^d + \alpha_1 y_{t-1}^d + \alpha_2 y_{t-2}^d + \alpha_3 y_{t-3}^d$$

As before, we have to somehow eliminate the unobserved variables x_t^* and y_t^d. Since

---

[18] D. W. Jorgenson, "Rational Distributed Lag Functions," *Econometrica*, Vol. 34, January 1966, pp. 135–149.

the algebraic details are similar to those in Section 10.7, we will not pursue them here.[19] Lucas and Rapping[20] use the RDL model for price expectations, instead of the adaptive expectations model, but they estimate it in the autoregressive form ignoring serial correlation.

The rational distributed lag model and its use in expectations should not be confused with the rational expectations models we discuss in the next section.

10.10 RATIONAL EXPECTATIONS

In Sections 10.2 and 10.3 we discussed some naive models of expectations and the adaptive expectations model. We also saw how the latter can be generalized using some polynomial lags. During the last decade a new theory, that of "rational expectations," has taken a strong hold in almost all econometric work on expectations.

The basic idea of "rational expectations" comes from a pathbreaking paper by John Muth,[21] who observed that the various expectational formulas that were used in the analysis of dynamic economic models had little resemblance to the way the economy works. If the economic system changes, the way expectations are formed should change, but the traditional models of expectations do not permit any such changes. The adaptive expectations formula, for instance, says that economic agents revise their expectations upward or downward based on the most recent error. The formula says

$$y_t^* - y_{t-1}^* = \lambda(y_{t-1} - y_{t-1}^*) \qquad 0 < \lambda < 1$$

where y_t^* is the expectation for y_t as formed at time $t-1$. In this formula λ is a constant. Of course, one can modify this formula so that λ depends on whatever variables produce changes in the economic system.

There are some reasonable requirements that y_t^* or the predicted value of y_t should satisfy. Consider the prediction error

$$\varepsilon_t = y_t - y_t^*$$

It is reasonable to require that expectations be unbiased, that is,

$$E(\varepsilon_t) = 0$$

Otherwise, there is a systematic component in the forecast error which forecasters should be able to correct.

Muth also required that the prediction error be uncorrelated with the entire information set that is available to the forecaster at the time the prediction is made.

[19] The estimation of the RDL model in the distributed lag form is discussed in G. S. Maddala, *Econometrics* (New York: McGraw-Hill, 1977), pp. 366–367.

[20] R. E. Lucas, Jr., and L. A. Rapping, "Price Expectations and the Phillips Curve," *The American Economic Review*, Vol. 59, 1969, pp. 342–350. They warn that this should not be confused with the "rational expectations" model as defined by Muth (which we discuss in the next section).

[21] John F. Muth, "Rational Expectations and the Theory of Price Movements," *Econometrica*, Vol. 29, 1961, pp. 315–335.

If we denote by I_{t-1} the information available at time $(t-1)$ and write

$$y_t = y_t^* + \varepsilon_t \tag{10.30}$$

then y_t^* depends on I_{t-1} and y_t^* is uncorrelated with ε_t. One implication of this equation is that $\text{var}(y_t) = \text{var}(y_t^*) + \text{var}(\varepsilon_t)$ and hence $\text{var}(y_t) \geq \text{var}(y_t^*)$. If the prediction error is correlated with any variables in I_{t-1}, it implies that the forecaster has not used all the available information. Taking (mathematical) expectations of all variables in (10.30), we get

$$y_t^* = E(y_t | I_{t-1}) \tag{10.31}$$

The left-hand side of (10.31) should be interpreted as the *subjective* expectation and the right-hand side of (10.31) as the *objective* expectation conditional on data available when the expectation was formed. Thus there is a connection between the subjective beliefs of economic agents and the actual behavior of the economic system.

Formula (10.31) forms the basis of almost all the econometric work on rational expectations. There are three assumptions involved in the use of formula (10.31).

1. There exists a unique mathematical expectation of the random variable y_t based on the given set of information I_{t-1}.
2. Economic agents behave *as if* they know this conditional expectation and equate their own subjective expectation of y_t to this conditional expectation. Note that this implies that the economic agents behave *as if they have full knowledge* about the model that the econometrician is estimating, that is, they behave as if they know not only the structure of the model but the parameters as well.
3. The econometrician, however, does not know the parameters of the model but has to make inferences about them based on assumption 2 about the behavior of economic agents and the resulting stochastic behavior of the system.

There have been many criticisms of the rational expectations hypothesis as implied by equation (10.31). The basic argument is that "rational" economic agents need not behave this way. We will not go through these criticisms here. The whole controversy surrounding the rational expectations hypothesis could have been avoided if the term "rational" was not used to describe the mechanism of expectation formation given by (10.31). A more appropriate term to characterize (10.31) is *model consistent*, because the expression for y_t^* derived from (10.31) depends on the particular model we start with. The coinage of the term "rational" is rather unfortunate. We will, however, continue to use the word "rational" to describe "model consistent" or Muthian expectations formed using (10.31).

The requirement that y_t^* should completely summarize the information in I_{t-1} has led Lovell[22] to suggest the term "sufficient expectations" because it is related to the statistical concept of a "sufficient estimator" which may be loosely defined as an estimator that utilizes all the information available in the sample.

---

[22] M. C. Lovell, "Tests of the Rational Expectations Hypothesis," *The American Economic Review*, Vol. 76, March 1986, pp. 110–124.

There are, basically, two methods of estimation for rational expectations models. The first method involves using the definition (10.31) and writing

$$y_t^* = y_t - v_t$$

where v_t is uncorrelated with all the variables in the information set I_{t-1}. We then estimate this model using the instrumental variable methods using the appropriate instruments. This method is very easy to apply and gives consistent, though not efficient estimators. We will illustrate this using the hyperinflation model discussed in Section 10.5.

The second method uses information on the structure of the model to derive an explicit expression for y_t^*. This method involves the following steps:

1. Derive the equation for y_t from the model you start with.
2. Take expectations of y_t conditional on I_{t-1} and substitute the resulting expression for y_t^* in the model.
3. Reestimate the model with this substitution.

We will illustrate this with a simple demand and supply model in Section 10.12. We will also present the results from the instrumental variable method for purposes of comparison.

The instrumental variable method, although not efficient, gives consistent estimators of the parameters in all rational expectations models and is worth using at least as an initial step. Consider, for instance, Cagan's model of hyperinflation. The model is

$$m_t - p_t = a + b(p_{t+1}^* - p_t) + u_t$$

Now substitute $p_{t+1} - v_{t+1}$ for p_{t+1}^*, where v_{t+1} is uncorrelated with all variables in the information set I_t. We can write the model as

$$m_t - p_t = a + b(p_{t+1} - p_t) + u_t - bv_{t+1}$$

This equation cannot be estimated by OLS because p_{t+1} is correlated with v_{t+1} and p_t with u_t. If m_t and p_t are known at time t, then v_{t+1} will be uncorrelated with these variables. One needs an instrument that is uncorrelated with u_t and v_{t+1}. Valid instruments are m_{t-1}, p_{t-1}, and higher-order lags of m_t and p_t. One can regress $p_{t+1} - p_t$ on lagged values of m_t and p_t and use the 2SLS method.

The estimation of the hyperinflation model under rational expectations using the above-mentioned instrumental variable method using the data in Tables 10.1 and 10.2 is left as an exercise.

10.11 TESTS FOR RATIONALITY

There is a considerable amount of literature on what is known as "tests for rationality." In this literature we do not start with any economic model. Usually, we have observations on y_t^* from survey data or other sources and we test whether the forecast error $y_t - y_t^*$ is uncorrelated with variables in the information set I_{t-1}. It is customary to start with a test of unbiasedness by estimating the regression equation

$$y_t = \beta_0 + \beta_1 y_t^* + \varepsilon_t$$

and testing the hypothesis $\beta_0 = 0$, $\beta_1 = 1$.

Further, since y_{t-1} is definitely in the information set I_{t-1}, the following equation is estimated:

$$y_t - y_t^* = \alpha_0 + \alpha_1 y_{t-1} + \varepsilon_t$$

and the hypothesis $\alpha_0 = 0$, $\alpha_1 = 0$ is tested. Rationality implies that $\alpha_1 = 0$. An alternative equation that can be estimated is

$$y_t - y_t^* = \alpha_0 + \alpha_1(y_{t-1} - y_{t-1}^*) + \varepsilon_t$$

Again, rationality implies that $\alpha_1 = 0$. If the forecast errors exhibit a significant nonzero mean and serial correlation (significant α_1), then this implies that the information contained in past forecast errors was not fully utilized in forming future predictions.

Tests based on y_{t-1} and $(y_{t-1} - y_{t-1}^*)$ examine what is known as the *weak version of the rational expectations hypotheses* and are tests for weak rationality. The strong version says that the forecast error $(y_t - y_t^*)$ is uncorrelated with all the variables known to the forecaster.

Yet another test for rationality is that var$(y_t) >$ var(y_t^*). As we saw earlier if

$$y_t = y_t^* + \varepsilon_t$$

and ε_t is uncorrelated with y_t^*, then var$(y_t) =$ var$(y_t^*) +$ var(ε_t). Hence var$(y_t) \geq$ var(y_t^*).

Lovell[23] considers these two tests:

1. Tests based on y_{t-1}.
2. Tests based on var$(y_t) >$ var(y_t^*).

He examines the evidence from a number of surveys on sales and inventory expectations, price expectations, wage expectations, data revisions, and so on, and argues that in a majority of cases the tests for rationality reject the hypothesis of rationality.

Some studies that test for rationality of survey forecasts like those by Pesando, Carlson, and Mullineaux for price expectations[24] and tests by Friedman for

[23] Lovell, "Tests."

[24] J. E. Pesando, "A Note on the Rationality of the Livingston Price Expectations," *Journal of Political Economy*, Vol. 83, August 1975, pp. 849–858; J. A. Carlson, "A Study of Price Forecasts," *Annals of Economic and Social Measurement*, Vol. 6, Winter 1977, pp. 27–56; D. J. Mullineaux, "On Testing for Rationality: Another Look at the Livingston Price Expectations Data," *Journal of Political Economy*, Vol. 86, April 1978, pp. 329–336.

interest-rate expectations [25] use a different procedure. What they do is the following:

1. Regress y on the variables in the informtion set I_{t-1}.

2. Regress y^* on the same variables in the information set I_{t-1}.

3. Test the equality of coefficients in the two regressions using the Chow test described in Chapter 4.

However, note that the variance of the error terms in the two equations are likely to be unequal, since $\text{var}(y_t)$ is expected to be greater than $\text{var}(y_t^*)$. Hence some adjustment should be made for this before applying the Chow test. (Divide each data set by the estimated standard deviation of the error term.)

This test is formally identical to the test suggested earlier of regressing the forecast error $y_t - y_t^*$ on the variables in I_{t-1} and checking that their coefficients are zero. Without any loss of generality, suppose that there are two variables z_1 and z_2 in the information set I_{t-1} (z_1 and z_2 can be sets of variables). We can write

$$y = \beta_1 z_1 + \beta_2 z_2 + u$$

$$y^* = \beta_1^* z_1 + \beta_2^* z_2 + u^*$$

Then

$$(y - y^*) = (\beta_1 - \beta_1^*)z_1 + (\beta_2 - \beta_2^*)z_2 + (u - u^*) \tag{10.32}$$

Thus a regression of $(y - y^*)$ on z_1 and z_2 and testing whether the coefficients of z_1 and z_2 are significantly different from zero is the same as testing the equality of the coefficients of z_1 and z_2 in the regressions of y and y^* on these variables. There is something to be said in the favor of the test based on (10.32) instead of the one based on separate regressions for y and y^*. With the test based on (10.32), the fact that $\text{var}(u)$ and $\text{var}(u^*)$ are different does not matter.

What happens if in the tests for rationality we use only a subset of the variables in the information set I_{t-1}? For instance, in equation (10.32) we just regress $y - y^*$ on z_1 only and test whether the coefficient of z_1 is significantly different from zero. Recall that this is what we do in tests for weak rationality where we regress $y_t - y_t^*$ on y_{t-1}.

Suppose that $(y - y^*)$ is uncorrelated with z_1 but not with z_2, so that in equation (10.32), $\beta_2 - \beta_2^* \neq 0$. This implies that the expectations y^* are not rational. Now suppose that z_1 and z_2 are uncorrelated. We can still get the result that the coefficient of z_1 in a regression of $y - y^*$ on z_1 is zero. Thus if we do not reject the hypothesis that this coefficient is zero, it does not necessarily mean that we can accept the hypothesis of rationality. [26] This implies that tests of weak rationality are indeed weak. However, in practice, it is highly unlikely that the variables in the information set I_{t-1} are uncorrelated. Hence one can have sufficient confidence in the weak tests and one need not worry that all the variables in the information set I_{t-1} are not included in the tests.

[25] B. M. Friedman, "Survey Evidence on the 'Rationality' of Interest Rate Expectations," *Journal of Monetary Economics*, Vol. 6, October 1980, pp. 453–466.

[26] A. Abel and F. S. Mishkin, "An Integrated View of Tests of Rationality, Market Efficiency and Short-Run Neutrality of Monetary Policy," *Journal of Monetary Economics*, Vol. 11 1983, pp. 3–24.

10.12 ESTIMATION OF A DEMAND AND SUPPLY MODEL UNDER RATIONAL EXPECTATIONS

We will illustrate the estimation of econometric models with rational expectations using equations (10.30) and (10.31) by considering a simple demand and supply model. Consider the following model (all variables considered as deviations from their means):

$$q_t = \beta_1 p_t + \gamma_1 z_{1t} + u_{1t} \qquad \text{demand function} \qquad (10.33)$$

$$q_t = \beta_2 p_t^* + \gamma_2 z_{2t} + u_{2t} \qquad \text{supply function} \qquad (10.34)$$

where q_t = quantity demanded or supplied (both are same by the assumption of equilibrium)

p_t = market price

p_t^* = market price at time t as expected at time $(t-1)$; we assume that there is one period lag between production decisions and market supply

z_{1t}, z_{2t} = exogenous variables

u_{1t}, u_{2t} = serially uncorrelated disturbances with the usual properties (zero mean, constant variances, and constant covariance)

We consider two cases: z_{1t} and z_{2t} known, and unknown, at time $(t-1)$.

Case 1

z_{1t} and z_{2t} are known at time $(t-1)$, that is, they are in the information set I_{t-1}. In this case the estimation of the model is very simple. The rational expectations hypothesis implies that

$$p_t = p_t^* + \varepsilon_t$$

where $E(\varepsilon_t) = 0$ and $\text{cov}(\varepsilon_t, z_{1t}) = \text{cov}(\varepsilon_t, z_{2t}) = 0$. Thus ε_t has the same stochastic properties as u_{1t} and u_{2t}. Now substituting $p_t^* = p_t - \varepsilon_t$ in (10.34) we get

$$q_t = \beta_2 p_t + \gamma_2 z_{2t} + (u_{2t} - \beta_2 \varepsilon_t) \qquad (10.34')$$

The composite error in this equation has the same properties as the error term in (10.34) (zero mean, and zero correlation with z_{1t} and z_{2t}).

Thus the implication of the "rational" expectations hypothesis is that all we have to do is to substitute p_t for p_t^* and proceed with the estimation as usual. Thus the rational expectations hypothesis greatly simplifies the estimation procedures. This conclusion holds good in any simultaneous equations model involving expectations of current endogenous variables if the current exogenous variables are assumed to be known at time $(t-1)$ (or at the time expectations are formed), and the errors are serially independent.

There is, however, one problem that the "rational" expectations hypothesis creates. Suppose that the variable z_{2t} is missing in equation (10.34). Then with any exogenous specification of the expectational variable p_t^* (as in the adaptive expectations formulation), the equation system would be identified. On the other hand, under the "rational" expectations hypothesis the demand function is not identified. Thus, in the general simultaneous-equations model with expectations of current endogenous variable, the identification properties will depend on the identification properties of the simultaneous equations model resulting from the substitution of y_t for y_t^*, where y_t^* is the expectation of the endogenous variable y_t. This result makes intuitive sense since what the rational expectations hypothesis does is to make the expectations endogenous.

Case 2

z_{1t} and z_{2t} are not known at time $(t - 1)$. That is, the exogenous variables at time t have to be forecast at time $(t - 1)$. What will happen if we just substitute $p_t^* = p_t - \varepsilon_t$ as before? Since ε_t is not uncorrelated with z_{1t} and z_{2t} [they are not in the information set at time $(t - 1)$], the composite error term in (10.34') will be correlated with z_{1t} and z_{2t}.

How do we estimate this model, then? What we have to do is to add equations for z_{1t} and z_{2t}. A common procedure is to specify them as autoregressions. For simplicity we will specify them as first-order autoregressions. Then we have

$$z_{1t} = \alpha_1 z_{1,t-1} + v_{1t}$$
$$z_{2t} = \alpha_2 z_{2,t-1} + v_{2t} \tag{10.35}$$

We now estimate equations (10.33), (10.34'), and (10.35) together.[27]

An alternative way of looking at this is to say that we estimate the demand and supply model given by (10.33) and (10.34) by replacing p_t^* by p_t and using lagged values of z_{1t} and z_{2t} as instrumental variables.

There is an alternative method of estimating the model with rational expectations which is somewhat more complicated. This is called the *substitution method* (SM). In this method we derive an expression for p_t^* using the relationship

$$p_t^* = E(p_t | I_{t-1})$$

and substitute it in the model and then estimate the model. For this we proceed as follows.

Equating demand and supply we get the equilibrium condition.

$$\beta_1 p_t + \gamma_1 z_{1t} + u_{1t} = \beta_2 p_t^* + \gamma_2 z_{2t} + u_{2t} \tag{10.36}$$

Now take expectations throughout, conditional on the information set I_{t-1}. Note that $E(u_{1t} | I_{t-1}) = 0$ and $E(u_{2t} | I_{t-1}) = 0$. Hence we get

$$\beta_1 p_t^* + \gamma_1 z_{1t}^* = \beta_2 p_t^* + \gamma_2 z_{2t}^* \tag{10.37}$$

---

[27] See M. R. Wickens, "The Efficient Estimation of Econometric Models with Rational Expectations," *Review of Economic Studies*, Vol. 49, 1982, pp. 55–67, who calls this method the "errors in variables method" (EVM).

where

$$z_{1t}^* = E(z_{1t} \mid I_{t-1}) \qquad \text{and} \qquad z_{2t}^* = E(z_{2t} \mid I_{t-1})$$

These are, respectively, the expectations of z_{1t} and z_{2t} as of time $(t-1)$. Let us define

$$z_{1t} = z_{1t}^* + w_{1t}$$

$$z_{2t} = z_{2t}^* + w_{2t}$$

Subtracting (10.37) from (10.36), we get

$$\beta_1(p_t - p_t^*) + \gamma_1 w_{1t} + u_{1t} = \gamma_2 w_{2t} + u_{2t}$$

or

$$p_t^* = p_t + \frac{1}{\beta_1}(\gamma_1 w_{1t} - \gamma_2 w_{2t} + u_{1t} - u_{2t}) \tag{10.38}$$

We now substitute this expression in (10.34) and get

$$q_t = \beta_2 p_t + \gamma_2 z_{2t} + \frac{\gamma_1 \beta_2}{\beta_1} w_{1t} - \frac{\gamma_2 \beta_2}{\beta_1} w_{2t} + u_{2t}^* \tag{10.39}$$

where

$$u_{2t}^* = u_{2t} + \frac{\beta_2}{\beta_1}(u_{1t} - u_{2t})$$

The error term u_{2t}^* has the same properties as the error term u_{2t} except in the special case where u_{1t} and u_{2t} are independent. Thus the consequence of the Muthian rational expectations hypothesis is the inclusion of the extra variables w_{1t} and w_{2t} in the supply function and the constraints on the parameters. (Note that the coefficients of w_{1t} and w_{2t} involve no new parameters.) This is an omitted variable interpretation of the rational expectations models.

If the nature of the autoregressions for z_{1t} and z_{2t} is specified, one can derive an alternative expression for p_t^*. For purpose of simplicity of exposition, let us assume that z_{1t} and z_{2t} are first-order autoregressive as in equations (10.35). We then have

$$z_{1t}^* = \alpha_1 z_{1,t-1}$$

$$z_{2t}^* = \alpha_2 z_{2,t-1}$$

Substituting these in (10.37), we get

$$p_t^* = \frac{1}{\beta_1 - \beta_2}(\gamma_2 \alpha_2 z_{2,t-1} - \gamma_1 \alpha_1 z_{1,t-1})$$

Now we substitute this expression in (10.34) and get

$$q_t = \frac{\beta_2 \gamma_2 \alpha_2}{\beta_1 - \beta_2} z_{2,t-1} - \frac{\beta_2 \gamma_1 \alpha_1}{\beta_1 - \beta_2} z_{1,t-1} + \gamma_2 z_{2t} + u_{2t} \tag{10.40}$$

We now estimate this equation along with equation (10.33) and equations (10.35). Again, note that the coefficients of $z_{1,t-1}$ and $z_{2,t-1}$ in equation (10.40) do not involve any new parameters. If higher-order autoregressions are used for z_{1t} and z_{2t}, then p_t^* will involve more of the lagged values of these variables.

Note that even if estimates α_1 and α_2 are obtained from (10.35) and substituted in (10.40), we still have to deal with cross-equation constraints. Tests of these cross-equation constraints have been often referred to as "tests for the rational expectations hypothesis."[28] The restrictions, however, arise because the exogenous variables z_{1t} and z_{2t} are not known at time $(t-1)$ and not from the rational expectations hypothesis as such. Moreover, the number of restrictions depends on the specification of the order of autoregression of the exogenous variables z_{1t} and z_{2t}. In view of this, it might be inappropriate to name the tests for the restrictions as tests of the rational expectations hypothesis. Note also that if equation (10.39) is used, the restrictions do not depend on the specification of the order of autoregression of the exogenous variables.

We have used a simple demand and supply model to outline the problems that are likely to arise in the Muthian rational expectations models if the exogenous variables are not known at time $(t-1)$.

Summary

There are three procedures we have outlined.

1. Just substitute p_t for p_t^* and use lagged exogenous variables as instruments. This can be done for all expectational variables.
2. Estimate autoregressions for z_{1t} and z_{2t}. Get the estimated residuals $\hat{w}_{1t}$ and $\hat{w}_{2t}$. Use these as additional regressors as in equation (10.39) after substituting p_t for p_t^*. Estimate the equations using the parameter constraints (computer programs like TSP do this).
3. Get an expression for p_t^* based on the structure of the model *and* the structure of the exogenous variables as in equation (10.40). Estimate the equations using the parameter constraints.

Note that method 1 uses equation (10.30), which says that $p_t = p_t^* + \varepsilon_t$. Methods 2 and 3 use equation (10.31), which says that

$$p_t^* = E(p_t \,|\, I_{t-1})$$

The latter methods use the structure of the model in deriving an expression for p_t^*. Method 3 uses the structure of the exogenous variables as well.

Illustrative Example[29]

We will illustrate the methods we have described, with the estimation of a demand and supply model. In Table 10.5 we present data for the 1964–1984 growing seasons

[28] K. F. Wallis, "Econometric Implications of the Rational Expectations Hypotheses," *Econometrica*, Vol. 48, 1980, pp. 49–74; N. S. Revankar, "Testing of the Rational Expectations Hypothesis," *Econometrica*, Vol. 48, 1980, pp. 1347–1363; D. L. Hoffman and P. Schmidt, "Testing the Restrictions Implied by the Rational Expectations Hypothesis," *Journal of Econometrics*, February 1981, pp. 265–288.
[29] I would like to thank my colleague, J. Scott Shonkwiler, for the data, model, and computations.

Table 10.5 Data on Florida Fresh Strawberries, 1964–1984

Year	P_t	Q_t	d_t	C_t	N_t	X_t
1964	378	2134	0.74	78.97	192	651.04
1965	397	1742	0.76	77.84	194	675.26
1966	395	1467	0.79	81.16	197	685.28
1967	346	1267	0.80	81.89	199	688.44
1968	391	1333	0.84	78.97	201	706.47
1969	553	1200	0.88	79.76	203	719.21
1970	419	1467	0.93	74.67	205	731.71
1971	379	1667	0.95	72.31	208	725.96
1972	516	1575	1.00	67.41	210	738.10
1973	457	1467	1.12	68.66	212	721.70
1974	508	1650	1.28	82.98	214	710.28
1975	506	1750	1.37	100.69	216	722.22
1976	493	1817	1.41	98.93	218	752.29
1977	689	2417	1.46	100.00	220	777.27
1978	692	3200	1.60	98.90	223	771.30
1979	706	3958	1.77	99.50	225	782.22
1980	498	5600	1.91	103.87	228	793.86
1981	644	8125	2.07	108.58	230	786.96
1982	614	8550	2.16	112.89	232	784.48
1983	538	7225	2.20	118.63	234	807.69
1984	694	8833	2.28	121.03	237	818.57

on fresh strawberries in Florida. The variables in the table are

P_t = price (cents per flat)
Q_t = number of flats (thousands)
d_t = food price deflator (1972 = 1.00)
C_t = production cost index (1977 = 100)
N_t = U.S. population (millions)
X_t = real per capita food expenditures (dollars per year)

The model estimated was the following.

$$Q_t = \alpha_0 + \alpha_1(P_t^* - C_t) + \alpha_2 Q_{t-1} + u_{1t} \qquad \text{supply}$$

$$P_t - d_t = \beta_0 + \beta_1(Q_t - N_t) + \beta_2 X_t + \beta_3 t + u_{2t} \qquad \text{demand}$$

All variables are in logs except the time trend t. (Note that the data in Table 10.5 are *not* in logs.) P_t^* is the expected price (as expected at time $t - 1$). The different estimation methods depend on different specifications of P_t^*.

Five different models have been estimated (except for the first model, the other models assume rational expectations):

1. *The Cobweb model.* In this model we substitute P_{t-1} for P_t^* and estimate the demand and supply functions by OLS.

2. *The 2SLS (Two-Stage Least Squares) method.* This is the procedure for the rational expectations model if the exogenous variables are assumed to be known at time $t - 1$ and the errors are not serially correlated. Since the rational expectations hypothesis implies

$$P_t^* = P_t - v_t$$

where v_t is an error uncorrelated with the variables in the information set I_{t-1}, we just substitute $P_t - v_t$ for P_t^* and combine the error v_t with the error in the supply function. Since v_t has the same properties as u_{1t}, we just estimate the model by two-stage least squares (2SLS).

3. *The IV (Instrumental Variable) method.* This is the method we use to get consistent estimators of the parameters under rational expectations when the exogenous variables at time t are not known at time $(t - 1)$. In this case, the error v_t can be correlated with the exogenous variables. We used the lagged exogenous variables as instruments.

4. *The OV (Omitted-Variable) method.* In this method we first estimated first-order autoregressions for the exogenous variables and used the residuals as additional explanatory variables in the supply function [estimating an equation like (10.39)], imposing no parameter constraints. After obtaining initial estimates of the parameters in the demand and supply functions the predicted value of P_t^* was obtained as in equation (10.38). This was introduced in the supply function which was then reestimated by OLS. This is just a two-stage method of imposing the parameter constraints in (10.39).

5. *The joint estimation method.* In this model the explicit expression for the rational expectation P_t^* is derived and then equation (10.40) is estimated jointly with the demand function imposing parameter constraints.

The results from these five methods of estimation are presented in Tables 10.6 and 10.7. Regarding the estimates of the supply function, the price coefficient is significant only when the estimation is done by the 2SLS method or the joint estimation method. The IV and OV methods which are less efficient methods for the estimation of rational expectations models gave rather worse results (the results,

Table 10.6 Estimates of the Parameters of the Supply Function[a]

	Cobweb	2SLS	IV	OV	Joint Estimation
α_0	−0.997	−1.593	−1.427	−1.371	−1.815
	(0.594)	(0.741)	(0.762)	(0.726)	(0.747)
α_1	0.310	0.604	0.520	0.515	0.713
	(0.213)	(0.301)	(0.318)	(0.308)	(0.315)
α_2	1.070	1.080	1.078	1.071	1.085
	(0.057)	(0.058)	(0.057)	(0.057)	(0.054)
DW[b]	1.573	1.642	1.326	1.440	—

[a] Figures in parentheses are standard errors.
[b] DW is the Durbin–Watson test statistic.

Table 10.7 Estimates of the Parameters of the Demand Function[a]

	Cobweb	2SLS	IV	OV	Joint Estimation
β_0	−9.796	−9.476	−14.896	−9.561	−9.531
	(9.848)	(9.871)	(11.643)	(9.860)	(9.720)
β_1	−0.121	−0.139	−0.136	−0.134	−0.133
	(0.075)	(0.079)	(0.078)	(0.077)	(0.077)
β_2	2.513	2.468	3.302	2.480	2.477
	(1.513)	(1.516)	(1.789)	(1.515)	(1.493)
β_3	−0.047	−0.045	−0.053	−0.045	−0.046
	(0.017)	(0.018)	(0.020)	(0.017)	(0.017)
DW[b]	2.286	2.315	2.306	2.245	—

[a] Figures in parentheses are standard errors.
[b] DW is the Durbin–Watson test statistic.

however, for the two methods are very close to each other). The Cobweb model gave the worst results. Of some concern is the fact that the coefficient α_2 of Q_{t-1} is not significantly different from 1, and the DW statistic is low for a model with a lagged dependent variable. Both these results indicate that the model is misspecified.

Regarding the estimates of the demand function (presented in Table 10.7), the Cobweb model and the 2SLS, OV, and joint estimation methods for the rational expectations model, all gave very similar results. It is only the IV method that gives slightly different results. The results are not very encouraging, although β_1 and β_2 both have expected signs. The negative coefficient of β_3 implies a gradual downward shift of the demand function.

Overall, we cannot say that the data are very informative about the models. All we can say, perhaps, is that the rational expectations model appears to be more appropriate than the Cobweb model. Many coefficients are not significant (although they have signs that one would expect a priori). The computations, however, illustrate the methods described. In estimating the rational expectations models, we used progressively more information about the models in the four methods described. Although the results are not much different in this case, one would be able to find differences in other cases. The estimation of the hyperinflation model described in Section 10.5 is left as an exercise.

10.13 THE SERIAL CORRELATION PROBLEM IN RATIONAL EXPECTATIONS MODELS

Until now we have assumed that the errors are serially uncorrelated. If they are serially correlated, we cannot use variables in the information set I_{t-1} as instruments. The following example illustrates the problem. Consider the model

$$y_t = \alpha x_t^* + \beta z_t + u_t \tag{10.41}$$

z_t is an exogenous variable, but x_t can be an exogenous or endogenous variable. We will assume that z_t is *not* a part of the information set I_{t-1}. This means that z_t should also be treated as endogenous if we substitute x_t for x_t^*. Finally, u_t follow a first-order autoregressive process

$$u_t = \rho u_{t-1} + v_t \qquad |\rho| < 1 \quad \text{and} \quad v_t \sim \text{IN}(0, \sigma^2)$$

Let us write, as usual, equation (10.41) as

$$y_t = \rho y_{t-1} + \alpha x_t^* - \alpha \rho x_{t-1}^* + \beta z_t - \beta \rho z_{t-1} + v_t$$

Using the rational expectations assumption and substituting $x_t^* = x_t - \varepsilon_t$, we get

$$y_t = \rho y_{t-1} + \alpha x_t - \alpha \rho x_{t-1} + \beta x_t - \beta \rho z_{t-1} + w_t \tag{10.42}$$

where $w_t = v_t - \alpha(\varepsilon_t - \rho \varepsilon_{t-1})$.

We would like to estimate this equation by instrumental variables. Note that x_{t-1} is correlated with ε_{t-1} and hence w_t. Thus although y_{t-1}, x_{t-1}, and z_{t-1} are definitely in the information set I_{t-1}, we cannot use them as instrumental variables.

The solution to the problem is to use the set of variables in I_{t-2} rather than I_{t-1}. Thus we obtain the predicted values $\tilde{x}_t$, $\tilde{x}_{t-1}$, $\tilde{z}_t$, $\tilde{z}_{t-1}$, $\tilde{y}_{t-1}$ by regressing each of these variables on the variables in the information set I_{t-2} and use these as instruments for estimating equation (10.42). Note that if the degree of autoregression in u_t is of a higher order, we have to use the variables in the information set of a higher order of lag. For instance, if u_t is a second-order autoregression, we use I_{t-3}, and so on.

Thus with serial correlation in errors we should not use the variables in the information set I_{t-1} to construct the instrumental variables in models with rational expectations.[30]

SUMMARY

1. In this chapter we have discussed three types of models of expectations:
(a) Naive models of expectations.
(b) The adaptive expectations model.
(c) The rational expectations model.
Naive models merely serve as benchmarks against which other models or survey data on expectations are judged.

2. Two methods of estimation of the adaptive expectations model have been discussed:

---

[30] A concise discussion of methods of obtaining consistent estimates of the parameters in single-equation models with rational expectations can be found in B. T. McCallum, "Topics Concerning the Formulation, Estimation and Use of Macroeconomic Models with Rational Expectations," *Proceedings of the Business and Economic Statistics Section*, American Statistical Association, 1979, pp. 65–72.

(a) Estimation in the autoregressive form.

(b) Estimation in the distributed lag form.

The first method is easy to use because one can use an OLS regression program. However, this method is not advisable. The second method is the better one. It can be implemented with an OLS regression program by using a search method (see Section 10.4).

3. Many economic variables when disturbed from their equilibrium position do not adjust instantly to their new equilibrium position. There are some lags in adjustment. The partial equilibrium model has been suggested to handle this problem. Recently, a generalization of this model, the error correction model, has been found to be more useful (see Section 10.6). One can combine these partial adjustment models with the adaptive (or any other) model of expectations (see Section 10.7).

4. Besides the partial adjustment and error correction models, two other models are commonly used in the literature on adjustment lags. These are:

(a) The polynomial lag (also known as the Almon lag) (Section 10.8).

(b) The rational lags (Section 10.9).

The latter should not be confused with the rational expectations model. Rational here means the ratio of two polynomials.

5. In the polynomial lags one has to choose the length of the lag and the degree of the polynomial. Given the lag length, some procedures have been suggested for these two choices. All lag distributions imply some restrictions on the coefficients. Before imposing these restrictions, it is always best to estimate unconstrained lag models by OLS.

6. The rational expectations model suggested by Muth has been very popular. The idea behind the rational expectations hypothesis is that the specification of expectations should be consistent with the rest of the model rather than being ad hoc. A proper terminology for this is "model-consistent expectations" rather than "rational expectations," Two investigators starting with two different models can arrive at two different expressions of the "rational expectation" of the same variable. However, we continued to use the word "rational" rather than "model consistent" because the former is the commonly used term.

7. The essence of the rational expectations hypothesis is that the difference between the realized value and the expected value should be uncorrelated with all the variables in the information set at the time the expectation is formed. Based on this, several tests for "rationality" have been applied to survey data on expectations. These tests are described in Section 10.11. In a large number of cases these tests reject the "rationality" of survey data on expectations.

8. There are, broadly speaking, two methods of estimation for rational expectations models. One procedure involves substitution of the realized value for the expected value and using some appropriate instrumental variables. The other procedure involves obtaining an explicit expression for the expected value from the model, substituting this in the model and then estimating the model using any parameter constraints that are implied. These procedures are illustrated with reference to a demand and supply model in Section 10.12.

9. With serially correlated errors one has to be careful in the choice of

appropriate instruments when estimating rational expectations models. A careful examination of which variables are correlated or uncorrelated with errors will reveal what variables are valid instruments. This is illustrated with a first-order autoregression in Section 10.13.

10. Some empirical examples are provided for the Almon lag, but computation of the Koyck model and some rational expectations models are left as exercises.

EXERCISES

1. Explain the meaning of each of the following terms.
    (a) Adaptive expectations.
    (b) Regressive expectations.
    (c) Rational expectations.
    (d) Koyck lag.
    (e) Almon lag.
    (f) Rational lags.
    (g) Partial adjustment model.
    (h) Error correction model.
    (i) Testing rationality.
    (j) Estimation in autoregressive form.
    (k) Estimation in distributed lag form.
2. What are the problems one encounters in the OLS estimation under adaptive expectations in the following models?
    (a) Models of agricultural supply.
    (b) Models of hyperinflation.
    (c) Partial adjustment models.
    (d) Error correction models.
3. Answer Exercise 2 if, instead of assuming adaptive expectations, we assume the following.
    (a) Naive expectations $y_t^* = y_{t-1}$.
    (b) Rational expectations.
4. In the demand and supply model for pork discussed in Section 9.3 (data are in Table 9.1), assume that supply depends on expected price, P_t^*. Estimate the model assuming the following.
    (a) Naive expectations $P_t^* = P_{t-1}$. This is the Cobweb model.
    (b) Adaptive expectations.
    (c) Rational expectations.
5. Estimate the hyperinflation model for Hungary and Germany using the data in Tables 10.1 and 10.2 and assuming the following.
    (a) Naive expectations $P_{t-1}^* = P_t$.
    (b) Adaptive expectations.
    (c) Rational expectations.
6. Answer Exercise 4 with the Australian wine data discussed in Section 9.5 (data are in Table 9.2). Assume that the supply depends on expected price.

7. Explain tests for rationality based on
   (a) y_{t-1}.
   (b) var y_t^* and var y_t.
   (c) Tests for equality of coefficients.
8. What is meant by weak tests for rationality? Are these tests really weak?
9. Future prices have often been used as a proxy for expected prices in the case of estimation of supply functions for agricultural commodities. How do you test whether the expectations implied in the future prices are rational?

11

Errors in Variables

11.1 INTRODUCTION

Since the early 1970s there has been a resurgence of interest in the topic of errors in variables models and models involving latent variables.[1] This late interest is perhaps surprising since there is no doubt that almost all economic variables are measured with error.

Part of the neglect of errors in variables is due to the fact that consistent estimation of parameters is rather difficult. During the 1970s this attitude changed

---

[1] Three early papers that sparked interest in this area are: A. Zellner, "Estimation of Regression Relationships Containing Unobservable Independent Variables," *International Economic Review*, October 1970, pp. 441–454; A. S. Goldberger, "Maximum Likelihood Estimation of Regression Models Containing Unobservable Variables," *International Economic Review*, January 1972, pp. 1–15; and Zvi Griliches, "Errors in Variables and Other Unobservables," *Econometrica*, November 1974, pp. 971–998.

because of the following developments:

1. It was realized that sometimes we can use some extra information available in the dynamics of the equation or the structure of other equations in the model to get consistent estimates of the parameters.
2. The fact that we cannot get consistent point estimates of the parameters does not imply that no inference is possible. It was realized that one can obtain expressions for the direction of the biases and one can also obtain consistent "bounds" for the parameters.

We will now discuss how consistent estimation of equations which contain variables that are measured with errors can be accomplished. We start our discussion with a single-equation model with one explanatory variable measured with error. This is known as the "classical" errors in variable model. We then consider a single equation with two explanatory variables. Next we apply these results to the problem of "reverse regression," which has been a suggested technique in the analysis of wage discrimination by race and sex.

Before we proceed, we should make it clear what we mean by "errors in variables." Broadly speaking, there are two types of errors that we can talk about.

1. Recording errors.
2. Errors due to using an imperfect measure of the true variable. Such imperfect measures are known as "proxy" variables. The true variables are often not measurable and are called "latent" variables.

What we will be concerned with in this chapter are errors of type 2.

A commonly cited example of a proxy variable is years of schooling (S), which is a proxy for education (E). In this case, however, the error $S - E$ is likely to be independent of S rather than of E. Another example is that of expectational variables, which must be replaced by proxies (either estimates generated from the past or measures obtained from survey data). Examples of this were given in Chapter 10.

We start our discussion with the classical errors-in-variables model and then progressively relax at least some of the restrictive assumptions of this model.

11.2 THE CLASSICAL SOLUTION FOR A SINGLE-EQUATION MODEL WITH ONE EXPLANATORY VARIABLE

Suppose that the true model is

$$y = \beta x + e \tag{11.1}$$

Instead of y and x, we measure

$$Y = y + v \quad \text{and} \quad X = x + u$$

u and v are measurement errors, x and y are called the systematic components. We will assume that the errors have zero means and variances σ_u^2 and σ_v^2, respectively.

We will also assume that they are mutually uncorrelated and are uncorrelated with the systematic components. That is,

$$E(u) = E(v) = 0 \qquad \text{var}(u) = \sigma_u^2 \qquad \text{var}(v) = \sigma_v^2$$

$$\text{cov}(u, x) = \text{cov}(u, y) = \text{cov}(v, x) = \text{cov}(v, y) = 0$$

Equation (11.1) can be written in terms of the observed variables as

$$Y - v = \beta(X - u) + e$$

or

$$Y = \beta X + w \tag{11.2}$$

where $w = e + v - \beta u$. The reason we cannot apply the OLS method to equation (11.2) is that $\text{cov}(w, X) \neq 0$. In fact,

$$\text{cov}(w, X) = \text{cov}(-\beta u, x + u) = -\beta \sigma_u^2$$

Thus one of the basic assumptions of least squares is violated. If only y is measured with error and x is measured without error, there is no problem because $\text{cov}(w, X) = 0$ in this case. Thus given the specification (11.1) of the true relationship, it is errors in x that cause a problem.

If we estimate β by OLS applied to (11.2) we have

$$b_{YX} = \frac{\sum XY}{\sum X^2} = \frac{\sum (x + u)(y + v)}{\sum (x + u)^2}$$

$$\text{plim } b_{YX} = \frac{\text{cov}(xy)}{\text{var}(x) + \text{var}(u)} = \frac{\sigma_{xy}}{\sigma_x^2 + \sigma_u^2}$$

since all cross products vanish. Since $\beta = \sigma_{xy}/\sigma_x^2$, we have

$$\text{plim } b_{YX} = \frac{\beta}{1 + \sigma_u^2/\sigma_x^2} \tag{11.3}$$

Thus b_{YX} will underestimate β. The degree of underestimation depends on σ_u^2/σ_x^2.

If we run a reverse regression (i.e., regress X on Y), we have

$$b_{XY} = \frac{\sum XY}{\sum Y^2} = \frac{\sum (x + u)(y + v)}{\sum (y + v)^2}$$

Hence

$$\text{plim } b_{XY} = \frac{\sigma_{xy}}{\sigma_y^2 + \sigma_v^2}$$

But from (11.1)

$$\sigma_y^2 = \beta^2 \sigma_x^2 + \sigma_e^2 \qquad \text{and} \qquad \sigma_{xy} = \beta \sigma_x^2$$

Hence

$$\text{plim } \frac{1}{b_{XY}} = \frac{\beta^2 \sigma_x^2 + \sigma_e^2 + \sigma_v^2}{\beta \sigma_x^2} = \beta \left(1 + \frac{\sigma_e^2 + \sigma_v^2}{\beta^2 \sigma_x^2} \right) \tag{11.3$'$}$$

Thus $1/b_{XY}$ overestimates β, and we have

$$\text{plim } b_{YX} \le \beta \le \frac{1}{\text{plim } b_{XY}}$$

We can use the two regression coefficients b_{YX} and b_{XY} to get bounds on β (at least in large samples).

In the preceding discussion we have implicitly assumed that $\beta > 0$. If $\beta < 0$, then

$$\text{plim } b_{YX} > \beta \qquad \text{and} \qquad (\text{plim } b_{XY})^{-1} < \beta$$

and thus the bounds have to be reversed, that is,

$$(\text{plim } b_{XY})^{-1} < \beta < \text{plim } b_{YX}$$

Note that since $b_{XY} \cdot b_{YX} = R_{XY}^2$, the higher the value of R^2 the closer these bounds are. Consider, for instance, the data in Table 7.3.[2] We have the equation

$$Y = 0.193 X_1 - 15.86 \qquad R^2 = 0.969$$

$$X_1 = 5.008 Y + 86.87 \qquad R^2 = 0.969$$

The second equation when solved for Y gives

$$Y = 0.199 X_1 = 17.32$$

Hence we have the bounds $0.193 < \beta_1 < 0.199$. Such consistent estimates of the bounds have been studied by Frisch and Schultz.[3]

The general conclusion from (11.3) is that the least squares estimator of β is biased toward zero and if (11.1) has a constant term, α, the least squares estimator of α is biased away from zero.[4]

If we define

$$\lambda = \frac{\sigma_u^2}{\sigma_u^2 + \sigma_x^2}$$

then from (11.3) we get the result that the bias in the least squares estimator of β is $\beta\lambda$.

11.3 THE SINGLE-EQUATION MODEL WITH TWO EXPLANATORY VARIABLES

In Section 11.2 we derived the bias in the least squares estimator and also some consistent bounds for the true parameter. We will now see how these two results can be extended to the case of several explanatory variables. Since it is instructive to consider some simple models, we discuss a model with two explanatory variables in some detail:

[2] These data are from E. Malinvaud, *Statistical Methods of Econometrics*, 3rd ed. (Amsterdam; North-Holland, 1980), p. 19.
[3] R. Frisch, *Statistical Confluence Analysis by Means of Complete Regression Systems*, Publication 5 (Oslo: University Economics Institute, 1934); H. Schultz, *The Theory and Measurement of Demand* (Chicago: University of Chicago Press, 1938).
[4] In the discussion that follows we mean by bias, asymptotic bias or more precisely plim $\hat{\theta} - \theta$, where $\hat{\theta}$ is the estimator of θ.

Two Explanatory Variables: One Measured with Error

Let us consider the case of two explanatory variables only one of which is measured with error. The equation is

$$y = \beta_1 x_1 + \beta_2 x_2 + e$$

The observed variables are

$$Y = y + v \qquad X_1 = x_1 + u \qquad X_2 = x_2$$

As before we will assume that the errors u, v, e are mutually uncorrelated and also uncorrelated with y, x_1, x_2. Note that we can combine the errors e and v into a single composite error in Y. Let $\text{var}(u) = \sigma_u^2$ and $\text{var}(v + e) = \sigma^2$. The regression equation we can estimate in terms of observables is

$$Y = \beta_1 X_1 + \beta_2 X_2 + w$$

where

$$w = e + v - \beta_1 u$$

To save on notation (and without any loss in generality) we will normalize the observed variables X_1 and X_2 so that $\text{var}(X_1) = 1$, $\text{var}(X_2) = 1$, and $\text{cov}(X_1, X_2) = \rho$. Note that

$$\text{cov}(X_1, w) = -\beta_1 \sigma_u^2 = -\beta_1 \lambda$$

where

$$\lambda = \frac{\sigma_u^2}{\text{var}(X_1)} = \sigma_u^2 \quad \text{since } \text{var}(X_1) = 1.$$

Hence we get

$$\text{var}(Y) = \beta_1^2 + \beta_2^2 + 2\rho\beta_1\beta_2 + \sigma^2 - \beta_1^2\lambda$$

$$\text{cov}(X_1, Y) = \beta_1 + \beta_2\rho - \beta_1\lambda$$

$$\text{cov}(X_2, Y) = \beta_1\rho + \beta_2$$

It is important to note that in this model there are some limits on λ that need be imposed for the analysis to make sense. This is because the condition

$$\text{var}(x_1)\,\text{var}(x_2) - [\text{cov}(x_1, x_2)]^2 \geq 0$$

needs to be satisfied.

Since $\text{var}(X_1) = 1$ we have $\text{var}(x_1) = 1 - \lambda$. Also, $\text{var}(X_2) = \text{var}(x_2) = 1$ and $\text{cov}(x_1, x_2) = \text{cov}(X_1, X_2) = \rho$. Hence we have the condition

$$1 - \lambda - \rho^2 \geq 0 \qquad \text{or} \qquad \lambda \leq 1 - \rho^2$$

This condition will turn out to be very stringent if ρ^2 is large or there is high collinearity between X_1 and X_2. For instance, if $\rho^2 = 0.99$, we cannot assume that $\lambda > 0.01$. If $\lambda = 0.01$, this implies that x_1 and x_2 are perfectly correlated.

What this implies is that we cannot use the classical errors in variables model if X_1 and X_2 are highly correlated and we believe that the variance of the error in x_1 is high.

We will see the implications of this condition when we derive the probability limits of the least squares estimators $\hat{\beta}_1$ and $\hat{\beta}_2$. The least squares estimators $\hat{\beta}_1$ and $\hat{\beta}_2$ of β_1 and β_2 are obtained by solving the equations

$$\sum X_1^2 \hat{\beta}_1 + \sum X_1 X_2 \hat{\beta}_2 = \sum X_1 Y$$
$$\sum X_1 X_2 \hat{\beta}_1 + \sum X_2^2 \hat{\beta}_2 = \sum X_2 Y$$

Dividing by the sample size throughout and taking probability limits, we get

$$\text{var}(X_1)\,\text{plim}\,\hat{\beta}_1 + \text{cov}(X_1, X_2)\,\text{plim}\,\hat{\beta}_2 = \text{cov}(X_1, Y)$$
$$\text{cov}(X_1, X_2)\,\text{plim}\,\hat{\beta}_1 + \text{var}(X_2)\,\text{plim}\,\hat{\beta}_2 = \text{cov}(X_2, Y)$$

That is,

$$\text{plim}\,\hat{\beta}_1 + \rho\,\text{plim}\,\hat{\beta}_2 = \beta_1 + \beta_2\rho - \beta_1\lambda$$
$$\rho\,\text{plim}\,\hat{\beta}_1 + \text{plim}\,\hat{\beta}_2 = \beta_1\rho + \beta_2$$

Solving these equations, we get [5]

$$\text{plim}\,\hat{\beta}_1 = \beta_1 - \frac{\beta_1\lambda}{1 - \rho^2} = \beta_1\left(1 - \frac{\lambda}{1 - \rho^2}\right)$$

$$\text{plim}\,\hat{\beta}_2 = \beta_2 + \frac{\beta_1\lambda\rho}{1 - \rho^2} \qquad\qquad (11.4)$$

Thus bias in $\hat{\beta}_2 = -\rho(\text{bias in } \hat{\beta}_1)$. This result also applies if there is more than one explanatory variable with no errors. For instance, if the regression equation is

$$y = \beta_1 x_1 + \beta_2 x_2 + \cdots + \beta_k x_k + e$$

and only x_1 is measured with error, the first formula in (11.4) remains the same except that ρ^2 is now the square of the multiple correlation coefficient between X_1 and $(X_2, X_2, \ldots, X_k)$. As for the biases in the other coefficients, we have

$$\text{bias in } \hat{\beta}_j = -\gamma_j(\text{bias in } \hat{\beta}_1)$$

where γ_j are the regression coefficients from the "auxiliary" regression of X_1 on $X_2, X_3, \ldots, X_k$:

$$E(X_1 \mid X_2, X_3, \ldots, X_k) = \gamma_2 X_2 + \gamma_3 X_3 + \cdots + \gamma_k X_k$$

Note that we are normalizing all the observed variables to have a unit variance. [6]

---

[5] These results are derived in Z. Griliches and V. Ringstad, *Economies of Scale and the Form of the Production Function* (Amsterdam: North-Holland, 1971), App. C.

[6] Similar formulas have been derived in M. D. Levi, "Errors in Variables Bias in the Presence of Correctly Measured Variables," *Econometrica*, Vol. 41, 1973, pp. 985–986, and Steven Garber and Steven Klepper, "Extending the Classical Normal Errors in Variables Model," *Econometrica*, Vol. 48, No. 6, 1980, pp. 1541–1546. However, these papers discuss the biases in terms of the variances and covariances of the *true* variables, $x_1, x_2, \ldots, x_k$ as well as auxiliary regression of the *true* variable x_1 on $x_2, \ldots, x_k$. The formulas stated here are in terms of the correlations of the *observed* variables. The only unknown parameter is thus λ. The formulas presented here are practically more useful since they are in terms of the correlations of the *observed* variables.

Returning to equations (11.4), note that if $\rho = 0$, the bias in β_1 is $-\beta_1\lambda$ as derived in (11.3). Whether or not $\hat{\beta}_1$ is biased toward zero as before depends on whether or not $\lambda < (1 - \rho^2)$. As we argued earlier, this condition has to be imposed for the classical errors in variables model to make sense. Thus, even in this model we can assume that $\hat{\beta}_1$ is biased toward zero. As for $\hat{\beta}_2$ the direction of bias depends on the sign of $\beta_1\rho$. The sign of ρ is known from the data and the sign of β_1 is the same as the sign of $\hat{\beta}_1$.

Consider now the regression of X_1 on Y and X_2. Let the equation be

$$X_1 = \gamma_1 Y + \gamma_2 X_2 + w^*$$

Then

$$\gamma_1 = \frac{1}{\beta_1} \qquad \gamma_2 = \frac{-\beta_2}{\beta_1} \qquad w^* = -\frac{w}{\beta_1}$$

The least squares estimators $\hat{\gamma}_1$ and $\hat{\gamma}_2$ for γ_1 and γ_2 are obtained from the equations

$$\left(\sum Y^2\right)\hat{\gamma}_1 + \left(\sum YX_2\right)\hat{\gamma}_2 = \left(\sum X_1 Y\right)$$
$$\left(\sum YX_2\right)\hat{\gamma}_1 + \left(\sum X_2^2\right)\hat{\gamma}_2 = \left(\sum X_1 X_2\right)$$

Divide throughout by the sample size and take probability limits. That is, we substitute population variances for sample variances and covariances. We get

$$(\beta_1^2 + \beta_2^2 + 2\rho\beta_1\beta_2 + \sigma^2 - \beta_1^2\lambda)\operatorname{plim}\hat{\gamma}_1 + (\beta_1\rho + \beta_2)\operatorname{plim}\hat{\gamma}_2 = \beta_1 + \beta_2\rho - \beta_1\lambda$$
$$(\beta_1\rho + \beta_2)\operatorname{plim}\hat{\gamma}_1 + \operatorname{plim}\hat{\gamma}_2 = \rho$$

Hence

$$\operatorname{plim}\hat{\gamma}_1 = \frac{1}{\Delta}[\beta_1(1 - \rho^2 - \lambda)]$$

$$\operatorname{plim}\hat{\gamma}_2 = \frac{1}{\Delta}[-\beta_1\beta_2(1 - \rho^2 - \lambda) + \rho\sigma^2]$$

where

$$\Delta = \beta_1^2(1 - \rho^2 - \lambda) + \sigma^2$$

Hence the estimates $(\tilde{\beta}_1, \tilde{\beta}_2)$ of (β_1, β_2) from the equations

$$\tilde{\beta}_1 = \frac{1}{\hat{\gamma}_1} \qquad \tilde{\beta}_2 = -\frac{\hat{\gamma}_2}{\hat{\gamma}_1}$$

have the probability limits

$$\operatorname{plim}\tilde{\beta}_1 = \beta_1 + \frac{\sigma^2}{\beta_1(1 - \rho^2 - \lambda)} = \beta_1\left[1 + \frac{\sigma^2}{\beta_1^2(1 - \rho^2 - \lambda)}\right]$$

$$\operatorname{plim}\tilde{\beta}_2 = \beta_2 - \frac{\rho\sigma^2}{\beta_1(1 - \rho^2 - \lambda)}$$

(11.5)

Again the bias in $\tilde{\beta}_2 = -\rho(\text{bias in } \tilde{\beta}_1)$. Also, if $\lambda < (1 - \rho^2)$ or $(1 - \rho^2 - \lambda) > 0$, we have the result that $\tilde{\beta}_1$ is biased away from zero. Hence

$$\text{plim } \hat{\beta}_1 < \beta_1 < \text{plim } \tilde{\beta}_1 \qquad \text{if } \beta_1 > 0$$

and   (11.6)

$$\text{plim } \hat{\beta}_1 > \beta_1 > \text{plim } \tilde{\beta}_1 \qquad \text{if } \beta_1 < 0$$

As for $\tilde{\beta}_2$ the bias will depend on the sign of $\rho\beta_1$.
   If $\rho\beta_1 > 0$, we have

$$\text{plim}\tilde{\beta}_2 < \beta_2 < \text{plim } \hat{\beta}_2 \qquad (11.7a)$$

and if $\rho\beta_1 < 0$, we have

$$\text{plim } \tilde{\beta}_2 > \beta_2 > \text{plim } \hat{\beta}_2 \qquad (11.7b)$$

Illustrative Example

Consider the data in Table 7.3 and a regression of imports (Y) on domestic production (X_1) and consumption (X_3). Note that X_1 and X_3 are very highly correlated, $\rho^2 = 0.99789$ or $1 - \rho^2 = 0.00211$. Let us assume that X_3 has no measurement error but that there is measurement error in X_1. As mentioned earlier, we have to have $\lambda \le 1 - \rho^2$ or $\lambda \le 0.00211$. This implies that the variance of the measurement error in X_1 cannot be greater than 0.211% of the variance of X_1. Thus we have to make a very stringent assumption on λ to do any sensible analysis of the data.
   The regression equation in this case is

$$Y = \underset{(0.1907)}{0.043X_1} + \underset{(0.2913)}{0.230X_3} - 18.63 \qquad R^2 = 0.970$$

(Figures in parentheses are standard errors.) The reverse regression is

$$X_1 = 0.078Y + 1.503X_3 - 16.37 \qquad R^2 = 0.998$$

which, when normalized with respect to Y, gives

$$Y = 12.81X_1 - 19.28X_3 + 2.09$$

If $\lambda < 0.00211$, we come to the conclusion that $\beta_1 > 0$, and hence from (11.6) the consistent estimates of bounds are

$$0.043 < \beta_1 < 12.81$$

Also, from (11.7) the consistent bounds for β_2 are (since $\rho\beta_1 > 0$)

$$-19.28 < \beta_2 < 0.23$$

All this merely indicates that the coefficients β_1 and β_2 are not estimable with any precision, which is what one would also learn from the high multicollinearity between X_1 and X_2 and the large standard errors reported. What the errors in variables analysis shows is that even very small errors in measurement can make a great deal of difference to the results, that is, the multicollinearity may be even more serious than what it appears to be and that the confidence intervals are perhaps wider than those reported.

Note that the consistent bounds are not comparable to a confidence interval. The estimated bounds themselves have standard errors since $\hat{\beta}_1$ and $\tilde{\beta}_1$ are both subject to sampling variation. If there are no errors in variables, even with multicollinearity, the least squares estimators are unbiased. But with errors in measurement they are not, and the estimated bounds yield (large sample) estimates of the biases.

One important thing to note is that the bounds are usually much too wide and making some special assumptions about the errors, one can get a range of consistent estimates of the parameters. We will illustrate this point.

Consider the regression of Y on X_1 and X_2 with the data in Table 7.3. Let us assume that stock formation is subject to error but X_1 is not.[7]

In this case we have $r_{12}^2 = 0.046$. The regression of Y on X_1 and X_2 gives

$$Y = 0.191X_1 + 0.405X_2 - 16.78 \qquad R^2 = 0.972$$
$$\quad\;\; (0.0087) \qquad (0.319)$$
$$\hat{\sigma}^2 = 155.8$$

The reverse regression gives (note we use X_2 as the regressand)

$$X_2 = 0.239Y - 0.040X_1 + 6.07 \qquad R^2 = 0.139$$

which, when normalized with respect to Y, gives

$$Y = 0.169X_1 + 4.184X_2 - 25.35$$

We thus get the bounds

$$0.169 < \beta_1 < 0.191 \qquad \text{and} \qquad 0.405 < \beta_2 < 4.184$$

The bounds for β_2 are very wide and we can learn more by studying the first equation in (11.4).[8] Suppose that $\lambda = 0.477$, that is, the error variance is 47.7% of the variance of X_2, which is a very generous assumption. In this case, a consistent estimate of β_2 is $2 \times 0.405 = 0.81$, which is far below the upper bound of 4.184. If $\lambda = 0$, that is, there is no error in X_2 a consistent estimate of β_2 is, of course, 0.405. Since $(1 - \rho^2) = 0.954$ in this case, we have to have $\lambda \simeq 0.86$ or the error variance about 86% of the variance of X_2 to say that a consistent estimate of β_2 is 4.184.

Thus, in many problems, any analysis of bounds should be supplemented by some estimates based on some plausible assumptions of error variances, especially when the bounds are very wide. Many of the comments made here regarding the use of bounds in errors in variables models apply to more general models. The purpose of analyzing a specialized model is to show some of the uses and shortcomings of the

---

[7] We will apply the formulas in (11.6) and (11.7) except that we have to interchange the subscripts 1 and 2.
[8] Note that since it is x_2 that we are assuming to have an error, we have to interchange the subscripts 1 and 2.

analysis in terms of bounds and these would not be as transparent when we consider a k-variable model with all variables measured with error.[9]

Two Explanatory Variables: Both Measured with Error

Consider the case where both x_1 and x_2 are measured with error. Let the observed variables be

$$Y = y + v \qquad X_1 = x_1 + u_1 \qquad X_2 = x_2 + u_2$$

We continue to make the same assumptions as before, that is, u_1, u_2, v are mutually uncorrelated and uncorrelated with x_1, x_2, y. As before, we use the normalization $\text{var}(X_1) = 1$, $\text{var}(X_2) = 1$, and $\text{cov}(X_1, X_2) = \rho$. Define

$$\lambda_1 = \frac{\text{var}(u_1)}{\text{var}(X_1)} \qquad \lambda_2 = \frac{\text{var}(u_2)}{\text{var}(X_2)} \qquad \sigma^2 = \text{var}(e + v)$$

We have the equation in observable variables:

$$Y = \beta_1 X_1 + \beta_2 X_2 + w$$

where

$$w = e + v - \beta_1 u_1 - \beta_2 u_2$$

Thus

$$\text{cov}(X_1, w) = -\beta_1 \lambda_1$$

$$\text{cov}(X_2, w) = -\beta_2 \lambda_2$$

We thus have

$$\sigma_{1y} = \text{cov}(Y, X_1) = \beta_1 + \beta_2 \rho - \beta_1 \lambda_1$$

$$\sigma_{2y} = \text{cov}(Y, X_2) = \beta_1 \rho + \beta_2 - \beta_2 \lambda_2 \qquad (11.8)$$

$$\sigma_y^2 = \text{var}(Y) = \beta_1^2 + \beta_2^2 + 2\rho \beta_1 \beta_2 + \sigma^2 - \beta_1^2 \lambda_1 - \beta_2^2 \lambda_2$$

As before, we can derive the probability limits of $\hat{\beta}_1$ and $\hat{\beta}_2$, the least squares estimators of β_1 and β_2. We get

$$\text{plim } \hat{\beta}_1 = \beta_1 - \frac{\beta_1 \lambda_1 - \rho \beta_2 \lambda_2}{1 - \rho^2}$$

$$\qquad (11.9)$$

$$\text{plim } \hat{\beta}_2 = \beta_2 - \frac{\beta_2 \lambda_2 - \rho \beta_1 \lambda_1}{1 - \rho^2}$$

These equations correspond to (11.4) considered earlier (which were for $\lambda_2 = 0$).

---

[9] The case of only one variable measured with error has also been considered by M. D. Levi, "Measurement Errors and Bounded OLS Estimates," *Journal of Econometrics*, Vol. 6, 1977, pp. 165–171. However, considering the two variable case discussed here, it is easy to see that the formulae he gives depend on the variances and covariance of the true variables x_1 and x_2, and σ_u^2. We have presented the results in terms of the sample variances and covariance of X_1 and X_2, as done by Griliches and Ringstad. In this case all we have to do is to make some assumption about λ, the proportion of error variance to total variance in X_1 to derive the bounds.

We will not present the detailed calculations here (because they are tedious), but the equations corresponding to (11.5) obtained from a regression of X_1 on Y and X_2 and normalizing with respect to Y are

$$\text{plim } \tilde{\beta}_1 = \beta_1 + \frac{1}{\Delta}[\beta_2\lambda_2(\beta_2 + \rho\beta_1 - \beta_2\lambda_2) + \sigma^2]$$

$$\text{plim } \tilde{\beta}_2 = \beta_2 - \frac{1}{\Delta}[\beta_2\lambda_2(\beta_1 - \rho\beta_2 - \beta_1\lambda_1) + \rho\sigma^2]$$

(11.10)

where

$$\Delta = \beta_1(1 - \rho^2 - \lambda_1) + \beta_2\lambda_2\rho = \beta_1(1 - \rho^2) - (\beta_1\lambda_1 - \rho\beta_2\lambda_2)$$

[Substituting $\lambda_2 = 0$, we get the results in (11.5).]

If $\bar{\beta}_1$ and $\bar{\beta}_2$ are the estimators of β_1 and β_2 obtained from a regression of X_2 on X_1 and Y, then plim $\bar{\beta}_1$ and plim $\bar{\beta}_2$ are obtained by just interchanging the subscripts 1 and 2 in equations (11.10).

It is easy to see from equations (11.9) and (11.10) that the direction of biases are rather difficult to evaluate. Further, we saw earlier in the case of equations (11.4) and (11.5) that the derived bounds are in many cases rather too wide to be of any practical use and it is better to use equations (11.4) to get a range of consistent estimates based on different assumptions about λ. The problem with equations (11.5) or (11.10) is that they depend on a further unknown parameter σ^2.

In this case, we cannot get any bounds on the parameters using the procedures of calculating probability limits as in equations (11.9) and (11.10). There is an alternative procedure due to Klepper and Leamer[10] but its discussion beyond our scope.

Here we will illustrate the range of consistent estimates of β_1 and β_2 using equations (11.8) or (11.9) with different assumptions about λ_1 and λ_2. This method is useful when we have some rough idea about the range of possible values for λ_1 and λ_2. There is the problem, however, that not all these estimates are valid because the implied estimate of σ^2 obtained from the third equation in (11.8) should be positive and also $\text{var}(x_1)\text{var}(x_2) - [\text{cov}(x_1, x_2)]^2 \geq 0$. This last condition implies that $(1 - \lambda_1)(1 - \lambda_2) - \rho^2 > 0$. Using equations (11.9) we obtain consistent estimates β_1^* and β_2^* of β_1 and β_2 by solving the equations

$$(1 - \rho^2 - \lambda_1)\beta_1^* + \rho\lambda_2\beta_2^* = (1 - \rho^2)\hat{\beta}_1$$

$$\rho\lambda_1\beta_1^* + (1 - \rho^2 - \lambda_2)\beta_2^* = (1 - \rho^2)\hat{\beta}_2$$

(11.11)

The estimate of σ^2 is obtained from the last equation in (11.8). It is

$$\hat{\sigma}^2 = \hat{\sigma}_y^2 - (\beta_1^{*2} + \beta_2^{*2} + 2\rho\beta_1^*\beta_2^* - \lambda_1\beta_1^{*2} - \lambda_2\beta_2^{*2})$$

(11.12)

As an example, let us consider the data in Table 7.3 and a regression of Y on X_1 and X_2. The correlation coefficient between X_1 and X_2 is 0.2156. Hence $\rho = 0.2156$. Also, $\hat{\sigma}_{1y} = 11.9378$ and $\hat{\sigma}_{2y} = 3.2286$.

[10] S. Klepper and E. E. Leamer, "Consistent Sets of Estimates for Regressions With Errors in All Variables," *Econometrica*, Vol. 52, 1984, pp. 163–183.

Table 11.1 Estimates of Regression Parameters and
Error Variance Based on Different Assumptions About
Error Variances

λ_1	λ_2	β_1	β_2	σ^2
0.01	0.10	0.1817	0.4519	155.5
0.01	0.20	0.1687	0.5119	155.5
0.01	0.30	0.1516	0.5903	155.5
0.01	0.40	0.1284	0.6970	155.4
0.02	0.10	0.1837	0.4514	155.5
0.02	0.20	0.1705	0.5114	155.5
0.02	0.30	0.1533	0.5898	155.5
0.02	0.40	0.1298	0.6965	155.4
0.05	0.10	0.1898	0.4500	155.5
0.05	0.20	0.1762	0.5099	155.5
0.05	0.30	0.1585	0.5882	155.5
0.05	0.40	0.1343	0.6949	155.4
0.10	0.10	0.2010	0.4473	155.5
0.10	0.20	0.1867	0.5071	155.5
0.10	0.30	0.1680	0.5853	155.5
0.10	0.40	0.1424	0.6920	155.4

It is reasonable to assume that X_1 (gross domestic production) has smaller measurement errors than X_2 (stock formation). Hence we consider

$$\lambda_1 = 0.01, 0.02, 0.05, 0.10$$

$$\lambda_2 = 0.10, 0.20, 0.30, 0.40$$

Note that for all these values, the condition $(1 - \lambda_1)(1 - \lambda_2) - \rho^2 > 0$ is satisfied. The results of solving equations (11.11) are presented in Table 11.1. The range of consistent estimates of β_1 is (0.128, 0.201) and the range of consistent estimates of β_2 is (0.447, 0.697). Note that the OLS estimates were $\hat{\beta}_1 = 0.191$ and $\hat{\beta}_2 = 0.405$. Thus with the assumptions about error variances we have made, the OLS estimate $\hat{\beta}_2$ is not within the consistent bounds for β_2 that we have obtained.

Note that assuming only X_2 (and not X_1) was measured with error we obtained earlier the bounds

$$0.169 < \beta_1 < 0.191 \quad \text{and} \quad 0.405 < \beta_2 < 4.184$$

The OLS estimates are at the extremes of these bounds. With the assumptions about error variances we have made, the bounds for β_1 are wider but the bounds for β_2 are much narrower.

The important conclusion that emerges from all this discussion and illustrative calculations is that in errors in variables models, making the most general assumptions about error variances leads to very wide bounds for the parameters, thus making no inference possible. On the other hand, making some plausible assumptions about the variances of the errors in the different variables, one could get more reasonable bounds for the parameters. A sensitivity analysis based on reasonable assumptions about error variances would be more helpful than obtaining bounds on very general assumptions.

11.4 REVERSE REGRESSION

In Sections 11.2 and 11.3 we considered two types of regressions. When we have the variables y and x both measured with error (the observed values being Y and X), we consider two regression equations:

1. Regression of Y on X, which is called the "direct" regression.
2. Regression of X on Y, which is called the "reverse" regression.

Reverse regression has been frequently advocated in the case of analysis of salary discrimination.[11] Since the problem is one of the usual errors in variables, both regressions need to be computed and whether reverse regression alone gives the correct estimates depends on the assumptions one makes.

The usual model, in its simplest form, is that of two explanatory variables, one of which is measured with error.

$$y = \beta_1 x_1 + \beta_2 x_2 + u \tag{11.13}$$

where y = salary
x_1 = true qualifications
x_2 = gender (in sex discrimination)
= race (in race discrimination)

What we are interested in is the coefficient of x_2. The problem is that x_1 is measured with error. Let

$$X_1 = \text{measured qualifications}$$

$$X_1 = x_1 + v$$

Suppose we adopt the notation that

$$x_2 = \begin{cases} 1 & \text{for men} \\ 0 & \text{for women} \end{cases}$$

Then $\hat{\beta}_2 > 0$ implies that men are paid more than women with the same qualifications and thus there is sex discrimination. A direct least squares estimation of equation (11.13) with X_1 substituted for x_1, and $\hat{\beta}_2 > 0$ has been frequently used as evidence of sex discrimination.

In the reverse regression

$$X_1 = \gamma_1 y + \gamma_2 x_2 + w \tag{11.14}$$

we are asking whether men are more or less qualified than women having the same

---

[11] There is a large amount of literature on this issue, many papers arguing in favor of "reverse regression." For a survey and different alternative models, see A. S. Goldberger, "Reverse Regression and Salary Discrimination," *Journal of Human Resources*, Vol. 19, No. 3, 1984, pp. 293–318.

salaries. The proponents of the reverse regression argue that to establish discrimination, one has to have $\hat{\gamma}_2 < 0$ in equation (11.14); that is, among men and women receiving equal salaries, the men possess lower qualifications.

The evidence from the reverse regression has been mixed. In some cases $\hat{\gamma}_2 < 0$ but not significant and in some others $\hat{\gamma}_2 > 0$. Conway and Roberts[12] consider data for 274 employees of a Chicago bank in 1976. In their analysis $y = \log$ salary and they get $\hat{\beta}_2 = 0.148$ (standard error 0.036), thus indicating that men are overpaid by about 15% compared with women with the same qualifications. In the reverse regression they get $\hat{\gamma} = -0.0097$ (standard error 0.0202), thus showing no evidence of discrimination one way or the other. In another study by Abowd, Abowd, and Killingsworth,[13] who compare wages for whites and several ethnic groups, the direct regression gave $\hat{\beta}_2 > 0$ and the indirect regression gave $\hat{\gamma}_2 > 0$ (indicating that whites are disfavored). Thus the direct regression showed discrimination and the reverse regression showed reverse discrimination.

Of course, in all these studies, there is no single measure of qualifications and x_1 is a set of variables rather than a single variable. In this case what they do in reverse regression is take the estimated coefficients from the direct regression and take the linear combination of these variables based on these estimated coefficients as the dependent variable and regress it on y and x_2. Since the direct regression gives biased estimates of these coefficients, what we have here is a biased index of qualifications.

The usual errors in variables result in equations (11.4) and (11.5) show that one should not make inferences on the basis of $\hat{\beta}_2$ and $\hat{\gamma}_2$ but obtain bounds for β_2, from the direct regression and reverse regression estimates. As shown in equation (11.7), these bounds depend on the sign of $\rho\beta_1$, where $\rho =$ correlation between X_1 and x_2. Normally, one would expect $\rho > 0$ and $\beta_1 > 0$ and hence we have

$$\text{plim } \tilde{\beta}_2 < \beta_2 < \text{plim } \hat{\beta}_2$$

where $\tilde{\beta}_2$ is the implied estimate of $\hat{\beta}_2$ from the reverse regression.

Note also from equations (11.4) and (11.5) that the (asymptotic) biases depend on two factors: $\lambda = \sigma_u^2/\text{var}(X_1)$ and $\rho =$ correlation between X_1 and x_2. λ is unknown but ρ can be computed from the data. Thus one can generate different estimates of β_2 from these equations based on different assumptions about the value of λ. We will not, however, undertake this exercise here.

11.5 INSTRUMENTAL VARIABLE METHODS

Consider equation (11.2). The reason we cannot use OLS is because the error w_i is correlated with x_i. The instrumental variable method consists of finding a variable

[12] Delores A. Conway and Harry V. Roberts, "Reverse Regression, Fairness and Employment Discrimination," *Journal of Business and Economic Statistics*, Vol. 1, January 1983, pp. 75–85.
[13] A. M. Abowd, J. M. Abowd, and M. R. Killingsworth, "Race, Spanish Origin and Earnings Differentials Among Men: The Demise of Two Stylized Facts," NORC Discussion Paper 83–11, The University of Chicago, Chicago, May 1983.

z_i that is uncorrelated with w_i but correlated with x_i, and estimating β by $\hat{\beta}_{IV} = \sum y_i z_i / \sum x_i z_i$. The variable z_i is called an "instrumental variable."

Note that in the usual regression model $y = \beta x + w$, the normal equation for the OLS estimation of β is

$$\sum x(y - \hat{\beta}x) = 0 \qquad (11.15)$$

This is the sample analog of the assumption we make that $\text{cov}(x, u) = 0$. If this assumption is violated, we cannot use the normal equation (11.15). However, if we have a variable z such that $\text{cov}(z, w) = 0$, we replace the normal equation (11.15) by

$$\sum z(y - \hat{\beta}x) = 0$$

or

$$\hat{\beta}_{IV} = \frac{\sum yz}{\sum xz}$$

which is the instrumental variable (IV) estimator. We can show that the IV estimator is consistent.

$$\text{plim } \hat{\beta}_{IV} = \text{plim} \frac{\sum(\beta x_i + w_i)z_i}{\sum x_i z_i}$$

$$= \beta + \text{plim}\left[\left(\frac{1}{n}\sum w_i z_i\right) \Big/ \frac{1}{n}\sum x_i z_i\right]$$

$$= \beta + \frac{\text{cov}(z, w)}{\text{cov}(z, x)} = \beta$$

since $\text{cov}(z, w) = 0$ and $\text{cov}(z, x) \neq 0$. The reason we want z to be uncorrelated with w but correlated with x is that we want $\text{cov}(z, w) = 0$ but $\text{cov}(z, x) \neq 0$. It is often suggested that z is a "good" instrument if it is highly correlated with x.

In practice it is rather hard to find valid instrumental variables. Usually, the instrumental variables are some variables that are "around," that is, whose data are available but do not belong in the equation. An illustration of this is the study by Griliches and Mason[14] who estimate an earnings function of the form

$$y = \alpha + \beta s + \gamma a + \delta x + u$$

where y is the log wages, s the schooling, a the ability, x the other variables, and u the error term. They substituted an observed test score t for the unobserved ability variable and assumed that it was measured with a random error. They then used a set of instrumental variables such as parental status, regions of origin, and so on. The crucial assumption is that these variables do not belong in the earnings function

[14] Z. Griliches and W. M. Mason, "Education, Income and Ability," *Journal of Political Economy*, Vol. 80, No. 3, Part 2, May 1972, pp. S74–S103.

explicitly, that is, they enter only through their influence on the ability variable. Some such assumption is often needed to justify the use of instrumental variables.

In the Griliches–Mason study the OLS estimation (the coefficients of the "other variables" x are not reported) gave

$$y = \text{const.} + \underset{(0.0458)}{0.1982}(\text{race}) + \underset{(0.0067)}{0.0331}(\text{schooling}) + \underset{(0.00038)}{0.00298}(\text{test score})$$

(Figures in parentheses are standard errors.) The IV estimation gave

$$y = \text{const.} + \underset{(0.0468)}{0.0730}(\text{race}) + \underset{(0.0065)}{0.0483}(\text{schooling}) + \underset{(0.00078)}{0.00889}(\text{test score})$$

The IV estimation thus gave a much higher estimate of the ability coefficient and lower estimate of the race coefficient.

In the case of time series data, lagged values of the measured X_t are often used as instrumental variables. If $X_t = x_t + u_t$ and the measurement errors u_t are serially uncorrelated but the true x_t are serially correlated, then X_{t-1} can be used as an instrumental variable. This suggestion was made as early as 1941 by Riersol. [15]

As an illustration, consider the model

$$Y_t = \beta x_t + e_t$$

$$X_t = x_t + u_t$$

$$x_t = \rho x_{t-1} + v_t$$

(There is no error of observation in Y_t.) Then

$$\text{var}(X_t) = \sigma_{xx} + \sigma_{uu}$$

$$\text{var}(Y_t) = \beta^2 \sigma_{xx} + \sigma_{ee}$$

$$\text{cov}(X_t, Y_t) = \beta \sigma_{xx}$$

$$\text{cov}(X_t, X_{t-1}) = \rho \sigma_{xx}$$

$$\text{cov}(Y_t, Y_{t-1}) = \beta^2 \rho \sigma_{xx}$$

$$\text{cov}(Y_t, X_{t-1}) = \text{cov}(X_t, Y_{t-1}) = \beta \rho \sigma_{xx}$$

Thus we can estimate β by

$$\hat{\beta}_1 = \frac{\text{cov}(Y_t, X_{t-1})}{\text{cov}(X_t, X_{t-1})} \qquad \text{or} \qquad \hat{\beta}_2 = \frac{\text{cov}(Y_t, Y_{t-1})}{\text{cov}(X_t, Y_{t-1})}$$

The former amounts to using X_{t-1} as the instrumental variable, and the latter amounts to using Y_{t-1} as the instrumental variable.

One other instrumental variable method is the *method of grouping*. Three main grouping methods have been suggested in the literature, by Wald, Bartlett, and

---

[15] O. Riersol, "Confluence Analysis by Means of Lag Moments and Other Methods of Confluence Analysis," *Econometrica*, 1941, pp. 1–24.

Durbin.[16] In Wald's method we rank the X's and form those above the median X into one group and those below the median into another group. If the means in the two groups are, respectively, $\bar{Y}_1, \bar{X}_1$ and $\bar{Y}_2, \bar{X}_2$, we estimate the slope β by

$$\beta^* = (\bar{Y}_2 - \bar{Y}_1)/(\bar{X}_2 - \bar{X}_1)$$

This amounts to using the instrumental variable

$$Z_i = \begin{cases} 1 & \text{if } X_i > \text{median} \\ -1 & \text{if } X_i < \text{median} \end{cases}$$

and using the estimator $\beta^* = \sum Y_i Z_i / \sum X_i Z_i$. Bartlett suggested ranking X's, forming three groups, and discarding the $n/3$ observations in the middle group. His estimator of β is

$$\beta^* = \frac{\bar{Y}_3 - \bar{Y}_1}{\bar{X}_3 - \bar{X}_1}$$

This amounts to using the instrumental variable

$$Z_i = \begin{cases} +1 & \text{for the top } n/3 \text{ observations} \\ -1 & \text{for the bottom } n/3 \text{ observations} \end{cases}$$

Durbin suggests using the ranks of X_i as the instrumental variables. Thus

$$\beta^* = \frac{\sum i Y_i}{\sum i X_i}$$

where the X_i are ranked in ascending order and the Y_i are the values of Y corresponding to the X_i. If the errors are large, the ranks will be correlated with the errors and the estimators given by Durbin's procedure will be inconsistent. Since the estimators given by Wald's procedure and Bartlett's procedure also depend on the ranking of the observations, these estimators can also be expected to be inconsistent. Pakes[17] investigates the consistency properties of the grouping estimators in great detail and concludes that except in very few cases they are inconsistent, quite contrary to the usual presumption that they are consistent (although inefficient).

Thus the grouping estimators are of not much use in errors in variables models.

11.6 PROXY VARIABLES

Often, the variables we measure are surrogates for the variables we really want to measure. It is customary to call the measured variable a "proxy" variable—it is a proxy for the true variable. Some commonly used proxies are years of schooling for

---

[16] A. Wald, "The Fitting of Straight Lines If Both Variables Are Subject to Errors," *Annals of Mathematical Statistics*, 1940, pp. 284–300; M. S. Bartlett, "Fitting of Straight Lines When Both Variables Are Subject to Error," *Biometrics*, 1949, pp. 207–212; J. Durbin, "Errors in Variables," *Review of International Statistical Institute*, 1954, pp. 23–32.
[17] Ariel Pakes, "On the Asymptotic Bias of Wald-Type Estimators of a Straight Line When Both Variables Are Subject to Error," *International Economic Review*, Vol. 23, 1982, pp. 491–497.

level of education, test scores for ability, and so on. If we treat the proxy variable as the true variable with a measurement error satisfying the assumptions of the errors in variables model we have been discussing, the analysis of proxy variables is just the same as the one we have been discussing. However, there are some other issues associated with the use of proxy variables that we need to discuss.

Sometimes, in multiple regression models it is not the coefficient of the proxy variable that we are interested in but the other coefficients. An example of this is the earnings function in Section 11.5, where our interest may be in estimating the effect of years of schooling on income and not the coefficient of ability (for which we use the test score as a proxy). In such cases one question that is often asked is whether it is not better to omit the proxy variable altogether. To simplify matters, consider the two-regressor case:

$$y = \beta x + \gamma z + u \tag{11.16}$$

where x is observed but z is unobserved. We make the usual assumption about x, z and the error term u. Instead of z we observe a proxy $p = z + e$. As in the usual errors-in-variables literature, we assume that e is uncorrelated with z, x and u. Let the population variances and covariances be denoted by M_{xx}, M_{xz}, M_{xp}, and so on.

If we omit the variable z altogether from (11.16) and the estimator of β is $\hat{\beta}_{ov}$, then using the omitted-variable formula [Equation (4.17)], we get

$$\text{plim } \hat{\beta}_{ov} = \beta + \gamma \frac{M_{xz}}{M_{xx}} \tag{11.17}$$

On the other hand, if we substitute the proxy p for z in equation (11.16) and the estimator of β is $\hat{\beta}_p$, it can be shown that [18]

$$\text{plim } \hat{\beta}_p = \beta + \gamma \frac{M_{xz}}{M_{xx}} \left[\frac{\sigma_e^2}{\sigma_e^2 + M_{zz}(1 - \rho^2)} \right] \tag{11.18}$$

where ρ is the correlation between x and z. The bias due to omission of the variable z is $\gamma(M_{xz}/M_{xx})$. The bias due to the use of the proxy p for z is the same multiplied by the ratio in brackets of (11.18). Since this ratio is less than 1, it follows that the bias is reduced by using the proxy. McCallum and Wickens have argued on the basis of this result that it is desirable to use even a poor proxy.

However, there are four major qualifications to this conclusion:

1. One should look at the variances of the estimators as well and not just at bias. Aigner [19] studied the mean-square errors of the two estimators $\hat{\beta}_{ov}$ and $\hat{\beta}_p$ and derived a sufficient condition under which $\text{MSE}(\hat{\beta}_p) \geq \text{MSE}(\hat{\beta}_{ov})$. This

[18] G. S. Maddala, *Econometrics* (New York: McGraw-Hill, 1977), p. 160. This result was derived in B. T. McCallum, "Relative Asymptotic Bias from Errors of Omission and Measurement," *Econometrica*, July 1972, pp. 757–758 and M. R. Wickens, "A Note on the Use of Proxy Variables," *Econometrica*, July 1972, pp. 365–372.

[19] D. J. Aigner, "MSE Dominance of Least Squares with Errors of Observation," *Journal of Econometrics*, Vol. 2, 1974, 365–372.

condition is

$$\frac{1 - (1 - \lambda n)\rho^2}{[1 - (1 - \lambda)\rho^2]^2} \frac{\lambda}{n} > \rho^2$$

where

$$\lambda = \frac{\sigma_e^2}{\sigma_e^2 + M_{zz}}$$

and ρ is as defined earlier. From this he concludes that the use of a proxy, although generally advisable may not be a superior strategy to dropping the error-ridden variable altogether. Kinal and Lahiri[20] analyze this problem in greater detail and generality. They give several alternative expressions to Aigner's. They conclude that including even a poor proxy is advisable under a wide range of empirical situations when the alternative is to discard it altogether.

2. The second major qualitifcation is that the proxy variable does not always fall in the pure errors-in-variables case. Usually, the proxy variable is "some variable" that also depends on the same factors, that is, p is of the form

$$p = \alpha x + \delta z + \varepsilon$$

Since z is unobserved and does not have any natural units of measurement, we will assume that $\delta = 1$. We can then write

$$p = \alpha x + z + e \qquad (11.19)$$

We will also assume that M_{ue} is not zero. Now it does not necessarily follow that including the proxy p leads to a smaller bias in the estimator of β in equation (11.16).[21] Thus, except in cases where the proxies fall in the category of pure errors in variables, it does not follow that using even a poor proxy is better than using none at all.

3. The third qualification is that the reduction-in-bias argument does not apply if the proxy variable is a dummy variable.[22] This is the case where we do not observe z but we know when it is in different ranges. For instance, we do not know how to measure "effective education" but we use dummies for the amount of education (e.g., grade school, high school, college). In this case it does not necessarily follow that using the proxy results in a smaller bias compared with the omission of z altogether.

4. The reduction-in-bias argument also does not apply if the other explanatory variables are measured with error.[23] In equation (11.16) suppose that the variable x is measured with error so that what we observe is $X = x + v$. We

---

[20] T. Kinal and K. Lahiri, "Specification Error Analysis with Stochastic Regressors," *Econometrica*, Vol. 51, 1983, pp. 1209–1219.

[21] Maddala, *Econometrics*, p. 161.

[22] See Maddala, *Econometrics*, pp. 161–162, for an example due to D. M. Grether.

[23] See Maddala, *Econometrica*, pp. 304–305 referring to the results from the papers by Welch and Griliches on estimation of the effects of schooling on income.

will assume that $\text{cov}(x, v) = \text{cov}(x, z) = \text{cov}(v, e) = 0$. We can consider two estimates of β, one using the proxy p and the other omitting it. Now we cannot say anything about the direction of the biases, nor about whether the bias will increase or decrease with the introduction of p.[24]

Coefficient of the Proxy Variable

The preceding discussion referred to a situation where our interest was in the coefficients of variables other than the proxy variable. There are also many situations where our interest is in the coefficient of the unobserved variable y in (11.16). Since z is not observed, we cannot think of any natural units of measurement for z. Thus it is not the magnitude of y but the sign of y with which we are concerned. A question we would like to ask is under what conditions the use of the proxy p will give us the correct sign for y. To answer this question we need a method of combining subjective assessments of how good the proxies are with objective information on the observed variables.

This problem has been analyzed by Krasker and Pratt.[25] Consider equation (11.16). Let the correlation coefficient between the unobserved variable z and the proxy variable p be r^*. The condition that the coefficient of the proxy variables has the same sign as y the coefficient of the unobserved variable in (11.16) is

$$(r^*)^2 > R^2_{p \cdot x} + 1 - R^2_{p \cdot yx} \tag{11.20}$$

As an example they consider the determinants of motor vehicle deaths. The data are cross-section data in 1960 for the 48 contiguous states in the United States. The variables are:

y_i = logarithm of the number of motor vehicle deaths per capita in the ith state in 1960

x_{1i} = dummy variable defined to be 1 if the ith state had mandatory motor vehicle inspection, 0 otherwise

x_{2i} = logarithm of per capital gasoline consumption in state i in 1960

x_{3i} = logarithm of the fraction of the ith state's population that was 18–24 in 1960

x_{4i} = logarithm of the number of automobiles (per capita) older than 9 years in state i in 1960

The estimated regression equation (with standard errors in parentheses) is

---

[24] Finis Welch, "Human Capital Theory: Education, Discriminations and Life Cycles," *American Economic Review*, May 1975, p. 67; Zvi Griliches, "Estimating the Returns to Schooling: Some Econometric Problems," *Econometrica*, Vol. 45, 1977, p. 12.

[25] W. S. Krasker and J. W. Pratt, "Bounding the Effects of Proxy Variables on Regression Coefficients," *Econometrica*, Vol. 54, 1986, pp. 641–655.

$$\hat{y}_i = -4.53 - 0.23x_{1i} + 1.17x_{2i} + 1.49x_{3i} + 0.04x_{4i}$$
$$\phantom{\hat{y}_i = }(1.77)(0.06)(0.23)(0.37)(0.12)$$

x_{2i} is considered a proxy variable for an unobserved variable z which is "per capita exposure to situations that create the possibility of fatal accidents." The question is whether the proxy has the same sign as the coefficient of this unobserved variable z. The R^2 from a regression of x_{2i} on x_{1i}, x_{3i}, x_{4i} is 0.3895. The R^2 from a regression of x_{2i} on $y_i, x_{1i}, x_{3i}, x_{4i}$ is 0.6193. Hence, according to (11.20), we can be sure that the coefficient of x_{2i} has the same sign as the coefficient of z, regardless of other correlations, if we are sure that the correlation between x_{2i} and z exceeds

$$(0.3895 + 1 - 0.6193)^{1/2} = 0.878$$

Krasker and Pratt conclude that "To ensure that the signs of the coefficients coincide with the signs of the unobservable true variables, the proxies must be of much higher quality than could be hoped for in the actual context."

Krasker and Pratt also give alternative formulas and methods of determining the correctness of the sign for the other coefficient β in (11.16) as well. Since these expressions are somewhat complicated, we will not reproduce them here. The condition given in (11.20) would enable us to judge the sign of γ. One reason why they get such a stringent condition is that they relax the usual assumptions made in the errors-in-variables models. They do not make the assumption that the error e in p is independent of z, x, or u.

To compute the Krasker–Pratt criterion (11.20) we have to compute the R^2's from a regression of the proxy on the other explanatory variables, and a regression of the proxy on the other explanatory variables *and* the dependent variable.

11.7 SOME OTHER PROBLEMS

We introduced the simple errors in variables model in Section 11.2 as a starting point of our analysis. This simple model may not be applicable with most economic data because of the violation of some of the assumptions implied in this simple model. The crucial assumptions made in that model are:

1. The errors have zero mean.
2. The covariances between the errors and the systematic parts are zero.
3. The covariances between the errors themselves are zero.

Based on these conclusions, we showed that the OLS estimator $\hat{\beta}$ is not consistent and is biased toward zero. We will now show that:

1. The problem of obtaining consistent estimators can be solved in some cases if we have more equations in which the same error-ridden variable occurs.
2. If we consider correlated errors, the least squares estimators need not be biased toward zero. In fact, the OLS estimator $\hat{\beta}$ may overestimate (rather than underestimate) β.

Thus the conclusions derived in Section 11.2 will not be correct.

The Case of Multiple Equations

The case of multiple equations can be illustrated as follows. Suppose that

$$y_1 = \beta_1 x + e_1$$

$$y_2 = \beta_2 x + e_2$$

x is not observed. Instead, we observe $X = x + u$. Suppose that e_1, e_2, and u are mutually uncorrelated and also uncorrelated with x. Also, let $\text{var}(e_1) = \sigma_1^2$, $\text{var}(e_2) = \sigma_2^2$, $\text{var}(u) = \sigma_u^2$, and $\text{var}(x) = \sigma_x^2$. Then we have

$$\text{var}(y_1) = \beta_1^2 \sigma_x^2 + \sigma_1^2$$

$$\text{var}(y_2) = \beta_2^2 \sigma_x^2 + \sigma_2^2$$

$$\text{cov}(y_1 y_2) = \beta_1 \beta_2 \sigma_x^2$$

$$\text{cov}(y_1, X) = \beta_1 \sigma_x^2$$

$$\text{cov}(y_2, X) = \beta_2 \sigma_x^2$$

$$\text{var}(X) = \sigma_x^2 + \sigma_u^2$$

These six equations can be solved to get estimates of β_1, β_2, σ_x^2, σ_u^2, σ_1^2, and σ_2^2. Specifically, we have

$$\hat{\beta}_1 = \frac{\text{cov}(y_1, y_2)}{\text{cov}(X, y_2)} \quad \text{and} \quad \hat{\beta}_2 = \frac{\text{cov}(y_2, y_1)}{\text{cov}(X, y_1)}$$

In effect, this is like using y_2 as an instrumental variable in the equation $y_1 = \beta_1 X + w_1$ and y_1 as an instrumental variable in the equation $y_2 = \beta_2 X + w_2$. Further elaboration of this approach of solving the errors-in-variables (and unobservable variables) problem by increasing the number of equations can be found in Goldberger.[26]

As an illustration, suppose that

$$y_1 = \text{expenditures on automobiles}$$

$$y_2 = \text{expenditures on other durables}$$

$$x = \text{permanent income}$$

$$X = \text{measured income}$$

If we are given only y_1 and X (or y_2 and X), we are in the single-equation errors-in-variables problem and we cannot get consistent estimators for β_1 (or β_2). But if we are given y_1, y_2, and X, we can get consistent estimators for both β_1 and β_2.

Correlated Errors

Until now we have assumed that the errors of observation are mutually uncorrelated and also uncorrelated with the systematic parts. If we drop these

[26] A. S. Goldberger, "Structural Equation Methods in the Social Sciences," *Econometrica*, 1972, pp. 979–1002.

assumptions, things will get more complicated. For example, consider the model $y = \beta x + e$.

The observed values are $X = x + u$ and $Y = y + v$, where u and v are the measurement errors. Let σ_{xy} denote the covariance between x and y, with a similar notation for all the other covariances. If the least squares estimate of β from a regression of Y on X is $\hat{\beta}$, then

$$\text{plim } \hat{\beta} = \frac{\text{cov}(YX)}{\text{var}(X)} = \frac{\text{cov}(x+u)(y+v)}{\text{var}(x+u)}$$

$$= \frac{\sigma_{xy} + \sigma_{xv} + \sigma_{yu} + \sigma_{uv}}{\sigma_{xx} + 2\sigma_{xu} + \sigma_{uu}}$$

$$= \frac{\beta\sigma_{xx} + \sigma_{xv} + \sigma_{yu} + \sigma_{uv}}{\sigma_{xx} + 2\sigma_{xu} + \sigma_{uv}}$$

Since $\sigma_{yu} = \beta\sigma_{xu}$ and $\sigma_{xv} = \text{cov}[(y-e)/\beta, v] = \sigma_{yv}/\beta$, we have

$$\text{plim } \hat{\beta} = \frac{\beta(\sigma_{xx} + \sigma_{xu}) + \sigma_{yv}/\beta + \sigma_{uv}}{\sigma_{xx} + 2\sigma_{xu} + \sigma_{uu}}$$

Now even if there is no error in x (i.e., $u = 0$), we find that plim $\hat{\beta} \neq \beta$ since $\sigma_{yv} \neq 0$. Thus it is not just errors in x that create a problem as in the earlier case.

One can calculate the nature of the bias in $\hat{\beta}$ making different assumptions about the different covariances. We need not pursue this further here. What is important to note is that one can get either underestimation or overestimation of β. With economic data where such correlations are more the rule than an exception, it is important not to believe that the slope coefficients are always underestimated in the presence of errors in observations, as is suggested by the classical analysis of errors-in-variables models.

We have all along omitted the intercept term. If there is an intercept term α, i.e., our true relationship is $y = \alpha + \beta x + e$, and instead we estimate $Y = \alpha + \beta X + w$, then the least squares estimator $\hat{\beta}$ underestimates β and consequently the least squares estimator $\hat{\alpha}$ will overestimate α. If, however, the errors do not have a zero mean [i.e., $X = x + u$ and $E(u) \neq 0$], these conclusions need not hold.

SUMMARY

1. In the single-equation model with a single explanatory variable that is measured with error, the least squares estimator of β underestimates the true β. Specifically, the bias is $\beta\lambda$, where λ is the proportion of the error variance in the variance of x. This result is based on the assumption that the errors have zero means and have zero covariance with the systematic parts and among themselves.

2. We can obtain bounds for the true coefficient β by computing the regression coefficient of y on x and the reciprocal of the regression coefficient of x on y (Section 11.2).

3. In a model with two explanatory variables x_1 and x_2 with coefficients β_1 and β_2

where only x_1 is measured with error, we can show that the bias in the estimator of β_1 is $(-\beta_1\lambda)/(1-\rho^2)$, where ρ is the correlation between the *measured* values of x_1 and x_2. Also, the bias in the estimator of $\beta_2 = -\rho$ (the bias in the estimator of β_1). Similar results can be derived when there are many explanatory variables. Some papers in the literature derive the expressions for the bias in terms of the correlations between the true unobserved variables. These expressions are not very useful in practice. Here we derive the expressions in terms of the correlations of the observed variables. The only unknown factor is λ, the proportion of error variance in the variance of the error-ridden variable (Section 11.3).

4. As with the model with a single explanatory variable, we can derive bounds for the true coefficients by running two regressions. These bounds are given in equations (11.6) and (11.7). However, these bounds are not comparable to confidence intervals. The estimated bounds themselves have standard errors. We have illustrated with an example that these bounds can sometimes, be so wide as to be almost useless. In many problems, therefore, it is better to supplement them with estimates based on some plausible assumptions about the error variances.

5. In the model with two explanatory variables, if both the variables are measured with error, the direction of biases in the OLS estimators cannot be easily evaluated [see equations (11.9) and (11.10)]. Making the most general assumptions about error variances often leads to wide bounds for the parameters, thus making no inference possible. On the other hand, making some plausible assumptions about the error variances, one can get more reasonable bounds for the parameters. This point is illustrated with an example.

6. In the application of the errors-in-varaibles model to problems of discrimination, the "reverse regression" has often been advocated. The arguments for and against this procedure are reviewed in Section 11.4.

7. One method for obtaining consistent estimators for the parameters in errors-in-variables models is the instrumental variable method. In practice it is rather hard to find valid instrumental variables. In time-series data lagged values of the measured x_t are often used as instrumental variables. Some grouping methods are often suggested for the estimation of errors-in-variables models. These methods can be viewed as instrumental variable methods. However, their use is not recommended. Except in special cases, the estimators they yield are not consistent.

8. Often in econometric work it is customary to use some surrogate variables for the variables we cannot measure. These surrogate variables are called proxy variables. In an equation like

$$y = \beta x + \gamma z + u$$

where we use a proxy p for z, a question that has often been asked is whether it is better to leave out p completely if we are interested in estimating β. Assuming that p falls in the category of the usual errors in variables, it has been shown that the bias in the estimator for β is reduced if we leave p in the equation. On the basis of this result it has been argued that even a poor proxy is better than none. However, this conclusion does not necessarily hold good if we take into account the variances of the estimators, or if the proxy is a dummy variable, or if the proxy does not fall in the category of the usual errors in variables. The conclusion also does not follow if x itself is measured with error.

9. In case we are interested in the coefficient γ, a question often arises whether the use of the proxy p gives us the correct sign. A criterion for determining this is given in equation (11.20)

10. If there are many explanatory variables that depend on the same error-ridden variable, sometimes we can use the dependent variables in the other equations as instrumental variables for the estimation of the parameters in each equation. An example of this is given in Section 11.7. Furthermore, all these assumptions about bias are invalid in the presence of correlated errors (see Section 11.7).

EXERCISES

1. Explain the meaning of each of the following terms.
   (a) Errors in variables bias.
   (b) Bounds for parameters.
   (c) Reverse regression.
   (d) Grouping methods.
   (e) Proxy variables.
2. Examine whether the following statements are true, false, or uncertain. Give a short explanation. If a statement is not true in general but is true under some conditions, state the conditions.
   (a) Errors in variables lead to estimates of the regression coefficients that are biased toward zero.
   (b) In errors-in-variables models we can always get two estimators $\hat{\beta}_1$ and $\hat{\beta}_2$ such that

   $$\text{plim } \hat{\beta}_1 < \beta < \text{plim } \hat{\beta}_2$$

   Thus, even though we cannot get a confidence interval, we can get bounds for the parameters that will serve the same purpose.
   (c) Grouping methods give consistent (although inefficient) estimators for the regression parameters in errors-in-variables models. Since they are very easy to compute, they should be used often.
   (d) It is always desirable to use even a poor proxy than to drop an error-ridden variable from an equation.
   (e) If we have an unobserved variable in an equation and we are interested in the sign of its coefficient, we should always use a proxy, since the estimated coefficient of the proxy variable will give us the correct sign.
   (f) In regressions of income on schooling where schooling is measured with error, omitting variables that measure ability will overestimate the effect of schooling on income.
   (g) In part (f) the bias in the estimator of the effect of schooling on income can be reduced if we include a proxy like test score for ability.
   (h) In part (g), if ability is measurable, then we should *always* include the measure available, in the earnings functions.
   (i) In an analysis of discrimination in salaries an investigator finds that the direct regression shows discrimination, whereas the reverse regression shows reverse discrimination. This proves that there is no evidence of discrimination in salaries.

3. Consider a regression model

$$y = \alpha_0 + \alpha_1 x_1 + \alpha_2 x_2 + \alpha_3 x_3 + u$$

The variable x_1 is not observed, but we use a proxy p for it. Let $\hat{\alpha}_1$ be the estimator of α_1 obtained from the multiple regression equation. If you are told that the correlation between x_1 and p is at least 0.8, explain how you will determine whether $\hat{\alpha}_1$ has the correct sign (same sign as α_1).

4. Consider the regression model

$$y = \beta_1 x_1 + \beta_2 x_2 + u$$

x_1 is not observed. The observed value is $X_1 = x_1 + e$, where e is uncorrelated with x_1, x_2, and u. Let $\gamma = \mathrm{var}(e)/\mathrm{var}(X_1)$. Suppose that we drop x_2 from the equation. Let the OLS estimator of β_1 be $\hat{\beta}_1$. Show that

$$\mathrm{plim}\,\hat{\beta}_1 = \beta_1 - \gamma\beta_1 + \beta_2 b_{21}$$

where b_{21} is the regression coefficient from a regression of x_2 on X_1. If $\tilde{\beta}_1$ is the estimator of β_1 from a regression of y on X_1 and x_2, show that

$$\mathrm{plim}\,\tilde{\beta}_1 = \beta_1 - \frac{\gamma\beta_1}{1 - r^2}$$

where r is the correlation between X_1 and x_2. [This is equation (11.4) derived in the text.]

5. In Exercise 4 compute the two probability limits if the true equation is

$$y = 1.0x_1 + 0.5x_2 + u$$

$$\gamma = 0.1 \qquad \mathrm{var}(X_1) = \mathrm{var}(x_2) = 9 \qquad r = 0.5$$

What do you conclude from these results?

12

Diagnostic Checking, Model Selection, And Specification Testing

12.1 INTRODUCTION

The early developments in econometrics were concerned with the problems of estimation of an econometric model once the model was specified. The major preoccupation of econometricians was with devising methods of estimation that produced consistent and efficient estimates of the parameters. These are the methods we discussed in the previous chapters. Sometimes some simplified methods like two-stage least squares were suggested because some other methods like limited-information maximum likelihood (LIML) were complicated to compute. With the recent developments in computer technology, such search for simplified methods of estimation is no longer worthwhile, at least in a majority of problems.

During recent years the attention of econometricians has been diverted to the problems of:

1. Checking the adequacy of the specification of the model. This is called "diagnostic checking" and "specification testing."
2. Choosing between alternative specifications of the model. This is called "model selection."
3. Devising methods of estimation based on weaker assumptions about the error distributions. This is called "semiparametric estimation."

The last area is well beyond the scope of this book and will not be discussed at all. The first two areas are also very vast in scope. Hence what we will do is to consider only a few of the major developments.

It is, of course, true that the problem of diagnostic checking has not been completely ignored. In fact, we discussed some tests for this purpose in the earlier chapters. For instance:

1. Tests for parameter stability in Chapter 4.
2. Tests for heteroscedasticity in Chapter 5.
3. Tests for autocorrelation in Chapter 6.

However, these tests are all based on least squares residuals, and during recent years some alternative residuals have been suggested. Also, tests for diagnostic checking have been more systematized (and incorporated in computer programs like the SAS regression program). The limitations of some standard tests have been noticed and further modifications have been suggested. For instance, in Chapter 6 we discussed the limitations of the DW test, which has been the most commonly used "diagnostic test" for many years.

We begin our discussion with diagnostic tests based on the least squares residuals. Here we summarize the tests discussed in the earlier chapters and discuss some other tests. We will then present some alternatives to least squares residuals and the diagnostic tests based on them. Next, we discuss some problems in model selection and specification testing. Many of the specification tests involve "expanded regressions," that is, the addition of residuals or some other constructed variables as regressors to the original model and testing for the significance of the coefficients of these added variables. Thus most of these tests can be easily implemented using the standard regression packages.

12.2 DIAGNOSTIC TESTS BASED ON LEAST SQUARES RESIDUALS

Diagnostic tests are tests that are meant to "diagnose" some problems with the models that we are estimating. The least squares residuals play an important role in many diagnostic tests. We have already discussed some of these tests, such as tests for parameter stability in Chapter 4, tests for heteroscedasticity in Chapter 5, and tests for autocorrelation in Chapter 6. Here we discuss two other tests using least squares residuals.

Tests for Omitted Variables

Consider the linear regression model

$$y_t = \beta x_t + u_t$$

To test whether the model is misspecified by the omission of a variable z_t, we have to estimate the model

$$y_t = \beta x_t + \gamma z_t + u_t$$

and test the hypothesis $\gamma = 0$.

If data on z_t are available, there is no problem. All we do is regress y_t on x_t and z_t and test whether the coefficient of z_t is zero. Suppose, on the other hand, that we use the following procedure:

1. Regress y_t on x_t and get the residual $\bar{u}_t$.
2. Regress $\bar{u}_t$ on z_t. Let the regression coefficient be $\hat{\gamma}$. Test the hypothesis $\gamma = 0$ using this regression equation.

What is wrong with this procedure?

The answer is that $\tilde{\gamma}$ is an inconsistent estimator of γ unless $\gamma = 0$. Furthermore, the distribution of $\tilde{\gamma}$ is complex and the standard errors provided by the least squares estimation of step 2 will not be the correct ones. If the least squares residuals at step 1 are to be used, we should regress them on z_t *and* x_t and then test whether the coefficient of z_t is zero.[1]

Thus if we are to use the residuals $\bar{u}_t$ from a regression of y_t on x_t for testing specification errors caused by omitted variables, it is advisable to regress $\bar{u}_t$ on z_t *and* x_t and not z_t only, and test the hypothesis that the coefficient of z_t is zero.

When observations on z are not available, we use a proxy $\tilde{z}$ for z. The preceding results apply to this case as well.[2] That is, an appropriate test for omitted variables is to estimate the model

$$y_t = \beta x_t + \gamma \tilde{z}_t + v_t$$

and test the hypothesis $\gamma = 0$. Alternatively, if we are using the residuals $\bar{u}_t$ from a regression of y_t on x_t, we have to regress $\bar{u}_t$ on $\tilde{z}_t$ *and* x_t and then test whether the coefficient of $\tilde{z}_t$ is zero. Of course, we need not go through this circuitous procedure, but the reason for discussing this is to make clear the distinction between tests for heteroscedasticity discussed in Chapter 5 and tests for omitted variables.

---

[1] We are omitting the detailed proofs. They can be found in the paper by A. R. Pagan and A. D. Hall, "Diagnostic Tests as Residual Analysis" with discussion, *Econometric Reviews*, Vol. 2, 1983, pp. 159–218.
[2] The only problem is that if $\tilde{z}$ is uncorrelated with z, the test would have low power, but cases where $\tilde{z}$ is uncorrelated with z are rare.

Ramsey[3] suggests the use of $\hat{y}_t^2$, $\hat{y}_t^3$ and $\hat{y}_t^4$ as proxies for z_t, where $\hat{y}_t$ is the predicted value of y_t from a regression of y_t on x_t.
The test procedure is as follows:

1. Regress y_t on x_t and get $\hat{y}_t$.
2. Regress y_t on x_t, $\hat{y}_t^2$, $\hat{y}_t^3$ and $\hat{y}_t^4$ and test the hypothesis that the coefficients of the powers of $\hat{y}_t$ are zero.

Note that this test is slightly different from Ramsey's test for heteroskedasticity discussed in Section 5.2. That test proceeds as follows:

1. Regress y_t on x_t and get the residual $\hat{u}_t$.
2. Regress $\hat{u}_t$ on $\hat{y}_t^2$, $\hat{y}_t^3$, and $\hat{y}_t^4$ and test that the coefficients of these variables are zero.

As explained earlier, if we want to use $\hat{u}_t$ to test for omitted variables, we have to include x_t as an extra explanatory variable. This is the difference between the two Ramsey tests.

Tests for ARCH Effects

In econometric models, the uncertainty in the economic relationship is captured by the variance σ^2 of the error term u_t. It has been found that it is important to model this error variance because it affects the behavior of economic agents. One such model is the ARCH model (Autoregressive Conditionally Heteroscedastic model) suggested by Engle.[4] In this model the unconditional variance $E(u_t^2)$ is constant but the conditional variance $E(u_t^2 \mid x_t)$ is not. Denoting this conditional variance by σ_t^2, the model suggested by Engle is

$$\sigma_t^2 = \sigma^2 + \gamma u_{t-1}^2 \qquad \gamma > 0$$

that is, the variance of the current error term u_t is higher if the past error term is higher. An unusually high disturbance term in one period results in an increase in uncertainty for the next period. If $\gamma = 0$, there is no ARCH effect and the usual methods of estimation apply. If $\gamma \neq 0$, we have to use more complicated maximum likelihood procedures to estimate the model.

A test for ARCH effect using the least squares residuals proceeds as follows:

1. Regress y_t on x_t. Obtain $\hat{u}_t$.
2. Regress $\hat{u}_t^2$ on $\hat{u}_{t-1}^2$ and test whether the regression coefficient is zero.

A large number of studies, particularly those of speculative prices, have reported significant ARCH effects. However, one has to be careful in interpreting the results

---

[3] J. B. Ramsey, "Tests for Specification Errors in Classical Linear Least Squares Regression Analysis," *Journal of the Royal Statistical Society, Series B*, Vol. 31, 1969, pp. 350–371.
[4] R. F. Engle, "Autoregressive Conditional Heteroscedasticity with Estimates of the Variance of United Kingdom Inflation," *Econometrica*, Vol. 50 1982, pp. 987–1007. See also Section 6.11.

because $\hat{u}_{t-1}^2$ might be acting as a proxy for omitted lagged values of y_t and x_t from the equation. (Note that $\hat{u}_{t-1} = y_{t-1} - \hat{\beta}x_{t-1}$.) Thus the ARCH test should be performed after including a sufficient number of lagged values of y_t and x_t in the equation. [5]

12.3 PROBLEMS WITH LEAST SQUARES RESIDUALS

In our discussion of heteroskedasticity in Chapter 5 and autocorrelation in Chapter 6, we considered only the least squares residuals $\hat{u}_i$ obtained from the least squares regression. The problem with these residuals, as we will demonstrate, is that they are heteroskedastic and autocorrelated *even if* the true errors have a common variance and are serially independent. This heteroskedasticity and autocorrelation depends on the particular values of the explanatory variables in the sample. That is why the Durbin–Watson test gives an inconclusive region. Durbin and Watson obtained lower and upper bounds for their test statistic that are valid irrespective of what values the explanatory variables take. Presumably, the bounds can be improved with a knowledge of the explanatory variables. In fact, we argued that with most economic variables, the upper limit is the one to use. An alternative solution is to construct residuals that have the same properties as the true errors. That is, if the errors have mean zero and constant variance σ^2 and are serially independent, the residuals also exhibit these same properties. One such set of residuals is the "recursive residuals" which are discussed in Section 12.4. First we demonstrate the problems with the least squares residuals.

During recent years separate books have been written on just the topic of residuals. [6] This is because an analysis of residuals is very important for all diagnostic tests.

The *least squares residuals* are obtained from the least squares regression. For simplicity of exposition let us assume that there is only one explanatory variable and no constant term, so that the regression equation is

$$y_i = \beta x_i + u_i$$

The least squares residuals are

$$\hat{u}_i = y_i - \hat{\beta}x_i \qquad \text{where} \quad \hat{\beta} = \frac{\sum x_i y_i}{\sum x_i^2}$$

---

[5] The point is similar to the one made in Section 6.9, where it was argued that sometimes the observed serial correlation in the residuals could be a consequence of misspecified dynamics (i.e., omission of lagged values of y_t and x_t from the equation).

[6] For instance, C. Dubbelman, *Disturbances in the Linear Model: Estimation and Hypothesis Testing* (The Hague: Martinus Nihjoff, 1978), and R. D. Cook and S. Weisberg, *Residuals and Influence in Regression* (London: Chapman & Hall, 1982).

These residuals satisfy the relationship [7]

$$\sum x_i \hat{u}_i = 0$$

Defining $S_{xx} = \sum x_i^2$, we can write $\hat{u}_i$ as

$$\hat{u}_i = y_i - \hat{\beta} x_i$$

$$= y_i - \frac{1}{S_{xx}}(x_1 y_1 + x_2 y_2 + \cdots + x_n y_n) x_i$$

Let us define $h_{ij} = x_i x_j / S_{xx}$. Thus $h_{ij} = h_{ji}$. Then we get [8]

$$\hat{u}_i = y_i - (h_{i1} y_1 + h_{i2} y_2 + \cdots + h_{in} y_n)$$

$$= (1 - h_{ii}) y_i + \sum_{j \neq i} h_{ij} y_j \tag{12.1}$$

Note that

$$\sum_j h_{ij}^2 = x_i^2 \frac{\left(\sum_j x_j^2\right)}{S_{xx}^2} \tag{12.2}$$

$$= \frac{x_i^2}{S_{xx}} = h_{ii}$$

From (12.1) we get (since the y_i are independent)

$$\text{var}(\hat{u}_i) = (1 - h_{ii})^2 \sigma^2 + \sum_{j \neq i} h_{ij}^2 \sigma^2$$

$$= (1 - 2h_{ii} + h_{ii}^2) \sigma^2 + \sum_{j \neq i} h_{ij}^2 \sigma^2$$

$$= (1 - 2h_{ii}) \sigma^2 + \sum_j h_{ij}^2 \sigma^2$$

Hence, using (12.2) we have

$$\text{var}(\hat{u}_i) = (1 - h_{ii}) \sigma^2 = \left(1 - \frac{x_i^2}{S_{xx}}\right) \sigma^2 \tag{12.3}$$

This shows that the least squares residuals are heteroskedastic. The variance of $\hat{u}_i$ depends on the particular values of the explanatory variable x. Also, from (12.1) it is easy to see that the least squares residuals are correlated (because of the occurrence of the common y's in the different $\hat{u}_i$).

Thus there are two problems with the least squares residuals:

1. They are correlated.
2. They are heteroskedastic.

---

[7] See equations (4.20). We do not have $\sum \hat{u}_i = 0$ because we do not have a constant term in the regression equation.

[8] The quantities h_{ij} play an important role in the analysis of residuals. The matrix of values h_{ij} is called a "*hat matrix*" because of the relationship $\hat{y}_i = h_{i1} y_1 + h_{i2} y_2 + \cdots + h_{in} y_n$.

This is so even if the true errors u_i are uncorrelated and have a common variance σ^2. The other residuals we will talk about are designed to solve these problems.

12.4   SOME OTHER TYPES OF RESIDUALS

We will discuss four other types of residuals:

1. Predicted residuals.
2. Studentized residuals.
3. BLUS residuals.
4. Recursive residuals.

The predicted and studentized residuals both have the same problems as the least squares residuals. However, some statisticians have found the predicted and studentized residuals useful in choosing between different regression models and detection of outliers, respectively. Hence we will discuss them briefly. The BLUS and recursive residuals both have the property that they have mean zero and constant variance σ^2 and are serially independent. Thus they solve the problems of least squares residuals. However, the BLUS residuals are more difficult to compute and have been found to be less useful than recursive residuals. Hence we will discuss them only briefly.

Predicted Residuals

Suppose that we take sample data of n observations and estimate the regression equation with $(n - 1)$ observations at a time by omitting one observation and then use this estimated equation to predict the y-value for the omitted observation. Let us denote the prediction error by $u_i^* = y_i - \hat{y}(i)$. The u_i^* are the *predicted residuals*.

By $\hat{y}(i)$ we mean a prediction of y_i from a regression equation that is estimated from all observations except the ith observation. This is in contrast to $\hat{y}_i$, which is the predicted value of y_i from a regression equation that is estimated using all the observations.

There is a simple relationship between least squares residuals $\hat{u}_i$ and predicted residuals u_i^*. This is [9]

$$u_i^* = \frac{\hat{u}_i}{1 - h_{ii}}$$

Since $V(\hat{u}_i) = (1 - h_{ii})\sigma^2$, we have

$$V(u_i^*) = \frac{\sigma^2}{1 - h_{ii}}$$

[9] We will not be concerned with the proof here. Proofs can be found in Cook and Weisberg, *Residuals* referred to earlier.

Thus the predicted residuals are also heteroskedastic. It has also been proved that the predicted residuals have the same correlation structure as the least squares residuals.

Although the predicted residuals have properties similar to the least squares residuals, some statisticians have found them more useful than the least squares residuals in problems of choosing between different regression models.[10] The criterion they use is that of the *predicted residual sum of squares* (PRESS), which is defined as

$$\text{PRESS} = \sum (u_i^*)^2$$

The more common criterion used is (the rationale for this is discussed in Section 12.6)

$$\text{RSS} = \sum \hat{u}_i^2$$

Since $u_i^* = \hat{u}_i/(1 - h_{ii})$, from the definition of h_{ii} we note that PRESS as a criterion for selection of regression models results in a preference for models that fit relatively well at remote values of the explanatory variables.

The predicted residuals can be computed by using the dummy variable method described in Chapter 8 (see Section 8.6). We will describe it after discussing studentized residuals, because the two are closely related.

Studentized Residuals

The studentized residual is just the predicted residual divided by its standard error. Thus if we are using the dummy variable method to get the ith studentized residual, we do the following. Estimate the regression equation with an extra variable D defined as

$$D = \begin{cases} 1 & \text{for the } i\text{th observation} \\ 0 & \text{for all others} \end{cases}$$

Then the estimate of the coefficient of D is the predicted residual and the t-ratio for this coefficient is the studentized residual. Thus to generate predicted and studentized residuals, the regressions involve all the observations in the sample and we create dummy variables in succession for the first, second, third, ... observations. Studentized residuals are usually used in the detection of outliers. Suppose that there is an outlier. In the case of the least squares residual, it might not be detected because we use the outlier as well in computing the regression equation. In the case of predicted and studentized residuals, we use all the other observations in computing the regression equation and try to use it in predicting this particular (outlying) observation. Thus there is a better chance of detecting outliers with this method.

---

[10] See, for instance, R. L. Anderson, D. M. Allen, and F. Cady, "Selection of Predictor Variables in Multiple Linear Regression," in T. A. Bancroft (ed.), *Statistical Papers in Honor of George W. Snedecor* (Ames. Iowa: Iowa State University Press, 1972).

The least squares and the predicted residuals both suffer from two problems. They are correlated and heteroskedastic even if the errors u_i are uncorrelated and have the same variance. There have been several methods suggested for the construction of residuals that do not have these shortcomings. We discuss only two of them: the BLUS residuals suggested by Theil[11] and recursive residuals.

BLUS Residuals

The BLUS (which stands for "best linear unbiased scalar") residuals are constructed from the least squares residuals so that they have the same properties as the errors u_i; that is, they have zero mean (they are unbiased), are uncorrelated, and have the same variance σ^2 as the errors u_i.

The computation of BLUS residuals is too complicated to be described here. However, we need not be concerned with this because it has been found that in tests for heteroskedasticity and autocorrelation, there is not much to be gained by using the BLUS residuals as compared with the least squares residuals.[12] Hence we will not discuss the BLUS residuals further.

Recursive Residuals

Recursive residuals have been suggested by Brown, Durbin, and Evans,[13] for testing the stability of regression relationships. However, these residuals can be used for other problems as well, such as tests for autocorrelation and tests for heteroskedasticity. Phillips and Harvey[14] use recursive residuals for testing serial correlation. Since the recursive residuals are serially uncorrelated and have a common variance σ^2, we can use the von neumann ratio tests (described in Chapter 6). There is no inconclusive region as with the Durbin–Watson test.

We will now describe the construction of recursive residuals. First, we order observations sequentially. This is not a problem with time-series data. The recursive residual can be computed by forward recursion or backward recursion. We describe forward recursion only. Backward recursion is similar. The idea behind recursive residuals is this: Let us say that we have T observations and the regression

[11] H. Theil, "The Analysis of Disturbances in Regression Analysis," *Journal of the American Statistical Association*, Vol. 60, 1965, pp. 1067–1079.

[12] Cook and Weisberg, *Residuals*, p. 35.

[13] R. L. Brown, J. Durbin, and J. M. Evans, "Techniques for Testing the Constancy of Regression Relationships" (with discussion), *Journal of the Royal Statistical Society, Series B*, Vol. 37, 1975, pp. 149–163. This paper gives algorithms for the construction of recursive residuals. Farebrother gives algorithms for the construction of BLUS and recursive residuals. See R. W. Farebrother, "BLUS Residuals: Algorithm A5104" and "Recursive Residuals: A Remark on Algorithm A75: Basic Procedures for Large, Sparse or Weighted Least Squares Problems," *Applied Statistics*, Vol. 25, 1976, pp. 317–319 and 323–324.

[14] G. D. A. Phillips and A. C. Harvey, "A Simple Test for Serial Correlation in Regression Analysis," *Journal of the American Statistical Association*, Vol. 69, 1974, pp. 935–939.

equation is

$$y_t = \beta x_t + u_t \qquad t = 1, 2, \ldots, T$$

Let $\hat{\beta}_i$ be the estimate of β from the first i observations. Then we use this to predict the next observation y_{i+1}. The prediction is

$$\tilde{y}_{i+1} = \hat{\beta}_i x_{i+1}$$

The prediction error is

$$e_{i+1} = y_{i+1} - \tilde{y}_{i+1}$$

Let us denote $V(e_{i+1})$ by $d_{i+1}^2 \sigma^2$. (The variance of prediction error in multiple regression has been discussed in Section 4.7.) Then the recursive residuals, which will denote by $\tilde{u}_{i+1}$, are

$$\tilde{u}_{i+1} = \frac{e_{i+1}}{d_{i+1}}$$

Note that $\operatorname{var}(\tilde{u}_{i+1}) = \sigma^2$. Now we add one more observation, estimate β using $(i + 1)$ observations, and use this to predict the next observation, y_{i+2}. Thus

$$\tilde{y}_{i+2} = \hat{\beta}_{i+1} x_{i+2}$$

and if $e_{i+2} = y_{i+2} - \tilde{y}_{i+2}$ and $V(e_{i+2}) = d_{i+2}^2 \sigma^2$, then

$$\tilde{u}_{i+2} = \frac{e_{i+2}}{d_{i+2}}$$

We continue this process until we get to the last observation. If we have k explanatory variables, since we have to estimate $k + 1$ parameters (including the constant term) and obtain their variances, we need at least $(k + 2)$ observations. Thus the recursive residuals start with the observation $(k + 3)$ and we have $T - k - 2$ recursive residuals.

The recursive residuals have been shown to have the following properties.[15]

1. They are uncorrelated.
2. They have a common variance σ^2.
3. Their sum of squares is equal to RSS, the residual sum of squares from the least squares regression.

The third property is useful in checking the accuracy of the calculations.

There are algorithms for calculating the regression coefficients $\hat{\beta}_i$ and also the prediction variance $d_i^2 \sigma^2$, in a recursive fashion.[16] There is, however, an alternative method that we can use for the recursive residuals as we have done for the predicted residuals described earlier. Note that recursive residuals are similar to predicted residuals except that the predictions are sequential.

---

[15] Proofs are omitted. These properties are proved in Brown, Durbin, and Evans, "Techniques for Testing."
[16] Phillips and Harvey, "A Simple Test."

Suppose that we use n observations and want to get the prediction error and the variance of the prediction error for the $(n + 1)$th observation. Then all we have to do is to create a dummy variable D which is defined as

$$D = \begin{cases} 1 & \text{for the } (n + 1)\text{th observation} \\ 0 & \text{for all others} \end{cases}$$

We have discussed this procedure in Chapter 8.

Now we just run a multiple regression with all the $(n + 1)$ observations and this extra variable D. The estimate of the coefficient of this variable D is the prediction error e_{n+1} and its standard error is $\hat{\sigma} d_{n+1}$. This result has been proved in Chapter 8. Thus we get from the regression program e_{n+1} and $d_{n+1}\hat{\sigma}$ or t_{n+1} the t-ratio, which is $e_{n+1}/d_{n+1}\hat{\sigma}$. But for the recursive residuals we need e_{n+1}/d_{n+1}. Thus all we have to do is multiply the t-ratio we get for the coefficient of D by $\hat{\sigma}$. This gives us the recursive residual.

The calculation of recursive residuals by the dummy variable method is similar to that for predicted residuals except that the regressions for predicted residuals involve all the observations in the sample and for recursive residuals the observation set is sequential and the dummy variable is also sequential.

Illustrative Example

In Table 12.1 we present the OLS residual, the forward recursive, and the backward recursive residuals for the production function (4.25). The sum of squares of the recursive residuals should be equal to the sum of squares of the OLS residuals, but there are small discrepancies which are due to rounding errors.

The recursive residuals are useful for:

1. Tests for heteroskedasticity described in Chapter 5.
2. Tests for autocorrelation described in Chapter 6.
3. Tests for stability described in Chapter 4.

For stability analysis, Brown, Durbin, and Evans suggest computing the cumulative sums (CUSUM) and cumulative sums of squares (CUSUMSQ) of the recursive residuals and comparing them with some percentage points that they have tabulated. A discussion of this is beyond the scope of this book. [17] Instead, we will apply some simple t-tests. If a test of the hypothesis that the mean of the recursive residual is zero gives us a significant t-statistic, this is an indication of instability of the coefficients. In Table 12.1 we present these t-ratios. With the forward recursive residuals we do not reject the hypothesis of zero mean. With the backward recursive residuals, we do reject at the 5% level, the hypothesis of zero mean. Thus the conclusions from the recursive residuals are similar to the conclusions we arrived at earlier in Chapter 4 from the predictive tests for stability.

---

[17] Those interested in this detail can refer to the paper by Brown, Durbin, and Evans, "Techniques for Testing."

Table 12.1 Different Residuals for the Production Function (4.25) (Multiplied by 100)

Year	OLS Residual	Forward Recursive	Backward Recursive
1929	−1.27		−1.304
1930	−4.29		−4.530
1931	−3.99		−4.710
1932	−1.30		−3.044
1933	−3.04	−1.975	−6.187
1934	−1.99	−0.809	−6.476
1935	−0.79	0.512	−6.440
1936	1.04	1.115	−4.246
1937	−0.26	−1.040	−4.359
1938	4.55	3.824	−2.900
1939	4.93	4.163	−2.224
1940	4.37	4.182	−2.668
1941	1.84	1.335	−2.971
1942	−1.74	−1.456	−4.775
1943	0.13	1.609	−3.110
1944	6.59	6.065	3.502
1945	11.11	8.487	8.844
1946	1.34	−4.811	5.452
1947	−6.59	−10.322	−1.531
1948	−5.90	−7.172	−1.884
1949	−2.06	−1.601	−0.132
1950	0.12	1.343	2.331
1951	−2.68	−0.884	0.273
1952	−3.24	−0.667	−0.702
1953	−2.38	0.883	−0.716
1954	1.10	4.137	1.293
1955	1.48	3.540	2.917
1956	−1.52	0.186	0.826
1957	−1.00	0.772	0.764
1958	1.43	2.917	0.912
1959	0.00	1.083	0.989
1960	−1.39	−0.367	−0.854
1961	0.38	1.400	−2.372
1962	1.21	1.963	−1.994
1963	2.51	2.865	−1.793
1964	2.31	2.297	
1965	1.85	1.561	
1966	0.00	−0.328	
1967	−2.97	−3.160	
Mean	0.00	0.618	−1.252
SD	3.379	3.506	3.338
Range	17.70	18.81	15.32
SS	433.8	431.3	433.6
t	0.00	1.04	−2.22

12.5 DFFITS AND BOUNDED INFLUENCE ESTIMATION

In Section 3.8 we discussed briefly the problem of outliers. The usual approach to outliers based on least squares residuals is as follows:

1. Look at the OLS residuals.
2. Delete the observations with large residuals.
3. Reestimate the equation.

Two major problems with this approach are that the OLS residuals (as we showed earlier) do not all have the same variance and furthermore the OLS residuals do not give us any idea of how important this particular observation is for the overall results. The idea behind the studentized residual is to allow for these differences in the variances and to look at the prediction error resulting from the deletion of this observation. Using a plus or minus 2σ rule of thumb, the studentized residuals shown in Table 12.2 suggest that the observations for the years 1945 and 1947 are outliers. With the OLS residuals in Table 12.1 we might have included 1944 and 1948 as well.

One other measure that is used to detect outliers is to see the change in the fitted

Table 12.2 Regression Diagnostics for Detecting Outliers for the Production Function (4.25)

Year	Studentized Residual	DFFITS	Year	Studentized Residual	DFFITS
1929	−0.38	−0.08	1949	−0.61	−0.16
1930	−1.28	−0.35	1950	0.04	0.01
1931	−1.21	−0.39	1951	−0.79	−0.19
1932	−0.42	−0.21	1952	−0.96	−0.22
1933	−0.97	−0.46	1953	−0.70	−0.15
1934	−0.61	−0.22	1954	0.32	0.06
1935	−0.24	−0.07	1955	0.43	0.08
1936	0.31	0.08	1956	−0.45	−0.09
1937	−0.08	−0.02	1957	−0.29	−0.06
1938	1.36	0.37	1958	0.42	0.10
1939	1.46	0.37	1959	0.01	0.00
1940	1.29	0.29	1960	−0.41	−0.11
1941	0.54	0.12	1961	0.11	0.03
1942	−0.51	−0.12	1962	0.37	0.11
1943	0.04	0.01	1963	0.75	0.23
1944	1.94	0.46	1964	0.70	0.22
1945	3.28	0.88	1965	0.56	0.18
1946	0.42	0.17	1966	0.02	0.01
1947	−2.04	−0.85	1967	−0.91	−0.33
1948	−1.80	−0.66			

value $\hat{y}$ of y that results from dropping a particular observation. Let $\hat{y}_{(i)}$ be the fitted value of y if the ith observation is dropped. The quantity $(\hat{y} - \hat{y}_{(i)})$ divided by its standard error is called DFFITS.

It has been shown that [18]

$$\text{DFFITS} = \left(\frac{h_{ii}}{1 - h_{ii}} \right)^{1/2} \tilde{u}_i$$

where $\tilde{u}_i$ is the ith studentized residual and h_{ii} is the quantity that figures repeatedly in equations (12.1)–(12.3). (It is also known as the ith diagonal term of the "hat matrix.")

There are many computer programs available to compute studentized residuals and DFFITS. For instance, the SAS regression program gives these statistics. The results in Table 12.2 have been obtained from the SAS regression program.

Belsley, Kuh, and Welsch suggest that DFFITS is a better criterion to detect outliers and influential observations. DFFITS is a standardized measure of the difference in the fitted value of y due to deleting this particular observation. Further, they suggest that observations with large studentized residuals or DFFITS should not be deleted. Their influence should be minimized. This method of estimation is called *bounded influence estimation*. The details of this method are complicated but a simple one-step bounded influence estimator suggested by Welsch [19] is as follows: Minimize $\sum w_i(y_i - \beta x_i)^2$, where

$$w_i = \begin{cases} 1 & \text{if } |\text{DFFITS}_i| \le 0.34 \\ \dfrac{0.34}{|\text{DFFITS}_i|} & \text{if } |\text{DFFITS}_i| > 0.34 \end{cases}$$

Illustrative Example

As an illustration, consider again, the production function (4.25). The values of DFFITS are shown in Table 12.2. There are nine observations (all before 1948) that have $|\text{DFFITS}_i| > 0.34$. These observations receive a weight < 1 in the bounded influence estimation.

Using this weighing scheme, we obtained the following results:

Estimate of:	Bounded Influence	OLS	OLS with Outlier Deletion
α	−3.987	−3.938	−3.980
β_1	1.468	1.451	1.466
β_2	0.375	0.384	0.376

[18] D. A. Belsley, E. Kuh, and R. E. Welsch, *Regression Diagnostics: Identifying Influential Data and Sources of Collinearity* (New York: Wiley, 1980).

[19] Roy E. Welsch, "Regression Sensitivity Analysis and Bounded Influence Estimation," in J. Kmenta and J. B. Ramsay (eds.), *Evaluation of Econometric Models* (New York: Academic Press, 1980), pp. 153–167.

For comparison we also present the estimates from the OLS regression (4.25) and also estimates using OLS after deleting the observations for 1944, 1945, 1947, and 1948, the years for which the OLS residuals in Table 12.1 are large.

In this example there was not much difference in the estimated coefficients. In fact, the bounded influence method and OLS with outlier deletion gave almost identical results. The data set we have used is perhaps not appropriate for the illustration of the bounded influence method. The problem of parameter instability and autocorrelated errors seems to be more important with this data set than that of detection of outliers.

In any case the preceding discussion gives an idea of what "bounded influence estimation" is about. The basic point is that the OLS residuals are not appropriate for detection of outliers. Further, outliers should not be all discarded. Their influence on the least squares estimates should be reduced (bounded) based on their magnitude.

As mentioned earlier, the data set we have used has not turned out to be appropriate for illustrating the method. Other data sets in the book can be used to check out the usefulness of the method.

Krasker[20] gives an interesting example of the use of bounded influence estimation. The problem is a forecasting problem faced by Korvett's Department Stores in 1975. The company has to choose between two locations, A and B to start a new store. Data are available for 25 existing stores on the following variables.

y = sales per capita

x_1 = medium home value ($\times 10^{-6}$)

x_2 = average family size ($\times 10^{-2}$)

x_3 = percent of population which is black or hispanic ($\times 10^{-4}$)

The regression results were (dependent variable: sales) (figures in parentheses are standard errors) as follows:

	Constant	x_1	x_2	x_3	$\hat{\sigma}$
OLS	−0.13	2.70	2.5	0.22	0.014
	(0.05)	(0.51)	(1.1)	(3.1)	
WLS	−0.05	1.00	1.7	−4.1	0.010
	(0.04)	(0.52)	(1.0)	(2.9)	

Note the change in the coefficient for x_3. The WLS estimator is the weighted least squares.[21] Krasker argues that there are two outliers (observations 2 and 11 in this sample). The other 23 observations are "well described by an OLS regression whose estimates are essentially those of the WLS." Thus again in this example the bounded

[20] W. S. Krasker, "The Role of Bounded Influence Estimation in Model Selection," *Journal of Econometrics*, Vol. 16, 1981, pp. 131–138.
[21] The weighting scheme is slightly different from the weighting scheme discussed in Welsch, "Regression Sensitivity," quoted earlier.

influence estimator does not appear to be different from the OLS with the two outliers omitted. (Results from OLS with 23 observations are not presented here).

Krasker suggests that site A is similar to observations 2 and if the model cannot be used to predict observation 2, it should not be used to make predictions for site A (with 50.8% of the population from minorities). The model (OLS with 23 observations or WLS with all observations) can be used to make predictions for site B.

12.6 MODEL SELECTION

In the usual textbook econometrics, the statistical model underlying the data is assumed to be known at the outset and the problem is merely one of obtaining good estimates of the parameters in the model. In reality, however, the choice of a model is almost always made after some preliminary data analysis. For instance, in the case of a regression model, we start with a specification that seems most reasonable a priori. But after examining the coefficients, their standard errors and the residuals, we change the specification of the model. Purists would consider this "data mining" as an illegitimate activity, but it is equally unreasonable to assume that we know the model exactly at the very outset.

The area of model selection comprises of:

1. Choice between some models specified before any analysis.
2. Simplification of complicated models based on the data (data-based simplification).
3. Post-data model construction.

The area of model selection is quite vast in its scope and includes diagnostic checking and specification testing (the other two areas we are discussing in this chapter). There are many references on the topic, some of which are a book by Leamer,[22] a paper by Mizon,[23] the dissertation by Sawyer,[24] and a special volume of the *Journal of Econometrics.*[25] Since it is impossible to cover this vast area, we discuss Leamer's classification of the different types of model searches usually attempted, and also Hendry's ideas behind data-based-simplification of models. In Sections 12.7 to 12.9 we go through two particular aspects of model selection:

1. Selection of regressors.
2. Use of cross-validation techniques.

Leamer talks of six types of specification searches that are usually undertaken in the process of model selection. The differences between the different searches are very minor. However, they are useful for organization of our ideas. The different

[22] E. E. Leamer, *Specification Searches* (New York: Wiley, 1978).
[23] G. E. Mizon, "Model Selection Procedures," in M. J. Artis and A. R. Nobay (eds.), *Studies in Current Economic Analysis* (Oxford: Basil Blackwell, 1977), Chap. 4.
[24] K. R. Sawyer, "The Theory of Econometric Model Selection," unpublished doctoral dissertation, Australian National University, 1980.
[25] G. S. Maddala (ed.), "Model Selection," *Journal of Econometrics*, Vol. 16, 1981.

searches are:

Type of Search	Purpose
(1) Hypothesis-testing search	Choosing a "true model"
(2) Interpretive search	Interpreting the sample evidence on many intercorrelated variables
(3) Simplification search	Constructing a "fruitful" model
(4) Proxy variable search	Choosing between different measures of the same set of hypothetical variables
(5) Data selection search	Selecting the appropriate data set for estimation and prediction
(6) Post-data model construction	Improving an existing model

Many of these searches have been discussed in previous chapters. But we will give further examples:

Hypothesis-Testing Search

Suppose that we estimate a Cobb–Douglas production function as in Section 4.11, and test the hypothesis of constant returns to scale ($\alpha + \beta = 1$ in that example). If the hypothesis is rejected, as in that example, we do not change the specification of the model. If it is not rejected, we change the specification and estimate a production function with constant returns to scale.

Interpretive Search

Sometimes the coefficients of the model do not make economic sense but the imposition of some constraints does. For instance, based on data for 150 house-holds, Leamer[26] estimated the demand for oranges as

$$\log D_i = 3.1 + 0.83 \log E_i + 0.01 \log P_i - 0.56 \log \pi_i \qquad R^2 = 0.20$$
$$\quad\;\; (1.0) \quad\;\; (0.20) \qquad\;\; (0.15) \qquad\;\; (0.60)$$

where D_i = purchases of oranges by household i
$\quad E_i$ = total expenditures by household i
$\quad P_i$ = price of oranges
$\quad \pi_i$ = price of grapefruit (a substitute commodity)

(Figures in parentheses are standard errors.) The coefficients of the price variables are insignificant and have the "wrong" sign. Also, the sum of the coefficients ($0.83 + 0.01 - 0.56 = 0.28$) is rather far from zero. If there is no money illusion, then multiplying E_i, P_i and π_i by the same factor should not produce any change in D_i. This implies that the sum of the coefficients of these variables should be zero. (This is known as the "homogeneity postulate.") Imposing this condition, Leamer gets the result:

$$\log D_i = 4.2 + 0.52 \log E_i - 0.61 \log P_i + 0.09 \log \pi_i \qquad R^2 = 0.19$$
$$\quad (0.9) \quad\;\; (0.19) \qquad\;\; (0.14) \qquad\;\; (0.31)$$

[26] Leamer, *Specification Searches*, p. 8.

The R^2 has fallen only slightly and the coefficients all have the right signs. Income Y_i and price P_i are significant. The constraint has improved the specifications, and the interpretation.

Simplification Search

In the equation above the coefficient of $\log \pi_i$ is not significant. Dropping this variable and imposing the homogeneity constraint, that is, assuming the other two coefficients to be equal in value and opposite in sign, we get

$$\log D_i = 3.7 + 0.58 \log (E_i/P_i) \qquad R^2 = 0.18$$
$$\quad (0.8) \qquad (0.18)$$

The R^2 is only slightly smaller and we have a simplified equation. This is called a simplification search. The purpose of this search is to find a simple but useful model.

Proxy Variable Search

In econometric work an investigator is faced with several definitions of the same variable. There are several definitions of money supply, several definitions of income, and so on. Further, some variables like education, ability, and risk are not directly measurable and we have to use some proxies for them. We are thus left with the problem of choosing among the different proxies. In the example of demand for oranges that Leamer considered, one has to choose between money income Y_i and expenditures E_i as measures of the household's true income. The estimated equations he gets are

$$\log D_i = 6.2 + 0.85 \log Y_i - 0.67 \log P_i \qquad R^2 = 0.15$$
$$\quad (1.1) \qquad (0.21) \qquad (0.13)$$

and

$$\log D_i = 5.2 + 1.1 \log E_i - 0.45 \log P_i \qquad R^2 = 0.18$$
$$\quad (1.0) \qquad (0.18) \qquad (0.16)$$

The R^2 has increased with the use of E_i, suggesting that E_i is a better proxy then Y_i for "true income."

Data Selection Search

Often, in econometric work we have different data sets from which we can estimate the same relationship. A question often arises as to whether we can pool the different data sets and get more efficient estimates of the parameters. In Section 4.6 we gave some examples where the data sets referred to prewar and postwar years. There we found significant differences in the coefficients between the two periods which suggested that the data should not be pooled. This is an example of a data-selection search.

Post-data Model Construction

This is what Leamer calls "Sherlock Holmes" inference. In response to a question by Dr. Watson about the likely perpetrators of the crime, Sherlock Holmes replied: "No data yet.... It is a capital mistake to theorize before you have all the evidence. It biases the judgments." According to the traditional statistical theory, on the other hand, it is a "capital mistake to view the facts before you have all the theories. It biases the judgments." Any theory that is postulated after looking at a particular data set cannot be tested using the same data set, because doing so would amount to double counting. On the other hand, Sherlock Holmes would argue that the set of viable alternative hypotheses is immense and the set of hypotheses formulated before the data set is observed can be incomplete. There is always the risk that the data favor some unspecified hypothesis. Hence the data evidence is used to construct a set of "empirically relevant" hypotheses, thereby reducing the cost of formulating a comprehensive set of hypotheses and the risk of not identifying the "best" hypothesis.

In almost all econometric work investigators do something similar to what Sherlock Holmes does. They formulate some hypotheses, then observe that the coefficients of some variables have wrong signs or implausible magnitudes or that the residuals have a peculiar pattern. Then they introduce more explanatory variables or impose some constraints on the parameters. A question arises as to whether this type of Sherlock Holmes inference can be brought within the scope of statistical inference.

Leamer's answer to this is that we have to view this new "data-instigated hypothesis" as something that was in the back of our mind all the time. We did not consider it explicitly because we thought it to be unimportant but now we change our mind after observing the data. Suppose that the model we want to consider is $y = \beta x + \gamma z + u$. Initially, we consider z to be uncorrelated with x or that γ is negligibly small. So we start with the model $y = \beta x + u$. If the resulting estimate of β has the wrong sign or the pattern of estimated residuals is peculiar, we change our mind and observe z. If the problem is viewed in this form of a decision problem, Leamer argues that we can attach the appropriate standard errors to the coefficients when the model $y = \beta x + \gamma z + u$ is estimated.

In all cases of specification searches, there is the question of what the appropriate standard errors should be for the final model estimated. There is no easy answer to this question except that the standard errors are higher than those obtained from the estimation of the final model. The inference problem is more straightforward in the case of a simplification search. That is why David Hendry suggests starting with an extremely general model and then simplifying it progressively. We will, therefore, discuss this approach in greater detail.

Hendry's Approach to Model Selection

The approach to model building suggested by David Hendry,[27] which is mainly applicable to dynamic time-series models, can be summarized as: *intended over-parametrization with data-based simplification*. By contrast most of empirical

---

[27] This approach is originally due to J. D. Sargan but has been popularized and expounded by David Hendry. Some representative papers are: D. F. Hendry, "Predictive Failure and Econometric Modelling in Macroeconomics: The Transactions Demand for Money," in Paul Ormerod (ed.), *Economic Modelling* (London: Heinemann, 1979), Chap. 9, pp. 217–242; and Mizon, "Model Selection Procedures" quoted earlier.

econometric work can be characterized as *excessive presimplification with inade-quate diagnostic testing*. The latter method consists of the following steps:

1. Commence from theories which are drastic abstractions of reality.
2. Formulate highly parsimonious relationships to represent the theories.
3. Estimate the equations from the available data using techniques which are "optimal" only on the assumptions that the highly restricted model is correctly specified.
4. Test a few of the assumptions explicitly or implicitly (such as the conventional Durbin–Watson test for autocorrelation).
5. Revise the specification in the light of evidence acquired.
6. Reestimate accordingly.

According to Hendry, this approach to model building, which is a "specific to general" approach or a "bottoms-up" approach, has three main drawbacks:

1. Every test is conditional on arbitrary assumptions which are to be tested *later*, and if these are rejected, all earlier inferences are invalidated.
2. The significance levels of the unstructured sequence of tests actually conducted is unknown. For instance, suppose that we estimate an equation by OLS, find a significant DW statistic, and then reestimate the equation adjusting for the serial correlation. What are the significance levels for the estimated coefficients from this transformed equation? This is not very clear.
3. It is not always possible to end up with the best model by using this iterative method. We might get sidetracked by using the wrong (or inadequate) diagnostic tests. For instance, we might start with the equation $y = \beta x + u$ and observing a significant DW test statistic, we reestimate the equation in a ρ-differenced form. If we now find that the coefficients of our equation are of the correct sign, we might rest satisfied. However, this procedure might lead us to the wrong model because as discussed in Section 6.9 the DW statistic could be significant not because of serial correlation in errors but because of misspecified dynamics. The model with serially correlated errors

$$y_t = \beta x_t + u_t \qquad u_t = \rho u_{t-1} + e_t$$

implies the model

$$y_t = \rho y_{t-1} + \beta x_t - \beta \rho x_{t-1} + e_t$$

which is the same as

$$y_t = \beta_1 y_{t-1} + \beta_2 x_t + \beta_3 x_{t-1} + e_t$$

with the restriction $\beta_1 \beta_2 = -\beta_3$. Now the true model could be the last one but with the restriction $\beta_1 \beta_2 = -\beta_3$ *not* satisfied. But there is no way of our arriving at this model by the modeling approach adopted. When we estimate the model $y_t = \beta x_t + u_t$, we would observe serial correlation in the residuals because y_{t-1} and x_{t-1} are "missing." But this does not mean that we have a model with serially correlated errors.

By contrast, the approach suggested by Hendry, which is a "top-down" or "general to specific" approach, starts with a very general dynamic model, which is "overparametized," that is, has more lags than you would consider necessary. The model is then progressively simplified with a sequence of "simplification tests." The significance levels for the sequence of tests is known unlike the case of the sequence of tests we perform in the "specific-to-general" approach. The significance level for jth test is[28]

$$1 - \prod_{i=1}^{j} (1 - \gamma_i)$$

where γ_i is the significance level for the ith test in the sequence. The sequential testing procedures are used to select a "data coherent specialization."

Hendry argues that only after these steps should one test economic theories. "Until the model characterizes the data generation process, it seems rather pointless trying to test hypotheses of interest in economic theory."[29]

12.7 SELECTION OF REGRESSORS

In Section 12.6 we outlined some general approaches to the model selection problem. We now concentrate on a specific issue, the problem of selection of regressors.

In Chapter 4 we considered a multiple regression of an explained variable y on a set of k explanatory variables $x_1, x_2, \ldots, x_k$. It was assumed that the set of variables to be included in the equation is given. In practice this is rarely the case. There is typically a very large number of potential explanatory variables or regressors and one is faced with a problem of choosing a subset of these. This is the problem often referred to as the problem of *selection of regressors.*

Suppose that there is a potential set of k regressors from which we have to select a smaller number. In the 1960s a number of stepwise regression methods were suggested.[30] Some of these started with a regression, including all the k variables and successively proceeded to eliminate variables with t-ratios less than a prespecified value (say, 1). This is called a backward selection procedure. Others started with a single variable which had the highest correlation with y and then picked at each stage the variable with the highest partial correlation coefficient (this is called forward selection procedure). Some procedures combined the elements of the forward and backward selection procedures at each stage (i.e., deleted some variables and added some others).

---

[28] This result was derived by T. W. Anderson in the paper cited in Section 10.8. This result has been proved for dynamic econometric models by J. D. Sargan (in an unpublished London School of Economics discussion paper).

[29] Hendry, "Predictive Failure," p. 226.

[30] These methods are not popular at present. However, those interested in a discussion of stepwise procedures can refer to N. Draper and H. Smith, *Applied Regression Analysis*, 2nd ed. (New York: Wiley, 1981), Chap. 6.

Table 12.3 Some Criteria for Choice Among Regression Models

Criterion	Minimize[a]
Theil's $\bar{R}^2$ (1961)	$RSS_j/(n - k_j)$
Hocking's S_p (1976)	$RSS_j/[(n - k_j)(n - k_j - 1)]$
Mallows' C_p (1973)	$RSS_j + 2k_j\hat{\sigma}_m^2$
Amemiya's PC (1980)	$RSS_j(n + k_j)/(n - k_j)$
Akaike's AIC (1973, 1977)	$RSS_j \exp[2(k_j + 1)/n]$

[a] k_j, number of explanatory variables; RSS_j, residual sum of squares for the jth model; $\hat{\sigma}_m^2$, (residual sum of squares)/$(n - k)$ in the model that includes *all* the k explanatory variables.

This sort of mechanical picking of variables by the computer is no longer popular among econometricians. Fortunately, although economists do not have an *exact* idea of all the variables that have to be included in an equation, they do have an idea of what variables are likely to be very important and what variables are doubtful. In this case we can specify a small number of alternative models and then we need to choose one of these alternatives. Since theory cannot give us any guidance at this stage we have to make a choice on statistical grounds.

There are many criteria that have been suggested in the literature. Some of these are listed in Table 12.3. We discuss them briefly. The criteria that we have chosen in Table 12.3 are applicable to regression models only and we have chosen those criteria that depend on some summary measures commonly used like residual sum of squares.

Let RSS denote the residual sum of squares from the jth model with k_j explanatory variables. We define

$$\hat{\sigma}_j^2 = \frac{RSS_j}{n - k_j}$$

an estimate of σ^2 from the jth model. We denote $\hat{\sigma}_m^2$ as the estimate of σ^2 from a model that includes *all* the k explanatory variables.

We now discuss briefly the criteria listed in Table 12.3.

Theil's $\bar{R}^2$ Criterion

Theil's criterion [31] is based on the assumption that one of the models considered is the correct model. In this case if $\hat{\sigma}_j^2 = RSS_j/(n - k_j)$ is the estimate of σ^2 from the jth model, then $E(\hat{\sigma}_j^2) = \sigma^2$ for the correct model but is $\geq \sigma^2$ for the misspecified model. [32] Thus, choosing the model with the minimum $\hat{\sigma}^2$ will *on the average* lead us to pick the correct model. Since minimizing $\hat{\sigma}^2$ is the same as maximizing $\bar{R}^2$ [see equation (4.22)], we refer to the rule alternatively as the maximum $\bar{R}^2$ rule.

[31] H. Theil, *Economic Forecasts and Policy*, 2nd ed. (Amsterdam: North-Holland, 1961).
[32] The proof of this result can be found in several books. See, for instance, G. S. Maddala, *Econometrics* (New York: McGraw-Hill, 1977), pp. 461–462. It is shown there that a model that has all the explanatory variables of the correct model but also a number of irrelevant variables will also give $E(\hat{\sigma}^2) = \sigma^2$.

A major problem with this rule is that a model that has all the explanatory variables of the correct model but also a number of irrelevant variables will also give $E(\hat{\sigma}^2) = \sigma^2$. Thus the rule will not help us pick the correct model in this case. This indeed is confirmed by the results in Schmidt and Ebbeler[33] concerning the power function of the maximum $\bar{R}^2$ criterion. The probability of picking the correct model is considerably below 1 when the alternative model includes a number of irrelevant variables.

Criteria Based on Minimizing the Mean Square Error of Prediction

Theil's criterion is based on minimizing the standard error of the regression. The following three criteria are based on minimizing the mean-square error of prediction:

1. Mallows' C_p criterion.[34]
2. Hocking's S_p criterion.[35]
3. Amemiya's PC criterion.[36]

Suppose that the correct equation involves k variables and the equation we consider involves k_1 ($< k$) variables. The problem is how to choose the number k_1, as well as the particular set of k_1 variables. In the prediction criteria we are considering this is done by minimizing the mean-squared error of prediction $E(y_f - \hat{y}_f)^2$, where y_f is the future value of y_f and $\hat{y}_f$ is the predicted value. If we denote the future values of the explanatory variables by x_{if}, then $E[(y_f - \hat{y}_f)^2 | x_{if}]$ is called the conditional MSE (mean-square error) of prediction and $E(y_f - \hat{y}_f)^2$ is called the unconditional MSE of prediction.

To get the unconditional MSE of prediction we have to make some assumptions about x_{if}. Amemiya assumes that the regressors for the prediction period are stochastic and that the values of x_{if} have the same behavior as the variables x_{it}

[33] P. Schmidt, "Calculating the Power of the Minimum Standard Error Choice Criterion," *International Economic Review*, February 1973, pp. 253–255. The numerical errors in Schmidt's paper are corrected in D. H. Ebbeler, "On the Probability of Correct Model Selection Using the Maximum $\bar{R}^2$ Choice Criterion," *International Economic Review*, June 1975, pp. 516–520. There are three types of misspecifications considered in these papers: omitted variables, irrelevant variables, and wrong variables. For the first two cases, Ebbeler shows that some simple analytical results are available.

[34] C. L. Mallows, "Some Comments on C_p," *Technometrics*, November 1973, pp. 661–676. The criterion was first suggested by Mallows in 1964 in an unpublished paper.

[35] R. R. Hocking, "The Analysis and Selection of Variables in Multiple Regression," *Biometrics*, March 1976, pp. 1–49. This has been further discussed in two papers by M. L. Thompson, "Selection of Variables in Multiple Regression. Part 1: A Review and Evaluation" and "Part 2: Chosen Procedures, Computations and Examples," *International Statistical Review*, Vol. 46, 1978, pp. 1–19 and pp. 129–146. Also se U. Hjorth, "Model Selection and Forward Validation," *Scandinavian Journal of Statistics*, Vol. 9, 1982, pp. 1–49.

[36] T. Amemiya, "Selection of Regressors," *International Economic Review*, Vol. 21, 1980, pp. 331–354.

during the sample period. Under this assumption he shows that[37]

$$\text{estimate of } E(y_f - \hat{y}_f)^2 \simeq \frac{2k_1}{n}\sigma^2 + \frac{\text{RSS}_1}{n}$$

where RSS_1 is the residual sum of squares from the model with k_1 regressors.

Now σ^2 has to be estimated. If we use $\hat{\sigma}_m^2 = \text{RSS}/(n-k)$, where RSS is the residual sum of squares from the complete model with k explanatory variables, we get Mallows' C_p criterion. On the other hand, if we use $\hat{\sigma}_1^2 = \text{RSS}_1/(n-k_1)$, then we get Amemiya's PC criterion. Note, however, that $\text{RSS}_1/(n-k_1)$ is an upward-biased estimate of σ^2 because of the fact that it is an estimate from a misspecified regression.[38] On the other hand, $\hat{\sigma}_1^2$ is an unbiased estimate of σ^2 if it is assumed that the model with k_1 variables is the correct model and the model with k variables includes a number of irrelevant variables. This is the "optimistic" assumption that Amemiya makes. However, if we are comparing different models with different sets of variables by the PC criterion, we cannot make the "optimistic" assumption that every one of these is the true model. This is one of the major problems with Amemiya's PC criterion. It is more reasonable to assume that $\hat{\sigma}_m^2$ is the appropriate estimate of σ^2 as assumed in Mallows' C_p criterion.

The important thing to note in the discussion above is that the regressors in the sample period are assumed nonstochastic, whereas they are assumed stochastic in the prediction period. Hocking, by contrast, assumes the regressors to have a multivariate normal distribution and derives the S_p criterion given in Table 12.3 by minimizing the unconditional MSE of prediction. Kinal and Lahiri[39] show that in the stochastic regressor case Amemiya's PC and Mallows' C_p both reduce to Hocking S_p criterion. Breiman and Freedman[40] give an alternative justification for Hocking's S_p criterion. It is not necessary for us to go through the different ways in which the criteria C_p and S_p have been derived and justified. This discussion can be found in the papers by Thompson cited earlier. The important thing to note is that Amemiya's PC and Mallows' C_p depend on the assumption of nonstochastic regressors, whereas Hocking's S_p depends on the assumption of stochastic regressors. A consequence of this assumption is that (as noted by Kinal and Lahiri) both the C_p and PC criteria require an estimate of the variance σ^2 of the disturbance in the true model, whereas S_p does not. It just requires an estimate of the variance of the disturbance term in the restricted model.

One more important thing to note is that the maximum $\bar{R}^2$ criterion and the predictive criteria C_p, S_p, and PC answer two different questions. In the case of the maximum $\bar{R}^2$ criterion, what we are trying to do is pick the "true" model, assuming that one of the models considered is the "true" one. In the case of the prediction criteria, we are interested in "parsimony" and we would like to omit some of the

---

[37] We will not be concerned with the proof here. It can be found in Amemiya, "Selection of Regressors."
[38] This is in fact the basis for the maximum $\bar{R}^2$ rule.
[39] T. Kinal and K. Lahiri, "A Note on 'Selection of Regressors,'" *International Economic Review*, Vol. 25, No. 3, October 1984.
[40] L. Breiman and D. Freedman, "How Many Variables Should Be Entered in a Regression Equation?" *Journal of the American Statistical Association*, March 1983, pp. 131–136.

regressors (even if a model that includes them is the true model) if this improves the MSE of prediction. For the latter problem, the question is whether we need to assume the existence of a true model or not. For the C_p and PC criteria, as we have seen, we do need to think in terms of a "true" model. For the S_p criterion (or in the stochastic regressor case), we do not have to worry about whether one of the models is the true model or not and what regressors are there in the "true" model.

Akaike's Information Criterion

Akaike's information criterion[41] (AIC) is a more general criterion that can be applied to any model that can be estimated by the method of maximum likelihood. It suggests minimizing

$$\frac{-2 \log L}{n} + \frac{2k}{n}$$

where k is the number of parameters in L. For the regression models this criterion implies minimizing $[\text{RSS} \exp(2k/n)]$, which is the criterion listed in Table 12.3.

We have included AIC in our list because it is the one that is commonly used (at least in nonlinear models) and like the other criteria listed in Table 12.3, it involves RSS_j and k_j only. Thus it can be computed using the standard regression programs.

12.8 IMPLIED *F*-RATIOS FOR THE VARIOUS CRITERIA

We saw earlier (Section 4.10) that maximizing $\bar{R}^2$ implies deletion of variables with an *F*-ratio < 1. We can derive similar conditions for the C_p, S_p, and PC criteria discussed in Section 12.7.

Consider the restricted model with k_1 ($< k$) variables, so that k_2 variables are deleted ($k = k_1 + k_2$). Define $\lambda = \text{RRSS}/\text{URSS}$, where RRSS and URSS are the residual sum of squares from the restricted and unrestricted models, respectively.

Then, as derived in Section 4.8, the *F*-ratio for testing the hypothesis that the coefficients of the k_2 excluded variables are zero is

$$F = \frac{(\text{RRSS} - \text{URSS})/k_2}{\text{URSS}/(n - k)} = \frac{(\lambda - 1)(n - k)}{k_2} \tag{12.4}$$

If the restricted model is chosen, then for the $\bar{R}^2$ criterion, this means that

$$\frac{\text{RRSS}}{n - k_1} < \frac{\text{URSS}}{n - k} \quad \text{or} \quad \lambda < \frac{n - k_1}{n - k} \tag{12.5}$$

---

[41] This criterion is derived in H. Akaike, "Information Theory and an Extension of the Maximum Likelihood Principle," in B. N. Petrov and F. Csaki (eds.), *2nd International Symposium on Information Theory*, (Budapest: Akadémiai Kiadó, 1973) and H. Akaike, "On Entropy Maximization Principle," in P. R. Krishniah (e.d.), *Applications of Statistics* (Amsterdam: North-Holland, 1977).

Substituting in (12.4) and noting that $k = k_1 + k_2$, we get the condition $F < 1$. For Amemiya's PC criterion we have

$$\lambda < \frac{n - k_1}{n + k_1} \frac{n + k}{n - k} \tag{12.6}$$

Substituting this in (12.4) and simplifying, we get

$$F < \frac{2n}{n + k_1} \tag{12.7}$$

For the C_p criterion we have

$$\lambda < 1 + \frac{2k_2}{n - k} \tag{12.8}$$

and thus $F < 2$. For the S_p criterion

$$\lambda < \frac{(n - k_1)(n - k_1 - 1)}{(n - k)(n - k - 1)} \tag{12.9}$$

and thus

$$F < 2 + \frac{k_2 + 1}{n - k - 1} \tag{12.10}$$

For the AIC criterion

$$\lambda < \frac{\exp(k/n)}{\exp(k_1/n)} \tag{12.11}$$

Substituting this in (12.4), we do not get any easy expression as in the other cases, but we can tabulate the values for different values of k/n and k_1/n.

For n large relative to k, we have

$$\exp\left(\frac{k}{n}\right) = 1 + \frac{k}{n}$$

and hence

$$\lambda < \frac{n + k}{n + k_1} \tag{12.12}$$

Substituting this in (12.4), we get

$$F < \frac{n - k}{n + k_1} \qquad \text{which is} < 1 \tag{12.13}$$

The F-values for deletion of the k_2 variables implied by the different criteria are shown in Table 12.4. They stand in the following relation:

$$F(\text{AIC}) < F(\bar{R}^2) = 1 < F(\text{PC}) < F(C_p) = 2 < F(S_p) \tag{12.14}$$

If n is large relative to k, note that PC, C_p and S_p all imply a cutoff value of $F = 2$.

Table 12.4   *F*-Values for Different Criteria

Criterion	Choose the Restricted Model if the F-Ratio for Testing the Restrictions Gives
Maximum $\bar{R}^2$	$F < 1$
Mallows' C_p	$F < 2$
Amemiya's PC	$F < \dfrac{2n}{n + k_1}$
Hocking's S_p	$F < 2 + \dfrac{k_2 + 1}{n - k - 1}$
Akaike's AIC (for n large relative to k)	$F < \dfrac{n - k}{n + k_1}$

The choice between the restricted and unrestricted models is based on an *F*-test for the restrictions. The use of the *F*-ratios in Table 12.4 implies two things:

1. The significance level that we use for the *F*-tests, for testing the restrictions, is not the conventional 5% level of significance. In fact, we use a much higher level of significance.
2. The significance level used, in general, decreases with the sample size. This is particularly true for the cases where we use a constant *F*-ratio like 1 or 2, irrespective of the sample size. It is also true of Amemiya's PC criterion, where the *F*-ratio is less than 2 for small samples and approaches 2 as $n \to \infty$. However, with Hocking's S_p criterion, the cutoff point of *F* declines toward 2 as the sample size increases. Thus in this case we cannot say unambiguously that the significance level decreases with sample size.

The common procedure of using a constant level of significance in hypothesis testing irrespective of sample size has been often criticized on grounds that with a sufficiently large sample every null hypothesis can be rejected. The procedure increasingly distorts the interpretation of data against a null hypothesis as the sample size grows. The significance level should, consequently, be a decreasing function of sample size. [42] As we have seen, the criteria for choice of regressors imply a decreasing significance level as the sample size increases. However, some Bayesian arguments have led to more substantial changes in the significance levels with sample size than are implied by the criteria in Table 12.4. We will discuss one such criterion, that of Leamer, [43] but before that we will explain briefly what the Bayesian approach is.

[42] This argument was made in D. V. Lindley, "A Statistical Paradox," *Biometrika*, Vol. 44, 1957, pp. 187–192, and since then in many Bayesian papers on model selection.
[43] Leamer, *Specification Searches*, pp. 114–116.

Bayes' Theorem and Posterior Odds for Model Selection

Bayes' theorem is based on the definition of conditional probability. Let E_1 and E_2 be two events. Then by the definition of conditional probability, we have

$$P(E_1 \mid E_2) = \frac{P(E_1 E_2)}{P(E_2)} \quad \text{and} \quad P(E_2 \mid E_1) = \frac{P(E_1 E_2)}{P(E_1)}$$

Hence

$$P(E_1 \mid E_2) = \frac{P(E_2 \mid E_1)P(E_1)}{P(E_2)}$$

Now substitute H (hypothesis about the model that generated the data) for E_1 and D (observed data) for E_2. Then we have

$$P(H \mid D) = \frac{P(D \mid H)P(H)}{P(D)} \tag{12.15}$$

Here $P(D \mid H)$ is the probability of observing the data given that H is true. This is usually called the *likelihood*. $P(H)$ is our probability that H is true *before* observing the data (usually called the *prior probability*). $P(H \mid D)$ is the probability that H is true *after* observing the data (usually called the *posterior probability*). $P(D)$ is the unconditional probability of observing the data (whether H is true or not). Often $P(D)$ is difficult to compute. Hence we write the relation above as

$$P(H \mid D) \propto P(D \mid H)P(H)$$

That is: Posterior probability varies with (or is proportional to) likelihood times prior probability.

If we have two hypothesis H_1 and H_2, then

$$P(H_1 \mid D) = \frac{P(D \mid H_1)P(H_1)}{P(D)} \quad \text{and} \quad P(H_2 \mid D) = \frac{P(D \mid H_2)P(H_2)}{P(D)}$$

Hence

$$\frac{P(H_1 \mid D)}{P(H_2 \mid D)} = \frac{P(D \mid H_1)}{P(D \mid H_2)} \frac{P(H_1)}{P(H_2)} \tag{12.16}$$

The left-hand side is called *posterior odds*. The first term on the right-hand side is called the *likelihood ratio*, and the second term on the right-hand side is called the *prior odds*. Thus we have:

Posterior odds equals likelihood ratio times prior odds.

In the problem of choice of regressors, H_1 and H_2 involve some parameters, say β and γ. The likelihood ratio is computed by a weighting procedure, the weights being determined by the prior distributions of these parameter sets. Thus we have

$$\frac{P(H_1 \mid \text{Data})}{P(H_2 \mid \text{Data})} = \frac{\int L_1 P_1(\beta)\,d\beta}{\int L_2 P_2(\gamma)\,d\gamma} \frac{P(H_1)}{P(H_2)} \tag{12.17}$$

where L_1 and L_2 are the respective likelihoods and P_1 and P_2 are the respective prior distributions for the parameters in models 1 and 2. The first term on the right-hand side is sometimes called the *Bayes factor*.

There have been many suggestions in the literature for P_1 and P_2 and thus for the computation of Bayesian posterior odds.[44] Since our purpose here is to illustrate how the implied *F*-ratio changes with the sample size according to some Bayesian arguments, we will present one formula suggested by Leamer. He suggests that the posterior probabilities should satisfy the following properties:

1. There must be no arbitrary constants.
2. The posterior probability of a model should be invariant to linear transformations of the data.
3. There should be a degrees of freedom adjustment: of two models that both yield the same residual sum of squares, the one with the fewer explanatory variables should have the higher posterior probability.

Based on these criteria, Leamer suggests prior distributions P_1 and P_2 and computes the posterior odds as prior odds times the Bayes factor given by (in the notation we are using)

$$B = \left(\frac{RRSS}{URSS}\right)^{n/2} n^{k_2/2} \tag{12.18}$$

Table 12.5 Critical *F*-Values Implied by Bayesian Posterior Odds Criterion

	$n - k$	5	10	50	100
$k_2 = 1$	$k = 1$	1.74	2.44	4.01	4.68
	3	1.48	2.18	3.89	4.60
	5	1.29	1.98	3.78	4.53
	10	0.99	1.62	3.53	4.37
	5% point of *F*	6.60	4.96	4.03	3.94
$k_2 = 3$	$k = 1$	2.42	3.08	4.34	4.90
	3	1.97	2.69	4.20	4.82
	5	1.66	2.40	4.07	4.74
	10	1.20	1.89	3.79	4.56
	5% point of *F*	5.41	3.71	2.79	2.70
$k_2 = 5$	$k = 1$	3.45	3.95	4.70	5.13
	3	2.67	3.36	4.54	5.05
	5	2.16	2.93	4.40	4.96
	10	1.47	2.23	4.07	4.76
	5% point of *F*	5.05	3.33	2.40	2.30

Source: E. E. Leamer, *Specification Searches*, Wiley, New York, 1978, p. 116.

---

[44] An early survey is in K. M. Gaver and M. S. Geisel, "Discriminating Among Alternative Models: Bayesian and Non-bayesian Methods," in P. Zarembka (ed.), *Frontiers of Econometrics* (New York; Academic Press, 1974).

We say that the evidence favors the restricted model if $B < 1$. Using the F-ratio defined in (12.4), we get the condition as

$$F < \frac{n - k}{k_2}(n^{k_2/n} - 1) \tag{12.19}$$

Compared with the F-ratios presented in Table 12.4, this criterion produces large changes in the F-ratios as the sample size n changes. The F-ratios Leamer's criterion implies are presented in Table 12.5.

12.9 CROSS-VALIDATION

One of the major criticisms of the different criteria for selection of regressors that we discussed in the preceding section is that a model we choose may be the best for the period used in estimation but may not be the best when we use it for prediction in future periods. To handle this criticism, it is often suggested that we use only part of the data for the purpose of estimation and save the rest for the purpose of prediction and to check the adequacy of the model chosen. We estimate the different models using the first part and then use the estimated parameters to generate predictions for the second part. The model that minimizes the sum of squared prediction errors is then chosen as the best model.

This procedure of splitting the data into two parts—one for estimation and the other for prediction—is called *cross-validation*. Actually, we have two sets of prediction errors. The prediction errors for the first part (estimation period) are known as *within sample* prediction errors. The sum of squares of these prediction errors is the usual residual sum of squares. The prediction errors from the second part are known as the *out-of-sample* prediction errors. Different criteria in cross-validation depend on different weights given to the sums of squares of these two sets of prediction errors. A criterion often used is to give equal weights to these two sets of prediction errors.

What the cross-validation procedure does is to impose a penalty for parameter instability. If the parameters are not stable between the estimation period and prediction period, the sum-of-squared out-of-sample prediction errors will be large even if the sum of squares of within-sample prediction errors is small. Thus the procedure of model selection by cross-validation implies choosing the model that minimizes: the usual residual sum of squares plus a penalty for parameter instability.

Instead of splitting the data into two sets and using one for estimation and the other for prediction, we can follow the procedure of using one observation at a time for prediction (and the remaining observations for estimation). That is, in fact, the idea behind "predicted residuals" discussed earlier in Section 12.4. There the sum of squares of the predicted residuals, PRESS, was suggested as a criterion for model choice. Note that at each stage $(n - 1)$ observation are within sample (i.e., used for estimation) and the remaining observation is out-of-sample (i.e., used for prediction). PRESS is the sum of squares of out-of-sample prediction errors.

Instead of using PRESS (the sum of squares of predicted residuals) as a criterion for model choice, we can consider the sum of squares of studentized residuals as a criterion of model choice.[45] As discussed in Section 12.4, the studentized residual is just the predicted residual divided by its standard error. The sum of squares of studentized residuals can be denoted by SSSR and the sum of squares of predicted residuals as SSPR. This would be a better terminology, in keeping with the use of the term "residual" for an "estimated error." From the derivatives in Section 12.3 we note that both SSPR and SSSR are weighted sums of squares of the least squares residuals $\hat{u}_i$. The $\bar{R}^2$ criterion also involves minimizing a weighted sum of squares of least squares residuals (we minimize $\sum \hat{u}_i^2 / \text{d.f.}$). To be a valid criterion of model choice we should be able to show that the expected value of the quantity minimized is less for the true model than for the alternative models. If this is not the case, the criterion does not consistently select the true model. Leamer[46] shows that the $\bar{R}^2$ criterion, and the SSSR criterion, which minimizes sum of squares of studentized residuals (this is Schmidt's SSPE criterion), satisfy this test and are valid criteria, but that the PRESS criterion and other criteria suggested in cross-validation are not valid by this test. Thus if one is interested in using predicted residuals for model choice, the best procedure appears to be not one of splitting the sample into two parts but to derive studentized residuals (the SAS regression program gives them) and consider minimization of the sum of squares of studentized residuals (SSSR) as a criterion of model choice (i.e., use Schmidt's SSPE criterion).

12.10 HAUSMAN'S SPECIFICATION ERROR TEST

Hausman's specification error test[47] is a general and widely used test for testing the hypothesis of no misspecification in the model.

Let H_0 denote the null hypothesis that there is no misspecification and let H_1 denote the alternative hypothesis that there is a misspecification (of a particular type). For instance, if we consider the regression model

$$y = \beta x + u \tag{12.20}$$

in order to use the OLS procedure, we specify that x is independent of u. Thus the null and alternative hypotheses are:

$$H_0: \quad x \text{ and } u \text{ are independent}$$

$$H_1: \quad x \text{ and } u \text{ are not independent}$$

To implement Hausman's test, we have to construct two estimators $\hat{\beta}_0$ and $\hat{\beta}_1$, which

---

[45] This is the criterion proposed in Peter Schmidt, "Choosing Among Alternative Linear Regression Models," *Atlantic Economic Journal*, 1974, pp. 7–13.

[46] E. E. Leamer, "Model Choice and Specification Analysis," in Z. Griliches and M. D. Intrilligator (eds.), *Handbook of Econometrics*, Vol. 1 (Amsterdam: North-Holland, 1983), Chap. 5, pp. 285–330.

[47] J. A. Hausman, "Specification Tests in Econometrics," *Econometrica*, Vol. 46, No. 6, November 1978, pp. 1251–1271.

have the following properties:

$\hat{\beta}_0$ is consistent and efficient under H_0 but is not consistent under H_1.

$\hat{\beta}_1$ is consistent under *both* H_0 and H_1 but is not efficient under H_0.

Then we consider the difference $\hat{q} = \hat{\beta}_1 - \hat{\beta}_0$. Hausman first shows that

$$\text{var}(\hat{q}) = V_1 - V_0$$

where $V_1 = \text{var}(\hat{\beta}_1)$ and $V_0 = \text{var}(\hat{\beta}_0)$, both variances being computed under H_0. Let $\hat{V}(\hat{q})$ be a consistent estimate of $\text{var}(\hat{q})$. Then we use

$$m = \frac{\hat{q}^2}{\hat{V}(\hat{q})}$$

as a χ^2 with 1 d.f. to test H_0 against H_1. This is an asymptotic test.

We have considered only a single parameter β. In the general case where β is a vector of k parameters, V_1 and V_0 will be matrices, $\hat{\beta}_1, \hat{\beta}_0$, and $\hat{q}$ will all be vectors and the Hausman test statistic is

$$m = \hat{q}'[\hat{V}(\hat{q})]^{-1}\hat{q}$$

which has (asymptotically) a χ^2-distribution with degrees of freedom k.

Since a consideration of the k-parameter case involves vectors and matrices, we discuss the single-parameter case. The derivations in the k-parameter case are all similar.

To prove the result $\text{var}(\hat{q}) = V_1 - V_0$, we first have to prove the result that

$$\text{cov}(\hat{\beta}_0, \hat{q}) = 0$$

The proof proceeds as follows. Under H_0, both $\hat{\beta}_0$ and $\hat{\beta}_1$ are consistent estimates for β. Hence we get

$$\text{plim } \hat{q} = \text{plim } \hat{\beta}_1 - \text{plim } \hat{\beta}_0 = \beta - \beta = 0$$

Consider a new estimator for β defined by

$$\hat{d} = \hat{\beta}_0 + \lambda\hat{q}$$

where λ is any constant. Then plim $\hat{d} = \beta$. Thus $\hat{d}$ is a consistent estimator of β for all values of λ.

$$V(\hat{d}) = V_0 + \lambda^2 \text{var}(\hat{q}) + 2\lambda \text{cov}(\hat{\beta}_0, \hat{q}) \geq V_0$$

Since $\hat{\beta}_0$ is efficient. Thus

$$\lambda^2 \text{var}(\hat{q}) + 2\lambda \text{cov}(\hat{\beta}_0, \hat{q}) \geq 0 \tag{12.21}$$

for all values of λ. We will show that the relationship (12.21) can be satisfied for all values of λ only if $\text{cov}(\hat{\beta}_0, \hat{q}) = 0$.

Suppose that $\text{cov}(\hat{\beta}_0, \hat{q}) > 0$. Then by choosing λ negative and equal to $-\text{cov}(\hat{\beta}_0, \hat{q})/\text{var}(\hat{q})$, we can show that the relationship (12.21) is violated. Thus $\text{cov}(\hat{\beta}_0, \hat{q})$ is not greater than zero.

Similarly, suppose that $\text{cov}(\hat{\beta}_0, \hat{q}) < 0$. Then by choosing λ positive and equal to

$-\text{cov}(\hat{\beta}_0, \hat{q})/\text{var}(\hat{q})$, we show that the relationship (12.21) is violated. Thus $\text{cov}(\hat{\beta}_0, \hat{q})$ cannot be greater than or less than zero. Hence we get $\text{cov}(\hat{\beta}_0, \hat{q}) = 0$.

Now since $\hat{\beta}_1 = \hat{\beta}_0 + \hat{q}$ and $\text{cov}(\hat{\beta}_0, \hat{q}) = 0$, we get

$$\text{var}(\hat{\beta}_1) = \text{var}(\hat{\beta}_0) + \text{var}(\hat{q})$$

or

$$\text{var}(\hat{q}) = \text{var}(\hat{\beta}_1) - \text{var}(\hat{\beta}_0) = V_1 - V_0$$

which is the result on which Hausman's test is based.

An Application: Testing for Errors in Variables or Exogeneity

Consider now the model given by equation (12.20). The model can be regarded as an errors-in-variables model (Chapter 11), where x is correlated with the error term u because it is an error-ridden explanatory variable. In this case our interest is in testing whether there is an error in this variable or not.

Alternatively, equation (12.20) can be regarded as one equation in a simultaneous equations model (Chapter 9) and x is correlated with u because it is an endogenous variable. We are interested in testing whether x is exogenous or endogenous. If x is not correlated with u, we are justified in estimating the equation by OLS.

Under H_1, $\hat{\beta}_0$ is not consistent. To get a consistent estimator for β we have to use the instrumental variable (IV) method. Let us denote the instrumental variable by z. Then the IV estimator is

$$\hat{\beta}_1 = \frac{\sum yz}{\sum xz} = \beta + \frac{\sum uz}{\sum xz}$$

$$V_1 = \text{var}(\hat{\beta}_1) = \sigma^2 \frac{\sum z^2}{(\sum xz)^2}$$

$\hat{\beta}_1$ is consistent under both H_0 and H_1. It is, however, less efficient than $\hat{\beta}_0$.

Defining $\hat{q} = \hat{\beta}_1 - \hat{\beta}_0$, we have

$$\text{var}(\hat{q}) = V_1 - V_0 = \sigma^2 \left[\frac{\sum z^2}{(\sum xz)^2} - \frac{1}{\sum x^2} \right]$$

$$= \frac{\sigma^2}{\sum x^2} \left[\frac{\sum x^2 \sum z^2}{(\sum xz)^2} - 1 \right] = \frac{\sigma^2}{\sum x^2} \left(\frac{1}{r^2} - 1 \right)$$

$$= V_0 \frac{1 - r^2}{r^2}$$

where r^2 is the squared correlation between x and the instrumental variable z.[48]

---

[48] Note that both V_1 and V_0 depend on σ^2. But when we get an estimate of $\text{var}(\hat{q})$, the estimate of σ^2 we use is the one obtained under H_0.

The test statistic is

$$m = \frac{\hat{q}^2 r^2}{(1 - r^2)\hat{V}_0}$$

which we use as χ^2 with 1 d.f.

Some Illustrative Examples

As an illustration, let us consider the data on Australian wine industry in Chapter 9 (Table 9.2). Let us consider the equation (all variables in log form)

$$Q_t = \alpha + \beta p_t^w + u_t$$

We are interested in testing the hypothesis that p_t^w is exogenous. The OLS estimator of β is

$$\beta_0 = \frac{1.78037}{0.507434} = 3.5085$$

Using the index of storage costs s as an instrumental variable, we get the IV estimator as

$$\hat{\beta}_1 = \frac{2.75474}{0.500484} = 5.4862$$

$$\hat{q} = \hat{\beta}_1 - \hat{\beta}_0 = 1.9777$$

The squared correlation coefficient between p_t^w and s_t is $r^2 = 0.408$. We also have

$$\hat{\sigma}^2 = 0.09217 \quad \text{and} \quad \hat{V}_0 = \frac{0.09217}{0.507434} = 0.18164$$

The test statistic is

$$m = \frac{(\hat{q}r)^2}{(1 - r^2)\hat{V}_0} = 14.84$$

This is significant at the 1% level (from the χ^2-tables with 1 d.f.). Thus we cannot treat p^w as exogenous and we have to consider a simultaneous equations model.

Let us see what happens if we use per capita disposable income y_t as the instrumental variable. In this case we have

$$\hat{\beta}_1 = \frac{2.215}{0.4592} = 4.8236$$

$$r^2 = 0.624$$

$$\hat{q} = 4.8236 - 3.5085 = 1.3151$$

The test statistic is now

$$m = \frac{(1.3151)^2(0.624)}{0.376(0.18164)} = 15.80$$

Again, this is significant at the 1% level, indicating that we have to treat p^w as endogenous.

As yet another example, consider the demand and supply model for pork considered in Chapter 9 (data in Table 9.1). Let us consider the hypothesis that Q is exogenous in the demand function(normalized with respect to P).

$$P = \alpha + \beta Q + \gamma Y + u$$

The OLS estimate of β is

$$\hat{\beta} = -1.2518 \text{ with SE} = 0.1032$$

The 2SLS estimate of β is

$$\tilde{\beta} = -1.2165$$

Thus

$$\hat{q} = \tilde{\beta} - \hat{\beta} = 0.0353$$
$$\hat{V}_0 = (0.1032)^2 = 0.01065$$

The instrumental variable that is implied by the use of the 2SLS is $\hat{Q}$, the predicted value of Q from the reduced form. The squared correlation between Q and $\hat{Q}$ is the R^2 from the reduced-form equation for Q, which is 0.898. Hence the test statistic is

$$\overset{.}{m} = \frac{(0.0353)^2(0.898)}{(1 - .898)(0.01065)} = 1.03$$

which is not significant even at the 25% level (from the χ^2-tables with 1 d.f.).

Thus we can treat Q as exogenous and estimate the demand equation by OLS. Note that this was our conclusion in Section 9.3.

An Omitted Variable Interpretation of the Hausman Test

There is an alternative way of implementing the Hausman test. Returning to equation (12.20), let $\hat{x}$ be the predicted value of x from a regression of x on the instrumental variable z, and $\hat{v}$ the estimated residual. That is, $\hat{v} = x - \hat{x}$. Then estimate by OLS the equation

$$y = \beta x + \gamma \hat{x} + \varepsilon$$

or

$$y = \beta x + \gamma \hat{v} + \varepsilon$$

and test the hypothesis $\gamma = 0$. These equations are known as *expanded regressions*. This test is identically the same as the test based on the statistic m derived earlier.

We will not prove this result[49] but we will explicitly state what the OLS estimate $\hat{\gamma}$

---

[49] For a proof, see Hausman, "Specification Tests," p. 1261.

will turn out to be. We have

$$\hat{\gamma} = \frac{\hat{\beta}_1 - \hat{\beta}_0}{1 - r^2} = \frac{\hat{q}}{1 - r^2}$$

where r^2 is the squared correlation between x and z. Also,

$$\text{var}(\hat{\gamma}) = \frac{V_0}{r^2(1 - r^2)}$$

Thus

$$\frac{\hat{\gamma}^2}{\text{var}(\hat{\gamma})} = \frac{\hat{q}^2 r^2}{(1 - r^2)V_0} = m$$

the statistic obtained earlier.

This omitted variable interpretation enables us to generalize the test to the case where we have more variables whose exogeneity we are interested in testing.

Suppose that one of the equations in a simultaneous equations model is

$$y_1 = \beta_2 y_2 + \beta_3 y_3 + \alpha_1 z_1 + u_1 \tag{12.22}$$

We want to test the hypothesis that y_2 and y_3 are exogenous (i.e., independent of u_1), the alternative hypothesis being that they are not. The variable z_1 is considered exogenous.

To apply the test, we need to have at least two instrumental variables, say z_2 and z_3. But there could be more in the system. Then what we do is regress y_2 and y_3 on the other exogenous variables in the system and obtain the predicted values $\hat{y}_2$ and $\hat{y}_3$. Now we estimate the *expanded regression equation*

$$y_1 = \beta_2 y_2 + \beta_3 y_3 + \alpha_1 z_1 + \gamma_2 \hat{y}_2 + \gamma_3 \hat{y}_3 + \varepsilon \tag{12.23}$$

by ordinary least squares and test the hypothesis $\gamma_2 = \gamma_3 = 0$ (by the methods described in Chapter 4). This is the Hausman test for exogeneity.

Let us define $\hat{v}_2 = y_2 - \hat{y}_2$ and $\hat{v}_3 = y_3 - \hat{y}_3$. Then, instead of (12.23), we can also estimate

$$y_1 = \beta_2 y_2 + \beta_3 y_3 + \alpha_1 z_1 + \gamma_2 \hat{v}_2 + \gamma_3 \hat{v}_3 + \varepsilon \tag{12.24}$$

by OLS and test the hypothesis $\gamma_2 = \gamma_3 = 0$.

This procedure applies *only* if we are testing the exogenity of all the variables under question and does not apply for testing the exogeneity of a subset of these variables. For instance, in equation (12.22) suppose we assume that y_2 is endogenous and z_1 is exogenous. What we want to do is test the hypothesis that y_3 is exogenous. Now we cannot just estimate equations like (12.23) and (12.24) and just test $\gamma_3 = 0$. Nor does the equivalence between (12.23) and (12.24) apply anymore.[50]

In this case we have to obtain the 2SLS estimates of β_3 under two assumptions:

1. y_3 *is exogenous.* Call this estimate $\hat{\beta}_3$ with variance V_0.
2. y_3 *is endogenous.* Call this estimate $\tilde{\beta}_3$ with variance V_1.

---

[50] This is pointed out in Alberto Holly, "A Simple Procedure for Testing Whether a Subset of Endogenous Variables Is Independent of the Disturbance Term in a Structural Equation," discussion paper, University of Lausanne, November 1982.

Then $\hat{q} = \tilde{\beta}_3 - \hat{\beta}_3$ and $\text{var}(\hat{q}) = V_1 - V_0$. We now apply the Hausman test as explained earlier. Note that both V_1 and V_0 depend on $\sigma^2 = \text{var}(u_1)$. However, when we get an estimate of $\text{var}(\hat{q})$ we have to use the estimate of σ^2 under H_0, that is, from the 2SLS estimation treating y_3 as exogenous.

The omitted variable method in this case is somewhat complicated, but consists of the following steps:

1. First we get the reduced-form residuals for the endogenous variables y_2 and y_3 as before. Call these residuals $\hat{v}_2$ and $\hat{v}_3$. However, we do not use these as the omitted variables. We construct linear combinations of these as explained in the next step.

2. Form the covariance matrix of these residuals and get its inverse. Denote this by

$$\begin{pmatrix} C_{22} & C_{23} \\ C_{32} & C_{33} \end{pmatrix}$$

In our simple case we have

$$C_{22} = \frac{\sum \hat{V}_3^2}{\Delta} \qquad C_{33} = \frac{\sum \hat{V}_2^2}{\Delta} \qquad C_{23} = C_{32} = -\frac{\sum \hat{V}_2 \hat{V}_3}{\Delta}$$

where $\Delta = \sum \hat{V}_2^2 \sum \hat{V}_3^2 - (\sum \hat{V}_2 \hat{V}_3)^2$.

3. Define

$$x_2 = C_{22} \hat{V}_2 + C_{23} \hat{V}_3$$
$$x_3 = C_{32} \hat{V}_2 + C_{33} \hat{V}_3$$

These are the missing variables we use.

4. Estimate the following equation by OLS.

$$y_1 = \beta_2 y_2 + \beta_3 y_3 + \alpha_1 z_1 + \gamma_2 x_2 + \gamma_3 x_3 + \varepsilon$$

and test the hypothesis $\gamma_3 = 0$. This is the required test for the hypothesis that y_3 is exogenous.

The test is actually not very complicated. In fact, step 1 has to be used in any 2SLS estimation. Only step 2 involves matrix inversion. Once this is done, step 3 is easy and step 4 is just OLS estimation.

12.11 THE PLOSSER–SCHWERT–WHITE DIFFERENCING TEST

The Plosser–Schwert–White (PSW) differencing test [51] is, like the Hausman test, a general test for model misspecification, but is applicable for time-series data only. The test involves estimation of the regression models in levels and in first differences.

---

[51] C. I. Plosser, G. W. Schwert, and H. White, "Differencing as a Test of Specification," *International Economic Review*, October 1982, pp. 535–552.

If the model is correctly specified, the estimators from the differenced and undifferenced models have the same probability limits and hence the results should corroborate one another. On the other hand, if there are specification errors, the differenced regression should lead to different results. The PSW test, like the Hausman test, is based on a comparison from the differenced and undifferenced regressions.

Davidson, Godfrey, and MacKinnon[52] show that, like the Hausman test, the PSW test is equivalent to a much simpler omitted variables test, the omitted variables being the sum of the lagged and one-period forward values of the variables.

Thus if the regression equation we are considering is

$$y_t = \beta_1 x_{1t} + \beta_2 x_{2t} + u_t$$

the PSW test involves estimating the expanded regression equation

$$y_t = \beta_1 x_{1t} + \beta_2 x_{2t} + \gamma_1 z_{1t} + \gamma_2 z_{2t} + u_t$$

where

$$z_{1t} = x_{1,t+1} + x_{1,t-1}$$

$$z_{2t} = x_{2,t+1} + x_{2,t-1}$$

and testing the hypothesis $\gamma_1 = \gamma_2 = 0$ by the usual F-test.

If there are lagged dependent variables in the equation, the test needs a minor modification. Suppose that the model is

$$y_t = \beta_1 y_{t-1} + \beta_2 x_t + u_t$$

Now the omitted variables would be defined as

$$z_{1t} = y_t + y_{t-2}$$

and

$$z_{2t} = x_{t+1} + x_{t-1}$$

There is no problem with z_{2t} but z_{1t} would be correlated with the error term u_t because of the presence of y_t in it. The solution would be simply to transfer it to the left-hand side and write the expanded regression equation as

$$(1 - \gamma_1)y_t = \beta_1 y_{t-1} + \beta_2 x_t + \gamma_1 y_{t-2} + \gamma_2 z_{2t} + u_t$$

This equation can be written as

$$y_t = \beta_1^* y_{t-1} + \beta_2^* x_t + \gamma_1^* y_{t-2} + \gamma_2^* z_{2t} + u_t^*$$

where all the starred parameters are the corresponding unstarred ones divided by $(1 - \gamma_1)$.

The PSW test now tests the hypothesis $\gamma_1^* = \gamma_2^* = 0$. Thus, in the case where the

---

[52] R. Davidson, L. G. Godfrey, and J. G. MacKinnon, "A Simplified Version of the Differencing Test," *International Economic Review*, October, 1985, pp. 639–647.

model involves the lagged dependent variable y_{t-1} as an explanatory variable, the only modification needed is that we should use y_{t-2} as the omitted variable, not $(y_t + y_{t-2})$. For the other explanatory variables, the corresponding omitted variables are defined as before. Note that it is only y_{t-1} that creates a problem, not higher-order lags of y_t, like y_{t-2}, y_{t-3}, and so on.

12.12 TESTS FOR NONNESTED HYPOTHESES

Consider the problem of testing two hypotheses:

$$H_0: \quad y = \beta x + u_0 \qquad u_0 \sim IN(0, \sigma_0^2) \tag{12.25}$$

$$H_1: \quad y = \gamma z + u_1 \qquad u_1 \sim IN(0, \sigma_1^2) \tag{12.26}$$

The hypotheses are said to be *nonnested* since the explanatory variables under one of the hypotheses are not a subset of the explanatory variables in the other.

It is a common occurrence in economics that there are many competing economic theories trying to explain the same variable (consumption, investment, etc.), and the explanatory variables in the different theories contain nonoverlapping variables. An extreme example is the paper by Friedman and Meiselman[53] around which there was a considerable amount of controversy in the 1960s. The Keynesian and monetarist theories were formulated in their simplified form as

$$C_t = \alpha_0 + \beta_0 A_t + u_{0t} \qquad \text{(Keynesian)}$$

$$C_t = \alpha_1 + \beta_1 M_t + u_{1t} \qquad \text{(Monetarist)}$$

where C_t = consumption expenditure in constant dollars
   A_t = autonomous expenditure in constant dollars
   M_t = money supply

The Davidson and MacKinnon Test

There have been several tests that have been suggested for testing such nonnested hypotheses.[54] The first such test is the Cox test. However, we will outline some simple alternative and asymptotically equivalent tests suggested by Davidson and MacKinnon[55] that are easy to apply. Their test procedure for testing H_0 against H_1

[53] M. Friedman and D. Meiselman, "The Relative Stability of Monetary Velocity and the Investment Multiplier in the U.S. 1897–1958," in *Stabilization Policies* (Commission on Money and Credit) (Englewood Cliffs, N. J.: Prentice-Hall), 1963).

[54] Two surveys of this extensive literature are: J. G. MacKinnon, "Model Specification Tests Against Non-nested Alternatives" (with discussion), *Econometric Reviews*, Vol. 2, 1983, pp. 85–158 and M. McAleer and M. H. Pesaran, "Statistical Inference in Non-nested Econometric Models," *Applied Mathematics and Computation*, 1986.

[55] R. Davidson and J. G. MacKinnon, "Several Tests for Model Specification in the Presence of Alternative Hypotheses," *Econometrica*, Vol. 49, 1981, pp. 781–793. The survey paper by MacKinnon contains additional references to the papers by Davidson and MacKinnon.

(H_0 is the maintained hypothesis) is as follows:

1. Estimate (12.26) by OLS. Let $\hat{y}_1 = \hat{\gamma}z$ be the predicted value of y.
2. Estimate the regression equation

$$y = \beta x + \alpha \hat{y}_1 + u \tag{12.27}$$

and test the hypothesis $\alpha = 0$.

If the hypothesis is not rejected, then H_0 is not rejected by H_1. If the hypothesis is rejected, then H_0 is rejected by H_1.

A test of H_1 against H_0 would be based on analogous steps.

1. Estimate (12.25) by OLS. Let $\hat{y}_0 = \hat{\beta}x$ be the predicted value of y.
2. Estimate the regression equation

$$y = \gamma z + \delta \hat{y}_0 + v \tag{12.28}$$

and test the hypothesis $\delta = 0$.

If the hypothesis is not rejected, then H_1 is not rejected by H_0. If the hypothesis is rejected, then H_1 is rejected by H_0.

The outcome of these two tests can be summarized as follows:

Hpothesis: $\delta = 0$	Hypothesis: $\alpha = 0$	
	Not Rejected	*Rejected*
Not rejected	Both H_0 and H_1 are acceptable	H_1 is acceptable H_0 is not
Rejected	H_0 is acceptable H_1 is not	Neither H_0 nor H_1 is acceptable

The motivation behind the tests suggested by Davidson and MacKinnon is the following: The models given by H_0 and H_1 can be combined into a single model

$$y = (1 - \alpha)\beta x + \alpha(\gamma z) + u \tag{12.29}$$

and testing $\alpha = 0$ versus $\alpha = 1$. However, there is no way of estimating β, γ, and α from this model. All we get are estimates of $(1 - \alpha)\beta$ and $\alpha\gamma$. Davidson and MacKinnon show that we can substitute $\hat{y}_1 = \hat{\gamma}z$ for γz in (12.29) and then test $\alpha = 0$. They show that under H_0, $\hat{\alpha}$ from (12.27) is asymptotically $N(0, 1)$. They call this the *J*-test (because α and β are estimated *jointly*). Note that the *J*-tests are one degree of freedom tests irrespective of the number of explanatory variables in H_0 and H_1.

The relationship between the *J*-test and optimum combination of forecasts is as follows: We have two forecasts of y from the two models (12.25) and (12.26). Call these $\hat{y}_0$ and $\hat{y}_1$, respectively. The two forecasts can be combined to produce a forecast with a smaller forecast error.[56] The combination can be written as

$$\hat{y} = (1 - \alpha)\hat{y}_0 + \alpha\hat{y}_1$$

---

[56] See C. W. J. Granger and P. Newbold, *Forecasting Economic Time Series*, 2nd ed. (New York: Academic Press, 1986), pp. 266–267 on combination of forecasts.

The value of α that gives the minimum forecast error is

$$\alpha = \frac{\lambda_1^2 - \rho\lambda_1\lambda_2}{\lambda_1^2 + \lambda_2^2 - 2\rho\lambda_1\lambda_2}$$

λ_1^2 and λ_2^2 are, respectively, the variances of the forecast errors $(y - \hat{y}_0)$ and $(y - \hat{y}_1)$ and ρ is the correlation between these forecast errors. Also,

$$\alpha \gtreqless 0 \quad \text{if and only if} \quad \frac{\lambda_1}{\lambda_2} \gtreqless \rho$$

Corresponding to the optimum combination of forecasts, equation (12.29) can also be written as

$$y = (1 - \alpha)\hat{y}_0 + \alpha\hat{y}_1 + v$$

where v is the error term. This can also be written as

$$y - \hat{y}_0 = \alpha(\hat{y}_1 - \hat{y}_0) + v$$

If we estimate this equation and the estimate of α is not significantly different from zero, we can say that H_1 does not add anything to explaining y over H_0. If α is significantly different from zero, H_1 explains y over and above H_0.

We will not pursue the extensions of the J-test here.[57] We will, however, discuss a few of the limitations.[58] One limitation of the test is that sometimes it rejects both H_0 and H_1 or accepts H_0 and H_1. Although this conclusion suggests that we should go back and examine both models, in many cases we would like to have some ranking of the models.

An alternative procedure is to embed the two models given by H_0 and H_1 into a comprehensive model

$$y = \beta x + \gamma z + u \tag{12.30}$$

and testing H_0 by testing $\gamma = 0$ and testing H_1 by testing $\beta = 0$. When there are more than one variable in x and z, these tests will be F-tests. This is in contrast to the J-test, which is a one-degree-of-freedom test whatever the number of explanatory variables in H_0 and H_1.

The Encompassing Test

At first sight it would appear that there is no relationship between the F-tests and the J-test. This is not so. Mizon and Richard[59] suggest a more general test called the

---

[57] McAleer and Pesaran, "Statistical Inference." G. R. Fisher and M. McAleer, "Alternative Procedures and Associated Tests of Significance for Non-nested Hypotheses," *Journal of Econometrics*, Vol. 16 (1981), pp. 103–119, suggest what is known as the *JA* test. Unlike the *J*-test, which is asymptotic, the *JA* test is a small-sample test (if x and z are fixed in repeated samples).

[58] A good review and discussion of the limitations of nonnested tests is L. G. Godfrey, "On the Use of Misspecification Checks and Tests of Non-nested Hypotheses in Empirical Econometrics," *Economic Journal*, Supplement, 1985, pp. 69–81.

[59] G. E. Mizon and J. F. Richard, "The Encompassing Principle and Its Application to Testing Non-nested Hypotheses," *Econometrica*, Vol. 54, 1986, pp. 657–678.

"encompassing test" of which the F-test and J-test are special cases. The encompassing principle is based on the idea that a model builder should analyze whether his model can account for salient features of rival models.[60] The encompassing test is a formulation of this principle. If your model is specified by H_0 and the rival model by H_1, a formal test of H_0 against H_1 is to compare $\hat{\gamma}$ and $\hat{\sigma}_1^2$ obtained under H_1 from equation (12.26), with the probability limits of these parameters under your hypothesis H_0. Comparing $\hat{\gamma}$ with plim $\hat{\gamma} \mid H_0$ gives the *mean encompassing test*. Comparing $\hat{\sigma}_1^2$ with plim $\hat{\sigma}_1^2 \mid H_0$ gives the *variance encompassing test*. Mizon and Richard show that the F-test is a mean encompassing test and the J-test is a variance encompassing test. This explains why the J-test is a one-degree-of-freedom test no matter how many explanatory variables there are in the models given by H_0 and H_1. The complete encompassing test (CET) suggested by Mizon and Richard is a *joint* test that compares $\hat{\gamma}_1$ and $\hat{\sigma}_1^2$ with their probability limits under H_0. A discussion of this joint test is beyond the scope of this book. Further, there is not much empirical evidence on it. The F-test and J-test, on the other hand, can be very easily implemented.

In summary, to test the nonnested hypothesis H_0 against H_1, we need to apply two tests:

1. The J-test testing $\alpha = 0$ based on equation (12.27).
2. The F-test testing $\gamma = 0$ in the comprehensive model (12.30).

As to how these tests perform in small samples, some experimental evidence suggests that the one-degree-of-freedom J-test is better than the F-test at rejecting the false model. However, this is no consolation because it has also been found that the J-test tends to reject the true model too frequently with the estimated small-sample significance levels being so large that it is often difficult to justify asymptotically valid critical values.[61] Yet another shortcoming of the nonnested tests is that if both H_0 and H_1 are false, these tests are inferior to standard diagnostic tests (discussed in earlier sections of this chapter.)[62]

What all this suggests is that in testing nonnested hypotheses, one should use the J-test with higher significance levels and supplement it with the F-test on the comprehensive model and standard diagnostic tests.

A Basic Problem in Testing Nonnested Hypotheses

The specification implied by equations (12.25) and (12.26) does not by itself enable us to make a valid comparison of the two models. In fact, this is the problem with testing nonnested models. Equation (12.25) specifies the conditional distribution of y *given* x. Similarly, equation (12.26) specifies the condition distribution y *given* z.

---

[60] J. E. H. Davidson and D. F. Hendry, "Interpreting Econometric Evidence: The Behavior of Consumers' Expenditures in the U.K.," *European Economic Review*, Vol. 16, 1981, pp. 179–198.

[61] Godfrey, "On the Use," p. 76.

[62] Godfrey "On the Use," p. 79. Godfrey quotes N. R. Erickson's Ph.D. thesis (1982) at the London School of Economics, which provides a numerical example in which F and one-degree-of-freedom tests reject only one of the two competing models, but misspecification tests decisively reject H_0, H_1, and the comprehensive model.

How can we compare these two conditional distributions unless the role of z under H_0 and the role of x under H_1 are specified? What we are given are two non-comparable conditional distributions. H_0 does not specify anything about the relationship between y and z. H_1 does not specify anything about the relationship between y and x. Thus to compare the two models given by (12.25) and (12.26), we should be able to derive the conditional distributions of $f(y|x)$ and $g(y|z)$ under both H_0 and H_1. To do this we have to supplement equations (12.25) and (12.26) by more equations. This is what is done by Mizon and Richard.

SUMMARY

1. Diagnostic tests are tests that "diagnose" specific problems with the model we are estimating. The least squares residuals can be used to diagnose the problems of heteroskedasticity, autocorrelation, omission of relevant variables, and ARCH effects in errors (see Section 12.2). Tests for heteroskedasticity and autocorrelation have been discussed in Chapters 5 and 6, respectively. To test for omitted variables, we first estimate the equation by OLS and use $\hat{y}_t^2$ and higher powers of $\hat{y}_t$ as additional variables, reestimate the equation, and test that the coefficients of these added variables are zero. A test based on a regression of $\hat{u}_t$ the estimated residual on $\hat{y}_t^2$ and higher powers of $\hat{y}_t$ is not a valid test. To test for ARCH effects, we estimate the regression

$$\hat{u}_t^2 = \gamma_0 + \gamma_1 \hat{u}_{t-1}^2 + e_t$$

and test $\gamma_1 = 0$.

2. There are two problems with the least squares residuals. They are heteroskedastic and autocorrelated even if the true errors are independent and have a common variance of σ^2 (see Section 12.3). To solve these problems, some alternative residuals have been suggested (see Section 12.4). Two such residuals, which are uncorrelated and have a common variance, are the BLUS residuals and recursive residuals. The BLUS residuals are more difficult to compute than the recursive residuals; moreover, in tests of heteroskedasticity and autocorrelation, their performance is not as good as that of least squares residuals. Hence we consider only recursive residuals. Two other types of residuals are the predicted residuals and studentized residuals. Both of these are, like the least squares residuals, heteroskedastic and autocorrelated. However, some statisticians have found the predicted residuals useful in choosing between regression models and the studentized residuals in the detection of outliers. The predicted residuals, studentized residuals, and recursive residuals can all be computed using the dummy variable method.

3. The usual approach to outliers based on least squares residuals involves looking at the OLS residuals, deleting the observations with large residuals, and reestimating the equation. During recent years an alternative criterion has been suggested. This is based on a criterion called DFFITS which measures the change in the fitted value $\hat{y}$ of y that results from dropping a particular observation. Further, we do not drop outliers. We merely see that their influence is minimized. This is what

is known as bounded influence estimation (Section 12.5). The SAS regression program computes DFFITS.

4. According to Leamer, the process of model building involves several types of specification searches. These can be classified under the headings: hypothesis-testing search, interpretive search, simplification search, proxy variable search, data selection search, and post-data model construction.

5. Hendry argues that most of empirical econometric work starts with very simplified models and that not enough diagnostic tests are applied to check whether something is wrong with the maintained model. His suggested strategy is to start with a very general model and then progressively simplify it by applying some data-based simplification tests. (The arguments for this are discussed in Section 12.6).

6. A special problem in model selection that we often encounter is that of selection of regressors. Several criteria have been suggested in the literature: the maximum $\bar{R}^2$ criterion and the predictive criteria PC, C_p, and S_p. These criteria are summarized in Section 12.7. There is, however, some difference in these criteria. In the case of the maximum $\bar{R}^2$ criterion what we are trying to do is pick the "true" model assuming that one of the models considered is the "true" one. In the case of prediction criteria, we are interested in parsimony and we would like to omit some of the regressors if this improves the MSE of prediction. For this problem the question is whether or not we need to assume the existence of a true model. For the PC and C_p criteria we need to assume the existence of a true model. For the S_p criterion we do not. For this reason the S_p criterion appears to be the most preferable among these criteria.

7. In Section 12.8 we discuss the critical F-ratios implied by the different criteria for selection of regressors. We show that

$$F(\bar{R}^2) = 1 < F(\text{PC}) < F(C_p) = 2 < F(S_p)$$

We also present the F-ratios implied by Leamer's posterior odds analysis. This method implies that the critical F-ratios used should be higher for higher sample sizes. For most sample sizes frequently encountered, F-ratios are > 2, which is another argument against $\bar{R}^2$ criterion and the PC and C_p criteria.

8. Cross-validation methods are often used to choose between different models. These methods depend on splitting the data into two parts: one for estimation and the other for prediction. The model that minimizes the sum-of-squared prediction errors is chosen as the best model. A better procedure than splitting the data into two parts is to leave out one observation at a time for prediction, derive the studentized residuals (the SAS regression program gives these), and use the sum of squares of the studentized residuals as a criterion of model choice.

9. A general test for specification errors that is easy to use is the Hausman test. Let H_0 be the hypothesis of no specification error and H_1 the alternative hypothesis that there is a specification error (of a particular type). We compute two estimators $\hat{\beta}_0$ and $\hat{\beta}_1$ of the parameter β. $\hat{\beta}_0$ is consistent *and* efficient under H_0 but is not consistent under H_1. $\hat{\beta}_1$ is consistent under both H_0 *and* H_1 but is not efficient under H_0. If $d = \hat{\beta}_1 - \hat{\beta}_0$, then $V(d) = V(\hat{\beta}_1) - V(\hat{\beta}_0)$. Hausman's test depends on comparing d with $V(d)$. If we are interested in testing for errors in variables or for exogeneity, Hausman's test reduces to a test of omitted variables.

10. Another general specification test (applicable in time-series models) is the PSW differencing test. In this test we compare the estimators from levels and first difference equations. The idea is that if the model is correctly specified, the estimates we get should not be widely apart. This test can also be viewed as an omitted-variable test (Section 12.11).

11. Very often, the comparison of two economic theories implies the testing of two nonnested hypotheses. The earliest test for this is the Cox test, but the alternative (and asymptotically equivalent) J-test is easier to apply. It can also be viewed as an omitted-variable test. There are, however, some conceptual problems with nonnested tests. The two hypotheses H_0 and H_1 specify two conditional distributions with different conditioning variables [e.g., $f(y|x)$ and $g(y|z)$] and it does not really make sense to compare them. A proper way is to derive the conditional distributions $f(y|x)$ and $g(y|z)$ under both H_0 and H_1 and compare them, that is, we have to have the same conditioning variables under both the hypotheses. This is the idea behind the encompassing test. What it amounts to is supplementing the J-test with an F-test based on a comprehensive model.

EXERCISES

1. Explain the meaning of each of the following terms.
   - (a) Least squares residual.
   - (b) Predicted residual.
   - (c) Studentized residual.
   - (d) Recursive residual.
   - (e) BLUS residual.
   - (f) DFFITS.
   - (g) Bounded influence estimation.
   - (h) ARCH errors.
   - (i) Post-data model construction.
   - (j) Overparametrization with data-based simplification.
   - (k) Posterior odds ratio.
   - (l) Cross validation.
   - (m) Selection of regressors.
   - (n) Diagnostic checking.
   - (o) Specification testing.
   - (p) Hausman's test.
   - (q) J-test.
   - (r) Encompassing test.
   - (s) Differencing test.

2. Examine whether the following statements are true, false, or uncertain. Give a short explanation. If a statement is not true in general but is true under some conditions, state the conditions.
   - (a) Since the least squares residuals are heteroskedastic and autocorrelated, even when the true errors are independent and homoskedastic, tests for

homoskedasticity and serial independence based on least squares residuals are useless.

(b) There is a better chance of detecting outliers with predicted residuals or studentized residuals than with least squares residuals.

(c) In tests of significance we should not use a constant level of significance. The significance level should be a decreasing function of the sample size.

(d) To test for omitted variables, all we have to do is get some proxies for them, regress the least squares residual $\hat{u}_t$ on the proxies, and test whether the coefficients of these proxies are zero.

(e) The procedure of estimating the regression equation

$$\hat{u}_t^2 = \gamma_0 + \gamma_1 \hat{u}_{t-1}^2$$

where $\hat{u}_t$ are the least squares residuals, does not necessarily test for ARCH effect.

(f) The $\bar{R}^2$ criterion of deciding whether to retain or delete certain regressors in an equation implies using a 5% significance level for testing that the coefficients of these regressors are zero.

(g) The criteria for selection of regressors proposed by Amemiya, Hocking, and Mallows imply using a higher significance level for testing the coefficients of regressors than the $\bar{R}^2$ criterion.

(h) The $\bar{R}^2$, C_p, and PC criteria for selection of regressors depend on the assumption that one of the models considered is a "true" model, whereas the S_p criterion does not. Hence given the choice between these criteria, we should use only the S_p criterion.

(i) The maximum $\bar{R}^2$ criterion and the predictive criteria PC, C_p, and S_p for selection of regressors are not really comparable since they answer different questions.

(j) For comparing different models we should always save part of the sample for prediction purposes.

(k) In the model

$$y_1 = \beta_2 y_2 + \beta_3 y_3 + \gamma_1 x_1 + u_1$$

where x_1 is exogenous, to test whether y_2 and y_3 are endogenous, we estimate the equation

$$y_1 = \beta_2 y_2 + \beta_3 y_3 + \gamma_1 x_1 + \alpha_2 \hat{v}_2 + \alpha_3 \hat{v}_3 + w$$

($\hat{v}_2$ and $\hat{v}_3$ are the estimated residuals from the reduced form equations for y_2 and y_3).

(l) In the model in part (k), if x_1 is specified as exogenous and y_2 as endogenous, to test whether y_3 is endogenous, we estimate the equation

$$y_1 = \beta_2 y_2 + \beta_3 y_3 + \gamma_1 x_1 + \alpha_3 \hat{v}_3 + w$$

and test $\alpha_3 = 0$.

3. Comment on the following: In a study on the demand for money, an economist regressed real cash balances on permanent income. To test whether the interest rate has been omitted, she regressed the residual from this regression on the interest rate and found that the coefficient was not significantly different from

zero. She therefore concluded that the interest rate does not belong in the demand for money function.

4. Explain how each of the following tests can be considered as a test for the coefficients of some extra variables added to the original equation.

    (a) Test for serial correlation.

    (b) Test for omitted variables.

    (c) Test for errors in variables.

    (d) Test for exogeneity.

    (e) *J*-test.

    (f) PSW differencing test.

In each case explain how you would interpret the results of the test and the actions you would take.

A

Tables

Table A.1 Ordinates of the Normal Density Function

$$\phi(x) = \frac{1}{\sqrt{2\pi}} e^{-x^2/2}$$

x	.00	.01	.02	.03	.04	.05	.06	.07	.08	.09
.0	.3989	.3989	.3989	.3988	.3986	.3984	.3982	.3980	.3977	.3973
.1	.3970	.3965	.3961	.3956	.3951	.3945	.3939	.3932	.3925	.3918
.2	.3910	.3902	.3894	.3885	.3876	.3867	.3857	.3847	.3836	.3825
.3	.3814	.3802	.3790	.3778	.3765	.3752	.3739	.3725	.3712	.3697
.4	.3683	.3668	.3653	.3637	.3621	.3605	.3589	.3572	.3555	.3538
.5	.3521	.3503	.3485	.3467	.3448	.3429	.3410	.3391	.3372	.3352
.6	.3332	.3312	.3292	.3271	.3251	.3230	.3209	.3187	.3166	.3144
.7	.3123	.3101	.3079	.3056	.3034	.3011	.2989	.2966	.2943	.2920
.8	.2897	.2874	.2850	.2827	.2803	.2780	.2756	.2732	.2709	.2685
.9	.2661	.2637	.2613	.2589	.2565	.2541	.2516	.2492	.2468	.2444
1.0	.2420	.2396	.2371	.2347	.2323	.2299	.2275	.2251	.2227	.2203
1.1	.2179	.2155	.2131	.2107	.2083	.2059	.2036	.2012	.1989	.1965
1.2	.1942	.1919	.1895	.1872	.1849	.1826	.1804	.1781	.1758	.1736
1.3	.1714	.1691	.1669	.1647	.1626	.1604	.1582	.1561	.1539	.1518
1.4	.1497	.1476	.1456	.1435	.1415	.1394	.1374	.1354	.1334	.1315
1.5	.1295	.1276	.1257	.1238	.1219	.1200	.1182	.1163	.1145	.1127
1.6	.1109	.1092	.1074	.1057	.1040	.1023	.1006	.0989	.0973	.0957
1.7	.0940	.0925	.0909	.0893	.0878	.0863	.0848	.0833	.0818	.0804
1.8	.0790	.0775	.0761	.0748	.0734	.0721	.0707	.0694	.0681	.0669
1.9	.0656	.0644	.0632	.0620	.0608	.0596	.0584	.0573	.0562	.0551

2.0	.0540	.0529	.0519	.0508	.0498	.0488	.0478	.0468	.0459	.0449
2.1	.0440	.0431	.0422	.0413	.0404	.0396	.0387	.0379	.0371	.0363
2.2	.0355	.0347	.0339	.0332	.0325	.0317	.0310	.0303	.0297	.0290
2.3	.0283	.0277	.0270	.0264	.0258	.0252	.0246	.0241	.0235	.0229
2.4	.0224	.0219	.0213	.0208	.0203	.0198	.0194	.0189	.0184	.0180
2.5	.0175	.0171	.0167	.0163	.0158	.0154	.0151	.0147	.0143	.0139
2.6	.0136	.0132	.0129	.0126	.0122	.0119	.0116	.0113	.0110	.0107
2.7	.0104	.0101	.0099	.0096	.0093	.0091	.0088	.0086	.0084	.0081
2.8	.0079	.0077	.0075	.0073	.0071	.0069	.0067	.0065	.0063	.0061
2.9	.0060	.0058	.0056	.0055	.0053	.0051	.0050	.0048	.0047	.0046
3.0	.0044	.0043	.0042	.0040	.0039	.0038	.0037	.0036	.0035	.0034
3.1	.0033	.0032	.0031	.0030	.0029	.0028	.0027	.0026	.0025	.0025
3.2	.0024	.0023	.0022	.0022	.0021	.0020	.0020	.0019	.0018	.0018
3.3	.0017	.0017	.0016	.0016	.0015	.0015	.0014	.0014	.0013	.0013
3.4	.0012	.0012	.0012	.0011	.0011	.0010	.0010	.0010	.0009	.0009
3.5	.0009	.0008	.0008	.0008	.0008	.0007	.0007	.0007	.0007	.0006
3.6	.0006	.0006	.0006	.0005	.0005	.0005	.0005	.0005	.0005	.0004
3.7	.0004	.0004	.0004	.0004	.0004	.0003	.0003	.0003	.0003	.0003
3.8	.0003	.0003	.0003	.0003	.0003	.0002	.0002	.0002	.0002	.0002
3.9	.0002	.0002	.0002	.0002	.0002	.0002	.0002	.0002	.0001	.0001

Source: Reprinted from A. M. Mood, F. A. Graybill, and D. C. Boes, *Introduction to the Theory of Statistics*, 3rd ed., McGraw-Hill, New York, 1973, by permission of the publishers.

Table A.2 Cumulative Normal Distribution

$$\Phi(x) = \int_{-\infty}^{x} \frac{1}{\sqrt{2\pi}} e^{-t^2/2}\, dt$$

x	.00	.01	.02	.03	.04	.05	.06	.07	.08	.09
.0	.5000	.5040	.5080	.5120	.5160	.5199	.5239	.5279	.5319	.5359
.1	.5398	.5438	.5478	.5517	.5557	.5596	.5636	.5675	.5714	.5753
.2	.5793	.5832	.5871	.5910	.5948	.5987	.6026	.6064	.6103	.6141
.3	.6179	.6217	.6255	.6293	.6331	.6368	.6406	.6443	.6480	.6517
.4	.6554	.6591	.6628	.6664	.6700	.6736	.6772	.6808	.6844	.6879
.5	.6915	.6950	.6985	.7019	.7054	.7088	.7123	.7157	.7190	.7224
.6	.7257	.7291	.7324	.7357	.7389	.7422	.7454	.7486	.7517	.7549
.7	.7580	.7611	.7642	.7673	.7704	.7734	.7764	.7794	.7823	.7852
.8	.7881	.7910	.7939	.7967	.7995	.8023	.8051	.8078	.8106	.8133
.9	.8159	.8186	.8212	.8238	.8264	.8289	.8315	.8340	.8365	.8389
1.0	.8413	.8438	.8461	.8485	.8508	.8531	.8554	.8577	.8599	.8621
1.1	.8643	.8665	.8686	.8708	.8729	.8749	.8770	.8790	.8810	.8830
1.2	.8849	.8869	.8888	.8907	.8925	.8944	.8962	.8980	.8997	.9015
1.3	.9032	.9049	.9066	.9082	.9099	.9115	.9131	.9147	.9162	.9177
1.4	.9192	.9207	.9222	.9236	.9251	.9265	.9279	.9292	.9306	.9319
1.5	.9332	.9345	.9357	.9370	.9382	.9394	.9406	.9418	.9429	.9441
1.6	.9452	.9463	.9474	.9484	.9495	.9505	.9515	.9525	.9535	.9545
1.7	.9554	.9564	.9573	.9582	.9591	.9599	.9608	.9616	.9625	.9633
1.8	.9641	.9649	.9656	.9664	.9671	.9678	.9686	.9693	.9699	.9706
1.9	.9713	.9719	.9726	.9732	.9738	.9744	.9750	.9756	.9761	.9767

x									
2.0	.9772	.9778	.9783	.9788	.9793	.9798	.9803	.9808	.9812	.9817
2.1	.9821	.9826	.9830	.9834	.9838	.9842	.9846	.9850	.9854	.9857
2.2	.9861	.9864	.9868	.9871	.9875	.9878	.9881	.9884	.9887	.9890
2.3	.9893	.9896	.9898	.9901	.9904	.9906	.9909	.9911	.9913	.9916
2.4	.9918	.9920	.9922	.9925	.9927	.9929	.9931	.9932	.9934	.9936
2.5	.9938	.9940	.9941	.9943	.9945	.9946	.9948	.9949	.9951	.9952
2.6	.9953	.9955	.9956	.9957	.9959	.9960	.9961	.9962	.9963	.9964
2.7	.9965	.9966	.9967	.9968	.9969	.9970	.9971	.9972	.9973	.9974
2.8	.9974	.9975	.9976	.9977	.9977	.9978	.9979	.9979	.9980	.9981
2.9	.9981	.9982	.9982	.9983	.9984	.9984	.9985	.9985	.9986	.9986
3.0	.9987	.9987	.9987	.9988	.9988	.9989	.9989	.9989	.9990	.9990
3.1	.9990	.9991	.9991	.9991	.9992	.9992	.9992	.9992	.9993	.9993
3.2	.9993	.9993	.9994	.9994	.9994	.9994	.9994	.9995	.9995	.9995
3.3	.9995	.9995	.9995	.9996	.9996	.9996	.9996	.9996	.9996	.9997
3.4	.9997	.9997	.9997	.9997	.9997	.9997	.9997	.9997	.9997	.9998

x	1.282	1.645	1.960	2.326	2.576	3.090	3.291	3.891	4.417
$\Phi(x)$	.90	.95	.975	.99	.995	.999	.9995	.99995	.999995
$2[1 - \Phi(x)]$	.20	.10	.05	.02	.01	.002	.001	.0001	.00001

Source: Reprinted from A. M. Mood, F. A. Graybill, and D. C. Boes, *Introduction to the Theory of Statistics*, 3rd ed., McGraw-Hill, New York, 1973, by permission of the publishers.

Table A.3 Cumulative χ^2-Distribution

$$F(u) = \int_0^u \frac{x^{(n-2)/2} e^{-x/2}}{2^{n/2}\Gamma(n/2)}\, dx$$

n \ F	.005	.010	.025	.050	.100	.250	.500	.750	.900	.950	.975	.990	.995
1	$.0^4393$	$.0^3157$	$.0^3982$	$.0^2393$	.0158	.102	.455	1.32	2.71	3.84	5.02	6.63	7.88
2	.0100	.0201	.0506	.103	.211	.575	1.39	2.77	4.61	5.99	7.38	9.21	10.6
3	.0717	.115	.216	.352	.584	1.21	2.37	4.11	6.25	7.81	9.35	11.3	12.8
4	.207	.297	.484	.711	1.06	1.92	3.36	5.39	7.78	9.49	11.1	13.3	14.9
5	.412	.554	.831	1.15	1.61	2.67	4.35	6.63	9.24	11.1	12.8	15.1	16.7
6	.676	.872	1.24	1.64	2.20	3.45	5.35	7.84	10.6	12.6	14.4	16.8	18.5
7	.989	1.24	1.69	2.17	2.83	4.25	6.35	9.04	12.0	14.1	16.0	18.5	20.3
8	1.34	1.65	2.18	2.73	3.49	5.07	7.34	10.2	13.4	15.5	17.5	20.1	22.0
9	1.73	2.09	2.70	3.33	4.17	5.90	8.34	11.4	14.7	16.9	19.0	21.7	23.6
10	2.16	2.56	3.25	3.94	4.87	6.74	9.34	12.5	16.0	18.3	20.5	23.2	25.2
11	2.60	3.05	3.82	4.57	5.58	7.58	10.3	13.7	17.3	19.7	21.9	24.7	26.8
12	3.07	3.57	4.40	5.23	6.30	8.44	11.3	14.8	18.5	21.0	23.3	26.2	28.3
13	3.57	4.11	5.01	5.89	7.04	9.30	12.3	16.0	19.8	22.4	24.7	27.7	29.8
14	4.07	4.66	5.63	6.57	7.79	10.2	13.3	17.1	21.1	23.7	26.1	29.1	31.3
15	4.60	5.23	6.26	7.26	8.55	11.0	14.3	18.2	22.3	25.0	27.5	30.6	32.8

16	5.14	5.81	6.91	7.96	9.31	11.9	15.3	19.4	23.5	26.3	28.8	32.0	34.3
17	5.70	6.41	7.56	8.67	10.1	12.8	16.3	20.5	24.8	27.6	30.2	33.4	35.7
18	6.26	7.01	8.23	9.39	10.9	13.7	17.3	21.6	26.0	28.9	31.5	34.8	37.2
19	6.84	7.63	8.91	10.1	11.7	14.6	18.3	22.7	27.2	30.1	32.9	36.2	38.6
20	7.43	8.26	9.59	10.9	12.4	15.5	19.3	23.8	28.4	31.4	34.2	37.6	40.0
21	8.03	8.90	10.3	11.6	13.2	16.3	20.3	24.9	29.6	32.7	35.5	38.9	41.4
22	8.64	9.54	11.0	12.3	14.0	17.2	21.3	26.0	30.8	33.9	36.8	40.3	42.8
23	9.26	10.2	11.7	13.1	14.8	18.1	22.3	27.1	32.0	35.2	38.1	41.6	44.2
24	9.89	10.9	12.4	13.8	15.7	19.0	23.3	28.2	33.2	36.4	39.4	43.0	45.6
25	10.5	11.5	13.1	14.6	16.5	19.9	24.3	29.3	34.4	37.7	40.6	44.3	46.9
26	11.2	12.2	13.8	15.4	17.3	20.8	25.3	30.4	35.6	38.9	41.9	45.6	48.3
27	11.8	12.9	14.6	16.2	18.1	21.7	26.3	31.5	36.7	40.1	43.2	47.0	49.6
28	12.5	13.6	15.3	16.9	18.9	22.7	27.3	32.6	37.9	41.3	44.5	48.3	51.0
29	13.1	14.3	16.0	17.7	19.8	23.6	28.3	33.7	39.1	42.6	45.7	49.6	52.3
30	13.8	15.0	16.8	18.5	20.6	24.5	29.3	34.8	40.3	43.8	47.0	50.9	53.7

Source: Abridged from Tables of Percentage Points of the Incomplete Beta Function and of the Chi-Square Distribution," *Biometrika*, Vol. 32, 1941. It is here published with the kind permission of its author, Catherine M. Thompson, and the editor of *Biometrika*.

one tail.

Table A.4 Cumulative Student's t-Distribution

$$F(t) = \int_{-\infty}^{t} \frac{\Gamma\left(\dfrac{n+1}{2}\right)}{\Gamma(n/2)\sqrt{\pi n}\left(1 + \dfrac{x^2}{n}\right)^{(n+1)/2}} \, dx$$

n \ F	.75	.90	.95	.975	.99	.995	.9995
1	1.000	3.078	6.314	12.706	31.821	63.657	636.619
2	.816	1.886	2.920	4.303	6.965	9.925	31.598
3	.765	1.638	2.353	3.182	4.541	5.841	12.941
4	.741	1.533	2.132	2.776	3.747	4.604	8.610
5	.727	1.476	2.015	2.571	3.365	4.032	6.859
6	.718	1.440	1.943	2.447	3.143	3.707	5.959
7	.711	1.415	1.895	2.365	2.998	3.499	5.405
8	.706	1.397	1.860	2.306	2.896	3.355	5.041
9	.703	1.383	1.833	2.262	2.821	3.250	4.781
10	.700	1.372	1.812	2.228	2.764	3.169	4.587
11	.697	1.363	1.796	2.201	2.718	3.106	4.437
12	.695	1.356	1.782	2.179	2.681	3.055	4.318
13	.694	1.350	1.771	2.160	2.650	3.012	4.221
14	.692	1.345	1.761	2.145	2.624	2.977	4.140
15	.691	1.341	1.753	2.131	2.602	2.947	4.073
16	.690	1.337	1.746	2.120	2.583	2.921	4.015
17	.689	1.333	1.740	2.110	2.567	2.898	3.965
18	.688	1.330	1.734	2.101	2.552	2.878	3.922
19	.688	1.328	1.729	2.093	2.539	2.861	3.883
20	.687	1.325	1.725	2.086	2.528	2.845	3.850
21	.686	1.323	1.721	2.080	2.518	2.831	3.819
22	.686	1.321	1.717	2.074	2.508	2.819	3.792
23	.685	1.319	1.714	2.069	2.500	2.807	3.767
24	.685	1.318	1.711	2.064	2.492	2.797	3.745
25	.684	1.316	1.708	2.060	2.485	2.787	3.725
26	.684	1.315	1.706	2.056	2.479	2.779	3.707
27	.684	1.314	1.703	2.052	2.473	2.771	3.690
28	.683	1.313	1.701	2.048	2.467	2.763	3.674
29	.683	1.311	1.699	2.045	2.462	2.756	3.659
30	.683	1.310	1.697	2.042	2.457	2.750	3.646
40	.681	1.303	1.684	2.021	2.423	2.704	3.551
60	.679	1.296	1.671	2.000	2.390	2.660	3.460
120	.677	1.289	1.658	1.980	2.358	2.617	3.373
∞	.674	1.282	1.645	1.960	2.326	2.576	3.291

Source: Abridged from R. A. Fisher and Frank Yates, *Statistical Tables*, Oliver & Boyd, Edinburgh and London, 1938. It is here published with the kind permission of the authors and their publishers.

Table A.5 Durbin–Watson Statistic (d): Significance Points of d_L and d_U: 5%[a]

n	$k' = 1$		$k' = 2$		$k' = 3$		$k' = 4$		$k' = 5$	
	d_L	d_U	d_L	d_U	d_L	d_U	d_L	d_U	d_L	d_U
15	1.08	1.36	0.95	1.54	0.82	1.75	0.69	1.97	0.56	2.21
16	1.10	1.37	0.98	1.54	0.86	1.73	0.74	1.93	0.62	2.15
17	1.13	1.38	1.02	1.54	0.90	1.71	0.78	1.90	0.67	2.10
18	1.16	1.39	1.05	1.53	0.93	1.69	0.82	1.87	0.71	2.06
19	1.18	1.40	1.08	1.53	0.97	1.68	0.86	1.85	0.75	2.02
20	1.20	1.41	1.10	1.54	1.00	1.68	0.90	1.83	0.79	1.99
21	1.22	1.42	1.13	1.54	1.03	1.67	0.93	1.81	0.83	1.96
22	1.24	1.43	1.15	1.54	1.05	1.66	0.96	1.80	0.86	1.94
23	1.26	1.44	1.17	1.54	1.08	1.66	0.99	1.79	0.90	1.92
24	1.27	1.45	1.19	1.55	1.10	1.66	1.01	1.78	0.93	1.90
25	1.29	1.45	1.21	1.55	1.12	1.66	1.04	1.77	0.95	1.89
26	1.30	1.46	1.22	1.55	1.14	1.65	1.06	1.76	0.98	1.88
27	1.32	1.47	1.24	1.56	1.16	1.65	1.08	1.76	1.01	1.86
28	1.33	1.48	1.26	1.56	1.18	1.65	1.10	1.75	1.03	1.85
29	1.34	1.48	1.27	1.56	1.20	1.65	1.12	1.74	1.05	1.84
30	1.35	1.49	1.28	1.57	1.21	1.65	1.14	1.74	1.07	1.83
31	1.36	1.50	1.30	1.57	1.23	1.65	1.16	1.74	1.09	1.83
32	1.37	1.50	1.31	1.57	1.24	1.65	1.18	1.73	1.11	1.82
33	1.38	1.51	1.32	1.58	1.26	1.65	1.19	1.73	1.13	1.81
34	1.39	1.51	1.33	1.58	1.27	1.65	1.21	1.73	1.15	1.81
35	1.40	1.52	1.34	1.58	1.28	1.65	1.22	1.73	1.16	1.80
36	1.41	1.52	1.35	1.59	1.29	1.65	1.24	1.73	1.18	1.80
37	1.42	1.53	1.36	1.59	1.31	1.66	1.25	1.72	1.19	1.80
38	1.43	1.54	1.37	1.59	1.32	1.66	1.26	1.72	1.21	1.79
39	1.43	1.54	1.38	1.60	1.33	1.66	1.27	1.72	1.22	1.79
40	1.44	1.54	1.39	1.60	1.34	1.66	1.29	1.72	1.23	1.79
45	1.48	1.57	1.43	1.62	1.38	1.67	1.34	1.72	1.29	1.78
50	1.50	1.59	1.46	1.63	1.42	1.67	1.38	1.72	1.34	1.77
55	1.53	1.60	1.49	1.64	1.45	1.68	1.41	1.72	1.38	1.77
60	1.55	1.62	1.51	1.65	1.48	1.69	1.44	1.73	1.41	1.77
65	1.57	1.63	1.54	1.66	1.50	1.70	1.47	1.73	1.44	1.77
70	1.58	1.64	1.55	1.67	1.52	1.70	1.49	1.74	1.46	1.77
75	1.60	1.65	1.57	1.68	1.54	1.71	1.51	1.74	1.49	1.77
80	1.61	1.66	1.59	1.69	1.56	1.72	1.53	1.74	1.51	1.77
85	1.62	1.67	1.60	1.70	1.57	1.72	1.55	1.75	1.52	1.77
90	1.63	1.68	1.61	1.70	1.59	1.73	1.57	1.75	1.54	1.78
95	1.64	1.69	1.62	1.71	1.60	1.73	1.58	1.75	1.56	1.78
100	1.65	1.69	1.63	1.72	1.61	1.74	1.59	1.76	1.57	1.78

[a] n, number of observations; k', number of explanatory variables.

Source: Reproduced from *Biometrika*, Vol. 41, p. 173, 1951, with the permission of the Trustees.

Table A.6   Durbin–Watson Statistic (d): Significance Points of d_L and d_U: 1%[a]

n	$k' = 1$		$k' = 2$		$k' = 3$		$k' = 4$		$k' = 5$	
	d_L	d_U	d_L	d_U	d_L	d_U	d_L	d_U	d_L	d_U
15	0.81	1.07	0.70	1.25	0.59	1.46	0.49	1.70	0.39	1.96
16	0.84	1.09	0.74	1.25	0.63	1.44	0.53	1.66	0.44	1.90
17	0.87	1.10	0.77	1.25	0.67	1.43	0.57	1.63	0.48	1.85
18	0.90	1.12	0.80	1.26	0.71	1.42	0.61	1.60	0.52	1.80
19	0.93	1.13	0.83	1.26	0.74	1.41	0.65	1.58	0.56	1.77
20	0.95	1.15	0.86	1.27	0.77	1.41	0.68	1.57	0.60	1.74
21	0.97	1.16	0.89	1.27	0.80	1.41	0.72	1.55	0.63	1.71
22	1.00	1.17	0.91	1.28	0.83	1.40	0.75	1.54	0.66	1.69
23	1.02	1.19	0.94	1.29	0.86	1.40	0.77	1.53	0.70	1.67
24	1.04	1.20	0.96	1.30	0.88	1.41	0.80	1.53	0.72	1.66
25	1.05	1.21	0.98	1.30	0.90	1.41	0.83	1.52	0.75	1.65
26	1.07	1.22	1.00	1.31	0.93	1.41	0.85	1.52	0.78	1.64
27	1.09	1.23	1.02	1.32	0.95	1.41	0.88	1.51	0.81	1.63
28	1.10	1.24	1.04	1.32	0.97	1.41	0.90	1.51	0.83	1.62
29	1.12	1.25	1.05	1.33	0.99	1.42	0.92	1.51	0.85	1.61
30	1.13	1.26	1.07	1.34	1.01	1.42	0.94	1.51	0.88	1.61
31	1.15	1.27	1.08	1.34	1.02	1.42	0.96	1.51	0.90	1.60
32	1.16	1.28	1.10	1.35	1.04	1.43	0.98	1.51	0.92	1.60
33	1.17	1.29	1.11	1.36	1.05	1.43	1.00	1.51	0.94	1.59
34	1.18	1.30	1.13	1.36	1.07	1.43	1.01	1.51	0.95	1.59
35	1.19	1.31	1.14	1.37	1.08	1.44	1.03	1.51	0.97	1.59
36	1.21	1.32	1.15	1.38	1.10	1.44	1.04	1.51	0.99	1.59
37	1.22	1.32	1.16	1.38	1.11	1.45	1.06	1.51	1.00	1.59
38	1.23	1.33	1.18	1.39	1.12	1.45	1.07	1.52	1.02	1.58
39	1.24	1.34	1.19	1.39	1.14	1.45	1.09	1.52	1.03	1.58
40	1.25	1.34	1.20	1.40	1.15	1.46	1.10	1.52	1.05	1.58
45	1.29	1.38	1.24	1.42	1.20	1.48	1.16	1.53	1.11	1.58
50	1.32	1.40	1.28	1.45	1.24	1.49	1.20	1.54	1.16	1.59
55	1.36	1.43	1.32	1.47	1.28	1.51	1.25	1.55	1.21	1.59
60	1.38	1.45	1.35	1.48	1.32	1.52	1.28	1.56	1.25	1.60
65	1.41	1.47	1.38	1.50	1.35	1.53	1.31	1.57	1.28	1.61
70	1.43	1.49	1.40	1.52	1.37	1.55	1.34	1.58	1.31	1.61
75	1.45	1.50	1.42	1.53	1.39	1.56	1.37	1.59	1.34	1.62
80	1.47	1.52	1.44	1.54	1.42	1.57	1.39	1.60	1.36	1.62
85	1.48	1.53	1.46	1.55	1.43	1.58	1.41	1.60	1.39	1.63
90	1.50	1.54	1.47	1.56	1.45	1.59	1.43	1.61	1.41	1.64
95	1.51	1.55	1.49	1.57	1.47	1.60	1.45	1.62	1.42	1.64
100	1.52	1.56	1.50	1.58	1.48	1.60	1.46	1.63	1.44	1.65

[a] n, number of observations; k', number of explanatory variables.

Source: Reproduced from *Biometrika*, Vol. 41, p. 175, 1951, with the permission of the Trustees.

Table A.7 F-distribution, upper 5% points $(F_{0.95})^a$

Degrees of freedom for numerator

denom \ num	1	2	3	4	5	6	7	8	9	10	12	15	20	24	30	40	60	120	∞
1	161	200	216	225	230	234	237	239	241	242	244	246	248	249	250	251	252	253	254
2	18.5	19.0	19.2	19.2	19.3	19.3	19.4	19.4	19.4	19.4	19.4	19.4	19.4	19.5	19.5	19.5	19.5	19.5	19.5
3	10.1	9.55	9.28	9.12	9.01	8.94	8.89	8.85	8.81	8.79	8.74	8.70	8.66	8.64	8.62	8.59	8.57	8.55	8.53
4	7.71	6.94	6.59	6.39	6.26	6.16	6.09	6.04	6.00	5.96	5.91	5.86	5.80	5.77	5.75	5.72	5.69	5.66	5.63
5	6.61	5.79	5.41	5.19	5.05	4.95	4.88	4.82	4.77	4.74	4.68	4.62	4.56	4.53	4.50	4.46	4.43	4.40	4.37
6	5.99	5.14	4.76	4.53	4.39	4.28	4.21	4.15	4.10	4.06	4.00	3.94	3.87	3.84	3.81	3.77	3.74	3.70	3.67
7	5.59	4.74	4.35	4.12	3.97	3.87	3.79	3.73	3.68	3.64	3.57	3.51	3.44	3.41	3.38	3.34	3.30	3.27	3.23
8	5.32	4.46	4.07	3.84	3.69	3.58	3.50	3.44	3.39	3.35	3.28	3.22	3.15	3.12	3.08	3.04	3.01	2.97	2.93
9	5.12	4.26	3.86	3.63	3.48	3.37	3.29	3.23	3.18	3.14	3.07	3.01	2.94	2.90	2.86	2.83	2.79	2.75	2.71
10	4.96	4.10	3.71	3.48	3.33	3.22	3.14	3.07	3.02	2.98	2.91	2.85	2.77	2.74	2.70	2.66	2.62	2.58	2.54
11	4.84	3.98	3.59	3.36	3.20	3.09	3.01	2.95	2.90	2.85	2.79	2.72	2.65	2.61	2.57	2.53	2.49	2.45	2.40
12	4.75	3.89	3.49	3.26	3.11	3.00	2.91	2.85	2.80	2.75	2.69	2.62	2.54	2.51	2.47	2.43	2.38	2.34	2.30
13	4.67	3.81	3.41	3.18	3.03	2.92	2.83	2.77	2.71	2.67	2.60	2.53	2.46	2.42	2.38	2.34	2.30	2.25	2.21
14	4.60	3.74	3.34	3.11	2.96	2.85	2.76	2.70	2.65	2.60	2.53	2.46	2.39	2.35	2.31	2.27	2.22	2.18	2.13
15	4.54	3.68	3.29	3.06	2.90	2.79	2.71	2.64	2.59	2.54	2.48	2.40	2.33	2.29	2.25	2.20	2.16	2.11	2.07
16	4.49	3.63	3.24	3.01	2.85	2.74	2.66	2.59	2.54	2.49	2.42	2.35	2.28	2.24	2.19	2.15	2.11	2.06	2.01
17	4.45	3.59	3.20	2.96	2.81	2.70	2.61	2.55	2.49	2.45	2.38	2.31	2.23	2.19	2.15	2.10	2.06	2.01	1.96
18	4.41	3.55	3.16	2.93	2.77	2.66	2.58	2.51	2.46	2.41	2.34	2.27	2.19	2.15	2.11	2.06	2.02	1.97	1.92
19	4.38	3.52	3.13	2.90	2.74	2.63	2.54	2.48	2.42	2.38	2.31	2.23	2.16	2.11	2.07	2.03	1.98	1.93	1.88
20	4.35	3.49	3.10	2.87	2.71	2.60	2.51	2.45	2.39	2.35	2.28	2.20	2.12	2.08	2.04	1.99	1.95	1.90	1.84
21	4.32	3.47	3.07	2.84	2.68	2.57	2.49	2.42	2.37	2.32	2.25	2.18	2.10	2.05	2.01	1.96	1.92	1.87	1.81
22	4.30	3.44	3.05	2.82	2.66	2.55	2.46	2.40	2.34	2.30	2.23	2.15	2.07	2.03	1.98	1.94	1.89	1.84	1.78
23	4.28	3.42	3.03	2.80	2.64	2.53	2.44	2.37	2.32	2.27	2.20	2.13	2.05	2.01	1.96	1.91	1.86	1.81	1.76
24	4.26	3.40	3.01	2.78	2.62	2.51	2.42	2.36	2.30	2.25	2.18	2.11	2.03	1.98	1.94	1.89	1.84	1.79	1.73
25	4.24	3.39	2.99	2.76	2.60	2.49	2.40	2.34	2.28	2.24	2.16	2.09	2.01	1.96	1.92	1.87	1.82	1.77	1.71
30	4.17	3.32	2.92	2.69	2.53	2.42	2.33	2.27	2.21	2.16	2.09	2.01	1.93	1.89	1.84	1.79	1.74	1.68	1.62
40	4.08	3.23	2.84	2.61	2.45	2.34	2.25	2.18	2.12	2.08	2.00	1.92	1.84	1.79	1.74	1.69	1.64	1.58	1.51
60	4.00	3.15	2.76	2.53	2.37	2.25	2.17	2.10	2.04	1.99	1.92	1.84	1.75	1.70	1.65	1.59	1.53	1.47	1.39
120	3.92	3.07	2.68	2.45	2.29	2.18	2.09	2.02	1.96	1.91	1.83	1.75	1.66	1.61	1.55	1.50	1.43	1.35	1.25
∞	3.84	3.00	2.60	2.37	2.21	2.10	2.01	1.94	1.88	1.83	1.75	1.67	1.57	1.52	1.46	1.39	1.32	1.22	1.00

Degrees of freedom for numerator

^{a} Interpolation should be performed using reciprocals of the degrees of freedom.

Source: Reproduced from M. Merrington, C. M. Thompson, "Tables of Percentage Points of the Inverted Beta (F) Distribution," *Biometrika*, Vol. 33, 1943, p. 73, with the permission of the Biometrika Trustees.

Table A.8 F-distribution, upper 1% points $(F_{0.99})^a$

Degrees of freedom for numerator

	1	2	3	4	5	6	7	8	9	10	12	15	20	24	30	40	60	120	∞
1	4,052	5,000	5,403	5,625	5,764	5,859	5,928	5,982	6,023	6,056	6,106	6,157	6,209	6,235	6,261	6,287	6,313	6,339	6,366
2	98.5	99.0	99.2	99.3	99.3	99.3	99.4	99.4	99.4	99.4	99.4	99.4	99.5	99.5	99.5	99.5	99.5	99.5	99.5
3	34.1	30.8	29.5	28.7	28.2	27.9	27.7	27.5	27.3	27.2	27.1	26.9	26.7	26.6	26.5	26.4	26.3	26.2	26.1
4	21.2	18.0	16.7	16.0	15.5	15.2	15.0	14.8	14.7	14.5	14.4	14.2	14.0	13.9	13.8	13.7	13.7	13.6	13.5
5	16.3	13.3	12.1	11.4	11.0	10.7	10.5	10.3	10.2	10.1	9.89	9.72	9.55	9.47	9.38	9.29	9.20	9.11	9.02
6	13.7	10.9	9.78	9.15	8.75	8.47	8.26	8.10	7.98	7.87	7.72	7.56	7.40	7.31	7.23	7.14	7.06	6.97	6.88
7	12.2	9.55	8.45	7.85	7.46	7.19	6.99	6.84	6.72	6.62	6.47	6.31	6.16	6.07	5.99	5.91	5.82	5.74	5.65
8	11.3	8.65	7.59	7.01	6.63	6.37	6.18	6.03	5.91	5.81	5.67	5.52	5.36	5.28	5.20	5.12	5.03	4.95	4.86
9	10.6	8.02	6.99	6.42	6.06	5.80	5.61	5.47	5.35	5.26	5.11	4.96	4.81	4.73	4.65	4.57	4.48	4.40	4.31
10	10.0	7.56	6.55	5.99	5.64	5.39	5.20	5.06	4.94	4.85	4.71	4.56	4.41	4.33	4.25	4.17	4.08	4.00	3.91
11	9.65	7.21	6.22	5.67	5.32	5.07	4.89	4.74	4.63	4.54	4.40	4.25	4.10	4.02	3.94	3.86	3.78	3.69	3.60
12	9.33	6.93	5.95	5.41	5.06	4.82	4.64	4.50	4.39	4.30	4.16	4.01	3.86	3.78	3.70	3.62	3.54	3.45	3.36
13	9.07	6.70	5.74	5.21	4.86	4.62	4.44	4.30	4.19	4.10	3.96	3.82	3.66	3.59	3.51	3.43	3.34	3.25	3.17
14	8.86	6.51	5.56	5.04	4.70	4.46	4.28	4.14	4.03	3.94	3.80	3.66	3.51	3.43	3.35	3.27	3.18	3.09	3.00
15	8.68	6.36	5.42	4.89	4.56	4.32	4.14	4.00	3.89	3.80	3.67	3.52	3.37	3.29	3.21	3.13	3.05	2.96	2.87
16	8.53	6.23	5.29	4.77	4.44	4.20	4.03	3.89	3.78	3.69	3.55	3.41	3.26	3.18	3.10	3.02	2.93	2.84	2.75
17	8.40	6.11	5.19	4.67	4.34	4.10	3.93	3.79	3.68	3.59	3.46	3.31	3.16	3.08	3.00	2.92	2.83	2.75	2.65
18	8.29	6.01	5.09	4.58	4.25	4.01	3.84	3.71	3.60	3.51	3.37	3.23	3.08	3.00	2.92	2.84	2.75	2.66	2.57
19	8.19	5.93	5.01	4.50	4.17	3.94	3.77	3.63	3.52	3.43	3.30	3.15	3.00	2.92	2.84	2.76	2.67	2.58	2.49
20	8.10	5.85	4.94	4.43	4.10	3.87	3.70	3.56	3.46	3.37	3.23	3.09	2.94	2.86	2.78	2.69	2.61	2.52	2.42
21	8.02	5.78	4.87	4.37	4.04	3.81	3.64	3.51	3.40	3.31	3.17	3.03	2.88	2.80	2.72	2.64	2.55	2.46	2.36
22	7.95	5.72	4.82	4.31	3.99	3.76	3.59	3.45	3.35	3.26	3.12	2.98	2.83	2.75	2.67	2.58	2.50	2.40	2.31
23	7.88	5.66	4.76	4.26	3.94	3.71	3.54	3.41	3.30	3.21	3.07	2.93	2.78	2.70	2.62	2.54	2.45	2.35	2.26
24	7.82	5.61	4.72	4.22	3.90	3.67	3.50	3.36	3.26	3.17	3.03	2.89	2.74	2.66	2.58	2.49	2.40	2.31	2.21
25	7.77	5.57	4.68	4.18	3.86	3.63	3.46	3.32	3.22	3.13	2.99	2.85	2.70	2.62	2.53	2.45	2.36	2.27	2.17
30	7.56	5.39	4.51	4.02	3.70	3.47	3.30	3.17	3.07	2.98	2.84	2.70	2.55	2.47	2.39	2.30	2.21	2.11	2.01
40	7.31	5.18	4.31	3.83	3.51	3.29	3.12	2.99	2.89	2.80	2.66	2.52	2.37	2.29	2.20	2.11	2.02	1.92	1.80
60	7.08	4.98	4.13	3.65	3.34	3.12	2.95	2.82	2.72	2.63	2.50	2.35	2.20	2.12	2.03	1.94	1.84	1.73	1.60
120	6.85	4.79	3.95	3.48	3.17	2.96	2.79	2.66	2.56	2.47	2.34	2.19	2.03	1.95	1.86	1.76	1.66	1.53	1.38
∞	6.63	4.61	3.78	3.32	3.02	2.80	2.64	2.51	2.41	2.32	2.18	2.04	1.88	1.79	1.70	1.59	1.47	1.32	1.00

Degrees of freedom for numerator

a Interpolation should be performed using reciprocals of the degrees of freedom.

Source: Reproduced from M. Merrington, C. M. Thompson, "Tables of Percentage Points of the Inverted Beta (F) Distribution," *Biometrika*, Vol. 33, 1943, p. 73, with the permission of the Biometrika Trustees.

Author Index

Subject Index